G000152335

International Trade
Volume II

The International Library of Critical Writings in Economics

Series Editor: Mark Blaug

Professor Emeritus, University of London
Professor Emeritus, University of Buckingham
Visiting Professor, University of Exeter

This series is an essential reference source for students, researchers and lecturers in economics. It presents by theme an authoritative selection of the most important articles across the entire spectrum of economics. Each volume has been prepared by a leading specialist who has written an authoritative introduction to the literature included.

A full list of published and future titles in this series is printed at the end of this volume.

International Trade Volume II

Production Structure, Trade and Growth

Edited by

J. Peter Neary

Professor of Political Economy
University College Dublin, Ireland

THE INTERNATIONAL LIBRARY OF CRITICAL WRITINGS IN ECONOMICS

An Elgar Reference Collection
Aldershot, UK • Brookfield, US

© J. Peter Neary 1995. For copyright of individual articles please refer to the Acknowledgements.

All rights reserved. No part of this publication may be reproduced, stored in a retrieval system, or transmitted in any form or by any means, electronic, mechanical, photocopying, recording, or otherwise without the prior permission of the publisher.

Published by
Edward Elgar Publishing Limited
Gower House
Croft Road
Aldershot
Hants GU11 3HR
UK

Edward Elgar Publishing Company
Old Post Road
Brookfield
Vermont 05036
US

British Library Cataloguing in Publication Data
International Trade. – (International
Library of Critical Writings in Economics;
No. 59)
  I. Neary, J. Peter II. Series
  382

Library of Congress Cataloguing in Publication Data
International trade / edited by J. Peter Neary.
     p. cm. — (International library of critical writings in
  economics ; 59) (Elgar reference collection)
  Includes bibliographical references and index.
  Contents: v. 1, Welfare and trade policy
  1. International trade. 2. International economic relations.
3. Competition, International. 4. Commercial policy. I. Neary, J.
Peter. II. Series. III. Series: Elgar reference collection.
HF1379.I578 1995
382—dc20

95–32856
CIP

ISBN 1 85278 361 3 (2 volume set)

Printed in Great Britain by Galliard (Printers) Ltd, Great Yarmouth

Contents

Acknowledgements

The editor and publishers wish to thank the following who have kindly given permission for the use of copyright material.

Academic Press Inc. for article: Elhanan Helpman (1987), 'Imperfect Competition and International Trade: Evidence from Fourteen Industrial Countries', *Journal of the Japanese and International Economies*, **1**, 62–81.

American Economic Association for articles: R. Dornbusch, S. Fischer and P.A. Samuelson (1977), 'Comparative Advantage, Trade, and Payments in a Ricardian Model with a Continuum of Goods', *American Economic Review*, **67** (5), December, 823–39; Ronald Findlay (1980), 'The Terms of Trade and Equilibrium Growth in the World Economy', *American Economic Review*, **70** (3), June, 291–9; Paul Krugman (1980), 'Scale Economies, Product Differentiation, and the Pattern of Trade', *American Economic Review*, **70** (5), December, 950–59; Harry P. Bowen, Edward E. Leamer and Leo Sveikauskas (1987), 'Multicountry, Multifactor Tests of the Factor Abundance Theory', *American Economic Review*, **77** (5), December, 791–809; Peter Neary (1988), 'Determinants of the Equilibrium Real Exchange Rate', *American Economic Review*, **78** (1), March, 210–15; Gene M. Grossman and Elhanan Helpman (1990), 'Comparative Advantage and Long-Run Growth', *American Economic Review*, **80** (4), September, 796–815; Sweder van Wijnbergen (1992), 'Trade Reform, Policy Uncertainty, and the Current Account: A Non-Expected-Utility Approach', *American Economic Review*, **82** (3), June, 626–33.

Basil Blackwell Ltd for articles: Richard E. Caves (1971), 'International Corporations: The Industrial Economics of Foreign Investment', *Economica*, **XXXVIII** (149), February, 1–27; J. Peter Neary (1978), 'Short-Run Capital Specificity and the Pure Theory of International Trade', *Economic Journal*, **88** (351), September, 488–510.

Canadian Journal of Economics for article: James R. Melvin (1969), 'Increasing Returns to Scale as a Determinant of Trade, *Canadian Journal of Economics*, **II** (3), August, 389–402.

Economic Record for article: W.E.G. Salter (1959), 'Internal and External Balance: The Role of Price and Expenditure Effects', *Economic Record*, **XXXV** (71), August, 226–38.

Elsevier Science B.V. for excerpts and articles: F.H. Gruen and W.M. Corden (1970), 'A Tariff that Worsens the Terms of Trade', in I.A. McDougall and R.H. Snape (eds), *Studies in International Economics*, 55–8; Ronald W. Jones (1971), 'A Three-Factor Model in Theory, Trade, and History', in Jagdish Bhagwati, Ronald W. Jones, Robert A. Mundell and Jaroslev Vanek (eds), *Trade, Balance of Payments and Growth: Papers in International Economics in Honor of Charles P. Kindleberger*, Chapter 1, 3–21; Rudiger Dornbusch (1974), 'Tariffs and Nontraded Goods', *Journal of International Economics*, **4** (2), May, 177–85; Wilfred Ethier (1974), 'Some of the Theorems of International Trade with Many Goods and Factors', *Journal of International Economics*, **4** (2), May, 199–206; Wilfred Ethier (1979), 'Internationally Decreasing Costs and World Trade', *Journal of International Economics*, **9** (1), February, 1–24; James A. Brander (1981), 'Intra-Industry Trade in Identical Commodities', *Journal of International Economics*, **11** (1), February, 1–14; James E. Anderson (1981), 'The Heckscher–Ohlin and Travis–Vanek Theorems Under Uncertainty', *Journal of International Economics*, **11** (2), May, 239–47; James R. Markusen (1983), 'Factor Movements and Commodity Trade as Complements', *Journal of International Economics*, **14** (3/4), May, 341–56; Alasdair Smith (1987), 'Strategic Investment, Multinational Corporations and Trade Policy', *European Economic Review*, **31**, 89–96; Paul Krugman (1987), 'The Narrow Moving Band, the Dutch Disease, and the Competitive Consequences of Mrs. Thatcher: Notes on Trade in the Presence of Dynamic Scale Economies', *Journal of Development Economics*, **27**, 41–55; Avinash Dixit (1987), 'Trade and Insurance with Moral Hazard', *Journal of International Economics*, **23**, 201–20; Anthony J. Venables (1990), 'International Capacity Choice and National Market Games', *Journal of International Economics*, **29**, 23–42; Igantius J. Horstmann and James R. Markusen (1992), 'Endogenous Market Structures in International Trade (Natura Facit Saltum)', *Journal of International Economics*, **32**, 109–29.

Elsevier Science S.A. for article: Wilfred J. Ethier (1982), 'The General Role of Factor Intensity in the Theorems of International Trade', *Economics Letters*, **10**, 337–42.

Helbing & Lichtenhahn Verlag AG, Basel and Frankfurt/M for article: Jaroslav Vanek (1968), 'The Factor Proportions Theory: The N–Factor Case', *Kyklos*, **XXI** (fasc. 4), 749–55.

Kluwer Academic Publishers for article: Elhanan Helpman (1988), 'Growth, Technological Progress, and Trade', *Empirica – Austrian Economic Papers*, **12**, 5–25.

MIT Press and Harvester Wheatsheaf for excerpt: Elhanan Helpman and Paul R. Krugman (1985), 'Single-Product Firms', in Elhanan Helpman and Paul R. Krugman (eds), *Market Structure and Foreign Trade: Increasing Returns, Imperfect Competition, and the International Economy*, Chapter 12, 227–45.

MIT Press Journals for article: Colin Lawrence and Pablo T. Spiller (1983), 'Product Diversity, Economies of Scale, and International Trade', *Quarterly Journal of Economics*, **XCVIII** (1), February, 63–83.

Review of Economic Studies Ltd for articles: Paul A. Samuelson (1953–54), 'Prices of Factors and Goods in General Equilibrium', *Review of Economic Studies*, **XXI** (1), 54, 1–20; David M.G. Newbery and Joseph E. Stiglitz (1984), 'Pareto Inferior Trade', *Review of Economic Studies*, **LI** (1), 164, January, 1–12.

University of Chicago Press for articles: Ronald W. Jones (1965), 'The Structure of Simple General Equilibrium Models', *Journal of Political Economy*, **LXXIII** (6), December, 557–72; Elhanan Helpman and Assaf Razin (1978), 'The Protective Effect of a Tariff Under Uncertainty', *Journal of Political Economy*, **86** (6), December, 1131–41; Edward E. Leamer (1980), 'The Leontief Paradox, Reconsidered', *Journal of Political Economy*, **88** (3), June, 495–503; Alan V. Deardorff (1980), 'The General Validity of the Law of Comparative Advantage', *Journal of Political Economy*, **88** (5), October, 941–57; Richard A. Brecher and Ehsan U. Choudhri (1982), 'The Leontief Paradox, Continued', *Journal of Political Economy*, **90** (4), August, 820–23; Robert C. Feenstra and Kenneth L. Judd (1982), 'Tariffs, Technology Transfer, and Welfare', *Journal of Political Economy*, **90** (6), December, 1142–65; Lars E.O. Svensson and Assaf Razin (1983), 'The Terms of Trade and the Current Account: The Harberger-Laursen-Metzler Effect', *Journal of Political Economy*, **91** (1), February, 97–125; Paul Krugman (1991), 'Increasing Returns and Economic Geography', *Journal of Political Economy*, **99** (3), June, 483–99.

Every effort has been made to trace all the copyright holders but if any have been inadvertently overlooked the publishers will be pleased to make the necessary arrangement at the first opportunity.

In addition the publishers wish to thank the Library of the London School of Economics and Political Science, the Marshall Library, Cambridge University and the Photographic Unit of the University of London Library for their assistance in obtaining these articles.

Introduction to Volume II

This is the second volume of a collection of readings in the theory of international trade. The criteria which guided the choice of articles were discussed in the introduction to Volume I and that volume contained a selection of papers broadly concerned with the normative theory of international trade. In the present volume most of the chapters are concerned with positive issues and in this introduction I discuss the chapters in Volume II and their relationship to the recent literature.

I Production Structure and Comparative Statics

The volume begins in Part I with questions which have been central in international trade theory at least since the work of Heckscher (1919) and Ohlin (1933). These writers are associated with a particular theory of the determinants of international trade, which is not considered explicitly until Part II. Their work also initiated an exploration of the implications of different assumptions concerning the structure of an economy for its comparative statics responses to exogenous shocks. One of the most complete, and still one of the most general, studies in this vein is Chapter 1 by Paul Samuelson. This discusses the behaviour of a very general competitive model of an open economy, examining such issues as the relative numbers of goods and factors in equilibrium; the implications of competitive behaviour; and the 'reciprocity' property, which links, on the one hand, the responses of outputs to changes in factor endowments and, on the other, the responses of factor prices to changes in goods prices. The Appendix to this chapter also introduces a new technical tool, later to become known as the 'revenue' or 'GNP' function, which is now widely used in presentations of the production side of competitive general equilibrium models. (See the textbooks by Dixit and Norman (1980) and Woodland (1982).[1])

Samuelson's paper was unusual for its day in breaking out of the straitjacket of the simple two-factor, two-sector version of the Heckscher–Ohlin model, which was the major laboratory for the study of issues in trade theory from the late 1940s to the 1970s (including Samuelson's own 1948 and 1949 papers on factor-price equalization). Even today, despite its many recognized deficiencies, this model remains an important tool of trade theory, all the more so because of its use in general equilibrium models of monopolistic competition, outlined in Part II. Chapter 2, by Ronald Jones, is one of the major statements of the basic properties of this model and the notation and style it introduced have been widely adopted. Jones and Samuelson were also instrumental, in two 1971 papers, in focusing attention on an alternative model, variously labelled the 'specific-factors' or 'Ricardo–Viner' model, which provides a more plausible description of short-run changes in resource allocation and income distribution. Jones's 1971 paper (reprinted as Chapter 3) also suggested that a plausible description of the time-path of adjustment to shocks in an open economy is obtained by combining the specific-factors model (representing short-run equilibria) and the Heckscher–Ohlin model (representing long-run equilibria). This suggestion was taken up in a number of papers, including Mayer (1974), Mussa (1974) and Chapter 4 by myself.[2] Here the predictions of the two models are compared and the transitional dynamics are outlined with special emphasis on the likely pattern of political support for tariff changes.

Just as the specific-factors model is the simplest which does not exhibit factor-price equalization, so the Gruen–Corden model, reprinted as Chapter 5, is the simplest which exhibits general equilibrium complementarity in production. Constructed to mimic the stylized facts of the Australian economy, the model is used by the authors to illustrate the paradoxical possibility that a tariff can worsen the terms of trade. From a formal perspective, the model combines a specific-factors structure for one industry (textiles) with a Heckscher–Ohlin structure for two others (labour-intensive grain and land-intensive wool). With labour mobile between all three sectors, the implication that a rise in the relative price of textiles induces an increase in the output of wool is immediate and makes the model a useful addition to the trade theorist's tool-kit.

Small-scale models such as those in Chapters 2 to 5, with relatively few factors and sectors, provide an important laboratory for the study of many important issues in international trade theory.[3] However, their usefulness in this respect would be reduced if the insights obtained from them bore no relation to the properties exhibited by models of higher dimensions. With this in mind, a highly technical literature evolved in the 1960s and 1970s, which attempted, with little success, to generalize the properties of the two-by-two Heckscher–Ohlin model to models with large numbers of goods and factors.[4] This literature probably erred, however, in attempting to derive answers to extremely detailed questions in large-scale models. More recent writings have shown that the essence of the propositions which hold in the two-by-two Heckscher–Ohlin model can be salvaged by adopting alternative approaches. Chapter 6 by Bill Ethier is in this vein and shows that many of the properties of the two-by-two model generalize provided they are expressed in terms of the responses of individual but unspecified variables. Consider, for example, the two-by-two Stolper–Samuelson prediction that protection will raise the real return of the scarce factor and lower the real return of the abundant factor.[5] Earlier writers concentrated on deriving stringent and technical conditions which would guarantee a 'strong' generalization of this theorem, such that an increase in the relative price of each good would raise the real return of only one factor and lower the real return of all other factors. By contrast, Ethier shows simply that, under general conditions, an increase in the relative price of each good must raise the real return of *at least* one factor and lower the real return of *at least* one other factor.[6]

II   Theories of International Trade

Part II turns to the central question in the positive theory of international trade, the determinants of trade patterns themselves, and explores it under a variety of assumptions about market structure.

A   Trade Based on Comparative Advantage

The first chapters in this section deal with trade patterns in models with perfect competition, and so make use of some of the models from Part I. However, they are included in a separate section because of their more explicit focus on the determinants of trade patterns, which leads them to concentrate on the implications of production structure for the world economy rather than on the comparative statics responses of a single small open economy facing exogenous world prices.

Most of the readings in this section reflect the supplanting of the Ricardian paradigm of constant production costs by neoclassical models of the Heckscher–Ohlin type. However, interest in the Ricardian model has been revived in recent years by its generalization to the case of a continuum of commodities by Rudiger Dornbusch, Stan Fischer and Paul Samuelson in Chapter 7.[7] The continuum assumption allows a general but tractable consideration of issues such as the endogenous determination of which goods are exported, imported or non-traded; and the model's Ricardian focus on the importance of international differences in technology makes it a useful vehicle for studying issues of trade and growth which are considered in Part VII below.[8]

While the Ricardian model remains of interest, its assumption of constant costs is clearly restrictive. However, the applicability of the law of comparative advantage in more general contexts remained an open question for some time. This issue was resolved in Chapter 8 by Alan Deardorff, who showed that the law of comparative advantage generalizes straight-forwardly, provided it is restated in terms of correlations between net exports and autarky relative prices.[9]

Turning to Heckscher–Ohlin-based models, Chapter 9 by Jaroslav Vanek is an important early contribution which noted that, provided factor prices are equalized internationally, then the Heckscher–Ohlin theorem may be reinterpreted as predicting the *factor content* of inter-national trade, irrespective of the numbers of goods and factors. Of course, the assumption of international factor-price equalization is highly restrictive. Moreover, it is desirable to obtain results in terms of actual trade volumes rather than just their factor contents. As with generalizations of the law of the comparative advantage, progress in this area has come by restating the Heckscher–Ohlin theorem in terms of correlations between international differences in factor endowments, factor prices and patterns of output and trade.[10] Results of this kind were obtained by Dixit and Norman (1980) and Deardorff (1982) and they are synthesized and extended by Bill Ethier in Chapter 10.

B Trade Based on Increasing Returns

All the readings in Part II.A retain two key assumptions of traditional trade theory, constant returns to scale and perfect competition. The potential importance for trade patterns of relaxing these assumptions has long been appreciated but formal analysis along these lines is of more recent vintage.[11]

The oldest strand of this tradition allows for increasing returns to scale but retains the assumption of perfect competition by assuming that they are external to the firm.[12] Chapter 11 by Jim Melvin illustrates this approach by considering a stylized model in which two countries are identical in all respects. Notwithstanding this symmetry of assumptions, the presence of external returns to scale in both industries leads to an asymmetry of outcomes with each country specializing completely in one industry. Moreover, the pattern of production and hence of trade is indeterminate, suggesting that tiny differences in initial conditions (perhaps induced by government intervention) may have enormous long-term consequences. This view of the implications of increasing returns remains influential: see, for example, Chapters 26 and 36 by Krugman below. However, Chapter 12 by Bill Ethier shows that it derives from the assumption that unit costs depend on the scale of the national industry. He argues instead that returns to scale are more often 'international', depending on the size of the industry worldwide. This assumption avoids the tendency towards specialization implied by national returns to scale and also generates incentives for intra-industry trade in intermediate goods.[13]

While Ethier's model is consistent with internal as well as external returns to scale, his assumption that the outputs of different manufacturing firms are homogeneous precludes any intra-industry trade in final goods. The development of models to explain this phenomenon has taken a different route, drawing on the formalizations of Chamberlin's model of monopolistic competition by Spence (1976) and Dixit and Stiglitz (1977). Chapter 13 by Paul Krugman presents such a model, in which consumer preferences reflect a 'taste for diversity'; internal returns to scale ensure that the number of products supplied depends on the scale of the market; and free entry drives profits to zero. The model predicts that identical countries will engage in mutually beneficial intra-industry trade and that, when transport costs are allowed, countries will tend to export those goods for which they have relatively large home markets.[14]

While Krugman's model isolates the role of increasing returns and imperfect competition, it leaves open the issue of how their influence interacts with the traditional explanation of inter-industry trade based on comparative advantage. The task of integrating the two approaches has been accomplished by a number of papers, of which Chapter 14 by Colin Lawrence and Pablo Spiller is an interesting example.[15] They demonstrate what has since become a widely-accepted generalization: that international differences in *factor endowments* explain the pattern and volume of *inter-industry* trade but that, because of their effects on the potential for producing a greater variety of differentiated products, it is international differences in *country size* which explain the pattern and volume of *intra-industry* trade.

C Trade Based on Oligopolistic Competition

So far, all the chapters in Part II deal with general equilibrium models in which profits are driven to zero by free entry and exit of firms and in which factor prices are endogenously determined. As a result they provide an endogenous explanation of why production costs differ between countries, a desirable feature of any complete explanation of trade patterns. Nonetheless, recent work has shown that a partial equilibrium perspective which treats costs as exogenous but pays careful attention to the strategies adopted by oligopolistic firms can also be of interest. In particular, Chapter 15 by Jim Brander was the first to point out that oligopolistic competition between firms in different countries is an independent source of trade. Indeed, such trade can occur in *identical* commodities, despite which, it is welfare-improving (unless transport costs are high) because it is pro-competitive.[16] This finding has been criticized by Ben-Zvi and Helpman (1992) because it relies on the assumption that national markets are fully segmented. However, Chapter 16 by Tony Venables shows that the basic predictions continue to hold under a more plausible assumption, whereby firms first choose their capacities and then choose how much to supply to each national market.

III Tests of Trade Theories

Part III turns from the formulation to the testing of trade theories. In fact, formal tests of any trade theory are extremely difficult to implement and the many 'tests' carried out in emulation of the pioneering work of MacDougall (1951 and 1952), Leontief (1954) and Baldwin (1971) have a shaky methodological basis, a point stressed by Deardorff (1984).[17] Chapter 17 by Ed Leamer points out some of the difficulties with the Leontief Paradox. Using Vanek's extension of the Heckscher–Ohlin model (Chapter 9 above) he shows that Leontief's procedure of inferring US factor abundance by comparing the capital per worker embodied in exports with that embodied in imports is erroneous except in a two-commodity world. By contrast, the theoretically correct comparison of the capital intensity of exports with that of domestic consumption reveals the US to be relatively capital abundant. However, Chapter 18 by Rick Brecher and Ehsan Choudhri notes that another feature of Leontief's data is not so easily explained. The data show that the US was a net exporter of labour services but also that expenditure per worker in the US was substantially greater than in the rest of the world. The joint occurrence of these two outcomes is inconsistent with the Heckscher–Ohlin–Vanek model.

A particular difficulty with testing the predictions of the Heckscher–Ohlin model is that it is necessary in principle to have independent estimates of the factor endowments in all countries whose trade is considered. This approach was first pursued by Leamer (1984) whose results were broadly consistent with the Heckscher–Ohlin–Vanek theorem. Using the same data set but more sophisticated econometric techniques, Leamer along with Harry Bowen and Leo Sveikauskas reexamine the issue in Chapter 19. This time the Heckscher–Ohlin–Vanek theorem fares less well. However, recent work by Trefler (1993) shows that the empirical failure of both the Heckscher–Ohlin–Vanek theorem and the factor-price equalization theorem can be explained by plausible international differences in factor productivity.

Finally, although the theories of trade based on imperfect competition were prompted by the empirical observation that a high percentage of world trade is intra-industry (as documented, in particular, by Grubel and Lloyd (1975)), they have as yet inspired relatively little formal econometric testing. An exception is the paper by Elhanan Helpman, Chapter 20, which provides an excellent concise summary of the theory and implements a partial test of its predictions. The paper's results confirm the prediction that relative country size has a major influence on the volume of intra-industry trade.

IV International Factor Movements and Multinational Corporations

All the chapters in this volume so far have concentrated on the Classical case where goods are internationally mobile but factors are not.[18] This nineteenth-century view of the world continues to dominate much of trade theory but many authors have attempted to go beyond it. One of the earliest attempts in this direction was that of Mundell (1957), who considered the effects of international factor movements in the two-sector Heckscher–Ohlin model. However, his paper highlighted an implausible implication of that model: international trade and international factor mobility are perfect substitutes in the sense that permitting one removes any incentive for the other. This result seems incompatible with the explosion in both trade and factor flows in recent decades. Fortunately, as Chapter 21 by Jim Markusen shows, the result does not hold under almost any other set of assumptions. (See also Wong (1986).) If trade is due to taxes, returns to scale or sector-specific factors, then it is likely to be encouraged when barriers to international factor flows are removed.

The papers by Mundell and Markusen belong to a tradition which models international capital movements as a reallocation of a given stock of mobile capital.[19] A different, though not necessarily incompatible, tradition views foreign direct investment as arising from the decisions of multinational corporations. Chapter 22 by Richard Caves contributed to both these traditions. On the one hand, it develops a competitive model of international capital mobility, extending the specific-factors model of Jones (Chapter 3 above) to allow for international but not intersectoral mobility of capital. As a result, rates of return are equalized internationally across industries but may differ permanently between industries in a given country. This model avoids the indeterminacy of trade patterns and factor movements found in models of the Heckscher–Ohlin type.[20] On the other hand, Caves argues that foreign direct investment by multinational corporations is most likely to occur in oligopolistic markets where products are differentiated. This industrial organization view of foreign investment is pursued in Chapter 23 by Elhanan Helpman and Paul Krugman, which draws on Helpman (1984). Here, as in Markusen (1984) and Helpman (1985), a multinational corporation is viewed as a vertically integrated firm which produces final output using both primary factors and an internally produced input called 'headquarter services'. These services represent activities such as management, marketing and R&D, and they can service more than one final goods plant. Helpman and Krugman show how this model can be appended to the two-sector Heckscher–Ohlin model in which one sector is monopolistically competitive, and they derive the implications for intra-industry and intra-firm trade.

While Helpman and Krugman view multinational activity as arising from economies of multi-plant activity, their assumption of Chamberlinian behaviour precludes any strategic motive for producing in more than one country. Such a motive is considered by Alasdair Smith in Chapter 24. Here the choice by a foreign firm between exporting to and producing in a country is shown to depend on its fixed costs (which are both firm- and plant-specific) and on the policy environment.[21] A tariff many induce entry by a home firm which deters direct investment by the foreign firm. Similar results were found by Horstmann and Markusen (1987) and in Chapter 25 the same authors show how a variety of different market structures, with or without multinational production, may emerge. Moreover, by altering the equilibrium market structure, a small change in an exogenous variable may bring about a discontinuous jump in outputs and welfare.

The final chapter in this section, by Paul Krugman, returns to the case of pure factor mobility but combines it with the assumption of increasing returns.[22] He constructs a model of two regions (which can of course be interpreted as countries) in which manufacturing firms tend to locate in the larger region in order to benefit from increasing returns and to minimize transport costs. Depending on parameters, a 'core-periphery' pattern, with manufacturing concentrated in one region, may or may not emerge. The results are suggestive of a general approach to economic geography, which Krugman has explored in a number of other papers. (See Krugman (1991a and 1991b) and Krugman and Venables (1990).)

V Uncertainty

The remainder of Volume II is concerned with papers on three disparate topics. The first of these is the implications of uncertainty for international trade. Early approaches to this question tended simply to graft uncertainty onto existing models without investigating how the implications of uncertainty would be affected by the availability of alternative market institutions. A major departure from this tradition was the work of Elhanan Helpman and Assaf Razin which showed that the effect of uncertainty depends crucially on whether international trade in equities is possible. In Chapter 27, they apply this insight to the protective effects of a tariff in a small open economy. In their model, resource allocation is determined by equity prices rather than commodity prices. With free trade in equities, the distinction matters little: protection raises the domestic price of equity in the protected sector and so has the usual effects. However, if equities are non-traded, domestic risk cannot be shared on world markets and the effect of protection on equity prices is unpredictable. Helpman and Razin construct an example where, because equities are non-traded, protection para- doxically contracts the import-competing sector.

In other work (1978) Helpman and Razin also explored the implications of uncertainty for patterns of international trade and concluded that the Heckscher–Ohlin theorem did not generalize even with free trade in equities. However, Jim Anderson shows in Chapter 28 that a mild restriction on preferences under uncertainty – essentially the stochastic equivalent of homothetic preferences which are needed to prove the Heckscher–Ohlin theorem in the absence of uncertainty – is sufficient to rescue the Heckscher–Ohlin theorem and its variants. Of course, it is best to see these papers not as a vindication of standard deterministic theory but rather as a clarification of the logical conditions under which its results extend to stochastic environments.

Returning to normative issues, an important issue raised by the uncertainty literature but left unanswered by Helpman and Razin is how alternative policies can be ranked when free trade in equities is *not* allowed. David Newbery and Joe Stiglitz in Chapter 29 give an example where free trade may be Pareto-inferior to autarky if markets are incomplete. This result, along with the demonstration by Eaton and Grossman (1985) that tariffs may be justified as a means of providing insurance when markets are incomplete, suggests a presumption that uncertainty severely restricts the applicability of standard normative theory. However, these papers do not address the underlying reason for the lack of complete markets. Avinash Dixit shows in Chapter 30 that, if moral hazard is the source, then trade policy may not be able to improve on the market outcome given the *actual* range of instruments that is available. In related work (Dixit, 1989a and 1989b), he shows that similar considerations apply when markets are incomplete because outcomes can only be imperfectly observed or because of adverse selection. Taken together, these papers suggest that the existence of uncertainty *per se* does not justify abandoning the standard principles of normative international trade theory.

VI Real Foundations of International Macroeconomics

Part VI deals with topics which could just as easily be found in a volume of readings on international macroeconomics. However, they belong here because they examine ways in which the real side of the economy influences macroeconomic questions and because their results do not hinge on the existence of money or on the presence of nominal rigidities.

Chapter 31 by W.E.G. Salter presents a classic exposition of how internal and external balance (full employment and balance-of-payments equilibrium) are attained in a small open economy where some goods are non-traded. Salter uses standard tools of trade theory to show how equilibrium will be determined at what he calls the 'kissing-tangency point' between the production possibilities frontier and the highest attainable social indifference curve. He also notes that 'such an equilibrium is a rare and delicate creature' and he examines how exogenous shocks disturb it and how short-run rigidities influence the adjustment process. Models with non-traded goods have since been studied by many authors.[23] Chapter 32 by Rudiger Dornbusch gives an algebraic version of the same model and applies it to analyse the effects of a tariff on the relative and absolute prices of traded and non-traded goods. Chapter 33 by myself extends this approach to allow for many non-traded goods and shows that the model throws light on a number of different policy issues, including the effects of international transfers, cross-section deviations from purchasing power parity and the 'Dutch Disease' whereby a sectoral boom leads to a real appreciation which reduces the competitiveness of other traded sectors. (See also Corden and Neary (1982), van Wijnbergen (1984) and Neary and van Wijnbergen (1986).)

The traded–non-traded margin is one route whereby the structure of the real economy influences macroeconomic performance. Another is the margin between present and future consumption. Chapter 34 by Lars Svensson and Assaf Razin develops a tractable model of intertemporal choice in a small open economy. With perfect international mobility of financial capital, the current balance of payments deficit or surplus arises from rational intertemporal allocation of resources.[24] Svensson and Razin apply their model to consider the effects of changes in the terms of trade on the current account, and show how previous views on this question can be reconciled. Their framework has also been applied to other issues, including the effects of trade liberalization.[25] In this context, the model implies that a permanent tariff cut affects current and future prices equally and so should have no effect on private savings and the current account. However, Chapter 35 by Sweder van Wijnbergen notes that this prediction is inconsistent with the actual experience following recent episodes of trade liberalization. He resolves this conflict by developing a more general model which predicts that savings will fall (so worsening the current account) both because the trade liberalization is expected to be reversed and because it increases the degree of policy uncertainty. In doing so he provides an interesting application to trade policy of the non-expected-utility approach to decision-making under uncertainty.

Many other aspects of real trade models have been used to throw light on the links between the structure of the real economy and macroeconomic performance, often inspired by actual real-world developments.[26] The reverse chain of causation, from macro performance to the real structure of the economy, is illustrated in Chapter 36 by Paul Krugman. He constructs a model with dynamic returns to scale by grafting learning by doing onto the Ricardian model of Dornbusch, Fischer and Samuelson (Chapter 7 above). The model implies that patterns of specialization and trade are self-reinforcing and can be permanently affected by temporary shocks, whether real (such as infant-industry protection or resource discoveries) or monetary (such as an exchange rate appreciation caused by contractionary monetary policy).

VII Trade, Technology and Growth

The final part turns to issues of long-run growth and technical change in open economies. Early work in this area explored how the two-sector neoclassical growth model could be extended to open-economy contexts. (See, for example, Oniki and Uzawa (1965), Bardhan (1970), Findlay (1970), and Smith (1977). Chapter 37 by Ron Findlay is an example of a different tradition, dealing with 'North–South' models which explicitly model asymmetries between developed and less-developed countries.[27] He assumes that the developed 'North' enjoys full-employment growth in accordance with a standard Solow one-sector growth model; whereas the less-developed 'South' exhibits more Classical features: only profits are saved, and the wage rate is exogenous as in Lewis's model of 'unlimited supplies of labour'. Findlay shows how the terms of trade serve to equilibrate the model, ensuring that the growth rate of the South adjusts to equal the exogenously given long-run growth rate of the North.[28]

A different source of asymmetry between North and South is access to technology. Drawing on Vernon's (1966) suggestive analysis of the product cycle, Findlay (1978) and Krugman (1979) developed models of international technology transfer. However, they took the rates of innovation and technology transfer as given. Chapter 38 by Rob Feenstra and Ken Judd endogenizes the latter in a model of monopolistic competition and explores the implications for trade policy.[29]

Models of technology transfer throw light on how growth rates of different countries may converge. However, they cannot explain continued growth in per capita incomes unless technical progress is appended. Chapter 39 by Elhanan Helpman reviews the work of Romer (1986 and 1990) on endogenous growth and explores their implications for open economies.[30] He also shows that endogenizing research and development suggests how the pattern of trade may evolve in growing economies. This aspect is explored more formally in Chapter 40 by Gene Grossman and Elhanan Helpman. They construct a two-country model of trade and growth in which endogenous technological progress occurs in response to profit incentives, and generates an externality in the form of knowledge spillovers. Here, and in their other work (1991), they show that trade policies can interact with comparative advantage to influence the long-run rate of growth.

Concluding Remarks

In conclusion, the papers in this collection demonstrate the breadth of contemporary thinking on international trade theory. Forecasting future research topics is always hazardous, but it seems likely that the internal evolution of the subject will prompt continued research on such topics as the dynamic consistency of strategic trade policy, political economy, economic geography and endogenous growth; while real-world policy concerns will encourage work on such topics as trade and the environment, regional trading arrangements and anti-dumping measures. I hope that these readings will stimulate others to reconsider the legacy of the existing literature and to tackle the many problems which remain inadequately addressed.

Notes

1. References to texts, surveys and collections of readings are given in Part 0 of the bibliography to the introduction to Volume I.
2. Related papers include Mussa (1978), where an optimizing approach to factor reallocation, modelling adjustment costs explicitly, is examined; Neary (1982), which introduces transitional unemployment and discusses the implications for adjustment assistance; Grossman (1983), which allows for differential degrees of mobility by both capital and labour; and Barry (1987), which reinterprets the specific-factors model as predicting the response to unanticipated shocks whereas the Heckscher–Ohlin model predicts the response to anticipated shocks.
3. This case is argued at greater length in Jones and Neary (1984).
4. Ethier (1984) provides a definitive survey of this literature.
5. See Stolper and Samuelson (1941) and, for a fiftieth anniversary appreciation, Deardorff and Stern (1994).
6. For later developments along these lines, see Diewert and Woodland (1977), Jones and Scheinkman (1977) and Chang (1979). Alternative approaches to generalizing the core propositions of Heckscher–Ohlin theory have worked with aggregate variables (see Neary (1985)) or with correlations between variables (see the work by Deardorff and Dixit and Norman discussed in Part II.A).
7. See also the generalization of the law of comparative advantage to a classical constant-cost model with many goods and countries by Jones (1961).
8. For other applications and extensions of the continuum approach, see Wilson (1980), Krugman (1985 and Chapter 36 below) and Taylor (1993).
9. This approach was independently initiated by Dixit and Norman (1980, pp. 94–100). See also Helpman (1984) and Neary and Schweinberger (1986).
10. The difficulties of generalizing the Heckscher–Ohlin theorem to many commodities, even with only two factors, are illustrated by Jones (1956 and 1974), Melvin (1968), Bhagwati (1972) and Deardorff (1979).
11. For surveys of this area, see Helpman (1984) and Krugman (1987).
12. The positive properties of models with external returns to scale are considered by Jones (1968), Herberg and Kemp (1969), Mayer (1974) and Panagariya (1981). Policy aspects are explored by Ethier in Chapter 18 of Volume I.
13. The microeconomic underpinnings of such trade in intermediate goods are spelt out by Ethier (1982) in a model with monopolistically competitive producers.
14. For related work, see Krugman (1979), Dixit and Norman (1980, Chapter 9) and Lancaster (1980).
15. Syntheses along similar lines have been presented by Krugman (1981) and Helpman (1981). Krugman's model makes the interesting point that trade liberalization is more likely to be Pareto-improving the more it takes the form of intra-industry specialization. In his model, comparative advantage derives from international differences in the relative endowments of two industry-specific factors, whereas Helpman, like Lawrence and Spiller, adopts a standard two-by-two Heckscher–Ohlin specification. Unlike most of the other papers in this area, Helpman does not use the 'taste for diversity' specification of preferences due to Dixit and Stiglitz (1977). Instead, he develops an alternative approach, more akin to the work of Hotelling on spatial competition. Both approaches imply that aggregate demand is diversified and their implications for positive questions such as trade patterns are broadly similar. These issues are considered in detail in Helpman and Krugman (1985); see also Chapter 20 below.
16. See also Brander and Krugman (1983).
17. This suggests that the criticisms directed at trade theorists by de Marchi (1976) and Blaug (1980, Chapter 12) for sticking with the Heckscher–Ohlin model despite Leontief's findings seem unjustified. In any case, no alternative model is fully consistent with the evidence either. MacDougall's findings, which appeared consistent with the Ricardian theory, are criticized by Bhagwati (1964). See also Falvey (1981) and Neary (1985), who show that empirical tests may appear to confirm Ricardian predictions even if trade is actually determined by factor endowments.
18. Of course, the models considered so far can easily be adapted to examine the effects of *exogenous*

international factor movements. However, as argued in Neary and Ruane (1988), the effects of such movements are an unreliable guide to the implications of *endogenous* factor mobility.

19. Normative issues in models of this type are examined by Kemp (1966), Jones (1967), Grossman (1984) and Neary (1993); positive questions are considered in Neary (1985) and Ethier and Svensson (1986).

20. Factor flows in the specific-factors model are examined in more detail by Jones, Neary and Ruane (1983) and Neary (1995).

21. A deficiency of the Helpman–Markusen approach to modelling multinational corporations is that it predicts that trade and multinational investment are substitutes. Ethier (1986) explores a different approach to endogenizing the choice between national and multinational production which avoids this counterfactual prediction.

22. Melvin in Chapter 11 above also looks at international capital mobility and increasing returns, though assuming perfect competition and a Heckscher–Ohlin production structure.

23. The simple model with one traded and one non-traded good is sometimes called the 'Australian' model, since Salter was one of a number of Australian-based economists who developed similar ideas around the same time (e.g., Pearce (1961) and Swan (1963)). This model is further explored by Jones (1974) and Bruno (1976), while Komiya (1967) and Ethier (1972) consider the implications of adding a third, non-traded, sector, to the Heckscher–Ohlin model.

24. For a related approach, see Sachs (1981).

25. See, for example, Razin and Svensson (1983), Edwards and van Wijnbergen (1986) and Edwards (1989).

26. An example is the persistence of the US trade deficit following the dollar's fall from its 1985 high. In the event, the deficit declined sharply from 1988, but not before it had prompted an interesting literature, focusing on the failure of foreign exporters to pass-through exchange rate changes into import prices. Explanations proposed for this behaviour included monopolistic pricing (Dornbusch (1987)), habit persistence in consumption (Froot and Klemperer (1989)) and sunk costs (Baldwin (1988), Baldwin and Krugman (1989) and Dixit (1989)).

27. Dixit (Chapter 5 in Volume I) deals with similar issues in a static context.

28. For a review of related work, see Findlay (1984, Section 3).

29. Related models are presented by Dollar (1986, 1987), Flam and Helpman (1987) and Jensen and Thursby (1987). The strategic use of R&D and trade policies is considered by Spencer and Brander (1983) in an oligopoly model similar to those reviewed in Volume I, Part II.B.

30. See also Rivera-Batiz and Romer (1991) and Taylor (1994).

Further Reading

I Production Structure and Comparative Statics

Barry, F.G. (1987), 'Fiscal policy in a small open economy: An integration of the short-run, Heckscher–Ohlin and capital accumulation models', *Journal of International Economics*, **22**, 103–21.

Chang, W. (1979), 'Some theorems of trade and general equilibrium with many goods and factors', *Econometrica*, **47**, 709–26.

Deardorff, A. and R.M. Stern (eds) (1994), *The Stolper–Samuelson Theorem: A Golden Jubilee*, Ann Arbor: University of Michigan Press.

Diewert, E. and A.D. Woodland (1977), 'Frank Knight's theorem in linear programming revisited', *Econometrica*, **45**, 375–98.

Ethier, W.J. (1984), 'Higher dimensional issues in trade theory', in R.W. Jones and P.B. Kenen (eds), *Handbook of International Economics: Volume I International Trade*, Amsterdam: North-Holland, 131–84.

Flam, H. and M.J. Flanders (eds) (1991), *Heckscher–Ohlin Trade Theory*, Cambridge, Mass.: MIT Press.

Grossman, G.M. (1983), 'Partially mobile capital: A general approach to two-sector trade theory', *Journal of International Economics*, **15**, 1–17.

Heckscher, E. (1919), 'The effect of foreign trade on the distribution of income', *Ekonomisk Tidskrift*, **11**, 497–512; reprinted in Ellis and Metzler (1950) and in Flam and Flanders (1991).

Jones, R.W. and J.P. Neary (1984), 'The positive theory of international trade', in R.W. Jones and P.B. Kenen (eds), *Handbook of International Economics: Volume 1 International Trade*, Amsterdam: North-Holland, 1–62.

Jones, R.W. and J. Scheinkman (1977), 'The relevance of the two-sector production model in trade theory', *Journal of Political Economy*, **85**, 909–35.

Mayer, W. (1974), 'Short run and long run equilibrium for a small open economy', *Journal of Political Economy*, **88**, 941–57.

Mussa, M. (1974), 'Tariffs and the distribution of income: The importance of factor specificity, substitutability and intensity in the short and long run', *Journal of Political Economy*, **82**, 1191–203.

Mussa, M. (1978), 'Dynamic adjustment in the Heckscher–Ohlin–Samuelson model', *Journal of Political Economy*, **86**, 775–92.

Neary, J.P. (1982), 'Intersectoral capital mobility, wage stickiness and the case for adjustment assistance', in J.N. Bhagwati (ed.), *Import Competition and Response*, Chicago: Chicago University Press, 39–67.

Neary, J.P. (1985), 'Two-by-two international trade theory with many goods and factors', *Econometrica*, **53**, 1233–47.

Ohlin, B. (1933), *Interregional and International Trade*, Cambridge, Mass.: Harvard University Press.

Samuelson, P.A. (1948), 'International trade and the equalisation of factor prices', *Economic Journal*, **58**, 163–84.

Samuelson, P.A. (1949), 'International factor-price equalisation once again', *Economic Journal*, **59**, 181–97; reprinted in Caves and Johnson (1968) and Bhagwati (1987).

Samuelson, P.A. (1971), 'Ohlin was right', *Swedish Journal of Economics*, **73**, 365–84.

Stolper, W. and P.A. Samuelson (1941), 'Protection and real wages', *Review of Economic Studies*, **9**, 58–73; reprinted in Ellis and Metzler (1950) and Bhagwati (1969).

II Theories of International Trade

A TRADE BASED ON COMPARATIVE ADVANTAGE

Bhagwati, J.N. (1972), 'The Heckscher–Ohlin theorem in the multi-commodity case', *Journal of Political Economy*, **80**, 1052–5.

Deardorff, A.V. (1979), 'Weak links in the chain of comparative advantage', *Journal of International Economics*, **9**, 197–209; reprinted in Bhagwati (1981) and (1987).

Deardorff, A.V. (1982), 'The general validity of the Heckscher–Ohlin theorem', *American Economic Review*, **72**, 683–94.

Helpman, E. (1984), 'The factor content of foreign trade', *Economic Journal*, **94**, 84–94.

Jones, R.W. (1956), 'Factor proportions and the Heckscher–Ohlin theorem', *Review of Economic Studies*, **24**, 1–10.

Jones, R.W. (1961), 'Comparative advantage and the theory of tariffs: A multi-country, multi-commodity model', *Review of Economic Studies*, **28**, 161–75.

Jones, R.W. (1974), 'The small country in a many commodity world', *Australian Economic Papers*, **13**, 225–36.

Krugman, P.R. (1985), 'A "technology gap" model of international trade', in K. Jungenfelt and D. Hague (eds), *Structural Adjustment in Developed Open Economies*, Proceedings of IEA Conference, London: Macmillan, 35–61.

Melvin, J. (1968), 'Production and trade with two factors and three goods', *American Economic Review*, **58**, 1249–68.

Neary, J.P. and A.G. Schweinberger (1986), 'Factor content functions and the theory of international trade', *Review of Economic Studies*, **53**, 421–32.

Taylor, M.S. (1993), '"Quality ladders" and Ricardian trade', *Journal of International Economics*, **34**, 225–43.

Wilson, C. (1980), 'On the general structure of Ricardian models with a continuum of goods: Applications to growth, tariff theory and technical change', *Econometrica*, **48**, 1675–702.

B TRADE BASED ON INCREASING RETURNS

Dixit, A.K. and J.E. Stiglitz (1977), 'Monopolistic competition and optimum product diversity', *American Economic Review*, **67**, 297–308.

Ethier, W. (1982), 'National and international returns to scale in the theory of international trade', *American Economic Review*, **72**, 389–405; reprinted in Grossman (1992).

Helpman, E. (1981), 'International trade in the presence of product differentiation, economies of scale, and monopolistic competition: A Chamberlin–Heckscher–Ohlin model', *Journal of International Economics*, **11**, 305–40; reprinted in Grossman (1992).

Helpman, E. (1984), 'Increasing returns, imperfect markets and trade theory', in R.W. Jones and P.B. Kenen (eds), *Handbook of International Economics: Volume 1 International Trade*, Amsterdam: North-Holland, 325–65.

Herberg, H. and M.C. Kemp (1969), 'Some implications of variable returns to scale', *Canadian Journal of Economics*, **2**, 403–15.

Jones, R.W. (1968), 'Variable returns to scale in general equilibrium theory', *International Economic Review*, **9**, 261–72.

Krugman, P.R. (1979), 'Increasing returns, monopolistic competition and international trade', *Journal of International Economics*, **9**, 469–79; reprinted in Bhagwati (1987).

Krugman, P.R. (1981), 'Intraindustry specialization and the gains from trade', *Journal of Political Economy*, **89**, 959–73.

Krugman, P.R. (1987), 'Increasing returns and the theory of international trade', in T.F. Bewley (ed.), *Advances in Economic Theory: Fifth World Congress*, Cambridge: Cambridge University Press, 301–28.

Lancaster, K.J. (1980), 'Intraindustry trade under perfect monopolistic competition', *Journal of International Economics*, **10**, 151–75.

Mayer, W. (1974), 'Variable returns to scale in general equilibrium: A comment', *International Economic Review*, **15**, 225–35.

Panagariya, A. (1981), 'Variable returns to scale in production and patterns of specialization', *American Economic Review*, **71**, 221–30.

Spence, A.M. (1976), 'Product selection, fixed costs, and monopolistic competition', *Review of Economic Studies*, **43**, 217–36.

C TRADE BASED ON OLIGOPOLISTIC COMPETITION

Ben-Zvi, S. and E. Helpman (1992), 'Oligopoly in segmented markets', in G. Grossman (ed.), *Imperfect Competition and International Trade*, Cambridge, Mass.: MIT Press, 31–53.

Brander, J. and P. Krugman (1983), 'A "reciprocal dumping" model of international trade', *Journal of International Economics*, **15**, 313–21.

III Tests of Trade Theories

Baldwin, R.E. (1971), 'Determinants of the commodity structure of U.S. trade', *American Economic Review*, **61**, 126–46.

Bhagwati, J.N. (1964), 'The pure theory of international trade: A survey', *Economic Journal*, **74**, 1–84.

Blaug, M. (1980), *The Methodology of Economics, or How Economists Explain*, Cambridge: Cambridge University Press.

Deardorff, A.V. (1984), 'Testing trade theories and predicting trade flows', in R.W. Jones and

P.B. Kenen (eds), *Handbook of International Economics: Volume 1 International Trade*, Amsterdam: North-Holland, 467–517.

de Marchi, N. (1976), 'Anomaly and the development of economics: The case of the Leontief paradox', in S.J. Latsis (ed.), *Method and Appraisal in Economics*, Cambridge: Cambridge University Press. 109–27.

Falvey, R.E. (1981), 'Comparative advantage in a multi-factor world', *International Economic Review*, **22**, 401–13.

Grubel, H.G. and P.J. Lloyd (1975), *Intra-Industry Trade: The Theory and Measurement of International Trade in Differentiated Products*, London: Macmillan.

Leamer, E.E. (1984), *Sources of International Comparative Advantage: Theory and Evidence*, Cambridge, Mass.: MIT Press.

Leontief, W. (1954), 'Domestic production and foreign trade: The American capital position re-examined', *Economia Internazionale*, **7**, 3–32; reprinted (in part) in Caves and Johnson (1968) and Bhagwati (1969).

MacDougall, G.D.A. (1951), 'British and American exports: A study suggested by the theory of comparative costs, Part I', *Economic Journal*, **61**, 697–724; reprinted in Caves and Johnson (1968).

MacDougall, G.D.A. (1952), 'British and American exports: A study suggested by the theory of comparative costs, Part II', *Economic Journal*, **62**, 487–521.

Neary, J.P. (1985), 'The observational equivalence of the Ricardian and Heckscher–Ohlin explanations of trade patterns', *Oxford Economic Papers*, **37**, 142–7.

Trefler, D. (1993), 'International factor price differences: Leontief was right', *Journal of Political Economy*, **101**, 961–87.

IV International Factor Movements and Multinational Corporations

Ethier, W.J. (1986), 'The multinational firm', *Quarterly Journal of Economics*, **100**, 805–33; reprinted in Grossman (1992).

Ethier, W.J. and L.E.O. Svensson (1986), 'The theorems of international trade with factor mobility', *Journal of International Economics*, **20**, 21–42.

Grossman, G.M. (1984), 'The gains from international factor movements', *Journal of International Economics*, **17**, 73–83.

Helpman, E. (1984), 'A simple theory of international trade with multinational corporations', *Journal of Political Economy*, **92**, 451–71; reprinted in Bhagwati (1987) and Casson (1990).

Helpman, E. (1985), 'Multinational corporations and trade structure', *Review of Economic Studies*, **52**, 443–58; reprinted in Grossman (1992).

Horstmann, I. and J.R. Markusen (1987), 'Strategic investments and the development of multinationals' *International Economic Review*, **28**, 109–21; reprinted in Casson (1990).

Jones, R.W. (1967), 'International capital movements and the theory of tariffs and trade', *Quarterly Journal of Economics*, **81**, 1–38.

Jones, R.W., J.P. Neary and F.P. Ruane (1983), 'Two-way capital flows: Cross-hauling in a model of foreign investment', *Journal of International Economics*, **14**, 357–66.

Kemp, M.C. (1966), 'The gain from international trade and investment: A neo-Heckscher–Ohlin approach', *American Economic Review*, **66**, 788–809.

Krugman, P. (1991a), 'History versus expectations', *Quarterly Journal of Economics*, **106**, 651–67.

Krugman, P. (1991b), *Economic Geography*, Cambridge, Mass.: MIT Press.

Krugman, P. and A.J. Venables (1990), 'Integration and the competitiveness of peripheral industry' in C. Bliss and J. de Macedo (eds), *Unity with Diversity in the European Community*, Cambridge Cambridge University Press, 56–75..

Markusen, J.R. (1984), 'Multinationals, multi-plant economies and the gains from trade', *Journal of International Economics*, **16**, 205–26; reprinted in Bhagwati (1987).

Mundell, R.A. (1957), 'International trade and factor mobility', *American Economic Review*, **4'** 321–35; reprinted in Caves and Johnson (1968) and Bhagwati (1987).

Neary, J.P. (1985), 'International factor mobility, minimum wage rates and factor-price equalization: A synthesis', *Quarterly Journal of Economics*, **100**, 551–70.

Neary, J.P. (1993), 'Welfare effects of tariffs and investment taxes', in W.J. Ethier, E. Helpman and J.P. Neary (eds), *Theory, Policy and Dynamics in International Trade: Essays in Honor of Ronald W. Jones*, Cambridge: Cambridge University Press, 131–56.

Neary, J.P. (1995), 'Factor mobility and international trade', *Canadian Journal of Economics* (forthcoming).

Neary, J.P. and F.P. Ruane (1988), 'International factor mobility, shadow prices and the cost of protection', *International Economic Review*, **21**, 571–85.

Wong, K. (1986), 'Are international trade and factor mobility substitutes?', *Journal of International Economics*, **21**, 25–44; reprinted in Bhagwati (1987).

V Uncertainty

Dixit, A. (1989a), 'Trade and insurance with imperfectly observed outcomes', *Quarterly Journal of Economics*, **104**, 195–203.

Dixit, A. (1989b), 'Trade and insurance with adverse selection', *Review of Economic Studies*, **56**, 235–47.

Eaton, J. and G.M. Grossman (1985), 'Tariffs as insurance: Optimal commercial policy when domestic markets are incomplete', *Canadian Journal of Economics*, **18**, 258–72.

Helpman, E. and A. Razin (1978), *The Theory of International Trade under Uncertainty*, New York: Academic Press.

VI Real Foundations of International Macroeconomics

Baldwin, R. (1988), 'Hysteresis in import prices: The beachhead effect', *American Economic Review*, **78**, 773–85.

Baldwin, R. and P. Krugman (1989), 'Persistent trade effects of large exchange rate shocks', *Quarterly Journal of Economics*, **104**, 635–54.

Bruno, M. (1976), 'The two-sector open economy and the real exchange rate', *American Economic Review*, **66**, 566–77.

Corden, W.M. and J.P. Neary (1982), 'Booming sector and deindustrialisation in a small open economy', *Economic Journal*, **92**, 825–48.

Dixit, A. (1989), 'Hysteresis, import penetration and exchange rate pass-through', *Quarterly Journal of Economics*, **104**, 384–406.

Dornbusch, R. (1987), 'Exchange rates and prices', *American Economic Review*, **77**, 93–106.

Edwards, S. (1989), 'Tariffs, capital controls and equilibrium real exchange rates', *Canadian Journal of Economics*, **22**, 79–92.

Edwards, S. and S. van Wijnbergen (1986), 'The welfare effects of trade and capital market liberalisation', *International Economic Review*, **27**, 141–8.

Ethier, W. (1972), 'Non-traded goods and the Heckscher–Ohlin model', *International Economic Review*, **13**, 132–47.

Froot, K.A. and P.D. Klemperer (1989), 'Exchange rate pass-through when market share matters', *American Economic Review*, **79**, 637–54.

Jones, R.W. (1974), 'Trade with non traded goods: The anatomy of inter connected markets', *Economica*, **41**, 121–38.

Komiya, K. (1967), 'Non-traded goods and the pure theory of international trade', *International Economic Review*, **8**, 132–52.

Neary, J.P. and S. van Wijnbergen (eds) (1986), *Natural Resources and the Macroeconomy*, Oxford: Basil Blackwell and Cambridge, Mass.: MIT Press.

Pearce, I.F. (1961), 'The problem of the balance of payments', *International Economic Review*, **2**, 1–28.

Razin, A. and L.E.O. Svensson (1983), 'Trade taxes and the current account', *Economics Letters*, **13**, 55–7.

Sachs, J.D. (1981), 'The current account and macroeconomic adjustment in the 1970s', *Brookings Papers on Economic Activity*, **1**, 201–68.

Swan, T.W. (1963), 'Longer-run problems of the balance of payments', in H.W. Arndt and W.M. Corden (eds), *The Australian Economy: A Volume of Readings*, Melbourne: Cheshire Press, 384–95; reprinted in Caves and Johnson (1968).

van Wijnbergen, S. (1984), 'The Dutch Disease: A disease after all?', *Economic Journal*, **94**, 41–55.

VII Trade, Technology and Growth

Bardhan, P.K. (1970), *Economic Growth, Development and Foreign Trade*, New York: Wiley.

Dollar, D. (1986), 'Technological innovation, capital mobility, and the product cycle in North–South trade', *American Economic Review*, **76**, 177–90.

Dollar, D. (1987), 'Import quotas and the product cycle', *Quarterly Journal of Economics*, **102**, 615–32.

Findlay, R. (1970), 'Factor proportions and comparative advantage in the long run', *Journal of Political Economy*, **78**, 27–34; reprinted in Bhagwati (1981) and (1987).

Findlay, R. (1978), 'Relative backwardness, direct foreign investment and the transfer of technology: A simple dynamic model', *Quarterly Journal of Economics*, **92**, 1–16.

Findlay, R. (1984), 'Growth and development in trade models', in R.W. Jones and P.B. Kenen (eds), *Handbook of International Economics: Volume 1 International Trade*, Amsterdam: North-Holland, 185–236.

Flam, H. and E. Helpman (1987), 'Vertical product differentiation and North–South trade', *American Economic Review*, **77**, 810–22.

Grossman, G.M. and E. Helpman (1991), *Innovation and Growth in the World Economy*, Cambridge, Mass.: MIT Press.

Jensen, R. and M. Thursby (1987), 'A decision theoretic model of innovation, technology transfer and trade', *Review of Economic Studies*, **55**, 631–48.

Krugman, P. (1979), 'A model of innovation, technology transfer and the world distribution of income', *Journal of Political Economy*, **87**, 253–66.

Oniki, H. and H. Uzawa (1965), 'Patterns of trade and investment in a dynamic model of international trade', *Review of Economic Studies*, **32**, 15–38.

Rivera-Batiz, L.A. and P.M. Romer (1991), 'Economic integration and endogenous growth', *Quarterly Journal of Economics*, **106**, 531–55; reprinted in Grossman (1992).

Romer, P.M. (1986), 'Increasing returns and long-run growth', *Journal of Political Economy*, **94**, 1002–37.

Romer, P.M. (1990), 'Endogenous technological change', *Journal of Political Economy*, **98**, S71–S102.

Smith, M.A.M. (1977), 'Capital accumulation in the open two-sector economy', *Economic Journal*, **87**, 273–82; reprinted in Bhagwati (1981) and (1987).

Spencer, B.J. and J.A. Brander (1983), 'International R&D rivalry and industrial strategy', *Review of Economic Studies*, **50**, 707–22.

Taylor, M.S. (1994), '"Once-off" and continuing gains from trade', *Review of Economic Studies*, **61**, 589–601.

Vernon, R. (1966), 'International investment and international trade in the product cycle', *Quarterly Journal of Economics*, **80**, 190–207.

Part I
Production Structure and
Comparative Statics

[1]

Prices of Factors and Goods in General Equilibrium

INTRODUCTION

1. The effects on factor prices of free international trade in goods is now fairly well understood in the case of few goods and factors.[1] This paper attempts to sketch briefly the general case of any number of goods and factors. At the same time a gap in the modern English literature can be partially filled by a succinct summary of the Walrasian statical model of general equilibrium in its competitive aspects. Purely technical details are briefly noted in the Mathematical Appendix, and more difficult sections of the text that can be skipped without penalty are starred.

2. I assume that each of n goods $X_1, \ldots, X_n$ is produced within a given country or region as a given function of the inputs devoted to it. Throughout I make the simplifying assumption most appropriate for viable perfect competition—namely constant-returns-to-scale or homogeneous production functions of the first order ; under this strict assumption the composition of industry output among firms becomes indeterminate and of no importance, so that the factors can be thought of as hiring each other in a Darwinian process of ruthless natural selection which severely punishes any momentary deviation from the statical optimum. In the main text I limit myself to the classical case where outputs and inputs are distinct : actually, as is shown in the Mathematical Appendix, the *same results* would follow if I supposed, with Leontief and others, that each good requires in its production every *other good* as an input. Goods would then have a double function—as inputs as well as outputs, as inter-mediate as well as final goods. Moreover, the only way to characterise a " primary factor " in such a system would be by the fact that it cannot be produced and repro-duced by a homogeneous production function.

For simplicity, then, I sharply distinguish inputs from outputs, and write the region's totals of r factors of production as $V_1, \ldots, V_r$. Each such input, such as V_j, is allocated among the n different industries, and we let V_{ij} stand for the amount of the jth input used by the ith industry. We can now write down the production functions for each industry in the following equivalent forms :

$$X^i \left(\frac{V_{i1}}{X_i}, \ldots, \frac{V_{ir}}{X_i} \right) = 1 \qquad (i = 1, 2, \ldots, n) \ldots\ldots\ldots\ldots\ldots(1)$$

$$X_i = X^i (V_{i1}, \ldots, V_{ir}), \ldots\ldots\ldots\ldots\ldots\ldots\ldots\ldots\ldots\ldots\ldots\ldots(1)'$$

[1] See Heckscher, E., " The Effect of Foreign Trade on the Distribution of Income," *Ekonomisk Tidskrift*, Vol. XXI, 1919, pp. 497–512, reprinted in *Readings in the Theory of International Trade*, Blakiston, Philadelphia, 1949. Ohlin, B., *Interregional and International Trade*, Harvard University Press, Cambridge, 1935. Stolper, W. F., and Samuelson, P. A., " Protection and Real Wages," REVIEW OF ECONOMIC STUDIES, Vol. IX (November, 1941), pp. 58–73. Reprinted in *Readings in the Theory of International Trade*, Blakiston, Philadelphia, 1949. Samuelson, P. A., " International Trade and the Equalisation of Factor Prices," *Economic Journal*, Vol. LVIII, June, 1948, pp. 163–84. Samuelson, P. A., " International Factor-Price Equalisation Once Again," *Economic Journal*, Vol. LIX, June, 1949, pp. 181–97. Tinbergen, J., " The Equalisation of Factor Prices between Free Trade Areas," *Metroeconomica*, Vol. I, July, 1949, pp. 40–47. Meade, J. E., " The Equalisation of Factor Prices: The Two-Country Three-Product Case," *Metroeconomica*, Vol. II, December, 1950, pp. 129–33. James, S. F., and Pearce, I. F., " The Factor Price Equalisation Myth," THE REVIEW OF ECONOMIC STUDIES, Vol. XIX (2), No. 49, 1951–52, pp. 111–20. See also P. A. Samuelson, " A Comment on Factor Price Equalisation," ibid., pp. 121–22. A. P. Lerner, " Factor Prices and International Trade," *Economica*, Vol. XIX, No. 73, February, 1952, pp. 1–15. See also I. F. Pearce, " A Note on Mr. Lerner's Paper," ibid., pp. 16–8.

all homogeneous functions of the first order. It will be convenient to use the usual symbols for " coefficients of production " $a_{ij} = V_{ij}/X_i$, and the reader can think of these as the input requirements for one unit of output ; (1) completely summarises the production function since it gives us the shape of one equal-product contour, and simply by changing scale we can get any other production configuration.

Some typographical errors in Walras have led to considerable confusion concerning the equivalence of (1) and (1)', and there have been unwarranted adverse comparisons of his views with the rather confused views of Pareto relative to production and marginal productivity. I should mention explicitly that (1) makes no assumptions concerning the smoothness of the production surface : e.g. if $X^i =$ minimum of $(V_{i1}/\bar{a}_{i1} \ldots, V_{ir}/\bar{a}_{ir})$, we have the early-Walras, Wieser, Cassel, Leontief case of fixed-proportions and so-called constant coefficients of production, the $\bar{a}$'s being the technological constants—or, strictly speaking, the constants of minimum requirement, since we may have more of an input without physical penalty.

THE LAW OF DIMINISHING RETURNS

3. If the production functions are everywhere smooth, then marginal productivities can be defined in the usual manner as partial derivatives $\partial X_i/\partial V_{ij}$. In terms of these the usual law of diminishing returns may be stated : e.g. certain curvatures or second derivatives are negative, and the same must be true for certain combinations of such terms. In common-sense terms we are assuming :

> Successive equal increments of any input or of any composite dose of inputs must *never* give rise to increasing increments of final output.

Note that this is supposed to hold *from the very beginning* and not simply after a certain stage. Note, too, that certain composite dose changes—such as varying all factors together must result in *non-increasing* returns but may result in the border-line case of constant returns rather than in strictly decreasing returns.

*4. We may simply assume that this generalised law of diminishing returns is an observed empirical hypothesis or we may try to deduce it from another empirical hypothesis that may seem more immediately plausible.

> Alternative hypothesis : We can always *independently* carry on production in two separate processes and there will not be any necessary " external " inter-action between these processes that prevents us from getting as a total *the sum* of their separate outputs.

Like the assumption of constant-returns-to-scale this is an empirical hypothesis rather than a truism ; not only are both of these hypotheses conceptually refutable, but in addition there is considerable empirical evidence, in connection with technology and the breakdown of perfect competition, that in large realms of economic life these are poor hypotheses to make. Together, our hypotheses can be expressed :

$$X^i (V_{i1}' + V_{i1}'', \ldots, V_{ir}' + V_{ir}'') \geqq X^i (V_{i1}', \ldots, V_{ir}') + X^i (V_{i1}'', \ldots, V_{ir}''),$$

the equality sign necessarily holding if V_{ij}' and V_{ij}'' differ only in scale. This assures what the mathematician calls convexity of the production surface. In connection with some confusions in the literature between laws of diminishing *average* productivity and laws of diminishing *marginal* productivity, let me emphasise that this formulation definitely refers to the marginal version. But, because of the constant-returns-to-scale and no-over-saturation assumption, there is also implied diminishing average productivity to any composite dose that does not include *all* the really-productive inputs.

PRICES OF FACTORS AND GOODS 3

CONDITIONS OF EQUILIBRIUM FOR FACTOR ALLOCATION

5. If competition is perfect, and if factors are perfectly mobile between industries within a region, then equilibrium requires that the *value marginal productivity* of a factor (which is the good's price times $\partial X_i/\partial V_{ij}$) must be equal in every line where it is actually used, this common value being its market wage. Denoting commodity prices by $p_1, \ldots, p_n$ and factor prices by $w_1, \ldots, w_r$, we have as our conditions of equilibrium :

$$w_j \geqq p_i \partial X^i (a_{i1}, \ldots, a_{ir})/\partial V_{ij} \quad (i = 1, 2, \ldots, n) \text{ and } (j = 1, 2, \ldots, r) \ \ldots \ldots (2)$$

$$p_i \leqq a_{i1}w_1 + a_{i2}w_2 + \ldots + a_{ir}w_r \quad \ldots\ldots\ldots\ldots\ldots\ldots\ldots\ldots\ldots\ldots\ldots\ldots(2)'$$

Note that the inequality signs can be disregarded if every good is actually being produced and if every factor is actually being used by every industry. However, if a good is not being produced at all, its unit cost may exceed the market price ; hence, the inequality sign can hold in (2)′ only if $X_i = 0$. Similarly, the value marginal productivity of a factor may fall short of its market wage, but then it will not be used ; hence, the inequality sign in (2) can hold only where $V_{ij} = 0$. Note, too, that any marginal productivity is an intensive magnitude dependent only upon relative proportions and not upon extensive scale ; that is why we can denote it in terms of the a's rather than the V's, if we want to. Finally, note that (2)′, which says that price cannot exceed unit cost of production, cannot be regarded as an additional condition to all that have gone before. Actually, if (1) holds and if (2) everywhere holds, then (2)′ must assuredly hold and it is redundant to list it separately. Why ? Because the scale of assumptions about (1) implies the truth of Euler's theorem on homogeneous functions ; this in turn assures us that the separate value marginal products add up to exhaust all the revenue, so that (2)′ is already implied by all the marginal conditions of (2). Alternatively, we can for one last residual factor omit the marginal conditions of (2) and deduce from (2)′ what its " rent " must be, and then from Euler's theorem we would know what its marginal product must be. To put all this mathematically, for any i we can multiply each jth equality in (2) by a_{ij}, then sum them, and then from (1)'s Euler theorem deduce (2)′. It is to be emphasised that the inequalities in (2) and (2)′ will never vitiate this dependence ; if a factor is not used in an industry, we lose its equation in (2), but its a also becomes zero in (2)′, etc.

By themselves, equations (1) and (2) are incomplete and are clearly insufficient to determine the final position of general equilibrium. For one thing, (1) and (2) are purely intensive, never telling us anything at all about the extensive scales of any process. For another, we have said nothing about factor endowments or supply, and nothing about tastes with respect to goods and services. Even a rough count of the number of unknown X's, V's, a's, p's and w's will show : to get a determinate system we must adjoin, to the $n + nr$ independent conditions of (1) and (2), new relations—such as domestic demands for goods and supplies of factors, or international prices, etc. Depending upon what new relations we adjoin, we end up with different versions of general equilibrium or of international trade theory ; so we can consider various possibilities in turn.

FROM FACTOR PRICES TO COMMODITY PRICES : THE CLASSICAL CASE

6. Suppose we took the w's as somehow prescribed to us. Then it would be child's play to deduce what commodity prices must be. Certainly Adam Smith in Book I of the Wealth of Nations had proceeded this far and beyond, and every thinking man since antiquity must have had a roughly correct notion of the process. In the simplest

4   THE REVIEW OF ECONOMIC STUDIES

case where the a's are all constants, (2)' alone gives us the conditions for competitive prices. In the general case of continuous or discontinuous substitutability, the conditions of minimum costs of production, as embodied in (2) or in more general inequalities, serve to determine optimal sets of a's and from this the restriction on competitive prices follow.

We can note one peculiar feature of this unilateral determination of commodity prices from factor prices : doubling all factor prices cannot make any substantive change in best factor proportions and hence must exactly double the competitive costs of producing every good. This shows the homogeneity " dualism " between prices and quantities. Just as the scale of goods is left undetermined by (1) and (2), so, too, is scale of prices left a matter of indifference.

Now one interpretation of the classical writers is to assume that they had in mind a unilateral specification of factor prices or w's. These were supposed to come from broad margins of supply or " disutility " : e.g. the minimum of subsistence or comfort determining population growth of labour ; the effective interest rate at which people cease to save, etc. However, note that if you take the w's as given in money terms, there will result money p's. Therefore, the system itself will determine your " real w's," and it is surely these that even a classical writer would want to specify in advance rather than trivial monetary levels. But, without knowing technology, you simply *cannot* specify all real w's arbitrarily : the result may simply not be feasible or may be grossly conservative.

This was dimly realised by the classical writers and explains why they had to single out a resource such as land and treat it differently from the other factors. Instead of specifying a broad margin remuneration which land must earn, Malthus and the classicists would specify its total quantity as given by nature. (The varying *qualities* of land was an empirical and analytic red-herring that both helped and hindered the classical writers' basic understanding.) In this case you can hope to specify the real remuneration of all the remaining factors : if you prescribe a higher real wage than can ever be produced by any labour-land combination, you will end up with race-suicide and a depopulated island ; if your specified real w's are simultaneously feasible at some level, then the economic process is feasible and can be expected dynamically to grow up to the point where the real w's become exactly equal to their prescribed figures. At this point of stationary equilibrium, there is no reason why the w for land, generated by equations (1) and (2) and by the adjoined real w's for all non-land factors and the adjoined inelastic supply of land, should be zero. Generally, it will be positive and there will be a *well-determined residual rent* for land. It can be proved that all this will be as true in the cases of fixed proportions or discontinuous substitutability as it will be in the case of smooth marginal productivities ! Many, perhaps most, versions of the classical theory are logically faulty, often containing too many residuals so that the system is undetermined. But it is wrong to think that there is not a valid (albeit empirically bizarre) version of the classical system.

From the standpoint of interregional trade theory, a more realistic application of the unilateral theory of w's determining p's can be found. Imagine one small firm or region imbedded in a great world, and with factors mobile between the rest of the world. Then all w's will be given, presumably in actual money terms, to this firm or region and (1) and (2) show its determinate responses : if the p's are also given, the inequalities will determine the pattern of specialisations ; if p's are not given, the equalities show the possible p's at which production can take place. This is a partial equilibrium aspect of the more general equilibrium.

PRICES OF FACTORS AND GOODS   5

SMALLNESS OF INDUCED CHANGES IN METHODS

*7. Before leaving the effects of w's on p's, I must briefly call attention to a fairly remarkable phenomenon concerning substitution in the Walras-Clark marginal productivity set-up. If the coefficients of production a_{ij} were constants, as in Walras' first edition of the *Elements* in the 1870's, then it would be very easy to predict the effects on the p's of any given change in the w's. When the a's change with the w's, we would be tempted at first glance to think that a similar prediction as to the rate at which any w_i will be inducing change in each p_i would be very difficult ; we would suspect that the resulting price changes will depend upon the substitutions that changing w_j makes mandatory. This first thought would actually be wrong—because of a fairly remarkable " envelope theorem " of what I call, in *Foundations of Economic Analysis*, the Wong-Viner type.

*8. Let us plot the relation between any p_i and any change in w_j from some previous equilibrium configuration. We may make two such plots : the first holding the a's strictly constant as in the Walras-Wieser theory, and the second letting the a's vary in an optimal way so as to keep costs down to a minimum. These curves will, of course, give the same p_i at the equilibrium point prior to any change in w_j ; but elsewhere, it is obvious that the varying a's must give us lower unit costs and a lower curve ; hence, the two curves must touch but not cross, and must, therefore, be tangential with equal slopes $\partial p_i / \partial w_j$ at the equilibrium point. This tangency means that we can always infer from the observed a's what the effects of a given small change in w will be on the p's, treating the a's as if they were constants. The substitution effects are of a higher order of smallness, influencing curvatures rather than first-order slopes.[1]

FROM COMMODITY PRICES TO FACTOR PRICES : THREE CASES

9. Returning to the quest for new conditions to complete those of (1) and (2), we consider what happens when the p's are adjoined as arbitrary prescribed constants. To go from commodity prices to factor prices is much more difficult than to go from factor to commodity prices. We must now distinguish three cases : the number of goods (i) equal to, (ii) greater than, or (iii) less than the number of factors ; i.e. $n = r$, $n > r$, and $n < r$. Also we shall first assume that the prescribed p's are not such as to cause specialisation with production of some goods becoming zero, thereby vitiating some of (2)'s equalities.

Case (i) : *Equal Goods and Factors.* Together (1) and (2) represent $nr + n$ independent relations to determine the nr unknown a's plus the r unknown w's. With $n = r$ and with the p's given to us (say, by international markets), we can hope for a determinate system in which the a's and the factor prices, $w_1, \ldots, w_r$, are uniquely determined. Of course, it is not always enough to compare the number of our equations with the number of our unknowns : the *quality* of our equations as well as their quantity is important in determining whether the relevant schedules intersect at least once and only once.

Later in connection with the discussion of factor intensities, I shall specify in detail a set of conditions sufficient to achieve uniqueness, so no more need be said here concerning the nature of the equations. But it is to be noted that the equalisation of factor prices between countries as a result of free trade between them is implied by (1) and (2) and our assumptions. This is rather a remarkable phenomenon : without mentioning factor endowments of the country or the scale of production of any good, we have uniquely determined its factor prices from knowledge of its commodity

---

[1] See Section 3 of the Mathematical Appendix, and *Foundations*, p. 66.

6 THE REVIEW OF ECONOMIC STUDIES

prices alone. Thus, if two different countries have the same production functions, and if they do produce in common as many different goods as there are factors, and if the goods differ in their " factor intensities," and if there are no barriers to trade to produce commodity price differentials, then the absolute returns of every factor must be fully equalised !

Case (ii) : *More Goods than Factors*. What happens if we consider the case where $n > r$? Now (1) and (2) give us $n - r$ equations *in excess* of the number of our unknowns. The situation is apparently over-determined. We seem to be imposing more conditions than the data can adjust themselves to. Something must apparently give. If the commodity prices are truly given to us in a completely arbitrary manner, it can be demonstrated that the system will then show a wisdom in deciding what commodities should *cease to be produced altogether*! Thus, the unit costs of food might turn out always to be higher than the unit costs of clothing. If, none the less, we insist upon imposing equal prices for the two goods, then by the same reasoning involved in the Ricardian theory of comparative advantage it can be shown that competition will act so as to cause the more expensive commodity, food, to be not produced at all : the equality between the price of food and its domestic cost is now replaced by the inequality stating that for any good, price can be less than unit and marginal cost provided that it is not produced at all. In the case of each industry that shuts down, we, of course, lose as many marginal productivity conditions in (2) as there are zero inputs.

Generally speaking, therefore, we can expect that when more than r commodity prices are given to us perfectly arbitrarily, there will result complete specialisation in a number of industries, with the remaining number shut down completely. (Indeed, with the right factor intensities, it is possible for all but one industry to shut down completely.) However, if commodity prices are not given to us arbitrarily, but are determined by international trading between countries with the same production function as ours and with factor endowments not too different from ours, then there is a *presumption* that the international commodity prices will be such as to permit us to produce something of at least r different goods. If this should be true, then the reasoning of the previous section, where the number of goods and factors were equal, again permits us to infer complete equalisation of factor prices.

10. But with complete equalisation of factor prices here and abroad, an even stronger statement can be made : there is now no reason why in our own country we should not produce something of *every* good. What the final scales of production will be cannot, of course, be told until we say something about factor endowments. But a little reflection will suggest that whatever be the world endowment of factors, so long as factor prices have been everywhere equalised, and as long as the number of goods exceeds the number of factors, and as long as we strictly adhere to the assumption of zero transport costs—then there will be a considerable *zone of indifference* as to how production of different goods is allocated between different regions ; there are no longer *any* differences in comparative advantage, and to the extent that there exists more than one way to produce any desired world total of all goods, there will necessarily be an inessential indeterminacy of the production pattern. If we introduced ever-so-little transport costs, this indeterminacy might disappear.

11. We may summarise the case of more goods than factors by saying that an apparent over-determinacy in our equations and unknowns will resolve itself under competition by having certain industries shut down, taking with them the extra number of equations. On the other hand, if commodity prices are not given to us in a perfectly arbitrary fashion, but are determined elsewhere by cost of production, then the over-determinacy may resolve itself by virtue of the fact that the prices of

PRICES OF FACTORS AND GOODS 7

$n - r$ of the goods will already have adjusted themselves to the prices of any r goods. In this case, our country can be expected to produce at least r goods in common with the rest of the world and thus to achieve full factor price equalisation. Just how many goods we will produce in addition to these r goods cannot be determined without knowing our factor endowments. And at the world level there is an inessential indeterminacy of the exact geographical production pattern, since with equal factor prices everywhere there are no longer any differences in comparative advantage, and there will usually be $n - r$ degrees of freedom in the geographical pattern of any given world totals to be produced.[1]

Case (*iii*) : *More Factors than Goods*. When $n < r$, we have in some ways the most interesting analytical case. Factor prices then will usually *not* be equalised. In fact, at first glance, it would seem that our equations are less than our unknowns by at least $r - n$ so that the equilibrium is under-determined. But our intuition tells us that something determinate must actually happen in any economy that faces given international prices for all goods. Our difficulty is resolved by the fact that although equations (1) and (2) are not sufficient to determine all our unknowns, once we go on to add the equations relating to factor endowments, the situation will then determine itself.

We could write total factor endowments for a country as a function of all prices of goods and services ; but it will be simpler for the present purpose to consider the case where all such supply functions are completely *inelastic* so that $V_1, \ldots, V_r$ can be regarded completely as constants. Our new equations are :

$$\Sigma V_{ij} = a_{1j}X_1 + a_{2j}X_2 + \ldots + a_{nj}X_n = V_j, \qquad (j = 1, 2, \ldots, r) \ \ldots\ldots(3)$$

expressing the fact that all non-free factors must be fully employed. If a w_j becomes zero, we can replace the $=$ sign by $\leqslant$ in the jth equation.

With (3) we have added n X's as new variables, but we have also added r new equations ; so we have exactly $r - n$ surplus equations to make up for the $r - n$ deficiency of (1) and (2). Or to put the same thing in a different way : together (1), (2) and (3) are $n + nr + r$ independent relations to determine the $nr + r + n$ unknown a's, w's and X's. Hence, regardless of the relative magnitudes of n and r, the equilibrium would seem to be determinate once the p's are prescribed.

However, in the present case where $n < r$, the intensive relations of (1) and (2) do have to be taken *in conjunction* with the scale or extensive relations of (3), with this result : the equilibrium values of the w's will certainly depend upon the factor endowments or V's, so two differently-endowed regions can face the same international commodity prices and still end up with different factor prices. Within the same region as we add more of any one factor such as labour, even if the region is too small to affect world prices, we may now expect the corresponding factor price to fall. (This is in contrast to the case where $n = r$ and where an increase in any one factor does not depress its price so long as (1) commodity prices all remain unchanged and (2) all goods continue to be produced in some amount, with changes in the relative importance of the different industries providing the only needed substitutions : e.g. when $n = r$ and we add labour, the importance of labour-intensive goods increases and this absorbs all the increase in labour with no change in factor proportions within

[1] For those who like to think geometrically it can be said that our equations define a production-possibility or transformation locus $T(X_1, \ldots, X_n, V_1, \ldots V) = 0$, which tells us the maximum we can get of any good when all other goods and all inputs are prescribed. This locus has nice convexity properties and its partial derivatives are proportional to marginal cost-ratios and marginal productivities. Given a trading ratio from abroad, our country will be forced by competition into tangency between this locus and the trading plane. With $n > r$, there will necessarily be flat planes and straight lines on the convex locus; and as with Ricardo, there will not be a unique tangency when the international trading ratio is exactly equal to one of these constant-cost ratios.

any industry being at all needed, and consequently there will be no diminishing returns to labour within a broad range.)

This non-equalisation of factor prices when there are more inputs than outputs is intuitively reasonable : if more capital in America made both labour and land twice as productive in the food and clothing industries as in the corresponding industries in Europe, the same food-clothing price-ratio would prevail in the two regions but with a lower American interest rate and higher wage and rent level.

OVER- AND UNDER-DETERMINACY

12. Now that we have written down the combined system (1), (2) and (3), we are able to throw additional light on the indeterminacy and apparent over-determinacy that enters when $n > r$.

In this case consider only those equations of (1) and (2) that hold for r rather than the full n of the industries. Together these are seen to be $r + r^2$ equations in $r^2 + r$ a's and w's, so that this subset can be expected to determine itself. But with *all* factor prices having been determined in this subset, the unit cost of production of every one of the remaining goods is also determined. If the prices of these goods were really prescribed at random and in an arbitrary fashion, they can hardly be expected to equal these unit costs : hence, the equations of (1) and (2) are over-determined and inconsistent, having so to speak $n - r$ *negative degrees of freedom*. It is true that (3) seems to possess $n - r$ positive degrees of freedom ; but these *cannot* be used to cancel out the over-determinacy.

13. There are different possible escapes from this simultaneous over- and under-determinacy. The first escape applies when prices are prescribed from abroad completely arbitrarily. As in the Ricardian theory of comparative advantage, the competitive system will then abandon those goods whose unit costs of production exceed the world-prescribed price. Thus $n - r$ industries will shut down, taking with them the surplus $n - r$ equations of (2).

The reader may wonder what will happen if it should turn out that the price of some one of the remaining $n - r$ goods were to be *greater* than the unit costs of production as determined from the factor prices set in the r industry subset. The answer in that case must be that we picked in the first place the *wrong set* of r goods that will actually be produced. Again, the theory of comparative advantage (or more precisely what is to-day called the mathematical theory of " linear programming ") guarantees that the *best* r goods will always be produced—best in the sense of maximising the total value of national product $p_1 X_1 + \ldots + p_n X_n$. It will then follow that for the remaining $n - r$ goods which cannot be produced, the p's must all exceed the unit costs of production.

Note that this pattern of optimal specialisation, which succeeds in getting rid of the over-determinacy in (2) does at the same time also get rid of the under-determinacy of (3). This is because in (3) we must set equal to zero the $n - r$ X's corresponding to the shut-down industries, leaving us with r equations in the remaining r unknown X's.

A still different escape from the over-determinacy dilemma applies when from r of the prescribed prices, it turns out that we are able to predict correctly the other $n - r$ in conformity with calculated costs of production. If all p's could be thought of as being drawn from an urn at random, this agreement of prediction would be a very singular case indeed. But if our country is imbedded in a world rather like itself and not differing too much in factor proportions from itself, then this singular case is likely to be the rule rather than the exception. (This can be proved rigorously by considering the full international conditions of equilibrium when factor endowments are the same abroad and at home, and then by considering the same relations as we

PRICES OF FACTORS AND GOODS 9

let the factor endowments *gradually* differ from each other. Until they differ so much as to necessitate a pattern of world specialisation in which some industries in some country or countries shut down completely, the commodity prices of $n - r$ goods will be dependent upon those of r goods.)

In this singular case where $n - r$ p's are dependent upon r p's, our extra $n - r$ equations in (2) cease to be inconsistent and we are no longer plagued with over-determinacy. But this time in making our escape from over-determinacy, we have not at the same time been relieved of the concomitant indeterminacy of $n - r$ degrees of freedom in (3). But as Meade and our earlier literary discussion showed, this residual indeterminacy is intrinsic and should not disappear. For with factor prices equalised both here and abroad, we are now in the Ricardian case of strictly equal advantage, and so there is a broad zone of indifference as to the division of production between different regions. Within any country there is more than one configuration of X's that will maximise the value of the national product and also keep employment of all resources full at the well-determined equilibrium factor prices. While the division between different countries is indeterminate, the world-wide totals may be well-determined by the full conditions of equilibrium : only there are many different ways of reaching this same world-wide total.

FACTOR INTENSITIES AND STRICT DETERMINATENESS

14. I have now completed the survey of the interrelations between commodity and factor prices in the general case of any number of factors and goods. The results seem to depend in a very essential way upon the exact relation of n to r. The thoughtful reader will no doubt be somewhat worried by this result ; for after all, the number of commodities or of factors is not always such a definite thing. If we wished, we might call blue-eyed people different factors from brown-eyed ones and simply by reclassification make r go from less than to greater than n. Or we could call all autos with even-number serial listings a different good from those with odd-numbers, and thereby change the relation of n to r. Moreover, it is possible that Nature has already done one of the above things. From a production viewpoint two quite different commodities might turn out to have the same a's or to require the same proportions of inputs. Or two apparently different inputs might turn out to be perfect substitutes for each other in every line.

It is clear then that $n = r$ is not really enough to guarantee equalisation of factor prices ; and this was pointed out in some of my earlier papers. It was also shown that *differences in factor intensities of the different goods* was a crucial part of the rigorous proof in the two-input two-output case.

15. I must now examine carefully the *quality* as well as the quantity of the equilibrium equations to see if they do indeed determine a unique solution. This can be a delicate mathematical task, and I shall be content to give overly-strong sufficiency conditions for a unique equilibrium in the case of $n = r$, and where all production relations have smooth regular properties. The details of the proof may be omitted by the non-specialist and are relegated to the Mathematical Appendix, Section 3.

Theorem of Determinateness : If $n = r$, and if for all w's, we have a numbering of the goods and factors for which

$$a_{11} \neq 0, \quad \begin{vmatrix} a_{11} & a_{12} \\ a_{21} & a_{22} \end{vmatrix} \neq 0, \ldots, \quad \begin{vmatrix} a_{11} & \ldots & a_{1n} \\ & \cdot & \\ & \cdot & \\ a_{n1} & \ldots & a_{nn} \end{vmatrix} \neq 0,$$

then equations (1) and (2) have a unique solution for the w's in terms of the p's.

16. In the case of food and clothing and land and labour, this merely says that we should be able to recognise one of the goods as being always relatively labour-using and the other goods as being relatively land-using. In the case of many factors and goods the literary interpretation becomes more difficult, although in the very special case in which each factor had associated with it a single good in terms of which it was " especially important," an interpretation might be given.

It will be noted that the above conditions do rule out the case where more than one factor or more than one good are really exactly the same but hiding under different names. It also rules out more complicated cases of concealed identity between various bundles of goods or factors.

RECIPROCITY RELATIONS

*17. At this point also, two fairly interesting " reciprocity " or symmetry relations might be briefly indicated. First, there is the by-now standard case where increasing the amount of V_j, with X's and other V's held constant, will have *exactly the same effect* on w_k (as measured in any numeraire) as will a similar change in V_k have on the price of V_j, w_j. A similar relation holds between two X's or between a change in an input and an output. Thus, along any country's optimum production-possibility locus, inputs and outputs are unambiguously either substitutes or complements to each other.

*18. A less well-known reciprocity relation holds when we ask for the effects on X_i or on w_j of a given change in prescribed p's or in prescribed V's. Because our equilibrium situation can always be thought of as maximising national product or of minimising its " dual," national expense, we can derive the identities :

National Product = National Expense

$$= N(p_1, \ldots, p_n, V_1, \ldots, V_r)$$

$$X_i = \partial N(p_1, \ldots, V_r)/\partial p_i \qquad\qquad , (i = 1, 2, \ldots, n)$$

$$w_j = \partial N(p_1, \ldots, V_r)/\partial V_j \qquad\qquad , (j = 1, 2, \ldots, r)$$

and

$$\partial X_i/\partial p_k = N_{p_i p_k} = N_{p_k p_i} = \partial X_k/\partial p_i$$

$$\partial w_j/\partial V_k = N_{v_j v_k} = N_{v_k v_j} = \partial w_k/\partial V_j$$

$$\partial X_i/\partial V_j = N_{p_i v_j} = N_{v_j p_i} = \partial w_j/\partial p_i$$

The last of these states the conclusion : If an increase in a given factor such as land will cause a good like food to be increased in production within a country facing fixed international prices, then an increase in the relative price of food can be expected to raise the rent of that kind of land. The reader may give his own interpretation of the other relations.

FULL GENERAL EQUILIBRIUM

19. It is well now to drop the assumption of p's as being given and show how the p's as well as the V's are actually determined. Assuming that we deal with a " closed economy," we must now add to (1), (2) and (3) n new equations to help determine the n p's and r new equations to help determine the r V's. These new equations we get by aggregating the demands of all households for goods and by aggregating the supplies of all factors offered by households on the market-place. Within each family or household, there can be thought to go on a balancing and weighing of the ordinal desirability of different goods purchasable for the p's, and of different services saleable in the market-

PRICES OF FACTORS AND GOODS 11

place for the w's. We may take for granted the ordinal-utility-disutility or marginal-rates-of-substitution conditions that guarantee that the family is spending the money it earns from all the productive services it sells in the way most suited to its indifference curves—so that it no longer pays anyone to substitute butter for oil, strawberries for further work, and teaching for ditch-digging. The indifference contours between the X's and V's may in many cases have corners so that the generalised tangency conditions of maximum well-being may have to be expressed in terms of inequalities rather than marginal equalities. This is of no consequence : a well-determining set of inequalities plays the same logical role as a well-determining set of equalities.

20. Just as the family demands and supplies can be expressed in terms of all the p's and w's, so too can be their sum for the whole community—Veblenesque external consumption effects being ignored. And disregarding for every individual any possibility of saving for the future, so that his total consumption of X's equals in value his total provision of V's to the market, we can know in advance that a similar identity must hold for the totals in the market-place. It will simplify our task if we do not try to go behind the total demands and supplies in the market-place and concentrate simply on the well-determined totals. These can be written as the following functions :

$$X_i = D^i (p_1, \ldots, p_n, w_1, \ldots, w_r) \qquad (i = 1, 2, \ldots, n) \qquad \ldots\ldots\ldots(4a)$$
$$V_j = S^j (p_1, \ldots, p_n, w_1, \ldots, w_r) \qquad (j = 1, 2, \ldots, r) \qquad \ldots\ldots\ldots(4b)$$

where not all of these are independent functions, by virtue of the known identity (at all p's and w's) of earnings and expenditures, or $\Sigma p_i D^i = \Sigma w_j S^j$. Also, it is clear that changing all p's and w's in the same proportion will have no effects on any individual's choices and hence no effects on any of the totals : consequently the functions in (4) like those in (2) are homogeneous of the zeroth order in the p's and w's and our system can only be solved for relative values, or for p's and w's expressed in terms of any *numeraire* good whose price is by convention set equal to unity.

21. We are now in a position to make a final audit of our complete system. Equations (1) to (4) are equivalent in number to $n + nr + r + n + r - 1$. The minus one comes in because one of the equations in our system can be shown to be dependent on the rest and, therefore, redundant. This follows from the fact that each consumer and hence all consumers spend only what they earn, and because our assumption of constant-returns-to-scale in the production sphere does through Euler's theorem lead to the same equivalence. Thus, if we wish we can drop any one equation in either (4a) or (4b) and still predict what it would have told us from the rest of the equations. Walras (and Cournot before him in a special connection) noted this very important redundancy.

When we come to count the number of our unknowns—the a's, the w's, the p's, and the X's and V's—we find they are $nr + r + n + n + r$ in all: i.e. both a price and total quantity for each input or output and in addition the unknown best proportions in which the factors should be used.[1] This total is seen to be one greater than the total of our *independent* equations. But when we recall that all of our equations depend only on ratios of p's and w's, our perplexity and despair gives way to joy and wonder : we do have just as many independent equations as there are unknowns. (If we wish to make some non-homogeneous monetary assumption, such as $p_1 = 1$, or $w_r = 1$, or $\Sigma p_i X_i =$ some constant called MV or anything else, then we have an extra equation to determine all absolute prices rather than simply price ratios.)

[1] In his early work, Walras replaced the least-cost marginal conditions of (2) by the simpler conditions that all the a's are fixed constants. In the second edition of the late 1880's, he indicated that the a's are to be determined by least-cost conditions, and in the third and later editions he formally included the marginal conditions. Thus Walras ended up with all that is valid in the simplified marginal productivity theory of pricing.

LOCALISATION AND INTERNATIONAL TRADE

22. The time has come to consider explicitly the interrelations between two or more separate economies. There are a variety of ways by which we can split our system up into separate parts, with a geographical division being perhaps the most common. In accordance with the classical tradition, it is often said that we must assume that factors of production are (almost by definition of what we mean by an economic region or country) perfectly mobile within the country and perfectly immobile between countries. Especially in a world of nationalism (and where national boundaries have some correspondence with geographical discontinuities) there may be some small semblance of realism in this assumption. But few would deny that there is a great divergence in reality from such a strict assumption in real life, factors within a country are to an important degree immobile, and to some degree at least some factors are mobile between countries.

Fortunately most of the apparatus of international trade theory is *not* intimately dependent upon any special mobility assumptions. The same methods can be applied to an analysis of the trading relations and changes in well-being of groups within a country (such as men and women, Negroes and whites, or right-handed and left-handed people). One of the criticisms that might be made of traditional international trade theory is that it almost completely neglects the role of space as such, and that a separate theory of location has had to grow up parallel with it.

23. For the present purpose, one might introduce international trade by postulating a geographical location initially for all resources, along with certain data on the transport costs of moving each different good and resource between geographical points. The simplest preliminary assumptions along these lines is to make the transport cost of each resource infinite and of each good zero ; but there is no reason why we should not then go on to make more complex assumptions (such as domestic finished goods that are perfectly immobile, certain categories of factors that move freely, and specified transport costs or tariff barriers for a wide range of products).

In the simplest case where we break the world into two parts, each with arbitrary factor endowments not subject to change and each producing goods that move perfectly freely in international trade, our earlier analysis shows that within a considerable range of unequal geographical endowments, the configuration of equilibrium will be *exactly the same* as if there were no space problems : factor prices are the same everywhere, and world production is exactly the same as it would be if we were dealing with a single closed economy. All this follows under ideal conditions where the production functions are everywhere the same and where there are at least as many commodities produced in both regions as there are factors, the factor intensities of the commodities being quite different in comparison with the difference in factor endowments.

But if the factor endowments become very different, there will be substantive effects of location on pricing of the inputs and on production. One or both regions will begin to shut down certain industries completely, in accordance with comparative advantage as determined by all the conditions of technology and tastes. In effect we have doubled our problem : for each country a set of a's, X's, V's, p's and w's must be determined, taking into account the trading relations between the two countries.

24. In the simplest case, equations (1) describing technology apply to each country as before. For each country we have a set of relations like (2), but with each country's w's inserted ; with zero transport costs for X's, the same international p's may be inserted. For each country, we have a set of relations like those of (3), it being understood that the variables now relate to that country alone. Each country

PRICES OF FACTORS AND GOODS 13

has a set of demand and supply relations like that of (4a) and (4b), it being understood that the w's and other variables of that country enter into the functions.

But now it is no longer true that production and consumption of each good are equal within a country. If we continue to use X_i as the symbol for production, we must introduce a new symbol, C_i, to represent our new unknown consumption variable for any good in a particular country, and in equations (4a) it is the C's and not the X's that must be inserted. Of course we must somewhere find new equations to help us determine the new unknowns : these must come from the fact that for every good, the *world*'s physical total of production must just balance the world's physical total of consumption ; and from the fact that for every country, there must be a value balance between total exports and total imports—or what is the same thing, a value balance between the total value of consumption and the total value of domestic production (as measured from the $\Sigma p_i X_i$ or $\Sigma w_j V_j$ aspect).

I shall use a superscript in front of each symbol to typify country I, 2, . . ., k, . . ., m : thus we have such things as $^2a_{15}$, meaning by this the amount of the fifth input needed in the second country to produce a unit of the first good ; the reader can supply the meaning for $^2w_5$, $^ka_{ij}$, ^kX_i, ^kC_i, ^kV_j, ^kw_j, and finally p_i without a country designation. For each country we have nr unknown a's, $2r$ unknown factor amounts and prices, $2n$ unknown amounts of production and consumption of goods—or altogether $(nr + 2r + 2n) \times m$ unknowns. In addition there are n unknown world prices, it being understood that all p's can be thought of as ratios to the price of the *numeraire* good whose price is to be set equal to unity.

25. The independent equations sufficient to determine all of our unknowns may be briefly written down for each and every country :

$$X^i\,(^ka_{i_1}, \ldots, {}^ka_{ir}) = \mathrm{I} \qquad (i = \mathrm{I}, 2, \ldots, n) \text{ and } (k = \mathrm{I}, 2, \ldots, m) \quad ..(\mathrm{I})$$
$$^kw_j \gtreqless p_i X^i{}_j\,(^ka_{i_1}, \ldots, {}^ka_{ir}) \qquad (i = \mathrm{I}, 2, \ldots, n ; \; j = \mathrm{I}, 2, \ldots r) \text{ and}$$
$$(k = \mathrm{I}, 2, \ldots, m) \quad \ldots \ldots \ldots \ldots \ldots \ldots (2)$$
$$^ka_{1j}\,{}^kX_1 + \ldots + {}^ka_{nj}\,{}^kX_n \lesseqgtr {}^kV_j \qquad (j = \mathrm{I}, 2, \ldots, r) \text{ and } (k = \mathrm{I}, 2, \ldots, m) \quad \ldots (3)$$
$$^kC_i = {}^kD^i\,(p_1, \ldots, p_n, {}^kw_1, \ldots, {}^kw_r) \qquad (i = \mathrm{I}, 2, \ldots, n) \text{ and } (k = \mathrm{I}, 2, \ldots, m) \quad ..(\text{4a})$$
$$^kV_j = {}^kS^j\,(p_1, \ldots, p_n, {}^kw_1, \ldots, {}^kw_r) \qquad (j = \mathrm{I}, 2, \ldots, r \text{ and } k = \mathrm{I}, 2, \ldots, m) \ldots .(\text{4b})$$

For the world as a whole we may add the relations :

$$^1C_i + {}^2C_i + \ldots + {}^mC_i = {}^1X_i + {}^2X_i + \ldots + {}^mX_i \qquad (i = \mathrm{I}, 2, \ldots, n) \quad \ldots \ldots (5)$$

and also the balance of payments equations for each country :

$$p_1\,{}^kC_1 + \ldots + p_n\,{}^kC_n = p_1\,{}^kX_1 + \ldots + p_n\,{}^kX_n \qquad (k = \mathrm{I}, 2, \ldots, m) \ldots \ldots (6)$$

Now it is clear that for each country equations (4) are so arranged in relationship to the previous equations that equations (6) will be automatically satisfied ; hence these are dependent and redundant and may be omitted. (Incidentally, if each right-hand term in (6) is subtracted from the corresponding left-hand term, the result will show that the algebraic total of the values of all imports must be zero, which is the more familiar form in which balances of international trade are usually presented.)

Because all of our equations are homogeneous of order zero in all p's and w's, we can only hope to solve for price ratios ; and hence we may add the *numeraire* equation to pin down the representation of our system :

$$p_1 = \mathrm{I} \quad \ldots \ldots \ldots \ldots \ldots \ldots \ldots \ldots \ldots \ldots \ldots \ldots \ldots \ldots \ldots \ldots \ldots \ldots \ldots \ldots \ldots \ldots (7)$$

26. Let us now count our equations and unknowns. To determine our $(nr + 2n + 2r)\,(m) + n$ unknowns, we have in (1) to (5) $(n + nr + r + n + r)\,(m) + n$ equations. If we add (7) to this, we seem to have one too many equations. Alternatively, if we decide only to work with price ratios, we have one too few unknowns. Either

THE REVIEW OF ECONOMIC STUDIES

way we seem to be in trouble, facing an over-determined situation. The way out of the dilemma must by now be clear. Scrutiny of our system shows that if (1) to (5) holds, and if all but one of the commodities in (5) show a balance between total world production and consumption, then the remaining commodity cannot fail to be in balance. The interested reader may verify this in the general case or in the case of a few goods, factors and countries. With one of our equations dependent and redundant, our worries over the over-determinacy of the system are at an end.

27. Of course the quality as well as the quantity of our equations must be taken into account. It is for this reason that the inequality signs were included in (2) and (3). When comparative advantage or technology decree that the amount of some input is to be zero in some industry, we lose a marginal productivity equality, replacing it by the statement that the wage must not be less than the value of marginal productivity. Similarly, if supply and demand should cause a factor to become a free-good with zero w, we would no longer in (3) require more than that its sum in all uses should not exceed the total available. Within the production sphere we could perhaps rule out all indeterminacy if the production functions all had nice regular curvature properties, with every marginal productivity running the gamut from infinity to zero.

So long as we are no longer striving to prove the geographical equalisation of factor prices, it is no longer necessary to require that there be as many goods as factors, or that the goods differ in their factor intensities ; but if we do assume inelastic supplies of the factors and fixed coefficients of production, singular cases can arise in the production sphere where inelastic supplies may overlap with inelastic demands with a resulting indeterminacy of pricing. But contrary to what some of the older writers thought, the inequalities in our equations make it quite impossible that negative prices or negative production should ever result.

28. Our equations are not complete if we do not go beyond the production sphere. The demand-supply relations of (4) were shown by Walras and Marshall to be quite capable of intersection more than once, so that multiple equilibria are possible both in the domestic and international sphere. In terms of a rudimentary theory of dynamics, or the laws of motion that govern the way a system out of equilibrium behaves, we could distinguish between locally-stable and locally-unstable equilibrium points.

CONCLUSION

37. I need scarcely add the caution that the above description is of a very idealised, statical, competitive situation, where monetary considerations scarcely raise their ugly heads. Yet, both from the standpoint of insight into the nature of pricing and into the normative aspects of *laissez-faire* not here discussed, I think that this particular set of idealised assumptions has much to be said for it—not only for quasi-aesthetic reasons, but also for the light it casts on so many of the often-confused issues of economic theory.

Cambridge, Mass. PAUL A. SAMUELSON.

PRICES OF FACTORS AND GOODS 15

MATHEMATICAL APPENDIX

1. Equations (1) and (2) are conditions for minimum unit cost for each good. Omitting the i designation, we may write for a typical good :

Subject to $X(V_1, \ldots, V_r) = X$ or $X(a_1, \ldots, a_r) = 1$, and to given w's minimise $A = \Sigma w_j V_j / X = \Sigma w_j a_j$.

This minimum unit cost must depend uniquely on the w's and can be written $A = A(w_1, \ldots, w_r)$. Intuition assures us that this must be a continuous function of the w's ; also, since doubling all w's will make no substantive difference in methods, this must be a homogeneous function of order 1 of its variables, just as the production function is homogeneous in terms of its variables. A further dualism between the A and X functions is less intuitively obvious but nonetheless true : $A(w_1, \ldots, w_r)$ can be shown to be subject to the same " generalised law of diminishing returns " in terms of its variables as was described in the text with respect to the production functions. Indeed, it is easy to verify that the equilibrium correspondences between the w's and a's, which we may write as w_a or a_w, can be defined by the following dual-minimum problem to the above original one :

Subject to $A(w_1, \ldots, w_r) = A$, and given V's or a's, pick w's so as to minimise $\Sigma w_j V_j$ or $\Sigma w_j a_j$.

It can be shown that if the X contours are flat, as in the case of infinite substitutability where many alternative configurations are indifferent, then at the corresponding places on the A contours there will be corners ; and vice versa in a perfectly dual fashion. Nonetheless, regardless of lack of uniqueness or smoothness of the relations, for all observed optimum points, we always have $\Sigma \triangle w_j \triangle V_j \lessgtr 0$ and $\Sigma \triangle w_j \triangle a_j \lessgtr 0$. It can also be shown that at all points where the functions do not have the requisite smoothness to give a unique definition to partial derivatives such as $\partial a_k / \partial w_j$ or $\partial w_k / \partial a_j$, their ranges of indeterminacy are restricted to satisfy *reciprocity* relations that represent generalisations of the *integrability* conditions holding in the regular case.

In the case of a regular smooth interior minimum, to define $(V_1, \ldots, V_r, A)$ in terms of given $(w_1, \ldots, w_r, X)$ we have :

$$A \frac{\partial X(V_1, \ldots, V_r)}{\partial V_j} = w_j, \quad \begin{bmatrix} \partial V_k/\partial w_j & \partial V_k/\partial X \\ \partial A/\partial w_j & \partial A/\partial X \end{bmatrix} = \begin{bmatrix} A\partial^2 X/\partial V_k \partial V_j & \partial X/\partial V_k \\ \partial X/\partial V_j & 0 \end{bmatrix}^{-1} \quad (1.1)$$

$$X(V_1, \ldots, V_r) = X$$

where $(\partial V_k/\partial w_j)$ must be negative semi-definite and is seen to be symmetric. The dual relations defining $(w_1, \ldots, w_r, X)$ in terms of $(V_1, \ldots, V_r, A)$ are :

$$X \frac{\partial A(w_1, \ldots, w_r)}{\partial w_j} = V_j = X a_j, \quad \begin{bmatrix} \partial w_k/\partial V_j & \partial w_k/\partial A \\ \partial X/\partial V_j & \partial X/\partial A \end{bmatrix} = \begin{bmatrix} \partial V_k/\partial w_j & \partial V_k/\partial X \\ \partial A/\partial w_j & \partial A/\partial X \end{bmatrix}^{-1}$$

$$A(w_1, \ldots, w1) = A,$$

$$= \begin{bmatrix} X\partial^2 A/\partial w_k \partial w_j & \partial A/\partial w_k \\ \partial A/\partial w_j & 0 \end{bmatrix}^{-1} \quad \ldots\ldots\ldots\ldots (1.2)$$

where similar reciprocity and semi-definiteness conditions hold in the dual.

2. The Wong-Viner envelope type theorem, that the changes in production resulting from changes in factor prices are of a smaller order than are the direct changes in unit cost of production as of fixed a's, is already proved by (1.2), since this says that $\partial A/\partial w_j = a_j$. A general proof of the phenomenon in question is given in *Foundations*, p. 34, equation (32). To reinforce the above two proofs, calculate $\partial \Sigma w_k a_k/\partial w_j = a_j + \Sigma w_k \partial a_k/\partial w_j = a_j + \Sigma w_k \partial a_j/\partial w_k = a_j + 0$, where the last term is

seen to vanish by virtue of Euler's theorem applied to the homogeneous function of order *zero* representing a_i and where the reciprocity relations have been utilised.

3. We may use the above result to calculate the Jacobian matrix of goods prices expressed in terms of factor prices, as given in (2)'. Confining ourselves to goods actually produced, and restoring the industry superscripts, we can re-write (2)' :

$$p_i = A^i (w_1, \ldots, w_r) \text{ and } \left[\partial p_i / \partial w_j \right] = \left[a_{ij} \right], \ i = 1, 2, \ldots, n \gtreqless r \ \ldots \ldots (3.1)$$

The problem of special interest to us is the following : when $n = r$ and the goods p's are given to us and we have one resulting set of non-negative w's as a solution to (2)' or (3.1), under what conditions can we be sure that this solution is *unique* and that there exists *no other* factor price solution ?

The problem of uniqueness of solution is mathematically a delicate and rarely discussed one. In the case of $n = 2 = r$, the solution will be unique if one good is *always* more " intensive " in its use of one of the factors ; as shown in my 1949 *Economic Journal* discussion, p. 188, n. 1, if the goods should ever exchange their relative factor intensities, multiplicities of solutions *must* result. In that same discussion, I gave as a mathematical sufficiency condition for uniqueness that the Jacobian determinant of the equations to be inverted must not vanish. I am indebted to A. Turing, a mathematician friend of Professor Pigou, for pointing out that this statement was faulty and it has since been corrected in the literature. Actually, the non-vanishing Jacobian and the usual version of the Implicit Function Theorem does not guarantee uniqueness of solution *in the large*, but only that multiple solutions—if they occur—will be locally isolated. Fortunately, the economics of the situation was clearer than my mathematical analysis ; because all the elements of the Jacobian represented inputs or a's, they were essentially one-signed ; and this condition combined with the non-vanishing determinant, turns out to be sufficient to guarantee uniqueness in the large.

There appears to be a slight gap in the mathematical literature. What is needed is a slight extension of the Implicit Function Theorem that will suffice to guarantee uniqueness of solution in the large in the case of any number of implicit equations. From the nature of the case, no convenient *necessary* and sufficient conditions seem possible. But a convenient set of *sufficient* conditions can be inferred from the usual proofs of the usual Implicit Function Theorem. I presume the theorem that I am about to state is not a new result, but I have not been able to find a reference to it in the mathematical literature.

Theorem : If there exists some re-numbering of the p's and w's so that the n implicit and differentiable equations $p_i = A^i (w_1, \ldots, w_n)$ have successive principal minors that are non-vanishing *for all* w's :

$$D_1 = \left| \partial A^1 / \partial w_1 \right| \neq 0, \ D_2 = \begin{vmatrix} \partial A^1 / \partial w_1 & \partial A^1 / \partial w_2 \\ \partial A^2 / \partial w_1 & \partial A^2 / \partial w_2 \end{vmatrix} \neq 0, \ldots, D_n = \begin{vmatrix} \partial A^1 / \partial w_1 & \ldots & \partial A^1 / \partial w_n \\ \cdot & & \cdot \\ \cdot & & \cdot \\ \partial A^n / \partial w_1 & \ldots & \partial A^n / \partial w_n \end{vmatrix} \neq 0,$$

then there cannot be a second w solution for given p's.

The proof is by mathematical induction. The theorem is certainly true in the simplest case of $n = 1$, since every function possessing a one-signed derivative must always have a unique inverse. If the theorem holds for $n = k$, it is not hard to show that it must hold for $n = k + 1$. For we may always solve the first k of our $k + 1$ equations for the first k w's in terms of $(p_1, p_2, \ldots, p_k, w_{k+1})$. Then substituting

PRICES OF FACTORS AND GOODS   17

into the last equation and remembering that all the p's are known, we end up with a single implicit equation in w_{k+1} alone :

$$f(w_{k+1}) = 0, \text{ with } f'(w_{k+1}) = D_{k+1}/D_k \neq 0,$$

and hence with a *unique* solution. Thus, the proof by induction proceeds smoothly.

4. We may now investigate the consequences of dropping the assumption of no intermediate goods. With Leontief we may assume that every good may be needed in the production of every other good ; however, in contrast to the simpler versions of his system, we may entertain the possibility that there are more than one " primary " or non-reproducible-at-constant-returns factors ; as before, we shall assume $r \geq 1$ such primary inputs. As before we assume statical conditions so that none of the problems of capital and interest arise.

Some revisions of notation are desirable. As before $(X_1, \ldots, X_n)$ refer to *net* production of each of the goods actually available for consumption : since something of each good may be required as intermediate inputs used up in production of other goods, it is clear that the net output, X_i, of any industry will usually be less than the *gross* output, which we may call x_i, and which is what is actually given to us by the production function. To gain the advantages of the symmetrical Leontief notations, which treat inputs simply as if they were negative outputs, we may re-write what we have called $(V_1, \ldots, V_r)$ in terms of the new symbols $(-X_{n+1}, \ldots, -X_{n+r})$. Finally, our symbol for the amount of the jth good used in the production of the ith good is x_{ij}. To test his understanding of the new notation, the reader can verify that up until now we had been assuming that $x_{ij} = 0$ for $n \geq i$; also, that what we previously called a_{ij} would now be called $x_{i,\,n+j}/x_i$ and must not be confused with what we shall now define as a_{ij}, namely x_{ij}/x_i. We may now write down the production functions of any good in terms of *all* inputs, and then write down the amount of net product left over after subtraction of all used up intermediate goods.[1]

$$x_i = x^i(x_{i_1}, \ldots, x_{in}, \ldots, x_{i,\,n+r}), \quad (i=1,\ldots,n), \text{ with } x^i(a_{i_1}, \ldots, a_{in}, \ldots, a_{i,\,n+r})) = 1$$
$$= 0 = x_{ij} \qquad\qquad , \quad (i = n+1, \ldots, n+r) \text{ and any } j$$

$$X_i = x_i - x_{1i} - x_{2i} - \ldots - x_{ni}$$
$$= x^i(x_{i_1}, \ldots, x_{in}, \ldots x_{i,\,n+r}) - \overset{n}{\underset{1}{\Sigma}} x_{ji}. \quad\ldots\ldots\ldots\ldots\ldots\ldots\ldots\ldots\ldots\ldots (4.1)$$

Adhering to our previous assumptions concerning scale and diminishing returns, and re-writing what we called $(p_1, \ldots, p_n, w_1, \ldots, w_r)$ as $(p_1, \ldots, p_n, \ldots, p_{n+r})$, we may write down the same competitive equalities of marginal value product in every input use, previously given in (2) and (2'), in the new form :

$$p_i \frac{\partial x_i(a_{i_1}, \ldots, a_{in}, \ldots, a_{i,\,n+r})}{\partial x_{ij}} \leq p_j \ (i = 1, \ldots, n), (j = 1, \ldots, n, \ldots, n+r) \ \ldots (4.2)$$

$$p_i \leq A^i(p_1, \ldots, p_n, \ldots, p_{n+r}) = \overset{n+r}{\underset{1}{\Sigma}} a_{ij} p_i \ \ldots\ldots\ldots\ldots\ldots\ldots\ldots\ldots\ldots\ldots (4.2)'$$

As before, because of our homogeneous production functions, (4.2)' is redundant being implied by (4.1) and (4.2). The inequalities have the same interpretation as before. Note, too, that the minimum cost of production A^i of the ith good now depends upon *all* market p's, including probably its own p_i. Even if the a's were technological con-

---

[1] These equations represent a generalisation to any number of primary factors of the version of the Leontief system, admitting of substitutions, given in my Chapter VII of T. C. Koopmans (ed.), *Activity Analysis of Production and Allocation* (Wiley, New York, 1951). Note that C_i there is equivalent to X_i here and my functions x^i here are written as F_i there.

stants or already determined at their optimum levels, (4.2)' would involve a set of circular simultaneous equations for the p's. Only non-negative p's are admissible, and the invisible hand will guarantee that only that subset of goods will be produced which is compatible with non-negative prices. If there exists no such set—e.g. because every good requires more than one unit of itself in production, or indirectly requires so much of other goods and they in turn require so much of it that the same exceeding of unity and violation of the so-called Hawkins-Simon conditions results—then all production will shut down.

Actually, the marginal productivity conditions of (4.2) can be given two, separate but related, " optimising " interpretations : if we are given *all* p's arbitrarily and told to maximise $\Sigma p_j X_j$, where both algebraic goods and services are included, then (4.2) tells us what production methods are optimal ; of course, if the best methods will result in $\Sigma p_j X_j < 0$, all production will be zero ; if $\Sigma p_j X_j = 0$, then the final scale will be indeterminate until we fix one or more of the X's ; if $\Sigma p_j X_j > 0$, the best scale would grow indefinitely—until some X were given a finite limit or until some change in the arbitrarily prescribed p's were made.

A second optimising interpretation of the marginal productivity conditions is as follows : if we arbitrarily prescribe all but one X, some being prescribed at negative levels in accordance with their interpretation as primary inputs, then (4.2), with the right p's inserted as parameters or Lagrangean undertermined multipliers, represents a necessary and sufficient condition for the algebraic maximisation of the remaining X. For the case of $r = 1$, this was proved in *Activity Analysis* just cited, and the same reasoning holds for any r.

On the assumption that we can neglect the inequalities in (4.2), we can eliminate the Lagrangean prices, and write down the logical equivalent to (4.1) and (4.2) :

$$\frac{\partial x^1}{\partial x_{1i}} \frac{\partial x^i}{\partial x_{ij}} - \frac{\partial x^1}{\partial x_{ij}} = 0 \ (i = 2, \ldots, n) \text{ and } (j = 1, 2, \ldots, n, \ldots, n+r), \frac{\partial x^1}{\partial x_{11}} = 1. \quad \ldots (4.3)$$

These relations are all independent of scale and can be thought of as restrictions on the n $(n + r)$ a's. Clearly (4.3) involves $(n + r)$ $(n - 1) + 1$ restrictions, and the homogeneous production functions of (4.1) involve n more restrictions. After a little algebraic manipulation and comparison, we find that we have $(r - 1)$ more unknowns than we have restrictions. We cannot, therefore, expect (4.3) and (4.1) by themselves would determine all the unknown a's. Only in conjunction with some specified tastes or amounts of all but one of the X's will we find the missing $(r - 1)$ equations.

The Leontief case of a single primary factor can now be put in its proper perspective. The essence of the " substitutability theorem " for the Leontief system boils down in the regular smooth case to this : for $r = 1$ and $r - 1 = 0$, we can hope from the marginal conditions of social efficiency alone to deduce a unique configuration of productive methods, independently of the final specified bill-of-goods items X_i. (See *Activity Analysis*, Chapters VII, VIII, IX, X.)

When $r = 0$, we have the earlier Leontief " closed " economy with no primary factors. Here $r - 1 = -1$, and we seem to have *negative* degrees of freedom in (4.1) and (4.3). This corresponds to an *over-determined* situation, where there are more equations than unknown a's. The only way out of this dilemma—as Leontief has already indicated in the case of fixed a's—is to assume that the technological relations are *not* arbitrarily independent. On the contrary, (1) if *all* goods and services are readily reproducible out of each other, and (2) if only a finite bill of goods is to be producible out of a finite initial supply of goods and services so that stationary equilibrium is possible, then the different x^i functions must be such as to yield, for a sub-set of X's set equal to zero, at most zero *net* outputs of the other goods. This

PRICES OF FACTORS AND GOODS   19

imposes a strong restriction on the rank of the Jacobian of our implicit equations for the a's. (Cf. W. Leontief, *Structure of the American Economy* (New York, 1951), 2nd edition, for the corresponding vanishing of the determinant of Leontief's closed-system a's.) In summary, for $r = 0$, we are saved from over-determinacy by the singularity and linear dependencies that must exist between the separate equations for a's, by virtue of the assumption of the possibility of a stationary equilibrium. Incidentally, as Leontief has indicated, the resulting system is completely undetermined with respect to scale—unless or until we bring in an open-end non-homogeneous element, such as population size or Engel's laws of tastes that do *not* show unitary income elasticities for all X's.

For $r > 1$, we have a striking confirmation that the inter-industry circular whirlpools do not in any way affect the conclusions of my main text. As an example, consider the remarkable " flatnesses " of the social transformation function that must hold when there are more goods than factors, as discussed in the footnote of Section 11. Why are we never permitted to name arbitrarily the costs of production of n goods when $n > r$? This would involve our setting $n - 1$ ratios of costs or prices arbitrarily, and if a new unique configuration of a's and w's (or remaining p's) were to correspond to these $n - 1$ arbitrary parameters, we would find ourselves with more than $r - 1$ degrees of freedom—by virtue of the postulate, $n > r$. This contradicts our count of the maximum number of degrees of freedom, which is $r - 1$.[1]

5. Aside from the counting of equations and unknowns, there is another and more basic way of seeing that there are but $r - 1$ degrees of freedom possible in any general equilibrium system. (Conceptually, therefore, we might hope to determine the maximum number of primary factors in any observed systems.) Independently of all smoothness and derivatives of the production functions, we can assert the following :

Theorem : If $(p_{n+1}, \ldots, p_{n+r})$ are all given, then subject to the relations,

$$p_i = \sum_1^{n+r} a_{ij} p_j \qquad\qquad (i = 1, 2, \ldots, n)$$

$$x^i (a_{i_1}, \ldots, a_{in}, \ldots, a_{i,\, n+r}) = 1.$$

there exists one or more sets of best a's that will give a minimum cost $p_k = A^k$ of any one specified k good ; this minimum cost can be written as a continuous function $A^k (p_{n+1}, \ldots, p_{n+r})$, homogeneous of the first order and subject to the " generalised law of diminishing returns." Furthermore, a set of all the a's that minimises unit costs of one good will also minimise the cost of *each* other good. Where unique partial derivatives happen to be defined, Wong-Viner considerations require :

$$\left[\partial A^i / \partial p_{n+j} \right] = \begin{bmatrix} 1-a_{11} & -a_{12} \cdots & -a_{1n} \\ -a_{21} & 1-a_{22} \cdots & -a_{2n} \\ \cdot & \cdot & \cdot \\ -a_{n1} & -a_{n2} \cdots & 1-a_{nn} \end{bmatrix}^{-1} \begin{bmatrix} a_{1,\,n+1} \cdots a_{1,\,n+r} \\ \cdot & \cdot \\ a_{n,\,n+1} \cdots a_{n,\,n+r} \end{bmatrix} \quad ..(5.1)$$

which will be the product of two non-negative matrices, and its rank can never exceed r.

---

[1] The *actual* number may be less than this maximum number if special linear dependencies occur between the marginal productivities and a's. For example, suppose all goods had had *identical* production functions. Then instead of there being $r - 1$ degrees of freedom, there would turn out to be only 1 : all factors could in this singular case be grouped into a single composite " dose " of factors, giving us a Ricardo-Marx one-factor world.

It follows that if $n > r$, we cannot specify $n - 1$ price or cost ratios arbitrarily and expect all the goods to be produced and relative factor prices to be determinable by inverting the resulting equations. If $n = r$, it *may* be possible to infer a unique set of factor prices from a given set of goods, prices and costs ; sufficient conditions would be the existence of a numbering of goods and factors for which the leading principal minors of $\left[\partial A^i / \partial p_{n+j} \right]$ are all positive, exactly as in the case without inter-industry dependencies.

Most generally, we might imagine that some factors move freely in international trade and some goods do not. Out of the total of $n + r$ goods and services, we shall not expect absolute price equalisation between regions on the basis of less than half of $n + r$ prices being equalised by trade ; if *half or more* such prices are equalised by trade, the remaining ones will also be equalised provided that certain " constant-intensity " principal minors can be found.

6. The reader can also for the case of inter-industry dependencies derive all the dual relations and reciprocity relations discussed earlier. Also, he can verify that (3) becomes :

$$\sum_1^n x_i a_{ij} = x_j - X_j \qquad\qquad j = 1, 2, \ldots, n$$

$$\sum_1^n x_i a_{i,\,n+j} = 0 - X_{n+j} \qquad j = 1, 2, \ldots, r \quad \ldots\ldots\ldots\ldots\ldots(5.2)$$

and that all the relations of (1) through (3), can be summed up in a transformation or efficiency locus :

$$T (X_1, \ldots, X_n, \ldots, X_{n+r}) = 0, \text{ with } p_i \text{ proportional to } \partial T / \partial X_i$$

and with scale being of no importance, and generalised diminishing returns holding. For any set of p's being given and quantities of the remaining variables being given, there will be a maximum value for $\Sigma p X$, where the summation is over the prescribed p's. This maximum value can be written as $V (p ; X)$ where it is understood that no good ever has both its p and X specified. V is a continuous and homogeneous function of the first order in the p variables alone and in the X variables alone. The vector $\partial V / \partial p$ is proportional to the X's and $\partial V / \partial X$ is proportional to the corresponding p's. Just as the X's maximise V as of the production relations and given p's, the p's minimise V as of given X's and competitive price relations—so here is the case of a minimax or saddlepoint, with all the implied duals of linear programming theory. Moreover, associated with this V is a similar expression $\Sigma p X$ where the summation now is over the indices *not* contained in the previous definition of V ; V plus the new complementary V always add up to a constant.

7. Still other analogies can be found with the duality and saddlepoint theorem of the type met with in the fields of linear programming and games theory.

THE JOURNAL OF
POLITICAL ECONOMY

| *Volume LXXIII* | DECEMBER 1965 | *Number 6* |

THE STRUCTURE OF SIMPLE GENERAL EQUILIBRIUM MODELS[1]

RONALD W. JONES
University of Rochester

I. INTRODUCTION

IT IS difficult to find any major branch of applied economics that has not made some use of the simple general equilibrium model of production. For years this model has served as the workhorse for most of the developments in the pure theory of international trade. It has been used to study the effects of taxation on the distribution of income and the impact of technological change on the composition of outputs and the structure of prices. Perhaps the most prominent of its recent uses is to be found in the neoclassical theory of economic growth.

Such intensive use of the simple two-sector model of production suggests that a few properties are being retranslated in such diverse areas as public finance, international trade, and economic growth. The unity provided by a com-

mon theoretical structure is further emphasized by the dual relationship that exists between sets of variables in the model itself. Traditional formulations of the model tend to obscure this feature. My purpose in this article is to analyze the structure of the simple competitive model of production in a manner designed to highlight both the dual relationship and the similarity that exists among a number of traditional problems in comparative statics and economic growth.

The model is described in Sections II and III. In Section IV I discuss the dual nature of two theorems in the theory of international trade associated with the names of Stolper and Samuelson on the one hand and Rybczynski on the other. A simple demand relationship is added in Section V, and a problem in public finance is analyzed—the effect of excise subsidies or taxes on relative commodity and factor prices. The static model of production is then reinterpreted as a neoclassical model of economic growth by letting one of the outputs serve as the capital good. The dual of the "incidence" problem in public finance in the static

[1] I am indebted to the National Science Foundation for support of this research in 1962–64. I have benefited from discussions with Hugh Rose, Robert Fogel, Rudolph Penner, and Emmanuel Drandakis. My greatest debt is to Akihiro Amano, whose dissertation, *Neo-Classical Models of International Trade and Economic Growth* (Rochester, N.Y.: University of Rochester, 1963), was a stimulus to my own work.

model is shown to have direct relevance to the problem of the stability of the balanced growth path in the neoclassical growth model. In the concluding section of the paper I show how these results can be applied to the analysis of technological progress. Any improvement in technology or in the quality of factors of production can be simply viewed as a composite of two effects, which I shall term the "differential industry" effect and the "differential factor" effect. Each effect has its counterpart in the dual problems discussed in the earlier part of the paper.

II. THE MODEL

Assume a perfectly competitive economy in which firms (indefinite in number) maximize profits, which are driven to the zero level in equilibrium. Consistent with this, technology in each of two sectors exhibits constant returns to scale. Two primary factors, labor (L) and land (T), are used in producing two distinct commodities, manufactured goods (M) and food (F). Wages (w) and rents (r) denote the returns earned by the factors for use of services, whereas p_M and p_F denote the competitive market prices of the two commodities.

If technology is given and factor endowments and commodity prices are treated as parameters, the model serves to determine eight unknowns: the level of commodity outputs (two), the factor allocations to each industry (four), and factor prices (two). The equations of the model could be given by the production functions (two), the requirement that each factor receive the value of its marginal product (four), and that each factor be fully employed (two). This is the format most frequently used in the theory of international trade and the neoclassical theory of growth.[2] I consider,

instead, the formulation of the model suggested by activity analysis.

The technology is described by the columns of the A matrix,

$$A = \begin{pmatrix} a_{LM} & a_{LF} \\ a_{TM} & a_{TF} \end{pmatrix},$$

where a_{ij} denotes the quantity of factor i required to produce a unit of commodity j. With constant returns to scale total factor demands are given by the product of the a's and the levels of output. The requirement that both factors be fully employed is thus given by equations (1) and (2). Similarly, unit costs of production in each industry are given by the columns of A multiplied by the factor prices. In a competitive equilibrium with both goods being produced, these unit costs must reflect market prices, as in equations (3) and (4).[3] This formula-

$$a_{LM}M + a_{LF}F = L, \qquad (1)$$

$$a_{TM}M + a_{TF}F = T, \qquad (2)$$

$$a_{LM}w + a_{TM}r = p_M, \qquad (3)$$

$$a_{LF}w + a_{TF}r = p_F, \qquad (4)$$

tion serves to emphasize the dual relationship between factor endowments and commodity outputs on the one hand

[2] As an example in each field see Murray C. Kemp, *The Pure Theory of International Trade* (Englewood Cliffs, N.J.: Prentice-Hall, Inc., 1964), pp. 10–11; and J. E. Meade, *A Neo-Classical Theory of Economic Growth* (London: Allen & Unwin, 1961), pp. 84–86.

[3] These basic relationships are usually presented as inequalities to allow for the existence of resource(s) in excess supply even at a zero price or for the possibility that losses would be incurred in certain industries if production were positive. I assume throughout that resources are fully employed, and production at zero profits with positive factor and commodity prices is possible. For a discussion of the inequalities, see, for example, R. Dorfman, Paul A. Samuelson, and Robert M. Solow, *Linear Programming and Economic Analysis* (New York: McGraw-Hill Book Co., 1958), chap. xiii; or J. R. Hicks, "Linear Theory," *Economic Journal*, December, 1960.

SIMPLE GENERAL EQUILIBRIUM MODELS 559

(equations [1] and [2]) and commodity prices and factor prices on the other (equations [3] and [4]).

In the general case of variable coefficients the relationships shown in equations (1)–(4) must be supplemented by four additional relationships determining the input coefficients. These are provided by the requirement that in a competitive equilibrium each a_{ij} depends solely upon the ratio of factor prices.

III. THE EQUATIONS OF CHANGE

The comparative statics properties of the model described in Section II are developed by considering the effect of a change in the parameters on the unknowns of the problem. With unchanged technology the parameters are the factor endowments (L and T) and the commodity prices (p_M and p_F), the right-hand side of equations (1)–(4).

Let an asterisk indicate the relative change in a variable or parameter. Thus p_F^* denotes dp_F/p_F and L^* denotes dL/L.[4] The four equations in the rates of change are shown in (1.1) through (4.1):

$$\lambda_{LM}M^* + \lambda_{LF}F^* \quad (1.1)$$
$$= L^* - [\lambda_{LM}a_{LM}^* + \lambda_{LF}a_{LF}^*],$$

$$\lambda_{TM}M^* + \lambda_{TF}F^* \quad (2.1)$$
$$= T^* - [\lambda_{TM}a_{TM}^* + \lambda_{TF}a_{TF}^*],$$

$$\theta_{LM}w^* + \theta_{TM}r^* \quad (3.1)$$
$$= p_M^* - [\theta_{LM}a_{LM}^* + \theta_{TM}a_{TM}^*],$$

$$\theta_{LF}w^* + \theta_{TF}r^* \quad (4.1)$$
$$= p_F^* - [\theta_{LF}a_{LF}^* + \theta_{TF}a_{TF}^*].$$

The λ's and θ's are the transforms of the a's that appear when relative changes are shown. A fraction of the labor force is

used in manufacturing (λ_{LM}), and this plus the fraction of the labor force used in food production (λ_{LF}) must add to unity by the full-employment assumption (shown by equation [1]). Similarly for λ_{TM} and λ_{TF}. The θ's, by contrast, refer to the factor shares in each industry. Thus θ_{LM}, labor's share in manufacturing, is given by $a_{LM} w/p_M$. By the zero profit conditions, θ_{Lj} and θ_{Tj} must add to unity.

In this section I assume that manufacturing is labor-intensive. It follows that labor's share in manufacturing must be greater than labor's share in food, and that the percentage of the labor force used in manufacturing must exceed the percentage of total land that is used in manufacturing. Let λ and θ be the notations for the matrices of coefficients shown in ([1.1], [2.1]) and ([3.1], [4.1]).

$$\lambda = \begin{pmatrix} \lambda_{LM} \lambda_{LF} \\ \lambda_{TM} \lambda_{TF} \end{pmatrix}, \qquad \theta = \begin{pmatrix} \theta_{LM} \theta_{TM} \\ \theta_{LF} \theta_{TF} \end{pmatrix}.$$

Since each row sum in λ and θ is unity, the determinants $|\lambda|$ and $|\theta|$ are given by

$$|\lambda| = \lambda_{LM} - \lambda_{TM},$$
$$|\theta| = \theta_{LM} - \theta_{LF},$$

and both $|\lambda|$ and $|\theta|$ are positive by the factor-intensity assumption.[5]

If coefficients of production are fixed, equations (1.1)–(4.1) are greatly simpli-

---

[4] This is the procedure used by Meade, *op. cit.* The λ and θ notation has been used by Amano, *op. cit.* Expressing small changes in relative or percentage terms is a natural procedure when technology exhibits constant returns to scale.

[5] Let P and W represent the diagonal matrices,

$$\begin{pmatrix} p_M & 0 \\ 0 & p_F \end{pmatrix} \quad \text{and} \quad \begin{pmatrix} w & 0 \\ 0 & r \end{pmatrix},$$

respectively, and E and X represent the diagonal matrices of factor endowments and commodity outputs. Then $\lambda = E^{-1}AX$ and $\theta = P^{-1}A'W$. Since $|A| > 0$ and the determinants of the four diagonal matrices are all positive, $|\lambda|$ and $|\theta|$ must be positive. This relation among the signs of $|\lambda|$, $|\theta|$, and $|A|$ is proved by Amano, *op. cit.*, and Akira Takayama, "On a Two-Sector Model of Economic Growth: A Comparative Statics Analysis," *Review of Economic Studies*, June, 1963.

fied as every a_{ij}^* and, therefore, the λ and θ weighted sums of the a_{ij}^*'s reduce to zero. In the case of variable coefficients, sufficient extra conditions to determine the a^*'s are easily derived. Consider, first, the maximizing role of the typical competitive entrepreneur. For any given level of output he attempts to minimize costs; that is he minimizes unit costs. In the manufacturing industry these are given by $(a_{LM}\ w + a_{TM}r)$. The entrepreneur treats factor prices as fixed, and varies the a's so as to set the derivative of costs equal to zero. Dividing by p_M and expressing changes in relative terms leads to equation (6). Equation (7) shows the corresponding relationship for the food industry.

$$\theta_{LM}a_{LM}^* + \theta_{TM}a_{TM}^* = 0, \qquad (6)$$

$$\theta_{LF}a_{LF}^* + \theta_{TF}a_{TF}^* = 0. \qquad (7)$$

With no technological change, alterations in factor proportions must balance out such that the θ-weighted average of the changes in input coefficients in each industry is zero.

This implies directly that the relationship between changes in factor prices and changes in commodity prices is *identical* in the variable and fixed coefficients cases, an example of the Wong-Viner envelope theorem. With costs per unit of output being minimized, the change in costs resulting from a small change in factor prices is the same whether or not factor proportions are altered. The saving in cost from such alterations is a second-order small.[6]

A similar kind of argument definitely does *not* apply to the λ-weighted average of the a^*'s for each factor that appears in

[6] For another example of the Wong-Viner theorem, for changes in real income along a transformation schedule, see Ronald W. Jones, "Stability Conditions in International Trade: A General Equilibrium Analysis," *International Economic Review*, May, 1961.

the factor market-clearing relationships. For example, $(\lambda_{LM}a_{LM}^* + \lambda_{LF}a_{LF}^*)$ shows the percentage change in the total quantity of labor required by the economy as a result of changing factor proportions in each industry at unchanged outputs. The crucial feature here is that if factor prices change, factor proportions alter in the same direction in both industries. The extent of this change obviously depends upon the elasticities of substitution between factors in each industry. In a competitive equilibrium (and with the internal tangencies implicit in earlier assumptions), the slope of the isoquant in each industry is equal to the ratio of factor prices. Therefore the elasticities of substitution can be defined as in (8) and (9):

$$\sigma_M = \frac{a_{TM}^* - a_{LM}^*}{w^* - r^*}, \qquad (8)$$

$$\sigma_F = \frac{a_{TF}^* - a_{LF}^*}{w^* - r^*}. \qquad (9)$$

Together with (6) and (7) a subset of four equations relating the a^*'s to the change in the relative factor prices is obtained. They can be solved in pairs; for example (6) and (8) yield solutions for the a^*'s of the M industry. In general,

$$a_{Lj}^* = -\theta_{Tj}\sigma_j(w^* - r^*); \qquad j = M, F.$$

$$a_{Tj}^* = \theta_{Lj}\sigma_j(w^* - r^*); \qquad j = M, F.$$

These solutions for the a^*'s can then be substituted into equations (1.1)–(4.1) to obtain

$$\lambda_{LM}M^* + \lambda_{LF}F^* = L^* + \delta_L(w^* - r^*), \qquad (1.2)$$

$$\lambda_{TM}M^* + \lambda_{TF}F^* = T^* - \delta_T(w^* - r^*), \qquad (2.2)$$

$$\theta_{LM}w^* + \theta_{TM}r^* = p_M^*, \qquad (3.2)$$

$$\theta_{LF}w^* + \theta_{TF}r^* = p_F^*, \qquad (4.2)$$

where $\delta_L = \lambda_{LM}\theta_{TM}\sigma_M + \lambda_{LF}\theta_{TF}\sigma_F$,

$\delta_T = \lambda_{TM}\theta_{LM}\sigma_M + \lambda_{TF}\theta_{LF}\sigma_F$.

In the fixed-coefficients case, δ_L and δ_T are zero. In general, δ_L is the aggregate percentage saving in labor inputs at unchanged outputs associated with a 1 per cent rise in the relative wage rate, the saving resulting from the adjustment to less labor-intensive techniques in both industries as relative wages rise.

The structure of the production model with variable coefficients is exhibited in equations (1.2)–(4.2). The latter pair states that factor prices are dependent only upon commodity prices, which is the factor-price equalization theorem.[7] If commodity prices are unchanged, factor prices are constant and equations (1.2) and (2.2) state that changes in commodity outputs are linked to changes in factor endowments via the λ matrix in precisely the same way as θ links factor price changes to commodity price changes. This is the basic duality feature of the production model.[8]

IV. THE MAGNIFICATION EFFECT

The nature of the link provided by λ or θ is revealed by examining the solutions for M^* and F^* at constant commodity prices in (1.2) and (2.2) and for w^* and r^* in equations (3.2) and (4.2).[9] If both endowments expand at the same rate, both commodity outputs expand at identical rates. But if factor endowments

expand at different rates, the commodity intensive in the use of the fastest growing factor expands at a greater rate than either factor, and the other commodity grows (if at all) at a slower rate than either factor. For example, suppose labor expands more rapidly than land. With M labor-intensive,

$$M^* > L^* > T^* > F^* .$$

This *magnification effect* of factor endowments on commodity outputs at unchanged commodity prices is also a feature of the dual link between commodity and factor prices. In the absence of technological change or excise taxes or subsidies, if the price of M grows more rapidly than the price of F,

$$w^* > p_M^* > p_F^* > r^* .$$

Turned the other way around, the source of the magnification effect is easy to detect. For example, since the relative change in the price of either commodity is a positive weighted average of factor price changes, it must be bounded by these changes. Similarly, if input coefficients are fixed (as a consequence of assuming constant factor and commodity prices), any disparity in the growth of outputs is reduced when considering the consequent changes in the economy's demand for factors. The reason, of course, is that each good requires both factors of production.

Two special cases have been especially significant in the theory of international trade. Suppose the endowment of only one factor (say labor) rises. With L^* positive and T^* zero, M^* exceeds L^* and F^* is negative. This is the Rybczynski theorem in the theory of international

---

[7] Factor endowments come into their own in influencing factor prices if complete specialization is allowed (or if the number of factors exceeds the number of commodities). See Samuelson, "Prices of Factors and Goods in General Equilibrium," *Review of Economic Studies*, Vol. XXI, No. 1 (1953-54), for a detailed discussion of this issue.

[8] The reciprocal relationship between the effect of a rise in the price of commodity i on the return to factor j and the effect of an increase in the endowment of factor j on the output of commodity i is discussed briefly by Samuelson. *ibid*.

[9] The solutions, of course, are given by the elements of λ^{-1} and θ^{-1}. If M is labor-intensive, the diagonal elements of λ^{-1} and θ^{-1} are positive and exceed unity, while off-diagonal elements are negative.

562   RONALD W. JONES

trade: At unchanged commodity prices an expansion in one factor results in an absolute decline in the commodity intensive in the use of the other factor.[10] Its dual underlies the Stolper-Samuelson tariff theorem.[11] Suppose p_F^* is zero (for example, F could be taken as numeraire). Then an increase in the price of M (brought about, say, by a tariff on imports of M) raises the return to the factor used intensively in M by an even greater relative amount (and lowers the return to the other factor). In the case illustrated, the *real* return to labor has unambiguously risen.

For some purposes it is convenient to consider a slight variation of the Stolper-Samuelson theorem. Let p_j stand for the *market* price of j as before, but introduce a set of domestic excise taxes or subsidies so that $s_j p_j$ represents the price received by producers in industry j; s_j is one plus the ad valorem rate of subsidy to the industry.[12] The effect of an imposition of subsidies on factor prices is given in equations (3.3) and (4.3):

$$\theta_{LM} w^* + \theta_{TM} r^* = p_M^* + s_M^*, \quad (3.3)$$

$$\theta_{LF} w^* + \theta_{TF} r^* = p_F^* + s_F^*. \quad (4.3)$$

At fixed commodity prices, what impact

[10] T. M. Rybczynski, "Factor Endowments and Relative Commodity Prices," *Economica*, November, 1955. See also Jones, "Factor Proportions and the Heckscher-Ohlin Theorem," *Review of Economic Studies*, October, 1956.

[11] W. F. Stolper and P. A. Samuelson, "Protection and Real Wages," *Review of Economic Studies*, November, 1941. A graphical analysis of the dual relationship between the Rybczynski theorem and the Stolper-Samuelson theorem is presented in Jones, "Duality in International Trade: A Geometrical Note," *Canadian Journal of Economics and Political Science*, August, 1965.

[12] I restrict the discussion to the case of excise subsidies because of the resemblance it bears to some aspects of technological change, which I discuss later. In the case of taxes, $s_j = 1/(1 + t_j)$ where t_j represents the ad valorem rate of excise tax.

does a set of subsidies have on factor prices? The answer is that all the subsidies are "shifted backward" to affect returns to factors in a *magnified* fashion. Thus, if M is labor-intensive and if the M industry should be especially favored by the subsidy,

$$w^* > s_M^* > s_F^* > r^*.$$

The *magnification* effect in this problem and its dual reflects the basic structure of the model with fixed commodity prices. However, if a demand relationship is introduced, prices are determined within the model and can be expected to adjust to a change in factor endowments or, in the dual problem, to a change in excise subsidies (or taxes). In the next section I discuss the feedback effect of these induced price changes on the composition of output and relative factor prices. The crucial question to be considered concerns the extent to which commodity price changes can dampen the initial magnification effects that are produced at constant prices.

V. THE EXTENDED MODEL: DEMAND ENDOGENOUS

To close the production model I assume that community taste patterns are homothetic and ignore any differences between the taste patterns of laborers and landlords. Thus the ratio of the quantities consumed of M and F depends only upon the relative commodity price ratio, as in equation (5).

$$\frac{M}{F} = f\left(\frac{p_M}{p_F}\right). \quad (5)$$

In terms of the rates of change, (5.1) serves to define the elasticity of substitution between the two commodities on the demand side, σ_D.

$$(M^* - F^*) = -\sigma_D(p_M^* - p_F^*). \quad (5.1)$$

The effect of a change in factor endowments at constant commodity prices was considered in the previous section. With the model closed by the demand relationship, commodity prices adjust so as to clear the commodity markets. Equation (5.1) shows directly the change in the ratio of outputs consumed. Subtracting (2.2) from (1.2) yields the change in the ratio of outputs produced.

$$(M^* - F^*) = \frac{1}{|\lambda|}(L^* - T^*)$$
$$+ \frac{(\delta_L + \delta_T)}{|\lambda|}(w^* - r^*).$$

The change in the factor price ratio (with no subsidies or taxes) is given by

$$(w^* - r^*) = \frac{1}{|\theta|}(p_M^* - p_F^*),$$

so that, by substitution,

$$(M^* - F^*) = \frac{1}{|\lambda|}(L^* - T^*)$$
$$+ \sigma_S(p_M^* - p_F^*),$$

where

$$\sigma_S = \frac{1}{|\lambda||\theta|}(\delta_L + \delta_T).$$

σ_S represents the elasticity of substitution between commodities on the *supply* side (along the transformation schedule).[13] The change in the commodity price ratio is then given by the mutual interaction of demand and supply:

$$(p_M^* - p_F^*)$$
$$= -\frac{1}{|\lambda|(\sigma_S + \sigma_D)}(L^* - T^*). \quad (10)$$

Therefore the resulting change in the ratio of commodities produced is

$$(M^* - F^*)$$
$$= \frac{1}{|\lambda|} \cdot \frac{\sigma_D}{\sigma_S + \sigma_D}(L^* - T^*). \quad (11)$$

With commodity prices adjusting to the initial output changes brought about by the change in factor endowments, the composition of outputs may, in the end, not change by as much, relatively, as the factor endowments. This clearly depends upon whether the "elasticity" expression, $\sigma_D/(\sigma_S + \sigma_D)$, is smaller than the "factor-intensity" expression, $|\lambda|$. Although it is *large* values of σ_S (and the underlying elasticities of factor substitution in each industry, σ_M and σ_F) that serve to dampen the spread of outputs, it is *small* values of σ_D that accomplish the same end. This comparison between elasticities on the demand and supply side is familiar to students of public finance concerned with questions of tax (or subsidy) incidence and shifting. I turn now to this problem.

The relationship between the change in factor prices and subsidies is given by (3.3) and (4.3). Solving for the change in the ratio of factor prices,

$$(w^* - r^*)$$
$$= \frac{1}{|\theta|}\{(p_M^* - p_F^*) + (s_M^* - s_F^*)\}. \quad (12)$$

Consider factor endowments to be fixed. Any change in factor prices will nonethe-

---

[13] I have bypassed the solution for M^* and F^* separately given from (1.2) and (2.2). After substituting for the factor price ratio in terms of the commodity price ratio the expression for M^* could be written as

$$M^* = \frac{1}{|\lambda|}[\lambda_{TF}L^* - \lambda_{LF}T^*]$$
$$+ e_M(p_M^* - p_F^*),$$

where, e_M, the shorthand expression for $1/|\lambda||\theta|$ ($\lambda_{TF}\delta_L + \lambda_{LF}\delta_T$), shows the percentage change in M that would be associated with a 1 per cent rise in M's relative price along a given transformation schedule. It is a "general equilibrium" elasticity of supply, as discussed in Jones, "Stability Conditions . . . ," *op. cit.* It is readily seen that $\sigma_S = e_M + e_F$. Furthermore, $\theta_M e_M = \theta_F e_F$, where θ_M and θ_F denote the share of each good in the national income.

less induce a readjustment of commodity outputs. On the supply side,

$$(M^* - F^*)$$
$$= \sigma_S\{(p_M^* - p_F^*) + (s_M^* - s_F^*)\}.$$

The relative commodity price change that equates supply and demand is

$$(p_M^* - p_F^*) = -\frac{\sigma_S}{\sigma_S + \sigma_D}(s_M^* - s_F^*). \quad (13)$$

Substituting back into the expression for the change in the factor price ratio yields

$$(w^* - r^*)$$
$$= \frac{1}{|\theta|} \cdot \frac{\sigma_D}{\sigma_S + \sigma_D}(s_M^* - s_F^*). \quad (14)$$

This is a familiar result. Suppose M is subsidized more heavily than F. Part of the subsidy is shifted backward, affecting relatively favorably the factor used intensively in the M-industry (labor). Whether labor's relative return expands by a greater proportion than the spread in subsidies depends upon how much of the subsidy has been passed forward to consumers in the form of a relatively lower price for M. And this, of course, depends upon the relative sizes of σ_S and σ_D.

Notice the similarity between expressions (11) and (14). Factors produce commodities, and a change in endowments must result in an altered composition of production, by a magnified amount at unchanged prices. By analogy, subsidies "produce" returns to factors, and a change in the pattern of subsidies alters the distribution of income. In each case, of course, the extent of readjustment required is eased if commodity prices change, by a factor depending upon the relative sizes of demand and supply elasticities of substitution.

VI. THE AGGREGATE ELASTICITY OF SUBSTITUTION

The analysis of a change in factor endowments leading up to equation (11) has a direct bearing on a recent issue in the neoclassical theory of economic growth. Before describing this issue it is useful to introduce yet another elasticity concept—that of an economy-wide elasticity of substitution between factors.[14] With no subsidies, the relationship between the change in the factor price ratio and the change in endowments can be derived from (10). Thus,

$$(w^* - r^*)$$
$$= -\frac{1}{|\lambda||\theta|(\sigma_S + \sigma_D)}(L^* - T^*). \quad (15)$$

By analogy with the elasticity of substitution in a particular sector, define σ as the percentage rise in the land/labor endowment ratio required to raise the wage/rent ratio by 1 per cent. Directly from (15),

$$\sigma = |\lambda||\theta|(\sigma_S + \sigma_D).$$

But recall that σ_S is itself a composite of the two elasticities of substitution in each industry, σ_M and σ_F. Thus σ can be expressed in terms of the three *primary* elasticities of substitution in this model:

$$\sigma = Q_M\sigma_M + Q_F\sigma_F + Q_D\sigma_D,$$
$$\text{where } Q_M = \theta_{LM}\lambda_{TM} + \theta_{TM}\lambda_{LM},$$
$$Q_F = \theta_{LF}\lambda_{TF} + \theta_{TF}\lambda_{LF},$$
$$Q_D = |\lambda| \cdot |\theta|.$$

Note that σ is not just a linear expression in σ_M, σ_F, and σ_D—it is a weighted

[14] For previous uses see Amano, "Determinants of Comparative Costs: A Theoretical Approach," *Oxford Economic Papers*, November, 1964; and E. Drandakis, "Factor Substitution in the Two-Sector Growth Model," *Review of Economic Studies*, October, 1963.

average of these three elasticities as $\Sigma Q_i = 1$. Note also that σ can be positive even if the elasticity of substitution in each industry is zero, for it incorporates the effect of intercommodity substitution by consumers as well as direct intracommodity substitution between factors.

Finally, introduce the concept, σ, into expression (11) for output changes:

$$(M^* - F^*) = \frac{|\theta|\,\sigma_D}{\sigma}(L^* - T^*), \quad (11')$$

and into expression (14) for the change in factor prices in the subsidy case:

$$(w^* - r^*) = \frac{|\lambda|\,\sigma_D}{\sigma}(s^*_M - s^*_F). \quad (14')$$

One consequence is immediately apparent: If the elasticity of substitution between commodities on the part of consumers is no greater than the over-all elasticity of substitution between factors, the *magnification* effects discussed in Section IV are more than compensated for by the damping effect of price changes.

VII. CONVERGENCE TO
BALANCED GROWTH

The two-sector model of production described in Sections I–VI can be used to analyze the process of economic growth. Already I have spoken of increases in factor endowments and the consequent "growth" of outputs. But a more satisfactory growth model would allow for the growth of at least one factor of production to be determined by the system rather than given parametrically. Let the factor "capital" replace "land" as the second factor in the two-sector model (replace T by K). And let M stand for machines rather than manufacturing goods. To simplify, I assume capital does not depreciate. The new feedback

element in the system is that the rate of increase of the capital stock, K^*, depends on the current output of machines, M. Thus $K^* = M/K$. The "demand" for M now represents savings.

Suppose the rate of growth of the labor force, L^*, is constant. At any moment of time the rate of capital accumulation, K^*, either exceeds, equals, or falls short of L^*. Of special interest in the neoclassical theory of growth (with no technological progress) is the case of balanced growth where $L^* = K^*$. Balance in the growth of factors will, as we have seen, result in balanced growth as between the two commodities (at the same rate). But if L^* and K^* are not equal, it becomes necessary to inquire whether they tend toward equality (balanced growth) asymptotically or tend to diverge even further.

If machines are produced by labor-intensive techniques, the rate of growth of machines exceeds that of capital if labor is growing faster than capital, or falls short of capital if capital is growing faster than labor. (This is the result in Section IV, which is dampened, but not reversed, by the price changes discussed in Section V.) Thus the rate of capital accumulation, if different from the rate of growth of the labor supply, falls or rises toward it. The economy tends toward the balanced-growth path.

The difficulty arises if machines are capital intensive. If there is no price change, the change in the composition of outputs must be a magnified reflection of the spread in the growth rates of factors. Thus if capital is growing more rapidly than labor, machine output will expand at a greater rate than either factor, and this only serves to widen the spread between the rates of growth of capital and labor even further.[15] Once account is taken of price changes, however, the change in the composition of outputs may be sufficiently dampened to allow convergence to balanced growth despite the fact that machines are capital intensive.

Re-examine equation (11'), replacing T^* by K^* and recognizing that $|\theta|$ is negative if machines are capital intensive. If σ exceeds $-|\theta|\sigma_D$, on balance a dampening of the ratio of outputs as compared to factor endowments takes place. This suggests the critical condition that must be satisfied by σ, as compared with σ_D and $|\theta|$, in order to insure stability. But this is not precisely the condition required. Rather, stability hinges upon the *sign* of $(M^* - K^*)$ being opposite to that of $(K^* - L^*)$. There is a presumption that when $(M^* - F^*)$ is smaller than $(K^* - L^*)$ (assuming both are positive) the output of the machine sector is growing less rapidly than is the capital stock. But the correspondence is not exact.

To derive the relationship between $(M^* - K^*)$ and $(M^* - F^*)$ consider the two ways of expressing changes in the national income (Y). It can be viewed as the sum of returns to factors or the sum of the values of output in the two sectors. Let θ_i refer to the share of factor i or commodity i in the national income. In terms of rates of change,

$$Y^* = \theta_L(w^* + L^*) + \theta_K(r^* + K^*)$$
$$= \theta_M(p_M^* + M^*) + \theta_F(p_F^* + F^*).$$

But the share of a factor in the national income must be an average of its share in each sector, with the weights given by the share of that sector in the national income. This, and equations (3.2) and (4.2), guarantee that

$$\theta_L w^* + \theta_K r^* = \theta_M p_M^* + \theta_F p_F^*.$$

That is, the rates of change of the financial components in the two expressions for Y^* balance, leaving an equality between the physical terms:

$$\theta_L L^* + \theta_K K^* = \theta_M M^* + \theta_F F^*.$$

The desired relationship is obtained by observing that θ_K equals $(1 - \theta_L)$ and θ_M is $(1 - \theta_F)$. Thus

$$(M^* - K^*) = \theta_F(M^* - F^*)$$
$$- \theta_L(K^* - L^*)$$

With this in hand it is easy to see that (from [11']) $(M^* - K^*)$ is given by

$$(M^* - K^*) = \frac{\theta_L}{\sigma}$$

$$\times \left\{ -\frac{\theta_F|\theta|}{\theta_L}\sigma_D - \sigma \right\}(K^* - L^*). \tag{16}$$

It is not enough for σ to exceed $-|\theta|\sigma_D$, it must exceed $-(\theta_F/\theta_L)|\theta|\sigma_D$ for convergence to balanced growth.[16] It nonetheless remains the case that σ greater than σ_D is sufficient to insure that the expression in brackets in (16) is negative. For (16) can be rewritten as (16'):

$$(M^* - K^*) = -\frac{\theta_L}{\sigma}$$

$$\times \left\{ \sigma - \left[1 - \frac{\theta_{LM}}{\theta_L} \right]\sigma_D \right\}(K^* - L^*). \tag{16'}$$

[15] See Y. Shinkai, "On Equilibrium Growth of Capital and Labor," *International Economic Review*, May, 1960, for a discussion of the fixed-coefficients case. At constant commodity prices the impact of endowment changes on the composition of output is the same regardless of elasticities of substitution in production. Thus a necessary and sufficient condition in Shinkai's case is the factor-intensity condition. For the variable coefficients case the factor-intensity condition was first discussed by Hirofumi Uzawa, "On a Two-Sector Model of Economic Growth," *Review of Economic Studies*, October, 1961.

[16] The two requirements are equivalent if $\theta_F = \theta_L$, that is, if total consumption $(p_F F)$ is matched exactly by the total wages (wL). This equality is made a basic assumption as to savings behavior in some models, where laborers consume all and capitalists save all. For example, see Uzawa, *ibid*.

Thus it is overly strong to require that σ exceed σ_D.[17]

VIII. SAVINGS BEHAVIOR

A popular assumption about savings behavior in the literature on growth theory is that aggregate savings form a constant percentage of the national income.[18] This, of course, implies that σ_D is unity. In this case it becomes legitimate to inquire as to the values of σ or σ_M and σ_F as compared with unity. For example, if each sector's production function is Cobb-Douglas (σ_M and σ_F each unity), stability is guaranteed. But the value "unity" that has a crucial role in this comparison only serves as a proxy for σ_D. With high σ_D even greater values for σ_M and σ_F (and σ) would be required.

If σ_D is unity when the savings ratio is constant, is its value higher or lower than unity when the savings ratio depends positively on the rate of profit? It turns out that this depends upon the technology in such a way as to encourage convergence to balanced growth precisely in those cases where factor intensities are such as to leave it in doubt.

The capital goods, machines, are demanded not for the utility they yield directly, but for the stream of additional future consumption they allow. This is represented by the rate of return (or profit), which is linked by the technology to the relative price of machines according to the magnification effects implicit in the Stolper-Samuelson theorem. The assumption that the savings ratio (the fraction of income devoted to new machines) rises as the rate of profit rises

implies that the savings ratio rises as the relative price of machines rises (and thus that σ_D is less than unity) if and only if machines are capital intensive. Of course the savings assumption also implies that σ_D exceeds unity (that is, that the savings ratio falls as the relative price of machines rises) if machines are labor intensive, but convergence to balanced growth is already assured in this case.[19]

IX. THE ANALYSIS OF TECHNOLOGICAL CHANGE

The preceding sections have dealt with the structure of the two-sector model of production with a given technology. They nonetheless contain the ingredients necessary for an analysis of the effects of technological progress. In this concluding section I examine this problem and simplify by assuming that factor endowments remain unchanged and subsidies are zero. I concentrate on the impact of a change in production conditions on relative prices. The effect on outputs is considered implicitly in deriving the price changes.

Consider a typical input coefficient, a_{ij}, as depending both upon relative factor prices and the state of technology:

$$a_{ij} = a_{ij}\left(\frac{w}{r}, t\right).$$

In terms of the relative rates of change, a_{ij}^* may be decomposed as

$$a_{ij}^* = c_{ij}^* - b_{ij}^*.$$

c_{ij}^* denotes the relative change in the input-output coefficient that is called forth by a change in factor prices as of a given technology. The b_{ij}^* is a measure of

---

[17] A condition similar to (16'), with the assumption that $\sigma_D = 1$, is presented by Amano, "A Two-Sector Model of Economic Growth Involving Technical Progress" (unpublished).

[18] For example, see Solow, "A Contribution to the Theory of Economic Growth," *Quarterly Journal of Economics*, February, 1956.

[19] For a more complete discussion of savings behavior as related to the rate of profit, see Uzawa, "On a Two-Sector Model of Economic Growth: II," *Review of Economic Studies*, June, 1963; and Kenichi Inada, "On Neoclassical Models of Economic Growth," *Review of Economic Studies*, April, 1965.

technological change that shows the alteration in a_{ij} that would take place at constant factor prices. Since technological progress usually involves a *reduction* in the input requirements, I define b_{ij}^* as $-1/a_{ij} \cdot \partial a_{ij}/\partial t$.

The b_{ij}^* are the basic expressions of technological change. After Section III's discussion, it is not surprising that it is the λ and θ weighted averages of the b_{ij}^* that turn out to be important. These are defined by the following set of π's:

$$\pi_j = \theta_{Lj} b_{Lj}^* + \theta_{Tj} b_{Tj}^* \qquad (j = M, F),$$

$$\pi_i = \lambda_{iM} b_{iM}^* + \lambda_{iF} b_{iF}^* \qquad (i = L, T).$$

If a B^* matrix is defined in a manner similar to the original A matrix, π_M and π_F are the sums of the elements in each column weighted by the relative factor shares, and π_L and π_T are sums of the elements in each row of B^* weighted by the fractions of the total factor supplies used in each industry. Thus π_M, assumed non-negative, is a measure of the rate of technological advance in the M-industry and π_L, also assumed non-negative, reflects the over-all labor-saving feature of technological change.

Turn now to the equations of change. The c_{ij}^* are precisely the a_{ij}^* used in equations (6)–(9) of the model without technological change. This subset can be solved, just as before, for the response of input coefficients to factor price changes. After substitution, the first four equations of change (equations [1.1]–[4.1]) become

$$\lambda_{LM} M^* + \lambda_{LF} F^* = \pi_L + \delta_L(w^* - r^*), \qquad (1.4)$$

$$\lambda_{TM} M^* + \lambda_{TF} F^* = \pi_T - \delta_T(w^* - r^*), \qquad (2.4)$$

$$\theta_{LM} w^* + \theta_{TM} r^* = p_M^* + \pi_M, \qquad (3.4)$$

$$\theta_{LF} w^* + \theta_{TF} r^* = p_F^* + \pi_F. \qquad (4.4)$$

The parameters of technological change appear only in the first four relationships and enter there in a particularly simple form. In the first two equations it is readily seen that, in part, technological change, through its impact in reducing input coefficients, has precisely the same effects on the system as would a change in factor endowments. π_L and π_T replace L^* and T^* respectively. In the second pair of equations the improvements in industry outputs attributable to technological progress enter the model precisely as do industry subsidies in equations (3.3) and (4.3) of Section IV. Any general change in technology or in the quality of factors (that gets translated into a change in input coefficiencies) has an impact on prices and outputs that can be decomposed into the two kinds of parametric changes analyzed in the preceding sections.

Consider the effect of progress upon relative commodity and factor prices. The relationship between the changes in the two sets of prices is the same as in the subsidy case (see equation [12]):

$$(w^* - r^*)$$
$$= \frac{1}{|\theta|} \{ (p_M^* - p_F^*) + (\pi_M - \pi_F) \}. \qquad (17)$$

Solving separately for each relative price change,

$$(p_M^* - p_F^*) = -\frac{|\theta|}{\sigma}$$
$$\times \{ (\pi_L - \pi_T) + |\lambda| \sigma_S(\pi_M - \pi_F) \}, \qquad (18)$$

$$(w^* - r^*) = -\frac{1}{\sigma}$$
$$\times \{ (\pi_L - \pi_T) - |\lambda| \sigma_D(\pi_M - \pi_F) \}. \qquad (19)$$

For convenience I refer to $(\pi_L - \pi_T)$ as the "differential factor effect" and $(\pi_M -$

π_F) as the "differential industry effect."[20]

Define a change in technology as "regular" if the differential factor and industry effects have the same sign.[21] For example, a change in technology that is relatively "labor-saving" for the economy as a whole ($[\pi_L - \pi_T]$ positive) is considered "regular" if it also reflects a relatively greater improvement in productivity in the labor-intensive industry. Suppose this to be the case. Both effects tend to depress the relative price of commodity M: The "labor-saving" feature of the change works exactly as would a relative increase in the labor endowment to reduce the relative price of the labor-intensive commodity (M). And part of the differential industry effect, like a relative subsidy to M, is shifted forward in a lower price for M.

Whereas the two components of "regular" technological change reinforce each other in their effect on the commodity price ratio, they pull the factor price ratio in opposite directions. The differential factor effect in the above case serves to depress the wage/rent ratio. But part of the relatively greater improvement in the labor-intensive M industry is shifted backward to increase, relatively, the return to labor. This "backward" shift is more pronounced the greater is the elasticity of substitution on the demand side. There will be some "critical" value of σ_D, above which relative wages will rise despite the downward pull of the differential factor effect:

$$(w^* - r^*) > 0 \text{ if and only if } \sigma_D$$
$$> \frac{(\pi_L - \pi_T)}{|\lambda|(\pi_M - \pi_F)}.$$

If technological progress is not "regular," these conclusions are reversed. Suppose $(\pi_L - \pi_T) > 0$, but nonetheless $(\pi_M - \pi_F) < 0$. This might be the result, say, of technological change where the primary impact is to reduce labor requirements in food production. Labor is now affected relatively adversely on both counts, the differential factor effect serving to depress wages as before, and the differential industry effect working to the relative advantage of the factor used intensively in food production, land. On the other hand, the change in relative commodity prices is now less predictable. The differential factor effect, in tending to reduce M's relative price, is working counter to the differential industry effect, whereby the F industry is experiencing more rapid technological advance. The differential industry effect will, in this case, dominate if the elasticity of substitution between goods on the supply side is high enough.

$$(p_M^* - p_F^*) > 0 \text{ if and only if } \sigma_S$$
$$> -\frac{(\pi_L - \pi_T)}{|\lambda|(\pi_M - \pi_F)}.$$

The differential factor and industry effects are not independent of each other.

---

[20] The suggestion that a change in technology in a particular industry has both "factor-saving" and "cost-reducing" aspects has been made before. See, for example, J. Bhagwati and H. Johnson, "Notes on Some Controversies in the Theory of International Trade," *Economic Journal*, March, 1960; and G. M. Meier, *International Trade and Development* (New York: Harper & Row, 1963), chap. i. Contrary to what is usually implied, I point out that a Hicksian "neutral" technological change in one or more industries has, nonetheless, a "factor-saving" or "differential factor" effect. The problem of technological change has been analyzed in numerous articles; perhaps those by H. Johnson, "Economic Expansion and International Trade," *Manchester School of Economic and Social Studies*, May, 1955; and R. Findlay and H. Grubert, "Factor Intensities, Technological Progress and the Terms of Trade," *Oxford Economic Papers*, February, 1959, should especially be mentioned.

[21] Strictly speaking, I want to allow for the possibility that one or both effects are zero. Thus technological change is "regular" if and only if $(\pi_L - \pi_T)(\pi_M - \pi_F) \geqq 0$.

Some insight into the nature of the relationship between the two can be obtained by considering two special cases of "neutrality."

Suppose, first, that technological change is "Hicksian neutral" in each industry, implying that, at unchanged factor prices, factor proportions used in that industry do not change.[22] In terms of the B^* matrix, the rows are identical ($b_{Lj}^* = b_{Tj}^*$). As can easily be verified from the definition of the π's, in this case

$$(\pi_L - \pi_T) = |\lambda|(\pi_M - \pi_F),$$

and technological change must be "regular." If, over-all, technological change is "labor-saving" (and note that this can happen even if it is Hicksian neutral in each industry), the price of the relatively labor-intensive commodity must fall. Relative wages will, nonetheless, rise if σ_D exceeds the critical value shown earlier, which in this case reduces to unity.

The symmetrical nature of this approach to technological change suggests an alternative definition of neutrality, in which the columns of the B^* matrix are equal. This type of neutrality indicates that input requirements for any factor, i, have been reduced by the same relative amount in every industry. The relationship between the differential factor and industry effects is given by

$$(\pi_M - \pi_F) = |\theta|(\pi_L - \pi_T).$$

Again, technological change must be "regular." If the reduction in labor coefficients in each industry exceeds the reduction in land coefficients, this must filter through (in dampened form unless each industry uses just one factor) to affect relatively favorably the labor-intensive industry. The remarks made in

the case of Hicksian neutrality carry over to this case, except for the fact that the critical value which σ_D must exceed in order for the differential industry effect to outweigh the factor effect on relative wages now becomes higher. Specifically, σ_D must exceed $1/|\lambda||\theta|$, which may be considerably greater than unity. This reflects the fact that in the case of Hicksian neutrality $(\pi_L - \pi_T)$ is smaller than $(\pi_M - \pi_F)$, whereas the reverse is true in the present case.

With Hicksian neutrality the paramount feature is the difference between rates of technological advance in each industry. This spills over into a differential factor effect only because the industries require the two factors in differing proportions. With the other kind of neutrality the basic change is that the input requirements of one factor are cut more than for the other factor. As we have just seen, this is transformed into a differential industry effect only in dampened form.

These cases of neutrality are special cases of "regular" technological progress. The general relationship between the differential factor and industry effects can be derived from the definitions to yield

$$(\pi_L - \pi_T) = Q_M \beta_M + Q_F \beta_F \\ + |\lambda|(\pi_M - \pi_F), \quad (20)$$

and

$$(\pi_M - \pi_F) = Q_L \beta_L + Q_T \beta_T \\ + |\theta|(\pi_L - \pi_T). \quad (21)$$

In the first equation the differential factor effect is broken down into three components: the labor-saving bias of technical change in each industry (β_j is defined as $b_{Lj}^* - b_{Tj}^*$) and the differential industry effect.[23] In the second expres-

---

[22] See Hicks, *The Theory of Wages* (New York: Macmillan Co., 1932).

[23] Note that Q_M and Q_F are the same weights as those defined in Section VI. The analogy between

sion the differential industry effect is shown as a combination of the relatively greater saving in each factor in the M industry (β_L, for example, is $b_{LM}^* - b_{LF}^*$) and the differential factor effect.[24] With these relationships at hand it is easy to see how it is the possible asymmetry between the row elements and/or the column elements of the B^* matrix that could disrupt the "regularity" feature of technical progress.[25]

For some purposes it is useful to make the substitution from either (20) or (21) into the expressions for the changes in relative factor and commodity prices shown by (17)–(19). For example, if technological change is "neutral" in the sense described earlier, where the reduction in the input coefficient is the same in each industry (although different for each factor), β_L and β_T are zero in (21) and the relationship in (17) can be rewritten as

$$(w^* - r^*) = \frac{1}{|\theta|}(p_M^* - p_F^*) + (\pi_L - \pi_T).$$

To make things simple, suppose π_T is zero. The uniform reduction in labor input coefficients across industries might reflect, say, an improvement in labor quality attributable to education. Aside from the effect of any change in commodity prices on factor prices (of the Stolper-

Samuelson variety), relative wages are directly increased by the improvement in labor quality.

Alternatively, consider substituting (20) into (19), to yield (19′):

$$(w^* - r^*) = -\frac{1}{\sigma}\Big\{Q_M\beta_M + Q_F\beta_F \tag{19′}$$
$$+ Q_D(1 - \sigma_D)\frac{(\pi_M - \pi_F)}{|\theta|}\Big\}.$$

Will technological change that is Hicks neutral in every industry leave the factor price ratio unaltered at a given ratio of factor endowments? Equation (19′) suggests a negative answer to this query unless progress is at the same rate in the two industries ($\pi_M = \pi_F$) or unless σ_D is unity.[26]

There exists an extensive literature in the theory of international trade concerned with (a) the effects of differences in production functions on pre-trade factor and commodity price ratios (and thus on positions of comparative advantage), and (b) the impact of growth (in factor supplies) or changes in technological knowledge in one or more countries on the world terms of trade.[27] The analysis of this paper is well suited to the discus-

---

the composition of σ and that of $(\pi_L - \pi_T)$ becomes more apparent if $|\lambda|(\pi_M - \pi_F)$ is rewritten as $Q_D \cdot \{(\pi_M - \pi_F)/|\theta|\}$. The differential factor effect is a weighted average of the Hicksian factor biases in each industry and a magnified $(1/|\theta|)$ differential industry effect.

[24] Q_L equals $(\lambda_{LF}\theta_{LM} + \lambda_{LM}\theta_{LF})$, and Q_T is $(\lambda_{TF}\theta_{TM} + \lambda_{TM}\theta_{TF})$. Note that $Q_L + Q_T$ equals $Q_M + Q_F$.

[25] These relationships involve the *difference* between π_L and π_T, on the one hand, and π_M and π_F on the other. Another relationship involving *sums* of these terms is suggested by the national income relationship, as discussed in Section VII. With technical progress. $\theta_M\pi_M + \theta_F\pi_F$ equals $\theta_L\pi_L + \theta_T\pi_T$.

[26] Recalling n. 23, consider the following question: If the elasticity of substitution between factors is unity in every sector, will a change in the ratio of factor endowments result in an equal percentage change in the factor price ratio? From Section VI it is seen that this result can be expected only if σ_D is unity.

[27] See H. Johnson, "Economic Development and International Trade," *Money, Trade, and Economic Growth* (London: George Allen & Unwin, 1962), chap. iv, and the extensive bibliography there listed. The most complete treatment of the effects of various differences in production conditions on positions of comparative advantage is given by Amano, "Determinants of Comparative Costs . . . ," *op. cit.*, who also discusses special cases of Harrod neutrality. For a recent analysis of the impact of endowment and technology changes on the terms of trade see Takayama, "Economic Growth and International Trade," *Review of Economic Studies*, June, 1964.

sion of these problems. The connection between (*a*) and expressions (17)–(19) is obvious. For (*b*) it is helpful to observe that the impact of any of these changes on world terms of trade depends upon the effect in each country separately of these changes on production and consumption at constant commodity prices. The production effects can be derived from the four equations of change for the production sector (equations [1.1]–[4.1] or later versions) and the consumption changes from equation (5.1).[28] The purpose of this paper is not to reproduce the results in detail but rather to expose those features of the model which bear upon all of these questions.

[28] Account must be taken, however, of the fact that with trade the quantities of M and F produced differ from the amounts consumed by the quantity of exports and imports.

[3]

A THREE-FACTOR MODEL IN
THEORY, TRADE, AND HISTORY

Ronald W. JONES

1.1. Introduction

One of the fundamental results in the pure theory of international trade is the factor-price equalization theorem. This result has wider applicability than to the area of trade, for fundamentally it is a statement of the relationship between any economy's commodity prices and the returns to its productive factors, whether or not that economy is engaged in trade. It is not surprising that the prices of commodities into which factors enter as productive agents influence the returns earned by those factors in a competitive market. What *is* surprising is that (under appropriate conditions) the quantities of the factors available for employment in the economy — the factor endowments — have no independent role to play in influencing factor prices. This dependence of factor prices *only* upon commodity prices is the essence of the theorem.

Of course even under the stringent assumptions of the two-commodity, two-factor case, it is not really correct to say that factor endowments have no effect on factor prices independently of commodity prices, for factor prices are uniquely determined by commodity prices only for some *range* of the factor endowments. Should the endowment bundle lie outside this range, the economy would be driven to specialize completely in one of the commodities; with fewer commodities being produced than factors employed, the basis for the theorem disappears.

The two-factor, one-commodity case provides the simplest example of general equilibrium in which factor endowments bear directly upon factor returns[1]. To reach a wider variety of possible applications, however, it is

---

[1] The main field in which such a model is used is obviously not that of international trade but of neoclassical growth. In the one sector, growth model changing capital/labor ratios over time affect the real wage and the rate of profit.

3

necessary to introduce more than one commodity. In this paper I analyze a restricted version of the three-factor, two-commodity case. The restriction is that although three factors of production are employed, only *two* enter into the production of any one commodity. This still allows the straitjacket of the factor-price equalization theorem to be removed, while preserving most of the simple methods of analysis characteristic of the two-by-two model. Furthermore, it is precisely this form of the three-by-two model that has served as the basis for two interesting recent contributions to the literature in the fields of economic history [13] and the theory of capital and international trade [7].

The basic structure of this three-by-two model is developed in the next section, using the framework I employed recently in analyzing the two-commodity two-factor model [5]. Following that, in Section 1.3, I discuss the concept of a *factor-price frontier* for this extended model, as a basis for interpreting Peter Temin's remarks concerning American and British technology in the mid-nineteenth century. In Section 1.4 I turn to a question embedded in Peter Kenen's new concept of the role of capital in production and trade, namely, what is the influence of the rate of interest on relative commodity prices (and therefore on the patterns of comparative advantage). Finally, in Section 1.5, I briefly discuss possible extensions of the model.

1.2. Basic Structure of Model

Let X_1 and X_2 denote the two commodities produced. Sector i makes use of a factor specific to that sector V_i and a factor shared with the other sector, the mobile factor, V_N. If a_{ij} represents the quantity of factor i required per unit output of X_j, the basic competitive equilibrium relations can be set out as in eqs. (1.1) to (1.5). These fall into two groups. The first set, eqs. (1.1) to (1.3), states that the endowment of each factor

$$a_{11}X_1 = V_1 , \tag{1.1}$$

$$a_{22}X_2 = V_2 , \tag{1.2}$$

$$a_{N1}X_1 + a_{N2}X_2 = V_N \tag{1.3}$$

is fully employed in one or more productive sectors. The second set, eqs. (1.4) and (1.5), is a statement of the competitive profit relationships. Here R_i is the "rental" return for the use of one unit of factor i, and p_j is the price of commodity j.

$$a_{11}R_1 + a_{N1}R_N = p_1 , \qquad (1.4)$$

$$a_{22}R_2 + a_{N2}R_N = p_2 . \qquad (1.5)$$

I assume throughout that both commodities are produced in positive amounts so that costs per unit of output are reflected exactly in market prices.

In the examples I discuss later in the paper the V_i represent physically different factors of production. However, the model is also capable of reinterpretation as a two-factor, two-commodity model where one of the factors is completely immobile occupationally. For example, V_1 and V_2 may represent capital goods installed in each sector and incapable of being transferred. The crucial consideration is not physical identity but economic identity. With immobilities, the returns to factors R_1 and R_2 need not be equalized in the market.

Eqs. (1.1) to (1.5) could be taken to represent *all* the equilibrium relationships for a competitive economy with fixed factor endowments facing fixed commodity prices only if techniques of production are invariant[2]. Otherwise more information is required to determine which set of a_{ij}, out of all the ones available (shown by the unit isoquants), is chosen in the competitive equilibrium. With competition ensuring that unit costs are minimized, each a_{ij} depends upon the ratio of factor prices in industry j, as shown in eq. (1.6):

$$a_{ij} = a_{ij}\left(\frac{R_N}{R_j}\right). \qquad (1.6)$$

The basis for the factor-price equalization theorem is to be found in the competitive profit relations. Consider eqs. (1.4) and (1.5). If this were a model for two commodities and two perfectly mobile factors, R_1 and R_2 would be driven to equality. With the a_{ij} depending upon factor prices, two relationships to determine two factor prices are given once commodity prices are known[3]. However, if V_1 and V_2 are different factors, or specific factors, the profit conditions are insufficient to determine factor returns solely from a

---

[2] With fixed coefficients, however, the resource constraints eqs. (1.1) to (1.3) are overdetermined unless inequalities are introduced. I do not pursue this matter as in general I assume sufficient variability in the a_{ij} to allow all resources to be fully absorbed in productive use.

[3] Of course a factor intensity condition is required as well. It is sufficient in the 2×2 model to have factor proportions *different* in the two sectors. The classic source for a discussion of the intensity conditions, and especially for a general treatment of the case of uneven numbers of goods and factors, is the 1953 paper by Samuelson [10].

knowledge of commodity prices. Use must be made also of the full-employment conditions, with the information they contain as to factor endowments. Solve eqs. (1.1) and (1.2) for each X_j and substitute into eq. (1.3) to obtain eq. (1.3'):

$$\frac{a_{N1}}{a_{11}} V_1 + \frac{a_{N2}}{a_{22}} V_2 = V_N . \tag{1.3'}$$

Since the a_{ij} depend on factor prices, eqs. (1.4), (1.5) and (1.3') provide a set of three relationships in the three factor prices and, as parameters, the two commodity prices and *all* the factor endowments.

The structure of this 3×2 model is best revealed by considering the way in which the equilibrium is disturbed by arbitrary small changes in commodity prices and factor endowments. First I shall examine the equations of change that are derived from eqs. (1.4), (1.5) and (1.3') to focus on the impact of parametric changes upon the returns to factors of production. Following that I shall make use of relationships (1.1) and (1.2) to discuss the effect of changes on the composition of outputs.

The basic equations of change, revealed by differentiating eqs. (1.4), (1.5), and (1.3'), are given in eqs. (1.7) to (1.9).

$$\theta_{11}\hat{R}_1 + \theta_{N1}\hat{R}_N = \hat{p}_1 , \tag{1.7}$$

$$\theta_{22}\hat{R}_2 + \theta_{N2}\hat{R}_N = \hat{p}_2 , \tag{1.8}$$

$$\lambda_{N1}\sigma_1\hat{R}_1 + \lambda_{N2}\sigma_2\hat{R}_2 - \{\lambda_{N1}\sigma_1 + \lambda_{N2}\sigma_2\}\hat{R}_N$$
$$= \{\hat{V}_N - \lambda_{N1}\hat{V}_1 - \lambda_{N2}\hat{V}_2\} . \tag{1.9}$$

A '^' over a variable denotes the relative change in that variable (e.g., $\hat{R}_1$ is dR_1/R_1). The θ_{ij} refers to the distributive share of factor i in industry j, while λ_{Nj} is the fraction of the mobile factor V_N, absorbed by the j-th industry. In deriving eqs. (1.7) to (1.9) use has been made of two simple relationships involving the relative changes in the input-output coefficients $\hat{a}_{ij}$. Consider the first industry. With a_{i1} chosen so as to minimize unit cost, the distributive-share weighted average of the changes in the a_{i1} coefficients $\{\theta_{11}\hat{a}_{11} + \theta_{N1}\hat{a}_{N1}\}$ must be zero[4]. This directly yields, in eq. (1.7), the

---

[4] Geometrically this states that the slope of the isoquant equals the slope of the factor-cost line. For a more detailed treatment of these relationships, see Jones [5].

statement that the change in the market price of X_1 must be a positively weighted average of (and therefore trapped between) the changes in individual factor prices. In addition, the *definition* of the elasticity of substitution between factors in the first industry, σ_1, relates the change in the a_{N1}/a_{11} ratio to the change in the factor/price ratio. This, and the comparable definition of σ_2, suffice to yield eq. (1.9).

Formal solutions for the effects on factor returns of changes in commodity prices and factor endowments are provided in eqs. (1.10) to (1.12).

$$\hat{R}_1 = \frac{1}{\Delta}\left\{\left[\lambda_{N1}\frac{\sigma_1}{\theta_{11}} + \frac{1}{\theta_{11}}\lambda_{N2}\frac{\sigma_2}{\theta_{22}}\right]\hat{p}_1 - \frac{\theta_{N1}}{\theta_{11}}\cdot\lambda_{N2}\frac{\sigma_2}{\theta_{22}}\hat{p}_2 \right.$$

$$\left. + \frac{\theta_{N1}}{\theta_{11}}\left[\hat{V}_N - \lambda_{N1}\hat{V}_1 - \lambda_{N2}\hat{V}_2\right]\right\}, \tag{1.10}$$

$$\hat{R}_N = \frac{1}{\Delta}\left\{\lambda_{N1}\frac{\sigma_1}{\theta_{11}}\hat{p}_1 + \lambda_{N2}\frac{\sigma_2}{\theta_{22}}\hat{p}_2 + [\lambda_{N1}\hat{V}_1 + \lambda_{N2}\hat{V}_2 - \hat{V}_N]\right\}, \tag{1.11}$$

$$\hat{R}_1 - \hat{R}_2 = \frac{1}{\Delta}\left\{\left[\frac{1}{\theta_{22}}\lambda_{N1}\frac{\sigma_1}{\theta_{11}} + \frac{1}{\theta_{11}}\lambda_{N2}\frac{\sigma_2}{\theta_{22}}\right](\hat{p}_1 - \hat{p}_2)\right.$$

$$\left. + \frac{1}{\theta_{11}\theta_{22}}(\theta_{N1} - \theta_{N2})[\hat{V}_N - \lambda_{N1}\hat{V}_1 - \lambda_{N2}\hat{V}_2]\right\} \tag{1.12}$$

where

$$\Delta = \lambda_{N1}\frac{\sigma_1}{\theta_{11}} + \lambda_{N2}\frac{\sigma_2}{\theta_{22}}.$$

The solution for $\hat{R}_2$ is not explicitly shown, as it can be obtained by permuting subscripts in the solution for changes in the other specific factor R_1. Note that the expression σ_i/θ_{ii} occurs frequently. This is the elasticity of the marginal product curve of the mobile factor in industry i[5]. Thus Δ is a weighted average of these elasticities.

With more factors employed than commodities produced, factor endowments exercise an influence over factor returns independent of commodity prices. The relationships are simple. With commodity prices held constant an increase in the endowment of the mobile factor lowers the return to that

[5] For footnote see next page.

mobile factor and raises the return to both specific factors. By contrast, an increased endowment of either specific factor raises the return to the mobile factor and lowers both R_1 and R_2. Changes in endowments always alter the returns to the mobile factor in a direction *opposite* to the returns to *both* specific factors. This is true because with commodity prices constant, any increase in the return to a factor of production must lower the return to the other factor used in that industry. Thus in eqs. (1.7) and (1.8) an increase in R_N with p_i constant must lower both R_1 and R_2. Although R_1 and R_2 move in the same direction as endowments change, eq. (1.12) explicitly shows that R_1 will undergo a greater *relative* change than R_2 if the share of the mobile factor used in the first industry (θ_{N1}) exceeds its share in the second industry (θ_{N2}).

Turn, now, to the influence of commodity price changes on factor prices. Clearly an equiproportionate rise in both commodity prices (a "pure" inflation) changes all factor prices by the same proportionate amount. Of more

[5] Consider the first industry. The marginal physical product of the mobile factor is given by R_N/p_1. This declines as a_{N1}/a_{11}, the ratio of mobile to fixed factor use, rises. The elasticity of the marginal product curve (defined so as to be positive) is $(\hat{a}_{11} - \hat{a}_{N1})/(\hat{R}_N - \hat{p}_1)$. But by eq. (1.7), $(\hat{R}_N - \hat{p}_1)$ equals $\theta_{11}(\hat{R}_N - \hat{R}_1)$. Given the definition of σ_1, the result follows.

With the model characterized by each sector having a specific factor not used by the other sector, it is not surprising that it is the elasticities of the marginal product curves for the mobile factors that assume importance. A simple graphical device (Fig. 1.1) could be employed to derive some of the results in this model. The marginal

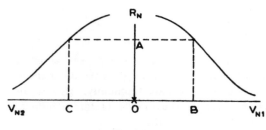

Fig. 1.1

product curves for the mobile factor are put back to back. With given commodity prices and factor endowments the diagram directly gives the solution for $R_N(OA)$ as dependent upon the total quantity of the mobile factor available to the two sectors (OB plus OC equals V_N). A change in V_i or p_i shifts the appropriate marginal product schedule. An increase in V_N moves both OB and OC outwards and lowers R_N.

interest is the case in which the system is disturbed by a change in *relative* commodity prices. Suppose the price of commodity 1 rises relatively to that of commodity 2. Then the following relationships hold:

$$\hat{R}_1 > \hat{p}_1 > \hat{R}_N > \hat{p}_2 > \hat{R}_2 \,.$$

The change in each commodity price must be trapped between the changes in the returns to factors used to produce that commodity. Furthermore, the changes in the returns to specific factors are more pronounced than in the return to the mobile factor. Indeed, as the solution in eq. (1.11) shows, $\hat{R}_N$ is a positively weighted average of the changes in each commodity price, a feature of the model that I shall require in Section 1.4.

Factor-price/commodity-price relationships in the standard two-commodity, two-factor model are characterized by what I have called the *magnification effect* [5]. With two mobile factors (and no specific factors), a relative rise in the price of commodity 1 would cause the return to one factor (the factor used more intensively in producing commodity 1) to rise by more (relatively) than either commodity price, and the return to the other factor to rise by less than either commodity price (or perhaps to fall). This is the basis for the Stolper-Samuelson theorem [12], whereby the *real* return to the factor used intensively in a tariff-protected industry is unambiguously raised, regardless of consumption patterns. This magnification effect is preserved in the present model for the specific factors but *not* for the mobile factor. Thus if labor is the single mobile factor, wages calculated in terms of one of the commodities might rise with protection but not in terms of the other commodity.

Note that whereas the fortunes of the specific factors wax or wane together with changes in factor endowments, they move in opposite directions (relative to any other prices) in the face of alterations in relative commodity prices.

Turning to the composition of outputs note from eqs. (1.1) and (1.2) that $\hat{X}_i$ equals $\hat{V}_i - \hat{a}_{ii}$. It would be an easy matter to solve for the change in each output, but consider, instead, the change in the *ratio* of outputs produced. This is given directly by eq. (1.13).

$$\hat{X}_1 - \hat{X}_2 = (\hat{V}_1 - \hat{V}_2) + (\hat{a}_{22} - \hat{a}_{11}) \,. \tag{1.13}$$

If coefficients of production are highly inflexible, output changes are limited to a large extent by changing available quantities of the specific factors. But the intensity with which the specific factors are used depends upon elasticities of substitution and upon changes in all the factor prices, which, by eqs. (1.10) and (1.11), are linked to commodity price and endowment changes. Substitution yields eq. (1.14) for the change in the ratio of outputs produced[6]:

$$(\hat{X}_1 - \hat{X}_2) = (\hat{V}_1 - \hat{V}_2) + \frac{1}{\Delta}\left[\theta_{N1}\frac{\sigma_1}{\theta_{11}} - \theta_{N2}\frac{\sigma_2}{\theta_{22}}\right](\hat{V}_N - \lambda_{N1}\hat{V}_1 - \lambda_{N2}\hat{V}_2)$$

$$+ \frac{\lambda_{N1}\theta_{N2} + \lambda_{N2}\theta_{N1}}{\Delta}\frac{\sigma_1}{\theta_{11}}\frac{\sigma_2}{\theta_{22}}(\hat{p}_1 - \hat{p}_2). \tag{1.14}$$

For given endowments the coefficient of $(\hat{p}_1 - \hat{p}_2)$ shows the elasticity of substitution along the transformation schedule. Of course this must be positive, and the transformation schedule exhibits the usual bowed-out shape. In the 2×2 case (both factors mobile), this result is also obtained *unless* the two industries use factors in the same proportion, in which case the production-possibilities curve is linear. Should this same proviso be applied to the present model? The first question that comes up in this connection is how to compare factor proportions when the two industries each use a factor not employed by the other industry. The answer is found by observing that both industries use the same mobile factor, and the distributive shares of that mobile factor in the two industries can be compared. Consider X_1 to be N-intensive if and only if θ_{N1} exceeds θ_{N2}[7]. As eq. (1.14) shows, even if factor intensities in the two industries are, in this sense, equal, the coefficient of $(\hat{p}_1 - \hat{p}_2)$ still remains finite and, indeed, can be quite small for low values of the elasticities of substitution. When both factors are mobile, the element leading to increasing opportunity costs is the fact that resources initially released by one industry are required in different proportions by the other industry. With some factors specific to an industry, however, expansion of output in that industry must entail adding more of the mobile factor to a fixed quantity of the specific factor (and less of the mobile factor in the other industry), which, by the law of diminishing returns, drives up relative costs in the expanding industry.

---

[6] To solve for $\hat{a}_{ii}$ use two relationships: (1) The θ-weighted average of the changes in input coefficients in the i-th industry is zero, and (2) the definition of σ_i. This yields $\hat{a}_{ii} = -\theta_{Ni}\sigma_i(\hat{R}_i - \hat{R}_N)$.

[7] Thus, referring to eq. (1.12), an increase in the endowment of the mobile factor at constant commodity prices raises, relatively, the return to the specific factor used in the industry making intensive use of the mobile factor. In my treatment of the 2×2 case [5], I showed that factor proportions are uniquely related to the size of θ_{ij} compared with θ_{ik} where $k \neq j$.

A question of great interest to trade theory and to the neoclassical theory of growth involves the way in which changes in factor endowments *shift* the transformation curve. The *magnification effect* discussed earlier in connection with price changes is also a feature of the dual relationship between endowment and output changes at constant commodity prices in the traditional 2×2 case[8]. For example, an increase in the endowment of only one productive factor would, at constant prices, raise the output of the commodity using that factor intensively by relatively a greater amount than the factor has increased, and reduce the output of the other commodity. To see how much of this relationship survives in the present 3×2 model, it is necessary to make a distinction between increases in the endowment of the mobile factor V_N and increases in the supply of either specific factor.

Consider the latter effect first. An increase in V_1 would result in greater production of X_1. Unlike the 2×2 case, however, factor prices are adjusting to this change even when commodity prices are being held constant. In particular, the return to the mobile factor rises relative to the return to either specific factor, and this serves to lower the ratio of mobile to specific factor used in the first industry. That is, $\hat{V}_{N1}$, although positive, would be less than $\hat{V}_1$, and therefore $\hat{X}_1$ must fall short of $\hat{V}_1$, thus invalidating this aspect of the magnification effect. However, it is still the case that the output of the other commodity falls, as V_2 is assumed unchanged and some of the mobile factor has been drawn into the expanding industry.

A less extreme change in the composition of outputs results from an increase only in the endowment of the mobile factor (at constant commodity prices). The relative cost of using the mobile factor is cut in both industries, and, since V_1 and V_2 are unchanged, more intensive use of factor N must increase outputs of both X_1 and X_2. As eq. (1.14) shows, this output expansion may not be uniform in the two industries. Two influences operate to alter the relative composition of output: (1) Differences between the two industries in the intensity with which the mobile factor is used. This effect is similar to the *only* explanation for changes in the composition of outputs in the 2×2 case. Other things equal, X_1 expands relatively to X_2 when V_N rises if the distributive share of the mobile factor in the first industry, θ_{N1}, exceeds θ_{N2}. By "other things equal" is meant (2) the elasticities of substitution in the two sectors. Even if factor intensities (as defined in terms of the θ's) are equal as between industries, high values for σ_1 relative to σ_2 allow X_1 to expand relatively to X_2. That is, to preserve the same value for R_N in the

---

[8] This relationship is usually referred to as the Rybczynski theorem. See [9], [4], and [5].

two sectors, most of the increase in N must go into the sector where large increases are required to lower the marginal product of N.

1.3. Factor-Price Frontier

This model can be used to shed light on some queries suggested by Peter Temin's [13] recent discussion of technology in Britain and America in the mid-nineteenth century[9]. The key question I wish to explore is whether one economy can be operating with the same production functions as another and still have higher real wages *and* higher interest rates. An examination of the factor-price frontier for the standard 2×2 model suggests a negative answer to this question. But what can be said if technology makes use of three factors of production with the restriction that each sector only uses two factors? This is precisely the model used by Temin; the general properties were discussed in the preceding section. My purpose in this section is to construct factor-price frontiers appropriate to Temin's model.

For this historical interpretation, let labor be the mobile factor, capital be represented by V_1, and land by V_2. Interpret X_1 as the output of manufacturing goods (including machines) and X_2 as the output of the agricultural sector. The special assumptions made are that no land is used in manufacturing activity and no capital is used in agriculture. The interest rate can be associated with the ratio between the returns to capital R_1 and the price of new machines p_1. How the "real wage" is defined makes a considerable difference to the results. To begin with, I make the extreme assumption that only agricultural goods enter into workers' consumption, so that wages R_N need be deflated only by the price of agricultural goods p_2.

A factor-price frontier is a locus of all combinations of factor prices allowed by an economy's given technology[10]. It is not an unambiguous concept. For example, if both factor prices are deflated by the price of the same commodity, the factor-price frontier is dependent only upon the production function for that sector. Thus in eq. (1.7), a relationship between R_1/p_1 and R_N/p_1 is implicitly given — a downward sloping curve whose elasticity is the ratio of distributive shares. If "real" wages were interpreted as R_N deflated

---

[9] I am indebted to Robert Fogel for bringing my attention to this literature. I have had many useful conversations with Fogel and with Stanley Engerman on the material covered in this section. For comments on Temin's article see [2] and [3].

[10] For an early discussion of the concept of a factor-price frontier see Samuelson [11].

by the price of manufactured goods, an economy employing only labor and capital to produce manufactured goods can raise real wages only at a sacrifice of lower rates of interest (rates of profit), regardless of how many factors are used in the rest of the economy. The mid-nineteenth century American economy must have had a superior technology *in manufacturing* if real wages, in this sense of the word, and the rate of interest were higher than in the United Kingdom. This is one extreme, and it is more interesting (and perhaps relevant) to look at the other — letting real wages be defined as R_N/p_2[11].

In a standard 2×2 model with capital and labor mobile, a downward sloping locus relates the wage rate deflated by the price of the consumption good to the rental on capital deflated by the price of the capital good[12]. Each point on the frontier corresponds to a particular commodity price ratio. An increase in the relative price of the labor intensive commodity would raise the real wage and lower the rate of interest. However, such a locus in the 3×2 model of this paper, is *upward sloping*. Suppose the relative price of manufactures rises, and consider the chain of inequalities for commodity and factor prices exhibited in the preceding section. The interest rate has risen $(\hat{R}_1 > \hat{p}_1)$ as has the real wage $(\hat{R}_N > \hat{p}_2)$. Two countries could have the same technology, but if transport costs or other impediments allowed a higher relative price for manufacturing goods in one of them (say America), both the rate of interest and real wages would have to be higher in that country[13].

But this is not the end of the story, for, unlike the standard 2×2 case, differences in factor endowments exert an independent influence on factor prices. At constant commodity prices, another factor price frontier is traced out if endowments change, and this frontier is negatively sloped. Suppose the supply of one of the specific factors, land, should rise[14]. At constant commodity prices this must raise the real wage and lower the rate of interest — the

[11] To the extent that workers also consumed manufactured goods, the appropriate deflator would be an index of both p_1 and p_2, with weights determined by the share of the two goods in the total budget. The appropriate factor price frontier would lie somewhere between the polar extremes considered in the text.

[12] Although the frontier must be negatively sloped, it *may* be bowed out (concave to the origin). The condition for this to occur is similar to the conditions under which convergence to balanced growth is jeopardized in two-sector growth models, viz. the capital good (manufactures) is capital intensive and elasticities of substitution are "sufficiently" low. For a discussion of this and related matters see the paper by Michael Bruno [1]. In the text, nothing hinges on the concavity of the frontier, only the slope.

[13] Of course *all* factor returns cannot be higher in one country than in another if technologies are identical. In the present example land rents would unambiguously be lower in America.

[14] For footnote, see next page.

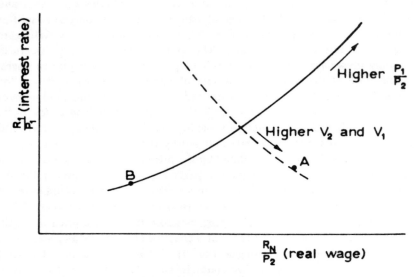

Fig. 1.2. Factor-price frontiers.

returns to mobile and specific factors are affected in opposite directions. In Fig. 1.2 I have shown this second kind of factor price frontier by the downward-sloping dotted curve. If the relative price of food was low in America, and if America was land (and capital) abundant (relative to the labor endowment) compared with Britain, both the real wage and rate of interest in America (say at A) could have been higher than in Britain (say at B). These stylized facts are consistent, in this model, with both countries having available the same basic technology.

1.4. Influence of Rate of Interest

In Kenen's treatment of "Nature, Capital, and Trade" [7] the mobile factor is capital. At first glance, Kenen's model seems rather complicated: five different productive activities are considered. However, all this activity can be

---

[14] From eq. (1.9) it is clear that a more complicated endowment change can just as easily be considered. A pure increase in the endowment of land would have the same kind of impact on factor prices as an increase in the weighted average of land and capital that exceeded any increase in the labor force.

decomposed into three groupings: (1) a standard 2×2 model of the Heckscher-Ohlin variety; (2) a standard two-factor, one-commodity process whereby the capital good is created; and (3) a three-factor, two-commodity model of the type with which this paper is concerned.

Consider, first, the 3×2 section of his model, where he introduces his novel theory of capital. Two factors of production exist in nature, land, and labor (V_1 and V_2). But these factors are inert until and unless they are made productive by an act of investment. In real terms, this can be thought of as, say, the addition of fertilizer to the land or education to the labor. In terms of the abstract model, Kenen posits two production functions ("factor service supply" functions), each of which combines a homogeneous kind of capital (let N equal K) with the specific inert factor (and none of the other factor). In Kenen's treatment, this interaction yields a stream of factor services for a finite number of periods, after which the "improved" factor reverts to its "inert" state unless further investment is undertaken. It is convenient for the present discussion to limit this amount of time (before sudden death depreciation) to one period. Thus at any point of time, the economy has the factor endowment bundle (V_1, V_2, V_K) and has, as outputs, the bundle (X_1, X_2), the quantities of "educated" labor and "fertilized" land[15].

Of course the "output" bundle (X_1, X_2) is really the input bundle for other productive activities. On the one hand, educated labor and improved land are each required to produce both of two commodities (say Y_1 and Y_2) that represent final consumer goods that enter into international trade. Capital is not directly required in these processes, although indirectly it is embodied in X_1 and X_2. On the other hand, the two improved factors are used to produce the capital good.

Kenen is especially concerned with the application of his model to the theory of international trade. Suppose that two countries have identical technologies and engage in free trade in the two goods Y_1 and Y_2. This serves to equalize the returns to the two factors X_1 and X_2 via the usual Heckscher-Ohlin theory. But equal p_1 and p_2 (the returns to the improved factors) do *not* imply the same returns to capital or the inert factors in both countries. As eqs. (1.10) and (1.11) illustrate, differences in factor endowments have an independent bite on R_1, R_2 and R_K. Other things equal, the country with relatively large quantities of capital will have lower

---

[15] Kenen makes stringent assumptions about the form of the factor-service supply function: each is a Cobb-Douglas function ($\sigma_i=1$) with equal shares of capital ($\theta_{K1}=\theta_{K2}$, a constant). See [7], p. 451, footnote 46 as corrected in the "erratum", p. 658. I am considering the general case.

values for R_K and lower interest rates. The latter follows since the cost of producing the capital good is equated as between countries despite the fact that capital does not enter into trade.

Perhaps the most subtle relationship embedded in Kenen's model connects the rate of interest to the relative price of commodities that enter into trade, and it is this aspect of his model I wish to discuss in this section. To erase the effects of differences in factor endowments per se suppose there exist two countries with identical endowments. Nevertheless, suppose that, before trade, one of the countries has a lower rate of interest than the other. With the opening up of trade, which commodity is exported by the low interest rate country? That is, in Kenen's model, what bias in comparative advantage is imparted by differences in the rate of interest? Equivalently one could reverse the procedure and ask about the effect of a change in the commodity terms of trade upon the rate of interest.

By introducing a make-believe production function, it is possible to get at this relationship and explain the link between relative commodity prices and interest rates using the standard Heckscher-Ohlin factor proportions account of relative prices valid for the 2×2 case. The improved factors X_1 and X_2 produce the traded goods Y_1 and Y_2 in a competitive setting. Therefore the relative price of Y_1 and Y_2 is determined in standard fashion by the relative factor price ratio p_1/p_2 or vice versa. It is as if the traded goods were really the improved factors. The hard question concerns the link between the factor price ratio p_1/p_2 and the rate of interest.

The price of the capital good p_K is determined in a competitive model by the cost of production and thus by the technology used and the factor prices p_1 and p_2. Considering small changes, relationship (1.15) connects $\hat{p}_i$ with $\hat{p}_k$, in the same fashion as eqs. (1.7) and (1.8) linked the $\hat{R}_i$ with the $\hat{p}_i$.

$$\theta_{1K}\hat{p}_1 + \theta_{2K}\hat{p}_2 = \hat{p}_K . \tag{1.15}$$

Now the rate of interest in this kind of model is the ratio of the returns for the use of capital R_K, and the price of the capital good p_K. If there existed a production process whose output was the "services" of capital, and using X_1 and X_2 as inputs, a relationship such as (1.15) for $\hat{R}_K$ could be obtained. Clearly no such physical process exists, but the pricing relationship connecting $\hat{R}_K$ with $\hat{p}_1$ and $\hat{p}_2$ that would be relevant for such a make-believe process *does* exist!

Consider the solution for $\hat{R}_K$ (replace N by K) in eq. (1.11). If endowments are held constant, relationship (1.16) emerges:

$$\theta_{1s}\hat{p}_1 + \theta_{2s}\hat{p}_2 = \hat{R}_K , \qquad (1.16)$$

where

$$\theta_{is} \equiv \frac{\lambda_{Ki}\dfrac{\sigma_i}{\theta_{ii}}}{\Delta}$$

and

$$\Delta = \lambda_{N1}\frac{\sigma_1}{\theta_{11}} + \lambda_{N2}\frac{\sigma_2}{\theta_{22}}.$$

The symbols θ_{1s} and θ_{2s} have been used to suggest the distributive shares that would be appropriate in such a make-believe production process. The point is that any increase in the returns to the improved factors filters down and affects, favorably, the return for the service of capital. Of course, by eq. (1.15), such a change would also raise the cost of capital. The change in the interest rate is $(\hat{R}_K - \hat{p}_K)$, and the link between this change and the change in p_1/p_2 (and therefore also the relative prices of the traded commodities) is given simply by comparing θ_{1s} and θ_{1K} (or θ_{1s}/θ_{2s} with θ_{1K}/θ_{2K}). An increase in the rate of interest raises the relative price of the commodity using educated labor relatively intensively (compared with improved land) if and only if educated labor is relatively more important in contributing to the rental on capital goods than it is in contributing to the costs of producing capital goods[16].

---

[16] As remarked in the preceding footnote 15 Kenen considers only the special case in which σ_1 is unity and θ_{K1} equals θ_{K2}. The appropriate comparison in the general case is θ_{1K}/θ_{2K} with θ_{1s}/θ_{2s}. The former exceeds the latter if and only if $p_1 X_{1K}/p_2 X_{2K}$ exceeds K_1/K_2. But if θ_{K1} equals θ_{K2}, K_1/K_2 must equal $p_1 X_1/p_2 X_2$. Therefore in Kenen's case the direction of change in commodity prices given by a change in the interest rate is linked to the comparison between the ratio of the two educated factors in producing $K(X_{1K}/X_{2K})$ and in the economy's endowment bundle (X_1/X_2). As is easily seen, this physical relationship as between factor proportions does not generalize. See Kenen [7], p. 449, and especially eq. (21).

Kenen's special assumptions as to the form of the factor-service supply functions also affect the way in which his transformation curve between X_1 and X_2 (his "gross factor-service frontier", [7], p. 445) shifts with the accumulation of capital. With $\sigma_1 = \sigma_2$ and θ_{K1} equal to θ_{K2} (and therefore θ_{11} also equal to θ_{22}), the coefficient of $\hat{V}_N$ in my eq. (1.14) is zero. An increase in K shifts the $X_1 - X_2$ transformation schedule uniformly outwards from the origin as Kenen demonstrates.

The feature of the 3×2 model that permits the financial counterpart of the make-believe production function for the services of capital is clearly (by eq. (1.11)) that the return to capital is derived from the market returns of the improved factors — and that changes in R_K must be a *positively* weighted average of changes in the p_i[17]. It is as if X_1 and X_2 were actually used to produce the services of capital in a competitive market, so that the zero-profit relationship appropriate to such a process would be given by eq. (1.16).

1.5. Possible Extensions of Model

The preceding two sections have served to illustrate two uses that have been made of the model analyzed in Section 1.2. In this concluding section, I suggest briefly how this model might be extended, still falling short of a completely general model in which all three factors can continuously be substituted for each other in producing each of the two commodities.

One suggestion involves allowing all three factors to be used in each industry but a pair of these to be fixed in proportion to each other — always the same pair, but not necessarily in the same proportion as between sectors[18]. Let a_{21} always equal αa_{11} and a_{12} equal βa_{22}. The a_{Ni} can be varied continuously with the bundle of (a_{1i}, a_{2i}). If $\alpha\beta$ is less than unity, the first commodity is distinguished from the second by a more intensive use of factor 1 relative to factor 2 (but not necessarily relative to factor N). The model of Section 1.2 is the special case in which $\alpha = \beta = 0$. Consider the other extreme: If $\alpha\beta = 1$, the model reduces to the familiar two-factor, two-commodity model, where the two factors are N and a particular bundle of factors 1 and 2 (always in the ratio $1/\alpha$ or, equivalently, β). From the production side of the model alone, it is not possible to determine R_1 and R_2 separately, only the return to the composite factor.

For intermediate cases, where $\alpha\beta < 1$, consider the two *different* composite factors: $(a_{11}, \alpha a_{11})$ and $(\beta a_{22}, a_{22})$, with returns R_1^* and R_2^*. In terms of these composite factors the special form of the 3×2 model in Section 1.2

---

[17] In either this 3×2 model, or in the standard 2×2 model, every factor price change is a weighted average of the changes in all commodity prices. However, except for the mobile factor in the 3×2 model, one of the weights in each case is *negative* (this is the magnification effect). Therefore such a pricing relationship could not be interpreted as having come from a productive process in which the two commodities are inputs and the service of the particular factor is the output.

[18] I am indebted to Murray Kemp for this suggestion.

is applicable[19]. For example, a change in commodity prices at unchanged endowments has a determinate effect on R_i^* and R_N (as given by a reinterpretation of eqs. (1.10) and (1.11)). These changes in the R_i^*, in turn, determine the changes in the R_i via a set of relationships equivalent to the zero-profit factor-price, commodity price equations of change in the standard 2×2 model:

$$\theta'_{11}\hat{R}_1 + \theta'_{21}\hat{R}_2 = \hat{R}_1^* ,$$

$$\theta'_{12}\hat{R}_1 + \theta'_{22}\hat{R}_2 = \hat{R}_2^* ,$$

where

$$\theta'_{ij} \equiv \frac{\theta_{ij}}{\theta_{1j} + \theta_{2j}} .$$

Thus by introducing the notion of composite factors it is possible to decompose a more general 3×2 case to the special form of the 3×2 model discussed in this paper and the standard 2×2 pricing relationships.

An alternative extension focuses on the relationship between V_1 and V_2 instead of introducing all three factors into the production process for any one commodity. Throughout the paper I have assumed that endowments of the specific factors are given as parameters. Suppose, instead, they are outputs of a productive process whereby V_2 can be "converted" into V_1 at increasing opportunity costs. Let the factor endowment ratio V_2/V_1 respond positively to relative returns, R_2/R_1[20]. The basic set of relations (1.7) to (1.9) is altered only in having $\lambda_{N1}\hat{V}_1 + \lambda_{N2}\hat{V}_2$ now depend upon the extent of the change in factor returns R_2/R_1 and the elasticity of substitution σ_V along the transformation locus connecting V_2 and V_1[21].

---

[19] For the concept of elasticity of substitution consider factor N in relation to the composite bundle. For example, define σ_1 as the relative change in (a_{11}/a_{N1}) divided by the relative change in (R_N/R_1^*). Eq. (1.3') changes to

$$\frac{a_{N1}}{a_{11}} \frac{(V_1 - \beta V_2)}{(1 - \alpha\beta)} + \frac{a_{N2}}{a_{22}} \frac{(V_2 - \alpha V_1)}{(1 - \alpha\beta)} = V_N .$$

R_1^* is merely $R_1 + \alpha R_2$, the cost of the bundle (a_{11}, a_{21}).

[20] In an unpublished manuscript [8], Howard Petith analyzes a two-sector vintage model. Each sector employs a different kind of machine, and these machines, in turn, are jointly produced subject to increasing opportunity costs.

[21] For footnote, see next page.

The model in this paper is the special case $\sigma_V = 0$. As the transformation curve between V_1 and V_2 becomes more elastic, the result of Section 1.2, whereby the change in the return to the mobile factor is trapped between the changes in the commodity prices, is altered to conform more closely with the "magnification" effect of the standard 2×2 model. That is, for sufficiently large σ_V, an increase in the relative price of the N-intensive commodity increases R_N by a proportionately greater amount.

These extensions serve to illustrate how more general cases can be decomposed into the kinds of results familiar from the 2×2 model and the results characteristic of the special form of the 3×2 model examined in this paper.

[21] If R_1/R_2 rises, V_1/V_2 also increases. The sign of $(\lambda_{N1} \hat{V}_1 + \lambda_{N2} \hat{V}_2)$ turns out to depend on a comparison of the distributive shares of the mobile factor V_N in the production of commodities X_1 and X_2. The implication of this is given by eq. (1.12). If the first commodity is N-intensive (in the sense that θ_{N1} exceeds θ_{N2}), compare the impact on the ratio R_1/R_2 of an increase in the endowment of the mobile factor (with constant commodity prices) under the alternative assumptions (1) that V_1 and V_2 remain constant, and (2) that V_1 and V_2 respond to changes in R_1/R_2. In both cases R_1/R_2 rises since X_1 is N-intensive. But in case (2) $\lambda_{N1} \hat{V}_1 + \lambda_{N2} \hat{V}_2$ is positive, thus damping the increase in R_1 and R_2, and in their spread. The possibility of having V_i respond to prices reduces the required extent of the change in prices. For a brief discussion in another context of the importance of terms such as $\lambda_{N1} \hat{V}_1 + \lambda_{N2} \hat{V}_2$ see R.W.Jones [6], p. 330.

References

[1] M.Bruno, "Fundamental Duality Relations in the Pure Theory of Capital and Growth", *Review of Economic Studies*, January 1969.

[2] I.M.Drummond, "Labor Scarcity and the Problem of American Industrial Efficiency in the 1850's: A Comment", *The Journal of Economic History*, September 1967.

[3] R.W.Fogel, "The Specification Problem in Economic History", *The Journal of Economic History*, September 1967.

[4] R.W.Jones, "Duality in International Trade: A Geometrical Note", *Canadian Journal of Economics and Political Science*, August 1965.

[5] R.W.Jones, "The Structure of Simple General Equilibrium Models", *The Journal of Political Economy*, December 1965.

[6] R.W.Jones, "Comments on Technical Progress", *The Philippine Economic Journal*, Second Semester, 1966.

[7] P.B.Kenen, "Nature, Capital, and Trade", *The Journal of Political Economy*, October 1965.

[8] H.Petith, "Substitution in a Vintage Capital Model", Unpublished.

[9] T.M.Rybczynski, "Factor Endowments and Relative Commodity Prices", *Economica*, November 1955.

[10] P.A.Samuelson, "Prices of Factors and Goods in General Equilibrium", *Review of Economic Studies*, XXI, 1953—54.

[11] P.A.Samuelson, "Parable and Realism in Capital Theory: The Surrogate Production Function", *Review of Economic Studies*, XXIX, 1962.

[12] W.F.Stolper and P.A.Samuelson, "Protection and Real Wages", *Review of Economic Studies*, IX, November 1941.

[13] P.Temin, "Labor Scarcity and the Problem of American Industrial Efficiency in the 1850's", *The Journal of Economic History*, September 1966.

[4]

The Economic Journal, **88** (*September* 1978), 488–510
Printed in Great Britain

SHORT-RUN CAPITAL SPECIFICITY AND THE PURE THEORY OF INTERNATIONAL TRADE*

I. INTRODUCTION

Among its many abstractions from reality, the pure theory of international trade, associated with the names of Heckscher, Ohlin, and Samuelson, assumes that both capital and labour are costlessly and instantaneously transferable between sectors. More recently, however, beginning with articles by Jones (1971 *b*) and Samuelson (1971 *a*, *b*), a number of writers have returned to an older tradition, traceable in the works of Marshall, Ohlin himself, and Harrod, which assumes that, in the short run at least, capital goods are sector-specific. In the light of this tradition, the Heckscher–Ohlin–Samuelson model is seen as describing positions of long-run equilibrium only. In the short run any disturbance will lead to a reallocation of the labour force between sectors. But capital in each sector is a fixed factor, and so differences emerge between the rentals in the two sectors. Over a longer time-horizon capital will flow between sectors in response to these rental differentials, tending eventually (unless another disturbance intervenes) to a new long-run equilibrium with all capital goods earning the same rental.

This view of the adjustment process, which I propose to call the "short-run capital specificity" hypothesis, is hardly novel; apart from the earlier writers already cited it is implicit, for example, in Harberger (1962) and Kemp and Jones (1962). However, as formalised in recent work, especially by Mayer (1974) and Mussa (1974), it provides a plausible hypothesis about the economy's response to exogenous disturbances. Moreover these writers have shown that it may be used to explain why there is no necessary contradiction between the somewhat counter-intuitive predictions of traditional international trade theory, and the more "commonsensical" views of politicians, businessmen and trade-union leaders.

The aim of this paper is threefold. First, it presents a new diagrammatic technique to illustrate the short-run capital specificity adjustment process in a small open economy. This technique is used in sections 2–4 to demonstrate the process of adjustment towards long-run equilibrium, following changes in commodity prices, population, and the level of factor market distortions. Sections 2 and 3 expound the findings of Mussa and Mayer on the effects of changes in the terms of trade and in total factor supplies, noting some extensions of these writers' analyses. Section 4 then applies the technique to the consideration of changes in the level of factor market distortions. It is shown that conflicts between long-run and short-run interests may arise in this case: for example, workers in a labour-intensive sector may have an incentive to press for higher wages, despite the fact that in the long run their action will lower wages in both sectors.

* At various stages of writing this paper, I benefitted from the comments and suggestions of John Black, Dermot McAleese, Alan Richeimer, Frances Ruane, Maurice Scott, Alasdair Smith, and Nick Stern.

Second, the implications of the short-run capital specificity adjustment process are examined in the context of an open economy with pre-existing factor market distortions. Much of the recent literature in this area (see especially Jones (1971 *a*) and Magee (1976)) has been concerned with the elucidation of a number of paradoxes which can arise in the presence of such factor market distortions, of which two of the more notable are a perverse price-output response and a perverse distortion-output response. Section 5 begins by giving a new diagrammatic exposition of these paradoxes, and then shows that, if the economy is assumed to adjust according to the short-run capital specificity hypothesis, then *these paradoxes will never be observed*, because they correspond to *dynamically unstable* long-run equilibria. For devotees of the Heckscher–Ohlin–Samuelson model, this is an encouraging conclusion, since it implies that the long-run predictions of that model in the presence of factor market distortions are much more consistent with simple economic intuition than had been thought. The analysis of this section complements that of a companion paper, Neary (1978*b*), where the same conclusions are shown to hold under a wider class of disequilibrium adjustment mechanisms.

The third aim of the paper is to point out the central role of the assumption of intersectoral capital mobility in traditional international trade theory. Section 6 surveys a number of cases, additional to those in sections 2–4, where this assumption is responsible for "paradoxical" or counter-intuitive conclusions. It is argued in section 7 that both common sense and the implications of observed self-interested behaviour on the part of market participants make this assumption inappropriate in the short run; and that the peculiar nature of the primary factor capital which it assumes – a fixed stock of homogeneous, infinitely long-lived, and perfectly mobile machines – makes it suspect in the long run.

2. SHORT-RUN AND LONG-RUN RESPONSE TO CHANGES IN THE TERMS OF TRADE

We begin by introducing the diagrammatic technique to be used in this paper. Essentially this combines two diagrams: the Edgeworth–Bowley production box, introduced to international trade theory by Stolper and Samuelson (1941), and the sector-specific capital diagram, familiar in writings on economic development, and used by Jones (1971 *b*) and Mussa (1974). As shown in Fig. 1, measuring the economy's labour force on the horizontal axis of the Edgeworth–Bowley box enables us to place the two diagrams vertically above one another, and thus to examine simultaneously the short-run and long-run consequences of any exogenous change.

The usual assumptions of the two-sector model of international trade are built into Fig. 1, where the initial equilibrium is indicated by the points A_0 and B_0 in the upper and lower parts of the figure respectively. The economy produces two goods, X and Y, under perfectly competitive conditions in both commodity and factor markets, using fixed supplies of the two factors, labour and capital, and subject to constant returns to scale. In the long run, both factors are completely mobile between sectors. In the short run, however, there are diminishing returns

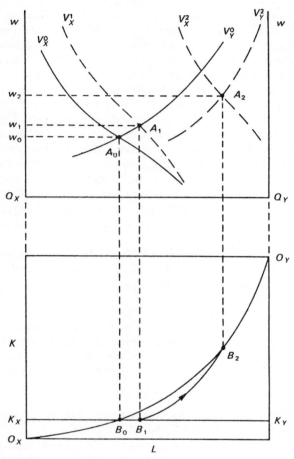

Fig. 1. Short-run and long-run adjustment to an increase in the relative price
of the labour-intensive good X.

to labour in each sector, because of the fixity of capital goods. Hence, entrepreneurs in each sector maximise profits by increasing employment until the value marginal product of labour equals the wage. Assuming that the wage rate adjusts to ensure full employment at all times, the initial wage rate and labour force allocation is therefore determined by the intersection of the two value marginal product of labour schedules, V_X^0 and V_Y^0, at A_0 in the upper part of Fig. 1. The location of these schedules depends on the initial commodity prices, and on the initial allocation of capital to each sector, with the latter represented by the distances $O_X K_X$ and $O_Y K_Y$ in the lower part of the figure. Finally, the fact that the initial position is one of long-run as well as of short-run equilibrium is shown by the fact that B_0, the point in the lower part of the diagram which corresponds to A_0, lies on the contract curve of the Edgeworth–Bowley box. This contract curve lies below the diagonal of the box, reflecting our last assumption, that X is the relatively labour-intensive sector.

Consider now the effect of a displacement of this initial equilibrium by a once-and-for-all change in the terms of trade, involving an increase in the relative price of X. With capital sector-specific in the short run, we may begin by examining the upper part of Fig. 1. Choosing good Y as numeraire, the value marginal product of labour in Y schedule, V_Y^0, is unaffected, whereas the corresponding schedule for the X sector shifts upwards, from V_X^0 to V_X^1, by the same proportional amount as the price increase. Therefore the new short-run equilibrium will be that represented by the points A_1 and B_1. (The latter point satisfies the restrictions that it lies vertically below A_1, and on the same capital allocation line, $K_X K_Y$, as B_0.) Labour has moved out of Y into X, and since the amount of capital in X is unchanged, the output of X has increased: thus even in the short run the economy responds to the rise in the relative price of X by expanding its output, to an extent determined by the slopes of the two value marginal product of labour schedules.

The short-run reactions of factor prices to this change have been considered in detail by Mussa (1974). The wage rate increases in terms of Y but falls in terms of X (this may be seen from the fact that the capital-labour ratio rises in sector Y but falls in sector X), so that the effect on the real income of wage earners is not independent of their consumption pattern. As for the rentals on capital, that in the X sector increases in terms of both goods, whereas that in the Y sector falls in terms of both. However, while all of these changes are of interest from the point of view of income distribution, the crucial fact from the point of view of resource allocation is that the capital rental in X has increased relative to that in Y. This may also be seen from the lower part of the diagram: since B_1 lies below the efficiency locus, it follows that the rental wage ratio is relatively higher in X, and since the same wage prevails in each sector this means that the rental must be higher in X than in Y. Given our assumed adjustment process therefore, competitive pressures will lead in the "medium run" to a reallocation of capital from the low to the high rental sector.[1] In the lower part of the diagram, this has the effect of causing the capital allocation line to shift upwards; in the upper part, both the V_X^1 and V_Y^0 schedules shift to the right, since an increase (decrease) in the quantity of capital in a sector must lead the marginal product of labour to rise (fall) at all levels of employment.

To establish the effects of this capital reallocation on factor rewards and on factor usage in each sector, we note first that the transfer of a given amount of capital from Y to X leads the former sector to seek to shed labour and the latter to try to acquire labour.[2] Since X is the relatively labour-intensive sector, the quantity of labour it wishes to acquire will, at the initial factor prices, exceed that which the Y sector is willing to give up. Excess demand for labour in the economy as a whole therefore develops, and so the wage rate is bid up. With both com-

---

[1] The timing and speed of this reallocation will depend on a variety of considerations including reallocation costs and entrepreneurial wage and price expectations. For a study which examines these aspects in greater detail, see Mussa (1975).

[2] I am very grateful to Alasdair Smith, whose comments suggested a major simplification of the remainder of this section.

modity prices constant, the increase in the wage must reduce the rental in each sector. This follows from the fact that the proportional change in the price of each good is a weighted average of the changes in factor prices in each sector, the weights being the share of each factor in the value of output of that sector:

$$\hat{p}_X = \theta_{LX}\,\hat{w} + \theta_{KX}\,\hat{r}_X, \tag{1}$$

$$\hat{p}_Y = \theta_{LY}\,\hat{w} + \theta_{KY}\,\hat{r}_Y. \tag{2}$$

Since the wage rental ratio rises in each sector as capital reallocates, both capital–labour ratios must also rise. The economy therefore moves away from B_1 in a north-easterly direction, along the path shown by a heavy line, which satisfies the properties that at every point along it the slope of the path is greater than the slope of the ray from O_X to that point, and less than the slope of the ray from O_Y to that point. This path may be called a "*labour-market equilibrium locus*", because although it is characterised throughout by disequilibrium in the capital market, the labour market is in equilibrium at all points along it (in the sense that full employment of labour and a uniform wage rate prevail).

Finally, what happens to the intersectoral rental differential as the economy moves along this locus? The fact that X is the relatively labour-intensive sector means that the distributive share of labour is greater in X than in Y; hence to keep relative commodity prices constant, it is necessary for the rental in X to fall by more than that in Y. This may be seen by setting the proportional changes in price in equations (1) and (2) equal to zero, and manipulating the equations to obtain:

$$\hat{r}_X - \hat{r}_Y = -\frac{\theta}{\theta_{KX}\theta_{KY}}\,\hat{w}, \tag{3}$$

where θ is the determinant of the matrix of sectoral shares, which is positive in this case, because X is relatively labour-intensive.[1] Equation (3) shows that, as a result of the transfer of capital between sectors and the consequent increase in the wage, the gap between the rentals in the two sectors has been partially closed. This process of capital reallocation continues until the gap is fully closed; at which time a new long-run equilibrium, corresponding to the points A_2 and B_2, is attained. This new equilibrium is exactly that predicted by Stolper and Samuelson (1941), at which, relative to the initial equilibrium at A_0 and B_0, the wage has risen and the rental common to both sectors has fallen in terms of each good. Thus the short run effect of the price change in increasing the rental on capital in the X sector is eroded, and eventually reversed, in the course of the adjustment process, as capital flows into the X sector in response to the higher return obtainable there.

Having examined the case where X is relatively labour-intensive, the case where it is relatively capital-intensive is straightforward. It is illustrated in Fig. 2. Perhaps the most important feature is that the initial reaction to the increase in the relative price of X is qualitatively identical to that in Fig. 1: as before, the wage rises initially in terms of Y, while the rentals on capital in X and Y rise and

---

[1] I.e. $\theta = \begin{vmatrix} \theta_{LX} & \theta_{LY} \\ \theta_{KX} & \theta_{KY} \end{vmatrix} = \begin{vmatrix} \theta_{LX} & \theta_{LY} \\ 1 - \theta_{LX} & 1 - \theta_{LY} \end{vmatrix} = \theta_{LX} - \theta_{LY}.$

fall respectively in terms of both goods. It is only in the course of the adjustment process that relative factor intensities play a role, as the verbal description above will have made clear. In this case, the movement of capital into the relatively capital-intensive sector reduces the demand for labour in the economy; hence the rental in both sectors rises, and the common wage rate falls, throughout the

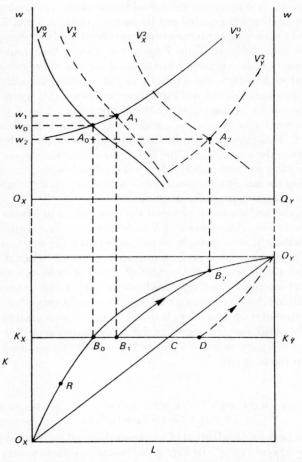

Fig. 2. Short-run and long-run adjustment to an increase in the relative price of the capital-intensive good X.

adjustment process. The capital–labour ratio in each sector therefore falls as capital reallocates, and so the path of adjustment from B_1 to B_2 is less steeply sloped at any point than the ray from O_X to that point, and more steeply sloped than the corresponding ray from O_Y. At the new long-run equilibrium (represented by A_2 and B_2) the wage will be lower than its initial value of w_0. But, despite this, it is possible for labour actually to favour the change on completely rational grounds, if its consumption pattern is sufficiently biased towards Y, and if either the speed of capital reallocation is sufficiently slow, or the rate at which labour discounts its future consumption to the present is sufficiently high.

The only additional qualification which must be made to the case where X is initially relatively capital-intensive, is that a sufficiently large price increase could cause the new short-run equilibrium point to lie to the right of C in the Edgeworth–Bowley box, thus reversing the initial factor intensity ranking of the two sectors. This possibility was pointed out by Mussa (1974, p. 1200, footnote 10), who claimed that such a factor intensity reversal would only be temporary, and that the factor allocation point in the Edgeworth–Bowley box would eventually recross the diagonal. However, this is incorrect: if the new short-run equilibrium occurs at a point such as D, to the right of C in Fig. 2, the factor allocation point will *not* recross the diagonal, but will move instead towards O_Y along the labour-market equilibrium locus indicated by the dashed line. The Y industry will eventually be completely eliminated, and the economy will specialise in the production of X. This follows from the fact (already established above) that, as capital reallocates, the expansion of the now labour-intensive sector X increases the wage rental ratio in both sectors. Hence the capital-labour ratio in sector Y cannot fall during the adjustment process, as it would have to if the labour-market equilibrium locus were to cross the diagonal.

In summary, this section has illustrated the conclusions of Mayer and Mussa that an increase in the relative price of X under the short-run capital specificity adjustment process will always imply a conflict between the short-run and long-run interests of at least one group of factor income recipients: when X is relatively labour-intensive, this is true of the owners of sector X capital, and when X is relatively capital-intensive it is true of both wage-earners and owners of sector Y capital. In addition it has been shown that, contrary to the suggestion of Mussa, a change in the terms of trade can never lead to a temporary reversal of the relative factor intensities of the two sectors, since the price change required to induce a short-run factor intensity reversal is more than sufficient to induce complete specialisation in the long run.

3. SHORT-RUN AND LONG-RUN RESPONSE TO CHANGES IN FACTOR ENDOWMENTS

The next case to be considered is that of a once-and-for-all increase in population, as examined by Mayer (1974). In Fig. 3 the initial equilibrium is at A_0 and B_0, with X the relatively capital-intensive sector. Suppose now that the labour force (assumed to be identical to the population) increases by an amount equal to the distance $Q_Y^0 Q_Y^1$. With unchanged capital allocations, the V_Y^0 schedule is shifted to the right by the full extent of the population increase, leading to a new short-run equilibrium at A_1, corresponding to the point B_1 in the production box.[1] It is clear from the diagram that the wage falls, and hence at constant (absolute and relative) commodity prices, the rental in each sector must rise. Moreover, from

---

[1] The point B_1 is above the new contract curve (not drawn) of the enlarged production box, since at B_1 the wage rental ratio in X exceeds that in Y.

equation (3) it follows that the rental must increase by a greater proportional amount in the relatively labour-intensive sector. Hence, in the "medium run", capital moves along the labour-market equilibrium locus $B_1 B_2$ from the capital-intensive sector X into the labour-intensive sector Y, causing the wage rate to increase steadily, and the rental to fall in each sector, with the gap between the two rentals narrowing and finally being eliminated.

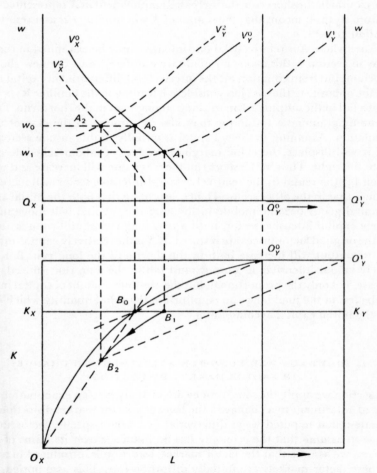

Fig. 3. Short-run and long-run adjustment to population growth.

From the Rybczynski theorem (Rybczynski, 1955) we know that the final long-run equilibrium must be at B_2 in the production box: with unchanged commodity prices and rentals equalised between sectors, relative factor prices, and hence factor proportions in each sector, must be identical to those which prevailed before the population increase. This may also be seen from the upper part of the diagram: the V_X and V_Y schedules have both shifted to the left to intersect at A_2, restoring the original wage w_0. Despite this long-run independence of the wage from the size of population, however, if workers have any positive discount rate, they will (for example) oppose immigration in a small open economy on perfectly rational grounds. Furthermore, the strong Rybczynski prediction, that at constant relative commodity prices the output of the capital-intensive sector must fall, is shown to be a long-run result only: with sector-specific capital in the short run, the increased employment in X represented by the move from A_0 to A_1 means that the output of X will initially *rise* as a result of the population growth.

The case where X is relatively labour-intensive may be examined in the same way. As in section 2, this makes no qualitative difference to the new short-run equilibrium; but from equation (3) the intersectoral differential in capital rentals will be the opposite to the case just considered, leading to the familiar Rybczynski result of a fall in the output of Y in the long (though not in the short) run. Finally, the same diagrammatic technique may also be applied to the case of capital accumulation. Assuming the new capital is initially usable in one sector only, say X, it will displace the value marginal product of labour schedule of that sector to the right. Thus in the short run the wage rate will increase and so from equation (3) the rental in the relatively capital-intensive sector will increase by more than that in the other sector. Hence, assuming that both the initial and the new capital goods become mobile in the long run, capital will move into the relatively capital-intensive sector, until a new long-run equilibrium is attained where the original factor prices are restored. If X is the relatively capital-intensive sector, its output will increase both in the short and the long run. But if it is relatively labour-intensive, its output must fall in the long run. Indeed, in the latter case, not only the proportional, but the absolute amount of capital in use in X will be less in the final long-run equilibrium than that quantity which it used before the initial capital accumulation.

4. SHORT-RUN AND LONG-RUN ADJUSTMENT TO CHANGES IN FACTOR MARKET DISTORTIONS[1]

In this section we apply the same framework of analysis to an examination of the process of adjustment to a change in the level of a factor market distortion, such as a trade-union imposed wage differential or a sector-specific factor tax. We continue to assume that the economy has no influence over its terms of trade. Moreover, we assume that the factor market distortion is introduced in a situation where factor markets are initially distortion-free. This assumption, of no pre-existing distortions, is a crucial one, and the consequences of relaxing it are examined in section 5.

We consider first the case of a wage differential, where the high-wage sector is relatively labour-intensive. In Fig. 4 the initial equilibrium is at A_0 and B_0, with the same wage rate prevailing in each sector.[2] Suppose now that workers in Y

[1] Since this section was written, I have found a somewhat similar analysis in Hu (1973).
[2] I am very grateful to Dermot McAleese, who pointed out a serious error in an earlier version of this diagram.

become unionised, and succeed in obtaining a wage which exceeds that in the X sector by a proportionate amount measured by the distortion parameter α:

$$w_Y = \alpha w_X \quad (\alpha > 1). \tag{4}$$

This change has no immediate effect on the V_X^0 and V_Y^0 schedules in the top half of Fig. 4: with an unchanged capital allocation they continue to represent the

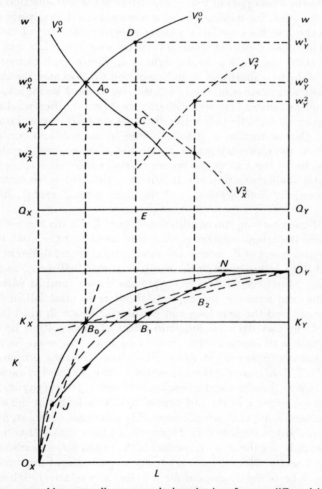

Fig. 4. Short-run and long-run adjustment to the introduction of a wage differential in favour of the labour-intensive sector Y.

value marginal product of labour in each sector. However, the effect of the union action is to drive a wedge between the value marginal products which can prevail in equilibrium in each sector. Faced with the obligation to pay higher wages, entrepreneurs in the Y sector will shed labour, and so a new short-run equilibrium will be established where the ratio between the value marginal product of labour in the two sectors – that is, the ratio between the distances DE and CE – equals the distortion parameter, α. Clearly, the initial impact of the differential is, in qualitative terms, independent of the relative factor intensities of the two sectors: the wage in the unionised sector rises and that in the X sector falls, and each of these changes is less, proportionately, than the change in the differential.

Turning to the lower part of Fig. 4, one effect of the introduction of the wage differential is to shift the contract curve downwards as shown, since in long-run equilibrium the X sector now faces a lower effective wage rental ratio than the Y sector. The new distorted contract curve must therefore cut the initial capital allocation line, $K_X K_Y$, to the right of B_0. However, it cannot cut it at or to the right of the new short-run equilibrium point B_1, because the short-run fall in the X sector wage rate combined with the rise in the Y sector wage rate must at constant output prices lead to an intersectoral rental differential in favour of sector X; hence B_1 must lie below the distorted contract curve. From a similar reasoning to that in section 2, it follows that in the medium run capital will reallocate from the unionised sector Y into the X sector, moving the economy upwards and to the right along the labour market equilibrium locus through B_1; and as capital reallocates into the relatively capital-intensive sector the wage rate is reduced in both sectors, and the intersectoral rental differential is narrowed.

Where will the new long run equilibrium occur? Evidently it must be at B_2, the intersection of the labour-market equilibrium locus and the distorted contract curve to the northeast of B_1, where the intersectoral rental differential is finally eliminated.[1] (The intersection to the southwest, at J, will be considered in the next section.) Moreover, as Magee (1971) has shown (and as will be demonstrated in the next section), the capital–labour ratio must fall in both sectors between the old and the new long-run equilibria; hence B_2 must lie above the ray $O_Y B_0$. It follows that the long-run effect of unionisation in the labour-intensive sector is to increase the rental and lower the wage in both sectors (implying that non-union wages must fall by more than the proportional wage differential[2]). This of course is the well-known result, derived in various ways by Harberger (1962), Johnson and Mieszkowski (1970), Jones (1971 a) and Magee (1971), that an increase in the differential paid to a factor in the sector which uses it intensively may, and, when commodity prices are constant, must, reduce the factor's reward in both sectors. However, we have shown that this result is a long-run one only, for the short-run effect of the union action was to increase the wage in the Y sector. Hence, contrary to the implication of the result just mentioned, it may be perfectly ratonal for a union in a relatively labour-intensive sector to press for higher wages, if its discount rate is high enough, and the process

[1] If the initial move from B_0 to B_1 had been caused by an increase in the relative price of X, the new long-run equilibrium would lie on the original efficiency locus at N. Thus, comparing a price change and a wage differential change, each of which has the same short-run effect, the long-run effect of the price change is greater than that of the wage differential change. This is intuitively plausible, since wage costs are a smaller percentage of variable costs in the long run than in the short run.

[2] This is another example of what Jones (1965) has called the "magnification effect" in the two sector model with intersectoral capital mobility, which does not arise when capital is sector-specific.

of capital reallocation sufficiently slow. Similar results may be derived for the case where the unionised sector is relatively capital-intensive: in the long run, labour in both sectors must gain, but once again a conflict between short-run and long-run interests arises, this time in the case of labour in X.

Finally, what can be said of distortions in the capital market, such as a corporate income tax of the kind studied by Harberger (1962)? The imposition of such a tax has no effect on resource allocation in the short run: since capital in the taxed sector is a fixed factor, its income amounts to a Marshallian quasi-rent, the taxation of which will have no immediate impact on behaviour.[1] However, the resulting differential between the net rentals in the two sectors will lead eventually to a reallocation of capital away from the taxed sector. This shows an important difference between the short-run consequences of a capital and a labour tax, which follows from our assumption about the relative adjustment speeds of the two factors: the imposition of a capital market distortion has no immediate effect on resource allocation, whereas that of a labour market distortion leads to an immediate contraction of the sector obliged to pay the higher wage. In the long run, on the other hand, there is a basic symmetry between the two types of distortion, at fixed commodity prices, in the sense that qualitatively the same effects will follow the imposition of a tax (or a trade union differential) on labour in sector Y as will follow the granting of a *subsidy* to capital in the other sector.

5. PRE-EXISTING DISTORTIONS AND THE REVERSAL OF VALUE AND PHYSICAL FACTOR INTENSITY RANKINGS

In the previous section we explicitly confined attention to the situation where a factor market distortion is introduced to factor markets which are initially undistorted. For "small" pre-existing distortions the analysis already given continues to hold without modifications. However, for a sufficiently large initial distortion (precisely how large depends in a complicated manner on various characteristics of the economy) many recent writers have shown that the long-run conclusions of the last section, as well as some other results of the Heckscher–Ohlin–Samuelson model, will no longer hold. (See, for example, Jones, 1971a; Bhagwati and Srinivasan, 1971; Magee, 1976.) The source of many (though not all) of these departures from orthodoxy is a particular feature which the economy may exhibit in the presence of initial factor market distortions, namely a lack of correspondence between the value and physical factor intensity rankings of the two sectors. The purpose of the present section is to show that, under the short-run capital specificity adjustment process, this feature is necessarily associated with *dynamic instability* of long-run equilibrium in a small open economy, which implies that the comparative static paradoxes discussed by the authors mentioned are theoretical *curiosa* which will "almost never" be observed.

We begin by elucidating the meaning and significance of the two senses of factor intensity. Sector X is said to be relatively labour-intensive in the *physical*

[1] As is well known, this statement is crucially dependent on the validity of the assumption of profit maximisation.

sense if its observed capital–labour ratio is lower (in equilibrium) than that of the other sector (which is represented in the diagrams above by the contract curve's lying below the diagonal of the Edgeworth–Bowley box); whereas sector X is said to be labour-intensive in the *value* sense if the share of payments to labour in the value of its output is higher than that in the other sector (which corresponds to a positive value of the determinant θ in equation (3)). When factor prices are equalised between sectors, that is, when factor markets are undistorted, the ranking of the sectors by these two concepts of factor intensity must be the same. But with an intersectoral divergence between marginal rates of substitution, either or both of these rankings can be reversed from their undistorted levels.[1] If *both* physical and value factor intensity rankings differ from their undistorted levels, the usual long-run predictions of the Hechscher–Ohlin–Samuelson model are unaffected. But if only one is changed, so that the rankings of the two sectors by physical and value factor intensity differ (i.e. one sector is capital-intensive in physical terms but labour-intensive in value terms), then many of the most familiar comparative static properties of the Heckscher–Ohlin–Samuelson model no longer hold. As Jones (1971 a) has emphasised, the reason for this is that it is the physical factor intensities which provide the link between the "real" variables of the model (i.e. factor endowments and output levels), while the value factor intensities link the "financial" variables (i.e. commodity and factor prices). When the rankings of the two sectors by these two factor intensity concepts differ, the link between the "real" and "financial" sides of the economy is broken, and various paradoxes can result.

Two of the most surprising of the paradoxes which appear when the value and physical factor intensity rankings of the sectors differ are: (1) a *perverse price–output response*: at constant factor market distortion levels, an increase in the relative price of one commodity will *lower* its output; and (2) a *perverse distortion–output response*: at constant commodity prices, an increase in the differential paid on either factor in one sector will *increase* the output of that sector.[2] While other authors have given algebraic proofs of these paradoxes, they may be demonstrated geometrically as follows, making use of the unit cost function diagrams in Figs. 5 and 6.[3] In Fig. 5, which assumes no initial factor market distortions, c_X and c_Y are the unit cost functions for sectors X and Y respectively, corresponding to the initial relative commodity prices. The *slope* of each of these curves at any point is the capital–labour ratio which will be adopted in the corresponding sector when costs are minimised subject to the factor prices represented by the co-ordinates of that point; similarly, the *elasticity* of each of these curves at any point is the ratio of capital's to labour's share in the value of output when the sector faces these factor prices. Therefore, at the initial equili-

---

[1] For example, while the undistorted efficiency locus must lie on one side of (or else coincide with) the diagonal in the Edgeworth–Bowley production box, a sufficiently large distortion may shift it to the other side of the diagonal, so changing the relative physical factor intensities of the two sectors.

[2] To appreciate the paradoxical nature of (2), note that it implies that, at constant commodity prices, an increase in a subsidy paid to one sector (whether an output or an input subsidy) will reduce the output of that sector and its employment of both factors. See Neary (1978a).

[3] This diagram may be viewed as the "dual" of the Lerner–Pearce diagram. For a recent exposition, which discusses its properties in detail and shows its usefulness in deriving many trade theorems, see Woodland (1977).

brium A, where both sectors pay the same factor prices, w^0 and r^0, sector X is relatively capital-intensive in both physical and value senses.

With no initial factor market distortions, the "normal" price–output and distortion–output responses of the economy may be demonstrated by combining Fig. 5 with the Edgeworth–Bowley boxes of Figs. 2 and 4. Thus, an increase in the

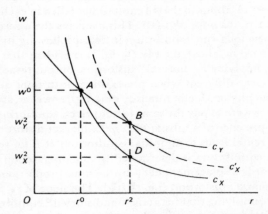

Fig. 5. Long-run effects of a change in relative prices and of the introduction of a wage differential, when factor markets are initially undistorted.

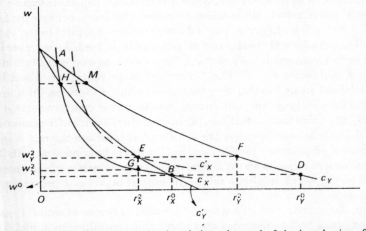

Fig. 6. Long-run effects of a change in relative prices and of the introduction of a wage differential, when initial factor market distortions are such that the value and physical factor intensity rankings of the two sectors differ.

price of X shifts c_X radially outwards from the origin, by an amount equal to the proportional magnitude of the price change. At the new long-run equilibrium, B, the usual Stolper–Samuelson conclusions of an increase in the real rental and a fall in the real wage (recalling that X is relatively capital-intensive) may be derived. Moreover, since the common wage rental ratio (represented by a ray from the origin to B) has fallen, the capital–labour ratio in each sector must also have fallen. Hence, in the lower part of Fig. 2, the new long-run production point must lie along the contract curve to the right of B_0, implying an increase in the output of X. Similarly, the introduction of a wage differential in favour of sector Y is represented in Fig. 5 by a movement from A to B for sector Y and from A to D for sector X. Once again the "effective" wage rental ratio (i.e. the ratio of the marginal product of labour to that of capital) has fallen in each sector, and so both capital–labour ratios must also fall. This confirms the assertion in section 4 above, that the new long-run equilibrium in Fig. 4 following the introduction of the differential must lie above the ray $O_Y B_0$. It is evident that the output of sector Y has fallen, implying a "normal" distortion–output response.

The situation is very different when pre-existing distortions are sufficient to reverse the value and physical factor intensity rankings, however, as Fig. 6 demonstrates. If each sector were to pay the same factor prices, equilibrium would be at A, but instead the presence of a substantial *capital* market distortion with sector Y paying a higher rental leads to an initial equilibrium at B for sector X and D for sector Y.[1] This equilibrium is determined by the intersection of c_X and c'_Y, where c'_Y is a leftwards displacement of c_Y by the same proportionate amount as the initial capital market distortion (i.e. r_Y^0 / r_X^0). The slope of c_X at B is greater than that of c_Y at D, implying that (as at the "undistorted" equilibrium A) sector X is relatively capital-intensive in the physical sense. However, the elasticity of c_X at B is *less* than that of c_Y at D, since it is easily checked that the latter is equal to the elasticity of c'_Y at B. Therefore, while X is relatively capital-intensive in the physical sense, it is relatively *labour*-intensive in the value sense, because the higher rental which sector Y is obliged to pay inflates the share of capital in the value of its output. The paradoxical conclusions are now easily derived. An increase in the price of X shifts c_X outwards to c'_X and implies a new long-run equilibrium with sector X at E and sector Y at F. The "effective" wage rental ratio, and hence the capital–labour ratio, has therefore increased in both sectors, and this implies that in Fig. 2 the new long-run equilibrium must lie on the contract curve, but to the left of B_0, at a point such as R. Thus, the increase in the price of the commodity which is relatively labour-intensive (in value terms) increases the real wage, by the usual Stolper–Samuelson mechanism; but for this to be consistent with factor market equilibrium requires an expansion of the sector which is labour-intensive in physical terms, which implies a fall in the output of X, i.e. a perverse price–output response.

Similarly, the introduction of a wage differential in favour of sector Y may be decomposed into a *Stolper–Samuelson effect* which shifts equilibrium in Fig. 6 from B and D to E and F; and a *pure wage differential effect*, which ensures that the equilibrium for sector X takes place not at E but at G, on the initial unit cost function, c_X. Hence, in the new long-run equilibrium, sector Y at F pays a higher wage *and* a higher rental than sector X at G; the "effective" wage rental ratio, and so the capital–labour ratio in each sector has risen; and therefore the economy must have moved in Fig. 4 to a point such as J on the new contract curve, implying a

---

[1] Note that the initial equilibrium could alternatively be at H and M, instead of at B and D. It will be shown below that the equilibrium at H and M is stable, whereas that at B and D is not.

perverse distortion–output response, since sector Y which was obliged to pay a higher wage has in fact expanded.

So far, I have simply provided a new exposition of the effects of a difference between the value and physical factor intensity rankings: Figs. 5 and 6 have been exclusively concerned with comparisons between long-run equilibria, and have given no attention to the passage from one such equilibrium to another. Referring, however, to the discussion in sections 2 and 4, it is easily seen that, under the short-run capital specificity adjustment process, the economy will *never* converge towards the new long-run equilibria indicated by the above comparative static

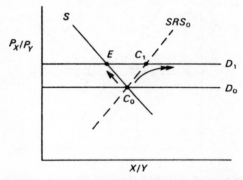

Fig. 7. Effects of a change in relative prices when the value and physical factor intensity rankings differ.

reasoning in the paradoxical cases. Consider, for example, the case of an increase in the relative price of X. The discussion in section 2 of the response to such a change is unaffected by a difference between value and physical rankings: when X is physically capital-intensive, the new short-run equilibrium will still occur at B_1 in Fig. 2, and since this point is below the contract curve of the box, there is an incentive for capital to reallocate from sector Y into sector X. Hence the capital allocation line $K_X K_Y$ in Fig. 2 will move upwards in the Edgeworth–Bowley box, and the factor allocation point will move along the labour-market equilibrium locus in the opposite direction to the new long-run equilibrium predicted by the comparative static analysis.

This constrast between the dynamic and the comparative static analyses is illustrated in relative output–relative price space in Fig. 7. The initial equilibrium is at C_0, the intersection of the demand curve D_0 (horizontal because of the small country assumption) and the supply curve S, which is downward sloping reflecting the perverse price–output response. An increase in the relative price of X, represented by an upward shift of the demand curve to D_1, should, according to the comparative static analysis, lead to a new long-run equilibrium at E, involving a fall in the relative output of X. But the dynamic adjustment process just outlined asserts to the contrary: the economy will first move along the short-run supply curve SRS_0 to the point C_1; and then, as capital reallocates into the X sector, that short-run supply curve will gradually move to the right, leading to a sequence of short-run equilibria as indicated by the double-headed arrow.

Eventually, as is clear from the production box analysis, a new long-run equilibrium will be attained either at a point where the long-run supply curve turns up again to intersect the new demand curve (this intersection would correspond to point B_2 in Fig. 2); or the supply curve never turns up, in which case the economy will be driven to specialise in the production of X (corresponding to a factor allocation at point O_Y in Fig. 2). In both cases the paradoxical price–output response will never be observed.

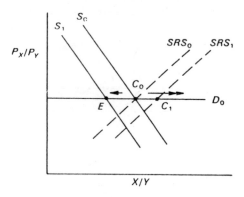

Fig. 8. Effects of a change in the level of a factor market distortion, when the value and physical factor intensity rankings differ.

An identical argument applies to the effects of a change in distortion levels. The comparative static analysis predicts that the new long run equilibrium in Fig. 4 will be at a point such as J; but, following the first move from B_0 to B_1, capital will move out of sector Y, and the factor allocation point will move in a north-easterly direction, towards a new equilibrium either at a point such as B_2 or (if no such point exists) at O_Y. In relative output–relative price space, as shown in Fig. 8, the long-run supply curve shifts to the left, reflecting a perverse distortion–output response. But the dynamic analysis shows that the equilibrium will initially move from C_0 to C_1, as the short-run supply curve shifts from SRS_0 to SRS_1; and following the reallocation of capital into sector X the equilibrium will move to the right along the demand curve, as indicated by the double-headed arrow.

Evidently a similar analysis could be carried out for the effect of any exogenous change in an economy where the value and physical factor intensity rankings differ. The common feature of all these cases is that every long-run equilibrium in the Edgeworth–Bowley box corresponds to an intersection of the contract curve and a labour–market equilibrium locus (both of which must be upward-sloping); but from the simple dynamic adjustment mechanism implicit in the short-run capital specificity hypothesis, such equilibria are stable only when the labour-market equilibrium locus is *more* steeply sloped than the contract curve. This condition in turn implies that the rankings of the two sectors by value and physical factor intensities must be the same. Hence, we may conclude that the long-run comparative static paradoxes which have received so much attention in recent writings are associated with unstable long-run equilbria only, and will therefore "almost never" be observed in practice.[1]

6. INTERSECTORAL CAPITAL MOBILITY AND "PARADOXES" IN INTERNATIONAL TRADE THEORY: A SURVEY

Sections 2–4 above examined three of the more striking predictions of the Heckscher–Ohlin–Samuelson model of a small open economy – that protection has an unambiguous effect on the real wage, population growth leaves wages unchanged and reduces the output of one sector, and unionisation in the relatively labour-intensive sector reduces both union and non-union wages – and showed that they do not hold when capital is assumed to be sector-specific. The purpose of the present section is to survey a number of additional cases where the assumption of sector-specific capital (SSC) leads to more intuitively plausible results than the assumption of intersectoral capital mobility (ICM). It will be seen that adopting this perspective serves to synthesise a substantial portion of international trade theory. (Needless to say, the list is not intended to be exhaustive.)[2]

(i) *Technological progress and income distribution.* Findlay and Grubert (1959) and Johnson (1970, pp. 46–7) showed that, with ICM, technological progress in the relatively capital-intensive sector must lower the real wage at constant commodity prices. With SSC, however, McCulloch (1976) has shown that technological progress in *either* sector must benefit labour (except in an extreme case where the technological progress is Hicksian labour-saving, and the potential for factor substitution in the progressing sector is implausibly low).

(ii) *Technological progress and the terms of trade.* Findlay and Grubert also showed that with ICM technological progress in one sector is not necessarily "ultra-biased" (i.e. the output of the other sector need not fall), and hence it has an ambiguous impact on the terms of trade, if it "saves" the factor which that sector uses relatively *less* intensively. (For example, if exportables are capital-intensive, the effect on the terms of trade of labour-saving progress in exportables or of capital-saving progress in importables cannot be predicted without a knowledge of domestic demand patterns.) By contrast, with SSC, technological progress in one sector is usually ultrabiased (except in the extreme case mentioned in (i) above), and hence its effect on the terms of trade is in the "expected" direction (i.e. they improve following progress in the import-competing sector and deteriorate following progress in exportables). Thus the assumption of SSC serves to rehabilitate partially the much-maligned claim of Hicks (1953) that import-biased technological progress in the United States would improve the U.S. terms of trade.

---

[1] Although this conclusion has only been demonstrated here for a particular adjustment mechanism, I have shown in Neary (1978b) that it continues to hold under a more general mechanism which allows for non-instantaneous adjustment in the labour market.

[2] Not all the results for the specific capital model mentioned in this list have been published. Where references are not given, substantiation of the assertions made may be obtained from the author.

(iii) *Income distribution and the offer curve.* Johnson (1959) showed that if labour and capital income recipients have different consumption patterns, it is possible with *ICM* for imports to behave as a Giffen good in aggregate consumption, implying complicated shapes for the offer curve, and introducing the possibilities of multiple trade equilibria and reversals of trade direction. From a purely formal point of view, this phenomenon is identical with the redistributive effect which endangers the uniqueness of momentary equilibrium in Uzawa's two sector model of economic growth (which, of course, assumes *ICM*); see Hahn (1965). In both cases the paradoxical outcomes are possible when each factor has a higher marginal propensity to consume the commodity in the production of which it is used relatively intensively. Once again, however, these problems do not arise with *SSC* (at least when full employment is assumed).

(iv) *Harris–Todaro model.* In their analysis of rural–urban migration in response to differences between the actual wage in agriculture and the expected wage in urban areas, Harris and Todaro (1970) assumed *SSC*. However, subsequent work has extended their model to allow *ICM*, and has discovered the possibility of a number of "paradoxes": an increase in the urban minimum wage can increase manufacturing output and employment (Corden and Findlay, 1975); urban unemployment may increase following capital accumulation and fall following population growth (*loc. cit.*); and the model is unstable if the urban sector is labour abundant relative to the rural sector (Neary, 1977). None of these pathological outcomes is possible in the original Harris–Todaro case with *SSC*.

(v) *Devaluation with rigid wages.* Jones and Corden (1976) have examined the effect of devaluation on the trade balance of a small open economy in a two-sector model which distinguishes between traded and non-traded goods rather than between exportables and importables. Assuming continual government intervention to maintain full employment and a constant nominal wage, they found that a devaluation always leads to a trade surplus under *SSC*, but (paradoxically) to a trade *deficit* under *ICM* when tradeables are relatively labour-intensive. Moreover, under the short-run capital specificity hypothesis, long-run equilibrium is unstable in the paradoxical case. Similar conclusions under *ICM* have been found by Helpman (1976) in a model which resembles that of Jones and Corden but allows the level of employment to vary.

(vi) *Variable factor supplies and specialisation.* The introduction into the *ICM* model of variable factor supplies which respond positively to their real return increases the likelihood that even a relatively small change in the terms of trade will lead the economy to specialise in one or other commodity (see Martin, 1976). In the limit, when one factor is in infinitely elastic supply at a given return (i.e. when the economy faces a binding minimum wage or rental constraint) there is only one relative commodity price ratio which is consistent with non-specialisation (see Brecher, 1974). With *SSC*, however, specialisation is much less likely: although Caves (1971, p. 18) claimed that if the capital goods specific to each sector were internationally mobile, one country would have to specialise, Amano (1977) has shown that this is not necessarily the case.

(vii) *Many-factor, many-commodity generalisations.* The elegance of the properties of the 2 × 2 model with *ICM* have led to many attempts to generalise them to models with many goods and factors (all of the latter being assumed to be perfectly mobile between all sectors). (See Ethier, 1974, for a recent survey and extension.) Without wishing to denigrate the intellectual activity which has been expended on this, it is probably fair to say that the results in this area have been disappointing: the properties of the two-good two-mobile-factor model do not appear to generalise in any simple way to the many-goods many-factors case. By contrast, the extension of the *SSC* model to many commodities is relatively straightforward (see Mussa, 1974; and Jones, 1975).

The preceding survey provides convincing evidence, if any were needed, that *ICM* is the source of many of the counter-intuitive results or "paradoxes" to be found in international trade theory.[1] Another way of expressing the same point is that *SSC* provides a rigorous general equilibrium foundation for partial equilibrium analysis as far as the supply side of the economy is concerned, whereas with *ICM* partial equilibrium reasoning will frequently be misleading (see Samuelson, 1971*a*). At the very least, these observations provide a convenient unifying principle for much of international trade theory.

7. A CRITIQUE OF THE ASSUMPTION OF INTERSECTORAL CAPITAL MOBILITY

The preceding sections have interpreted the assumption of *SSC* as referring to the short run, and the Heckscher–Ohlin–Samuelson assumption of *ICM* as referring to the long run. However, it is tempting to go further and to argue that there is *no* time horizon over which the assumption of *ICM* is appropriate. For short-run analysis it is clear that *SSC* is more satisfactory;[2] this is confirmed by the fact that it is more consistent with the apparent perceptions of industry and trade-union lobbyists (see Magee, 1977). Of course, for medium- and long-run analysis, *SSC* is quite unrealistic: changes in exogenous variables which give rise to intersectoral differences in quasi-rents must lead sooner or later to intersectoral resource reallocation if competitive pressures are allowed to operate. It is here, however, that a major difficulty with the assumption of *ICM* becomes apparent: in practice, medium-run resource reallocation does not for the most part take the form of a diversion of physical capital equipment from one use to another, with the total stock of homogeneous, infinitely long-lived machines remaining constant throughout. Rather it appears frequently to take the form of a slowing down in the rate of replacement of depreciating capital goods in the declining sector, coinciding with a rechannelling of new investment towards the expanding

---

[1] It may be conjectured that *ICM* is the source of *all* the paradoxes which are peculiar to international trade theory, with the exception of those which arise from the failure to adopt first-best policies, and which therefore fall under the head of the theory of the second best. The latter include both those paradoxes which arise from the failure to follow first best *trade* policies (such as the Metzler paradox and the Bhagwati (1958) form of immiserising growth), and those which arise from the failure to follow first best *domestic* policies (such as various welfare paradoxes which are possible in the presence of factor market distortions, all of which may be viewed as special cases of the immiserising growth phenomenon; see Bhagwati (1973)).

[2] This is not to say that the assumptions underlying the short-run capital specificity hypothesis are completely satisfactory: for example, though immobile between sectors, capital is assumed to be no less substitutable for labour in the short run than it is in the long run. However, since shift lengths are variable even in the very short run, this assumption may not be excessively unrealistic.

sector. Once it is recognised that investment requires abstinence from consumption, it is clear that, except under very strong assumptions, this process will lead to a change in the total capital stock between the old and the new long-run equilibria. Hence the usual long-run Heckscher–Ohlin–Samuelson predictions will not follow in general.[1] Pending the development of a more satisfactory way of modelling the process of medium-run intersectoral resource allocation, this suggests that the Heckscher–Ohlin–Samuelson model should be treated with more caution and less esteem than is currently the case in international trade theory.

8. SUMMARY AND CONCLUSION

This paper has presented a simple geometric technique to illustrate the process of adjustment towards long-run equilibrium in a two-sector economy where capital is sector-specific in the short run. The technique was used to show how such an economy would react to changes in commodity prices, in factor endowments, and in the level of factor market distortions. It was shown that the rational pursuit by market participants of their own self-interest could lead to behaviour very different from that implied by traditional "long-run" international trade theory.

The technique was also applied to analyse the behaviour of the Heckscher–Ohlin–Samuelson model of a small open economy with pre-existing factor market distortions. It was shown that if such an economy is assumed to adjust according to the short-run capital specificity adjustment process, then an equilibrium where the rankings of the two sectors by physical and value factor intensities differ must be dynamically unstable. This means that a number of paradoxes which have attracted much attention in recent writings, such as a perverse price–output response and a perverse distortion–output response, will "almost never" be observed.

Finally, attention was drawn to the pivotal role of the assumption of intersectoral capital mobility in international trade theory: this assumption was shown to be largely responsible for a propensity to generate paradoxes which is seen by many as an unattractive feature of the theory. It was argued that the assumption is inappropriate over any time horizon: in the short run capital goods are not mobile, while in the medium and long runs their total stock is not fixed.

It would perhaps be going too far to suggest, paraphrasing Jevons's remark about Ricardo, that the influence of Heckscher, Ohlin and Samuelson has shunted the car of international trade theory on to a wrong line.[2] Nevertheless, in a broader historical perspective, the concentration by trade theorists in the post-war period on an especially simple form of intersectoral capital mobility

---

[1] Even retaining the assumption of reallocation of a fixed stock of homogeneous machines between sectors, the Heckscher–Ohlin–Samuelson predictions will not hold in the long run if the two sectors face different costs of reallocation. See Mussa (1975).

[2] Such a suggestion would also be unfair to the originators of the theory. The analyses of Heckscher and Ohlin were considerably richer and less formalised than the theory which bears their name, while Ohlin at least can be interpreted as having assumed sector-specificity of capital, as Samuelson recently pointed out in his retraction of his own earlier views on factor price equalisation. See Samuelson (1971 b).

1978]   SHORT-RUN CAPITAL SPECIFICITY   509

may well be seen as a mistake, not merely because it is unrealistic (since this must be true to some extent of all assumptions) but because it focuses attention on a particular time horizon which bears little or no relation to any economically relevant time period. A more satisfactory way of conceptualising the effects of exogenous changes on medium run resource allocation is required.

Nuffield College, Oxford   J. PETER NEARY

Date of receipt of final typescript: November 1977

REFERENCES

Amano, A. (1977). "Specific Factors, Comparative Advantage, and International Investment." *Economica*, vol. 44, 131–44.
Bhagwati, J. N. (1958). "Immiserizing Growth: a Geometrical Note." *Review of Economic Studies*, vol. 25, 201–5.
—— (1973). "The Theory of Immiserizing Growth; Further Applications." In *International Trade and Money* (ed. M. Connolly and A. K. Swobada), pp. 45–54. London: George Allen & Unwin.
—— and T. N. Srinivasan (1971). "The Theory of Wage Differentials; Production Response and Factor Price Equalization." *Journal of International Economics*, vol. 1, 19–35.
Brecher, R. A. (1974). "Minimum Wage Rates and the Pure Theory of International Trade." *Quarterly Journal of Economics*, vol. 88, 98–116.
Caves, R. E. (1971). "International Corporations: the Industrial Economics of Foreign Investment." *Economica*, vol. 38, 1–27.
Corden, W. M. and Findlay, R. (1975). "Urban unemployment, intersectoral capital mobility and development policy." *Economica*, vol. 42, 59–78.
Ethier, W. (1974). "Some of the Theorems of International Trade with Many Goods and Factors." *Journal of International Economics*, vol. 4, 199–206.
Findlay, R. and Grubert, H. (1959). "Factor Intensities, Technological Progress and the Terms of Trade." *Oxford Economic Papers*, vol. 11, 111–21.
Hahn, F. H. (1965). "On Two Sector Growth Models." *Review of Economic Studies*, vol. 32, 339–46.
Harberger, A. C. (1962). "The Incidence of the Corporation Income Tax." *Journal of Political Economy*, vol. 70, 215–40
Harris, J. R. and Todaro, M. P. (1970). "Migration, Unemployment and Development: a Two-sector Analysis." *American Economic Review*, vol 60, 126–42.
Helpman, E. (1976). "Macroeconomic Policy in a Model of International Trade with a Wage Restriction." *International Economic Review*, vol. 17, 262–77.
Hicks, J. R. (1953). "An Inaugural Lecture: 2. The Long-run Dollar Problem." *Oxford Economic Papers*, vol. 5, 121–35.
Hu, S. C. (1973). "Capital Mobility and the Effects of Unionization." *Southern Economic Journal*, vol. 39, 526–34.
Johnson, H. G. (1959). "International Trade, Income Distribution and the Offer Curve." *Manchester School of Economic and Social Studies*, vol. 27, 241–60.
—— (1970). "The Efficiency and Welfare Implications of the International Corporation." In *The International Corporation: A Symposium* (ed. C. P. Kindleberger). Cambridge: M.I.T. Press.
—— and Mieszkowski, P. M. (1970). "The Effects of Unionization on the Distribution of Income: a General Equilibrium Approach." *Quarterly Journal of Economics*, vol. 84, 539–61.
Jones, R. W. (1965). "The Structure of Simple General Equilibrium Models." *Journal of Political Economy*, vol. 73, 557–72.
—— (1971a). "Distortions in Factor Markets and the General Equilibrium Model of Production." *Journal of Political Economy*, vol. 79, 437–59.
—— (1971b). "A Three-factor Model in Theory, Trade and History." In *Trade, Balance of Payments and Growth: Essays in Honor of C. P. Kindleberger* (ed. J. N. Bhagwati *et al.*). Amsterdam: North-Holland.
—— (1975). "Income Distribution and Effective Protection in a Multi-commodity Trade Model." *Journal of Economic Theory*, vol. 11, 1–15.
—— and Corden, W. M. (1976). "Devaluation, Non-flexible Prices, and the Trade Balance for a Small Country." *Canadian Journal of Economics*, vol. 9, 150–61.
Kemp, M. C. and Jones, R. W. (1962). "Variable Labour Supply and the Theory of International Trade." *Journal of Political Economy*, vol. 70, 30–6.
Magee, S. P. (1971). "Factor Market Distortions, Production, Distribution, and the Pure Theory of International Trade." *Quarterly Journal of Economics*, vol. 86, 623–43.

Magee, S. P. (1976). *International Trade and Distortions in Factor Markets*. New York: Marcel Dekker.
—— (1977). "Three Simple Tests of the Stolper–Samuelson Theorem." The University of Texas at Austin, Graduate School of Business, Working Paper 77–28, February.
Martin, J. P. (1976). "Variable Factor Supplies and the Heckscher–Ohlin–Samuelson Model." ECONOMIC JOURNAL, vol. 86, 820–31.
Mayer, W. (1974). "Short-run and Long-run Equilibrium for a Small Open Economy." *Journal of Political Economy*, vol. 82, 955–68.
McCulloch, R. (1976). "Technology, Trade and the Interests of Labor: a Short Run Analysis of the Development and International Dissemination of New Technology." Harvard Institute of Economic Research, Discussion Paper No. 489, June.
Mussa, M. (1974). "Tariffs and the Distribution of Income: the Importance of Factor Specificity, Substitutability, and Intensity in the Short and Long Run." *Journal of Political Economy*, vol. 82, 1191–204.
—— (1975). "Dynamic Adjustment to Relative Price Changes in the Heckscher–Ohlin–Samuelson Model." University of Rochester, Department of Economics, Discussion Paper No. 75–6, May.
Neary, J. P. (1977). "On the Harris–Todaro Model with Intersectoral Capital Mobility." Nuffield College, Oxford, mimeo, July.
—— (1978a). "Capital Subsidies and Employment in an Open Economy." *Oxford Economic Papers* (forthcoming).
—— (1978b). "Dynamic Stability and the Theory of Factor Market Distortions." *American Economic Review* (forthcoming).
Rybczynski, T. N. (1955). "Factor Endowments and Relative Commodity Prices." *Economica*, vol. 22, 336–41.
Samuelson, P. A. (1971a). "An Exact Hume–Ricardo–Marshall Model of International Trade." *Journal of International Economics*, vol. 1, 1–18.
—— (1971b). "Ohlin was right." *Swedish Journal of Economics*, vol. 73, 365–84.
Stolper, W. F. and Samuelson, P. A. (1941). "Protection and Real Wages." *Review of Economic Studies*, vol. 9, 58–73.
Woodland, A. D. (1977). "A Dual Approach to Equilibrium in the Production Sector in International Trade Theory." *Canadian Journal of Economics*, vol. 10, 50–68.

[5]

A tariff that worsens
the terms of trade

F. H. GRUEN

Monash University

W. M. CORDEN

Nuffield College, Oxford

It is a familiar proposition that the imposition of some level of tariff can raise a country's real income by improving its terms of trade. This argument is usually demonstrated by means of a two-product, two-factor and two-country model: e.g. [1, pp. 31–3].

In the past the terms of trade argument has been used on occasions as a justification for protecting manufacturing industry in Australia. Our paper seeks to show that, once a second export product is explicitly allowed for in the analysis, a favourable terms of trade effect of protection is less likely. In fact we shall show that in a particular world with three products and three factors and certain factor-intensity conditions not unlike those of Australia, a tariff may worsen the terms of trade by leading to increased production of one of the export products.

The model

Suppose we have an economy A operating under free trade where one product, textiles, is imported and two products, wool and grain, are exported. Initially we shall suppose that A is a small country confronted with an infinitely elastic demand for its exports. This assumption will of course be removed later, since otherwise there could be no terms of trade effect.

There are three factors of production, land, labour and capital. We assume that the production of both wool and grain require land and labour but not capital, and that textile production uses capital and labour but not land. Capital is therefore a specific input for the textile industry, land is specific for the two agricultural industries, whilst labour is mobile between all three industries. We assume perfect competition throughout, perfect divisibility of all factors and that all production functions are linear and homogeneous. Finally, and this assumption is crucial, we assume that grain production is always more labour-intensive than wool production. In other words, for any given ratio of the price of labour to the price of land the labour/land ratio is always higher in grain that in wool production.

The imposition of a tariff

We shall now examine the effect of the imposition of a tariff on the imported good, textiles. This will have two effects: (i) on the allocation of productive resources within the economy, and (ii) on the allocation of consumers' expenditures. We shall first examine the effect on the allocation of productive resources.

The imposition of a tariff will raise the domestic price of textiles. As a result textile production will become relatively more profitable and the value of the marginal product of labour and capital in textile production will increase. On the other hand, the marginal product of labour in wool and grain production has not altered. Some labour previously used in the production of wool and grain will therefore be attracted to textile production. The effect of protecting textile production will thus be to reduce the amount of labour which remains available for wool and grain production.

What will be the effect of a reduction in the supply of labour on the quantities of wool and grain? This question has in fact been answered by Rybczynski [2]. He shows that, in a two-factor, two-product model, if the quantity of one factor is increased with the quantity of the other remaining unchanged, the maintenance of the same factor–price ratio requires that there be an absolute expansion in the production of the commodity intensive in that factor and an absolute curtailment of production of the other commodity. In our model this means that if the quantity of labour available to agricultural industries is reduced while the quantity of land is fixed, and if the factor–price ratio is to stay unchanged, there must be an absolute reduction in the production of the labour-intensive good, grain, and an absolute increase in the production of the land-intensive good, wool. In this model, and at this stage of the argument, the factor–price ratio must stay unchanged, since, with constant returns to scale in both industries, there is a unique relation between the product–price ratio, which is given by the world prices of wool and grain, and the factor–price ratio. Hence the imposition of a tariff on textiles will increase the production of textiles *and of wool* and reduce the production of grain.

The effect of the imposition of a duty on textiles on consumers' expenditures will be to reduce consumption of textiles (since the local price has risen) and to increase the consumption of grain and wool.

If we look at the total effect of the duty on imports and exports of particular products, we obtain the following pictuie:

(a)   Imports of textiles will decline since local production of textiles increases whilst consumption declines.

(b)   Exports of grain will decline since local production declines whilst consumption increases.

(c)   The effect on exports of wool is uncertain. Both production and consumption will increase. Obviously if the increase in production exceeds the increase in consumption, exports of wool will increase and *vice versa*.

The terms of trade effect

We shall now drop the 'small country' assumption for wool exports and suppose that increased exports of wool would lead to a fall in the price of wool. We continue to assume that the country cannot affect the prices of grain and textiles. In the case of Australia there is some justification for this type of model.

The imposition of a duty on textiles may then lead to a deterioration of the country's terms of trade. The external prices of wheat and textiles have remained unchanged whilst the possible increase in wool exports would reduce local and world prices of wool and thus adversely affect the economy's terms of trade.

If our model were to represent a valid and useful simplification of the real world, what policy should country A adopt in order to improve its terms of trade? Obviously the first best policy would be to put an export tax on wool. Exactly the same result could be obtained by an appropriate export subsidy on grain combined with an import subsidy (negative tariff) at the same rate on textiles. If the only available policy instrument is a tariff on textiles (with an import subsidy ruled out) then the optimum tariff is zero. If taxes and subsidies on production and consumption of grain and textiles are feasible, then taxing production of textiles, subsidising production of grain, and taxing consumption of textiles and of grain would all improve the terms of trade.

Effect on the pattern of exports

Apart from this demonstration of a possible perverse terms-of-trade effect of protection, the model can be used to examine some interesting effects of protection on the allocation of resources between different export industries. In our example, with grain a closer substitute on the side of production for textiles than is wool, wool production increased and grain production decreased; factors of production moving from grain to wool. We might replace grain with another product M which can be taken to represent actual or potential exportable manufactures. A tariff will then shift resources out of industries producing manufactured exports into wool. Alternatively we might let M represent the domestic value-added element in exports of a processed (refined) mineral, say steel, and replace wool with the crude mineral iron ore. Exports consist then of iron ore and steel, the latter being a package of iron ore and the value added element in steel. A tariff will then increase the crude content of exports and reduce the processing or value added element in total exports. In this model protection will thus encourage more of our minerals to be exported *before* being processed.

References

[1] HARRY G. JOHNSON, *International Trade and Economic Growth* (Allen and Unwin, London, 1958).
[2] T. N. RYBCZYNSKI, 'Factor Endowments and Relative Commodity Prices', *Economica*, November 1965, pp. 336–341.

[6]

Journal of International Economics 4 (1974) 199–206. © North-Holland Publishing Company

SOME OF THE THEOREMS OF INTERNATIONAL TRADE WITH MANY GOODS AND FACTORS

Wilfred ETHIER*

University of Pennsylvania, Philadelphia, Penn. 19174, U.S.A.

The Heckscher–Ohlin model yields three important results beyond the Heckscher–Ohlin theorem itself: the Rybczynski, Stolper–Samuelson, and factor price equalization theorems. Recent years have witnessed many investigations of whether these results generalize to the case of n goods and n factors. This literature has succeeded both in clarifying our understanding of the neoclassical production model and in obtaining difficult and frequently elegant results. However, most of these results imply that the n by n generalizations of the simple and powerful 2 by 2 properties are true only subject to conditions on the relevant determinants that are at once stringent, complicated, and, frequently, economically arcane. A reader might not unnaturally conclude that the most significant implication is that the interesting 2 by 2 properties can not in practice be expected to hold in any essential way in the more general n by n environment and therefore reflect nothing more than the simplification to a world of two goods and two factors.[1] This I think would be a mistake. It is the primary intent of this note to argue that to a significant degree the powerful 2 by 2 results reflect essential properties of the neoclassical general equilibrium of production (as opposed to properties of a 2 by 2 model) and that therefore a central economic core of these results generalizes in a straightforward way to the n by n case.[2] These generalizations depend on no complicated matrix properties and indeed follow immediately from the most elementary properties of the model.

Secondarily, I shall argue that economic considerations suggest a somewhat different route for the n by n generalizations of the strongest properties than has thus far been taken, and I shall make some efforts in that direction.

---

*This paper owes much to the comments, criticisms, and suggestions of John Chipman and Murray Kemp; thanks are also due to David Humphrey and Ronald Jones.

[1] This impression would be reinforced by the fact that the conditions for many of the n by n results to hold can be interpreted as requiring that the $n \times n$ case reduce in some sense to the 2×2 case. See in particular Kemp and Wegge (1969), Uekawa (1971), and Uekawa, Kemp and Wegge (1973).

[2] For the contrary point of view see, for example, Pearce (1970).

Let me first present my notation by briefly setting out the basic model. All n goods are produced by means of the n factors according to strictly quasi-concave, linear homogeneous production functions: $1 = f_j(\theta_{1j}, \ldots, \theta_{nj})$, where $j = 1, \ldots, n$. θ_{ij} denotes the number of units of factor i being employed in the production of one unit of good j and depends upon factor prices: $\theta_{ij} = \theta_{ij}(w) \equiv \theta_{ij}(w_1, \ldots, w_n)$ for $i, j = 1, \ldots, n$, where w_j denotes the price of the jth factor. Assume always positive marginal products so that all resources are fully employed in equilibrium. Then if X, K, P, and w denote the (strictly positive) vectors of outputs, factor endowments, and commodity and factor prices respectively, and if all goods are produced,

$$K = \theta(w)X, \tag{1}$$

$$P = w\theta(w), \tag{2}$$

where $\theta(w)$ denotes the matrix of $\theta_{ij}(w)$'s. It can be shown [see, e.g., Samuelson (1953)] that

$$\left[\frac{\partial K_i}{\partial X_j}\right] = \theta(w), \tag{3}$$

$$\left[\frac{\partial P_j}{w_i}\right] = \theta(w), \tag{4}$$

or, in elasticity terms:

$$\left[\frac{X_j}{K_i}\frac{\partial K_i}{\partial X_j}\right] = \hat{K}^{-1}\left[\frac{\partial K_i}{\partial X_j}\right]\hat{X} = \hat{K}^{-1}\theta(w)\hat{X} \equiv [a_{ij}] \equiv A, \tag{5}$$

$$\left[\frac{w_i}{P_j}\frac{\partial P_j}{\partial w_i}\right] = \hat{w}\left[\frac{\partial P_j}{\partial w_i}\right]\hat{P}^{-1} = \hat{w}\theta(w)\hat{P}^{-1} \equiv [b_{ij}] \equiv B, \tag{6}$$

where $\hat{X}$ etc. denote the diagonal matrices formed from the vectors X etc. (i.e, $\hat{X}_{ii} = X_i$, $\hat{X}_{ij} = 0$ if $i \neq j$). It is easily seen that a_{ij} equals the proportion of the total supply of factor i devoted to industry j so that eq. (1) implies that $\Sigma_j a_{ij} = 1$ and so A is row stochastic. Similarly b_{ij} equals the distributive share of factor i in industry j so that as a consequence of Euler's theorem on homogeneous functions B is column stochastic. I shall assume that θ, A, and B have all strictly positive elements; the implications of zeroes are easily deduced.

In the 2 by 2 case[3] the Stolper–Samuelson and Rybczynski theorems are easily derived directly from eqs. (5) and (6). Since A and B are stochastic matrices A^{-1} and B^{-1} must each have one negative term and one term exceeding

---

[3]See, for example, Jones (1965) for an analysis of the 2 by 2 model. Also Ethier (1972) has a discussion of how these theorems are affected by nontraded goods.

unity in each row and each column. Thus it is possible to assign the goods and factors to each other in such a way that an increase in one commodity price increases by a greater proportion the corresponding factor reward while reducing absolutely the reward to the other factor, etc. The only condition is that A^{-1} and B^{-1} exist, i.e., that $\theta(w)$ be non-singular.

In the n by n case it is likewise desirable to know whether associations of factors and goods exist which lead to similar conclusions. But many different criteria are possible. Chipman (1969) has suggested two. The first, dubbed by Chipman the weak Stolper–Samuelson property, requires that for some numbering of goods and factors B^{-1} have diagonal elements that all exceed unity. Thus an increase in any commodity price would induce a change in the corresponding factor reward independent of index number considerations. Alternatively the strong Stolper–Samuelson property, as defined by Chipman, requires that for some numbering of goods and factors B^{-1} have elements exceeding unity along the diagonal and have all other elements negative, i.e., an increase in any commodity price must increase by a greater proportion the reward of the associated factor while reducing absolutely the rewards of all other factors. Inada (1971) has pointed out that an alternative non-equivalent strong property would be for B^{-1} to have negative elements along the diagonal and all other elements positive.

Considerable effort has been devoted to deriving necessary and sufficient conditions for these criteria.[4] However, it will be useful to first look more closely at the fundamental economic issues involved.

The basic problem is to establish the existence of one or more associations of *each* factor with *some* good and of one or more associations of *each* good with *some* factor that possess certain comparative statics properties of economic interest. I shall use S to refer to an association of each good (price) with some factor (price) and R to refer to an association of each factor (quantity) with some good (quantity). Also an association will be termed intensive if the changes in associated goods and factors are in the same direction, non-intensive if they are in opposite directions.

Taking the 2 by 2 case as an analogy, there seem to be two distinct economic properties that are of interest. First an association should be *unambiguous*. I call an S association, for example, unambiguous if an increase in any commodity price causes a change in the associated factor price that is independent of index number considerations, i.e., if the appropriate element of B^{-1} does not lie between zero and unity.

The second property of interest is *duality*. I say that an S intensive association, for example, is dual if an increase in any commodity price induces an unambiguous increase in the associated factor price *and* if, at constant prices, an increase in the supply of that factor induces an unambiguous rise in the output

[4]See in particular Chipman (1969), Kemp and Wegge (1969), Kemp (1969), Uekawa (1971), Wegge and Kemp (1969), Inada (1971), and Uekawa, Kemp and Wegge (1973).

of that commodity, i.e., the corresponding elements of A^{-1} and of B^{-1} both exceed unity.[5]

Chipman's weak criterion is concerned only with the first of these two properties and implies nothing about duality. The economic essence of this criterion seems to be that some unambiguous S association exist. Now, whereas the weak criterion in the specific matrix form originally stated by Chipman is not implied simply by the non-singularity of θ as in the 2 by 2 case, but instead requires strict additional conditions on B, it is true that a property actually stronger than the above general reformulation of the weak criterion does hold and that this property follows directly from eqs. (5) and (6) in as simple a fashion as in the 2 by 2 case.[6]

Theorem 1. Let $\theta(w)$ be non-singular. Then there exist:

(a)   unambiguous, dual R-non-intensive and S-non-intensive associations,

(b)   unambiguous, R-intensive and unambiguous, S-intensive associations.

Proof. Since θ is non-singular $AA^{-1} = I$, where I denotes the indentity matrix. Since A is row stochastic some positive weighted average of each column of A^{-1} equals zero; thus each such column must contain a negative element. Also some positive weighted average of each column equals unity; this together with a negative element in each column implies an element exceeding unity in each column. In like manner B^{-1} has a negative element and an element exceeding unity in each row. Finally, since $\hat{R}^{-1}$, $\hat{X}$, $\hat{w}$, and $\hat{P}^{-1}$ have strictly positive diagonals, θ^{-1}, A^{-1}, and B^{-1} have the same sign pattern.

Theorem 1 appears to me to be the strongest result obtainable without additional restrictions.[7] Immediate implications are that A has a dual R-intensive association if for some S-intensive association the total reward to each factor is at least as great as the output of its S-intensive good, and that B has a dual S-intensive association if for some R-intensive association the value of the total output of each good is at least as great as the total reward to its R-intensive factor.

Whereas I have thus far discussed 'weak' questions concerned with whether each good can be associated with some factor, etc., one can also follow the

[5]Duality and unambiguity represent the two general ideas that seem to be of interest although one could of course instead consider somewhat stronger or weaker alternative specific definitions. A stronger version of duality, for example, would be to require an S-intensive association to be the inverse of an R-intensive; a weaker version would be to require each factor to be S-intensive in some good.

[6]Murray Kemp has informed me that much of Theorem 1 was deduced by James Meade in private correspondence in 1968.

[7]Murray Kemp has shown that much of the theorem can be extended to the case of unequal numbers of goods and factors; see Kemp (1973). Also for a further discussion of duality see Kemp and Ethier (1973).

spirit of Chipman's discussion and investigate 'strong' questions concerned with whether each good can be associated with each factor, etc. Accordingly I say that a technology is strongly R-unambiguous if A^{-1} has no elements between zero and unity, strongly S-unambiguous if B^{-1} has no elements between zero and unity, and strongly dual if in addition all associations are dual. Note that a technology can be strongly R-unambiguous but neither strongly S-unambiguous nor strongly dual. However, since A^{-1} and B^{-1} must always have the same sign pattern, strong duality is equivalent to a technology being both strongly R-unambiguous and strongly S-unambiguous.

Now Chipman's strong criterion applied to B^{-1} is of course a particular example of a strongly S-unambiguous technology. But it also implies that the technology is strongly R-unambiguous and thus dual as well. This follows from the facts that A^{-1} must have the same sign pattern as B^{-1} and that the inverse of a row stochastic matrix also has unit row sums ($Au = u$ implies $u = A^{-1} u$, where u denotes the vector of ones) so that the positive diagonal elements of A^{-1} must also exceed unity. Thus Chipman's strong property is quite strong indeed.

It should be emphasized that the situation regarding Inada's alternative is, surprisingly enough, radically different from an economic point of view, despite a symmetry of mathematical results [for the latter see Inada (1971), and Uekawa, Kemp and Wegge (1973)]. For if B^{-1} has negative diagonal elements and positive off-diagonal elements the positive elements need not exceed unity (if n is greater than two) and thus B^{-1} need not be strongly S-unambiguous. And even if the positive elements are assumed to be greater than unity it does not follow that the technology is dual or strongly R-unambiguous. Thus despite the severe mathematical conditions necessary to establish Inada's criterion it is basically a 'weak' rather than a 'strong' result and indeed gives economic information of about the same value as that which Theorem 1 yields in 'almost all' cases.[8]

'Strong' properties need not hold 'almost always' and so additional necessary and sufficient conditions must be considered. Such conditions tend to be complicated and need not be of any interest because if they require one to perform tests involving an entire matrix one might just as well simply calculate the inverse in the first place. Attention thus focuses on conditions which can be given some intuitive interpretation, such as that the economy reduce to a 2 by 2 economy in some sense. Following Uekawa (1971), such a condition will be presented for the technology to be strongly unambiguous. In the 2 by 2 case good one is said to be intensive in factor one if $\theta_{11}/\theta_{21} > \theta_{12}/\theta_{22}$. An alternative statement of this condition would be to require that for each factor (say the first) there exists some good (in this case the first) and some positive proportional increases y_1 and y_2 in the present output levels X_1 and X_2 such that $\theta_{21}X_1y_1 = \theta_{22}X_2y_2$, $\theta_{11}X_1y_1 > \theta_{12}X_2y_2$ and $\theta_{11}X_1(y_1-\delta) < \theta_{12}X_2(y_2+\delta)$ for some positive $\delta \leqq y_1$.

[8]Inada's criterion is weaker than Theorem 1 in that it says nothing about intensive associations, stronger in that the nonintensive is unique and one to one.

It is in the context of this formulation of the factor intensity condition that the n by n economy will be required in a sense to reduce to a 2 by 2 economy. The following result is obtained easily enough.

Theorem 2. A non-singular positive $\theta(w)$ is strongly R-unambiguous if and only if for each factor k there exists some decomposition of the n goods into two groups J and $\bar{J}$ and some positive vector y such that if each industry output X_j is increased in the proportion y_j, then

(a) *the goods in J will together require exactly as much additional input of each factor other than k as will the goods in $\bar{J}$ together,*

(b) *the goods in J will together increase their use of factor k more than will the goods in $\bar{J}$ together,*

(c) *for some uniform reduction in the y_j of the J goods and increase in the y_j of the $\bar{J}$ goods, the latter will together require more additional units of k than will the former.*

Proof. The condition means that for some decomposition $J, \bar{J}$ of $\{1, \ldots, n\}$ and some positive y

$$\sum_{j\in J} a_{ij}y_j = \sum_{j\in\bar{J}} a_{ij}y_j, \qquad i \neq k, \tag{7}$$

$$\sum_{j\in J} a_{kj}y_j > \sum_{j\in\bar{J}} a_{kj}y_j, \tag{8}$$

$$\sum_{\in J} a_{kj}(y_j-\delta) < \sum_{j\in\bar{J}} a_{kj}(y_j+\delta), \quad \text{where } y_j-\delta \geq 0, j\in J. \tag{9}$$

Since A is row stochastic, eq. (9) can be rewritten as

$$\delta > \sum_{j\in J} a_{kj}y_j - \sum_{j\in\bar{J}} a_{kj}y_j,$$

or $\qquad 1 > \sum_{j\in J} a_{kj}\left(\frac{y_j}{\delta}\right) - \sum_{j\in\bar{J}} a_{kj}\left(\frac{y_j}{\delta}\right) \equiv m,$

or $\qquad 1 = \sum_{j\in J} a_{kj}z_j - \sum_{j\in\bar{J}} a_{kj}z_j, \quad \text{where} \quad z_j = y_j/\delta m. \tag{9'}$

Now eq. (8) implies that $1 > m > 0$, which together with $y_j-\delta \geq 0$ for $j\in J$ implies that $z_j > 1$ for $j\in J$. Let x be the vector such that $x_j = z_j$ for $j\in J$ and $x_j = -z_j$ for $j\in\bar{J}$. Thus eqs. (7) and (9') are equivalent to $Ax = e_k$, where e_k denotes the vector with the kth component equal to unity and all others zero. Then $A^{-1}e_k = x$, where x has no component between zero and unity. As the argument applies to each k this proves that the condition of the theorem is equivalent to A^{-1} having no element between zero and unity.[9]

[9]The method of Theorem 2 can also be applied to obtain an analogous condition for θ to be strongly *S*-unambiguous. Strong duality requires that the two conditions hold simultaneously.

In order to give some idea of how these 'strong' properties compare with Chipman's formulation of the strong criterion, it is desirable to have conditions for the latter based on that concept of factor intensity which motivated Theorem 2. The proof of this theorem immediately implies that A^{-1} has an element exceeding unity in each row and column and all other elements negative if and only if the set J in Theorem 2 has precisely one good. Also A^{-1} has a negative element in each row and column and all other elements greater than unity (i.e., the strengthened form of Inada's criterion) if and only if the set $\bar{J}$ in Theorem 2 has precisely one good.[10] Finally, it can easily be shown that a technology possesses Chipman's strong property if and only if for any set J of factors there exists a corresponding equal-sized set of goods and a positive vector y of proportional changes in outputs for which the goods in J will together use exactly as much additional input of each factor in $\bar{J}$ and uniformly more additional input of each factor in J than will the goods in $\bar{J}$ together.

I now turn briefly to the factor price equalization property. Most n by n treatments have been concerned[11] with the global univalence of the cost function (2). This problem is of interest in its own right and is central to whether complete diversification implies factor price equalization. But it is not relevant to what seems to me to be the essential message of factor price equalization: if trading countries have 'sufficiently similar' factor endowments commodity trade will completely substitute for factor movements whereas if the endowments are not 'sufficiently similar' factor prices can not possibly be equalized by trade regardless of the actual pattern of specialization. This result does not depend upon the global properties of the cost function and can easily be shown to generalize in full strength to the n by n case:

(a) For any P such that eq. (2) holds for some w there exists some closed cone $H(P)$ such that all countries with non-zero endowments in $H(P)$ will have equal factor prices if engaged in free trade at world prices P.

(b) For any K there exists a closed cone $G(K)$ such that for any positive $K' \in G(K)$ there exists a closed cone $M(K, K')$ such that countries with positive endowments K and K' will have equal factor prices if engaged in free trade at any world prices $P \in M(K, K')$.

(c) The cones $H(P)$ and $G(K)$ can be made exhaustive in the sense that $K \in H(P)$ and $K' \notin H(P)$ imply that countries with endowments K and K' can not have equal factor prices when trading at commodity prices P and that $K' \notin G(K)$ implies that countries with endowments K and K' can never have equal factor prices.[12]

[10]Note that if J contains but one good then part (c) of Theorem 2 must be trivially satisfied, i.e., it becomes a restriction only when J contains at least two goods.

[11]See, for example, Samuelson (1953, 1967), McKenzie (1955, 1960, 1967), Gale and Nikaido (1965), Pearce (1967), and Chipman (1969). For a notable exception see McKenzie (1955) and cf. also Pearce (1970, chs. 12 and 16).

[12]Proposition (a) is essentially McKenzie's (1955) Theorem 1 and propositions (b) and (c) can be proved in roughly similar fashion.

International Trade II

I have argued that the 2 by 2 Heckscher–Ohlin model is quite robust in the specific sense that an essential core of basic results generalizes in a straight-forward way to the *n* by *n* case. Indeed it is the Heckscher–Ohlin theorem itself which is apparently the least robust (and recall that this is quite fragile in the 2 by 2 case; see Jones' classic paper (1956–57) for example). Of course it must be a matter of opinion as to what is called the 'essential core'. But, once it is known that the strongest possible interpretations do not generalize without additional restrictions, there is reason to point out what does.

References

Chipman, S., 1969, Factor price equalization and the Stolper–Samuelson theorem, International Economic Review 10, 399–406.

Ethier, W., 1972, Non-traded goods and the Heckscher–Ohlin model, International Economic Review 13, 132–147.

Gale, D. and H. Nikaido, 1965, The Jacobian matrix and global univalence of mappings, Mathematische Annalen 159, 81–93.

Inada, Ken-Ichi, 1971, The production coefficient matrix and the Stolper–Samuelson condition, Econometrica 39, 219–240.

Jones, R.W., 1956–57, Factor proportions and the Heckscher–Ohlin theorem, Review of Economic Studies 24, 1–10.

Jones, R.W., 1965, The structure of simple general equilibrium models, Journal of Political Economy 73, 557–572.

Kemp, M.C., 1969, The pure theory of international trade and investment (Prentice-Hall, Englewood Cliffs).

Kemp, M.C., 1973, Relatively simple generalizations of the Stolper–Samuelson and Samuelson–Rybczynski theorems, unpublished.

Kemp, M. C. and W. Ethier, 1973, A note on joint production and the theory of international trade, Department of Economics Discussion Paper no. 265 (University of Pennsylvania, Philadelphia).

Kemp, M.C. and L.L. Wegge, 1969, On the relation between commodity prices and factor rewards, International Economic Review 10, 407–413.

McKenzie, L.W., 1955, Equality of factor prices in world trade, Econometrica 23, 239–257.

McKenzie, L.W., 1960, Matrices with dominant diagonals and economic theory, in: Arrow, Karlin and Suppes, eds., Mathematical methods in the social sciences, 1959 (Stanford University Press, Stanford) 47–62.

McKenzie, L.W., 1967, The inversion of cost functions: A counter-example, International Economic Review 8, 271–278.

Pearce, I., 1967, More about factor price equalization, International Economic Review 8, 255–270.

Pearce, I., 1970, International trade (Norton, New York).

Samuelson, P.A., 1953, Prices of factors and goods in general equilibrium, Review of Economic Studies 21, 1–20.

Samuelson, P.A., 1967, Summary on factor price equalization, International Economic Review 8, 286–295.

Uekawa, Y., 1971, Generalization of the Stolper–Samuelson theorem, Econometrica 39, 197–218.

Uekawa, Y., M.C. Kemp and L.L. Wegge, 1973, *P*- and *PN*-matrices, Minkowski- and Metzler-matrices, and generalization of the Stolper–Samuelson and Samuelson–Rybczynski theorems, Journal of International Economics 3, 53–76.

Wegge, L.L. and M.C. Kemp, 1969, Generalizations of the Stolper–Samuelson and Samuelson–Rybczynski theorems in terms of conditional input–output coefficients, International Economic Review 10, 414–425.

Part II
Theories of International Trade

A
Trade Based on Comparative Advantage

[7]

Comparative Advantage, Trade, and Payments in a Ricardian Model with a Continuum of Goods

By R. DORNBUSCH, S. FISCHER, AND P. A. SAMUELSON*

This paper discusses Ricardian trade and payments theory in the case of a continuum of goods. The analysis thus extends the development of many-commodity, two-country comparative advantage analysis as presented, for example, in Gottfried Haberler (1937), Frank Graham (1923), Paul Samuelson (1964), and Frank W. Taussig (1927). The literature is historically reviewed by John Chipman (1965). Perhaps surprisingly, the continuum assumption simplifies the analysis neatly in comparison with the discrete many-commodity case. The distinguishing feature of the Ricardian approach emphasized in this paper is the determination of the competitive margin in production between imported and exported goods. The analysis advances the existing literature by formally showing precisely how tariffs and transport costs establish a range of commodities that are not traded, and how the price-specie flow mechanism does or does not give rise to movements in relative cost and price levels.

The formal *real* model is introduced in Section I. Its equilibrium determines the *relative* wage and price structure and the efficient international specialization pattern. Section II considers standard comparative static questions of growth, demand shifts, technological change, and transfers. Extensions of the model to nontraded goods, tariffs, and transport costs are then studied in Section III. Monetary considerations are introduced in Section IV, which examines the price-specie mechanism under stable parities, floating exchange rate regimes, and also questions of unemployment under sticky money wages.

*Massachusetts Institute of Technology. Helpful comments from Ronald W. Jones are gratefully acknowledged. Financial support was provided by a Ford Foundation grant to Dornbusch, NSF GS-41428 to Fischer, and NSF 75-04053 to Samuelson.

I. The Real Model

In this section we develop the basic real model and determine the equilibrium relative wage and price structure along with the efficient geographic pattern of specialization. Assumptions about technology are specified in Section IA. Section IB deals with demand. In Section IC the equilibrium is constructed and some of its properties are explored. Throughout this section we assume zero transport costs and no other impediments to trade.

A. *Technology and Efficient Geographic Specialization*

The many-commodity Ricardian model assumes constant unit labor requirements $(a_1, \ldots, a_n)$ and $(a_1^*, \ldots, a_n^*)$ for the n commodities that can be produced in the home and foreign countries, respectively. The commodities are conveniently indexed so that relative unit labor requirements are ranked in order of diminishing home country comparative advantage,

$$a_1^*/a_1 > \ldots > \ldots > a_i^*/a_i > \ldots > a_n^*/a_n$$

where an asterisk denotes the foreign country.

In working with a continuum of goods, we similarly index commodities on an interval, say [0, 1], in accordance with diminishing home country comparative advantage. A commodity z is associated with each point on the interval, and for each commodity there are unit labor requirements in the two countries, $a(z)$ and $a^*(z)$, with relative unit labor requirement given by

$$(1) \qquad A(z) \equiv \frac{a^*(z)}{a(z)} \qquad A'(z) < 0$$

The relative unit labor requirement function in (1) is by strong assumption continuous, and by construction (ranking or indexing of goods), decreasing in z. The function $A(z)$ is shown in Figure 1 as the downward sloping schedule.

Consider now the range of commodities produced domestically and those produced abroad, as well as the relative price structure associated with given wages. For that purpose we define as w and w^* the domestic and foreign wages measured in *any* (common!) unit. The home country will efficiently produce all those commodities for which domestic unit labor costs are less than or equal to foreign unit labor costs. Accordingly, any commodity z will be produced at home if

$$(2) \qquad a(z)w \leq a^*(z)w^*$$

Thus

$$(2') \qquad\qquad \omega \leq A(z)$$

where (3) defines the parameter ω, fundamental to Ricardian analysis,

$$(3) \qquad\qquad \omega \equiv w/w^*$$

This is the ratio of our real wage to theirs (our "double-factoral terms of trade"). It follows that for a given relative wage ω the home country will efficiently produce the range of commodities

$$(4) \qquad\qquad 0 \leq z \leq \tilde{z}(\omega)$$

where taking (2') with equality defines the borderline commodity z, for which

$$(5) \qquad\qquad \tilde{z} = A^{-1}(\omega)$$

$A^{-1}(\ )$ being the inverse function of $A(\ )$. By the same argument the foreign country will specialize in the production of commodities in the range

$$(4') \qquad\qquad \tilde{z}(\omega) \leq z \leq 1$$

The minimum cost condition determines the structure of relative prices. The relative price of a commodity z in terms of any other commodity z', when both goods are produced in the home country, is equal to the ratio of home unit labor costs:

$$(6) \quad P(z)/P(z') = wa(z)/wa(z')$$
$$= a(z)/a(z');$$
$$z \leq \tilde{z}, z' \leq \tilde{z}$$

The relative price of home produced z in terms of a commodity z'' produced abroad is by contrast

$$(7) \quad P(z)/P(z'') = wa(z)/w^* a^*(z'')$$
$$= \omega a(z)/a^*(z'');$$
$$z < \tilde{z} < z''$$

In summarizing the supply part of the model we note that any specified relative real wage is associated with an efficient geographic specialization pattern characterized by the borderline commodity $\tilde{z}(\omega)$ as well as by a relative price structure. (The pattern is "efficient" in the sense that the world is out on, and not inside, its production-possibility frontier.)

B. *Demand*

On the demand side, the simplest Mill-Ricardo analysis imposes a strong homothetic structure in the form of J. S. Mill or Cobb-Douglas demand functions that associate with each ith commodity a *constant expenditure share*, b_i. It further assumes *identical* tastes for the two countries or *uniform* homothetic demand.

By analogy with the many-commodity case, which involves budget shares

$$b_i = P_i C_i / Y \qquad b_i = b_i^*$$

$$\sum_1^n b_i = 1$$

We therefore prescribe for the continuum case a given $b(z)$ profile:

$$(8) \qquad\qquad b(z) = P(z)C(z)/Y > 0$$
$$b(z) = b^*(z)$$
$$\int_0^1 b(z)\,dz = 1$$

where Y denotes total income, C demand for and P the price of commodity z.

Next we define the fraction of income spent (anywhere) on those goods in which the home country has a comparative advantage:

$$(9) \qquad \vartheta(\tilde{z}) \equiv \int_0^{\tilde{z}} b(z)\,dz > 0$$
$$\vartheta'(\tilde{z}) = b(\tilde{z}) > 0$$

where again $(0, \bar{z})$ denotes the range of commodities for which the home country enjoys a comparative advantage. With a fraction ϑ of each country's income, and therefore of world income, spent on home produced goods, it follows that the fraction of income spent on foreign produced commodities is

$$(9') \quad 1 - \vartheta(\bar{z}) \equiv \int_{\bar{z}}^{1} b(z)\,dz$$

$$0 \leq \vartheta(z) \leq 1$$

C. Equilibrium Relative Wages and Specialization

To derive the equilibrium relative wage and price structure and the associated pattern of efficient geographic specialization, we turn next to the condition of market equilibrium. Consider the home country's labor market, or equivalently the market for domestically produced commodities. With $\bar{z}$ denoting the *hypothetical* dividing line between domestically and foreign produced commodities, equilibrium in the market for home produced goods requires that domestic labor income wL equals world spending on domestically produced goods:

$$(10) \quad wL = \vartheta(\bar{z})(wL + w^*L^*)$$

Equation (10) associates with each $\bar{z}$ a value of the relative wage w/w^* such that market equilibrium obtains. This schedule is drawn in Figure 1 as the upward sloping locus and is obtained from (10) by rewriting the equation in the form:

$$(10') \quad \omega = \frac{\vartheta(\bar{z})}{1 - \vartheta(\bar{z})}\,(L^*/L) = B(\bar{z}; L^*/L)$$

where it is apparent from (9) that the schedule starts at zero and approaches infinity as $\bar{z}$ approaches unity.

To interpret the $B(\ )$ schedule we note that it is entirely a representation of the demand side; and in that respect it shows that if the range of domestically produced goods were increased at constant relative wages, demand for domestic labor (goods) would increase as the dividing line is shifted —at the same time that demand for foreign

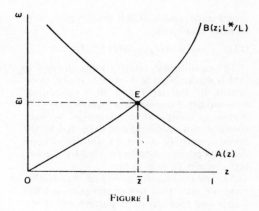

FIGURE 1

labor (goods) would decline.[1] A rise in the domestic relative wage would then be required to equate the demand for domestic labor to the existing supply.

An alternative interpretation of the $B(\ )$ schedule as the locus of trade balance equilibria uses the fact that (10) can be written in the balance-of-trade form:

$$(10'') \quad [1 - \vartheta(\bar{z})]wL = \vartheta(\bar{z})w^*L^*$$

This states that equilibrium in the trade balance means imports are equal in value to exports. On this interpretation, the $B(\ )$ schedule is upward sloping because an increase in the range of commodities hypothetically produced at home at constant relative wages lowers our imports and raises our exports. The resulting trade imbalance would have to be corrected by an increase in our relative wage that would raise our import demand for goods and reduce our exports, and thus restore balance.

The next step is to combine the demand side of the economy with the condition of efficient specialization as represented in equation (5), which specifies the competitive margin as a function of the relative wage. Substituting (5) in (10') yields as a solution the unique relative wage $\bar{\omega}$, at which the world is efficiently specialized, is in bal-

---

[1]Throughout this paper we refer to "domestic" goods as commodities produced in the home country rather than to commodities that are nontraded. The latter we call "nontraded" goods.

anced trade, and is at full employment with all markets clearing:

$$(11) \qquad \bar{\omega} = A(\bar{z}) = B(\bar{z}; L^*/L)$$

The equilibrium relative wage defined in (11) is represented in Figure 1 at the intersection of the $A(\ )$ and $B(\ )$ schedules.[2] Commodity $\bar{z}$ denotes the equilibrium borderline of comparative advantage between commodities produced and exported by the home country ($0 \leq z \leq \bar{z}$), and those commodities produced and exported by the foreign country ($\bar{z} \leq z \leq 1$).

Among the characteristics of the equilibrium we note that the equilibrium relative wages and specialization pattern are determined by technology, tastes, and relative size (as measured by the relative labor force).[3] The relative price structure associated with the equilibrium at point E is defined by equations (6) and (7) once (11) has defined the relative wage $\bar{\omega}$ and the equilibrium specialization pattern $\bar{z}(\bar{\omega})$.

The equilibrium levels of production $Q(z)$ and $Q^*(z)$, and employment in each industry $L(z)$ and $L^*(z)$, can be recovered from the demand structure and unit labor requirements once the comparative advantage pattern has been determined.

We note that with identical homothetic tastes across countries and no distortions, the relative wage $\bar{\omega}$ is a measure of the well-

---

[2]See the Appendix for the relation of the diagram to previous analyses.

[3]The construction of the $B(\ )$ schedule relies heavily on the Cobb-Douglas demand structure. If, instead, demand functions were identical across countries and homothetic, an analogous schedule could be constructed. In the general homothetic case, however, a set of relative prices is required at each z to calculate the equivalent of the $B(\ )$ schedule; the relative prices are those that apply on the $A(\bar{z})$ schedule for that value of z. In this case the independence of the $A(\ )$ and $B(\ )$ schedules is obviously lost. In the general homothetic case there is still a unique intersection of the $A(\ )$ and $B(\ )$ schedules. For more general nonhomothetic demand structures, it is known that an equilibrium exists; but even in the case of two Ricardian goods there may be *no* unique equilibrium even though there will almost always be a finite number of equilibria. See Gerard Debreu and Stephen Smale. Extensions of our analysis with respect to the demand structure and the number of countries are developed in unpublished work by Charles Wilson.

being of the representative person-laborer at home relative to the well-being of the representative foreign laborer.

II. Comparative Statics

The unique real equilibrium in Figure 1 is determined jointly by tastes, technology, and relative size, L^*/L. We can now exploit Figure 1 to examine simple comparative static questions.

A. *Relative Size*

Consider first the effect of an increase in the relative size of the rest of the world. An increase in L^*/L by (10) shifts the $B(\ )$ trade balance equilibrium schedule upward in proportion to the change in relative size and must, therefore, raise the equilibrium relative wage at home and reduce the range of commodities produced domestically. It is apparent from Figure 2 that the domestic relative wage increases *proportionally less* than the decline in domestic relative size.

The rise in equilibrium relative wages due to a change in relative size can be thought of in the following manner. At the initial equilibrium, the increase in the foreign relative labor force would create an excess supply of labor abroad and an excess demand for labor at home—or, correspondingly, a trade surplus for the home country. The resulting increase in domestic relative wages serves to eliminate the trade surplus while

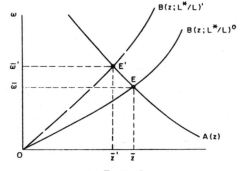

FIGURE 2

at the same time raising relative unit labor costs at home. The increase in domestic relative unit labor costs in turn implies a loss of comparative advantage in marginal industries and thus a needed reduction in the range of commodities produced domestically.

The welfare implications of the change in relative size take the form of an unambiguous improvement in the home country's real income and (under Cobb-Douglas demand) a reduction in real income per head abroad. We observe, too, that from the definition of the home country's share in world income and (10), we have

$$(12) \qquad wL/(wL + w^* L^*) = \vartheta(\bar{z})$$

It is apparent, as noted above, that a reduction in domestic relative size in raising the domestic relative wage (thereby reducing the range of commodities produced domestically) must under our Cobb-Douglas demand assumptions lower the home country's share in total world income and spending even though our per capita income rises.

B. *Technical Progress*

To begin with, we are concerned with the effects of uniform technical progress. By equation (1), a uniform proportional reduction in foreign unit labor requirements implies a reduction in $a^*(z)$ and therefore a proportional downward shift of the $A(z)$ schedule in Figure 1. At the initial relative wage $\bar{\omega}$, the loss of our comparative advantage due to a reduction in foreign unit labor costs will imply a loss of some industries in the home country and a corresponding trade deficit. The resulting induced decline in the equilibrium relative wage serves to restore trade balance equilibrium, and to offset in part our decline in comparative advantage.

The net effect is therefore a reduction in domestic relative wages, which must fall proportionally short of the decline in relative unit labor requirements abroad. The home country's terms of trade therefore improve as can be noted by using (7) for any two commodities z and z'', respectively, produced at home and abroad:

$$(13) \qquad \hat{P}(z) - \hat{P}(z'') = \hat{\bar{\omega}} - \hat{a}^*(z'') > 0$$

where a "hat" denotes a proportional change. Domestic real income increases, as does foreign real income.[4] The range of goods produced domestically declines since domestic labor, in efficiency units, is now relatively more scarce.

An alternative form of technical progress that can be studied is the international transfer of the least cost technology. Such transfers reduce the discrepancies in relative unit labor requirements— by lowering them for each z in the relatively less efficient country—and therefore flatten the $A(z)$ schedule in Figure 1. It can be shown that such harmonization of technology must benefit the innovating low-wage country, and that it may reduce real income in the high-wage country whose technology comes to be adopted. In fact, the high-wage country must lose if harmonization is complete so that relative unit labor requirements now become identical across countries and all our consumer's surplus from international trade vanishes.[5]

C. *Demand Shifts*

The case with a continuum of commodities requires a careful definition of a demand shift. For our purposes it is sufficient to ask: What is the effect of a shift from high z commodities toward low z commodities? It is apparent from Figure 2 that such a shift will cause the trade balance equilibrium schedule $B(\ )$ to shift up and to the left. It follows that the equilibrium domestic rela-

---

[4]The purchasing power of foreign labor income in terms of domestically produced goods is $w^* L^*/wa(z) = L^*/a(z)\bar{\omega}$ and in terms of foreign goods $L^*/a^*(z)$. The fact that foreigners' real income per head rises is guaranteed by our Cobb-Douglas demand assumption. In the general homothetic case, a balanced reduction in $a^*(z)$ can be immiserizing abroad if the real wage falls strongly in terms of all previously imported goods; however, the balanced drop in $a^*(z)$ in the general homothetic case *always* increases our real wage.

[5]Complete equilization of unit labor requirements implies that the $A(\ )$ schedule is horizontal at the level $\omega = A(z) = 1$. In this case geographic specialization becomes indeterminate and inessential.

tive wage will rise while the range of commodities produced by the home country declines. Domestic labor is allocated to a narrower range of commodities that are consumed with higher density while foreign labor is spread more thinly across a larger range of goods.

Welfare changes cannot be identified in this instance because tastes themselves have changed. It is true that domestic relative income rises along with the relative wage. Further we note that since $\bar{\omega}$ rises, the relative well-being of home labor to foreign labor (reckoned at the new tastes) is greater than was our laborers' relative well-being (reckoned at the old tastes).

D. *Unilateral Transfers*

Suppose foreigners make a continual unilateral transfer to us. With uniform homothetic tastes and no impediments to trade, neither curve is shifted by the transfer since we spend the transfer *exactly* as foreigners would have spent it but for the transfer. The new equilibrium involves a recurring trade deficit for us, equal to the transfer, but there is no change in the terms of trade. As Bertil Ohlin argued against John Maynard Keynes, here is a case where full equilibration takes place solely as a result of the spending transfers. When we introduce nontraded goods below, Ohlin's presumption will be found to require detailed qualifications, as it also would if tastes differed geographically.

III. Extensions of the Real Model

Extensions of the real model taken up in this section concern nontraded goods, tariffs, and transport costs. The purpose of this section is twofold. First we establish how the exogenous introduction of nontraded goods qualifies the preceding analysis. Next we turn to a particular specification of tariffs and transport costs to establish an equilibrium range of endogenously determined nontraded goods as part of the equilibrium solution of the model. Transfers are then shown to affect the equilibrium

relative price structure and the range of goods traded.

A. *Nontraded Goods*

To introduce nontraded goods into the analysis we assume that a fraction k of income is everywhere spent on internationally traded goods, and a fraction $(1 - k)$ is spent in each country on nontraded commodities. With $b(z)$ continuing to denote expenditure densities for traded goods, we have accordingly

$$(14) \qquad k \equiv \int_0^1 b(z)\,dz < 1$$

where z denotes traded goods.[6] As before the fraction of income spent on domestically exportable commodities is $\vartheta(z)$, except that ϑ now reaches a maximum value of $\vartheta(1) = k$.

Equation (1) remains valid for traded goods, but the trade balance equilibrium condition in $(10'')$ must now be modified to:

$$(15) \qquad [1 - \vartheta(\bar{z}) - (1 - k)]wL$$
$$= \vartheta(\bar{z})w^*L^*$$

since domestic spending on imports is equal to income less spending on *all* domestically produced goods including nontraded commodities. Equation (15) can be rewritten as

$$(15') \qquad \omega = \frac{\vartheta(\bar{z})}{k - \vartheta(\bar{z})}\,(L^*/L)$$

where k is a constant and therefore independent of the relative wage structure.

We note that $(15')$ together with (5) determines the equilibrium relative wage and efficient geographic specialization, $(\bar{\omega}, \bar{z})$. Further it is apparent that $(15')$ has exactly the same properties as $(10')$ and that accordingly a construction of equilibrium like that in Figure 1 remains appropriate. The equilibrium relative wage again depends on

---

[6] We can think of the range of nontraded goods as another [0, 1] interval with commodities denoted by x and expenditure fractions on those goods given by $c(x)$. With these definitions we have $\int_0^1 c(x)\,dx = 1 - k$, a positive fraction.

relative size, technology, and demand conditions. In this case demand conditions explicitly include the fraction of income spent on traded goods:

$$(11') \quad \bar{\omega} = \frac{\vartheta(\bar{z})}{k - \vartheta(\bar{z})} \frac{L^*}{L} = A(\bar{z})$$

This nicely generalizes our previous equilibrium of (11) to handle exogenously given nontraded goods.[7]

Two applications of the extended model highlight the special aspects newly introduced by nontraded goods. First consider a shift in demand (in each country) toward *nontraded* goods. To determine the effects on the equilibrium relative wage we have to establish whether this shift is at the expense of high or low z commodities. In the former case the home country's relative wage increases while in the latter case it declines. If the shift in demand in each country is uniform so that $b(z)$ is reduced in the same proportion for all z in both countries, then the relative wage remains unchanged.

Consider next a transfer received by the home country in the amount T measured in terms of foreign labor. As is well known, and already shown, with identical homothetic tastes and *no* nontraded goods, a transfer leaves the terms of trade unaffected. In the present case, however, the condition for balanced trade, inclusive of transfers, becomes:

$$(16) \quad T = (k - \vartheta)[\omega L + T]$$
$$- \vartheta[L^* - T]$$

or, in equilibrium,

(16')

$$\bar{\omega} = \frac{1 - k}{k - \vartheta(\bar{z})} (T/L) + \frac{\vartheta(\bar{z})}{k - \vartheta(\bar{z})} (L^*/L)$$

It is apparent from (16') that a transfer receipt by the home country causes the trade balance equilibrium schedule in Figure 1 to shift upward at each level of z. Accordingly, the equilibrium domestic relative wage increases and the range of commodities produced domestically is reduced. The steps in achieving this result are, first, that at the initial relative wage only a fraction of the transfer is spent on imports in the home country, while foreign demand for domestic goods similarly declines only by a fraction of their reduced income. The resulting surplus for the home country has to be eliminated by, second, an increase in the domestic relative wage and a corresponding improvement in the home country's terms of trade.[8]

The analysis of nontraded goods therefore confirms in a Ricardian model the "orthodox" presumption with respect to the terms of trade effects of transfers.[9]

B. *Transport Costs: Endogenous Equilibrium for Nontraded Goods*

The notion that transport costs give rise to a range of commodities that are nontraded is established in the literature and is particularly well stated by Haberler (1937). In contrast with the previous section we shall now endogenously determine the range of nontraded commodities as part of the equilibrium. We assume, following the "iceberg" model of Samuelson (1954), that transport costs take the form of "shrinkage" in transit so that a fraction $g(z)$ of commodity z shipped actually arrives. We further impose the assumption that $g = g(z)$ is identical for all commodities and the same for shipments in either direction.

The home country will produce commodities for which domestic unit labor cost falls short of foreign unit labor costs adjusted for shrinkage, and we modify (2') accordingly:

$$(17) \quad wa(z) \leq (1/g)w^*a^*(z)$$

or

$$\omega \leq A(z)/g$$

---

[7] Diagrams much like Figures 1 and 2 again apply: the descending $A(z)$ schedule is as before; and now the new rising schedule looks much as before. As before, a rise in L^*/L and a balanced drop in $a^*(z)$ will raise $\bar{\omega}$ and lower $\bar{z}$.

[8] At constant relative wages the current account worsens by $[(1 - k - \vartheta) + \vartheta]dT = (1 - k)dT$ which is less than the transfer, since it is equal to the fraction of income spent on nontraded goods.

[9] The pre-Ohlin orthodox view of Keynes, Taussig, Jacob Viner and other writers is discussed in Viner (1937) and Samuelson (1952, 1954). A recent treatment with nontraded goods is Ronald Jones (1975).

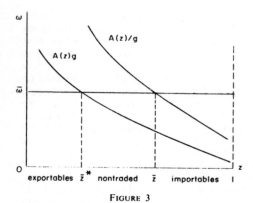

FIGURE 3

Similarly the foreign country produces commodities for which foreign unit labor cost falls short of adjusted unit labor costs of delivered imports:

(18) $w^*a^*(z) \leq (1/g)wa(z)$

or $A(z)g \leq \omega$

In Figure 3 we show the adjusted relative unit labor requirement schedules $A(z)/g$ and $A(z)g$. It is apparent from (17) and (18) that for any given relative wage the home country produces and exports commodities to the left of the $A(z)g$ schedule, both countries produce as nontraded goods commodities in the intermediate range, and the foreign country produces and exports commodities in the range to the right of $A(z)/g$.

To determine the equilibrium relative wage we turn to the trade balance equilibrium condition in (19)—together with (20) and (21)—which is modified to take account of the endogenous range of nontraded goods:

(19) $(1 - \lambda)wL = (1 - \lambda^*)w^*L^*$

The variable λ is the fraction of home country income spent on our domestically (or home) produced goods—exportables and nontraded—and λ^* is the share of foreigners' income spent on goods they produce. Both λ and λ^* are endogenously determined because the range of goods produced in each country depends on the relative wages.

(20) $\lambda(g\omega) \equiv \int_0^{\bar{z}} b(z)dz \quad \lambda'(g\omega) < 0$

$\lambda^*(\omega/g) \equiv \int_{\bar{z}}^1 b(z)dz \quad \lambda^{*\prime}(\omega/g) > 0$

The dependence of $\lambda( )$ and $\lambda^*( )$ on the variables specified in (20) and the respective derivatives follow from (21) below.

The limits of integration $\bar{z}$ and $\bar{z}^*$ are derived from the conditions for efficient production in (17) and (18) by imposing equalities and so defining the borderline commodities. Thus, in Figure 3, $\bar{z}$ is the borderline between domestic nontraded goods and imports for the home country, and $\bar{z}^*$ denotes the borderline between foreign nontraded goods and the home country's exports:

(21) $\bar{z}^* = A^{-1}(\omega/g) \quad d\bar{z}^*/d(\omega/g) < 0$
        $\bar{z} = A^{-1}(g\omega) \quad d\bar{z}/d(g\omega) < 0$

Of course, equilibrium $\bar{z}$ and $\bar{z}^*$ are yet to be determined by the interaction of technology and demand conditions.

From (21) an increase in the relative wage reduces the range of commodities domestically produced and therefore raises the fraction of income spent on imports. Abroad the converse holds. An increase in the domestic relative wage increases the range of goods produced abroad and therefore reduces the fraction of income spent on imports. It follows that we can solve:

(19') $\bar{\omega} = \dfrac{1 - \lambda^*(\bar{\omega}/g)}{1 - \lambda(g\bar{\omega})} (L^*/L)$

$\equiv \varphi(\bar{\omega}; L^*/L, g) \quad \partial\varphi/\partial\bar{\omega} < 0$

for the unique equilibrium relative wage as a function of relative size and transport costs:

(22) $\bar{\omega} = \bar{\omega}(L^*/L, g)$

Because (19')'s right-hand side declines as $\bar{\omega}$ rises, a rise in L^*/L must still raise $\bar{\omega}$; a rise in g can shift $\bar{\omega}$ in either direction, depending on the $B(z)$ and $A(z)$ profiles.

The equilibrium relative wage in (22), taken in conjunction with (21), determines the equilibrium geographic production pattern, $\bar{z}$ and $\bar{z}^*$. Since the range of nontraded goods $\bar{z}^* \leq z \leq \bar{z}$ depends in this formulation on the equilibrium relative wage, it is obvious that shifts in given parameters will shift the range of nontraded commodities. Thus, a transfer that raises the equilibrium relative wage at home causes previously exported commodities to become nontraded, and previously nontraded commodities to become importables.

C. Tariffs

We consider next the case of zero transport cost but where each country levies a uniform tariff on imports at respective rates t and t^*, with proceeds rebated in lump sum form. This case, too, leads to cost barriers to importing, and to a range of commodities that are not traded, with the boundaries defined by:

$$(23) \qquad \bar{z} = A^{-1}\left(\frac{\omega}{1+t}\right)$$

and

$$\bar{z}^* = A^{-1}(\omega(1+t^*))$$

From (23) it is apparent that the presence of tariffs in either or both countries must give rise to nontraded goods because in this case $\bar{z} \neq \bar{z}^*$.

The trade balance equilibrium condition at international prices becomes, in place of (19),

$$(24) \quad (1-\lambda)Y/(1+t) =$$
$$(1-\lambda^*)Y^*/(1+t^*)$$

where Y and Y^* denote incomes inclusive of lump sum tariff rebates. Using the fact that rebates are equal to the tariff rate times the fraction of income spent on imports, we arrive at the trade balance equilibrium condition in the form:[10]

$$(25) \qquad \omega = \left(\frac{1-\lambda^*}{1-\lambda}\right)\frac{1+t\lambda}{1+t^*\lambda^*}(L^*/L)$$

where λ and λ^* are functions of (ω, t, t^*).

[10]Tariff rebates in the home country are equal to $R = (1-\lambda)Yt/(1+t)$. With $Y = WL + R$ we therefore have $Y = WL(1+t)/(1+\lambda t)$ as an expression for income inclusive of transfers. From equations (20) and (23) we have $\lambda = \lambda[\omega/(1+t)]$ and $\lambda^* = \lambda^*[\omega(1+t^*)]$, having substituted the tariff instead of transport costs as the obstacle to trade.

The implicit relations (25) can be solved for the equilibrium relative wage as a function of relative size and the tariff structure:

$$(26) \qquad \bar{\omega} = \bar{\omega}(L^*/L, t, t^*)$$

From (26) and (23) it is apparent now that the range of nontraded goods will be a function of both tariff rates. It is readily shown that an increase in the tariff improves the imposing country's relative wage and terms of trade. Furthermore, as is well known, when all countries but one are free traders, then one country can always improve its own welfare by imposing a tariff that is not too large.

A further question suggested by (26) concerns the effect of a uniform increase in world tariffs. Starting from zero, a small uniform increase in tariffs raises the relative wage of the country whose commodities command the larger share in world spending. This result occurs for two reasons. First, at the initial relative wage a larger share of spending out of tariff rebates falls on the goods of the country commanding a larger share in world demand. Second, the tariff induces new nontraded goods and therefore increases net demand for the borderline commodity of the country whose residents have the larger income, or equivalently, the larger share in world income.

If countries are of equal size as measured by the share in world income, such a uniform tariff increase has zero effect on relative wages, but of course reduces well-being in both places. Multilateral tariff increases, in this case, unnecessarily create some nontraded goods, and artificially raise the relative price of importables in terms of domestically produced commodities in each country exactly in proportion to the tariff.

IV. Money, Wages, and Exchange Rates

In this section we extend the discussion of the Ricardian model to deal with monetary aspects of trade. Specifically we shall be interested in the determination of exchange rates in a flexible rate system, in the process of adjustment to trade imbalance under fixed rates, and in the role of wage stickiness. The purpose of the extension is to integrate real and monetary aspects of trade.

A. *Flexible Exchange Rates*

The barter analysis of the preceding sections is readily extended to a world of flexible exchange rates and flexible money wages. Assume a given nominal quantity of money in each country, M and M^*, respectively. Further, in accordance with the classical Quantity Theory, assume constant expenditure velocities V and V^*.[11] A flexible exchange rate, and our stipulating the absence of nonmonetary international asset flows, will assure trade balance equilibrium and therefore the equality of income and spending in each country. The nominal money supplies and velocities determine nominal income in each country:

(27) $WL = MV$ and $W^*L^* = M^*V^*$

where W and W^* (now in capital letters) denote domestic and foreign money wages in terms of the respective currencies. Further, defining the exchange rate e as the domestic currency price of foreign exchange, the foreign wage measured in terms of domestic currency is eW^*, and the relative wage therefore is $\omega \equiv W/eW^*$.

From the determination of the equilibrium real wage ratio $\bar{\omega}$ by our earlier "real" relations, we can now find an expression for the equilibrium exchange rates:

(28) $\bar{e} = (1/\bar{\omega})(\overline{W}/\overline{W}^*) =$
$$(1/\bar{\omega})(MV/M^*V^*)(L^*/L)$$

where (27′) defines equilibrium money wages:

(27′) $\overline{W} = MV/L$

and

$$\overline{W}^* = M^*V^*/L^*$$

In this simple structure and with wage flexibility, we can keep separate the determinants of all equilibrium real variables from all monetary considerations. Mone-

[11] This is a strong assumption since it makes spending independent of income and nonliquid assets even in the short run.

tary changes or velocity changes in one country will be reflected in equiproportionate changes in prices in that country and in the exchange rate in the fashion of the neutral-money Quantity Theory. However, a real disturbance, as (28) shows, definitely does have repercussions on the nominal exchange rate as well as on the real equilibrium.

Using the results of Section II, we see that an increase in the foreign relative labor force causes, under flexible exchange rates and given $\overline{M}$ and $\overline{M}^*$, a depreciation in the home country's exchange rate as does uniform technical progress abroad. A shift in real demand toward foreign goods likewise leads to a depreciation of the exchange rate as well as to a reduction in real $\bar{\omega}$. A rise in foreign tariffs will also cause our currency to depreciate. Each of these real shifts is assumed to take place while (M, M^*) are unchanged and on the simplifying proviso that real income changes leave V and V^* unchanged.

B. *Fixed Exchange Rates*

In the fixed exchange rates case we assume currencies are fully convertible at a parity pegged by the monetary authorities. In the absence of capital flows and sterilization policy, a trade imbalance is reflected in monetary flows. In the simplest metal money model, the world money supply is redistributed toward the surplus country at precisely the rate of the trade surplus. We assume that the world money supply is given and equal to $\overline{G}$, measured in terms of domestic currency. The rate of increase of the domestic quantity of money is therefore equal to the reduction in foreign money, valued at the fixed exchange rate $\bar{e}$:

(29) $\dot{M} = -\bar{e}\dot{M}^*$

where $\dot{M} \equiv dM/dt$.

For a fixed rate world we have to determine in addition to the real variables $\bar{\omega}$ and $\bar{z}$, the levels of money wages W and W^* as well as the equilibrium balance of payments associated with each short-run equilibrium. In the long run the balance of payments will be zero as money ends up redistributed internationally to the point where income equals spending in each country. In the short run an initial misallocation of money balances implies a discrepancy between income and spending and an associated trade imbalance. To characterize the preferred rate of adjustment of cash balances in the simplest and most manageable way, we assume that spending by each country is proportional to money holdings.[12] On the further simplifying assumption that velocities are equal in each country, $V = V^*$,[13] world spending is equal to

$$(30) \qquad VM + eV^*M^* \equiv V\bar{G}$$

For the tastes and technology specified in Section I, world spending on domestically produced goods is given by

$$(31) \qquad V\bar{G} \int_0^{\tilde{z}} b(z)dz \equiv \vartheta(\omega)V\bar{G}$$

$$\tilde{z} = A^{-1}(\omega)$$

In equilibrium, world spending on our goods must equal the value of our full-employment income WL:

$$(32) \qquad WL = \vartheta(\omega)V\bar{G}$$

Equilibrium requires, too, that world spending on foreign goods equals the value of foreign full-employment income:

$$(33) \qquad \bar{e}W^*L^* = [1 - \vartheta(\omega)]V\bar{G}$$

Equations (32) and (33) express what would seem to be the *joint* determination of real and monetary variables. But, in fact, we could have taken the shortcut of recognizing that the real equilibrium is precisely that of the barter analysis developed in Section I. Dividing (32) by (33) and substitut-

[12]The assumption that spending is proportional to cash balances is only one of a number of possible specifications. Conditions for this expenditure function to be optimal are derived in Dornbusch and Michael Mussa. In general, expenditure will depend on both income and cash balances.

[13]In the long-run equilibrium, higher V than V^* leaves us with a smaller share of the world money stock than foreigners, but with nominal and real income *shares* in the two countries the same as when $V = V^*$.

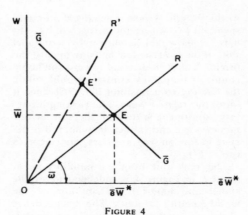

FIGURE 4

ing from (11) for the equilibrium relative wage $\bar{\omega}$, we can employ equations (32) and (33) to determine money wage levels.

The equilibrium determined by equations (32) and (33) can be analyzed in terms of Figure 4. The figure emphasizes the separation of real and monetary aspects of the equilibrium under our assumptions of traded goods only, and no distribution effects. From the ratio of (32) and (33) we obtain the equilibrium relative wage $\bar{\omega}$ as a function of tastes and technology solely from the barter model. This equilibrium relative wage is plotted as the ray OR in Figure 4.

The equality of world income and spending

$$(30') \qquad WL + \bar{e}W^*L^* = V\bar{G}$$

is shown as the downward sloping straight line $\bar{G}\bar{G}$, which is drawn for given velocity, world quantity of money, and labor forces. Point E is the equilibrium where relative prices and the level of wages and prices are such that all markets clear. At a level of wages and prices higher than point E, there would be a world excess supply of goods, and conversely at points below E.

Figure 4 immediately shows some comparative static results. Thus a doubling of both countries' labor forces, from the analysis of the barter model, will leave the relative wage unaffected but will double world output. Given unchanged nominal spending $V\bar{G}$, wages and prices will have to halve. This would be shown by a parallel shift of the $\bar{G}\bar{G}$ schedule halfway toward the origin. A shift in demand toward the home country's output by contrast would rotate the OR ray to a position like OR' since it raises our relative wage. The ensuing monetary adjustment is then an increase in our money wage and money income and a decline in foreign wages, prices, and incomes (point E').

The real and nominal equilibrium at point E in Figure 4 is independent of the short- and long-run distribution of the world quantity of money. The independence of the real equilibrium derives from the uniform homothetic tastes. The independence of the nominal equilibrium is implied by identical velocities. What does, however, depend on the short-run distribution of world money is the transition periods' balance of payments. As in the absorption approach of Sidney Alexander (1952), we know this: when goods markets clear, the trade surplus or balance of payments $\dot{M}$ of the home country is equal to the excess of income over spending, or:

$$(34) \qquad \dot{M} = \bar{W}L - VM$$

With the nominal wage independent of the distribution of world money, equation (34) therefore implies that the trade balance monotonically converges to equilibrium at a rate proportional to the discrepancy from long-run equilibrium:[14]

$$(34') \qquad \dot{M} = V(\bar{M} - M); \ \bar{M} = \vartheta(\bar{\omega})\bar{G}$$

The assumptions of this section were designed to render inoperative most of the traditional mechanisms discussed as part of

[14]Suppose $V > V^*$ and our share of the world money supply is initially larger than our equilibrium share. Then, as we lose M, total world nominal income and nominal GNP falls. Always our share of nominal world GNP stays the same under the strong demand assumptions. Total world real output never changes during the transition; only regional consumption shares change. Therefore, *both* countries' nominal price and wage levels fall in the transition, but such balanced changes have no real effects on either the transient or the final real equilibrium.

the adjustment process: changes in the terms of trade, in home and/or foreign price levels, in relative prices of traded and nontraded goods (there being none of the latter), in double factoral terms of trade; and any discrepancies in the price of the same commodity between countries. The features of the adjustment process of this section rely on 1) identical, constant expenditure velocities, 2) uniform-homothetic demand, and 3) the absence of trade impediments. If velocities were constant but differed between countries, the absolute *levels* of money wages and prices, though not *relative* wages or prices, would depend on the world distribution of money. Relaxation of the uniform-homothetic taste assumption would make equilibrium relative prices a function of the distributions of spending. Finally, the presence of nontraded goods would, together with Ricardo's technology, provide valid justification for some of the behavior of relative prices and price levels frequently asserted in the literature; this behavior is studied in more detail in the next section.

C. *The Price-Specie Flow Mechanism under More General Conditions*

We now discuss the adjustment process to monetary disequilibrium and enquire into the price effects associated with a redistribution of the world money supply when there are nontraded goods. Common versions of the Hume price-specie flow mechanism usually involve the argument that in the adjustment process, prices decline along with the money stock in the deficit country, while both rise in the surplus country. There is usually, too, an implication that the deficit country's terms of trade will necessarily worsen in the adjustment process and indeed have to do so if the adjustment is to be successful.

Section IVB demonstrated that the redistribution of money associated with monetary imbalance need have no effects on real variables (production, terms of trade, etc.) and on nominal variables other than the money stock and spending. While this is clearly a very special case, it does serve as a benchmark since it establishes that the monetary adjustment process would be effective even in a one-commodity world.

To approach the traditional view of the adjustment process more clearly and provide formal support for that view, we consider an extension to the monetary realm of our previous model involving nontraded goods. We return to the assumption that a fraction $(1 - k)$ of spending in each country falls on nontraded goods, and accordingly equations (32) and (33) become:

$$(32') \qquad WL = \vartheta(\omega) V\overline{G} + (1 - k)\gamma V\overline{G};$$
$$\gamma \equiv M/\overline{G}$$

$$(33') \quad \overline{e}W^*L^* = [k - \vartheta(\omega)]V\overline{G}$$
$$+ (1 - \gamma)(1 - k)V\overline{G}$$

These hold both in final equilibrium, and in transient equilibrium where specie is flowing. Equations (32') and (33') imply that the equilibrium relative wage does depend on the distribution of the world money supply. Solving these equations for the equilibrium relative wage we have:

$$(35) \qquad \overline{\omega} = \overline{\omega}(\gamma) \qquad \frac{\partial \overline{\omega}}{\partial \gamma} > 0$$

An increase in the home country's initial share in the world money supply γ raises our relative wage.

Using this extended framework, we can draw on the analysis of the transfer problem in Section II to examine the adjustment that follows an initial distribution of world money between the two countries that differs from the long-run equilibrium distribution.

Suppose our M is initially excessive, say from a gold discovery here. Assume also that the gold discovery occurred when the world was in long-run equilibrium with the previous world money stock. As a result of our excess M, we spend more than our earnings, incurring a balance-of-payments deficit equal to the rate at which our M is flowing out. In effect, the foreign economy is making us a real transfer to offset our deficit. As seen earlier, we, the deficit country, are devoting some of our excess spending to nontraded goods, shifting some of our resources to their production at the expense of our previous exports. We not only export fewer types of goods, but also import more types, and import more of each ($\overline{\omega}$ rises and $\overline{z}$ falls).

During the transition, while the real transfer corresponding to our deficit is taking place, our terms of trade are more favorable than in the long-run state. The new gold raises both their W^* and our W, but in addition, our W is up relative to their W^*. Therefore the price level of goods we continue to produce is up relative to the price level of goods they continue to produce. This is true both for our nontraded goods and for our exportables. The prices of goods we produce rise relative to the prices of goods they produce in proportion to the change in relative wages.

Thus the price levels in the two countries have been changed differentially by the specie flow and implied real transfer. But that does not mean that any traded good ever sells for different prices in two places. In fact the divergence in weighted average (consumer) price levels is due to nontraded goods. The price level will rise in the gold-discovering country relative to the other country the greater is the share of nontraded goods in expenditure, $1 - k$. It is a bit meaningless to say, "What accomplished the adjustment is the relative movements of price levels for nontraded goods in the two countries," since we have seen that the adjustment can and will be made even when there are no such nontraded goods. It is meaningful to say, "The fact that people want to direct some of their expenditure to nontraded goods makes it necessary for resources to shift in and out of them as a result of a real transfer, and such resource shifts take place only because the terms of trade (double-factoral and for traded goods) do shift in the indicated way."

The adjustment process to a monetary disturbance is stable in the sense that the system converges to a long-run equilibrium distribution of money with balanced trade. To appreciate that point, we supplement equations (32') and (33') with (34) that continues to describe the monetary adjustment process. We note, however, that now W and W^* are endogenous variables whose levels in the short run do depend on the distribution of the world money supply. A redistribution of money toward the home country would raise our spending and demand for goods, and reduce foreign spending and demand. As before, spending changes for traded goods offset each other precisely so that the net effect is an increase in demand for nontraded goods at home and a decline abroad. As a consequence our wages will rise and foreign wages decline. Therefore, starting from full equilibrium, a redistribution of money toward the home country will create a deficit equal to

$$(36) \quad d\dot{M}/dM = -V(1 - \delta) \quad 0 \le \delta < 1$$

where δ is the elasticity of our nominal wages with respect to the quantity of money and is less than unity.[15] Equation (36) implies that the price-specie flow mechanism is stable.

It is interesting to observe in this context that the presence of nontraded goods in fact *slows down* the adjustment process by comparison with a world of only traded goods (contrary to J. Laurence Laughlin's turn of the century worries). As we saw before, with all goods freely tradeable, wages are independent of the distribution of money, and accordingly $\delta = 0$. Further we observe that the speed of adjustment depends on the relative size of countries. Thus the more equal countries are in terms of size, the slower tends to be the adjustment process.

In concluding this section we note that nontraded goods (and/or localized demand) are essential to the correctness of traditional insistence that the adjustment process necessarily entails absolute and re-

lative price, wage, and income movements. They are, of course, in no way essential to the existence of a stable adjustment process, nor is there at any time a need for a discrepancy of prices of the same commodity across countries in either case.[16]

A final remark concerns the adjustment to real disturbances such as demand shifts or technical progress. It is certainly true that whether the exchange rate is fixed or flexible, real adjustment will have to take place and cannot be avoided by choice of an exchange rate regime. So long as wages and prices are flexible, it is quite false to think that fixed parities "put the whole economy through the wringer of adjustment" while in floating rate regimes "only the export and import industries have to make the real adjustment." It is true, however, that once we depart from flexible wages and prices there may well be a preference for one exchange rate regime over another. The next section is devoted to that question.

D. *Sticky Money Wages*

The last question we address in this section concerns the implications of sticky money wages. For a given world money supply, *downward* stickiness of money wages implies the possibility of unemployment. We assume upward flexibility in wages, once full employment is attained.

We start with a fixed exchange rate $\bar{e}$. The relation between wages and the world quantity of money is brought out in Figure 5. Denote employment levels in each country, as opposed to the labor force, by the new symbols $\bar{L}$ and $\bar{L}^*$, respectively; denote nominal incomes by Y and Y^*. The equality of world income and spending is again shown by the $\overline{GG}$ schedule, the equation of which now is

$$(37) \quad V\overline{G} = Y + \bar{e}Y^* \equiv \overline{W}\bar{L} + \bar{e}\overline{W}^*\bar{L}^*$$

---

[15] The value of δ can be calculated from equations (32′) and (33′) to be

$$\delta \equiv (1 - k)\frac{\gamma(1 - \gamma)}{\gamma(1 - \gamma) + \vartheta\epsilon}$$

where ϵ is the elasticity of the share of our traded goods in world spending, $\epsilon \equiv -\vartheta'\omega/\vartheta > 0$. The elasticity δ is evaluated at the long-run equilibrium where $\gamma \equiv \vartheta/k$. If $A'(z)$ falls slowly, ϵ will be large.

[16] The continuum Ricardian technology is special in that there can be no range of goods both imported and produced at home. Therefore, the cross elasticity of supply between nontraded goods and exports must be greater than the zero cross elasticity between nontraded goods and imports. Consequently, a transfer must shift the terms of trade (for goods and factors) in the stated orthodox way, favorably for the receiver.

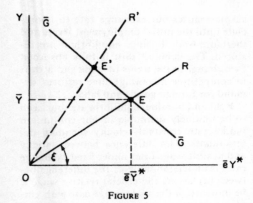

FIGURE 5

where $\overline{W}$ and $\overline{W}^*$ are the fixed money wages set at too high sticky levels. The schedule is drawn for given money wages, a given world quantity of money, and a pegged parity for $\bar{e}$. The ray OR now is predetermined by the given sticky relative wage $\bar{\omega} = \overline{W}/\bar{e}\overline{W}^*$. From equations (32) and (33) the ratio of money incomes $Y/\bar{e}Y^*$ is just a function of the relative wage now given exogenously by rigid money wages and the exchange rate:

$$(38) \quad Y/\bar{e}Y^* = \frac{\vartheta(\omega)}{1 - \vartheta(\omega)} \equiv \xi(\overline{W}/\bar{e}\overline{W}^*)$$

$$\xi'(\omega) < 0$$

Point E is the nominal equilibrium where by assumption the world quantity of money is insufficient relative to wage rates to ensure full employment. Although that equilibrium is one with unemployed labor, it is efficient in other respects. Specifically, geographic specialization follows comparative advantage as laid out above, but now labor employed adjusts to sticky wage patterns of specialization.

Employment levels $\overline{L}$ and $\overline{L}^*$ now are determined by (39)

$$(39) \quad \overline{L} = \overline{Y}/\overline{W}, \quad \overline{L}^* = \bar{e}\overline{Y}^*/\overline{W}^*$$

where $\overline{Y}$ and $\overline{Y}^*$ are the equilibrium levels of nominal income determined by equations (37) and (38) or by point E in Figure 5.

Consider now the impact of a foreign increase in money wages. The effect of the im-

plied reduction in our relative wages and the resulting increase in our relative income are shown in Figure 5 by the rotation from OR to OR'.

The new equilibrium is at E' where our money income and employment have risen while income and employment decline abroad. Thus an increase in the foreign wage rate, by moving the terms of trade against us, shifts comparative advantage and employment toward the home country. The extent to which the home country benefits from the adverse terms of trade shift in terms of employment will depend on both the substitutability in demand and the elasticity of the $A(z)$ schedule in Figure 1. We observe, too, that the move from E to E' will bring about a transitory balance-of-payments surplus. Given the initial distribution of money and hence of spending, the foreign decline in income and the increase at home implies that we will spend less than our income and therefore have a trade surplus. This surplus persists until money is redistributed to match the new levels of income at E'.

Next we move to flexible exchange rates. Under flexible rates an increase in the foreign money wage $\overline{W}^*$, given money supplies in each country, will similarly have real repercussion effects on relative prices and employment at home. Now employment in each country is determined by money supplies and prevailing wages:

$$(39') \quad \overline{L} = V\overline{M}/\overline{W}; \quad \overline{L}^* = V\overline{M}^*/\overline{W}^*$$

Given the employment levels thus determined, we know from the analysis of the earlier barter model that there is a unique relative wage at which the trade balance achieves equilibrium. The higher is $\overline{M}^*/\overline{W}^*$, the higher will be employment abroad—and, therefore, the higher will be our relative wage $\bar{\omega}$. It is thus apparent that an increase in the foreign money wage, $\overline{W}^*$, will reduce employment abroad. Employment declines only in proportion to the increase in wages and thus declines by less than it would under fixed exchange rates when specie is lost abroad.

We saw in the barter model that a reduction in effective foreign labor causes a decline in our relative wage, but that the decline in our relative wage falls proportionately short of the foreign reduction in labor. Now, at the initial exchange rate, the increase in foreign wages reduces our relative wage and their employment in the same proportion. The decline in our relative wage is therefore excessive. Domestic goods are underpriced and the exchange rate appreciates to *partly* offset the gain in cost competitiveness. The net effect is therefore a decline in our relative wage and an appreciation of our exchange rate (a decline in *e*) that falls short of the foreign increase in wages. Since our terms of trade unambiguously deteriorate without any compensating gain in employment, it must be true that welfare declines at home. Abroad, the loss in employment is offset by a gain in the terms of trade, but there too the net effect is a loss in welfare under our strong Mill-Ricardo assumption.

The adjustment to money wage disturbances under fixed and flexible rates differs in several respects. Under fixed rates employment effects are transmitted, while under flexible rates they are bottled up in the country initiating the disturbance. Under fixed rates the terms of trade move one for one with money wage, while under flexible rates exchange rate movements partly offset increases in the foreign money wage rate.

The difference between fixed and flexible rates in relation to the adjustment process is further brought out by an example of a real disturbance. Consider a shift in world demand toward our goods. Under fixed rates the resulting increase in our relative income will, from (38), move us in Figure 5 from *E* to *E'*. Employment rises at home and falls abroad. Demand shifts are fully reflected in employment changes. Under flexible rates, by contrast, with given wages and money, a demand shift has no impact on employment—as we observe from (39). At the initial exchange rate the demand shift would give rise to an excess demand for our goods and to an excess supply abroad. Domestic income and employment would tend to rise while falling abroad. The resulting trade

surplus causes our exchange rate to appreciate until the initial employment levels and therefore trade balance equilibrium are restored. The demand shift is fully absorbed by a change in the terms of trade and a shift in competitive advantage that restores demand for foreign goods and labor.

Real and nominal equilibria are thus seen to be uniquely definable in our continuum model with constant-velocity spending determinants. The difference between sticky and flexible wage rates under fixed exchange rates is understandable as the difference between (a) having the crucial relative wage $\bar{\omega}$ be imposed in the sticky wage case with employments having then to adjust; or (b) having the full employments be imposed and $\bar{\omega}$ having to adjust. Under floating exchange rates, sticky nominal wages impose employment levels in each country and the crucial relative wage $\bar{\omega}$ then adjusts to those employment levels.

APPENDIX

Historical Remark

Figure 1 seems to be new. G. A. Elliot (1950) gives a somewhat different diagram, one that makes explicit the meaning of Marshall's 1879 "bales" (which, by the way, happen to work only in the two-country constant labor costs case). In terms of the present notations, Elliott plots for the *U.S.* offer curve the following successive points traced out for all ω on the range $[0, \infty]$: on the vertical axis is plotted our total real imports valued in foreign labor units ("our demand for bales of their labor," so to speak), namely,

$$\int_z^1 [P^*(z)/w^*]C(z)dz = \int_z^1 a^*(z)C(z)dz$$

and on the horizontal axis, our total real exports valued in home labor units ("our supply of bales of labor to them"), namely,

$$\int_0^z [P(z)/w][Q(z) - C(z)]dz =$$

$$L - \int_0^z a(z)C(z)dz$$

It is to be understood that $\bar{z}$ is a function of ω, namely the inverse function $A^{-1}(\omega)$; also that $C(z)$ are the amounts demanded as a function of our real income L and of the $P(z)/W$ function defined for each, namely $\min[\omega a(z), a^*(z)]$. Because we have a continuum of goods, we avoid Elliott's branches of the offer curve that are segments of various rays through the origin. The reader will discern by symmetry considerations how the foreign offer curve is plotted in the same (L, L^*) quadrant, by varying ω to generate the respective coordinates

$$\left[\int_0^{\bar{z}} a(z) C^*(z) dz, \right.$$

$$\left. L^* - \int_{\bar{z}}^1 a^*(z) C^*(z) dz \right]$$

Our model forces the Elliott-Marshall diagram to generate a *unique* solution under uniform-homothetic demand. Unlike our Figure 1, the Elliott diagram can handle the general case of nonhomothetic demands in the two countries; but then, as is well known, multiple solutions are possible, some locally stable and some unstable. The price one pays for this generality is that, as Edgeworth observed, the Marshallian curves are the end products of much implicit theorizing, with much that is interesting having taken place offstage.

REFERENCES

S. Alexander, "The Effects of a Devaluation on the Trade Balance," *Int. Monet. Fund Staff Pap.*, Apr. 1952, *2*, 263–78.

J. S. Chipman, "A Survey of International Trade: Part I: The Classical Theory," *Econometrica*, July 1965, *33*, 477–519.

G. Debreu, "Economies with a Finite Set of Equilibria," *Econometrica*, May 1970, *38*, 387–92.

R. Dornbusch and M. Mussa, "Consumption, Real Balances and the Hoarding Function," *Int. Econ. Rev.*, June 1975, *16*, 415–21.

G. A. Elliott, "The Theory of International Values," *J. Polit. Econ.*, Feb. 1950, *58*, 16–29.

F. Graham, "The Theory of International Balances Re-Examined," *Quart. J. Econ.*, Nov. 1923, *38*, 54–86.

Gottfried Haberler, *The Theory of International Trade*, London 1937.

R. W. Jones, "Presumption and the Transfer Problem," *J. Int. Econ.*, Aug. 1975, *5*, 263–74.

James Laurence Laughlin, *Principles of Money*, New York 1903.

John S. Mill, *Principles of Political Economy*, London 1848.

David Ricardo, *On the Principles of Political Economy and Taxation*, 1817; edited by P. Sraffa, London 1951.

P. A. Samuelson, "The Transfer Problem and Transport Costs: The Terms of Trade When Impediments are Absent," *Econ. J.*, June 1952, *62*, 278–304; reprinted in Joseph Stiglitz, ed., *Collected Scientific Papers of Paul A. Samuelson*, Vol. 2, Cambridge, Mass., ch. 74.

———, "The Transfer Problem and the Transport Costs, II: Analysis of Effects of Trade Impediments," *Econ. J.*, June 1954, *64*, 264–89; reprinted in Joseph Stiglitz, ed., *Collected Scientific Papers of Paul A. Samuelson*, Vol. 2, Cambridge, Mass., ch. 75.

———, "Theoretical Notes on Trade Problems," *Rev. Econ. Statist.*, May 1964, *46*, 145–54; reprinted in Joseph Stiglitz, ed., *Collected Scientific Papers of Paul A. Samuelson*, Vol. 2, Cambridge, Mass., ch. 65.

S. Smale, "Structurally Stable Systems Are Not Dense," *Amer. J. Math.*, 1966, *88*, 491–96.

Frank W. Taussig, *International Trade*, New York 1927.

Jacob Viner, *Studies in the Theory of International Trade*, New York 1937.

C. Wilson, "On the General Structure of Ricardian Models with a Continuum of Goods: Applications to Growth, Tariff Theory and Technical Change," unpublished paper, Univ. Wisconsin-Madison, 1977.

[8]

The General Validity of the Law of Comparative Advantage

Alan V. Deardorff

Institute for International Economic Studies,
University of Stockholm, and University of Michigan

It is well known that the law of comparative advantage breaks down when applied to individual commodities or pairs of commodities in a many-commodity world. This paper shows that the law is nonetheless valid if restated in terms of averages across all commodities. Specifically, a theorem and several corollaries are derived which establish correlations between vectors of trade and vectors containing relative-autarky-price measures of comparative advantage. These results are proven in a general many-commodity model that allows for tariffs, transport costs, and other impediments to trade.

The purpose of this paper is to demonstrate, in a general model, the validity of a weak form of the Law of Comparative Advantage, that is, that the *pattern of international trade is determined by comparative advantage.* This is surely the oldest proposition in the pure theory of international trade and is common both to the Ricardian comparative-costs theory and the Heckscher-Ohlin factor-proportions theory, so long as comparative advantage is measured by relative autarky prices. As such, one might think that the proposition requires no further comment except in the basic textbooks whose job it is to explain important truths in simple terms.

Yet this proposition, like other more recent theorems of trade theory, has proven somewhat difficult to extend beyond the simple

I would like to thank Ted Bergstrom, Paul Courant, Ronald Jones, Robert Stern, Lars Svensson, and Hal Varian for their helpful comments on an earlier draft of this paper, originally titled "Comparative Advantage and Natural Trade in General Equilibrium."

[*Journal of Political Economy*, 1980, vol. 88, no. 5]
© 1980 by The University of Chicago. 0022-3808/80/8805-0003$01.50

models in which it was first formulated. Three examples should suffice to illustrate this difficulty. First, when Jones (1961) extended the doctrine of comparative advantage to a classical model with many goods and countries, he was forced to restate the concept of comparative costs in a form that lacked most of the simplicity and intuitive appeal of the original. Second, in the context of the Heckscher-Ohlin model, Melvin (1968) showed that if there are more goods than primary factors of production then the indeterminacy of the structure of production, that had been noted previously by Samuelson (1953), implies that any good may be exported by any country. This, it would seem, destroys altogether any determinate relationship between the pattern of trade and anything else. And third, Travis (1964, 1972) has argued that the introduction of impediments to trade, and particularly of tariffs, can alter the pattern of trade, causing goods that would have been exported to be imported and vice versa. Thus, it appears that if the two-commodity, two-country, free-trade model is extended or modified in plausible ways, it then ceases to be possible to explain the pattern of trade by simple comparisons of autarky prices. Most recently, this impossibility has been shown by Drabicki and Takayama (1979).

I will show in this paper, however, that a version of the comparative-advantage proposition *does* hold in a general model that allows for all of the complications just mentioned. This is not to say that the authors cited in the last paragraph were wrong. Instead, what is needed is to relax somewhat the rigidity of the proposition itself and require only that it hold in the sense of an appropriate average rather than for each commodity individually. While several forms of the proposition will be proved below, all may be summarized by the following statement: There must exist a negative correlation between any country's relative autarky prices and its pattern of net exports. Thus, on average, high autarky prices are associated with imports and low autarky prices are associated with exports.

This proposition will be demonstrated in a model that includes a variety of impediments to trade, as well as free trade, as special cases. I allow in a general way for transport costs, and I allow domestic and world prices to differ by additional amounts to reflect such artificial trade impediments as tariffs and quantitative restrictions. Unlimited interference with trade is not allowed, however, since it is clear that sufficient use of trade *subsidies* could lead to any pattern of trade and thus invalidate the law of comparative advantage. For ease of reference, and to distinguish it from the more restrictive case of free trade, I will refer to this combination of assumptions as defining "natural trade." Thus a natural trade equilibrium is one in which there are no trade subsidies or other artificial stimulants to trade, but in which trade impediments of any sort may or may not be present. Free trade is then a special case of natural trade.[1]

My treatment of transport costs is somewhat unusual and should therefore also be mentioned in this introduction. Rather than postulate an explicit form for transport costs, I will distinguish goods on the basis of where they are delivered and incorporate transportation technology into a more general specification of the technology of production. For each country, a single production possibility set will define the constraints on its ability to produce for delivery at home and for delivery abroad. Thus any resources used up in transportation will be taken into account when the competitive producers and traders of the economy maximize the value of net delivered output. In the body of the paper I will simplify notation somewhat by assuming that all world trade passes through a single international port, though in an Appendix I show that most of my results carry over to a world of any number of such ports.

With this introduction the analysis can proceed. In Section I, I will state and discuss the assumptions of the model, which are broad enough to encompass a wide variety of models that have appeared in the literature. In Section II, I will first prove a basic theorem, which uses autarky prices to value the vector of goods that a country trades in a natural trade equilibrium. This result then leads readily to four corollaries which provide alternative statements of the law of comparative advantage in the average sense discussed above. In Section III, I discuss several ways that these results can be strengthened or modified. Finally, I return in Section IV to the particular issues raised above and show how my results contribute to an understanding of the various phenomena noted by other authors.

I. The Model

Consider a world of m countries, $i = 1, \ldots, m$, and n goods, $j = 1, \ldots, n$. The list of goods includes all final goods, intermediate goods, and services of primary factors of production. Each good may be delivered either on the country's home market or at the international port. Let Q^i be an n-vector of net supplies to country i's home market and T^i be an n-vector of net supplies by country i to the international port. Thus positive elements of Q^i represent goods available for consumption in country i, while negative elements represent net use of goods or factor services by production processes in country i. Similarly, the elements of the vector T^i represent the country's trade in each of the n goods: exports if positive and imports if negative. The country's total

---

[1] Natural trade also includes autarky as another special case, though my results are, of course, of interest only in situations in which some trade actually does take place.

production, net of goods and resources used up in production and transport, is then $X^i = Q^i + T^i$.

Each country has its own net production possibility set, F^i, defined as the set of all feasible pairs of n-vectors, Q^i and T^i, given its technology and any constraints it may face on endowments of primary factors. Of the sets, F^i, I assume whatever is necessary to permit existence of the equilibria I will be studying. Thus, they must be closed, convex, and, in some weak sense, bounded from above.[2] In addition, I make the following assumption that says essentially that transport costs are nonnegative: If

$$(Q^i, T^i) \in F^i,$$ (1)

then

$$(Q^i + T^i, 0) \in F^i,$$

where 0 here represents an n-vector of zeros. This says that any total net output vector that is feasible with trade is also feasible without, since resources can only be used up, but never created, by transporting goods between the domestic market and the international port. Thus if it is feasible to produce a good and deliver it abroad, $T_j^i > 0$, then it is also feasible to produce it and deliver it at home. Likewise, if it is feasible to import a good, $T_j^i < 0$, then it is also feasible not to import it and to reduce deliveries on the home market by the same amount.[3]

To represent demand in each country, stronger assumptions will be used. I assume that preferences in each country can be represented by a family of n-dimensional community indifference curves, which it will be convenient to represent by a community utility function, U^i. These utility functions are assumed to have the property of local nonsatiation: For any Q^{i^0} there exists a Q^{i^1} arbitrarily close to Q^{i^0} such that

$$U(Q^{i^1}) > U(Q^{i^0}).$$ (2)

This assumption will be used to rule out "thick" indifference curves.

Both producers and consumers are assumed to behave competitively, so that they maximize, respectively, the value of net output and the utility of consumption, subject to the prices that they face in each country.[4] In autarky equilibrium, production is for the domestic

---

[2] It would be sufficient, though not necessary, to assume the existence of a vector $\bar{X}^i$ such that $Q + T \leqslant \bar{X}^i$ for all $(Q, T) \in F^i$.

[3] Note that this assumption includes, as a special case, the more explicit assumption made by Samuelson (1954), who specified that some fraction, α_j, of each good be used up in transport. If I let G be a more conventional production possibility set in which location of delivery is not specified, then my $F = \{(Q, T)$ such that $\bar{X} \in G$ where $\bar{X}_j = Q_j + T_j + \alpha_j|T_j|\}$. Assumption (1) then follows immediately.

[4] In order for producers to maximize the value of net output, I make the standard assumptions that domestic economies are competitive and that there are no externalities, production taxes, or other domestic distortions. Increasing returns to scale must also be ruled out.

LAW OF COMPARATIVE ADVANTAGE   945

market only, while with trade, producers maximize the sum of the
value of output delivered at home and the value of output delivered
abroad, the prices of which will in general be different due to transportation costs. The price of output delivered abroad will also in
general be different from the world price, due to impediments to
trade such as tariffs. Equilibrium in the home market requires that
the vector of net supplies to the home market be consumed. Equilibrium in international trade requires in addition that the sum of all
countries' net supplies to the international port be zero and that each
country's trade be balanced at world prices.

I begin by characterizing autarky equilibrium. Let Q^{ai} be a vector of
net outputs both supplied and demanded on the domestic market
of country i under autarky, and let p^{ai} be a corresponding vector of
autarky prices. Then the following three assumptions require that Q^{ai}
be feasible, maximal, and preferred, given the prices p^{ai}:

$$(Q^{ai}, 0) \in F^i, \tag{3}$$

$$p^{ai}Q^{ai} \geq p^{ai}Q \text{ for all } (Q, 0) \in F^i, \tag{4}$$

$$U^i(Q^{ai}) \geq U^i(Q) \text{ for all } Q \text{ such that } p^{ai}Q \leq p^{ai}Q^{ai}. \tag{5}$$

Here, and throughout the paper, all products of vectors represent
inner products.

To characterize a natural trade equilibrium, more notation is
needed. Let Q^{ni} and T^{ni} be vectors of net supply by country i to
domestic and foreign markets in a natural trade equilibrium. Let p^{qi}
and p^{ti} be corresponding vectors of prices facing domestic producers,
consumers, and traders in these markets, defined in terms of a single
international numeraire. Thus the elements of p^{qi} are simply the
domestic prices in country i, while those of p^{ti} are the prices paid or
received by domestic traders at the international port and will be
referred to as traders' prices. In particular, p^{ti} includes any tariffs that
must be paid on domestic imports and is net of any export taxes paid
on exports. The two vectors of prices will have to differ by enough to
cover transport costs if trade is to take place, but this will be assured by
the maximization assumption below. Assumptions analogous to those
above require that production, trade, and consumption be feasible,
maximal, and preferred given these prices:

$$(Q^{ni}, T^{ni}) \in F^i, \tag{6}$$

$$p^{qi}Q^{ni} + p^{ti}T^{ni} \geq p^{qi}Q + p^{ti}T \text{ for all } (Q, T) \in F^i, \tag{7}$$

$$U^i(Q^{ni}) \geq U^i(Q) \text{ for all } Q \text{ such that } p^{qi}Q \leq p^{qi}Q^{ni}. \tag{8}$$

Within the international port, there is also a vector of world prices,
p^w, also measured in terms of the international numeraire. It represents the price at which international exchange actually takes place

and may differ from the national traders' prices, p^{ti}, to the extent that countries levy tariffs or export taxes. Each country's trade is assumed to be balanced at these world prices:

$$p^w T^{ni} = 0. \tag{9}$$

The relationship between world prices and national traders' prices can in general be complicated, depending both on the precise nature of trade impediments and on the direction of trade itself. However, all I need to characterize natural trade is to rule out trade subsidies, and this is done by the following simple assumption:

$$(p_j^w - p_j^{ti}) T_j^{ni} \geq 0 \text{ for } \quad j = 1, \ldots, n. \tag{10}$$

What this says is that if a good is exported, $T_j^{ni} > 0$, then the world price must be at least as large as the price the exporter receives, any differences between the two representing an export tax levied by country i. And if a good is imported, $T_j^{ni} < 0$, then the world price must be no greater than the price the importer pays, any difference representing a tariff. Of course, if there were no policies interfering with trade, then (10) would be an equality.

Finally, I require that the world market for each good clear:

$$\sum_{i=1}^{m} T^{ni} = 0. \tag{11}$$

Assumptions (1) through (11) are sufficient for most of my results. However, later in the paper I will have occasion to make comparisons among autarky and world prices. For that purpose it will be convenient to normalize world prices and each country's autarky prices to lie on the unit simplex:

$$\sum_{j=1}^{n} p_j^w = \sum_{j=1}^{n} p_j^{ai} = 1 \quad i = 1, \ldots, m. \tag{12}$$

This is equivalent to taking, as numeraire, a bundle containing one unit of each good.

It may be well to note, before I proceed, that my list of assumptions does *not* include a number that are often made in trade theory. The utility functions have not been assumed to be differentiable and neither have the boundaries of the production possibility sets. The latter have not been assumed to be convex, nor the former to be homothetic. And neither have been assumed to be in any sense identical across countries. Thus the countries can differ arbitrarily in tastes, technologies, and factor endowments. None of this should be too surprising, however, since, while some of these assumptions may make certain modes of analysis more convenient, they are not really needed for establishing the role of comparative advantage.

LAW OF COMPARATIVE ADVANTAGE   947

More surprising, perhaps, is the limited amount I have had to say about the role of, and availability of, factor endowments in the model. Since the assumption of natural trade permits any of the "goods" to be nontraded, one can as well include the services of any or all factors of production as elements in the vector of n goods and even allow them to be in variable supply. One could even allow some or all of them to be traded internationally, so that the concept of comparative advantage is then extended to trade in the services of factors of production. Or, at the other extreme, one could identify as separate factors those which are employed in different industries and thus allow for various degrees of interindustry factor immobility. Finally, with some care one can allow for dynamic factor accumulation by interpreting the sets F as constraints on steady-state net output per capita.[5]

The point is that, while the list of assumptions earlier in this section was a long one, the assumptions themselves are much less restrictive than one often meets in models of international trade. With some care and ingenuity in interpreting the model, the results I am about to derive can shed light on the mechanism of international trade in quite a variety of contexts.

II. A Theorem and Its Corollaries

Now consider any one of the countries described in Section I. I will show first that if one uses autarky prices to evaluate its net trade vector in a natural trade equilibrium then that value must be less than or equal to zero. That is, the value of what a country gives up in trade is no greater, at autarky prices, than the value of what it acquires. While this may not seem to be a very surprising property, its proof uses most of the assumptions that were introduced in Section I. And once it is established, it leads fairly easily to a variety of results concerning comparative advantage.

The meaning of the theorem can be illustrated with the simple offer-curve diagram of figure 1. For a country which trades only two goods, the curve COC' shows the various possibilities for exports and imports of both goods with free trade. My theorem says that any trade which takes place will have a negative value when valued at autarky prices. But since autarky prices are given by the slope of the line tangent to the offer curve at the origin, POP', this means merely that

[5] Care is needed here in assuring that a competitive economy will still, in a dynamic context, maximize the steady-state value of net output per capita. If technology permits inputs and outputs at different times, then it is the discounted value of the input-output stream that is maximized by a competitive economy. This can be resolved for one's purposes either by assuming that the interest rate equals the natural rate of growth or, more generally, by making a distinction between rental markets for the services of stocks of goods and the markets for their flow as final sales.

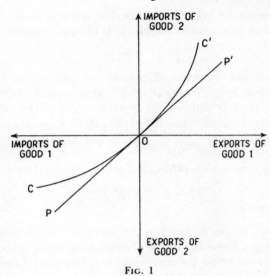

FIG. 1

COC' lies wholly to one side of this line. Well-behaved offer curves will
have this property, and the reader may recognize a number of my
assumptions as necessary to prevent the offer curve from "bending
backward." Of course my model is far more general than figure 1,
since it allows an arbitrary number of goods and does not require free
trade. Still, one can interpret the theorem as saying that autarky
prices provide a supporting hyperplane for the set of all possible
trades.

Theorem.—If prices and quantities in autarky and trade satisfy assumptions (1)–(10) for a particular country, i, then

$$p^{ai}T^{ni} \le 0. \tag{13}$$

Proof.—Since I am dealing with only a single country, I will omit the
country superscript in what follows. I begin by adding up the inequalities in (10) to get

$$p^{w}T^{n} - p^{t}T^{n} \ge 0, \tag{14}$$

from which, using (9),

$$p^{t}T^{n} \le p^{w}T^{n} = 0. \tag{15}$$

From (3) and (7) it then follows that

$$p^{q}Q^{a} \le p^{q}Q^{n} + p^{t}T^{n} \le p^{q}Q^{n}, \tag{16}$$

and this, from (8), implies

$$U(Q^{n}) \ge U(Q^{a}). \tag{17}$$

Thus the vector of goods consumed in natural trade is at least as preferred as that consumed in autarky. It follows from (2) and (5) that

$$p^a Q^n \geqslant p^a Q^a, \tag{18}$$

for if this were not the case, (2) would permit one to find another vector, $\bar{Q}$, in the neighborhood of Q^n, that would also cost less at autarky prices than Q^n but would be strictly preferred, violating (5).

Now (6) and (1) imply that $(Q^n + T^n, 0) \in F$, so that (4) implies

$$p^a Q^a \geqslant p^a (Q^n + T^n). \tag{19}$$

Rearranging and using (18) one gets the desired result:

$$p^a T^n \leqslant p^a Q^a - p^a Q^n \leqslant 0. \tag{20}$$

Q.E.D.

The theorem has been stated in the form of a weak inequality. Still it should be clear, from the chain of reasoning used in its proof, that there are many ways that the inequality can be strengthened. Some of these will be mentioned in Section III.

Consider, now, the issue of comparative advantage. My theorem is already very suggestive in this regard: For the autarky-price value of trade to be negative, it would have to be true that the autarky prices of exports are low compared with those of imports, and thus the country is exporting those goods with relatively low autarky prices as the principle of comparative advantage would suggest. To make this relationship more precise, I will now examine several correlations between particular vectors of relative autarky prices and net exports. By showing these correlations to be less than or equal to zero, I establish a *tendency* for high-autarky-priced items to be imported and for low-autarky-priced items to be exported. I do not attempt to say anything about the pattern of trade in any particular commodity, or pair of commodities, for it is known from the work of others that such statements are likely to be invalid in a model as general as mine. Still, if I can show a negative correlation such as just described, I will have demonstrated that comparative advantage is nonetheless valid as at least a partial determinant of the pattern of trade overall.

The sign of a correlation between two vectors is, of course, the same as the sign of their covariance. For any two n-vectors, x^1 and x^2, by definition

$$\text{cor}(x^1, x^2) = \frac{\text{cov}(x^1, x^2)}{\sqrt{\text{var}(x^1)\,\text{var}(x^2)}} \tag{21}$$

where

$$\text{cov}(x^1, x^2) = \sum_{j=1}^{n} (x_j^1 - \bar{x}^1)(x_j^2 - \bar{x}^2), \tag{22}$$

$$\text{var}\,(x^i) = \sum_{j=1}^{n} (x_j^i - \bar{x}^i)^2 \quad \text{for } i = 1, 2, \tag{23}$$

and

$$\bar{x}^i = \frac{1}{n} \sum_{j=1}^{n} x_j^i \quad \text{for } i = 1, 2. \tag{24}$$

Since the denominator of (21) is nonnegative (and nonzero if the correlation is defined), the correlation and covariance must have the same sign.[6] Furthermore, the covariance can be rewritten as follows:

$$\text{cov}\,(x^1, x^2) = x^1 x^2 - n\bar{x}^1\bar{x}^2. \tag{25}$$

Thus if either of the vectors sums to zero, so that it has zero mean, then the sign of their correlation is just the sign of their inner product. Since I will use this property several times, I state it formally for ease of reference: If

$$\sum_{j=1}^{n} x_j^i = 0 \quad \text{for } i = 1 \quad \text{or} \quad i = 2, \tag{26}$$

then

$$\text{cor}\,(x^1, x^2) \gtreqqless 0 \qquad \text{as } x^1 x^2 \gtreqqless 0.$$

In stating the role of comparative advantage, my first problem is to decide what is meant by "relative autarky prices." With many countries, there is no single set of foreign autarky prices with respect to which one country's can be compared. I will resolve this problem first by using world prices with trade as the basis for comparison. This gives corollaries 1 and 2 below. Then I show in corollary 3 that if in fact there are only two countries, so that a single vector of foreign autarky prices can be identified, then a comparison of the two vectors of autarky prices also yields the appropriate correlation with the vector of trade. Finally, in corollary 4 I establish a correlation between trade and autarky prices for a world of many countries without reference to world prices.

Corollary 1.—For any country let ρ be the vector of ratios of its autarky prices to the world prices that prevail with trade,

$$\rho_j = p_j^a / p_j^w \qquad j = 1, \dots, n, \tag{27}$$

---

[6] I ignore, in what follows, the possibility of either vector having a zero variance so that the correlation is undefined. When that happens, as it will when there is no trade or when relative autarky prices are all identical, my conclusions about correlations can be restated as conclusions about the corresponding covariances only.

and let e be the vector of the country's net exports, valued at world prices,

$$e_j = p_j^w T_j^n \qquad j = 1, \dots, n. \tag{28}$$

Then if assumptions (1)–(10) are satisfied for that country, it must be true that

$$\mathrm{cor}\,(p, e) \leq 0. \tag{29}$$

Proof.—From balanced trade (9),

$$\sum_{j=1}^{n} e_j = p^w T^n = 0 \tag{30}$$

so that (26) permits one to consider only the inner product, pe. But

$$pe = \sum_{j=1}^{n} \frac{p_j^a}{p_j^w} p_j^w T_j^n = \sum_{j=1}^{n} p_j^a T_j^n = p^a T^n \leq 0 \tag{31}$$

by the theorem. Q.E.D.

Here I have used ratios of autarky to world prices as the basis for comparison of industries. A slightly different comparison is also possible using the difference between autarky and world prices. For this difference to be meaningful, I assume that both price vectors are normalized to lie on the unit simplex, as stated in assumption (12).

Corollary 2.—If assumptions (1)–(10) are satisfied for any country and if prices are normalized as in (12), then

$$\mathrm{cor}\,(p^a - p^w, T^n) \leq 0. \tag{32}$$

Proof.—For the inner product I have

$$(p^a - p^w)T^n = p^a T^n - p^w T^n = p^a T^n \leq 0 \tag{33}$$

by (9) and the theorem. Since, by (12),

$$\sum_{j=1}^{n} (p_j^a - p_j^w) = \sum_{j=1}^{n} p_j^a - \sum_{j=1}^{n} p_j^w = 0, \tag{34}$$

(26) permits one to deduce (32) from (33). Q.E.D.

Notice that both of these results obtain for any particular country without any assumptions whatever about behavior in the rest of the world. Also, no use has been made of the requirement that world markets clear, assumption (11). This, of course, is because I have not yet tried to make comparisons across countries. I now make such a comparison for a two-country world.

Corollary 3.—If the world contains only two countries, $i = 1, 2$, both satisfying (1)–(10), and if (11) is also satisfied, then

$$\mathrm{cor}\,(p^{a1} - p^{a2}, T^{n1}) \leq 0, \tag{35}$$

where p^{a1} and p^{a2} are both normalized to the unit simplex (12).

Proof.—From (11) with $m = 2$ note that

$$T^{n1} = -T^{n2}. \tag{36}$$

Thus

$$(p^{a1} - p^{a2})T^{n1} = p^{a1}T^{n1} + p^{a2}T^{n2}, \tag{37}$$

which is seen to be nonpositive by applying the theorem to each of the two terms on the right-hand side separately. The normalization (12), together with (26), then implies (35). Q.E.D.

This result, though derived only for a two-country world, has the advantage of placing a clear restriction on the possible pattern of natural trade. Given the two vectors of autarky prices, it says that, of all the conceivable patterns of trade that might emerge, only those which yield the indicated nonpositive correlation will be observed. Corollaries 1 and 2, on the other hand, do not embody such a clear restriction on the pattern of trade, since they contain the world-price vector which must be determined simultaneously with the pattern of trade.

To obtain a similar restriction for a many-country world I now prove a final corollary which deals with all countries and industries simultaneously. Let P^a be a vector of length mn containing the autarky prices of all countries and all industries, and let E be a vector of the same length containing the net exports of all countries and all industries, arranged in the same order as in P^a.

Corollary 4.—If the world contains m countries, all satisfying assumptions (1)–(10), and if (11) is also satisfied, then

$$\text{cor}(P^a, E) \leq 0. \tag{38}$$

Proof.—From the construction of E, it is clear that

$$\sum_{k=1}^{mn} E_k = \sum_{j=1}^{n}\left(\sum_{i=1}^{m} T_j^{ni}\right) = 0 \tag{39}$$

by (11). Thus (26) allows one to look only at the inner product of P^a and E. But

$$P^a E = \sum_{k=1}^{mn} P_k^a E_k = \sum_{i=1}^{m}\left(\sum_{j=1}^{n} p_j^{ai} T_j^{ni}\right)$$

$$= \sum_{i=1}^{m} p^{ai} T^{ni}. \tag{40}$$

From the theorem, each term in this summation is nonpositive, implying (38). Q.E.D.

To summarize, the first two corollaries provide alternative explanations of a single country's trade, one in value terms, the other in terms of quantities, with comparative advantage measured by comparisons of autarky prices with world prices. The third corollary provides the general analogue to the traditional comparative-advantage proposition for two countries in terms of a good-by-good comparison of the two countries' autarky prices. Finally, the fourth and last corollary provides the most general statement of comparative advantage for the world as a whole.

III. Refinements

In this section I point out two ways that the proofs above can be modified, either to strengthen the results or to alter the assumptions needed for their validity.

Strong Inequalities

The theorem and its corollaries are stated in terms of weak inequalities. These can be strengthened by any of several additional assumptions which serve to contribute a strict inequality somewhere in the chain of reasoning used to prove the theorem. I leave it to the reader to verify that any of the following assumptions would serve this purpose. (1) Transport costs are strictly positive for nonzero trade. (2) Tariff or export tax revenues are strictly positive in the natural trade equilibrium. (3) The optimal consumption bundle given any positive price vector is unique and different in natural trade and autarky. (4) The production possibility set is strictly convex, and trade and autarky prices differ.

   While the first of these assumptions, especially, is realistic, I have chosen not to use any of them throughout the paper since they would exclude one of the best-known models and results of trade theory. That is the classical Ricardian constant-costs model with two countries of different size. In that model a trade equilibrium can arise in which the world prices equal the autarky prices of the large country, which then alters production, but not consumption, when it moves from autarky to trade. In that case the value of its trade at its own autarky prices is of course zero, as are the correlations of corollaries 1 and 2 for the large country. However, aside from this and perhaps other equally special cases, one can expect strictly negative correlations to be the normal result.

Relation to the Gains from Trade

The reader will already have noted that part of the proof of the theorem bears a marked similarity to the proof of the gains from

954   JOURNAL OF POLITICAL ECONOMY

trade (Samuelson 1939). I showed first that natural trade would be preferred to autarky (inequality [17]) and then that this implies the theorem. An alternative proof could have begun, then, with the assumption that trade is beneficial.

While this would not really be an improvement over the present analysis, since it would leave unanswered the question of whether there would indeed be gains from trade, this modification does suggest an alternative proof that does not rely on the fiction of community preferences.[7] Suppose that each country contains many individuals, each with his own preferences, and that a move from autarky to trade is accompanied by suitable redistribution of income so as to leave all individuals better off. Then an inequality like (18) can be obtained for each consumer individually, and (18) itself can be obtained by adding these up. The rest of the proof then follows.

IV. Discussion

At the beginning of the paper I noted that familiar simple statements about the role of comparative advantage become difficult or impossible when models are complicated in a variety of realistic ways. I have now developed an alternative way of representing the relationship between autarky prices and trade by looking at correlations between the two. This has enabled me to state a variety of simple propositions regarding comparative advantage, and I have proved these propositions in a very general model. I will now compare these results with others that have appeared in the literature.

Consider first the classical model of constant costs. Here it must be admitted that my contribution is limited, for the role of comparative advantage is already well understood in the classical model. The familiar proposition for a two-country world, that goods can be ranked in terms of comparative advantage with one end of the chain being exportable and the other importable, is considerably stronger than my own corollary 3 for the same case.[8] I note only what has sometimes been doubted: that while the classical theory predicts only the direction and not the magnitude of trade, it nonetheless permits one to infer a negative correlation between relative costs and net exports.[9]

[7] This alternative proof was suggested by Ted Bergstrom.
[8] The explanation of trade in terms of a chain of comparative advantage was apparently first demonstrated by Haberler (1936).
[9] Doubt that this should be true has been expressed, e.g., by Bhagwati (1964, p. 11) in criticizing empirical tests of the comparative-costs theory. Similar doubts in the context of the factor-proportions theory also led Harkness and Kyle (1975) to employ logit analysis, rather than least-squares regression, to test that theory. While my results do not deal directly with factor endowments or factor intensities, they nonetheless suggest that tests for simple correlations may not, after all, be inappropriate.

With both many countries and many goods, the classical model has been examined in detail by Jones (1961). His results, again, allow a much more precise determination of the pattern of international specialization than does, say, my corollary 4. Still, my results do show that a straightforward comparison of costs does have something to say about the pattern of trade without going all the way to the solution of a mathematical programming problem as is done by Jones.[10]

Turning now to generalizations of the factor-proportions theory of trade, one sees that my model is consistent with the 3-good, 2-factor model in which Melvin (1968) found the pattern of trade to be indeterminate. But this indeterminacy has not prevented me from obtaining meaningful correlations. What I have done, in a sense, is to exploit those limitations that Melvin *was* able to place, implicitly, on the pattern of trade, as he did in his elegant figure 8, and to show that these limitations are enough to assure that the pattern of trade still, in a general sense, follows the dictates of comparative advantage. In his figure, Melvin showed that trade could be represented by any of an infinite number of lines, connecting two other parallel lines and passing through a single point representing demand. The clue to the validity of my correlations is that the two parallel lines must lie on opposite sides of the demand point in a manner that is prescribed by relative autarky prices. Thus in Melvin's model, and in more general multicommodity, multifactor models, the law of comparative advantage is weakened but not destroyed by the indeterminacy of the pattern of production.

Finally, a great advantage of my model is that it allows for a considerable amount of interference with the free flow of trade by such impediments to trade as transport costs and tariffs. It is true, as Travis (1964, 1972) has suggested, that such impediments can cause particular goods to be exported that would have been imported and vice versa.[11] But while this is possible for particular goods, my analysis shows that it cannot be true of so many goods as to reverse the average relationship that must hold between comparative advantage and trade. Only by subsidies could this average relationship be made not to hold—subsidies either of production, which would violate my assumptions (4) and (7), or of trade, which could violate my assumption (10).

---

[10] In a further discussion of his results, Jones (1977) remarks that "alternative and equivalent criteria in two-by-two cases may not prove equivalent in more general settings. But knowledge of the general case can aid in recasting criteria in the simple model so that it can generalize." My results provide another example of this phenomenon, for my correlations, when applied to the two-by-two case, are equivalent to alternative statements of the comparative advantage criterion.

[11] An example of this is given in Deardorff (1979) and requires the presence of intermediate goods, as well as tariffs or transport costs, in a multicommodity model.

Appendix

Instead of the single international port assumed in the body of the paper, let there now be an arbitrary number of ports, l, indexed $h = 1, \ldots, l$. While it is not necessary, these could now be identified with the countries of the model, in which case one would have $l = m$. Instead of a single trade vector for each country, I must now distinguish trade vectors for each of the l destinations. Let $^h t^i$ represent country i's vector of net supplies to port h. Then the total trade vector, $T^i = \Sigma_{h=1}^l {}^h t^i$. In addition I must now distinguish separate world-price vectors at each port, $^h p^w$, and separate vectors of traders' prices facing country i's traders at each port, $^h p^{ti}$. A country's production possibilities set, F^i, now contains all feasible collections of the $l + 1$ vectors $(Q^i, {}^1 t^i, \ldots, {}^l t^i)$.

The following assumptions now replace those in Section I:

$$\text{If } (Q^i, {}^1 t^i, \ldots, {}^l t^i) \in F^i, \quad \text{then} \quad \left(Q^i + \sum_{h=1}^l {}^h t^i, 0, \ldots, 0 \right) \in F^i, \quad (A1)$$

$$(Q^{ai}, 0, \ldots, 0) \in F^i, \quad (A3)$$

$$p^{ai} Q^{ai} \geqslant p^{ai} Q \text{ for all } (Q, 0, \ldots, 0) \in F^i, \quad (A4)$$

$$(Q^{ni}, {}^1 t^{ni}, \ldots, {}^l t^{ni}) \in F^i, \quad (A6)$$

$$p^{ai} Q^{ni} + \sum_{h=1}^l {}^h p^{tih} {}^h t^{ni} \geqslant p^{ai} Q + \sum_{h=1}^l {}^h p^{tih} {}^h t \text{ for all } (Q, {}^1 t, \ldots, {}^l t) \in F^i, \quad (A7)$$

$$\sum_{h=1}^l {}^h p^{wh} {}^h t^{ni} = 0, \quad (A9)$$

$$({}^h p_j^w - {}^h p_j^{ti}) {}^h t_j^{ni} \geqslant 0 \quad \text{for } j = 1, \ldots, n; h = 1, \ldots, l, \quad (A10)$$

$$\sum_{i=1}^m {}^h t^{ni} = 0 \quad \text{for } h = 1, \ldots, l, \quad (A11)$$

$$\sum_{j=1}^n p_j^{ai} = 1 \quad i = 1, \ldots, m. \quad (A12)$$

The remaining assumptions are unchanged.

The statement of the theorem is unchanged, but its proof must be modified. Inequality (14) is obtained for each port individually, and thus from (A9), I get

$$^h p^{tih} {}^h t^n \leqslant 0 \quad \text{for } h = 1, \ldots, l. \quad (A15)$$

Inequality (16) then follows from (A7) as before; (17) and (18) are unchanged, while (19) follows from (A1), (A6), and (A4) as before; (20) follows, and the theorem is proved.

Corollaries 1 and 2 no longer make sense, as there are now many vectors of world prices. However, corollaries 3 and 4 can still be proved by using the theorem and (A11).

Thus most of the results of the paper continue to be valid in a world of many ports, and the fiction of a single port was needed only to simplify notation.

LAW OF COMPARATIVE ADVANTAGE   957

References

Bhagwati, Jagdish N. "The Pure Theory of International Trade: A Survey." *Econ. J.* 74 (March 1964): 1–84.

Deardorff, Alan V. "Weak Links in the Chain of Comparative Advantage." *J. Internat. Econ.* 9 (May 1979): 197–209.

Drabicki, John Z., and Takayama, Akira. "An Antinomy in the Theory of Comparative Advantage." *J. Internat. Econ.* 9 (May 1979): 211–23.

Haberler, Gottfried von. *The Theory of International Trade, with Its Applications to Commercial Policy.* London: Hodge, 1936.

Harkness, Jon, and Kyle, John F. "Factors Influencing United States Comparative Advantage." *J. Internat. Econ.* 5 (May 1975): 153–65.

Jones, Ronald W. "Comparative Advantage and the Theory of Tariffs: A Multi-Country, Multi-Commodity Model." *Rev. Econ. Studies* 28 (June 1961): 161–75.

———. " 'Two-ness' in Trade Theory: Costs and Benefits." Special Papers in International Economics no. 12, Princeton Univ., Internat. Finance Sec., April 1977.

Melvin, James R. "Production and Trade with Two Factors and Three Goods." *A.E.R.* 58 (December 1968): 1249–68.

Samuelson, Paul A. "The Gains from International Trade." *Canadian J. Econ. and Polit. Sci.* 5 (May 1939): 195–205.

———. "Prices of Factors and Goods in General Equilibrium." *Rev. Econ. Studies* 21 (February 1953): 1–20.

———. "The Transfer Problem and Transport Costs, II: Analysis of Effects of Trade Impediments." *Econ. J.* 64 (June 1954): 264–89.

Travis, William P. *The Theory of Trade and Protection.* Cambridge, Mass.: Harvard Univ. Press, 1964.

———. "Production, Trade, and Protection When There Are Many Commodities and Two Factors." *A.E.R.* 62 (March 1972): 87–106.

[9]

THE FACTOR PROPORTIONS THEORY:
THE N–FACTOR CASE

I

The economic literature—perhaps not surprisingly—is entirely devoid of a rigorous treatment of the well known HECKSCHER-OHLIN theorem in instances where the trading partners are endowed with more than two factors of production[1]. Without any doubt, the reason for this is the fact that in situations where more than two factors are involved, we cannot have a unique ordering of technologies according to relative factor intensity[2]. Coupled with an always unique ordering of factor endowments of two trading partners, this multiplicity renders statements and proofs of any meaningful theorems extremely difficult.

It will be recalled that the usual way of stating the HECKSCHER-OHLIN Theorem involves relative factor-endowments on the one hand, and relative factor-intensities of products on the other; and it is the latter that cause all the trouble when more than two factors are considered. But it is possible to restate the theorem for the two factor case with reference to amounts of factor-services embodied in goods traded, rather than with reference to products[3]: 'The country relatively better endowed with one productive factor will be net exporter of the services of that factor, and net importer of the services of the other factor.' While in the two-factor case this statement is just about equivalent to the more usual statement of the theorem, when more than two factors are present analogous statements (regarding trade-factor-contents rather than types of products traded) are far

1. For evidence of this, see a recent review article of J. BHAGWATI, 'The Pure Theory of International Trade', *Economic Journal*, March 1964.
2. Note that already in the 3-factor case one production function can be ordered with respect to another one in three different ways: taking land as a reference-input, it can be 1. either more or less labor intensive; 2. either more or less capital intensive; and with reference to labor it can be 3. either more or less capital intensive.
3. Note for example that the well known LEONTIEF-paradox is stated in these terms. Specifically, LEONTIEF compares aggregates of factor inputs in exports and imports, computed over a large number of products.

JAROSLAV VANEK

more manageable. And yet, such theorems are not only equally scientifically interesting but also just as useful for purposes of policy formulation. Clearly, the advantage of the approach here suggested is that instead of a multiple ordering of products we now have again a unique ordering of trade-factor-intensities. It is this approach that I take in this paper.

I will first state the assumptions and the conclusions and then proceed to the derivation of the results.

II

As found in economic literature, the rigorous proof of the factor proportions theory with two productive factors and two trading partners requires the following assumptions:

1. Identical and linearly homogeneous production functions for identical products in the two trading countries.
2. Identical preferences and either identical incomes (with trade) or unitary income elasticity for all products.
3. Product price equalization through free international trade.
4. No relative factor-intensity reversals; that is, impossibility to have more than one set of relative factor prices for one prescribed set of relative product prices.
5. At least as many products as productive factors.
6. Perfectly homogeneous and internationally immobile productive factors, fixed in supply in the two countries.
7. Perfect competition in factor as well as product markets.

Our generalization of the factor proportions theory for large numbers of productive factors (n) and products (m) is based on the same assumptions and one additional one, namely,

8. Specialization (in the two-country world) in no more than $m - n$ products.

While assumption 8. renders the idealized world of the factor proportions theory only slightly more restrictive (over and above what is implied by assumptions 1. through 7.), it reduces what other-

THE FACTOR PROPORTIONS THEORY

wise would have been a mamoth problem to very easily manageable dimensions. Actually, once it is realized that assumption 8. completes the set of assumptions needed for international factor price equalization, the problem may even appear to some as trivial.

Using X_i for supplies of domestic and x_i for supplies of foreign factors, the following relation between factor endowments is postulated to prevail:

$$\frac{X_1}{x_1} \geq \frac{X_2}{x_2} \geq \ldots \geq \frac{X_n}{x_n} \tag{1}$$

Then it can be concluded that with free international trade the following must hold:

1. The domestic economy will be a net exporter of services of X_1, $X_2, \ldots, X_j$ and a net importer of services of $X_{j+1}, X_{j+2}, \ldots,$ X_n, where $j \neq n$.
2. j can be exactly determined if, as an additional piece of information, the common factor prices are also given.
3. With factor prices known the net flow of each factor service through international trade can exactly be calculated.
4. If factor-income-shares in the world (the two countries taken together) are indentical for all factors, the ranking in relation (1) will exactly be reproduced in the ranking of net factor-flows through international trade.
5. If any two or more world factor income shares are identical, the rankings in (1) and of the corresponding net trade-flows will be identical.
6. Conclusions analogous to 4 and 5 hold if factor-shares are identical in only one country.
7. With different factor-income shares in the world, but following the same (reverse) ranking as (of) that given in relation (1), the ranking in (1) will be reproduced in the ranking of net factor-outflows (inflows).
8. If we measure the net trade-flows of individual factors as a share (in physical terms or in value) of the total world, or national (of either country) endowments of the corresponding factors, the ranking of flows thus measured will always match perfectly the ranking in (1).

JAROSLAV VANEK

III

The proofs of all these propositions are remarkably simple. Call X and x, the (n times one) vectors reflecting factor-endowments of the domestic economy and factor-endowments of the foreign economy respectively, and call W a diagonal ($n \times n$) matrix with the n factor prices on the diagonal, ordered as in relation (1). Then the vector V reflecting the factor content of total world output, each content being measured as a money-value, is

$$V = W (X + x) \tag{2}$$

and the vector reflecting the value-contents of the national output of the domestic economy, Y, is

$$Y = W X \tag{3}$$

Given the assumptions of the factor-proportions theory (1. through 8.) stated in II above, the value-factor-content of national expenditure of the domestic economy, y, is

$$y = m V \tag{4}$$

where m is a constant to be determined, measuring the share of expenditure of the domestic economy in total world output (expenditure). The trade-vector T reflecting the net factor-contents of trade then is

$$T = Y - y \tag{5}$$

and the constant m is to be determined from the condition

$$T'I = 0 \tag{6}$$

where I is a (n times one) vector, each of its elements being one. Now consider the j'th element of the vector T; it is

$$T_j = W_j [X_j (1 - m) - m x_j] \tag{7}$$

For values of m between zero and unity and prescribed values of X_j, x_j and W_j the function T_j is drawn in *Figure 1*. As indicated in

752

THE FACTOR PROPORTIONS THEORY

the diagram, the line reflecting T_j has one point independent of the corresponding wage rate; it is its intersection with the horizontal axis. On the other hand, the slope of the line, measured in absolute value, is nothing but the world income of the j'th factor. Note that the intercepts with $m = 0$ and $m = 1$ are $+ W_j X_j$ and $- W_j x_j$ respectively. The point invariant with respect to W_j, namely, m_j, is, as indicated in the diagram,

$$m_j = \frac{1}{1 + (x_j/X_j)} \tag{8}$$

Recalling relation (1) it is immediately apparent that for $j < i$, necessarily, $m_j \geq m_i$. This is indicated by the intersection of another net factor-content T_i with the m-axis.

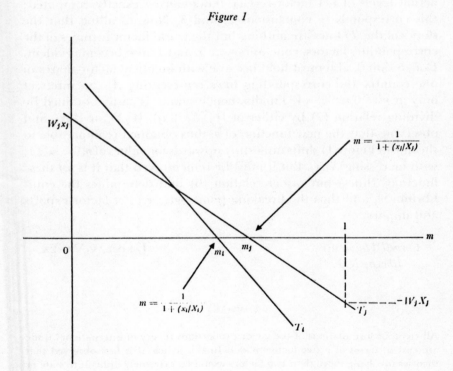

Figure 1

JAROSLAV VANEK

The actual level of m, the proportion of domestic expenditure in total world expenditure, is found from relation (6); referring to the diagram, the solution is such value of m that makes the sum of (positive and negative) vertical distances between the horizontal axis and all the n T-lines zero. For example, in the two-factor case, with only factors i and j, such a solution would be obtained somewhere between m_i and m_j. This is nothing but the situation described by the alternative version of the HECKSCHER-OHLIN theorem: the domestic economy must be a net exporter of services of the j-factor and importer of services of the i-factor. For more than two factors, it is immediately apparent that the solution m must be *inside* (not on the boundaries of) the range m_1 to m_n, and thus, recalling the perfect matching between the order in relation (1) and the order of the m_j's along the m-axis, our conclusion 1. becomes evident. Knowledge of the W_j's tells us the slopes of the T_j lines, and thus m, as well as the actual levels of net factor-service flows can be exactly computed; this corresponds to conclusions 2. and 3. Now recalling that the slopes of the T_j lines are nothing but the world factor incomes of the corresponding factors, conclusions 4., 5. and 7. also become evident. Conclusion 6. also must hold because with identical factor-shares in one country the corresponding lines representing A_i can intersect only at $m = 0$ or $m = 1$. Finally, conclusion 8. is easily obtained by dividing relation (7) by either of $W_j(X_j + x_j)$, $W_j X_j$, or $W_j x_j$, and observing that the new function of m thus obtained (comparable to the line in Figure 1) shifts uniformly upwards for values of m $0 < m < 1$, with increasing X_j/x_j. But it must be remembered that it is *not* these functions (lines) but rather relation (6) that determines the equilibrium m, and thus the breaking-point between net factor exports and imports.

Cornell University   JAROSLAV VANEK
Ithaca, N.Y.

SUMMARY

All rigorous formulations of the factor proportions theory of international trade are cast in terms of a two-factor model. In this article it is first observed that theories involving more than two factors would be extremely difficult to state or

THE FACTOR PROPORTIONS THEORY

prove with respect to the commodity structure of trade, because of the difficulty of ranking products according to factor intensity. However, if we are interested in the factor-content structure of trade rather than in the commodity structure, meaningful theorems still can be derived, irrespective of the number of productive factors actually involved in world production. Eight such theorems, otherwise based on the same assumptions as the traditional factor proportions theories, are stated and proved in the article. As an illustration, one of the theorems implies that a country better endowed in the j'th factor relative to the i'th factor with respect to the rest of the world (i.e. another country in a two-country model) could never be a net exporter of productive services of the i'th factor embodied in international barter exchange.

[10]

Economics Letters 10 (1982) 337–342
North-Holland Publishing Company

THE GENERAL ROLE OF FACTOR INTENSITY
IN THE THEOREMS OF INTERNATIONAL TRADE *

Wilfred J. ETHIER

University of Stockholm, S-106 91 Stockholm, Sweden

Received 1 April 1982

The pattern of factor intensities often allows predictions of directions of change in 2×2 trade theory, but the most general higher dimensional extensions have said little about analogous predictions. This paper obtains general results in an elementary way.

1. Introduction

The Stolper–Samuelson theorem (as does its Rybczynski analog) contains two assertions: that relative commodity price changes produce unambiguous changes in real factor rewards, and that the direction of the latter can be predicted from relative factor intensities. The Heckscher–Ohlin theorem likewise predicts trade flows on the basis of such intensities.

Higher dimensional generalization has followed two paths. That concerned with stronger results [1] has touched on both aspects of the theorems, with the existence of desired relations between goods and factors shown to be equivalent to the satisfaction of stringent factor intensity conditions. But the second, more general, path [2] has focused on the first aspect and ignored whether relative factor intensities allow a prediction

---

* Research for this paper was supported by the National Science Foundation. Lars Svensson and Avinash Dixit contributed valuable suggestions.

[1] See Uekawa (1971), and Kemp (1976, ch. 3).
[2] See Ethier (1974), Kemp (1976, chs. 4, 7), Jones and Scheinkman (1977) and Ethier (1983, app. One).

0165-1765/82/0000–0000/$02.75 © 1982 North-Holland

338   *W.J. Ethier / Factor intensity in international trade theorems*

of the direction of factor-reward responses or of trade flows. [3] This paper obtains general results in an elementary way.

2. Stolper–Samuelson type and Rybczynski type results

Allow any number of goods and factors. Consider a change in commodity prices, and denote by p^0 and p' the respective vectors of prices of those goods actually produced *both* before and after the change. Let $c(w) = wA(w)$ denote the cost functions of those goods, where w denotes the vector of factor rewards and $A(w)$ the matrix of least-cost techniques.

Thus $p^0 = c(w^0)$ and $p' = c(w')$. Define $b(w) = c(w)(p' - p^0)$. By the mean value theorem there exists some vector $\overline{w}$ of factor rewards such that

$$b(w') = b(w^0) + (w' - w^0)\,\mathrm{d}b(\overline{w}), \tag{1}$$

where $\mathrm{d}b(\overline{w})$, the Hessian matrix of b, equals $[A(\overline{w}) + \overline{w}\mathrm{d}A(\overline{w})](p' - p^0)$. Now $\overline{w}\mathrm{d}A(\overline{w}) = 0$ as a condition of cost minimization. Thus (1) can be written

$$\left[c(w') - c(w^0) \right](p' - p^0) = (w' - w^0)A(\overline{w})(p' - p^0). \tag{2}$$

Noting that $c(w') - c(w^0) = p' - p^0$, (2) implies

$$(w' - w^0)A(\overline{w})(p' - p^0) \geqslant 0. \tag{3}$$

This is the basic result: $(w' - w^0)$ is positively *correlated* with $A(\overline{w})(p' - p^0)$, or $(p' - p^0)$ is positively correlated with $(w' - w^0)A(\overline{w})$. Large values of $(w_i' - w_i^0)$ tend to accompany large values of a_{ij} and of $(p_j' - p_j^0)$; commodity price changes on average raise the most the rewards of the factors used most intensively by the goods whose prices increase the most, etc. In the two-by-two case (3) gives the usual rigid link, but when dimensionality increases the relation says nothing about the direction of change of individual factor rewards and merely describes *average* changes.

---

[3] Exceptions are Uekawa (1979), unrelated to the present paper, Deardorff (1981), and Dixit and Norman (1980), discussed below.

Note the great generality of (3). It follows directly from cost minimization without any special restriction on dimensionality, technology, or endowments. [4] The present proposition relates the direction of factor reward changes to the direction of changes in the prices of goods that continue to be produced. Goods not produced in either or both states contribute no information, although they would of course be relevant to the magnitude of changes in *real* rewards.

For sufficiently small changes, $\overline{w} = w^0$ will work in (3), but large changes could demand a $\overline{w}$ close to neither w^0 nor w', so that $A(\overline{w})$ could be quite distinct from observed techniques. But this is *not* a penalty of higher dimensions: the point can be grasped in a two-by-two world. Suppose that, because of a factor-intensity reversal, $p^0 = c(w^0) = c(w^{00})$, and $p' = c(w') = c(w'')$, with $w_2''/w_1'' > w_2^0/w_1^0 > w_2^{00}/w_1^{00} > w_2'/w_1'$. Then the movement from w^0 to w' involves the opposite direction of change of relative factor rewards to the movement from w^{00} to w''. $A\overline{w}$ satisfying (3) need imply the appropriate pattern of factor intensities in the former case, but the latter case requires a quite different $\overline{w}$ with the opposite intensity pattern. The ability to choose $\overline{w}$ appropriately is the reason I have a global Stolper–Samuelson-type result without ruling out factor intensity reversals or their higher dimensional analogs.

A similar Rybczynski type result is easily obtained. Let v^0 and v' be two endowment vectors and x^0 and x' the corresponding vectors of outputs of those goods actually produced in *both* states. Then, *if* $w^0 = w'$,

$$v' - v^0 = A(w^0)(x' - x^0) \tag{4}$$

and multiplying both sides by the vector $(v' - v^0)$

$$(v' - v^0)A(w^0)(x' - x^0) \geq 0. \tag{5}$$

This is a general Rybczynski-type result: on average, endowment changes cause the largest increases in the outputs of the goods which most intensively use the factors that have increased relatively the most in supply, etc. The requirement that $w^0 = w'$ limits applicability. The change $v' - v^0$ must not be large enough to depart from the relevant diversifica-

---

[4] Of course the mean value theorem must be applicable, so $b(w)$ should be continuously differentiable over some path of non-negative factor prices connecting w^0 and w'. But no restrictions are placed on production patterns over that path, endowments can change in any way between equilibria, and A need not even be non-singular. But constant returns to scale and no joint production are assumed.

tion cone. If $n \geqslant m$, where n and m denote the numbers of produced goods and factors, the factor-price-equalization theorem can be appealed to for $w^0 = w'$, and my result is again a direct consequence of cost minimization. But if $m > n$, the elements of $v' - v^0$ cannot be chosen at will: n of them may be specified arbitrarily, with the remaining $m - n$ then set to equilibrate factor markets at prices w_0 (as would be the case if $m - n$ factors were freely traded at world prices). This limits the result in a way not necessary with its Stolper–Samuelson analog. But such asymmetry should come as no surprise. [5]

3. Heckscher–Ohlin type theorems

Let w' and w^0 denote home and foreign autarky prices. Then define $d(w) = c(w)M$, where M denotes the vector of home free-trade imports. The same logic which produced (3) implies, for some $\overline{w}$,

$$(p' - p^0)M = (w' - w^0)A(\overline{w})M.$$

Now $(p' - p^0)M \geqslant 0$ by the general law of comparative advantage, [6] so

$$(w' - w^0)A(\overline{w})M > 0. \tag{6}$$

This correlation is a generalized price version of the Heckscher–Ohlin theorem: on average countries tend to import the goods most intensive in the use of the factors most abundant in a price sense, etc. [7] This is a very general result, depending only on cost minimization and requiring no restrictions on demand or on technology – including no exclusion of higher-dimensional analogs of factor intensity reversals.

Turning to the quantity version, let v' and v^0 denote home and foreign endowments and suppose at least as many produced goods as factors. With endowments given, commodity prices uniquely relate to factor

[5] See, for example, Kemp (1976, ch. 4) or Jones and Scheinkman (1977).
[6] See Deardorff (1980), Dixit and Norman (1980, pp. 94–96) or Ethier (1983, app. One).
[7] Deardorff (1981) obtains in a different way a similar result with $A(\overline{w})$ replaced by a matrix A^0, which can be obtained by using in each column the technique actually employed in free trade in the country of export of the respective goods. Thus $A(\overline{w})$ has the advantage of consistent comparison across industries since its techniques would actually be chosen under some common factor rewards, and A^0 the advantage of being constructed from observed (post-trade) techniques. See also Ethier (1983, app. One).

prices [see McKenzie (1955)], so I can write $w = f(p, v)$. Define $h(p, v) = f(p, v)(v' - v^0)$ and proceed as above to obtain, for some $\bar{w} = f(\bar{p}, \bar{v})$,

$$g(p', v') - g(p^0, v^0) = (p' - p^0)f_p(\bar{p}, \bar{v})(v' - v^0)$$
$$+ (v' - v^0)f_v(\bar{p}, \bar{v})(v' - v^0),$$

where f_p and f_v denote the appropriate matrices of partial derivatives. Now $f_v(\bar{p}, \bar{v}) = 0$ by the factor price equalization theorem and $f_p(\bar{p}, \bar{v}) = A^{-1}(\bar{w})$, where $A(\bar{w})$ is made square, if necessary, by arbitrarily deleting enough goods. Also it is known [8] that $(w' - w^0)(v' - v^0) \leq 0$, with identical homothetic tastes. So

$$(p' - p^0)A^{-1}(\bar{w})(v' - v^0) \leq 0. \tag{7}$$

This correlation is a generalized quantity version: countries tend on average to have a comparative advantage in those goods that most intensively employ the most relatively abundant factors. [9] Note the relation between the concepts of relative factor intensity in my price and quantity generalizations: the former interprets factor intensity as a matter of the relative magnitude of the elements of A whereas the latter looks at the elements of A^{-1}, and the two are likely evaluated at different factor prices. These two concepts become distinct when the numbers of goods and factors exceed two.

Next, assume that all countries have identical homothetic tastes and that in free trade factor-price equalization holds. Then it is well-known that the *factor content* of trade will reflect relative factor abundance in a quantity sense, [10] but there are no results on commodity composition. To obtain one, define, in (5), $x^0 = (1 - g)x^H$, $x' = gx^F$, $v^0 = (1 - g)v^H$, $v' = gv^F$, where v^H and v^F denote the home and foreign endowment vectors, x^H and x^F home and foreign free trade outputs, and g a scalar:

$$\left[gv^F - (1 - g)v^H \right] A(\bar{w}) \left[gx^F - (1 - g)x^H \right] \geq 0. \tag{8}$$

Now if g is set equal to free trade home income as a fraction of world

[8] See Dixit and Norman (1980, p. 99) or Ethier (1983, app. One).
[9] Dixit and Norman (1980, p. 100) obtain a result like (7) on the strong assumption that $c(w)$ is globally invertible. The present approach demonstrates that such an assumption is unnecessary, and the discussion following (3) explains why.
[10] See, for example, Vanek (1968).

income, identical homothetic tastes imply that $M = g(x^H + x^F) - x^H = gx^F - (1 - g)x^H$. Thus

$$\left[g(v^F + v^H) - v^H \right] A(\overline{w}) M \geqslant 0. \tag{9}$$

This correlation says that on average a country tends to import those goods which make most intensive use of the country's relatively scarce factors, where factor scarcity is measured in a quantity sense by comparing the national endowment to the world endowment scaled down by the aggregate value of national factor service supplies as a fraction of the aggregate value of world supplies.

References

Deardorff, A.V., 1980, The general validity of the law of comparative advantage, Journal of Political Economy 88, 941–957.

Deardorff, A.V., 1981, The general validity of the Heckscher-Ohlin theorem, processed.

Dixit, A.K. and V. Norman, 1980, Theory of international trade (Nisbet, Cambridge, London).

Ethier, W., 1974, Some of the theorems of international trade with many goods and factors, Journal of International Economics 4, 194–206.

Ethier, W., 1983, Modern international economics (Norton, New York).

Jones, R.W. and J. Scheinkman, 1977, The relevance of the two-sector production model in trade theory, Journal of Political Economy 85, 909–935.

Kemp, M.C., 1976, Three topics in the theory of international trade (North-Holland, Amsterdam).

McKenzie, L.W., 1955, Equality of factor prices in world trade, Econometrica 23, 239–257.

Uekawa, Y., 1971, Generalization of the Stolper-Samuelson theorem, Econometrica 39, 197–218.

Uekawa, Y., 1979, On the concepts of factor intensities and the relation between commodity prices and factor rewards, in: J.R. Green and J.A. Scheinkman, eds., General equilibrium, growth, and trade (Academic, New York).

Vanek, J., 1968, The factor proportions theory: The n-factor case, Kyklos 21, 749–755.

B
Trade Based on Increasing Returns

[11]

INCREASING RETURNS TO SCALE AS A DETERMINANT OF TRADE

JAMES R. MELVIN *University of Western Ontario*

Les rendements croissants à l'échelle pris comme déterminant du commerce international.
Presque tous les modèles récents de commerce international prennent comme point de
départ la différence des proportions dans l'utilisation des facteurs de production, et, même
s'il est juste d'attacher de l'importance à ces modèles, peu d'attention s'est portée sur la
possibilité que ces échanges pourraient être causés par un certain nombre d'autres facteurs.
Nous examinons ici l'effet d'un de ces facteurs, les rendements croissants à l'échelle.
Afin d'être certain de ne capturer que les effets des rendements croissants nous devons neu-
traliser toute autre influence. Ceci implique l'acceptation aussi bien des habituelles hypothèses
de Heckscher-Ohlin que de celle d'une dotation identique de facteurs entre les deux pays. Il
est par la suite démontré que des rendements croissants peuvent entraîner un échange de
biens d'un pays à l'autre; toutefois, il n'est plus certain que les deux pays y gagneraient et ce,
même si la production mondiale augmente. Nous montrons aussi qu'un tel commerce international aboutit à des prix inégaux pour les facteurs de production, ce qui mène à un
examen des effets de la mobilité de ces facteurs. Nous nous apercevons alors que la mobilité
des facteurs entraîne un nouvel équilibre (non unique) qui implique des gains additionnels
pour la production mondiale. La distribution de ces gains dépend du degré relatif de
mobilité des facteurs. Après ajustements sur le marché des facteurs nous constatons qu'un
pays relativement bien doté d'un facteur exportera le produit où ce facteur est employé
à sa plus haute intensité. Ainsi resurgit la conclusion de Heckscher-Ohlin même si l'échange
a été causé par des rendements croissants à l'échelle.
L'article se termine sur une brève discussion de quelques-unes des autres propositions
traditionnelles de la théorie du commerce international et de leurs relations au cas des
rendements croissants. Nous montrons, par exemple, que la formule habituelle du tarif optimum ne s'applique pas dans un monde où le commerce international est dû aux rendements
croissants.

I / Introduction

Since the pioneering work of Heckscher[1] and Ohlin,[2] the factor-proportions
explanation of trade has gained almost universal acceptance among international trade economists. While it is recognized that there are other variables,
such as tastes, returns to scale, production conditions, and market imperfections, which must be taken into account, the influence of these are usually
given subservient roles, and are viewed as troublesome conditions which could
possibly subvert the results of the so-called Heckscher-Ohlin theorem. Seldom
are they viewed as possible explanations of trade in their own right. The purpose of this paper is to discuss another possible explanation of trade, increasing
returns to scale, within the confines of the simple two-good, two-factor, two-
country world. We will also attempt to put the various possible determinants
of trade in a somewhat better perspective.

[1]Eli Heckscher, "The Effects of Foreign Trade on the Distribution of Income," in H. S.
Ellis and L. A. Metzler (eds.), *Readings in the Theory of International Trade* (Philadelphia, 1949).
[2]Bertil Ohlin, *Interregional and International Trade* (Cambridge, Mass., 1933).

Canadian Journal of Economics/Revue canadienne d'Economique, II, no. 3
August/août 1969. Printed in Canada/Imprimé au Canada.

In order to start from a completely neutral position, we will begin by constructing a situation in which there will be no trade. One such world has the two countries identical in all respects, and this situation can be achieved by making the following set of assumptions. (1) The two factors exist in equal amounts in both countries. (2) Tastes are identical in both countries. (3) Production functions differ between goods, but are identical in the two countries. (4) All production functions are homogeneous of the first degree, and concave. (5) Perfect competition prevails in both countries. It is clear that this list of assumptions describes a situation in which the two countries will be identical from both the demand and supply side, so that the autarky price ratios will be the same and thus there will be no basis for trade.

It is perhaps worthwhile to observe that a number of the usual international trade assumptions are not necessary for the no-trade result. We need make no assumptions about tariffs, since they can have no influence if there is no basis for trade. Also, because both factor and commodity prices will be equal in both countries, there is no tendency for factors or commodities to move. Therefore we need make no assumptions about the international mobility of factors or goods. Of course, we are assuming internal factor mobility.

The relaxation of any one of the assumptions 1 to 5 can provide a basis for trade. If assumption 1 is relaxed, and we assume that factors exist in different proportions, we have the familiar Heckscher-Ohlin theorem.[3] It is a well-known result that even if production conditions are identical, differences in tastes in the two countries can present a basis for trade.[4] Also, the fact that trade will be expected if production functions differ between countries forms the very earliest explanation of trade, for this is the basis for trade in the Ricardian model. The relaxation of assumption 5 could take many forms and we will not attempt even to enumerate what the many possibilities would be. Although space does not permit a discussion of this question here, it seems clear that such things as discriminatory taxation could be an important determinant of trade. Assumption 4 can be relaxed either by assuming decreasing or increasing returns to scale. For decreasing returns to scale there are no new results, for the production possibility curve still has the same basic shape. The case of increasing returns to scale has received some attention,[5] but the traditional treatment has not attempted to isolate the influence of increasing returns to scale from the influence of differences in factor endowments, nor have all the implications of increasing returns to scale been explored. This paper considers these questions.

II / A model with increasing returns to scale

In this section we construct the basic model. Assumption 4 is replaced with the alternative assumption that both goods are produced under increasing returns

[3]We must also add the assumption that there is no factor intensity reversal.
[4]For example see C. P. Kindleberger, *International Economics*, 4th ed., (Homewood, Ill., 1968), 50–1.
[5]The most well-known treatment is probably that of James Meade, *A Geometry of International Trade* (London, 1952), chap. v. For another excellent treatment see Murray Kemp, *The Pure Theory of International Trade* (Englewood Cliffs, 1964), chap. 8.

Increasing Returns to Scale 391

to scale to the industry. The firm, however, is assumed to operate under conditions of constant returns to scale, that is, the production functions of the firms are assumed to be homogeneous of the first degree. We retain all other assumptions with the result that the production possibility curves for the two countries will be identical. This approach is necessary to ensure that the results we derive are due to the presence of increasing returns to scale and not to some other cause or combination of causes.

For the case of increasing returns to scale, it is still possible that the traditional analysis will be appropriate, for the production possibility curve may still have the usual "bowed-out" shape over at least part of its length.[6] There are two things which influence the shape of the production possibility curve: differences in factor intensities and returns to scale. Different factor intensities tend to make the curve "bowed-out," while increasing returns to scale tend to make it "bowed-in," and the final shape will depend on the relative strengths of these two forces.

For our purposes, the interesting case is where returns are increasing enough to result in a "bowed-in" production possibility curve such as *BAC* in Figure 1. We assume that *A* represents the autarky equilibrium point for both countries.[7]

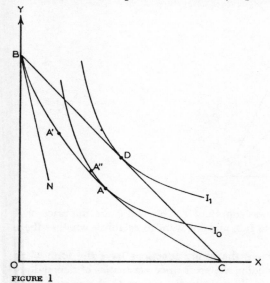

FIGURE 1

---

[6]For a proof that with increasing returns in both industries, the production possibility curve will be convex to the origin at points close enough to both axes, even though it may be concave to the origin throughout a large part of the interior of the output space, see Murray C. Kemp and Horst Herberg, "Some Implications of Variable Returns to Scale," this JOURNAL, II, 3 (Aug. 1969), 403.

[7]A question which can arise with respect to point *A* is whether or not it is stable. The answer to this question depends on what particular dynamic adjustment assumption we make. For a full discussion see Kemp, *The Pure Theory*, chap. 8. It has also been shown by Kemp and Herberg, "Variable Returns to Scale," and Ronald W. Jones, "Variable Returns to Scale in General Equilibrium Theory," *International Economic Review*, 9 (Oct. 1968), 269–71 that when returns are not constant it is no longer generally true that the equilibrium price ratio will be tangent to the production possibility curve at equilibrium,

392   JAMES R. MELVIN

Now suppose we allow international trade. The two countries are now no
longer restricted to producing at *A*, and we would expect one of them to produce at point *B* and the other to produce at point *C*. Let us further suppose
that we have the very special case where, with the price-ratio line *BC*, consumption for both countries is at the mid-point *D*. This is clearly an equilibrium position. Furthermore, given the shape of the indifference curves shown,
it is stable, for if the price of *X* increases relative to the price of *Y* there will
be excess supply of *X* and excess demand for *Y*, and equilibrium will be re-
established at *D*. Similarly if the price of *Y* increases. But of course, in general,
we could not expect the equilibrium point to be mid-way between *B* and *C*.
Suppose, for example, that with the price line *BC*, consumers in both countries
want to consume at *E* in Figure 2. This is clearly not an equilibrium, for there

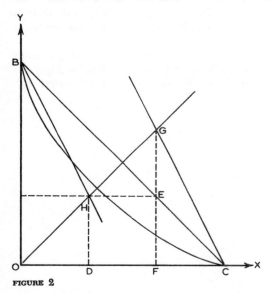

FIGURE 2

is excess demand for *X* and excess supply of *Y*. This will cause the price of *X*
to increase and the price of *Y* to fall, and we want to establish whether there
exists an equilibrium.

Consider the special case where the utility functions have the form $U =
X^2Y$. For this type of utility function, the cross-price elasticities of demand are
zero. Thus, as we rotate the price line clockwise around *C*, the consumers of
the country producing at *C* will increase their consumption of *Y*, but will not
change their consumption of *X*. Similarly, as we rotate the price line clockwise
around *B*, the consumers of the country producing at *B* will reduce their consumption of *X*, but will not change their consumption of *Y*. Clearly an equilibrium will eventually be reached (Figure 2) where the country producing at *C*

and indeed tangency will be achieved only if returns increase or decrease by the same
amount in both industries. In the Kemp-Herberg terminology this means that $\omega_1 = \omega_2 =$
constant. We will make this assumption throughout our analysis.

consumes at G and the country producing at B consumes at H. OD is equal to FC, and then, since BH and GC are parallel, demand is equal to supply for both goods, and trade is balanced. Furthermore, the equilibrium is stable, since further increases in the price of X will reduce the demand for X and increase the demand for Y. Then, since supply is fixed, the price of X will fall and the price of Y will rise, and the equilibrium position will be re-established. These same results hold for any utility functions which satisfy assumption 2, as long as the elasticity of substitution is greater than zero.[8] As long as the quantity demanded of Y can be made as large as desired by making the price of Y sufficiently low, we can always find a price ratio such that the quantity demanded is equal to the quantity supplied, which is fixed, and this, in turn, implies equality of the demand and supply of X.

III / The gains from trade

Figure 2 illustrates that while there will be trade, there is very little else that we can definitely conclude about the pattern of trade in the increasing-returns situation. We have no way of knowing, for example, which country will export which good. We know that one country will specialize in X and one in Y, but except for that the production pattern is indeterminate. Of even more importance, we cannot even be sure that both countries will gain from trade. In Figure 2, for example, the country producing at B and consuming at H is clearly worse off than it would be in autarky, for it is consuming inside its production possibility curve. Of course, this result is by no means certain, for it depends on the extent to which returns are increasing, the relative preferences of consumers for the two goods, and the elasticity of substitution in consumption. However, if the situation of Figure 2 occurs, it raises the interesting possibility that the country could be better off by imposing a prohibitive tariff. It is clear that in Figure 2 the country consuming at H could achieve a higher indifference curve by imposing a prohibitive tariff and returning to the autarky position. Such a case would seem to represent a legitimate economic justification for protection.[9]

The fact that we cannot be sure that there will be gains from trade for both countries when there are increasing returns to scale tends to illustrate the bias which our concentration on the Heckscher-Ohlin theorem has imparted to the analysis of theoretical questions in international trade. That there will be gains from trade is a well-established proposition in international trade theory. It depends on a number of assumptions, one of which is that there are constant returns to scale. But not only is the assumption of constant returns to

[8]For the case where the two goods are consumed in fixed proportions along the ray OE, i.e., the elasticity of substitution is zero, any increase in the price of X will reduce both the demand for X and the demand for Y, and since supply is fixed there does not exist any equilibrium position. The only exception is where the goods are consumed along the ray OD in Figure 1 where D is mid-way between B and C. In this case, however, all price ratios give rise to equilibrium situations.
[9]In this discussion we are defining "better off" to mean being on a higher community indifference curve.

394   JAMES R. MELVIN

scale crucial, in the sense that without it the theorem cannot be proved; it may also be that by the elimination of the possibility of increasing returns, we are abstracting from one of the more important reasons for the existence of trade in the first place. Of course, this is not to suggest that it is improper to investigate the conditions under which there will be gains from trade when there are differences in factor endowments among countries. The point is that differences in factor endowments is only one of the possible reasons for trade and that the other possible determinants of trade should be given equal time. After all, there seems to be no *a priori* reason for believing that different factor endowments is a more important determinant of trade than increasing returns to scale.

IV / Factor price equalization and the gains from factor mobility

In this section we will first consider the question of whether trade will result in the equalization of factor prices, and it is immediately clear that it will not, for with trade both countries specialize. Imagine, for example, that there are n firms in each industry, all of exactly the same size, so that in both countries each firm receives $1/n$ of the total capital and $1/n$ of the total labour. Call these quantities K_0 and L_0. In Figure 3, the point S represents the endowment of a typical firm in each country.[10] Through S will pass an isoquant for each industry, and the factor prices which will prevail in the two countries will be equal to the slopes of the two isoquants at S. It is clear that trade does

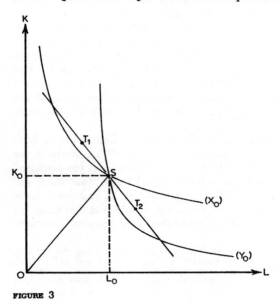

FIGURE 3

[10]Recall that the two countries are assumed to have identical endowments of both factors.

not equalize factor prices,[11] and in fact quite the opposite occurs, for if both countries are assumed to be at A in Figure 1 before trade, and since both countries are identical, factor prices must have been equal in the autarky situation.

The fact that factor price equalization will not take place in our model leads us to the consideration of how allowing factor mobility, which has been implicitly excluded to this point, would affect our results. In the Heckscher-Ohlin model, when a free-trade equilibrium is established at which factor prices are equal, there is clearly no tendency for factors to move. Furthermore, it is known that the same world production point could be achieved by complete mobility of factors and completely restricted trade.[12] It is in this sense that trade is a substitute for factor mobility.

Now consider the free-trade position for the increasing-returns-to-scale case shown in Figure 3. Factor prices in the two countries are equal to the slopes of the isoquants (X_0) and (Y_0) at point S. If country H is specializing in X and country F in Y, then when we allow factor mobility, capital will flow into country H, the country producing the capital-intensive commodity, and labour will move to country F, the country producing the labour-intensive good. We are now interested in knowing whether a new equilibrium, if it exists, will be stable and unique, and we are interested in comparing the total world output implied by this new equilibrium with the old equilibrium S.

With factor movements, while we cannot, in general, say what the new equilibrium endowments will be, we do know that a line joining the two endowment points will pass through S and that S will be the midpoint of this line.[13] Now consider any line through S with a slope which is between the slopes of the two isoquants at S. This line will be tangent to some X isoquant somewhere above and to the left of S, and tangent to some Y isoquant somewhere below and to the right of S. These two points are labelled T_1 and T_2 respectively in Figure 3.

Suppose that the distance T_1S in Figure 3 is equal to the distance ST_2. Then we have found an equilibrium-endowment configuration, for the line T_1ST_2 is the factor-price-ratio line, and since it is equal for both countries, there is no further tendency for factors to move. Each firm in country H produces the quantity of X associated with point T_1, and each firm in country F produces the quantity of Y associated with the point T_2. Furthermore, this equilibrium is stable, for if a small amount of capital is transferred to H and a small amount of labour is transferred to F, say in the ratio represented by

[11]The only case in which factor prices could be equal would be the case where there is factor intensity reversal and where the factor intensity reversal ray (the ray along which both sets of isoquants have the same slope) coincides with the endowment ray OS. For the remainder of our analysis we will assume that no factor intensity reversals occur.

[12]Because of free trade, and under the assumption that factor prices are equalized, factor proportions in the corresponding industries in the two countries will be equal. Then because of constant returns to scale, it makes no difference whether all the factors are assumed to be in one country, i.e., complete mobility of factors, or whether there are two (or many) countries.

[13]This is true since the amount of capital H gains must be equal to the amount F loses, and the amount of labour that F receives is the amount that leaves H. Recall that there are n firms in both countries, and with no loss of generality we can assume that there is a pairing up of these firms and that the transfer of factors occurs within each pair.

the slope of T_1ST_2, the wage-rental ratio will rise in H and fall in F with the result that the factor flow will be reversed and equilibrium re-established.[14]

Of course the possibility that this arbitrarily chosen line T_1ST_2 will result in a situation where T_1 and T_2 are equidistant from S is very remote, and we must consider the case where this does not occur. Suppose, for example, that the distance T'_1S is greater than the distance ST_2 so that we do not have an equilibrium. If we now rotate the line T_1ST_2 counter-clockwise around S, the distance T_1S becomes smaller, and the distance ST_2 becomes larger, and because the limit of the length of T_1S is zero as the slope of the line approaches the slope of (X_0) at S, we must eventually reach a position where ST_2 is equal to T_1S. Exactly the same kind of argument holds for the case where ST_2 is greater than T_1S, and thus we have established the existence of an equilibrium.

We now want to consider the question of whether this endowment equilibrium will be unique, and we are not long in discovering that it is not. The situation we have shown in Figure 3 is very special, for there is no reason why the equilibrium factor-price ratio should have the same slope as the line T_1T_2. In fact it is quite easy to show that for any line through S there will exist an equilibrium. In Figure 4 we have reproduced the line T_1ST_2, but have omitted the isoquants in order to keep the diagram as simple as possible. From the origin we have drawn the lines OT_1 and OT_2, and through T_1 and T_2 we have drawn the lines N_1T_1 and N_2T_2 parallel to OT_2 and OT_1 respectively.

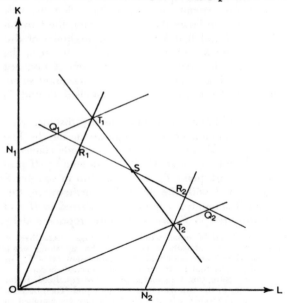

FIGURE 4

[14]As we will see presently, we cannot be sure that the same equilibrium will be achieved. And note that the equilibrium we are referring to here is an equilibrium in the factor market, i.e., a position at which there is no tendency for factors to move. In particular we are not making an argument about equilibrium in the product market.

Increasing Returns to Scale 397

The two pairs of cones with origins T_1 and T_2 (i.e., OT_1N_1, N_2T_2O and their images on the other side of T_1T_2) can be shown to contain all possible equilibrium points, as follows. Observe that for the line Q_1SQ_2, arbitrarily drawn except that it must go through S, Q_1S is equal to SQ_2 and R_1S is equal to SR_2. Consider Q_1 and Q_2 as candidates for equilibrium points. Because the production functions are homogeneous, the slope of the isoquant at Q_2 is equal to the slope of T_1T_2, while the slope of the isoquant at Q_1 is greater since the slope of the isoquant through R_1 is equal to the slope of T_1T_2. But this establishes that there are no equilibrium points further from S on the line Q_1Q_2, for as we move further from S along SQ_1 the slope of the isoquants becomes steeper, and as we move further from S along SQ_2 the slope of the isoquants becomes less steep and we are thus moving away from equality of factor prices. Exactly the same kind of argument shows that no equilibrium positions exist on the line R_1SR_2. It is now clear that there must exist a pair of points giving rise to equilibrium on the segments Q_1R_1 and Q_2R_2, for at R_1 the slope of the isoquant is equal to the slope of T_1T_2 and at R_2 it is greater, while at Q_2 the isoquant has the slope T_1T_2 and at Q_1 the slope is greater. Thus from continuity there exists a pair of points on these segments, equidistant from S, at which the slopes of the isoquants are the same. This is true for any line through S, and thus there are an infinite number of pairs of equilibrium points, and these trace out lines through T_1 and T_2.[15] All these equilibriums are stable by the same argument that we used previously.

We have thus established that when we allow factor mobility, a factor-market-equilibrium which is stable but not unique will be achieved. Furthermore it is clear from Figure 3 that for some of these equilibriums, the total world output of both goods will be larger than the free-trade position with no factor mobility. For example, the equilibrium points T_1 and T_2 imply a larger output of both X and Y than did the free-trade position S. This illustrates that with increasing returns to scale we must distinguish between gains from trade on the one hand, and gains from factor movements on the other. Simply allowing free trade does not permit the world to consume the maximum possible quantities of the two goods. We note, however, that trade is a necessary condition for any gain, for without trade in this model there will be no incentive for factors to move.

We have seen that the movement of factors can result in an increase in the level of output of both commodities, but we have not yet determined whether or not both countries will be expected to gain from this increase in output. That it is possible for both countries to gain is easily established by supposing, in Figure 2, that output increases by the same percentage for the firms of both countries. This will change the scale of the diagram, but since the utility functions are homogeneous, nothing else will change. The terms of trade will remain the same and the only difference will be that the points H and G now represent tangencies on higher community indifference curves for both countries.

---

[15]If the production functions for the two firms are Cobb-Douglas, these loci of equilibrium points will be linear. As this fact has no particular significance for our analysis the proof is left to the interested reader.

Now consider the case where the factor movements are such that there is an increase in the output of X, but no change in the output of Y.[16] In Figure 5, which reproduces Figure 2 except for the omission of the lines which for our

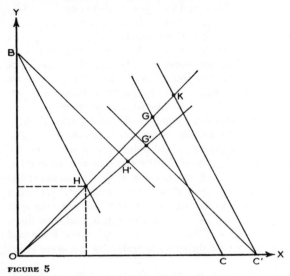

FIGURE 5

present purposes are non-essential, this change implies a shift in C to a position such as C'. If through C' we draw a line parallel to the original terms of trade CG, and assuming that the utility function is homogeneous, the tangency point with the highest indifference curve would be K. But consumption at K by country H (the country specializing in the production of X) and consumption at H by country F is not an equilibrium situation, for there is excess demand for Y and excess supply of X, and so in order to achieve equilibrium we must raise the price of Y. Now, since the quantity of Y produced does not change, the price of Y must be increased until consumers of both countries demand the same total amount of Y as previously, and if the elasticity of substitution in consumption is low, this price change might need to be substantial. For country F, an increase in the price of Y means an improvement in her terms of trade, and, with a low elasticity of substitution, F will want to consume more of both X and Y, with the result that country H will, in the final equilibrium, be consuming less Y than initially. It is even possible that the final equilibrium position for country H will contain less of both commodities as, for example, the situation of Figure 5, where G' and H' are the final consumption points for countries H and F respectively.

In our original discussion of Figure 2 we made the assumption that the utility functions were of the form $U = X^2Y$ for both countries. Thus, since the demand functions derived from this utility function have the property that all cross-price elasticities are zero, when the terms of trade for country F im-

[16]That such a situation is possible can be demonstrated in much the same way that we showed, in Figure 4, that there exists a pair of equilibrium points on every line through S.

prove, only the purchase of commodity X changes. If we were to make this assumption it would be impossible for either country to be made worse off by the particular kind of factor movement described here, for, in the final equilibrium, the consumption of Y for both countries would remain the same as before the increase in output, and the increase in the production of X would be divided between them. Thus we can conclude that, as long as the total output of both goods increases (or at least does not fall), both countries will be made better off by the factor movement as long as the cross-elasticities of demand are non-negative.

While it does not come as much of a surprise that some of the possible equilibrium positions resulting from the international movement of factors may make one of the countries worse off, it is a little more surprising that the only country which can suffer a loss is the one in which the expansion of output takes place. The other country will always be better off in the sense of being on a higher community indifference curve. Of course, this kind of situation is relevant not only for the case of international factor movements which are due to trade; it also illustrates one kind of result which is possible when economic expansion takes place in an increasing-returns-to-scale model. The situation of Figure 5 could represent a technological improvement in the X industry, or it could represent growth biased towards the X industry. With either such interpretation, Figure 5 shows that economic expansion may make a country worse off, or to use Bhagwati's terminology,[17] that growth can be immiserizing.

V / The characteristics of equilibrium

We have shown that when factor movements are allowed, there are an infinity of endowment-equilibrium positions possible, and that corresponding to each is a general equilibrium position. Further, the equilibrium achieved will depend on the relative quantities of the factors that migrate. This infinity of equilibrium positions will describe a locus in the output space, but this locus must be interpreted with some care. It does not correspond to a production-possibility locus of the usual kind, for the equilibrium does not require that there be a tangency between this locus and a world-indifference curve. As we have already observed, any one of these points could represent the world equilibrium production and consumption point. But while we do not know, in general, which of these points will be attained, there will be one which maximizes world utility. The point is that while an optimum consumption position exists, this optimum will not, except by pure chance, be reached by a perfectly competitive system. Of course, if we knew exactly where this optimum position was, and we presumably would if the utility function, the production functions, and the nature of the increasing returns were specified exactly, this optimum could be reached by appropriate intervention. Since the particular equilibrium position achieved depends on the ratio of the amount

[17]Jagdish Bhagwati, "Immiserizing Growth: A Geometrical Note," *Review of Economic Studies*, 25 (June 1958), 201–5.

of the one factor a country receives relative to the amount of the other factor that leaves, this intervention would take the form of restriction or encouragement of factor movements. Thus, in a world in which increasing returns to scale prevail, a policy of restricting immigration or capital outflows might be an appropriate policy to pursue. Of course, it must be remembered that the point which maximizes world utility need not be the point which maximizes the utility of the two countries taken separately.

This argument illustrates the importance that the relative degree of factor mobility can have, for if the market is allowed to operate freely, it is the speed with which the two factors respond to international differences in their returns which will determine the position of the final equilibrium. Thus if capital tends to adjust quickly to higher interest rates while labour responds slowly to different wage levels, the slope of the line through S will tend to be steep and we would expect the output of X, the capital-intensive good, to rise more than the output of Y. As we have already observed, however, this need not imply that the country producing X will be better off.

But there is another sense in which the degree of factor mobility may be important. In the construction of Figure 3, we first considered the special case where the slope of the factor-movement-ratio line (the line T_1ST_2) had the same slope as the equilibrium factor-price-ratio line. While we observed that this particular case was only one of an infinite number of possibilities, this is the only equilibrium for which $w/r = dK/dL$ (or $wdL = rdK$) where w and r are the prices of labour and capital respectively. This is the condition that the value of the factors leaving the country be equal to the value of the factors arriving, both valued at their equilibrium price, and is the analogy of the condition that commodity trade be balanced. If we feel that this condition should be imposed on the model, then the equilibrium achieved by the movement of factors will be unique.

The condition that the value of factor movements be equal is not very appealing when labour is one of the factors, for we usually think of labour moving on its own accord, not being exchanged for something else. For the other factors of production, however, such objections do not seem appropriate, for certainly when capitalists in one country supply firms in another with capital services, they expect something in return. Similarly, although we do not transfer coal mines or oil wells to foreign countries, we do send coal and oil, which can legitimately be considered as the services of these kinds of land, and we certainly expect something in exchange for these services.[18] Indeed one wonders if our failure to recognize that the international transfer of such things as coal and iron ore should be considered as movements of the services of land rather than commodity trade has not hindered our understanding of the process of international trade.

If we now think of our model as one in which the factors of production are capital and land it becomes not only reasonable that we should have an inter-

---

[18]The labour that we plug into a production function is not physical human beings, but rather labour services, and similarly the capital which we plug in is the services of capital. The treatment of coal and iron ore as the services of land seems to be quite analogous. An objection which could be raised to our approach is that coal and iron ore are not primary factors, for they require inputs of other factors before they can be used in the production process. But, of course, the same is true of capital.

national accounting for the movement of these factor services, but in fact essential.[19] In such a model, then, a stable unique equilibrium is ensured. Observe from Figure 3 that this equilibrium implies an increase in the output of both goods, which makes the possibility of gain by both countries more likely.

But since all we need is an overall balance in international payments, we could have a deficit in commodity trade made up by a surplus in the payments for factor services. This opens up the possibility that a further realignment of trade and factor movements could result in the achievement of an even higher level of world utility. Space does not permit the discussion of this question.

We have seen that, starting from a position where both countries are identical, trade would result in factor prices becoming unequal. Then, if factors are mobile, factors will move to the country where their return is highest, with the result that the relative factor endowments of the two countries will become unequal. Furthermore, in the new equilibrium we would observe that both countries export the good which uses their abundant factor intensively which, of course, is the statement of the Heckscher-Ohlin theorem. If the world is characterized by increasing returns to scale, then differences in factor endowments may be the result of trade rather than the cause. Thus if we find that countries which are well endowed with capital export capital-intensive goods there is no *a priori* way of telling whether trade has been caused by different factor endowments or by increasing returns to scale. This suggests that our preoccupation with the Heckscher-Ohlin result as *the* determinant of trade deserves a careful re-examination. The observation that the world is characterized by differences in factor endowments is not, contrary to popular belief, proof of the appropriateness of the Heckscher-Ohlin approach.

VI / Some other trade propositions

Some of the other international trade propositions which have been derived from the factor-endowment approach are basically unchanged when trade is caused by increasing returns to scale, while for others the questions asked no longer have much relevance. In the former category we have the transfer problem, which, because of the complete specialization in production, can be handled in the same way as the fixed production model.[20] In the second category we have the Rybczynski theorem which gives an answer to the question of how the outputs of the two commodities will change in one of the countries when the supply of one of the factors increases, the terms of trade being given. In the model being discussed here, both countries specialize, and so the question is not relevant. If we do not insist on the terms of trade remaining the same, and if factors are mobile, then it is possible that for small increases in the supply of one of the factors the price of this factor will fall so much

[19]Our assumption need not be so severe. We could consider a world in which there are three factors of production, land, labour, and capital, but in which only the services of land and capital are internationally mobile.
[20]The case where both countries have a single efficient production point has been thoroughly analysed by P. A. Samuelson, "The Transfer Problem and Transport Costs: The Terms of Trade when Impediments are Absent," *Economic Journal*, 62 (June 1952), 278–304.

that the output of the good intensive in the other factor may fall. Thus, if the world supply of labour goes up, it is possible (but by no means certain) that world production of the capital-intensive good may fall. The related problem of how a tariff will affect the real return of the factors, the Stolper-Samuelson result, is also not of much interest in our increasing-returns-to-scale model, for unless the tariff is prohibitive, production conditions will not change and thus relative factor returns will not change. Thus a tariff that increases the price of our import good relative to the price of our export good will make both factors better off in terms of exports, but worse off in terms of imports.

There is, however, one branch of tariff theory which deserves further comment. In the Heckscher-Ohlin model it is known that as long as the elasticity of the foreign offer curve is not infinite, there exists an optimum tariff. From an examination of the offer curve for the increasing-returns-to-scale case it can be shown that the optimum tariff will almost certainly involve specialization by the foreign country and thus the traditional formula, which relies on a tangency solution, will no longer be relevant. Furthermore, the terms of trade will be such that foreigners will be forced to consume inside their production possibility curve, making retaliation almost certain.

VII / Conclusions

Throughout our entire discussion we have maintained the assumption that in the initial situation the two countries are identical in all respects. Some might object to this on the grounds that allowing differences in factor endowments, tastes, or even size of the countries, might be expected to change some of our conclusions. But while this is doubtlessly true, the point of this analysis has been to isolate the effects of increasing returns to scale, and to do so we must neutralize all the other factors that could, themselves, cause trade. We have, in other words, taken exactly the same approach as is taken in the discussion of the Heckscher-Ohlin theorem.

The results of this paper should not be regarded as being in conflict with the results of the factor endowment approach, but rather as presenting information of a complementary nature which, hopefully, will enable us to consider certain questions which could not be dealt with within the framework of the Heckscher-Ohlin model. And of course the results presented here should not be regarded as providing, either separately or in conjunction with the traditional results, final answers to the questions which arise in international economics, for there are still assumptions to be relaxed. We really do not believe, for example, that perfect competition prevails everywhere, nor is it clear that production functions and demand conditions are the same throughout the world. And we have not yet even mentioned the implications of the assumption of two goods, two factors, and two countries. The theory of international trade will not be very useful for practical policy questions until the combined effects of all these influences can be determined. The simplest part of this job is determining how these various factors, taken separately, will influence trade, and even here there is work yet to be done.

[12]

Journal of International Economics 9 (1979) 1–24. © North-Holland Publishing Company

INTERNATIONALLY DECREASING COSTS AND
WORLD TRADE

Wilfred ETHIER*

University of Pennsylvania, Philadelphia, PA 19104, U.S.A.

Received September 1977, revised version received September 1978

This paper seeks to reformulate the existing theory of international trade and increasing returns by arguing that such returns depend upon the size of the world market rather than national output. The result is the disappearance of the tendency towards interindustry specialization and multiple equilibrium and the emergence of a theory of trade in intermediate goods. A new analytical tool – the allocation curve – is developed for this context.

1. Introduction

Increasing returns in production have long been recognized as determinants of international trade. Nonetheless they have never played a central theoretical role. In his survey John Chipman (1965, p. 737) noted, 'It is probably correct to say that economies of scale tend to be ignored in theoretical models not so much on empirical grounds as for the simple reason that the theoretical difficulties are considerable.... That this is a poor reason for excluding them is evident, especially if it is true that they constitute one of the principal sources of international trade.' Another reason is probably the conclusion to which decreasing costs have led. To quote Chipman (1965, p. 749) once again, 'the most important conclusion...was...that the presence of economies of large scale production leads to multiple equilibrium, and therefore introduces an intrinsic arbitrariness into the determination of the international pattern of specialization and trade.' Such arbitrariness[1] leaves the customary comparative-statics exercises unattractive. Furthermore the relevance of a theory yielding such conclusions

---

*I take pleasure in acknowledging the helpful comments of Bela Balassa, Herbert Grubel, Murray Kemp, Arvind Panagariya, Asaaf Razin, and the participants of seminars at the University of Pennsylvania and Johns Hopkins University.

[1]This characteristic, basically due to what Edgeworth (1894) termed 're-entrant' offer curves, is clear in the central modern treatments of the subject: Matthews (1949/50), Meade (1952), and Kemp (1969). For a slightly different point of view see Ethier (1978), and also see the interesting recent paper by Panagariya (1978).

to a world in which the lion's share of trade involves the exchange of manufactures and intermediate goods between similar economies is questionable at best, despite the fact that scale economies have repeatedly been shown to have empirical significance in such trade.

The purpose of this paper is to reformulate the traditional theory of international trade and increasing returns in a fundamental way. I shall argue that the result is the disappearance of the tendency towards specialization and 'arbitrariness,' and the emergence of a theory of trade in intermediate goods. My central theme is the interdependence of world industrial activity, and I shall fashion a new tool – the allocation curve – expressly for such a context.

2. Internationally decreasing costs

The central element in this reformulation is the idea of internationally decreasing costs – that average cost depends, with free trade, on the size of the international market rather than national output.

Consider the traditional example of the Swiss watch industry – frequently used to illustrate decreasing costs which are also external to the firm. An increase in watch output (presumably a large increase, with a long time allowed for adjustment) would allow the development of additional specialized crafts and so generate economics of scale. World production is thus most efficient when world output of watches is concentrated in one country.[2] This is the usual argument – basically Adam Smith's pin-factory parable writ large.

But note that international specialization is not really central to this argument, if free trade in intermediate goods is possible. Economies could be realized just as well by having Swiss craftsmen concentrate on one part of the watch and German craftsmen on another as by having two groups of Swiss concentrate on the two parts. That is, international specialization could be entirely confined to the detailed operations comprising watch production and need not extend at all to the industry level. This view of scale economies as largely, or at least substantially, a matter of the division of labor is central to Adam Smith and subsequent extensions, such as Young (1928), and is also prominent in contemporary investigations.[3] The key is the division of the production process into a large number of distinct operations and not the concentration of the overall industry to a single place. The distinct operations can just as profitably be dispersed over the globe.

---

[2]But note that the argument does not indicate why Switzerland should be that country. This is a facet of the 'arbitrariness' referred to above.
[3]See Balassa (1961, 1967), Daly, Key, and Spence (1968), and also the many references cited in these works.

The neoclassical writers would not have subscribed to this view. For they envisioned the realization of economies of scale as an organic process[4] involving learning-by-doing and extensive communication between industry participants. Thus geographical concentration was taken as a matter of course.

Though such a presumption may have been quite natural in the nineteenth century, it is surely not so today. Advances in communications and transport have nearly fused the major industrial countries into a singular integrated economy within which former boundaries retain only residual significance as determinants of channels of technological communication. The dominant form of industrial organization is now the multinational corporation, arranging the stages of production on a global scale and internalizing relevant information flows. These firms rely on international pools of bankers and managers (not infrequently members of international trade organizations) and operate in a milieu significantly influenced by international bureaucracies and international academic communities. To a large (and increasing) degree trade consists of exchanges of intermediate industrial goods, significantly classifiable as intraindustry trade even on a fairly disaggregated basis. I doubt that an observer unfamiliar with the existing literature on increasing returns and international trade would ever spontaneously advance that literature's central and universal premise: that decreasing costs depend upon national output and not international output.

Let me not push the case too strongly. As long as communication is not perfect mere propinquity must go for something. Add to this historical cultural barriers. Nevertheless, the assumption in what follows that (with free trade) decreasing costs are a function solely of world output need not rest entirely on the efficiency of a direct focus on the central concern of this paper.

Some economies do require by their very nature that industry production be concentrated at a single place. Balassa (1967, ch. 5) refers to these as "economies of scale in the traditional sense" in contrast to 'horizontal specialization' and 'vertical specialization,' which he regards as more important and which correspond to the economies I have discussed above as due to the division of labor. I shall not treat such 'traditional' economies in what follows. These economies are specific to particular, narrowly-defined products whereas my analysis will be in terms of the usual two-sector, general-equilibrium approach. The very existence of these narrowly-defined products can itself be thought of as a consequence of economies of scale. Recall that, while discussing his pin factory, Smith noted that pin-making itself had been rendered a distinct trade by the division of labor. Furthermore, I do not think that explicit consideration of these economies would much influence

---

[4]See, for example, Taussig (1927, pp. 84–86).

what follows. The analysis can proceed on the assumption that all such economies are always fully exploited. This is because this paper will not depend upon a distinction between internal and external economies.

Since Marshall, writers have assumed that economies of scale are external to the firm. Occasional deviants were severely taken to task, and much of the literature involved whether such economies exist, either logically[5] or empirically. The reasons were the beliefs that the conclusions of the theory required perfect competition and that the latter was inconsistent with increasing returns internal to the firm.

International economies and free entry do indeed imply that in equilibrium industry output will be concentrated in one firm. But costless entry will constrain that firm to choose efficient techniques and to sell at average cost – precisely how the industry would behave if the economies were external.[6] There may be only one firm in existence, but potential competitors are what count, and costless entry means there are always plenty of these. However, in a two-sector economy with one sector a single firm, free entry appears far more stringent than in a world of many small competitors.[7] At any rate I assume that the industry possessing increasing returns is characterized by average-cost pricing, regardless of the number of firms.

3. Production

Consider a world of two goods, manufactures (M) and wheat (W). Manufactures are subject to increasing returns. The domestic scale m of manufacturing operations is related to domestic wheat output by a concave production-possibility frontier $m = T(W)$ of the usual neoclassical sort. An analogous curve $m^* = S(W^*)$ applies to the rest of the world (I employ asterisks to refer to the foreign country). The extent k of scale economies in manufacturing is defined by $k \equiv M/m$, where M denotes the output of manufactures.[8] Similarly $k^* \equiv M^*/m^*$.

The key point of departure of the present paper is the argument that k and k^* depend upon world manufacturing activity. I suppose accordingly that a percentage increase in $m + m^*$ increases $M + M^*$ by α percent, assuming for simplicity that α is constant (and greater than unity). Thus[9] with free trade

$$k = k^* = (m + m^*)^{\alpha - 1}. \tag{1}$$

[5]See Chipman (1970) for a recent contribution.
[6]To my knowledge this has been recognized only by Murray Kemp (1969, 1976), and he appears to go to the opposite extreme of treating free entry as no more restrictive than usual.
[7]Thus one must not assume that Graham would have silenced Knight with such an argument.
[8]Note the assumption, common in the literature, that the production function for M is separable into m and k.
[9]The existing theory assumes by contrast that k depends on m alone and k^* on m^* alone. Note that I have simplified by assuming that k and k^* are identical functions of $m + m^*$.

The two countries are distinguished by the shapes of their production-possibility frontiers. Assume that $T' < S'$ whenever 'average outputs' are equal, $m/W = m^*/W^*$. This would be the case if the production-possibility frontiers were generated by a Heckscher–Ohlin production structure (without a separating factor-intensity reversal), and the home country was relatively abundant in the factor relatively intensive in the production of manufactures.

This assumption would ensure, with constant returns to scale ($k = 1 = k^*$), that the home country has a comparative advantage in manufactures, assuming away a 'demand reversal.' As the latter is of no concern, I suppose that the two countries possess identical Mill–Graham demand functions: everyone in the world always spends a constant proportion (γ) of his income on manufactures.

4. Efficient world output

Which allocations of production are efficient, in the sense that world outputs are on the world production-possibility frontier? Suppose that world wheat output $W + W^*$ is constrained to equal some feasible level. Then the problem is to find allocations of resources in the two countries which maximize the world output $M + M^*$ of manufactures subject to this constraint. But $M + M^* = (m + m^*)^\alpha$, so that maximizing $M + M^*$ is equivalent to maximizing $m + m^*$, regardless of the magnitude of α. In particular this is so if $\alpha = 1$; thus the efficient allocations with internationally decreasing costs are identical to those with constant returns to scale.

Proposition 1. Internationally increasing returns to scale have no effect upon the efficient patterns of production.

The efficient allocations are determined solely by the shapes of $T(W)$ and $S(W^*)$, and not at all by α. Therefore the home country has a comparative advantage in manufactures and the foreign country in wheat, if the term 'comparative advantage' is used in a purely normative sense.

From a technical point of view proposition 1 is trivial, once it has been formulated. Nonetheless it is fundamental, for it completely undercuts the standard model's pervasive tendency towards specialization and 'arbitrariness.'

Proposition 1 is basic, but I must be clear about what it does *not* say. (i) It does not mean that equilibrium output patterns, trade flows, and prices are independent of internationally increasing returns; the latter contribute to general equilibrium. (ii) Proposition 1 does not say anything about what will happen, only about what should happen for production efficiency. (iii) The proposition addresses only the allocation between manufactures and wheat, and not allocations within the manufacturing sector. As will subsequently become clear, intraindustry trade will in fact play an important role. (iv) 'Efficiency' refers, here and elsewhere, only to production efficiency. With average-cost pricing in manufactures, equilibrium will not in general be Pareto Optimal. This problem is familiar and I shall not subsequently allude to it. (But note that there are some interesting questions of national economic policy here, particularly if the increasing returns are due to economies external to the firm but internal to the *international* market.)

Formal illustrations[10]

In view of the importance of proposition 1 I briefly digress to illustrate it formally. The home production-possibility curve between manufactures and wheat is given by

$$M = kT(W) = [T(W) + m^*]^{\alpha - 1} T(W). \tag{2}$$

If the rest of the world produces only wheat, or if the home economy is in autarky, in the sense that it derives no scale economies from foreign manufacturing, this becomes $M = T(W)^{\alpha}$. This is a curve with negative slope and a second derivative given by

$$\frac{d^2 M}{dW^2} = \alpha m^{\alpha - 1} \left[T'' + (\alpha - 1) \frac{(T')^2}{T} \right]. \tag{3}$$

With 'Ricardian' constant costs ($T'' = 0$) the curve is convex to the origin; with constant returns to scale ($\alpha = 1$) it is concave; in general it may be either convex or concave or some combination, depending upon the size of α and shape of T. Eq. (3) simply illustrates the well-known expression in Tinbergen (1945, eq. (6)).

But all this changes in an open economy if the rest of the world produces some manufactures. No longer is it meaningful to speak of *the* production-possibility frontier, because, as is clear from (2), its very shape depends upon the foreign pattern of production, and vice-versa. But proposition 1 in effect refers to the world production-possibility frontier, which is still meaningful.

Let W_0 and W_0^* denote the maximum possible outputs of wheat at home and abroad, so that $T(W_0) = 0 = S(W_0^*)$, and let W_1 be the level of domestic wheat production for which $T'(W_1) = S'(W_0^*)$, with W_1 set equal to zero if T is everywhere steeper than all points on S. The world production possibility frontier is illustrated by the curve $ABCD$ in fig. 1. Along AB the foreign country specializes to wheat and the home economy produces both goods, between B and C both countries produce both goods, and between C and D

[10]Subsections (with *italic* headings) can be skipped without loss of continuity.

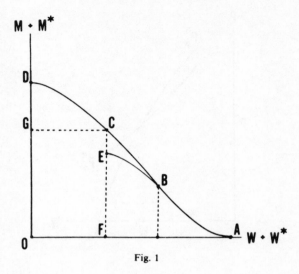

Fig. 1

the home country specializes to manufactures while the rest of the world diversifies. The domestic production bloc in autarky is $FABE$. This coincides with ABC on the world PPF when the foreign economy produces only wheat. The segment BC lies outside BE for two reasons: because the foreign economy is producing some manufactures (and less wheat), and also because foreign manufacturing shifts the domestic PPF upwards.

If T is everywhere steeper than all points of S (as in the Heckscher–Ohlin case if the two countries have sufficiently dissimilar relative factor endowments) points B and C coincide, so that one country always specializes, and FAB represents the domestic autarkic production block. However GCD does not represent the foreign block, because a movement from C towards D will increase the domestic output of manufactures. At $B(=C)$ the world PPF will now have a cusp, at which the ratio of the right-hand derivative to the left-hand derivative equals

$$\alpha T(0)^{\alpha-1}T'(0)/\alpha[T(0)+S(W_0^*)]^{\alpha-1}S'(W_0^*) = T'(0)/S'(W_0^*),$$

which is the size of the kink which the world PPF would have with constant returns to scale.

5. Autarkic equilibrium

In autarky international increasing returns must be indistinguishable from national increasing returns. Fig. 2 illustrates domestic autarkic equilibrium.

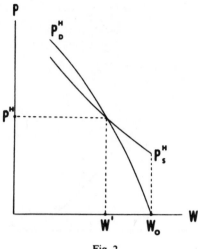

Fig. 2

P_D^H denotes the home relative demand price of wheat in terms of manufactures: the price that will equate demand to supply for any specific level of W and corresponding M. Thus $P_D^H = (1-\gamma)T(W)^\alpha/\gamma W$. Similarly P_S^H, the home relative supply price, denotes the price at which firms would willingly produce any specific level of W and corresponding M. Thus, with average-cost pricing in the manufacturing sector, $P_S^H = -kT'$ or $-T(W)^{\alpha-1}T'(W)$ in autarky. Intersection of the two curves determines equilibrium, so that the domestic relative autarkic price P^H is given by

$$P^H = -T(W')^{\bar{\alpha}-1}T'(W'),   \tag{4}$$

where W' is the solution to $-T'(W) = (1-\gamma)T(W)/\gamma W$.

The P_D^H curve has a negative slope and is cut from below by the P_S^H curve. Thus W' is unique and stable with respect to the 'Marshallian' adjustment process: output increases whenever demand price exceeds supply price.

Note from (4) that P^H depends positively upon the scale variable $T(W')$: thus a larger country is likely to have a higher relative autarkic price of wheat than a small country. This is familiar from the existing literature on national increasing returns.

It is now apparent that there are two contrasting influences at work. If comparative advantage is defined with respect to production efficiency, proposition 1 says it is determined in the same way as with constant returns to scale. But if comparative advantage is defined in terms of relative autarkic prices it is determined in the same way as with national increasing returns. To see how these two tendencies interact, and what determines comparative advantage in the sense of a predictor of trade patterns, requires an analysis of international equilibrium.

6. International equilibrium: Allocation curves

International equilibrium is commonly analyzed with offer curves, which are also used by Marshall, Matthews, Meade, and Kemp for their discussions of increasing returns. I could do the same now, but the resulting analysis would be exceedingly cumbersome: international increasing returns imply that a movement along one country's offer curve results in a shift of the other. Therefore I shall develop a new analytical technique, that of allocation curves, which allows a cleaner and more direct treatment.

Each point in the planes of fig. 3 corresponds to a particular allocation of resources in both countries: the coordinates indicate wheat outputs, and the manufacturing scales follow from $m = T(W)$ and $m^* = S(W^*)$. An allocation curve can be drawn for each country. The domestic allocation curve AB indicates for each level W of home wheat output that foreign allocation (or allocations) of resources W^* which will cause the domestic economy to be in equilibrium in world markets. That is, W and W^* are on the home allocation curve if the world demand price P_D, which clears world markets when wheat output is $W + W^*$ and manufacturing output is $[T(W) + S(W^*)]^\alpha$, is equal to the home supply price P_S^H, for which domestic firms willingly supply the quantity W of wheat and $kT(W)$ of manufactures. Such a curve is illustrated by AB in each panel of fig. 3.

On the allocation curve $P_D = P_S^H$. A rise of W^* above the curve must reduce the world demand price as it increases world wheat output and lowers manufacturing output, both directly through reducing m^* and indirectly through reducing k. The supply price also falls because of the reduction in k. But the reduction in P_S^H must be less than that in P_D because the former is not affected directly by the fact that fewer manufactures are

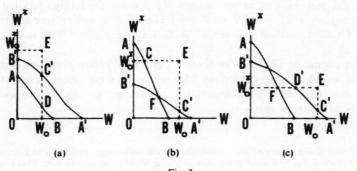

(a)   (b)   (c)

Fig. 3

being produced abroad. Thus $P_D < P_S^H$ above the allocation curve, and similarly $P_D > P_S^H$ below. Also the fall in demand price below supply price caused by a rise in W^* can be rectified for analogous reasons by a fall in W: the allocation curve must have a negative slope.

Point E in each panel of fig. 3 shows what wheat outputs in the two countries would be if both produce only wheat. Thus, with the given resources, only the rectangles $OW_0EW_0^*$ matter, and the portions of the curves lying outside these rectangles, such as the segment DB in fig. 3(a), are irrelevant. Also, if the domestic economy is specialized to wheat, domestic equilibrium is consistent with $P_D > P_S^H$, as there are no further resources to respond to the price differential by flowing from manufacturing to wheat. Similarly $P_D < P_S^H$ is consistent with domestic equilibrium if $W = 0$. Thus the complete domestic allocation curve, taking into account existing resources, is given by $W_0^*ADW_0$ in fig. 3(a), by CB in fig. 3(b), and by FB in fig. 3(c).

A foreign allocation curve relating W to W^* can be described in analogous fashion. International equilibrium requires an allocation W and W^* which enables each country to be in equilibrium in the world economy:

Proposition 2. International equilibrium is given by the intersection of the two allocation curves.

This is illustrated in fig. 3. The three panels depict the three qualitatively distinct cases, with equilibrium denoted by F in each panel. The home country is specialized in manufacturing in panel (a), the foreign economy to wheat in panel (c), and both countries diversify in panel (b). Each country's supply price is relatively more sensitive to its own level of wheat output than to foreign, and I have assumed internationally identical demand conditions. Thus the home allocation curve is steeper than the foreign, and equilibrium is unique.

The two curves need not have an interior intersection, as required for (b). If they do, then $P_S^H = P_S^F$ in equilibrium (P_S^F denotes the foreign relative supply price), so that $-kT' = -kS'$ or $T' = S'$. Thus if T is everywhere steeper than all points on S such an intersection does not take place.[11] This is depicted in panel (a).

International equilibrium involves a pattern of production consistent with efficient world output, regardless of relative autarkic prices. The latter are thus poor indicators of comparative advantage, to which Proposition 1 emerges as centrally relevant.

---

[11] If T and S are generated by a Heckscher–Ohlin technology without a separating factor-intensity reversal, fig. 3(b) illustrates a case implying factor-price equalization. This is precluded by sufficiently dissimilar relative factor endowments.

Proposition 3. With free trade international equilibrium necessarily involves an efficient pattern of world production.

If the foreign country is relatively large it might indeed have a higher autarkic relative price of wheat than the home country, but this will not influence the equilibrium pattern of international trade.

6.1. International equilibrium further considered

The argument of the previous section, culminating in propositions 2 and 3, requires formal justification.

If W and W^* are the respective wheat outputs, the world demand price, with free trade, is given by $P_D = (1-\gamma)[T(W) + S(W^*)]^a / \gamma[W + W^*]$. The home allocation curve is the collection of W and W^* for which $P_S^H = P_D$ and the foreign allocation curve the collection for which $P_S^F = P_D$. Substitution yields the following expressions for the interior parts of the home and foreign curves respectively:

$$(1-\gamma)[T(W) + S(W^*)] + \gamma T'(W)[W + W^*] = 0, \tag{5}$$

$$(1-\gamma)[T(W) + S(W^*)] + \gamma S'(W^*)[W + W^*] = 0. \tag{6}$$

Differentiation confirms that supply price exceeds demand price above a country's allocation curve and falls short below.

Let E denote the point in the W–W^* plane where the world specializes to wheat: $W = W_0$ and $W^* = W_0^*$. Consider the limiting value of P_D/P_S^H as point E is approached, with W converging to W_0 from below and W^* to W_0^* from below:

$$\lim \frac{P_D}{P_S^H} = \lim \frac{1-\gamma}{\gamma} \frac{T(W) + S(W^*)}{T'(W)[W + W^*]} = 0.$$

Similarly P_D/P_S^F converges to zero as E is approached from below. Thus, with $\gamma < 1$, the world demand price must exceed both supply prices near point E. This means that E lies above the interior parts of both allocation curves, so that the latter must pass through the rectangles $OW_0EW_0^*$ in fig. 3.

Implicit differentiation of (5) and (6) yields

$$\left.\frac{dW^*}{dW}\right|_{HA} = -\frac{T' + \gamma(W + W^*)T''}{\gamma T' + (1-\gamma)S'}, \tag{7}$$

$$\left.\frac{dW^*}{dW}\right|_{FA} = -\frac{\gamma S' + (1-\gamma)T'}{S' + \gamma(W + W^*)S''}, \tag{8}$$

which imply that both curves have negative slopes. Either the two curves intersect within $OW_0EW_0^*$ or not. Suppose they do. Then $P_S^H = P_S^F$ at the intersection, whence $T' = S'$. Then (7) and (8) imply that the home curve must be steeper at the intersection than the foreign. This means the intersection must be unique. It also means that the home allocation curve intersects the boundary OW_0^*E above and/or to the right of the foreign curve. This precludes an equilibrium on that boundary. Similarly the home allocation curve intersects the boundary OW_0E below and/or to the left of the foreign curve, ruling out an equilibrium on that boundary. The interior equilibrium is therefore unique; both countries diversify.

Suppose alternatively that the two allocation curves do not intersect in the interior of $OW_0EW_0^*$. Then one of the curves must lie outside the other everywhere inside the rectangle. Consider the point where the (interior) home allocation curve strikes the boundary OW_0E. There are two possibilities. (i) The intersection is on W_0E. Then at this point $W = W_0$ and W^* is the solution to $(1 - \gamma)S(W^*) = -\gamma T'(W_0)[W_0 + W^*]$. Thus

$$P_D - P_S^F = S(W^*)^{\alpha - 1}[(1 - \gamma)S(W^*) + \gamma S'(W^*)(W_0 + W^*)]$$

$$= (1 - \gamma)S(W^*)^\alpha \left[1 - \frac{S'(W^*)}{T'(W_0)} \right].$$

(ii) The intersection is on OW_0. Then $W^* = 0$ and W is the solution to $(1 - \gamma)[T(W) + S(0)] = -\gamma T'(W)W$. Thus

$$P_D - P_S^F = [T(W) + S(0)]^{\alpha - 1}[S'(0) - T'(W)].$$

In both cases the assumption I have made about the relative shapes of T and S implies that $P_D > P_S^F$. This means that the (interior) home allocation curve lies inside the foreign near OW_0E, and therefore throughout the rectangle as well. Accordingly there can be no equilibrium on OW_0E and there must be a unique equilibrium on OW_0^*E; in this equilibrium either the home country specializes to manufactures or the foreign country to wheat, or both.

6.2. The Ricardian case

The case where T' and S' are constant yields further insight and facilitates a more detailed analysis. Choose units so that $T' = -1$ and denote $-S'$ by s, which is less than unity. Then (7) and (8) reveal that the allocation curves are straight lines whose relative slopes reflect the pattern of 'comparative costs' s. The interior parts of the home and foreign curves are illustrated by the lines AB and $B'A'$ in fig. 4. The allocation curve technique allows all

W. Ethier, Decreasing costs and world trade   13

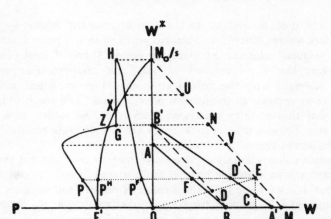

Fig. 4

relative country sizes W_0^*/W_0 to be considered without shifting the (interior) allocation curves. This is because, as (5) and (6) confirm, those curves are invariant as long as W_0 and W_0^* are constrained by a constant world capacity of manufacturing scale $M_0 = W_0 + sW_0^*$. This is depicted by the dashed line $(M_0/s)M_0$ in fig. 4. Specifying any endowment, such as E, determines the relevant rectangle $(OW_0^*EW_0)$ and completes the allocation curves (FB for the home country and $W_0^*D'C'$ for the foreign). Free-trade equilibrium is thus at F. Accordingly VM indicates the range of relative endowments for which the foreign country specializes to wheat and the home country diversifies, NV the range for which foreigners specialize to wheat and the home economy to manufactures, and $(M_0/s)N$ the range for which the foreign economy diversifies while domestic production is concentrated in manufacturing.

The dashed line $B'B$ – parallel to $(M_0/s)M_0$ but only the fraction $(1-\gamma)$ as far from the origin – indicates autarkic equilibria. Thus with endowment E the allocations in autarky are indicated by point D.

The three curves in the left-hand quadrant of fig. 4 depict the free trade and respective autarkic relative prices of wheat corresponding to each possible endowment E on $(M_0/s)M_0$. The curve $F'PGH$ indicates the free trade price, $F'P^H(M_0/s)$ the home autarkic price, and OP^FH the foreign autarkic price. Thus with endowment E, points P, P^H, and P^F denote the respective relative prices. The segment $U(M_0/s)$ depicts the range of endowments where comparative autarkic prices incorrectly predict comparative advantage.

Sliding E along $(M_0/s)M_0$ thus allows all possible free-trade and autarkic equilibria for both countries to be completely illustrated. A few of the resulting observations warrant explicit mention.

Note first that, in contrast to the case of constant returns to scale, free trade prices always differ from autarkic prices, with the possible exception of the two singular cases corresponding to points X and Z (and of course the cases where the world consists of only one country). Furthermore the country (foreign) with the comparative advantage in wheat must always experience an increase in the relative price of wheat as a result of trade. This implies that that country must gain from trade, no matter how large her relative size. Thus an international character to increasing returns invalidates an old argument against free trade.

The home country autarkic price curve may or may not cut the terms of trade curve and pass outside point G as illustrated (it will do so if and only if $s > \gamma^{\alpha - 1}$). If it does, there will exist a range of relative endowments, contained in the interval UV, yielding the conventional result that the terms of trade falls between the relative autarkic prices. Otherwise the relative price of wheat must rise in both countries as a result of trade (and this always happens in the intervals $(M_0/s)U$ and VM_0). This reflects the fact that merely opening the countries up to trade increases manufacturing productivity, even without reallocations of resources between the two sectors in either country.

7. Stability

The allocation curve simplifies the treatment of the Marshallian dynamic adjustment process, according to which an industry is expanding if demand price exceeds supply price. This is because the curves subdivide the plane on the basis of the relation between world demand price and supply price in each country. Thus it is easy to see that the equilibria in fig. 3 are in fact stable, with a noncyclical approach to equilibrium in each case.

A more complex and interesting situation is depicted in fig. 5 (where I have temporarily abandoned the assumption of identical Mill–Graham demand functions). The home allocation curve is $W_0^* A D W_0$ and the foreign $W_0 A' B'$. Equilibria are depicted at B', F', F, F'', and W_0; arrows depict the directions of movement. Clearly the equilibria are alternatively stable and unstable, with stable equilibria at B', F, and W_0, and unstable at F' and F''.

Fig. 5 suggests an interesting result. Imagine the allocation curves to be offer curves, with home and foreign wheat production playing the role of 'imports' and 'exports' respectively. Define ε as the domestic offer-curve elasticity in the usual way (percentage fall in W/percentage rise in (W^*/W)), with ε equal to minus infinity along $W_0^* A$ where an improvement in the 'terms of trade' is accompanied by a finite fall in 'exports.' Similarly ε^* denotes the elasticity of the foreign 'offer curve.' Then fig. 5 illustrates the following result, easily confirmed by experimenting with other hypothetical cases.

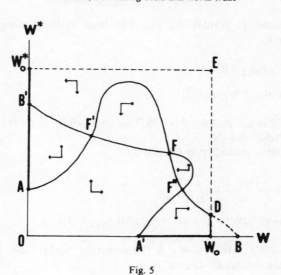

Fig. 5

Proposition 4. *If an equilibrium has a negative elasticity for a country producing both goods it is unstable. Otherwise stability is equivalent to the violation of the familiar Marshall–Lerner condition.*

Point F', where $\varepsilon < 0$ and $\varepsilon^* < 1$, illustrates the first sentence of proposition 4. The Marshall–Lerner condition is met at F'' and violated at B', F, and W_0.

Proof of proposition 4

Write $P_D = \phi(W, W^*)$, $P_S^H = \psi(W, W^*)$ and $P_S^F = \psi^*(W, W^*)$. I assume[12] that an increase in either country's wheat output reduces the demand price both absolutely and relatively to that country's supply price, and lowers the other country's supply price:

$$\phi_W, \phi_{W^*}, \phi_W - \psi_{W^*}^*, \phi_{W^*} - \psi_{W^*}^*, \psi_{W^*}, \psi_{W^*}^* < 0 \qquad (9)$$

The (interior) home and foreign allocation curves $W^* = A(W)$ and $W = A^*(W^*)$ are the respective solutions to $\phi = \psi$ and $\phi = \psi^*$. The dynamic adjustment process can be represented by:

$$\hat{W} = [\phi(W, W^*)/\psi(W, W^*)] - 1,$$
$$\hat{W} = [\phi(W, W^*)/\psi^*(W, W^*)] - 1,$$

[12]These assumptions are implied by, but much weaker than, the model of section 3.

where $\hat{W}$ denotes $(1/W)(dW/dt)$, etc. The local stability conditions of this system reduce to

$$a_{11} + a_{22} < 0, \tag{10}$$

$$a_{12}a_{21} - a_{11}a_{22} < 0, \tag{11}$$

where $a_{11} = W(\phi_w - \psi_w)/\phi$, $a_{22} = W^*(\phi_{w^*} - \psi^*_{w^*})/\phi$, $a_{12} = W(\phi_{w^*} - \psi_{w^*})/\phi$, and $a_{21} = W^*(\phi_w - \psi^*_w)/\phi$.

The 'offer-curve elasticity' is defined by

$$\varepsilon \equiv \frac{-(W^*/W)}{W} \frac{dW}{d(W^*/W)}$$

$$= W^*/(W^* - WA') = W^*a_{12}/(W^*a_{12} + Wa_{11}).$$

Similarly $\varepsilon^* = Wa_{21}/(Wa_{21} + Wa_{22})$. Substitution yields the following expression for the 'Marshall–Lerner' term:

$$\varepsilon + \varepsilon^* - 1 = \frac{\varepsilon\varepsilon^*}{a_{21}a_{22}}(a_{12}a_{21} - a_{11}a_{22}). \tag{12}$$

Assumption (9) implies that $a_{12} < 0$ and $a_{21} < 0$. The following possibilities exist. (i) $\varepsilon, \varepsilon^* < 0$. Then a_{11} and a_{22} are necessarily positive and the system is unstable. (ii) $\varepsilon > 0$, $\varepsilon^* < 0$. If $\varepsilon + \varepsilon^* < 1$, then (12) implies that (11) is violated. If $\varepsilon + \varepsilon^* > 1$, then necessarily $\varepsilon > 1$ and $\varepsilon^* < 0$, implying $a_{11} > 0$ and $a_{22} > 0$ so that (10) is violated. (iii) $\varepsilon < 1$, $\varepsilon^* > 0$. This is completely analogous to (ii). (iv) $\varepsilon, \varepsilon^* > 0$. Then (12) implies that $\varepsilon + \varepsilon^* > 1$ is equivalent to the violation of (11). If $\varepsilon + \varepsilon^* < 1$, (11) is met and furthermore $\varepsilon < 1$, $\varepsilon^* < 1$ which implies that $a_{11} < 0$, $a_{22} < 0$ so that (10) is met as well. This completes the proof of proposition 4 for an internal equilibrium. The boundary cases, which are tedious but straightforward, are left to the reader.[13]

The above dynamic process (not to be confused with that used by Marshall in his foreign-trade discussions (1930, 1960)) is straightforward enough. But note that it abstracts from both an irreversibility of increasing returns and any dynamic aspect to the realization of scale economies-notions prominent in the neoclassical literature.

8. Trade in intermediate goods

Thus far I have been concerned solely with the exchange of wheat for

---

[13]See Ethier (1978) for a complete proof (including boundary cases) of the special case of proposition 4 for which $\psi_{w^*} = 0 = \psi^*_w$ (which excludes internationally decreasing costs).

manufactures. But, since the source of internationally decreasing costs is world-wide specialization *within* the manufacturing sector, trade in intermediate manufactures must also be prominent. Indeed the principal argument of this paper is that in the modern world economy decreasing costs imply (intraindustry) trade in intermediate manufactures rather than 'arbitrary' patterns of industry specialization.

A complete description of such intermediate-goods trade requires details of the manufacturing sector beyond the scope of this paper. But some general conclusions can be drawn even with the present description of manufactures as a single, aggregate good produced by an integrated world-wide industry. If the foreign country specializes to wheat there is no trade in intermediates. Otherwise the volume of such trade must be at least as large as I_m, the smaller of the two national outputs of manufactures.

Proposition 5. The minimum possible volume of trade in intermediate goods is equal to the smaller of km and km*.

The line $E'E$ in fig. 6 below depicts the combinations of wheat outputs for which $T(W) = S(W^*)$. Thus domestic output of manufactures exceeds foreign output above $E'E$ and vice-versa below. The line HKN in panel (a) depicts

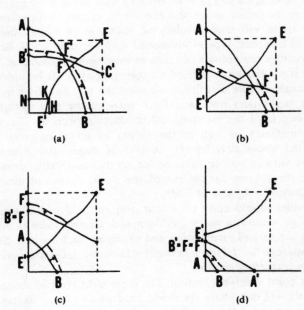

(a)

(b)

(c)

(d)

Fig. 6

an I_m contour: allocations of W and W^* yielding identical values of I_m. Movements away from the origin pass through contours corresponding to successively lower values of I_m, with K moving along $E'E$.

Two examples usefully illustrate the argument. Suppose first that the world manufacturing sector consists of the independent production of separate components which can be costlessly assembled into the single final manufactured good. The scale economies are associated with the number of components, with the two countries specializing, in free trade, in the production of distinct components. Then the volume of trade in intermediate goods must equal $M[M_c^*/(M + M^*)] + M^*[M_c/(M + M^*)]$, where M_c and M_c^* denote domestic and foreign consumption of (finished) manufactures. Since $M_c + M_c^* = M + M^*$, this volume equals I_m if $M = M^*$ and exceeds it otherwise. There need be no trade involving final manufactures, so that intermediates are exchanged for wheat as well as each other. Unless enough additional structure is put into the model to mandate the assignment of specific components to the two countries, the volume of intraindustry trade corresponding to any specific disaggregation of manufactures must be indeterminate.

For the second example suppose the world manufacturing sector has a vertical structure in which output passes through successive 'stages' to emerge as finished manufactures. The volume of trade in intermediates will be minimized (and equal to I_m) if the country with the smaller manufacturing sector performs the earlier stages and exports its output to the other country. International trade will then involve the exchange of wheat, finished manufactures, and a specific type of unfinished manufactured good. But without additional structure the volume of trade in intermediate goods, as well as of intraindustry trade (for any specified disaggregation), must be indeterminate, because the stages can be distributed between the two countries in any way: manufactures might pass back and forth between the two countries many times in the course of the international production process. The volume of trade in intermediates, as well as the variety of goods entering into such trade, is limited above only by the number of stages. But if this trade is measured only with respect to value-added, so that essentially entrepôt trade is netted out, the volume cannot exceed the world output of manufactures. Thus it is bounded by I_m and $M + M^*$.

These examples should make clear that proposition 5 is about as far as it is possible to go without a more specific model. Clearly there is much work to be done in the way of formulating and exploring such models. Such work would also address the relation between nationally increasing returns and internationally increasing returns.

One further point deserves mention. The more alike the two economies are, the more evenly will they share the world production of manufactures. While this limits the scope for the interindustry exchange of wheat and manufactures emphasized by the conventional theory, it enlarges that for intraindustry exchanges of intermediate manufactured goods.

Proposition 6. Internationally decreasing costs imply a presumption that a greater similarity of $T(W)$ and $S(W^*)$ results in a larger volume of trade in intermediate manufactured goods, both absolutely and relatively to the volume of interindustry trade.

If T and S are sufficiently different so that the foreign country specializes to wheat, international trade will consist entirely of the exchange of wheat for finished manufactures. At the other extreme, there is no basis at all for interindustry trade if T and S are identical, and international trade would consist of the exchange of intermediate (and perhaps finished) manufactures.

This can be looked at from a different point of view. Suppose T and S are generated by a Heckscher–Ohlin model, and that some capital is moved from the capital-abundant country to the other. This will substitute for international trade in wheat and manufactures, so that the volume of such trade will probably fall, as is well known. But, since this will probably also tend to equalize the sizes of the manufacturing sectors in the two countries, it will stimulate intraindustry trade in intermediates; if k is large such trade could be greatly stimulated.[14]

9. Tariffs on trade in intermediate goods

Assume that the world manufacturing sector is similar to that discussed in the second example of section 8. That is, manufactures are produced by a (timeless) integrated global process in which output passes through (a continuum of) successive stages before emerging as finished goods. An expansion of world activity raises k by allowing the employment of additional stages.

How is international equilibrium influenced by commercial policy? Many types of policy could be considered, but I shall focus on just one: a uniform tariff levied by both countries on all intermediate manufactures, with trade in wheat and finished manufactures remaining free, and with tariff revenues spent like other income. I consider this policy both because it applies to the distinct assumptions of this paper, and also because it is natural to wonder whether the results summarized in propositions 1–6 are in fact crucially dependent upon free trade in intermediates.

Suppose then that the two countries impose such a tariff on all imports of

[14]I leave to the reader the task of formalizing this by proving the present model's version of the Rybczynski Theorem. Clearly the magnitude of k and the sizes of the two manufacturing sectors will figure prominently in such a theorem.

intermediate goods.[15] World production of manufactures will then arrange itself[16] so that the country with the smaller manufacturing sector produces the earlier stages. Trade in intermediates will therefore equal I_m, and tariffs will actually be collected only by the country with the larger manufacturing sector. The tariff of the other country will appear redundant, but it will not in fact be so.

The world demand price P_D will still equal $(1-\gamma)(M+M^*)/\gamma(W+W^*)$, since the tariff does not apply to finished manufactures. Suppose first that the home country has the larger manufacturing sector: $T(W) > S(W^*)$. Then, with a tariff, output will consist of finished manufactures and perhaps wheat, both free of tax. Thus home supply price is still $P_S^H = -kT'$, so that the home allocation curve is not affected by the tariff. If, on the other hand, $T(W) < S(W^*)$, the home manufacturing sector produces intermediates which are subject to the foreign tariff. The home supply price is accordingly equal to $P_S^H = -kT'/(1+t)$, which implies that the allocation curve shifts out. Similar considerations apply to the foreign country.

Proposition 7. The imposition by both countries of a common tariff on intermediate manufactured goods shifts the home allocation curve out where $T < S$ and leaves it unchanged where $T > S$. The foreign allocation curve shifts out where $T > S$ and is unchanged where $S > T$. Also home manufacturing concentrates on earlier stages and foreign manufacturing on later stages when $T < S$, and vice versa where $T > S$.

The results are illustrated in fig. 6. The separate panels depict the four possible initial states of interest; if the foreign country initially specializes to wheat, intermediate goods do not enter trade and so the tariff has no effects.

If the home country specializes to manufactures but is small enough so that its manufacturing sector is nonetheless smaller than the foreign, as in panel (d), a small tariff has no effects beyond the international rearrangement of the stages of production. Supply price initially exceeds the world price, so the reduction in the former produced by the tariff does not matter. In all other cases a (small) tariff involves a shift of one allocation curve and movement along the other. Algebraic manipulation confirms that world wheat output increases while manufacturing production falls. If the home economy produces no wheat, as in panel (a), this is brought about entirely via a reallocation of resources in the foreign country, although domestic output also falls because of the reduction in k.

---

[15]It is easy to see that, if only one country levies the tariff, this country will produce the earlier stages and the other country the later stages, no tariffs will actually be collected, and the preceding analysis will be unchanged.

[16]It might be conjectured that the scale economies are due to some type of externalities that removes all incentives for the manufacturing sector to minimize its exposure to the tariff. I will not further consider this possibility.

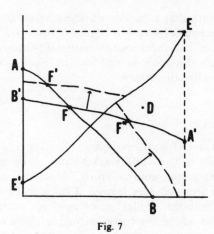

Fig. 7

If neither country specializes, the common tariff will also induce an international reallocation of manufacturing activity from the country with the smaller manufacturing sector to that with the larger. This produces the striking result that manufacturing production becomes more concentrated, not less, as a result of protection. This is clear in panels (a) and (b) of fig. 6. Note that the reallocation may run counter to the pattern of comparative advantage or not.

A large tariff can generate multiple equilibria, as illustrated in fig. 7. The two tariff-ridden equilibria differ with respect to which country has the larger manufacturing sector. Thus they imply opposite arrangements of the stages of production, and opposite directions for the reallocation of manufacturing activity.

If proposition 4 is applied to fig. 7, both F' and F'' are stable. But if F is the initial position, the economy will in fact converge to F' so that F'' is irrelevant and the above small-tariff discussion applies, with fig. 7 equivalent to fig. 6(a).

But there are two reasons to be sceptical about such a dynamic argument. First, if the economy is initially in autarkic equilibrium at D a movement from autarky to limited trade would establish equilibrium at F''.

Second, the dynamic adjustment process discussed in section 7 does not specifically involve the rearrangement of the stages of production implied by a tariff. In free trade the arrangement is indeterminate; suppose that in fact the home country produces the earlier stages and the foreign country the latter. As this is the same arrangement as at F'', and opposite that at F', one can easily imagine that a dynamic process incorporating this consideration would move the economy from F to F''. Apparently there is scope for considerable work involving adjustment in a tariff-ridden context.

One might conjecture that a barrier to intermediate-goods trade could in fact cause an overlapping of stages in the two countries, or the (partial or complete) development of independent nationally-integrated industries in addition to the effects discussed in this section. Such a conjecture is false. Space precludes a detailed discussion.

10. Concluding remarks

This paper has advanced and investigated the idea that increasing returns depend upon the scale of the world market rather than that of the national market. This consideration removes from the theory its emphasis upon multiple equilibrium and provides instead a basis for a theory of trade in intermediate goods between similar economies. A secondary purpose has been to illustrate the allocation-curve technique. Specific conclusions are summarized in the seven propositions and need not be repeated now; in general they clearly bring the theory into much closer resemblance to the facts of modern trade.[17]

In some ways this paper must be regarded as a preliminary treatment of the subject it raises. I have indicated several places above where further formal development appears warranted, and other instances should be apparent. Also those ideas should be further investigated in conjunction with those topics to which they have a natural affinity, such as international capital movements, the multinational firm, and the theory of time-phased systems.

The virtually complete concentration for so many years of the increasing-returns-and-trade literature upon the case of nationally increasing returns is a puzzle, in view of the great difference that assumption makes. One reason, as mentioned earlier, is that the ease of communication, the predominance of the international firm, and the integrated world economy have to a significant degree only recently appeared. But this can hardly be a complete explanation. The preoccupation of much of the earlier literature on the use of increasing returns as a justification for protection may also be part of the reason. But more important, I think, is the nature of the internal development of the theory of international trade.

The idea of internationally decreasing costs is at bottom an application to the world arena of Adam Smith's notion of the gains from the division of labor, independently of its geographical location. International trade theory has by contrast followed Ricardo in examining the international allocation of specified production processes. Cairnes (1874, pp. 297–302) clearly distinguished the two possible sources of gains from trade. But he argued that the former had little to do with international trade and indeed went so far as

---

[17] I have struggled manfully against the temptation to continually call attention to this fact.

to say that this was one of the principle factors distinguishing domestic trade from foreign trade. In this he was clearly influenced by his view of the world of his day. More recently, Grubel and Lloyd (1975) and Balassa (1975) have noted the tendency for trade liberalization to stimulate intraindustry trade rather than interindustry specialization, and have speculated that significant economies result. But the implication for the pure theory of international trade was not pursued. Harberler (1936, pp. 130–131) repeated Cairnes' argument and also linked it to the familiar examples of increasing returns and trade, but only on a national level.

The sole explicit reference to internationally decreasing costs which I have found in the literature is a single paragraph in Viner (1965, p. 480). As it is quite short I shall quote it in full (so that the present paper will contain the total existing literature on its subject):

> In the first place, if the external economies are a function of the size of the world industry, and not of the national portion of it, as may well be the case, they will still be retained by a national industry which shrinks in size if this shrinkage is offset by a corresponding expansion of the foreign industry. Suppose that as the watch industry as a whole expands and increases its purchases of watchmaking machinery, such machinery can consequently be obtained at lower unit prices. If there is free trade in machinery, this economy in machinery costs will not be lost to the watch industry in a particular country merely because it is shrinking in size, if there is no shrinkage in the size of the watch industry as a whole.

Viner is here advancing internationally decreasing costs as a reason to reject Frank Graham's argument for protection. Section 6.1 demonstrated that they can fulfill this role.

References

Balassa, B., ed., 1975, European economic integration (North-Holland, Amsterdam).
Balassa, B., 1961, The theory of economic integration (Irwin, Homewood).
Balassa, B., 1967, Trade liberalization among industrial countries (McGraw-Hill, New York).
Cairnes, J.E., 1874, Some leading principles of political economy newly expounded (Macmillan, London).
Chipman, J., 1970, External economies of scale and competitive equilibrium, Quarterly Journal of Economics 84, 347–385.
Chipman, J., 1965, A survey of the theory of international trade: Part 2, The neoclassical theory, Econometrica 33, 685–760.
Daly, D.J., B.A. Keys and E.J. Spence, 1968, Scale and specialization in Canadian manufacturing, Staff study no. 21, Economic Council of Canada.
Edgeworth, F.Y., 1874, The theory of international values, II, Economic Journal 4, 424–443.
Ethier, W., 1978, Increasing returns to scale and international trade, mimeo.
Grubel, H.G. and P.J. Lloyd, 1975, Intra-industry trade: The theory and measurement of international trade in differentiated products (Macmillan, London).
Haberler, G., 1936, The theory of international trade, with its applications to commercial policy (W. Hodge, London).

Kemp, M., 1976, Three topics in the theory of international trade: Distribution, welfare and uncertainty (North-Holland, Amsterdam).

Kemp, M., 1969, The pure theory of international trade and investment (Prentice-Hall, Englewood Cliffs).

Marshall, A., 1960, Money, credit, and commerce (Augustus Kelley, New York).

Marshall, A., 1930, The pure theory of foreign trade and the pure theory of domestic values (London School of Economics and Political Science, London).

Matthews, R.C.O., 1949/50, Reciprocal demand and increasing returns, Review of Economic Studies 17, 149–158.

Meade, J.E., 1952, A geometry of international trade (George Allen and Unwin, London).

Panagariya, A., 1978, Variable returns to scale in production and patterns of specialization, mimeo.

Taussig, F.W., 1927, International trade (Macmillan, New York).

Tinbergen, J., 1945, International economic cooperation (Elsevier, Amsterdam).

Viner, J., 1965, Studies in the theory of international trade (Augustus Kelley, New York).

Young, A., 1928, Increasing returns and economic progress, Economic Journal 38, 527–542.

[13]

Scale Economies, Product Differentiation, and the Pattern of Trade

By PAUL KRUGMAN*

For some time now there has been considerable skepticism about the ability of comparative cost theory to explain the actual pattern of international trade. Neither the extensive trade among the industrial countries, nor the prevalence in this trade of two-way exchanges of differentiated products, make much sense in terms of standard theory. As a result, many people have concluded that a new framework for analyzing trade is needed.[1] The main elements of such a framework—economies of scale, the possibility of product differentiation, and imperfect competition—have been discussed by such authors as Bela Balassa, Herbert Grubel (1967, 1970), and Irving Kravis, and have been "in the air" for many years. In this paper I present a simple formal analysis which incorporates these elements, and show how it can be used to shed some light on some issues which cannot be handled in more conventional models. These include, in particular, the causes of trade between economies with similar factor endowments, and the role of a large domestic market in encouraging exports.

The basic model of this paper is one in which there are economies of scale in production and firms can costlessly differentiate their products. In this model, which is derived from recent work by Avinash Dixit and Joseph Stiglitz, equilibrium takes the form of Chamberlinian monopolistic competition: each firm has some monopoly power, but entry drives monopoly profits to zero. When two imperfectly competitive economies of this kind are allowed to trade, increasing returns produce trade and gains

from trade even if the economies have identical tastes, technology, and factor endowments. This basic model of trade is presented in Section I. It is closely related to a model I have developed elsewhere; in this paper a somewhat more restrictive formulation of demand is used to make the analysis in later sections easier.

The rest of the paper is concerned with two extensions of the basic model. In Section II, I examine the effect of transportation costs, and show that countries with larger domestic markets will, other things equal, have higher wage rates. Section III then deals with "home market" effects on trade patterns. It provides a formal justification for the commonly made argument that countries will tend to export those goods for which they have relatively large domestic markets.

This paper makes no pretense of generality. The models presented rely on extremely restrictive assumptions about cost and utility. Nonetheless, it is to be hoped that the paper provides some useful insights into those aspects of international trade which simply cannot be treated in our usual models.

I. The Basic Model

A. *Assumptions of the Model*

There are assumed to be a large number of potential goods, all of which enter symmetrically into demand. Specifically, we assume that all individuals in the economy have the same utility function,

$$(1) \qquad U = \sum_i c_i^\theta \qquad\qquad 0 < \theta < 1$$

where c_i is consumption of the ith good. The number of goods actually produced, n,

*Yale University and Massachusetts Institute of Technology.

[1]A paper which points out the difficulties in explaining the actual pattern of world trade in a comparative cost framework is the study of Gary Hufbauer and John Chilas.

will be assumed to be large, although smaller than the potential range of products.[2]

There will be assumed to be only one factor of production, labor. All goods will be produced with the same cost function:

$$(2) \qquad l_i = \alpha + \beta x_i \qquad \alpha, \beta > 0$$

$$i = 1, \ldots, n$$

where l_i is labor used in producing the ith good and x_i is output of that good. In other words, I assume a fixed cost and constant marginal cost. Average cost declines at all levels of output, although at a diminishing rate.

Output of each good must equal the sum of individual consumptions. If we can identify individuals with workers, output must equal consumption of a representative individual times the labor force:

$$(3) \qquad x_i = Lc_i \qquad i = 1, \ldots, n$$

We also assume full employment, so that the total labor force must just be exhausted by labor used in production:

$$(4) \qquad L = \sum_{i=1}^{n} (\alpha + \beta x_i)$$

Finally, we assume that firms maximize profits, but that there is free entry and exit of firms, so that in equilibrium profits will always be zero.

B. Equilibrium in a Closed Economy

We can now proceed to analyze equilibrium in a closed economy described by the assumptions just laid out. The analysis proceeds in three stages. First I analyze consumer behavior to derive demand functions. Then profit-maximizing behavior by firms is derived, treating the number of firms as given. Finally, the assumption of free entry is used to determine the equilibrium number of firms.

[2] To be fully rigorous, we would have to use the concept of a continuum of potential products.

The reason that a Chamberlinian approach is useful here is that, in spite of imperfect competition, the equilibrium of the model is determinate in all essential respects because the special nature of demand rules out strategic interdependence among firms. Because firms can costlessly differentiate their products, and all products enter symmetrically into demand, two firms will never want to produce the same product; each good will be produced by only one firm. At the same time, if the number of goods produced is large, the effect of the price of any one good on the demand for any other will be negligible. The result is that each firm can ignore the effect of its actions on other firms' behavior, eliminating the indeterminacies of oligopoly.

Consider, then, an individual maximizing (1) subject to a budget constraint. The first-order conditions from that maximum problem have the form

$$(5) \qquad \theta c_i^{\theta-1} = \lambda p_i \qquad i = 1, \ldots, n$$

where p_i is the price of the ith good and λ is the shadow price on the budget constraint, that is, the marginal utility of income. Since all individuals are alike, (5) can be rearranged to show the demand curve for the ith good, which we have already argued is the demand curve facing the single firm producing that good:

$$(6) \qquad p_i = \theta \lambda^{-1} (x_i/L)^{\theta-1} \qquad i = 1, \ldots, n$$

Provided that there are a large number of goods being produced, the pricing decision of any one firm will have a negligible effect on the marginal utility of income. In that case, (6) implies that each firm faces a demand curve with an elasticity of $1/(1-\theta)$, and the profit-maximizing price is therefore

$$(7) \qquad p_i = \theta^{-1} \beta w \qquad i = 1, \ldots, n$$

where w is the wage rate, and prices and wages can be defined in terms of any (common!) unit. Note that since θ, β, and w are the same for all firms, prices are the same for all goods and we can adopt the shorthand $p = p_i$ for all i.

The price p is independent of output given the special assumptions about cost and utility (which is the reason for making these particular assumptions). To determine profitability, however, we need to look at output. Profits of the firm producing good i are

$$(8) \qquad \pi_i = p x_i - \{\alpha + \beta x_i\} w \qquad i = 1, \dots, n$$

If profits are positive, new firms will enter, causing the marginal utility of income to rise and profits to fall until profits are driven to zero. In equilibrium, then $\pi = 0$, implying for the output of a representative firm:

$$(9) \qquad x_i = \alpha / (p/w - \beta) = \alpha \theta / \beta (1 - \theta)$$

$$i = 1, \dots, n$$

Thus output per firm is determined by the zero-profit condition. Again, since α, β, and θ are the same for all firms we can use the shorthand $x = x_i$ for all i.

Finally, we can determine the number of goods produced by using the condition of full employment. From (4) and (9), we have

$$(10) \qquad n = \frac{L}{\alpha + \beta x} = \frac{L(1 - \theta)}{\alpha}$$

C. *Effects of Trade*

Now suppose that two countries of the kind just analyzed open trade with one another at zero transportation cost. To make the point most clearly, suppose that the countries have the same tastes and technologies; since we are in a one-factor world there cannot be any differences in factor endowments. What will happen?

In this model there are none of the conventional reasons for trade; but there will nevertheless be both trade and gains from trade. Trade will occur because, in the presence of increasing returns, each good (i.e., each differentiated product) will be produced in only one country—for the same reasons that each good is produced by only one firm. Gains from trade will occur because the world economy will produce a

greater diversity of goods than would either country alone, offering each individual a wider range of choice.

We can easily characterize the world economy's equilibrium. The symmetry of the situation ensures that the two countries will have the same wage rate, and that the price of any good produced in either country will be the same. The number of goods produced in each country can be determined from the full-employment condition

$$(11) \qquad n = L(1 - \theta)/\alpha; \qquad n^* = L^*(1 - \theta)/\alpha$$

where L^* is the labor force of the second country and n^* the number of goods produced there.

Individuals will still maximize the utility function (1), but they will now distribute their expenditure over both the n goods produced in the home country and the n^* goods produced in the foreign country. Because of the extended range of choice, welfare will increase even though the "real wage" w/p (i.e., the wage rate in terms of a representative good) remains unchanged. Also, the symmetry of the problem allows us to determine trade flows. It is apparent that individuals in the home country will spend a fraction $n^*/(n + n^*)$ of their income on foreign goods, while foreigners spend $n/(n + n^*)$ of their income on home country products. Thus the value of home country imports measured in wage units is $L n^* / (n + n^*) = L L^* / (L + L^*)$. This equals the value of foreign country imports, confirming that with equal wage rates in the two countries we will have balance-of-payments equilibrium.

Notice, however, that while the *volume* of trade is determinate, the *direction* of trade—which country produces which goods—is not. This indeterminacy seems to be a general characteristic of models in which trade is a consequence of economies of scale. One of the convenient features of the models considered in this paper is that nothing important hinges on who produces what within a group of differentiated products. There is an indeterminacy, but it doesn't matter. This result might not hold up in less special models.

Finally, I should note a peculiar feature of the effects of trade in this model. Both before and after trade, equation (9) holds; that is, there is no effect of trade on the scale of production, and the gains from trade come solely through increased product diversity. This is an unsatisfactory result. In another paper I have developed a slightly different model in which trade leads to an increase in scale of production as well as an increase in diversity.[3] That model is, however, more difficult to work with, so that it seems worth sacrificing some realism to gain tractability here.

II. Transport Costs

In this section I extend the model to allow for some transportation costs. This is not in itself an especially interesting extension although the main result—that the larger country will, other things equal, have the higher wage rate—is somewhat surprising. The main purpose of the extension is, however, to lay the groundwork for the analysis of home market effects in the next section. (These effects can obviously occur only if there are transportation costs.) I begin by describing the behavior of individual agents, then analyze the equilibrium.

A. *Individual Behavior*

Consider a world consisting of two countries of the type analyzed in Section I, able to trade but only at a cost. Transportation costs will be assumed to be of the "iceberg" type, that is, only a fraction g of any good shipped arrives, with $1-g$ lost in transit. This is a major simplifying assumption, as will be seen below.

[3] To get an increase in scale, we must assume that the demand facing each individual firm becomes more elastic as the number of firms increases, whereas in this model the elasticity of demand remains unchanged. Increasing elasticity of demand when the variety of products grows seems plausible, since the more finely differentiated are the products, the better substitutes they are likely to be for one another. Thus an increase in scale as well as diversity is probably the "normal" case. The constant elasticity case, however, is much easier to work with, which is my reason for using it in this paper.

An individual in the home country will have a choice over n products produced at home and n^* products produced abroad. The price of a domestic product will be the same as that received by the producer p. Foreign products, however, will cost more than the producer's price; if foreign firms charge p^*, home country consumers will have to pay the c.i.f. price $\hat{p}^*=p^*/g$. Similarly, foreign buyers of domestic products will pay $\hat{p}=p/g$.

Since the prices to consumers of goods of different countries will in general not be the same, consumption of each imported good will differ from consumption of each domestic good. Home country residents, for example, in maximizing utility will consume $(p/\hat{p}^*)^{1/(1-\theta)}$ units of a representative imported good for each unit of a representative domestic good they consume.

To determine world equilibrium, however, it is not enough to look at consumption; we must also take into account the quantities of goods used up in transit. If a domestic resident consumes one unit of a foreign good, his combined direct and indirect demand is for $1/g$ units. For determining total demand, then, we need to know the ratio of total demand by domestic residents for each foreign product to demand for each domestic product. Letting σ denote this ratio, and σ^* the corresponding ratio for the other country, we can show that

$$(12) \qquad \sigma=(p/p^*)^{1/(1-\theta)}g^{\theta/(1-\theta)}$$

$$\sigma^*=(p/p^*)^{-1/(1-\theta)}g^{\theta/(1-\theta)}$$

The overall demand pattern of each individual can then be derived from the requirement that his spending just equal his wage; that is, in the home country we must have $(np+\sigma n^*p^*)d=w$, where d is the consumption of a representative domestic good; and similarly in the foreign country.

This behavior of individuals can now be used to analyze the behavior of firms. The important point to notice is that the elasticity of *export* demand facing any given firm is $1/(1-\theta)$, which is the same as the elasticity of *domestic* demand. Thus transportation costs have no effect on firms' pricing policy; and the analysis of Section I can be carried out as before, showing that transportation costs also have no effect on the number of firms or output per firm in either country.

Writing out these conditions again, we have

(13) $\quad p = w\beta/\theta; \ p^* = w^*\beta/\theta$

$\quad n = L(1-\theta)/\alpha; \ n^* = L^*(1-\theta)/\alpha$

The only way in which introducing transportation costs modifies the results of Section I is in allowing the possibility that wages may not be equal in the two countries; the number and size of firms are not affected. This strong result depends on the assumed form of the transport costs, which shows at the same time how useful and how special the assumed form is.

B. Determination of Equilibrium

The model we have been working with has a very strong structure—so strong that transport costs have no effect on either the numbers of goods produced in the countries, n and n^*, or on the prices relative to wages, p/w and p^*/w^*. The only variable which can be affected is the relative wage rate $w/w^* = \omega$, which no longer need be equal to one.

We can determine ω by looking at any one of three equivalent market-clearing conditions: (i) equality of demand and supply for home country labor; (ii) equality of demand and supply for foreign country labor; (iii) balance-of-payments equilibrium. It will be easiest to work in terms of the balance of payments. If we combine (12) with the other equations of the model, it can be shown that the home country's balance of payments, measured in *wage units* of the *other* country, is

(14) $\quad B = \dfrac{\sigma^* n \omega}{\sigma^* n + n^*} L^* - \dfrac{\sigma n^*}{n + \sigma n^*} \omega L$

$\quad = \omega L L^* \left[\dfrac{\sigma^*}{\sigma^* L + L^*} - \dfrac{\sigma}{L + \sigma L^*} \right]$

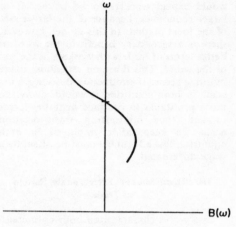

FIGURE 1

Since σ and σ^* are both functions of $p/p^* = \omega$, the condition $B = 0$ can be used to determine the relative wage. The function $B(\omega)$ is illustrated in Figure 1. The relative wage $\bar{\omega}$ is that relative wage at which the expression in brackets in (4) is zero, and at which trade is therefore balanced. Since σ is an increasing function of ω and σ^* a decreasing function of ω, $B(\omega)$ will be negative (positive) if and only if ω is greater (less) than $\bar{\omega}$, which shows that $\bar{\omega}$ is the unique equilibrium relative wage.

We can use this result to establish a simple proposition: *that the larger country, other things equal, will have the higher wage.* To see this, suppose that we were to compute $B(\omega)$ for $\omega = 1$. In that case we have $\sigma = \sigma^* < 1$. The expression for the balance of payments reduces to

(14') $\quad B = L L^* \left[\dfrac{1}{\sigma L + L^*} - \dfrac{1}{L + \sigma L^*} \right]$

But (14') will be positive if $L > L^*$, negative if $L < L^*$. This means that the equilibrium relative wage ω must be greater than one if $L > L^*$, less than one if $L < L^*$.

This is an interesting result. In a world characterized by economies of scale, one would expect workers to be better off in larger economies, because of the larger size of the local market. In this model, however, there is a secondary benefit in the form of better terms of trade with workers in the rest of the world. This does, on reflection, make intuitive sense. If production costs were the same in both countries, it would always be more profitable to produce near the larger market, thus minimizing transportation costs. To keep labor employed in both countries, this advantage must be offset by a wage differential.

III. "Home Market" Effects on the Pattern of Trade

In a world characterized both by increasing returns and by transportation costs, there will obviously be an incentive to concentrate production of a good near its largest market, even if there is some demand for the good elsewhere. The reason is simply that by concentrating production in one place, one can realize the scale economies, while by locating near the larger market, one minimizes transportation costs. This point—which is more often emphasized in location theory than in trade theory—is the basis for the common argument that countries will tend to export those kinds of products for which they have relatively large domestic demand. Notice that this argument is wholly dependent on increasing returns; in a world of diminishing returns strong domestic demand for a good will tend to make it an import rather than an export. But the point does not come through clearly in models where increasing returns take the form of external economies (see W. M. Corden). One of the main contributions of the approach developed in this paper is that by using this approach the home market can be given a simple formal justification.

I will begin by extending the basic closed economy model to one in which there are two industries (with many differentiated products within each industry). It will then be shown for a simple case that when two countries of this kind trade, each will be a net exporter in the industry for whose prod-ucts it has the relatively larger demand. Finally, some extensions and generalizations will be discussed.

A. A Two-Industry Economy

As in Section I, we begin by analyzing a closed economy. Assume that there are two classes of products, *alpha* and *beta*, with many potential products within each class. A tilde will distinguish *beta* products from *alpha* products; for example, consumption of products in the first class will be represented as $c_1, \ldots, c_n$ while consumption of products in second are $\tilde{c}_1, \ldots, \tilde{c}_n$.

Demand for the two classes of products will be assumed to arise from the presence of two groups in the population.[4] There will be one group with L members, which derives utility only from consumption of *alpha* products; and another group with $\tilde{L}$ members, deriving utility only from *beta* products. The utility functions of representative members of the two classes may by written

$$(15) \quad U = \sum_i c_i^\theta; \quad \tilde{U} = \sum_j \tilde{c}_j^\theta \qquad 0 < \theta < 1$$

For simplicity assume that not only the form of the utility function but the parameter θ is the same for both groups.

On the cost side, the two kinds of products will be assumed to have identical cost functions:

$$(16) \quad l_i = \alpha + \beta x_i \qquad\qquad i = 1, \ldots, n$$

$$\tilde{l}_j = \alpha + \beta \tilde{x}_j \qquad\qquad j = 1, \ldots, \tilde{n}$$

where, l_i, $\tilde{l}_j$ are labor used in production on typical goods in each class, and x_i, $\tilde{x}_j$ are total outputs of the goods.

The demand conditions now depend on the population shares. By analogy with (3),

---

[4] An alternative would be to have all people alike, with a taste for both kinds of goods. The results are similar. In fact, if each industry receives a fixed share of expenditure, they will be identical.

we have

(17) $x_i = Lc_i$ $i = 1, \ldots, n$

$\tilde{x}_j = \tilde{L}\tilde{c}_j$ $j = 1, \ldots, \tilde{n}$

The full-employment condition, however, applies to the economy as a whole:

(18) $\sum_{i=1}^{n} l_i + \sum_{j=1}^{\tilde{n}} \tilde{l}_j = L + \tilde{L}$

Finally, we continue to assume free entry, driving profits to zero. Now it is immediately apparent that the economy described by equations (15)–(18) is very similar to the economy described in equations (1)–(4). The price and output of a representative good—of either class—and the total number of products $n + \tilde{n}$ are determined just as if all goods belonged to a single industry. The only modification we must make to the results of Section I is that we must divide the total production into two industries. A simple way of doing this is to note that the sales of each industry must equal the income of the appropriate group in the population:

(19) $npx = wL; \quad \tilde{n}\tilde{p}\tilde{x} = \tilde{w}\tilde{L}$

But wages of the two groups must be equal, as must the prices and outputs of any products of either industry. So this reduces to the result $n/\tilde{n} = L/\tilde{L}$: the shares of the industries in the value of output equal the shares of the two demographic groups in the population.

This extended model clearly differs only trivially from the model developed in Section I when the economy is taken to be closed. When two such economies are allowed to trade, however, the extension allows some interesting results.

B. Demand and the Trade Pattern: A Simple Case

We can begin by considering a particular case of trade between a pair of two-industry countries in which the role of the domestic market appears particularly clearly. Suppose that there are two countries of the type just described, and that they can trade with transport costs of the type analyzed in Section II.

In the home country, some fraction f of the population will be consumers of *alpha* products. The crucial simplification I will make is to assume that the other country is a *mirror image* of the home country. The labor forces will be assumed to be equal, so that

(20) $L + \tilde{L} = L^* + \tilde{L}^* = \bar{L}$

But in the foreign country the population shares will be reversed, so that we have

(21) $L = f\bar{L}; \quad L^* = (1 - f)\bar{L}$

If f is greater than one-half, then the home country has the larger domestic market for the *alpha* industry's products; and conversely. In this case there is a very simple home market proposition: *that the home country will be a net exporter of the first industry's products if $f > 0.5$*. This proposition turns out to be true.

The first step in showing this is to notice that this is a wholly symmetrical world, so that wage rates will be equal, as will the output and prices of all goods. (The case was constructed for that purpose.) It follows that the ratio of demand for each imported product to the demand for each domestic product is the same in both countries.

(22) $\sigma = \sigma^* = g^{\theta/(1-\theta)} < 1$

Next we want to determine the pattern of production. The expenditure on goods in an industry is the sum of domestic residents' and foreigners' expenditures on the goods, so we can write the expressions

(23) $npx = \dfrac{n}{n + \sigma n^*} wL + \dfrac{\sigma n}{\sigma n + n^*} wL^*$

$n^* px = \dfrac{\sigma n^*}{n + \sigma n^*} wL + \dfrac{n^*}{\sigma n + n^*} wL^*$

where the price p of each product and the

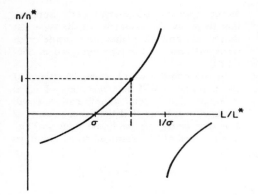

FIGURE 2

output x are the same in the two countries. We can use (23) to determine the relative number of products produced in each country, n/n^*.

To see this, suppose *provisionally* that some products in the *alpha* industry are produced in both countries; i.e., $n>0$, $n^*>0$. We can then divide the equations (23) through by n and n^*, respectively, and rearrange to get

(24) $L/L^* = (n+\sigma n^*)/(\sigma n+n^*)$

which can be rearranged to give

(25) $n/n^* = \dfrac{L/L^* - \sigma}{1 - \sigma L/L^*}$

Figure 2 shows the relationship (25). If $L/L^* = 1$, so does n/n^*; that is, if the demand patterns of the two countries are the same, their production patterns will also be the same, as we would expect. And as the relative size of either country's home market rises for *alpha* goods, so does its domestic production, as long as L/L^* lies in the range $\sigma < L/L^* > 1/\sigma$.

Outside that range, (25) appears to give absurd results. Recall, however, that the derivation of (24) was made on the provisional assumption that n and n^* were both nonzero. Clearly, if L/L^* lies outside the range

from σ to $1/\sigma$, this assumption is not valid. What the figure suggests is that if L/L^* is less than σ, $n=0$; the home country specialized entirely in *beta* products, producing no *alpha* products (while the foreign country produces only *alpha* products). Conversely, if L/L^* is greater than $1/\sigma$, $n^*=0$, and we have the opposite pattern of specialization.

We can easily demonstrate that this solution is in fact an equilibrium. Suppose that the home country produced no *alpha* products, and that a firm attempted to start production of a single product. This firm's profit-maximizing f.o.b. price would be the same as that of the foreign firm's. But its sales would be less, in the ratio

$$\frac{\sigma^{-1}L + \sigma L^*}{L + L^*} < 1$$

Thus such a firm could not compete.

This gives us our first result on the effect of the home market. It says that if the two countries have sufficiently dissimilar tastes each will specialize in the industry for which it has the larger home market. Obviously, also, each will be a net exporter of the class of goods in which it specializes. Thus the idea that the pattern of exports is determined by the home market is quite nicely confirmed.

We also get some illuminating results on the conditions under which specialization will be incomplete. Incomplete specialization and two-way trade within the two classes of products will occur if the relative size of the domestic markets for *alpha* goods lies in the range from σ to $1/\sigma$, where $\sigma = g^{\theta/(1-\theta)}$. But g measures transportation costs, while $\theta/(1-\theta)$ is, in equilibrium, the ratio of variable to fixed costs;[5] that is, it is an index of the importance of scale economies. So we have shown that the possibility of incomplete specialization is greater, the greater are transport costs and the less important are economies of scale.

A final result we can take from this special case concerns the pattern of trade when

[5]One can see this by rearranging equation (9) to get $\beta x/\alpha = \theta/(1-\theta)$.

specialization is incomplete. In this case each country will both import and export products in *both* classes (though not the same products). But it remains true that, if one country has the larger home market for *alpha* producers, it will be a *net* exporter in the *alpha* class and a net importer in the other. To see this, note that we can write the home country's trade balance in *alpha* products as

$$(26) \quad B_\alpha = \frac{\sigma n}{\sigma n + n^*} wL^* - \frac{\sigma n^*}{n + \sigma n^*} wL$$

$$= wL^* \left[\frac{\sigma n}{\sigma n + n^*} - \frac{\sigma n^*}{n + \sigma n^*} \frac{L}{L^*} \right]$$

$$= \frac{\sigma wL^*}{\sigma n + n^*} [n - n^*]$$

where we used (24) to eliminate the relative labor supplies. This says that the sign of the trade balance depends on whether the number of *alpha* products produced in the home country is more or less than the number produced abroad. But we have already seen that n/n^* is an increasing function of L/L^* in the relevant range. So the country with the larger home market for the *alpha*-type products will be a net exporter of those goods, even if specialization is not complete.

C. *Generalizations and Extensions*

The analysis we have just gone through shows that there is some justification for the idea that countries export what they have home markets for. The results were arrived at, however, only for a special case designed to make matters as simple as possible. Our next question must be the extent to which these results generalize.

One way in which generalization might be pursued is by abandoning the "mirror image" assumption: we can let the countries have arbitrary populations and demand patterns, while retaining all the other assumptions of the model. It can be shown that in that case, although the derivations become more complicated, the basic home market result is unchanged. Each country will be a net exporter in the industry for whose goods it has a relatively larger demand. The dif-

ference is that wages will in general not be equal; in particular, smaller countries with absolutely smaller markets for both kinds of goods will have to compensate for this disadvantage with lower wages.

Another, perhaps more interesting, generalization would be to abandon the assumed symmetry between the industries. Again, we would like to be able to make sense of some arguments made by practical men. For example, is it true that large countries will have an advantage in the production and export of goods whose production is characterized by sizeable economies of scale? This is an explanation which is sometimes given for the United States' position as an exporter of aircraft.

A general analysis of the effects of asymmetry between industries would run to too great a length. We can learn something, however, by considering another special case. Suppose that the *alpha* production is the same as in our last analysis, but that the production of *beta* goods is characterized by *constant* returns to scale and perfect competition. For simplicity, also assume that *beta* goods can be transported costlessly.

It is immediately apparent that in this case the possibility of trade in *beta* products will ensure that wage rates are equal. But this in turn means that we can apply the analysis of Part B, above, to the *alpha* industry. Whichever country has the larger market for the products of that industry will be a net exporter of *alpha* products and a net importer of *beta* products. In particular: if two countries have the same composition of demand, the larger country will be a net exporter of the products whose production involves economies of scale.

The analysis in this section has obviously been suggestive rather than conclusive. It relies heavily on very special assumptions and on the analysis of special cases. Nonetheless, the analysis does seem to confirm the idea that, in the presence of increasing returns, countries will tend to export the goods for which they have large domestic markets. And the implications for the pattern of trade are similar to those suggested by Steffan Linder, Grubel (1970), and others.

REFERENCES

Bela Balassa, *Trade Liberalization Among Industrial Countries*, New York 1967.

W. M. Corden, "A Note on Economies of Scale, the Size of the Domestic Market and the Pattern of Trade," in I. A. McDougall and R. H. Snape, eds., *Studies in International Economics*, Amsterdam 1970.

A. Dixit and J. Stiglitz, "Monopolistic Competition and Optimum Product Diversity," *Amer. Econ. Rev.*, June 1977, 67, 297–308.

H. Grubel, "Intra-Industry Specialization and the Pattern of Trade," *Can. J. Econ.*, Aug. 1967, 33, 374–388.

_____, "The Theory of Intra-Industry Trade," in I. A. McDougall and R. H. Snape, eds., *Studies in International Economics*, Amsterdam 1970.

G. Hufbauer and J. Chilas, "Specialization by Industrial Countries: Extent and Consequences," in Herbert Giersch, ed., *The International Division of Labor*, Tübingen 1974.

I. Kravis, "The Current Case for Import Limitations," in *United States Economic Policy in an Interdependent World, Commission on International Trade and Investment Policy*, Washington 1971.

P. Krugman, "Increasing Returns, Monopolistic Competition, and International Trade," *J. Int. Econ.*, Nov. 1979, 9, 469–80.

Steffan Linder, *An Essay on Trade and Transformation*, New York 1961.

[14]

PRODUCT DIVERSITY, ECONOMIES OF SCALE, AND INTERNATIONAL TRADE*

Colin Lawrence and Pablo T. Spiller

The paper develops new testable implications for monopolistic competition in the open economy. Within a two-sector model we explore how international trade affects plant size, the degree of product diversity, and excess capacity. The analysis then focuses on how trade affects the degree of domestic and international concentration, intersectoral capital mobility, and output in the competitive sector. Finally, we compare the model to the traditional Hecksher-Ohlin model and find that many of the central propositions still hold.

I. Introduction

Recently, a growing body of literature extending the traditional theory of international trade to the case of monopolistic competition has emerged.[1] This research has come about for two fundamental reasons. First, the traditional Hecksher-Ohlin (H-O) framework does not explain the bulk of international trade, which is essentially intraindustry trade. Second, during the last few years the relevance of introducing measures of foreign competition in empirical applications of industrial organization models has been highlighted.[2]

Previous theoretical work has mostly been concerned with analyzing the robustness of the traditional H-O propositions in the presence of returns to scale and product diversity. Our work, on the other hand, emphasizes the development of new testable implications of monopolistic competition in open economies. We explore how plant size, the number of plants, the degree of excess capacity, and prices in the monopolistic-competitive sector[3] depend upon the relative size of domestic—and foreign—markets and relative factor endowment differentials. We also analyze the impact of trade on the degree of domestic and international concentration, the average size of plants,

*We are grateful to Elhanan Helpman and to an anonymous referee of this *Journal* for their invaluable suggestions. Wilfred Ethier and Assaf Razin also made helpful suggestions. Needless to say, all the remaining errors are our responsibility. We are grateful to Ann Facciolo for her efficient typing. This research was partially financed by the Center for the Study of Organizational Innovation and by the Wharton Center for International Management Studies, both at the University of Pennsylvania.

1. See Ethier [1979a, 1979b], Helpman [1980], Krugman [1979], Lancaster [1980], and Venables [1980].
2. See Caves *et al.* [1980], Esposito and Esposito [1971], and Jacquemin [1979].
3. Throughout this paper the term "monopolistic competitive sector" will be freely interchanged with terms such as "product variety sector," "the diversified sector," or the "industrial sector."

© 1983 by the President and Fellows of Harvard College. Published by John Wiley & Sons, Inc.
The Quarterly Journal of Economics, February 1983   CCC 0033-5533/83/010063-21$03.10

64   *QUARTERLY JOURNAL OF ECONOMICS*

intersectoral capital mobility, the level of output in competitive sectors, and the implications for income distribution and welfare.

Our model is related to previous models in the following way. First, it differs from Krugman's [1979]—and in this way it is similar to Helpman's [1980]—in presenting a general equilibrium model of a two-sector economy (one sector is competitive, while the other is monopolistically competitive), with two factors of production (capital and labor) and full intersectoral factor mobility. On the other hand, it differs from Helpman's [1980] specification of the technology used in the monopolistic competitive sector. While Helpman specifies either a general production function or a homothetic one as a special case, we specify a nonhomothetic production function. Firms, in order to enter the industry, have to incur significant fixed costs in the form of a capital requirement (for example, Research and Development outlays). This assumption closely resembles ones used in models of industrial organization, where measures of "Minimum Efficient Size" are generally used.[4]

We establish several propositions. The opening of trade *increases* the degree of excess capacity in the labor country, while making the capital-abundant economy exploit its economies of scale. Furthermore, due to the opening of trade, the degree of international industrial concentration will fall. Thus, despite the lower number of firms in the labor-abundant country, its firms compete in a more competitive environment under free trade.

Although autarchic equilibria are characterized by a state that is not Pareto optimal, opening to trade benefits both countries, abstracting from the distribution of real income. The larger the partner country, the greater the gains from trade. The reason is that the larger country produces a larger array of diverse products. The importing of such variety increases the level of welfare for the home country. Also, the gains from trade seem to be the highest when factor proportions between countries are extremely different. Finally, Helpman [1980] has proved that for homothetic production functions, pretrade prices are useful for predicting the direction of trade, even under economies of scale. We show that for a particular class of nonhomothetic production functions, the post-trade equilibrium prices and factor proportions are bounded by the autarchic prices in each country.[5] Thus, pretrade prices in our model will predict the direction of trade.

4. See Scherer [1980] for a general discussion of returns to scale in different industries.
5. This proposition was kindly pointed out to us by Helpman.

II. THE CLOSED ECONOMY

IIA. *The Competitive Equilibrium*

Consider an economy composed of identical consumers whose preferences can be characterized by a utility function,[6]

$$(2.1) \qquad U = Y^{1-s} \left[\left(\sum_{i=1}^{n} X_i^{\theta} \right)^{1/\theta} \right]^s, \qquad 0 < \theta, s \leqslant 1.$$

Y is a homogeneous commodity produced in a competitive market. The X_i's are of a heterogeneous quality, where the elasticity of substitution between any X_i and Y,θ, is identical for all $i = 1,n$. There exists some substitutability between any X_i and X_j, $j \neq i$. The number of products being produced is represented by n. The production of any X_i involves some fixed costs and variable costs. It is produced in a monopolistic competitive market.

The production function of the competitive sector is assumed to be a Cobb-Douglas function,

$$(2.2) \qquad Y = K_y \, \epsilon \, L_y^{1-\epsilon},$$

where K_y is the capital input and L_y the labor input in the Y industry. The cost function for any $X_i (X_i > 0)$[7] is

$$(2.3) \qquad TC_i = \gamma r + w\beta X_i, \qquad \text{for all } i = 1, \dots, n,$$

where γ is the capital setup cost, r is the rental rate, w the wage rate, and $1/\beta$ the marginal product of labor. For simplicity, this has been set equal to the average product. We assume that there is free entry into both industries.

The first-order condition for utility maximization is

$$(2.4) \qquad P_i = \frac{s}{1-s} \, Y \, X_i^{\theta-1} \Big/ \sum_{i=1}^{n} X_i^{\theta}.$$

If n is sufficiently large, the elasticity of demand for each X_i is $-1/$

---

6. This utility function is a special case of the Dixit-Stiglitz [1977] model.
7. Hence, the production function for each X_i is

$$X_i = \begin{cases} 0 & \text{for } K_i < \gamma \\ \dfrac{1}{\beta} L_i & \text{for } K_i \geqslant \gamma. \end{cases}$$

A more general function would allow capital and labor to have both fixed and variable components. Our assumption is the limiting case of a production function where capital is used intensively as a fixed factor and labor as a variable one.

$(1 - \theta)$.[8] The utility function in (2.1) and cost function in (2.3) imply a symmetrical solution, so that $X = X_i$ and $P = P_i$ for all i. Expression (2.4) can then be written as

$$(2.4a) \qquad\qquad P = \frac{s}{1 - s}\, Y\, \frac{1}{Xn}\,.$$

Since there are increasing returns to scale in producing any X_i, no two firms will produce the same X_i. Moreover, since there are no economies of scope, we assume that each firm specializes in one product. Each firm entering the X industry will equalize marginal revenue to marginal costs. This condition is

$$(2.5) \qquad\qquad P = \beta w/\theta \qquad \text{for all } i.$$

Since the optimal price for each X_i is independent of other products being produced, zero profits equilibrium in the X sector will be achieved by increasing the number of products (firms) until the point where no abnormal profits can be earned. The zero profit equilibrium for all X_i is

$$(2.6) \qquad\qquad X = \frac{r}{w}\, \frac{\gamma}{\beta}\, \frac{\theta}{1 - \theta}\,.$$

Expression (2.6) implies that the higher the r/w ratio, the larger the plant size. This is so, since a larger r/w implies lower variable costs, and hence firms increase their output (and reduce their excess capacity). If the capital requirement γ rises, so will X, since a larger output of X is needed to cover the higher fixed costs.[9]

The first-order conditions for profit maximization in the Y industry are simply

$$(2.7) \qquad\qquad wL_y = (1 - \epsilon)Y; \qquad rK_y = \epsilon Y,$$

where L_y is the amount of labor and K_y the amount of capital utilized

8. In fact, the traditional Chamberlin tangency is obtained here. The tangency solution implies that $1 - \theta$ also measures the degree of economies of scale *in equilibrium* ($1 - \theta = (AC - MC)/AC$). The parameter θ also measures the elasticity of demand facing each firm. The assumption that the elasticity of demand is independent of the number of competitors is not intuitively appealing if there are a small number of competitors. A more general approach would let θ depend on total variety (n)—in particular, θ could be increasing in n ($0 < \theta < 1$). However, when n is large, the assumption of a constant θ is a plausible one. Throughout the paper we assume a large n, since its assumption significantly simplifies the analysis. The implications of θ being a variable are left for future research.

9. The parameter λ can be thought of as the counterpart of the minimum efficient size variable used in the industrial organization literature. See Scherer [1980] for a discussion.

in the Y industry. We assume that the stock of labor ($\overline{L}$) and capital ($\overline{K}$) are fixed. The endowment constraints are

$$(2.8) \qquad\qquad \overline{L} = L_y + nL_x$$

$$(2.9) \qquad\qquad \overline{K} = K_y + n\gamma,$$

where L_x is the amount of labor used in each X plant.

Using (2.4a), (2.5), and (2.6), (2.8), and (2.9), we obtain total variety:

$$(2.10) \qquad\qquad n = \frac{\overline{K}}{\gamma} \frac{s(1-\theta)}{z},$$

where $z = s(1-\theta) + \epsilon(1-s)$.

Product variety depends only on the capital stock, since we have assumed that the only fixed costs incurred are capital costs. z is the share of capital (out of income) utilized in the Y industry, and product variety is inversely related to it.

The Herfindahl index (H) is a measure of concentration of an industry. Since all firms are alike, $H = 1/n$. Hence, the degree of concentration depends positively on γ and negatively on $\overline{K}$.[10]

By utilizing (2.7), (2.8), (2.9), and (2.10), we can obtain the reduced-form equations of $K_x/L_x, w/r, X,$ and Y:

$$(2.11) \qquad k_X \equiv \frac{K_x}{L_X} = \frac{(1-\epsilon)(1-\theta)}{\epsilon\theta}\psi k; \qquad k_y \equiv \frac{K_y}{L_y}\psi k$$

$$(2.12) \qquad\qquad w/r = [(1-z)/z]k$$

$$(2.13) \qquad\qquad X = \frac{\gamma\epsilon\theta}{\beta(1-\epsilon)(1-\theta)\psi k}$$

$$(2.14) \qquad\qquad Y = \left(\frac{1-\epsilon}{1-z}\right)(1-s)(\psi k)^\epsilon \overline{L},$$

where k is the economy-wide capital-labor ratio, i.e., $\overline{K}/\overline{L}$, and $\psi = [\epsilon(1-z)]/[z(1-\epsilon)]$. Thus, as in the H-O model, the wage-rental ratio depends monotonically on the capital-labor ratio.[11] The size of any X plant is inversely related to the capital-labor ratio because any rise in k will lead to higher real variable costs. Recalling that diversity

10. The Herfindahl index is defined as $H = \Sigma_{i=1}^n S_i^2$, where S_i is the share of the ith firm's sales in total industry sales. The relationship between H and γ has been supported by most empirical studies on the concentration-profitability question. See Weiss [1971, 1974] for surveys of this literature. The relationship between H and $\overline{K}$ has not received much attention until very recently.

11. Note that the capital-labor ratios in both X and Y industries depend monotonically on the w/r ratio.

depends on the absolute capital stock, a country with both absolute and relative capital abundance will produce a large variety of goods with small-size plants. To investigate the degree of relative factor intensities, divide k_x by k_y in (2.11). If $\theta + \epsilon < 1$, then the product variety sector is the capital-intensive sector.[12] Throughout the remainder of this paper, we shall assume that $\theta + \epsilon < 1$. However, in footnotes, we shall also analyze the case where $\theta + \epsilon > 1$. Empirically we believe that $\theta + \epsilon$ will be less than unity.

Finally, it should be noted that any increase in w/r will lead to a higher wage in terms of y products. However, from (2.5) the real wage in terms of X goods remains constant at $1/\beta$. If w/r increases, rental on capital will fall in terms of both X and Y goods. Thus, as in the H-O model, w/r can be used as an index of income distribution between labor and capital.

IIB. Pareto Optimality and Factor Allocation

Since there are economies of scale, the competitive solution of factor allocation may be suboptimal. This is true, since firms will enter the industry only if profits are nonnegative. However, from society's point of view, a new product should be introduced whenever *producer plus consumer surplus* is nonnegative. The optimal solution is to find the values for n, X, and Y, which maximize the utility function in (2.1), subject to technological constraints (2.2) and (2.3) and factor endowment constraints (2.8) and (2.9). The optimal values of n and X are

$$(2.15) \qquad n^o = \frac{\overline{K}}{\gamma} \left(\frac{(1 - \theta)s}{(\theta\epsilon(1 - s) + s(1 - \theta))} \right)$$

$$(2.16) \qquad x^o = \frac{\gamma[\theta\epsilon(1 - s) + s(1 - \theta)]}{\beta k(1 - \theta)(1 - \epsilon(1 + s))}.$$

By comparing (2.15) and (2.16) to their counterparts in the competitive equilibrium, (2.10) and (2.6), we obtain the following results:

a. The optimal level of diversity exceeds the competitive level: $(n^o > n)$.

b. Optimal total output in the X industry is larger than the competitive level $(n^o X^o > nX)$. The budget constraint implies that Y^o is lower than the competitive equilibrium case.

c. The optimal size per plant may exceed or fall short of the

---

12. We are grateful to Helpman for pointing this out.

PRODUCT DIVERSITY AND SCALE ECONOMICS 69

competitive outcome, depending on the relative value of the parameters.[13]

 d. The percentage deviations of variety, plant size, and output Y are independent of the size of the economy. Hence, the larger the economy, the larger the absolute value of the distortion.

 We have now completed the description of the closed economy. The reason for its development is that it will be used as a yardstick in measuring the impact of trade on the structure of the economy and on its welfare. The next section develops these issues.

III. ANALYSIS OF THE OPEN ECONOMY

IIIA. *The Competitive Equilibrium*

 The utility functions in each country are

$$U = \tilde{y}^{1-s} \left[\sum_{i=1}^{n} \tilde{X}_{1i}^{\theta} + \sum_{i=1}^{n} \tilde{X}_{2i}^{\theta} \right]^{s/\theta};$$

(3.1)

$$U^* = \tilde{y}^{*1-s} \left[\sum_{i=1}^{n} \tilde{X}_{1i}^{*\theta} + \sum_{i=1}^{n^*} \tilde{X}_{2i}^{*\theta} \right]^{s/\theta},$$

where * refers to the foreign country and ~ to the levels of consumption. The subscripts 1 and 2 refer to the production location of the good: 1 is home production, while 2 is foreign production. For example, $\tilde{X}_{2j}^*$ is foreign consumption of product j produced in the foreign country. We define goods produced in the home country as X_1 and those in the foreign country as X_2^*.[14] Since the equilibrium is symmetrical, the budget constraint in each country can be represented as

(3.2)
$$P_1 \tilde{X}_1 n + P_2 \tilde{X}_2 n^* + \tilde{y} = P_1 n X_1 + y$$
$$P_1 \tilde{X}_1^* n + P_2 \tilde{X}_{2n}^* * + \tilde{y}^* = P_2 n^* X_2^* + y^*,$$

where P_1 and P_2 are the prevailing prices in the home and foreign country, respectively. Maximizing (3.1) subject to budget constraint (3.2) yields the following first-order condition:

(3.3) $\quad P_j = \dfrac{s}{1-s} \tilde{y} \dfrac{\tilde{X}_{ji}^{1-\theta}}{\sum_{i=1}^{n} \tilde{X}_{1i}^{\theta} + \sum_{i=1}^{n^*} \tilde{X}_{2i}^{\theta}} \qquad$ for $i = 1, \dots, n,$

---

 13. In the extreme case where $\epsilon = 1$, $x > x^0$, and vice versa for $\epsilon = 0$.
 14. To clarify the nomenclature, for production, the term X_1 is equivalent to X and the term X_2 to X^*.

and similarly for the foreign country. In the absence of taxes or tariffs and since the solution is symmetric, there will be factor-price equalization. Moreover, the size of plants will be equalized. The above two results hold also for more general cases of utility and cost functions. This has been proved by Helpman [1980, pp. 24–25]. In equilibrium then,

$$\text{(3.3a)} \quad P = \frac{s}{1-s}\,\tilde{y}\,\frac{1}{(n+n^*)\tilde{X}} = \frac{s}{1-s}\,\tilde{y}^*\,\frac{1}{(n+n^*)\tilde{X}^*} = P^*,$$

where $\tilde{X}^*$ represents the consumption of each X in the home (foreign country). When $n + n^*$ is large, from (3.3) the elasticity of demand for all products is $-1/(1-\theta)$. Therefore, the profit-maximizing solution of P is

$$\text{(3.4)} \qquad P = \beta\theta^{-1}w; \qquad P^* = \beta\theta^{-1}w^*.$$

The first-order profit-maximizing conditions in the competitive sector are

$$\text{(3.5)} \qquad \begin{array}{ll} w = (1-\epsilon)k_y^{\epsilon}; & w^* = (1-\epsilon)k_y^{*\epsilon}; \\ r = \epsilon k_y^{\epsilon-1}; & r^* = \epsilon K_y^{*\epsilon-1}. \end{array}$$

Using (3.3)–(3.5), we see that it follows that

$$\text{(3.6)} \qquad k_y = k_y^*$$

$$\text{(3.7)} \qquad \begin{array}{l} r = r^* \\ w = w^*; \end{array}$$

and moreover, the zero profit conditions imply that

$$\text{(3.8)} \qquad X = X^* = \frac{r}{w}\,\frac{\gamma\theta}{\beta(1-\theta)}\,.$$

IIIB. From Autarchy to Free Trade

In order to simplify the discussion, let us introduce the following relationships of differential factor endowments:

$$\bar{K}^* = a\gamma\bar{K}; \qquad \bar{L}^* = (2-a)\bar{\gamma}L; \qquad 0 \leqslant a \leqslant, \qquad \text{and } \lambda > 0,$$

where a is a measure of the capital-labor differential and λ is a measure of size. If $a < 1$, the home country is capital abundant, while for $a > 1$, the home country is labor abundant. If $\lambda < 1$, the home country is larger and vice versa for $\lambda > 1$. If $\lambda = 1$, the countries are of the same

PRODUCT DIVERSITY AND SCALE ECONOMICS 71

size, and if $a = 1$, the countries are endowed with identical relative factor endowments.[15]

The world capital and labor endowments are

$$\overline{K} = \overline{K} + \overline{K}^* \equiv [1 + a\lambda]\overline{K}; \qquad \overline{L} = \overline{L} + \overline{L}^* \equiv [1 + (2 - a)\lambda]\overline{L}.$$

The international capital-labor ratio $\overline{k}$ is

(3.9) $\qquad \overline{k} = \delta k, \qquad$ where $\delta = (1 + a\lambda)/[1 + (2 - a)\lambda]$,

and k is the domestic capital-labor ratio. Recalling the labor endowment constraints (2.8), we see that

(2.8) $\qquad \overline{L} = nX\beta + L_y; \qquad \overline{L}^* = n^*X^*\beta + L_y^*.$

Substitute both the consumption and production first-order conditions for each product ((3.3a), (3.4), and (3.5)) and the zero profit conditions (3.8) into (2.8). We obtain the reduced-form value of the international w/r ratio:

(3.10) $\qquad \dfrac{w}{r} = \dfrac{1 - z}{z} \overline{k}, \qquad 0 \leqslant z \leqslant 1.$

Compare (3.10) to the autarchic equilibrium (2.12) and obtain the following proposition.

PROPOSITION 1. The factor found in relative abundance in each country will experience an increase in its relative reward, while the factor that is relatively scarce will experience a decline in its reward.[16] Furthermore, the international w/r ratio is bounded by the autarchic w/r's.

The above proposition depends crucially on the specification of the production and utility functions. Helpman [1980] has proved that in a more general case, Proposition 1 *does not* necessarily hold. However, he has shown that it holds for the homothetic production functions. Thus, Proposition 1 shows that there is a class of nonhomothetic production functions, in addition to homothetic ones, for which the above H-O theorem holds under economies of scale.

---

15. This notation is introduced in order to have measures of size and factor proportion differentials. When a increases, the foreign country becomes relatively more capital abundant, but in order not to increase its size, it is necessary to reduce its labor stock. We are then implicitly defining size as the area of the Edgeworth box that would be equal to 2 if $\overline{K} = \overline{L}$. The correct (but intractable) definition of size should be related to the level of utility.

16. Note that wages in terms of the variety good X do not change, since the marginal product of labor in terms of X is fixed. The rental rate changes in terms of both goods.

The reduced-form equilibrium size of plant can be found by substituting (3.10) into (3.8):

$$(3.11) \qquad X = \frac{z}{(1-z)} \frac{\theta\gamma}{(1-\theta)\beta} \frac{1}{\overline{k}}.$$

Comparing (3.11) to plant size in the autarchic equilibrium (2.13), we obtain the following proposition:

PROSPOSITION 2. The capital-abundant country will experience an expansion in plant size, while the labor-abundant country will contract its plant size.

Again this result depends on our specified nonhomothetic production function. If instead of capital being the fixed factor, and labor the variable factor, we have the opposite case, then Proposition 2 will obviously be stated in the reverse. Consequently, a more general Proposition 2 would state that the country abundant in the fixed factor will experience an expansion in plant size, while the country abundant in the variable factor will contract its plant size. The intuition behind this result is that the cost of the variable input (labor) becomes cheaper, in the country abundant in the fixed factor (capital), providing an incentive for plant expansion. In contrast, the variable factor- (labor-) abundant country will decrease the size of its plants.[17]

In order to investigate the intersectoral mobility of inputs in each country, substitute (3.10) into the profit-maximizing conditions (3.5) and obtain

$$(3.12) \qquad k_y = \psi\overline{k} = k_y^*,$$

where[18]

$$\psi = [\epsilon(1-z)]/[z(1-\epsilon)], \qquad 0 \leqslant \psi \leqslant 1,$$

and k_y is the post-trade equilibrium capital-labor ratio in the competitive sector. The capital-labor ratio in the product variety sector is then

$$k_x = \gamma/\beta x = k_x^*.$$

---

17. This result also depends on our assumption of θ being a constant. See footnote 8 above.

18. The expression ψ lies between zero and one only if $\theta + \epsilon < 1$; i.e., if the diversity sector is capital abundant in equilibrium. If, on the other hand, $\theta + \epsilon > 1$ (but to obtain an interior solution $1 - \theta - \epsilon > -\epsilon/s$), i.e., the diversified sector is labor abundant in equilibrium, then ψ may exceed one. Throughout this paper we shall assume that $\theta + \epsilon < 1$, and shall present the implications of $\theta + \epsilon > 1$ in footnotes.

PRODUCT DIVERSITY AND SCALE ECONOMICS 73

Substitute (3.11) into the above and derive the reduced-form capital-labor ratio in the x sector:

$$(3.13) \qquad k_x = \frac{(1 - \theta)(1 - z)}{\theta z} \overline{k} = k_x^*.$$

Compare (3.12) and (3.13) to the autarchic equilibria and obtain the following result:

PROPOSITION 3. *The movement from autarchy to free trade implies that the capital- (labor-) abundant country will experience a decrease (increase) in the capital-labor ratios for all sectors.*

Much like the H-O model, the capital-abundant country faces a decline in relative labor costs. It will thus move toward more labor-intensive activity in all sectors. Consequently, in the product variety sector, the capital-abundant country increases its plant size and hence adds more labor to the fixed capital stock in each plant. Conversely, for the labor-abundant country, plant size is reduced, and hence the x sector will become more capital intensive. The capital- (labor-) abundant country will experience a decrease (increase) in the degree of excess capacity. A suitable measure for degree of capital utilization is the physical average product of capital, x/γ, which rises (falls) in the capital- (labor-) abundant country.[19]

The wage rate w and rental rate r can be found by substituting (3.12) into (3.5); that is,

$$(3.14) \qquad w = (1 - \epsilon)(\psi \overline{k})^\epsilon$$

$$(3.15) \qquad r = \epsilon(\psi \overline{k})^{\epsilon - 1}.$$

By comparing these to the autarchic case, we note that wages will fall in the capital-abundant country (in terms of Y goods) and rental rates will rise in terms of both X and y goods. Output in the Y sector can be found by substituting (3.14) and (3.15) and utilizing the production function (2.3):

$$(3.16) \qquad y = [\psi \overline{k}]^\epsilon [(1 - \epsilon)(1 - \theta) - \theta \epsilon / \psi \delta][1 - \theta - \epsilon]^{-1} \overline{L}.$$

Compare (3.16) to autarchic equilibrium condition (2.14) and obtain

PROPOSITION 4. *The labor-abundant country will expand production in the competitive sector, while the capital-abundant country*

---

19. This result is independent of which sector is the relatively capital intensive. It is derived from the assumption that capital is the fixed cost.

will contract the production of y—hence reallocating factors to the product variety sector.[20]

The price of x (in terms of y) can be found by substituting (3.14) into (3.4):

$$(3.17) \qquad P = \theta^{-1}\beta(1 - \epsilon)(\psi \bar{k})^{\epsilon}.$$

PROPOSITION 5. *The price of goods in the product variety sector* falls *in the capital-abundant country and rises in the labor-abundant country.*[21]

This proposition emanates from the specific nonhomothetic product fashion. Marginal costs must necessarily fall (rise) in the capital- (labor-) abundant country. The fall in price in the capital-abundant county reflects the greater exploitation of economies of scale.

To analyze the effect of trade on product variety, we substitute (3.16) into (3.5) and use the labor endowment constraint (2.9) to find the level of product variety in each country and the world:

$$(3.18) \qquad n = \frac{\bar{k}}{\gamma} s \frac{1 - \theta}{z} Q,$$

where

$$Q = (1 - \psi\delta)/(1 - \psi).$$

Similarly, in the foreign country,

$$(3.19) \qquad n^* = \frac{\bar{K}^*}{\gamma} s \frac{1 - \theta}{z} Q^*,$$

where

$$Q^* = \frac{1 - \psi(2 - a)\delta/a}{1 - \psi}.$$

The total number of different products in the world is

$$(3.20) \qquad n + n^* = (\bar{K}/\gamma s)(1 - \theta)/z.$$

Visual inspection of (3.18) and (3.19) and the autarchic values of n and n^* (2.15), shows that

20. Proposition 4 critically depends on whether $\theta + \epsilon < 1$. If $\theta + \epsilon > 1$, then Proposition 4 is reversed.

21. Note that P is not the terms of trade, since one of the countries exports *both* X and Y. However, it can be shown that $\bar{P}$, the terms of trade, which is a weighted average of X and Y goods, is monotonically related to P. Thus, for all useful purposes, changes in P can be thought of as changes in the terms of trade.

PRODUCT DIVERSITY AND SCALE ECONOMICS 75

(3.18′)
$$n = n^A Q$$

and

$$n* = n*^A Q*,$$

where n^A and $n*^A$ are the autarchic values of the number of products in each country. The Q terms depend on relative size and the degree of factor endowment differences. If capital-labor ratios were identical across countries and the countries were of the same size, $a = \delta = 1$, then $Q = Q*$. This implies that if the countries have identical factor endowments, trade will not change the number of firms operating in each country. If the home country is capital abundant, then $\delta < 1$, and therefore, $Q > 1$, and $Q* < 1$. This leads us to state our next proposition.

PROPOSITION 6. The number of firms operating in the product variety sector rises (falls), in the capital- (labor-) abundant country.[22]

Proposition 6 suggests that domestic industrial concentration should be higher in relatively labor-abundant countries (holding size constant). Moreover, the opening to international trade will increase the latter country's level of domestic concentration. This result implies that relatively labor-abundant countries, which pursue protectionist policies, will have a smaller degree of domestic concentration than will those countries experiencing free trade.

On the other hand, domestic concentration (a widely used variable in the conduct-structure-performance tests for open economies)[23] does not take foreign competition into account. If domestic and foreign firms have equal access to information (so that the possibility of collusion is the same among domestic or foreign firms), then the relevant concentration measure is the degree of concentration of the firms supplying the country (both domestic and foreigners). In our case the value of the Herfindahl (international) index is $1/(n + n*)$.

---

22. This proposition again depends on $\theta + \epsilon < 1$. Since it can be shown that $Q = 1 + [(1 + \delta)(1 - \theta - \epsilon)|\epsilon|(1 - z)]/s$, then $Q > 1$ if and only if $(1 - \delta)$ has the same sign as $(1 - \theta - \epsilon)$. Therefore, if the home country is capital abundant ($\delta < 1$), then the number of firms operating in the diversified sector under free international trade will exceed (fall short of) the number under autarchy if and only if $1 - \theta - \epsilon > 0$ ($1 - \theta - \epsilon < 0$). On the other hand, if the country is labor abundant ($\delta - 1$), the number of firms will rise (fall) only if $1 - \theta - \epsilon < 1$ ($1 - \theta - \epsilon > 0$). Therefore, the value of $\theta + \epsilon$ is crucial in determining the effect of opening to trade on the number of firms operating in each country.

23. See Caves *et al.* [1980] or Jacquemin *et al.* [1979] for examples of the aforementioned tests. Interested readers may look at the references provided by Caves *et al.* [1980].

The next proposition makes it clear that the degree of competition must rise when a country opens to trade.

PROPOSITION 7. The total number of products in the world $(n + n*)$ remains constant as economies move from autarchic to free trade equilibrium. Thus, opening to trade involves a relocation of production—the increase in variety production of the relatively capital-abundant country is exactly offset by the decrease in variety production in the relatively labor-abundant country.[24]

As we saw in equations (3.18) and (3.19), the percentage change in the number of firms $(n^T/n^A - 1)$, where T and A mean after and before trade, equals $Q - 1$. Therefore, the larger the difference (in absolute value) between a and 1, the larger the structural change resulting from opening the economy. However, the structural change—in the presence of different factor endowment ratios—depends on the relative sizes of the economies.

It can be shown that

$$(3.21) \qquad \frac{\partial Q}{\partial \lambda} = -\frac{2\psi(a-1)}{(1+\psi)(1+(2-a)\lambda)^2} \gtreqless 0 \qquad \text{if } a \gtreqless 1.$$

PROPOSITION 8. If a country is relatively capital- (labor-) abundant, an increase in its partner's size increases (decreases) the number of firms.[25]

The above proposition, for a capital-abundant country, is presented in Figure I.

For a relatively labor-abundant country, there is a critical size of the foreign country (let us call it $\hat{\lambda}$), such that for $\lambda \geq \hat{\lambda}$, the home country specializes in Y. Moreover, $\hat{\lambda}$ falls as the foreign country becomes more capital abundant. This can be seen from the definition of Q in (3.18). We obtain

$$\hat{\lambda} = \frac{s(1 - \theta - \epsilon)}{(a - 2)z - 2z\epsilon(1 - a) + a\epsilon}$$

and

$$\frac{\partial \hat{\lambda}}{\partial a} = \frac{s(1 - \theta - \epsilon)(z + 2z\epsilon + \epsilon)}{\Delta^2} < 0,$$

24. Proposition 7 is the result of our assumptions concerning both utility and the technology. In particular, if θ is not a constant (it could depend on the number of diverse products in the world), then this proposition may not hold. See footnote 8.

25. This proposition clearly depends on the assumption that $\epsilon + \theta < 1$. If $\theta + \epsilon > 1$, then the proposition would be reversed. This can be seen by differentiating Q with respect to λ. $\partial Q/\partial \lambda = 2\epsilon(1 - z)(1 - a)(1 - \theta - \epsilon)(1 + (2 - a)\lambda^2)$. The sign of $\partial Q/\partial \lambda$ depends on the sign of $(1 - \theta - \epsilon)(1 - a)$.

PRODUCT DIVERSITY AND SCALE ECONOMICS 77

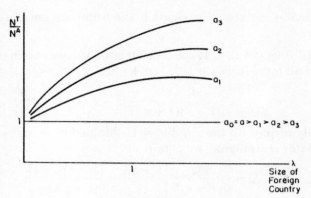

FIGURE I
Size, Factor Differentials, and the Degree of Diversity

where Δ is the denominator in the previous expression.

IIIC. *Patterns of Intersectoral and Intraindustry Trade*

Of particular importance is the division of trade into H-O trade or intraindustry trade. To analyze this, we first look at the volume of Y products traded. We call trade in Y, H-O trade, since its equilibrium volume depends on differences in factor endowments. Post-trade consumption can be found by substituting (3.2), (3.11), (3.17), and (3.20) into (3.3):

$$(3.22) \qquad \tilde{y} = (1 - s)(\psi \overline{k})^\epsilon (1 - \epsilon + \epsilon/\psi \delta)\overline{L}.$$

Post-trade production of y is found in (3.16). The deficit in trade of y goods is then

$$D_y \equiv \tilde{y} - y = \frac{[\psi \overline{k}]^\epsilon z(1 - \epsilon)(1 - \delta)}{\delta(1 - \theta - \epsilon)}.$$

From the above expression, it is clear that the sign of D_y depends upon the sign of $(1 - \delta)/(1 - \theta - \epsilon)$. Since the sign of $1 - \theta - \epsilon$ determines which sector (in equilibrium) is capital intensive, we can state the following proposition:

PROPOSITION 9. The capital-abundant country imports the relatively labor-intensive good and is a *net exporter* of the capital-intensive good.[26] If $\epsilon + \theta < 1$, the capital-abundant country will produce

---

26. This result is independent of our specific assumptions. Helpman [1980, pp. 27–28] proves this in a more general case.

a greater variety of products if the countries are of the same size.

By substituting (3.22), (3.17), and (3.20) into (3.3), we obtain the value of $\tilde{X}_i$ for all industries, $i = 1, \ldots, n + n^*$:

$$(3.23) \quad \tilde{X} = \frac{\gamma z \theta}{\beta(1 - c)(1 - \theta)(1 + a\lambda)} [1 - \epsilon + c(\psi\delta)^{-1}] \frac{1}{k}.$$

The trade surplus for the x industry is obtained by using (3.23) and (3.11). After rearranging, we obtain

$$(3.24) \qquad X - \tilde{X} = \frac{\gamma \theta z}{\beta(1 - \theta)k} \left[\frac{1 + a\lambda - (1 - z)\delta - z}{(1 - z)\delta(1 + a\lambda)} \right];$$

$$(3.24a) \qquad X - \tilde{X} = X^A \frac{[1 + a\lambda - (1 - z)\delta - z]}{\delta(1 + a\lambda)},$$

where X^A is value of both output and consumption in autarchy. Let us now explore how factor endowment differentials and size affect (3.24). Consider the special case where countries are of the same size and k ratio. From our analysis in Section IIIB we learned that under such conditions there would be no change in factor allocation when moving from autarchy to trade. However, there is an incentive to engage in intraindustry trade. Setting $a = \lambda = \delta = 1$ in (4.3a) (i.e., both countries are identical), we obtain

$$X - \tilde{X} = X^A/2.$$

Therefore, each country will export one half of its production in each plant. To observe how size affects this result, set $a = 1 = \delta$, but allow $0 < \lambda < 1$. Then from (3.24),

$$X - \tilde{X} = \frac{X^A}{1/\lambda + 1}.$$

As the home country expands $[\lambda \to 0]$, the value of exports decreases. In the limiting case $[\lim \lambda = 0]$ the value of exports would be zero. Large countries, as expected, export a small proportion of each good, while small countries export the bulk of their diverse products. The impact of differential factor endowments (captured by a), is ambiguous and depends on the structural parameters θ, s, z, and ϵ.

IIID. The Gains from Trade and Welfare Implications

It is not at all clear whether countries will gain from trade. Recall that the competitive solution for the case of autarchy implies an allocation of resources that is not consistent with Pareto optimality.

PRODUCT DIVERSITY AND SCALE ECONOMICS 79

Looking at the home country, we can show that the ratio of utility after trade to before trade is

$$(3.25) \quad \frac{U^T}{U^A} = \left[1 + \frac{z}{\delta(1-z)}\right] \delta^{\epsilon(1-s)} [1 + a\lambda] \frac{s(1-\theta)}{\theta} (1-z),$$

Let us first consider the case where countries are identical; i.e., $a = \lambda = \delta = 1$. This is a situation where only intraindustry trade takes place. Expression (3.25) becomes

$$\frac{U^T}{U^A} = 2^{s(1-\theta)/\theta} > 1.$$

Under such conditions both countries will gain from intraindustry trade. The larger the share of expenditure on the product variety sector and the smaller the elasticity of demand facing each product (or the elasticity of substitution between any two X-products), the larger will be the gains from trade.

Gains from trade depend on the relative size of the countries as well as on the factor endowment differential. To see how size matters, differentiate (3.25) by λ and obtain

$$(3.26) \quad \frac{\partial \log(U^T/U^A)}{\partial \lambda} \approx (2-a) \left[\frac{z}{1-z}(1-s)\right]$$

$$+ \left[\frac{s(1-\theta)}{\theta} + \epsilon(1-s)\right] a > 0.$$

Therefore,

PROPOSITION 10. The larger the trading partner (in relation to the country's size), the larger (in percentage terms) the gains from trade.

As in the H-O framework, factor proportions are relevant in determining the gains from trade. The following proposition states that relationship.

PROPOSITION 11. For any given size, the larger the differences in relative factor abundance, the larger are the gains in trade. Moreover, the maximum gains from trade for a country are obtained when the relative capital abundance of its partner is extremely large.

Because the proof of this proposition is in the Appendix, we shall simply outline it here. First, it is proved that there is a unique $\hat{a}$ ($0 < \hat{a} < 2$), such that the gains from trade are minimized. Second, as $|a$

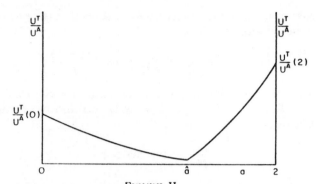

FIGURE II
The Gains from Trade with Varying K/L Endowments

$- \hat{a}|$ increases, the gains from trade also rise. That is, the home country is better off as the other country becomes extremely labor or capital abundant (i.e., as a tends to zero or to 2). Finally, we prove that the benefits from trade are larger when $a = 2$ than when $a = 0$.

We have shown that countries tend to gain the most from trade when relative factor proportions are extremely different. Moreover, it is not true that in the intermediate cases (i.e., a close to $\hat{a}$), an increase in factor diversity increases the gains from trade. For example, if $\hat{a} > 1$ and countries are identical in size, $\lambda = 1$, an increase (decrease) in a reduces (increases) the gain for the home country, and the opposite for its partner. There are two sources of gains. One is the pure intraindustry trade, that is, when $a = 1$, which is just the appearance of more variety, with no change in the structure and pattern of production. The other source arises whenever $a \neq 1$. If a is different from one, the relatively labor-abundant country gains, since it will tend to specialize in the competitive commodity, and most of the variety will be provided by its trading partner. On the other hand, the relatively capital-abundant country also gains, since trade allows it both to achieve higher economies of scale and to reduce the production of the competitive commodity.

Finally, combining (3.24) and (3.25), we obtain

PROPOSITION 12. For every value of the parameters, the gains from trade are always positive for both countries.

From (3.25) we learn that the gains from trade increase monotonically with the other country's size. Moreover, from (3.24) we observe that when $\lambda = 0$, $U^T/U^A = 1$. Therefore, for any positive size the home country gains from trade.

PRODUCT DIVERSITY AND SCALE ECONOMICS 81

TABLE I

	Values of					
	a	λ	ϵ	S	θ	U^{AT}/U^{BT}
Maximum	1.9	1.9	0.1	0.9	0.1	$9.435\,E4$
Minimum	1.5	0.1	0.1	1.0	0.8	1.002

Simulation results for U^{AT}/U^{BT}. Parameters were given values in their respective range (and were restricted to $0 < \lambda < 2$) that were increased by 0.1.

To provide an alternative proof, we simulated the model providing different values to the parameters. We searched for the maximum and minimum values of the gains from trade (U^T/U^A). From Table I we can see—as proved—that the maximum gain is obtained (for the home country) when the partner is extremely capital abundant and large. The minimum is obtained when the foreign country is small, and $\bar{a}$ turns out to be larger than 1. In this case, the gains are positive but very close to zero (only 2/1,000 percent).

IV. CONCLUSIONS

This paper has developed a framework in which to analyze the effects of fixed costs, and sizes of the domestic and foreign economy, as well as relative factor endowment differentials on the structure—and performance—of industries. We have derived several empirically testable hypotheses for industrial studies in open economies. First, we should expect domestic concentration to depend upon factor endowments. If capital is the major fixed cost, and labor is the major variable cost, then the capital- (labor-) abundant country will experience lower (higher) domestic industrial concentration. But, world concentration will be reduced by the introduction of free trade. Second, industries with relatively high concentration ratios will have a higher proportion of GNP, the larger the relative capital abundance. Finally, during the last few years a few less developed nations, generally of small size, have reversed their policy of infant industry protection. Our framework suggests that those countries will experience an increase in the degree of excess capacity in the industrial sector. Moreover, the larger the differences in relative factor endowments, the stronger the structural changes will be.

Most of the above results were derived on the basis of specific utility and technology functions. Empirical work would test the adequacy of the above specifications.

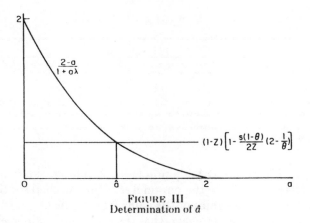

FIGURE III
Determination of $\hat{a}$

APPENDIX: PROOF OF PROPOSITION 11

If we take the logs of (3.25) and differentiate with respect to a, and make it equal to zero, we obtain

(A.1) $\dfrac{\partial \log(U^T/U^A)}{\partial a} \approx \lambda 2Z \left[1 - \dfrac{(2-a)}{(1-z)(1+a\lambda)} \right]$

$$- s(1-\theta)\left(2 - \frac{1}{\theta}\right) = 0.$$

Rearranging terms yields

(A.2) $\dfrac{2-a}{1+a\lambda} = (1-z)\left[\dfrac{s(1-\theta)}{2z}\left(2 - \dfrac{1}{\theta}\right) \right].$

Equation (A.2) is plotted in Figure III. Since the left-hand side of (A.2) is a monotonic decreasing function in a, which takes values between two and zero (for a between zero and two), if there is an interior solution, it is unique. Moreover, it is a minimum, since

$$\frac{\partial^2 \log(U^T/U^A)}{\partial a^2} \approx \frac{1+2\lambda}{(1+a\lambda)^2} > 0.$$

Therefore, the gains from trade as a function of a has a U shape, with the minimum at $a = a$, where a is the (interior) solution to (A.2) (see Figure II).

Finally, the gains from trade when $a = 2$ are larger than when $\theta = 0$, since $z < 1$:

$$\frac{U^T/U^A \ (a = 2)}{U^T/U^A \ a = 0)} = \frac{1 + 2\lambda - 2\lambda z}{1 + 2\lambda z}(1 + 2\lambda)^{2\epsilon(1-s)+(s(1-\theta)/\theta)-1}$$

$$> (1 + 2\lambda(1 - Z))(1 + 2\lambda)^{2\epsilon(1-s)+(s(1-\theta)/\theta)-1} > 1.$$

COLUMBIA GRADUATE SCHOOL OF BUSINESS
UNIVERSITY OF PENNSYLVANIA

PRODUCT DIVERSITY AND SCALE ECONOMICS 83

REFERENCES

Caves, R. E., M. E. Porter, A. M. Spence, with J. T. Scott, *Competition in the Open Economy* (Cambridge, MA: Harvard University Press, 1980).

Dixit, A. K., and J. E. Stiglitz, "Monopolistic Competition and Optimum Product Diversity," *American Economic Review*, XVII (1977), 297–308.

Esposito, L., and E. F. Esposito, "Foreign Competition and Domestic Industry Profitability," *Review of Economics and Statistics*, LIII (Nov. 1971), 343–55.

Ethier, W. J., "National and International Returns to Scale in the Modern Theory of International Trade," Discussion Paper #406, University of Pennsylvania, November 1979a.

——, "International Decreasing Costs and World Trade," *Journal of International Economics*, IX (1979b), 1–24.

Helpman, E., "International Trade in the Presence of Product Differentiation, Economics of Scale and Monopolistic Competition: A Chamberlin-Hecksher-Ohlin Approach," mimeo, Tel Aviv University, September 1980.

Jacquemin, A., E. de Ghellinck, and C. Huveneers, "Concentration and Profitability in a Small Open Economy," W. P. #7912, Université Catholique de Louvain, 1979.

Krugman, P., "Increasing Returns, Monopolistic Competition and International Trade," *Journal of International Economics*, IX (Nov. 1979), 496–79.

Lancaster, K., "Intra-industry Trade under Perfect Monopolistic Competition," *Journal of International Economics*, X (1980), 151–235.

Scherer, F. M., *Industrial Market Structure and Economic Performance* (Chicago: Rand McNally, 1980).

Spence, M., "Product Selection, Fixed Costs and Monopolistic Competition," *Review of Economic Studies*, XLIII (1976), 217–35.

Venables, A. J., "Monopolistic Competition and the Possible Losses from International Trade," mimeo, University of Sussex, April 1980.

Weiss, L., "Quantitative Studies of Industrial Organization," in M. D. Intriligator, ed., *Frontiers of Quantitative Economics* (Amsterdam: North-Holland, 1971).

——, "The Concentration and Profits Issue," in H. J. Goldschmidt *et al.*, eds., *Industrial Concentration and the New Learning* (Boston: Little, Brown, 1974).

C
Trade Based on Oligopolistic Competition

[15]

Journal of International Economics 11 (1981) 1–14. North-Holland Publishing Company

INTRA-INDUSTRY TRADE IN IDENTICAL COMMODITIES

James A. BRANDER*

Queen's University, Kingston, Ontario K7L3N6, Canada

Received June 1979, revised version received April 1980

The usual approach to intra-industry trade is to assume that such trade arises because slightly different commodities are produced and traded to satisfy consumers' tastes for variety. In this paper it is shown that there are reasons to expect two-way trade even in identical products, due to strategic interaction among firms.

1. Introduction

We observe that a substantial portion of world trade is in similar products and between similar countries. [See Grubel and Lloyd (1975)]. While such trade is not excluded by the Heckscher–Ohlin and Ricardian models of trade, neither is it well explained by them. The H–O and Ricardian models stress differences between countries as determinants of international trade. It is, however, possible to consider models that stress similarity among countries and increasing returns to scale as causes of trade. Such models are, perhaps, appropriate for analyzing this phenomenon known as intra-industry trade: trade in similar products.

Consider the export of ham from the United States to Denmark and from Denmark to the US. The natural argument is that American ham is slightly different from Danish ham, so it is not unreasonable that some consumers in each home market would prefer the foreign good.

What is not so widely recognized is that there are reasons to expect such trade even if the goods in question are identical. Two-way trade in identical products is sometimes referred to as cross-hauling and has been discussed in the basing-point-pricing literature [for example, Clark (1943)]. The context here is completely different: we examine the possibility of cross-hauling in a Cournot setting.

By a Cournot setting we mean that each firm assumes the output of other firms remains the same in each market. It may certainly be argued that the

*This paper is based on my Ph.D. dissertation at Stanford University. I would like to thank Ronald McKinnon and two anonymous referees for helpful comments. I would also like to thank Paul Krugman for pointing out an error in an earlier draft in the section on welfare improvement. Financial support from the Social Sciences and Humanities Research Council of Canada is gratefully acknowledged.

0022-1996/81/0001-0014/$02.50 © North-Holland Publishing Company

Cournot strategy is naive and that firms are unlikely to use it in fact. On the other hand, very sophisticated strategies are unlikely because they require that firms incur high information-gathering and information-processing costs. Consequently, limiting our attention to simple strategies is not necessarily bad. It is by no means clear, of course, that the Cournot strategy is superior to other simple strategies. We shall see, however, that the Cournot strategy may at least be more profitable than the limit-pricing strategy. It is worth emphasizing that firms must follow some strategy. The most frequently assumed strategy is the competitive strategy: firms are assumed to believe that they can sell as much output as they like at the going price. This is highly inappropriate for many of the industries characterized by intra-industry trade.

This paper is, then, intended to contribute to the theory of trade between similar countries, such as trade within the European Economic Community (EEC). Accordingly, different countries are assumed to be identical and the pattern of trade is determined by the interaction of increasing returns to scale, transport costs, and firms' imperfectly competitive behaviour.

2. The model

2.1. Production and cost

Increasing returns of a very simple form are assumed so that the cost function is

$$C(x) = F + cx,$$

where C = total cost, x = output, and c = marginal cost.

2.2. Transport costs

There are two countries, A and B. Transport costs are borne by producers. It is convenient to think of transport costs as shrinkage of the product [see Dornbusch et al. (1977)] so that if the quantity x is exported from A to B, quantity gx arrives in country B where $0 \leqq g \leqq 1$. Equivalently, per unit transport costs are $(1-g)/g$, using the commodity in question as the numeraire.

2.3. Firms' strategy and market structure

Firms employ a Cournot strategy. That is, each firm maximizes profit assuming the output of other firms in each market remains the same. As pointed out by a referee, it is important to distinguish this case from the case in which firms take total output by other firms (domestic + export) as given, but not output in each market separately as given. The assumption made here is a very special one, and a very important one for the analysis.

Firms stay in business only so long as they make non-negative profits. Also, to begin, we assume that there is at most one firm in each country.

2.4. Demand

The industry in question is assumed to be sufficiently small that income effects are negligible. We can think of a gross surplus function whose derivative is the inverse demand function:

$$\text{surplus} \quad W = W(X),$$

$$\text{demand} \quad W' = W'(X),$$

where W is assumed to be the same in both countries. W' is the price that clears quantity X.

2.5. The problem

Each firm must decide how much of the commodity to produce for domestic consumption and how much to export. We shall refer to the firm in A as the home firm and the firm in B as the foreign firm. Let

x = production by the home firm for domestic consumption,
y = production by the foreign firm for export to A,
u = production by the home firm for export to B,
v = production by the foreign firm for consumption in B,
X = total consumption in A, and
V = total consumption in B.

Then

$$X = x + gy \quad \text{and} \quad V = gu + v.$$

Let π = profits of the home firm and π^* = profits of the foreign firm.
Then

$$\pi = xW'(x+gy) - F - cx + guW'(gu+v) - cu \tag{1}$$

and

$$\pi^* = gyW'(x+gy) - F - cy + vW'(gu+v) - cv. \tag{2}$$

The home firm takes y and v as given and maximizes expression (1) with respect to x and u; the foreign firm takes x and u as given and maximizes expression (2) with respect to y and v. The four first-order conditions are the reaction functions and constitute four equations in four unknowns. Solutions to this system are Cournot equilibria, provided the second-order conditions are satisfied. The first-order conditions are:

$$\pi_x = 0 \rightarrow xW''(x+gy) + W'(x+gy) - c = 0, \tag{3}$$

$$\pi_y^* = 0 \rightarrow g^2yW''(x+gy) + gW'(x+gy) - c = 0, \tag{4}$$

$$\pi_u = 0 \rightarrow g^2uW''(gu+v) + gW'(gu+v) - c = 0, \tag{5}$$

$$\pi_v^* = 0 \rightarrow vW''(gu+v) + W'(gu+v) - c = 0. \tag{6}$$

This system of four equations in four unknowns can be partitioned into two separable subsystems. Eqs. (3) and (4) are two equations in two unknowns, x and y. Similarly, (5) and (6) are two equations in u and v. This separability property depends on the assumption of constant marginal cost, for if marginal cost depended on output, u would enter eq. (3), v would enter eq. (4), x would enter eq. (5), and y would enter eq. (6); so all four equations would be linked.

Also, the two subsystems are perfectly symmetric, so the set of solutions to the first is also the set of solutions to the second with $x=v$ and $y=u$. Therefore, we need consider only one subsystem. Let us consider the subsystem consisting of eqs. (1) and (2), which corresponds to the market in country A. We shall not consider the second-order conditions except to note that they are satisfied if the profit functions are continuous and concave. Given constant marginal cost, this is true in the positive quadrant if marginal revenue in each own product is downward sloping, which is certainly what we would expect. The only problem arises because profit is not continuous at zero output, due to fixed costs. Consequently, the local first- and second-order conditions are not sufficient to ensure a global maximum over the entire feasible range. Instead, each firm will calculate its local optimum and compare it with zero output. More simply, firms obey the first-order conditions provided that profits and output are non-negative at the solution. For most of the paper we shall assume this is the case.

We have two equations in two unknowns:

$$xW'' + W' - c = 0 = f(x,y)$$

and

$$g^2yW'' + gW' - c = 0 = h(x,y),$$

where f and h are two reaction functions in implicit form. There is no way of telling how many solutions exist, if any, and which are stable, if any, because the surplus function is unspecified. There are two strategies open. Either an explicit functional form for W may be specified or we can try to determine which minimum sets of restrictions on W imply which properties for the system. We shall follow the former course, chiefly because it is simpler.

2.6. Example

Assume W is quadratic. Then W' is linear and the two equations have a solution if the Jacobian matrix, J, associated with f and h, is non-singular:

$$J = \begin{bmatrix} f_1 & f_2 \\ h_1 & h_2 \end{bmatrix},$$

where the subscripts denote partial derivatives.

Surplus $\qquad W = aX - bX^2/2,$

where a and b are greater than zero.

Inverse demand $\qquad W' = a - bX,$

$$W'' = -b.$$

From the reaction functions f and h we have, using $X = x + gy$:

$$x + gy/2 + (c-a)/2b = 0 \qquad : \quad f(x,y) = 0,$$

$$x/2g + y + (c-ga)/2bg^2 = 0 \qquad : \quad h(x,y) = 0,$$

$$J = \begin{bmatrix} 1 & g/2 \\ 1/2g & 1 \end{bmatrix}.$$

Because the determinant of J is not zero, the equations have a solution. We have

$$J \cdot \begin{bmatrix} x \\ y \end{bmatrix} = \begin{bmatrix} (a-c)/2b \\ (ga-c)/2bg^2 \end{bmatrix}.$$

This Jacobian matrix is nothing more than the coefficient matrix of a linear system; the condition that the Jacobian be non-singular means that the two equations must be independent. We can solve the system using Cramer's rule:

$$x = (ga + c - 2gc)/3gb,$$

$$y = (ga + gc - 2c)/3g^2 b.$$

The only meaningful solutions are in the positive quadrant. Because negative production is ruled out we should have truncated the reaction functions at 0. We can at least read off the conditions on g and the parameters of the surplus function that imply a positive solution. For y to be positive we must have

$$g > 2c/(a + c).$$

Transport costs must be below a certain level before invasion will take place. (Transport costs fall as g rises.) If marginal cost were high relative to demand, $2c/(a+c)$ could be greater than one, in which case there would be no range of g that allowed invasion. However, if $2c/(a+c)$ actually were to exceed one, home production would not be profitable either. In other words, there is a range of g for which the home market is subject to invasion for any relevant level of demand.

This is a manifestation of the general result that, in a Cournot industry, low-cost firms do not drive out high-cost firms. In addition, as g approaches 1 (transport costs approach 0), x and y approach the Cournot equilibrium

$$x = y = (a - c)/3b.$$

It is easy to check the following derivatives:

$$dx/dg < 0,$$

$$d(gy)/dg > 0,$$

$$dX/dg > 0,$$

and that $x > gy$.

Thus, as transport costs fall, goods produced abroad make up a greater and greater share of domestic consumption, with the share approaching 1/2 as g approaches 1; also, total consumption rises as transport costs fall. As demand grows (a rises), the range of g for which invasion takes place increases, making cross-hauling more likely. Therefore, we can expect an increase in world income to increase the incidence of cross-hauling.

The two markets, one in country A and the other in country B, represented by the two subsystems of equations, are symmetric, as proven earlier. Therefore, there is two-way trade in this commodity despite the existence of transport costs. As pointed out by a referee, trade is arising from a 'dumping' or 'price discriminating' motivation. Imperfectly competitive firms set marginal revenue, not price, equal to marginal cost. Since each firm has a smaller share of the foreign market than of its domestic market, marginal revenue in the foreign market can exceed marginal revenue in the domestic market even when price is the same in both markets.

Thus, the firm can tolerate the higher effective marginal cost (including transport costs) of export production. This works in both directions, leading to cross-hauling. We shall now use this example to illustrate four characteristics of such trade:

(1) cross-hauling,
(2) inefficient scale,
(3) degree of competition, and
(4) variety

3. Characteristics of intra-industry trade

3.1. Cross-hauling

As just mentioned, the situation in country B is symmetric to that in A. The firm located in A exports to B and produces for its home market, while the firm in B exports to A and produces for its home market. In other words, the market equilibrium involves trade in spite of the fact that both countries produce exactly the same commodity, and there is an obvious loss due to transport costs. (We are assuming here that $2c/(a+c) < g < 1$ and that profits for each firm are non-negative. Clearly there are parameter values for which these assumptions are valid). This is the phenomenon of cross-hauling.

The same total consumption for each country could be achieved at lower total cost if each firm produced solely for its home market, which we might think of as a planning solution:

market solution

$$\text{total cost, } TC_m = 2F + 2(x+y)c;$$

planning solution

$$\text{total cost, } TC_p = 2F + 2(x+gy)c.$$

The difference between the two, $TC_m - TC_p$, is easily seen to be

$$(1-g)2y,$$

which is positive.

Allowing free entry has no particular bearing on the relevance of this result. Suppose, for example, that the two-firm equilibrium allowed, by coincidence, exactly normal profits. (There are certainly parameter values for which this is true.) Then there would be no incentive to enter and cross-hauling would exist even though there were no barriers to entry.

3.2. Inefficient scale

Average cost is strictly declining for both firms, yet there are two firms operating rather than one. If transport costs were sufficiently low the same consumption could be achieved at lower cost by concentrating all production in one country. Let the total costs in the market solution and the concentration solution be denoted TC_m and TC_c, respectively. Then

$$TC_m = 2F + 2(x+y)c,$$

$$TC_c = F + (x+gy)c + (x+gy)c/g,$$

$$TC_m > TC_c \Leftrightarrow F > c(gy + x/g - x - y).$$

The greater start-up costs are and the less transport costs are, the more likely concentration is to be efficient.

3.3. Degree of competition

It is fairly striking that trade is apparently inefficient and welfare-reducing. This welfare loss is with respect to a planning solution, however, and planning solutions generally have many hidden costs, not the least of which is the cost of gathering relevant information. If we compare market outcomes before and after trade, we find that trade can be welfare-improving because of increased competition.

Suppose initially that $g=0$, so there is no trade. Perhaps there are prohibitive tariffs. Each firm takes the other's output as zero and acts as a monopolist:

$$\pi = xW'(x) - F - cx,$$

$$\pi' = 0 \rightarrow x = (a-c)/2b.$$

Assuming that a exceeds c and that profits are non-negative, the total consumption in A (and in B for that matter) under autarky, X_a, is $(a-c)/2b$. Suppose now that g rises to a level at which trade is feasible. The total amount consumed in A under trade, X_t, is $x+gy$, where x and y are the solution values to the original problem.

$$X_t = x + gy = (ga + c - 2gc)/3gb + g(ga + gc - 2c)/3bg^2$$

$$= (2ga - gc - c)/3gb,$$

$$X_t - X_a = (2ga - gc - c)/3gb - (a - c)/2b$$

$$= gy/2.$$

In the range where $y > 0$, the trading range, we have $X_t > X_a$, so consumption of the commodity is unambiguously increased by trade. That is, trade has a production-creating effect which is welfare improving. A lower bound on the welfare improvement is $(p - c/g)gy/2$, using surplus measures. However, trade also has a production-diverting effect in that domestic production falls and is replaced by higher cost foreign production. The amount of production diversion is also $gy/2$ and the welfare cost is $(c/g - c)gy/2$. Therefore, a lower bound on the net welfare improvement is

$$(p - c/g)gy/2 - (c/g - c)gy/2 = pgy/2 - cy(2 - g)/2.$$

This must exceed 0 if $g > 2c/(p+c)$. Since $2c/(p+c) < 1$, there is a range of g for which trade is definitely welfare improving.

To restate: trade increases quantity consumed and decreases price, and consequently reduces the monopoly distortion. Welfare increases for sufficiently low transport costs despite the existence of cross-hauling. This can be offered as a possible justification of the claim that tariff reductions, within the EEC for example, have increased welfare by increasing the level of competition.

3.4. Variety

So far we have not been concerned about whether the commodity will be produced at all. It is quite possible that under autarky neither location could support production of the commodity by itself, but that after trade, one firm could be supported. In order to interpret this as an increase in variety, suppose that there are several products under consideration and that the surplus function is additive:

$$W(X_1, \ldots, X_n) = W_1(X_1) + \ldots + W_n(X_n).$$

In this context, the emergence of X_1 after trade opens can be interpreted as an increase in product variety. Such an increase unambiguously increases welfare: gross surplus exceeds gross revenue to the firm (revenue is taken from the surplus), and revenue must exceed cost in order for the firm to stay in business. Therefore, surplus exceeds cost and welfare is improved.

3.5. Limit pricing

In this section we see that the Cournot strategy may yield higher profits to both firms than another strategy, the limit-pricing strategy. The limit-pricing strategy involves having the domestic firm set price sufficiently low that the foreign firm cannot compete. In order to set the limit price efficiently, the domestic firm would like to know the foreign firm's strategy. However, if the domestic firm remains agnostic about the foreign firm's strategy it can prevent invasion by setting price at the foreign firm's marginal cost of selling one unit in the domestic firm's country. In our example, this marginal cost is c/g. That is to say, to sell a unit in the home country the foreign firm must produce $1/g$ units because only $g(1/g)=1$ unit survives transport. The marginal cost of producing $1/g$ units is, of course, c/g. Note that if the foreign firm follows the Cournot strategy then c/g is the true limit price.

Assume that the domestic firm sets price at c/g as its limit-pricing strategy. We then have

$$\pi = xW'(x) - F - cx,$$

where $W' = c/g$. We can calculate the implied x and π:

$$x = (ga - c)/bg,$$

$$\pi = c((1/g) - 1)(ga - c)/bg - F.$$

Observe that as g approaches 1, profits approach $-F$, because the limit price approaches marginal cost. Thus, it should not surprise us that the limit-pricing strategy should be inferior to the Cournot strategy for some parameter values. For example, suppose

$$c = 0.1; \qquad g = 0.9; \qquad a = 1.0; \qquad b = 0.1.$$

Under the limit-pricing strategy profits are $0.1 - F$ (assuming both firms limit price).

Under the Cournot strategy we have:

$$x = v = 3.04,$$

$$gy = gu = 2.93,$$

$$X = V = 5.97,$$

$$W' = 0.4$$

$$\pi = 1.76 - F.$$

Accepting the Cournot equilibrium is far better for the firms than limit pricing. This will be the case whenever $(a - c)$ is large, b is small, and g is close to 1. This is given as a (slight) defence of the Cournot strategy.

3.6. Behaviour as the number of firms increases

So far the analysis has been carried out under the assumption that there is exactly one firm in each country. We might wonder about the effects of assuming that more firms might enter. The behaviour of Cournot industries as the number of firms increases has been carefully studied. Friedman (1977) summaries the results and has an extensive bibliography. Of particular interest is an article by Ruffin (1971), in which the conditions under which Cournot industries converge to competitive equilibria are examined. Ruffin makes clear that the question of convergence to the competitive position should be distinguished from the question of quasi-competitiveness. An industry is said to be quasi-competitive if increasing the number of firms causes the quantity sold to increase (and the price to fall). Very few completely general things can be said about Cournot industries. They do not necessarily converge to competitive equilibria, they are not necessarily quasi-competitive, equilibria may not exist, and even if equilibria do exist they may not be stable. General statements can be made for certain classes of cost and demand functions, and the reader is referred to Friedman (1977) and the references cited there for further discussion of general results. Cournot industries are usually quasi-competitive in the relevant ranges but rarely converge to competitive equilibria.

We shall now examine the properties of the particular model under consideration here. Suppose, first, that we allow free entry in each country before trade takes place. Each firm sets marginal revenue equal to marginal cost and firms enter until profits are driven to their normal level. Let

x = output of a representative firm,

n = the number of firms, and

$X = nx$ = total output.

We shall examine the problem of a representative firm, assuming that the equilibrium is symmetric. Finding such an equilibrium ensures that a symmetric equilibrium exists, but does not rule out the possibility that asymmetric equilibria may exist. However, the solution to our model is the solution to n independent linear equations in n unknowns; consequently, the symmetric equilibrium is the only equilibrium. The solution is:

$x = (a-c)/b(n+1)$,

$X = n(a-c)/b(n+1)$,

$n = (a-c)/(bF)^{\frac{1}{2}} - 1$.

At this equilibrium each firm equates marginal cost and marginal revenue, which is below price, so price exceeds marginal cost. Let

$h = MC/p$.

Each country has the same equilibrium. If we now admit the possibility of trade, we observe that for sufficiently low transport costs, specifically for $g > h$, each firm has an incentive, under the Cournot perception, to invade the market in the other country. Therefore, the free entry no trade position cannot be an equilibrium. The new equilibrium will involve cross-hauling.

The next step is to consider the behaviour of the after-trade equilibrium as the number of firms increases. Consider a representative firm. The profit of this firm is:

$$\pi = px + gp^*x^* - cx - cx^* - F,$$

where

p = $a - bX$ = domestic price,

p^* = foreign price,

x = output for domestic market, and

x^* = output for foreign market.

Consider a representative domestic firm and a representative foreign firm operating in the domestic market. (The two markets can be considered separately.) We can write down the appropriate first-order condition for each. (By symmetry, x^* also equals the output of the foreign firm for export to the domestic market.)

$$p + x \, dp/dx - c = 0, \qquad \text{domestic firm,}$$

$$gp + gx^* \, dp/dx^* - c = 0, \quad \text{foreign firm.}$$

We can solve these two equations for x and x^* given $X = n(x + gx^*)$. The solution has the following properties:

(1) $x^* > 0$ (for $g > c(n+1)/(a+nc)$),

(2) $dX/dn > 0$, and

(3) $d(gx^*/x)/dn < 0$.

The first property indicates that cross-hauling may exist even if n is large. Property 2 shows that this model is quasi-competitive: as n increases quantity consumed increases and price falls. However, property 3 shows that the ratio of cross-hauling to domestic production falls as n increases. As transport costs fall, of course, the portion of cross-hauling rises. Thus, if we interpret a fall in transport costs as an increase in the extent of the market, we can say that cross-hauling increases as the extent of the market increases.

4. Conclusions

It is sometimes argued that trade in similar goods arises because of minor product differences, differences that are too fine to show in international trade data, but which are significant to consumers. Presumably France and Germany exchange Renaults and Porsches because the products are slightly different. For the sake of clarity, however, we should first consider whether trade might arise even in identical commodities. Apparently it might.

There are some caveats. The model here has been described and interpreted as a model of trade. However, as pointed out by a referee, we would obtain precisely the same result if each firm operated a low cost plant at home and a high cost plant abroad, without trade taking place.

Secondly, the assumption that each firm assumes the other firm keeps output in each of its markets constant is crucial and perhaps not realistic. An alternative assumption that could lead to different results is that firms expect other firms to keep total output fixed and divide total output in the most profitable way between the two markets.

Nevertheless, the paper demonstrates that if firms do act as Cournot firms in each market separately, cross-hauling can emerge even in identical products and also, that such trade can be welfare improving.

References

Clarke, J.M., 1943, Imperfect competition theory and basing point problems, American Economic Review 33, 283–300.

Dornbusch, R., Fischer, S. and Samuelson, P., 1977, Comparative advantage, trade and payments in a Ricardian model with a continuum of goods, American Economic Review 67, 823–839.

Friedman, J., 1977, Oligopoly and the theory of games (North-Holland, New York).

Giersch, H., 1979, On the economics of intra-industry trade: Symposium (Mohr, Tubingen).

Grubel, H. and Lloyd, P.J., 1975, Intra-industry trade (Wiley, New York).

Krugman, P., 1979, Increasing returns, monopolistic competition and international trade, Journal of International Economics 9, 469–479.

Ruffin, R.J., 1971, Cournot oligopoly and competitive behaviour, Review of Economic Studies 38, 493–502.

Spence, A.M., 1976, Product selection, fixed costs, and monopolistic competition, Review of Economic Studies 43, 217–235.

[16]

Journal of International Economics 29 (1990) 23–42. North-Holland

INTERNATIONAL CAPACITY CHOICE AND NATIONAL MARKET GAMES

Anthony J. VENABLES*

University of Southampton, Southampton, SO9 5NH, UK

Received August 1988, revised version received September 1989

International trade is modelled as a two-stage game between firms in different countries. At the first stage firms choose their capacity and at the second stage play a separate price game in each national market, given their worldwide capacity. It is established that firms use capacity strategically in order to manipulate the distribution of rivals' output between markets. The volume of intra-industry trade is intermediate between the cases of integrated and segmented market Cournot equilibria. Countries gain from small import tariffs and export subsidies, but these gains are less than in the segmented market Cournot equilibrium case.

1. Introduction

In order to model firms as oligopolists competing in international markets it is necessary to specify the set of strategies available to firms. One aspect of this is whether firms are assumed to be playing a game in quantities or prices; the non-cooperative Nash equilibrium leading to Cournot and Bertrand outcomes, respectively. A second aspect, peculiar to trade theory, is whether firms are permitted to select strategies for each national market, or merely to choose a strategy at the world level. The former case is referred to as the segmented market hypothesis, and the latter the integrated market hypothesis. Neither the integrated nor the segmented market hypothesis is entirely satisfactory. Integration implies that producers set a single quantity (or price) at the world level, and let arbitrageurs determine the distribution of sales to national markets [e.g. Markusen (1981)]. This does not seem a realistic representation of firms' sales decisions. At the other extreme, segmented market behaviour, when combined with constant marginal costs, implies that the game played between firms in one country is completely separate from the game that the firms are playing in other countries [e.g. Brander (1981), Brander and Krugman (1983), Dixit (1984)]. The total

*Much of this work was done while visiting the Faculty of Commerce at the University of British Columbia; I am grateful for their support. The paper has benefited from the comments of participants in seminars at the Universities of British Columbia, Southampton, Sussex, Warwick, the London School of Economics, and the Norwegian School of Economics and Business Administration, and from the comments of anonymous referees.

0022–1996/90/$03.50 © 1990—Elsevier Science Publishers B.V. (North-Holland)

absence of any interaction between national markets again seems unsatisfactory.

A more satisfactory treatment is to recognise that some of the firms' decisions are taken on an integrated, or worldwide, basis, and others on a segmented market basis. The most natural variable in the former category is firms' capacity choice, since a unit of capacity can be used to supply any country. In the latter category, we may wish to leave some of firms' market decisions (price or sales) to be taken on a national basis. Given a separation of capacity and market decisions it is also natural to model the former as preceding the latter. The goal of this paper is to model trade as the perfect Nash equilibrium of a two-stage game between firms located in different countries, in which each firm chooses world capacity at the first stage of the game, and at the second stage makes market decisions conditional upon this installed level of capacity.

Three models are presented in the paper. In all cases the first stage of the game involves choice of capacity under the integrated markets hypothesis. In the first model (model I) the second-stage game is also played under the integrated market hypothesis, and simply involves firms selling their entire capacity output on world markets. In the second model (model C) the second stage game is segmented market and Cournot, so firms choose the quantities they sell in each country, taking as given other firms' sales in each country. The final model (model B) has firms playing a segmented market price game at the second stage. This model is the most interesting of those presented. The characterisation of oligopoly as price competition subject to capacity constraints is intuitively appealing, and the model captures rich interaction between markets. This model constitutes a generalisation of the work of Kreps and Scheinkman (1983) to a two-market framework, a generalisation also undertaken by Ben-Zvi and Helpman (1988). Unlike these papers, the present paper works with differentiated products, so avoiding the discontinuities associated with capacity constrained price games with homogeneous products.

This paper is organised as follows. Section 2 sets out assumptions and notation used throughout the paper. Sections 3–5 characterise the perfect Nash equilibrium of games (I), (C) and (B), respectively. The equilibria are compared and discussed in section 6. It is established that the different equilibria support different volumes of trade, and possibly also different levels of output. Section 7 investigates the effects of import tariffs and export subsidies in the three different equilibria.

2. The model

There are two countries, denoted A and B. The model is one of partial equilibrium, and we denote the home and export sales of country A output by x and x^*, respectively, and the home and export sales of country B output by y and y^*. Demands are derived from a single strictly concave aggregate utility function in each country, $u^A(x, y^*)$ and $u^B(y, x^*)$. Prices of each good in each country are given by the partial derivatives u_x^A, u_y^A, u_x^B, and u_y^B. We permit products x and y to be differentiated, in order to ensure positive levels of trade in all cases, and to ensure continuity of firms' demand functions when prices are chosen non-cooperatively. Permitting the form of product differentiation to be quite general does not always yield transparent results, so the following assumption will sometimes be employed.

Assumption 1.

$$u^A(x, y^*) = \Phi(x + y^*) + \alpha x y^*, \qquad u^B(y, x^*) = \Phi(y + x^*) + \alpha y x^*,$$

$$\phi \equiv \Phi' \geq 0, \quad \alpha \geq 0, \quad \phi' \leq 0, \quad \phi' + \alpha \leq 0,$$

so that

$$u_x^A = \phi(x + y^*) + \alpha y^*, \qquad u_y^B = \phi(y + x^*) + \alpha x^*,$$

$$u_y^A = \phi(x + y^*) + \alpha x, \qquad u_x^B = \phi(y + x^*) + \alpha y,$$

$$u_{xx}^A = u_{yy}^A = \phi'(x + y^*), \qquad u_{yy}^B = u_{xx}^B = \phi'(y + x^*),$$

$$u_{xy}^A = \phi'(x + y^*) + \alpha, \qquad u_{yx}^B = \phi'(y + x^*) + \alpha.$$

Products are identical if $\alpha = 0$, in which case Assumption 1 imposes no restrictions on the utility function. If products are differentiated, then $\alpha > 0$ and $\phi' + \alpha < 0$, so that goods are substitutes, and cross elasticities of demand are of smaller absolute value than are own elasticities. The restriction imposed by Assumption 1 is that price differences $(u_x^A - u_y^A)$ are linear in quantity differences, so that second-order partial derivatives, u_{xx}^A and u_{xy}^A, differ only by a constant, and all third-order partial derivatives of the utility function are equal. Notice that if Φ is quadratic, then these preferences reduce to linear demands.

Each economy contains a single firm. The capacities of the firm in country A and of that in B are denoted X and Y, respectively, and the cost of installing a unit of capacity is k in both countries. Each firm can produce up to its capacity at zero marginal cost, and there are trade costs t_x associated with shipping a unit of x^* from A to B, and t_y for shipping y^* from B to A. The profits of the country A firm are:

$$\pi^A = x u_x^A(x, y^*) + x^* \{ u_x^B(y, x^*) - t_x \} - kX. \tag{1}$$

π^B is defined analogously.

Our method for analysing each of the equilibria below is as follows. First, the equilibrium of the second-stage game is characterised. This determines market sales, x, y, x^*, and y^*, given capacities X and Y. We then analyse the first-stage game in which each firm chooses its capacity given its rival's capacity, and incorporating the changes in x, y, x^*, and y^* which maintain equilibrium in the second-stage game. The first-order condition for the choice of capacity by the country A firm is an equation of the form:

$$\frac{d\pi^A}{dX} = \{u_x^A + xu_{xx}^A\} \cdot \frac{dx}{dX} + xu_{xy}^A \cdot \frac{dy^*}{dX}$$

$$+ \{u_x^B - t_x + x^*u_{xx}^B\} \cdot \frac{dx^*}{dX} + x^*u_{xy}^B \cdot \frac{dy}{dX} - k = 0, \qquad (2)$$

in which the terms dx/dX, dx^*/dX, dy/dX, and dy^*/dX are specific to the form of the second-stage game.

Some results will be evaluated around a symmetric equilibrium with full capacity utilisation. We refer to this as Assumption 2.

Assumption 2.   Symmetry: utility functions u^A and u^B are the same,

$$t_x = t_y = t, \quad \text{and} \quad X = x + x^*, \qquad Y = y + y^*.$$

At a symmetric equilibrium with full capacity utilisation it will be the case that

$$y = x, \qquad y^* = x^*, \qquad X = Y = x + x^* = y + y^*, \qquad (3)$$

and

$$u_x^A = u_y^B, \qquad u_y^A = u_x^B, \qquad u_{xx}^A = u_{yy}^B, \qquad u_{yy}^A = u_{xx}^B, \qquad u_{xy}^A = u_{xy}^B.$$

Notice that if we impose Assumptions 1 and 2, then the first-order condition for optimal choice of capacity is obtained by using Assumption 1 and (3) in eq. (2) to give:

$$\phi(X) + \alpha x + (X - x)\phi'(X) - t + [(X - 2x)(\alpha - \phi'(X)) + t] \cdot dx/dX$$

$$+ (X - 2x)(\phi'(X) + \alpha) \cdot dy/dX = k. \qquad (4)$$

We are now in a position to analyse equilibrium for each form of the second-stage game.

3. Integrated markets

The integrated market hypothesis means that each firm chooses a total volume of world sales, and the allocation of sales to markets is determined by an arbitrage condition stating that the domestic price of each good must equal the export price net of trade costs. Provided that marginal revenue at full capacity output is non-negative, capacity will be fully used so $x^* = X - x$, $y^* = Y - y$, and the second-stage equilibrium is characterised by the two equations:

$$u_x^A(x, Y - y) = u_x^B(y, X - x) - t_x,$$

$$u_y^B(y, X - x) = u_y^A(x, Y - y) - t_y. \qquad (5)$$

With Assumptions 1 and 2 [using eqs. (3)] these can be solved to derive an explicit expression for domestic sales in terms of capacity, trade costs, and a demand parameter:

$$x = [X + t/\alpha]/2, \begin{cases} \text{if } t/\alpha \leq X, \\ \\ \text{else } x = X. \end{cases} \qquad (6)$$

Domestic consumption is therefore one-half of output if products are differentiated and trade costs are zero. Higher trade costs or a lower value of α reduce the volume of intra-industry trade (raises x) up to a point where trade is zero.

In the first-stage game each firm chooses capacity. The effect of changes in capacity on sales is obtained by total differentiation of the two equilibrium conditions characterising the second stage. These differentials will be written as:

$$a_1 \, dx + a_2 \, dy + a_3 \, dX + a_4 \, dY = 0,$$

$$b_1 \, dy + b_2 \, dx + b_3 \, dY + b_4 \, dX = 0. \qquad (7)$$

This pair of equations can be solved to give:

$$dx/dX = \{a_2 b_4 - b_1 a_3\}/\{a_1 b_1 - a_2 b_2\},$$

$$dy/dX = \{b_2 a_3 - a_1 b_4\}/\{a_1 b_1 - a_2 b_2\}. \qquad (8)$$

With full capacity utilisation and Y constant we also have:

$$dx^*/dX = 1 - dx/dX, \qquad dy^*/dX = -dy/dX. \tag{9}$$

Under the integrated markets hypothesis the coefficients a_i and b_i are derived from total differentiation of eqs. (5), giving:

$$a_1 = u_{xx}^A + u_{xx}^B, \qquad b_1 = u_{yy}^B + u_{yy}^A,$$

$$a_2 = -u_{xy}^A - u_{xy}^B, \qquad b_2 = -u_{xy}^B - u_{xy}^A, \tag{10}$$

$$a_3 = -u_{xx}^B, \qquad b_3 = -u_{yy}^A,$$

$$a_4 = u_{xy}^A, \qquad b_4 = u_{xy}^B.$$

Using eqs. (10) in (8) and (9) gives the change in sales when firm A capacity, X, is perturbed. In general all sales change following the change in X, and the effects cannot, unambiguously, be signed. For example, the sign of dy/dX is equal to the sign of $\{u_{xx}^B u_{xy}^A - u_{xx}^A u_{xy}^B\}$. This depends on curvatures of two different utility functions, each evaluated at different points. Imposing symmetry alone does not resolve the ambiguity, as u_{xx}^A and u_{xx}^B are not equal. We therefore proceed with the central case in which Assumptions 1 and 2 hold. In this case eqs. (10) become:

$$a_1 = b_1 = 2\phi', \qquad a_3 = b_3 = -\phi', \tag{11}$$

$$a_2 = b_2 = -2(\phi' + \alpha), \qquad a_4 = b_4 = \phi' + \alpha,$$

so we derive [using eqs. (11) in (8)]:

$$dx/dX = dx^*/dX = 1/2 \quad \text{and} \quad dy/dX = dy^*/dX = 0. \tag{12}$$

The optimal capacity choice may now be obtained by using these derivatives in the first-order condition for profit maximisation, i.e. using (12) in (2), to give:

$$\frac{d\pi^A}{dX} = \frac{1}{2}[u_x^A + xu_{xx}^A] + \frac{1}{2}[u_x^B + (X - x)u_{xx}^B - t_x] - k = 0. \tag{13}$$

Using Assumptions 1 and 2 again [with eqs. (3)], this first-order condition reduces to:

$$\phi(X) + X[\alpha + \phi'(X)]/2 = k + t/2. \tag{14}$$

This equation implicitly defines the equilibrium capacity level, X. We assume that t/α is small enough for trade to occur, and that the left-hand side of the equation is strictly decreasing in X so that higher k reduces equilibrium capacity.

4. Cournot equilibrium with segmented markets

With segmented markets and Cournot behaviour firms choose the quantity of sales in each market, taking as constant the rival's sales in each market. In the second-stage game capacity is taken as given so the necessary conditions for profit maximisation are that firms equate the marginal revenue, net of trade costs, that they derive in each market. Assuming full capacity utilisation (i.e. non-negative marginal revenue), maximisation of profits gives the first-order condition:

$$d\pi^A/dx = u_x^A(x, Y - y) + x u_{xx}^A(x, Y - y)$$

$$- \{u_x^B(y, X - x) + (X - x)u_{xx}^B(y, X - x) - t_x\} = 0. \tag{15}$$

A similar equation holds for country B. Employing Assumptions 1 and 2, we may solve for the second-stage equilibrium level of domestic sales:

$$x = \{X + t/[\alpha - \phi']\}/2, \begin{cases} \text{if } t/(\alpha - \phi') \leqq X, \\ \text{else } x = X. \end{cases} \tag{16}$$

In order to find the equilibrium of the first-stage game we proceed as in the preceding section. Second-stage equilibrium conditions [eqs. (15)] are totally differentiated, and the coefficients a_i of eq. (7) are:

$$a_1 = 2u_{xx}^A + x u_{xxx}^A + 2u_{xx}^B + (X - x)u_{xxx}^B = 4\phi' + X\phi'',$$

$$a_2 = -[u_{xy}^A + x u_{xxy}^A + u_{xy}^B + (X - x)u_{xxy}^B] = -[2(\phi' + \alpha) + X\phi''],$$

$$a_3 = -[2u_{xx}^B + (X - x)u_{xxx}^B] = -[2\phi' + (X - x)\phi''], \tag{17}$$

$$a_4 = u_{xy}^A + x u_{xxy}^A = \phi' + \alpha + x\phi''.$$

The right-hand set of equations in (17) are by obtained imposing Assumptions 1 and 2. Coefficients b_i are symmetric to a_i, i.e. have superscripts A and B and subscripts x and y interchanged. As before we may solve for the change in sales when capacity changes by using these equations. dx/dX is non-zero, but since x has been optimised in the second-stage game, a small change dx is of no value to the country A firm [as may be confirmed by using (15) in (2)]; this term may therefore be ignored. The change in the country B firm's allocation of output between markets is complex, and we report it here for the case where Assumptions 1 and 2 are imposed:

$$\frac{dy}{dX} = \frac{\phi''(2x - X)}{4(\alpha - \phi')} = -\frac{dy^*}{dX}. \tag{18}$$

Country A capacity choice therefore has a strategic role in that it influences the second-stage equilibrium values of B's sales. Optimal capacity choice is now found by using eq. (18) in the first-order condition for profit maximisation, (4), and simplifying with (16). We find that the symmetric equilibrium value of X is implicitly defined by:

$$\phi(X) + \frac{X[\alpha + \phi'(X)]}{2} = k + \frac{t}{2} - \frac{\phi''(X)t^2(\phi'(X) + \alpha)}{4(\phi'(X) - \alpha)^3}. \tag{19}$$

The symmetric equilibrium is therefore characterised by eqs. (16) and (19). The final term on the right-hand side of eq. (19) gives the 'strategic' role of capacity, i.e. the incentive for firms to use capacity to change the distribution of rivals' output between markets. Interpretation of this term will be discussed in section 6.

Notice that if behaviour were non-strategic, i.e. firms ignore the effect of their capacity on the distribution of rivals' output so that dy/d$X = 0$, then the first-order condition for capacity choice is as in the preceding section, eq. (14). The non-strategic Cournot segmented market equilibrium which has been extensively analysed in the literature, [e.g. Brander (1981), Brander and Krugman (1983), Dixit (1984)] is therefore characterised by eqs. (16) and (14).

5. Bertrand equilibrium with segmented markets

We now consider the case in which the equilibrium of the second-stage game is a Nash equilibrium in prices. Each firm chooses its price in each market given capacity, and taking as given its rival's prices and capacity. We assume throughout this section that products are differentiated so that the demand for each firm's output is a strictly decreasing and continuous function of its own price. This permits the firm's optimisation problem to be modelled as a choice of quantities. Assuming full capacity utilisation, in the second-stage game firm A therefore chooses x to maximise profits:

$$\pi^A = x u_x^A(x, y^*) + [X - x]\{u_x^B(y, X - x) - t_x\} - kX, \tag{20}$$

subject to the following constraints:

$$u_y^B(y, X - x) = \bar{u}_y^B, \tag{21}$$

$$u_y^A(x, y^*) = \bar{u}_y^A, \tag{22}$$

where $\bar{u}_y^A$ and $\bar{u}_y^B$ are firm B's prices in the two markets. If constraints (21) and (22) hold, then a change dx must give rise to changes in y and y^* of the form:

$$dy/dx = u_{yx}^B/u_{yy}^B, \qquad dy^*/dx = -u_{yx}^A/u_{yy}^A. \tag{23}$$

Profit maximisation therefore gives the first-order condition

$$d\pi^A/dx = u_x^A + xu_{xx}^A - \{u_x^B - t_x + (X - x)u_{xx}^B\}$$

$$+ (X - x)u_{xy}^B\{u_{xy}^B/u_{yy}^B\} - xu_{xy}^A\{u_{yx}^A/u_{yy}^A\} = 0. \tag{24}$$

Before proceeding we need to establish the effect of the changes dy and dy^* on the total demand for firm B's output and check that this is consistent with firm B's capacity. From a point where both firms are at full capacity, B stays at full capacity as x is varied if $dy/dx + dy^*/dx = 0$. If this equation should fail, then firm A must take into account in its optimisation the fact that some consumers of firm B's output may be rationed. Assume Assumption 1; the derivatives (23) then take the form;

$$dy/dx = u_{yx}^B/u_{yy}^B = 1 + \alpha/\phi'(y + X - x),$$

$$dy^*/dx = -u_{yx}^A/u_{yy}^A = -\{1 + \alpha/\phi'(x + y^*)\}. \tag{25}$$

As is apparent from adding these equations, Assumption 1 plus Assumption 2 (implying that $y + X - x = x + y^*$), ensure that the change dx can induce changes in y and y^* which simultaneously hold both the rival's prices constant *and* leaves the total demand for its output unchanged. Rationing of consumers is avoided.

Assumption 1 will be maintained for the rest of this section. With this assumption the first-order condition, eq. (24), takes the form:

$$\phi(x + y^*) + (y^* - y)\alpha + x\phi'(x + y^*) - \phi(y + X - x)$$

$$+ t_x - (X - x)\phi'(y + X - x)$$

$$+ (X - x)\{\alpha + \phi'(y + X - x)\}^2/\phi'(y + X - x)$$

$$-x\{\alpha+\phi'(x+y^*)\}^2/\phi'(x+y^*)=0. \tag{26}$$

Further imposing Assumption 2 gives an explicit equation for the volume of trade, given capacity:

$$x=\tfrac{1}{2}\left[X+\frac{t\phi'(X)}{\alpha(3\phi'(X)+\alpha)}\right], \quad \text{if } \frac{t\phi'(X)}{\alpha(3\phi'(X)+\alpha)}\leq X,$$

$$\text{else } x=X. \tag{27}$$

In order to find the equilibrium of the first-stage game we proceed as before, totally differentiating the equilibrium conditions of the second-stage game, (26). Evaluating these derivatives at the symmetric equilibrium with full capacity utilisation gives:

$$a_1=b_1=2\phi'-2\alpha(2+\alpha/\phi')+X(\alpha/\phi')^2\phi'',$$

$$a_2=b_2=-2\phi'-2\alpha-X(\alpha/\phi')^2\phi'',$$

$$a_3=b_3=-\phi'+\alpha(2+\alpha/\phi')-(X-x)(\alpha/\phi')^2\phi'', \tag{28}$$

$$a_4=b_4=\phi'+\alpha+x(a/\phi')^2\phi''.$$

The effect of the change dX on the distribution of output between markets can be established by using these in eq. (8) to give:

$$\frac{dy}{dX}=\frac{(2x-X)\alpha\phi''}{4(3\phi'+\alpha)\phi'}=\frac{-dy^*}{dX},$$

$$\frac{dx}{dX}=\tfrac{1}{2}+\frac{(2x-X)\alpha\phi''}{4(3\phi'+\alpha)\phi'}. \tag{29}$$

Notice, that the change dX destroys symmetry, yet symmetry was used in the construction of the second-stage equilibrium in order to establish that the changes, dy/dx and dy^*/dx, which held firm B's prices constant also held the total demand for its output constant. However, eqs. (29) imply that

$$\frac{d(y+X-x)}{dX}=\frac{d(x+y^*)}{dX}=\tfrac{1}{2},$$

that is, the arguments of both countries' utility functions, $\Phi(y+X-x)$ and

$\Phi(x + y^*)$, change by identical amounts as X varies. The derivatives, dy/dx and dy^*/dx, given by eqs. (25) therefore sum to zero, not only at the symmetric equilibrium, but also as X is varied around this point. This means that firm A does not have to take into account the possibility that firm B's consumers become rationed as it changes either x, or X, in the neighbourhood of a symmetric equilibrium. This property depends on Assumption 1.

We may now complete characterisation of the first-stage equilibrium by using eqs. (29) in the first-order condition for capacity choice, eq. (4). After some rearrangement we find that the symmetric equilibrium value of X is implicitly defined by:

$$\phi(X) + \frac{X[\alpha + \phi'(X)]}{2} = k + \frac{t}{2} - \frac{\phi''(X)t^2(\phi'(X) + \alpha)}{4(3\phi'(X) + \alpha)^3}. \tag{30}$$

Once again, since dy/dX is non-zero, capacity choice has a strategic role which shows up as the final term in eq. (30).

6. Comparing the equilibria

Consider first the implications of the different second-stage equilibrium concepts for the allocation of output between markets, given capacity levels.

If Assumptions 1 and 2 are made, then we have explicit expressions for the volume of domestic sales and hence of trade. Using $x^* = X - x$ in eqs. (6), (16) and (27) gives:

$$x^*(\text{I}) = \max \{[X - t/\alpha]/2, 0\},$$

$$x^*(\text{B}) = \max \left\{ \left[X - \frac{t\phi'(X)}{\alpha(3\phi'(X) + \alpha)} \right]\tfrac{1}{2}, 0 \right\},$$

$$x^*(\text{C}) = \max \{[X - t/(\alpha - \phi'(X))]/2, 0\}.$$

Notice that if $t = 0$, then all cases are identical, with domestic and export sales being equal. If $t > 0$ and $\alpha \to 0$ (i.e. the degree of product differentiation goes to zero), then intra-industry trade is zero in cases (I) and (B) [as is established in Ben-Zvi and Helpman (1988)], but not in case (C). If products are differentiated, then increases in t reduce the volume of trade in all cases, but at different rates. Inspection of these equations reveals that for $t > 0$, $x^*(\text{I}) < x^*(\text{B}) < x^*(\text{C})$. This result can be stated in a manner which does not require Assumption 1.

Proposition 1 (Volume of trade). *Assume symmetry (Assumption 2), product* *differentiation, and that the utility function has the property* $x > y^* \Rightarrow$ $xu_{xx}(x, y^*) < y^* u_{yy}(x, y^*)$. *Suppose that capacity is the same in all cases, and that equilibria* (I), (C), *and* (B) *all have the same volume of trade with* $x > y^*$. *Then these equilibria must be supported by trade costs* $t(C) > t(B) > t(I) > 0$.

Proof. Under the terms of the proposition, utility functions are evaluated at the same quantities at all equilibria. We may therefore subtract equilibrium conditions for the second-stage equilibrium in cases (B) and (I) [eq. $(24)-(5)$] to give, [with (3)]:

$$t(B) - t(I) = \{(X - x)u_{yy}^A - xu_{yy}^B\}\{u_{xx}^A u_{yy}^A - u_{xy}^A u_{xy}^A\}/u_{yy}^A u_{yy}^B.$$

Similarly, subtracting second-stage equilibrium conditions in cases (C) and (B) [eq. $(24)-(15)$] gives:

$$t(C) - t(B) = \{(X - x)u_{yy}^A - xu_{yy}^B\}u_{xy}^B u_{xy}^B/\{u_{yy}^B u_{yy}^A\}.$$

With symmetry $(X - x)u_{yy}^A - xu_{yy}^B = y^* u_{yy}(x, y^*) - xu_{xx}(x, y^*)$ which is positive under the terms of the proposition. Using the strict concavity of the utility function, we have $t(B) - t(I) > 0$, and $t(C) - t(B) > 0$.

The direction of inequalities in Proposition 1 is of course dependent on the condition that $x > y^* \Rightarrow xu_{xx}(x, y^*) < yu_{yy}(x, y^*)$, and would be reversed if this inequality went the other way. This condition is not automatically satisfied by the restrictions of consumer theory or by any stability requirements. However, it is relatively weak, and is certainly satisfied if products are identical, or if Assumption 1 holds. It is best interpreted in the following way. Suppose there are Cournot duopolists supplying a single market, and the firm producing y^* has higher marginal cost than the firm producing x; the condition states that the difference between the firm's prices is less than the difference between their marginal costs, as may be readily verified by writing down the equality of marginal revenue to marginal cost for the two firms.

Since trade volumes are certainly decreasing in trade costs, Proposition 1 generalises the results that trade volumes are highest in case (C), followed by case (B) and lowest in case (I). The intuition behind these results is as follows. Suppose that the volume of trade is that of equilibrium (I), and consider the effect of switching one unit of country A output from domestic to export sales. In case (I) this can have no effect on prices or profits, as arbitrage occurs to hold the price difference between different markets equal to t. In case (B) the extra unit of export sales (given rival's prices) reduces firm A's export price and increases its price on domestic sales (by equal amounts in the case of linear demands). The fact that the volume of domestic sales is greater than the volume of export sales implies that profits are raised by such a change. In case (C) the extra unit of exports brings larger price changes, because the rival's sales in each market are conjectured to remain constant, and hence the rival's price will rise in market A, and fall in market B. The larger price changes associated with a unit increase in exports imply greater incentives to export and a higher equilibrium volume of trade.

The argument above is set out in terms of price changes. The quantity analogue is that, comparing cases (B) and (C), in the former each firm perceives that an increase in its exports will lead to an increase in imports to its home market, as the rival firm switches output between markets to hold prices constant. In the latter case, (C), this feedback effect is absent, increasing the incentive to export.

If capacity is the same at the three equilibria, then Proposition 1 has an immediate implication for welfare levels. Take as a country's welfare indicator, W, the sum of consumer surplus and profits, and suppose that trade costs, t, are real costs. With symmetry and holding capacity constant, the effect of an increase in the volume of trade, $dx^* = -dx = dy^* = -dy$, is:

$$dW/dx^* = -u_x^A + u_x^B - t. \tag{31}$$

This is zero at the integrated equilibrium [eq. (5)], and negative at equilibria with higher trade volumes (since u_x^A is increasing in x^* and u_x^B is decreasing in x^*), implying that $W(I) > W(B) > W(C)$. At the integrated equilibrium the difference between consumer prices in the two countries fully reflects the marginal cost of trade, whereas at (B) and (I) some of this cost is absorbed by firms, so there is more trade than is socially optimal (given capacity levels). Of course, this hinges on trade costs being real. If t were a transfer payment, then it would be deleted from eq. (31), and we would have $dW/dx^* > 0$ at all three equilibria, so $W(I) < W(B) < W(C)$.

We may now turn to considering the implications of the different equilibria for capacity. In general, cases (I), (C) and (B) support different levels of capacity, as summarised in the following proposition.

Proposition 2 (Capacity level). *Assume Assumptions 1 and 2. If $t > 0$ and the demand function is convex ($\phi'' > 0$) then $X(C) > X(B) > X(I)$. Inequalities are reversed if demand functions are concave.*

Proof. Equilibrium capacity levels are given by eqs. (14), (19) and (30), i.e.

$X(I)$ solves: $\phi(X) + X[\alpha + \phi'(X)]/2 = k + t/2,$

$X(B)$ solves: $\phi(X) + \dfrac{X[\alpha + \phi'(X)]}{2} = k + \dfrac{t}{2} - \dfrac{\phi''(X)t^2(\phi'(X) + \alpha)}{4(3\phi'(X) + \alpha)^3},$

$X(C)$ solves: $\phi(X) + \dfrac{X[\alpha + \phi'(X)]}{2} = k + \dfrac{t}{2} - \dfrac{\phi''(X)t^2(\phi'(X) + \alpha)}{4(\phi'(X) - \alpha)^3}.$

We assume that the left-hand side of these equations is decreasing in X, so the proposition is proved by comparison of the right-hand sides, noting that $\phi' < 0$, and $\phi' + \alpha < 0$.

The source of this result is that capacity has a strategic role, as it can influence the distribution of rivals' output between markets. To understand this, consider eqs. (29), giving the changes in x and y caused by a change in capacity X. Take $t > 0$, so $x > x^*$ and $2x - X > 0$. If demands are linear, then an increase in capacity, dX, causes an equal increase in sales of x in both markets, with $dx = dx^* = dX/2$. The increase in X therefore causes the difference, $x - x^*$, to remain constant, but reduces the ratio x/x^*. y and y^* remain unchanged. If demands are convex, then the increase in X raises x by more than x^*, so changing the difference, $x - x^*$, by more but the ratio x/x^* by less than was the case with linear demands. However, the fact that $dx > dx^*$ causes the reduction in y^* and increase in y. This reduction in foreign sales in firm A's domestic markets and the associated price change is of positive value to firm A, both because its home sales exceed its export sales, and because [in cases (C) and (B)] unit profits are higher on domestic sales than on export sales. If demands are concave this effect is reversed, since increasing X would increase x and x^* but reduces the difference between them, $x - x^*$, leading to an increase in y^* and reduction in y.

Fig. 1 is constructed from a numerical example computed to illustrate the quantitative difference between equilibria. The example takes an iso-elastic – and therefore convex – form for ϕ. Details of the example are given in appendix A. Curve $\tilde{X}$ in fig. 1 gives the level of capacity when there is no strategic interaction, but positive levels of trade [from eq. (14)]. $X(C)$ gives capacity when strategic interaction is recognised, and behaviour is Cournot [eq. (19)]. We see that the extra capacity induced by strategic behaviour is small, $X(C)$ reaching 105 percent of $\tilde{X}$ when trade costs are 30 percent of production costs. $X(B)$ (not illustrated) lies between $\tilde{X}$ and $X(C)$. The curves x^* trace out the volumes of intra-industry trade associated with each equilibrium, incorporating capacity differences between the equilibria. If $t = 0$, then the three equilibria coincide, but as t increases, the volume of trade

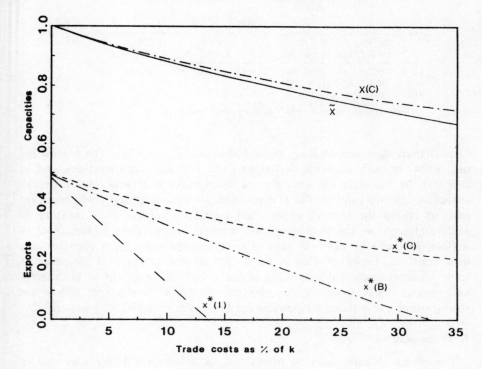

Fig. 1. Capacity and exports.

diminishes at very different rates. The different models therefore give quite different predictions about the volume of intra-industry trade, and about the effect of changes in tariffs or trade costs on this volume.

The numerical example also provides some illustrative information on the magnitudes of other variables of interest. For all values of trade costs given in fig. 1, profits, consumer surplus (*CS*) and their sum can be ranked as follows:

$$\pi(B) > \quad \pi(C) \quad > \pi(I),$$

$$CS(I) > \quad CS(C) \quad > CS(B),$$

$$CS(I) + \pi(I) > CS(B) + \pi(B) > CS(C) + \pi(C).$$

Profits are lowest when markets are integrated, as would be expected, as in this case firms do not have the ability to price discriminate. Second-stage quantity competition [case (C)] yields lower profits and higher consumer

Table 1

	du_x^A/dt_y $(=du_y^B/dt_x)$	du_y^A/dt_y $(=du_x^B/dt_x)$	du_x^B/dt_y $(=du_y^A/dt_x)$	du_y^B/dt_y $(=du_x^A/dt_x)$
(I)	$Db/2(b-\alpha)$	$D[3(b/(b-\alpha))^2-1]$	$Db/2(b-\alpha)$	$-D(b/(b-\alpha))^2$
(C)	$Db/(b-\alpha)$	$(1-D)/2$	0	0
(B)	$Db/(b-\alpha)$	$1/2$	0	$-D/2$

Note: $D=(b-\alpha)^2/(b+\alpha)(3b-\alpha)$, $1/3>D>0$, and $b-\alpha>0$.

surplus than does second-stage price competition [case (B)]. The reason for this is that in both cases the first-stage game is a game in quantities, and in case (C) the incentive for strategic use of capacity is greater, giving rise to somewhat greater total output (Proposition 2). Assuming that trade costs are real, so taking the sum of profits and consumer surplus as a measure of welfare change, we see that integrated markets supports the highest level of welfare, followed by case (B) then (C), as was the case when capacity was held constant. However, this is no longer a general result. Differences in trade volumes suggest this ranking of cases, but differences in total capacity and output levels work in the opposite direction. If strategic effects are strong enough it is therefore possible for the welfare ranking to be changed.

7. Trade policy

The effects of trade taxes on prices and on welfare are different in each of the above equilibria. In order to analyse policy we have to evaluate movements away from symmetric equilibria, and this is most easily done if attention is restricted to the case in which demand curves are linear. It is then possible to solve explicitly for equilibrium values of variables as functions of tax rates and other parameters. If demand is linear then Φ is quadratic, and we have:

Assumption 3.

$$u^A = a(x+Y-y)-b(x+Y-y)^2/2+\alpha x(Y-y),$$

$$u^B = a(y+X-x)-b(y+X-x)^2/2+\alpha y(X-x),$$

$$u_x^A = a-bx+(\alpha-b)(Y-y), \qquad u_y^A = a-b(Y-y)+(\alpha-b)x,$$

$$u_{xx}^A = u_{yy}^A = -b<0, \qquad u_{xy}^A = u_{yx}^A = \alpha-b<0.$$

Note that with linear demands ϕ'' is zero, so that strategic use of capacity is absent. Explicit solutions for variables in each of the equilibria are given in appendix B, together with notes on their derivation.

The effect of policy on prices can be obtained from eqs. (A5)–(A7) of the appendix. Equilibrium prices are linear in t_y and t_x, and their derivatives with respect to tax changes are set out in table 1.

A number of remarks may be made about table 1. First, the effect of a tariff change on a particular price never changes sign across equilibria.

Table 2

	C	B	I
Country A import tariff:			
$dW^A/dt_y =: Eb(3b-\alpha)$		$> E(5b^2-\alpha^2)/2$	$> Eb(5b-3\alpha)/2 > 0$
Country A export subsidy:			
$-dW^A/dt_x =: E(b-\alpha)^2$		$> E(b-\alpha)^2/2$	$> E(b^2-5\alpha b+2\alpha^2)/2$

Note: $E = (a-k)/\{(3b-\alpha)^2(b+\alpha)\} > 0$.

Second, in case (C) an import tariff only affects prices in the country employing the tariff. By contrast, in case (I) the effect of the tariff is felt in all markets, as it must be because of the arbitrage equations. Case (B) is intermediate, as the tariff changes both prices in the economy employing the tariff and, in addition, changes the domestic price of the good subject to the tariff. For example, the country A tariff on good y, dt_y, causes sales of y to be switched from country A to country B, reducing u_y^B. Notice also that the magnitudes of the price changes in case (B) always lie between the price changes in cases (I) and (C).

We evaluate the welfare effects of trade taxes using as welfare indicator the sum of profits, consumer surplus and government revenue for each country. Evaluated at the point where $t_x = t_y = 0$, the change in A's welfare caused by changes in country A import or export taxes is:

$$dW^A = x^* du_x^B - y^*(du_y^A - dt_y) + (u_x^A - k)\,dx + (u_x^B - k)\,dx^*.$$

The first two terms give terms of trade effects, and the second two the effect of the policy on changing the scale of domestic production, where this operates at price in excess of marginal cost. The welfare effects of small country A import tariffs and export subsidies can be obtained using price changes from table 1 above, together with quantity changes and levels of variables obtained from the appendix. Results are given in table 2.

The effect of a small tariff is to raise welfare in all cases. The export subsidy raises welfare in cases (C) and (B), but has an ambiguous effect in case (I), only raising welfare if products are relatively close substitutes, so α is small [for further discussion of the difference between cases (C) and (I), see Markusen and Venables (1988)]. Notice that the relative sizes of the welfare gains across equilibria have the same pattern for both policy instruments, with case (B) lying between cases (C) and (I).

8. Conclusions

Modelling the competitive interaction between firms located in different countries must be at the centre of the theory of trade under imperfect competition, yet most of the literature in this field has concentrated on two rather extreme cases – the cases of market integration and market segmentation. This paper proposes a new framework of analysis in which firms choose one strategic variable – capacity – at the world level, and others at the national market level. A two-stage game framework is developed, with capacity being chosen at the first stage, and three different types of second-stage game being studied. The most interesting of these cases is that in which worldwide capacity choice is followed by national market price competition. From analysis of this case three conclusions are derived. First, capacity has a strategic role in so far as choice of capacity at the first stage can influence the second-stage equilibrium distribution of firms' sales between markets. This result turns on curvature of demand functions, with equilibrium levels of capacity being higher if demand curves are convex. Second, if products are differentiated, then intra-industry trade occurs, and the volume of this trade is intermediate between the two cases most widely studied in the trade literature – integrated markets, and Cournot equilibrium with segmented markets. This means that an observed volume of trade is supported as an equilibrium with lower trade costs than would be the case if firms were playing a segmented market Cournot game. This has important implications for empirical research using models of imperfect competition to explain intra-industry trade [for example, Baldwin and Krugman (1988), Smith and Venables (1988)]. Third, policy analysis in this framework establishes that the effect of tariff policy is not restricted to the market in which the tariff is imposed, but spills over into other markets. There are welfare gains from the use of both import tariffs and export subsidies, and the size of the gains lie in between the gains achieved in the integrated market, and Cournot segmented market cases.

Appendix A: Numerical example

The example is computed with $\phi(x+y^*)=(x+y^*)^{-1/\varepsilon}$, $\varepsilon=2$, $\alpha=0.25$ and $k=1$. α measures product differentiation, and (given scaling of variables), $\alpha=0.25$ indicates a high (but variable) cross elasticity of demand. For example, at $t=10$ percent of k the export quantities illustrated in table 1 are supported by ratios of export prices to domestic prices of 1.014 (C), 1.026 (B) and 1.075 (I).

Appendix B

B.1. Second-stage equilibrium

We first solve the equations characterising equilibrium of the second-stage game in order to obtain sales as a function of parameters and firms' capacities. For the integrated market case, (I), use of Assumption 3 in eqs. (5) gives:

$$y(\text{I}) = [Y + \{bt_y + (b-\alpha)t_x\}/\{\alpha(2b-\alpha)\}]/2,$$

$$x(\text{I}) = [X + \{bt_x + (b-\alpha)t_y\}/\{\alpha(2b-\alpha)\}]/2. \tag{A.1}$$

In the Cournot case, (C) eq. (14), and the analogous equation for the firm in country B, can be solved to give:

$$y(\text{C}) = [Y + \{2bt_y + (b-\alpha)t_x\}/\{(3b-\alpha)(b+\alpha)\}]/2,$$

$$x(\text{C}) = [X + \{2bt_x + (b-\alpha)t_y\}/\{(3b-\alpha)(b+\alpha)\}]/2. \tag{A.2}$$

In the Bertrand case, (B), Assumption 3 implies that $dy/dx = -dy^*/dx = (b-\alpha)/b$. Even away from the symmetric equilibrium, changes in x therefore cause changes in y and y^* which hold $y + y^*$ constant. Eq. (24), and the analogous equation for the country B firm, can be solved to give:

$$y(\text{B}) = [Y + \{bt_y(2b^2 - (\alpha-b)^2) + b^2(b-\alpha)t_x\}/\{\alpha(2b-\alpha)(3b-\alpha)(b+\alpha)\}]/2,$$

$$x(\text{B}) = [X + \{bt_x(2b^2 - (\alpha-b)^2) + b^2(b-\alpha)t_y\}/\{\alpha(2b-\alpha)(3b-\alpha)(b+\alpha)\}]/2. \tag{A.3}$$

B.2. First-stage game

The effect of a change in capacity on market sales is the same in each of the second-stage equilibria, since in all cases $dy/dX = 0$ and $dx/dX = 1/2$ [eqs. (A.1)–(A.3)]. Use of this fact in eq. (2), together with Assumption 3 and eqs. (A.1)–(A.3), gives the first-order condition for firm A's capacity choice, X. A symmetric equation can be derived for choice of Y, and the pair solved to give:

$$X = \{2(a-k) + [(b-\alpha)t_y - 2bt_x]/(b+\alpha)\}/(3b-\alpha),$$

$$Y = \{2(a-k) + [(b-\alpha)t_x - 2bt_y]/(b+\alpha)\}/(3b-\alpha). \tag{A.4}$$

Capacity levels are the same in cases (I), (C), and (B).

Given quantities, we may now use Assumption 3 to derive explicit expressions for country A prices; analogous expressions may be obtained for country B prices:

$$u_x^A(\text{I}) = \{ab + (2b-\alpha)k + b[(b-\alpha)t_y - 2bt_x]/[2(b+\alpha)]\}/\{3b-\alpha\}, \tag{A.5}$$

$$u_y^\wedge(I) = \{ab + (2b - \alpha)k + [b(b - \alpha)t_x$$

$$+ 2t_y(2b^2 + 2\alpha b - \alpha^2)]/[2(b + \alpha)]\}/\{3b - \alpha\};$$

$$u_x^\wedge(C) = \{ab + (2b - \alpha)k + t_y b(b - \alpha)/(b + \alpha)\}/\{3b - \alpha\},$$

$$\text{(A.6)}$$

$$u_y^\wedge(C) = \{ab + (2b - \alpha)k + t_y[b^2 + 2\alpha b - \alpha^2]/(b + \alpha)\}/\{3b - \alpha\};$$

$$u_x^\wedge(B) = \{ab + (2b - \alpha)k + [bt_y - (b - \alpha)t_x/2](b - \alpha)/(b + \alpha)\}/\{3b - \alpha\},$$

$$\text{(A.7)}$$

$$u_y^\wedge(B) = \{ab + (2b - \alpha)k + t_y(3b - \alpha)/2\}/\{3b - \alpha\}.$$

References

Baldwin, R. and P.R. Krugman, 1988, Market access and international competition; A simulation study of 16k random access memories, in: R. Feenstra, ed., Empirical methods for international trade (MIT Press, Cambridge, MA).

Ben-Zvi, S. and E. Helpman, 1988, Oligopoly in segmented markets processed (Harvard).

Brander, J.A., 1981, Intra-industry trade in identical commodities, Journal of International Economics 11, 1–14.

Brander, J.A. and P.R. Krugman, 1983, A reciprocal dumping model of international trade, Journal of International Economics 15, 313–321.

Dixit, A.K., 1984, International trade policy for oligopolistic industries, Economic Journal, suppl., 1–16.

Kreps, D. and J. Scheinkman, 1983, Quantity precommitment and Bertrand competition yield Cournot outcomes, Bell Journal of Economics 14, 326–337.

Markusen, J.A., 1981, Trade and the gains from trade with imperfect competition, Journal of International Economics 11, 531–551.

Markusen, J. and A.J. Venables, 1988, Trade policy with increasing returns and imperfect competition; contradictory results from competing assumptions, Journal of International Economics 24, 299–316.

Shapiro, C., 1988, Theories of oligopoly behaviour, in: R. Schmalensee and R. Willig, eds., Handbook of international economics, forthcoming.

Smith, A. and A.J. Venables, 1988, Completing the internal market in the European community; Some industry simulations, European Economic Review 32, 1501–1525.

Part III
Tests of Trade Theories

[17]

The Leontief Paradox, Reconsidered

Edward E. Leamer

University of California, Los Angeles

Using the Heckscher-Ohlin-Vanek model of trade, it is shown that a country is revealed to be relatively well endowed in capital compared with labor if and only if one of the following three conditions holds, where K_x, K_m, L_x, L_m, K_c, L_c are capital and labor embodied in exports, imports, and consumption: (a) $K_x - K_m > 0$, $L_x - L_m < 0$; (b) $K_x - K_m > 0$, $L_x - L_m > 0$, $(K_x - K_m)/(L_x - L_m) > K_c/L_c$; (c) $K_x - K_m < 0$, $L_x - L_m < 0$, $(K_x - K_m)/(L_x - L_m) < K_c/L_c$. Leontief's data for the United States in 1947 satisfy b, and the United States is actually revealed by trade to be capital abundant. The comparison by Leontief of K_x/L_x with K_m/L_m is shown to be theoretically inappropriate.

The Leontief paradox (1954) rests on a simple conceptual misunderstanding. It makes use of the intuitively appealing but nonetheless false proposition that if the capital per man embodied in exports is less than the capital per man embodied in imports, the country is revealed to be poorly endowed in capital relative to labor. This is a true proposition if the net export of labor services is of the opposite sign of the net export of capital services, but when both are positive, as in Leontief's data, the proper comparison is between the capital per man embodied in *net* exports and the capital per man embodied in consumption. Leontief's figures, which produced the so-called paradoxical result that U.S. exports are less capital intensive than U.S. competing imports, can also be used to show that U.S. net exports are more capital intensive than U.S. consumption, which in fact implies

Written with the assistance of Harry P. Bowen and with the support of Ford Foundation grant 775-0692. Comments from Larry Kotlikoff and a referee are also gratefully acknowledged.

[*Journal of Political Economy*, 1980, vol. 88, no. 3]

© 1980 by The University of Chicago. 0022-3808/80/8803-0006$00.95

that capital is abundant relative to labor. There is no paradox if the conceptually correct calculations are made.

The first section of this paper shows that a country is revealed to be relatively well endowed in capital compared with labor if and only if one of the following three conditions holds, where $K_x, K_m, L_x, L_m, K_c,$ L_c are capital and labor embodied in exports, imports, and consumption:

a) $K_x - K_m > 0, L_x - L_m < 0.$

b) $K_x - K_m > 0, L_x - L_m > 0, (K_x - K_m)/(L_x - L_m) > K_c/L_c.$

c) $K_x - K_m < 0, L_x - L_m < 0, (K_x - K_m)/(L_x - L_m) < K_c/L_c.$

Although Leontief found that $K_x/L_x < K_m/L_m$, his data are shown in Section II to satisfy *b*, and therefore the United States is revealed to be capital abundant. In a largely overlooked article, Williams (1970) makes a related point.

I.   Trade-revealed Factor Abundance

This reconsideration of the Leontief paradox rests on the Heckscher-Ohlin-Vanek (HOV) theorem (Vanek 1968).

The Heckscher-Ohlin-Vanek Theorem

Given: (*a*) There are *n* commodities which are freely mobile internationally. (*b*) There are *n* factors which are perfectly immobile internationally. (*c*) All individuals have identical homothetic preferences. (*d*) Production functions are the same in all countries and exhibit constant returns to scale. (*e*) There is perfect competition in the goods and factors markets. (*f*) Factor prices are equalized across countries.

Then: There exists a set of positive scalars $\alpha_i, i = 1, \ldots, I$, such that the vector of net exports of country *i*, T_i, the vector of factor endowments of country *i*, E_i, and the $n \times n$ matrix of total factor requirements A, bear the following relationship to each other:

$$AT_i = E_i - E_w\alpha_i, \qquad i = 1, \ldots, I, \qquad (1)$$

where E_w is the world's endowment vector, $E_w = \sum_i E_i$.

Proof: The proof of this result is straightforward. The equalization of factor prices and constant-returns-to-scale production functions imply the matrix of total factor inputs A, where A_{jk} is the amount of factor *j* used to produce one unit of commodity *k*. If Q_i is the vector of outputs of country *i*, then equilibrium in the factor markets requires factor demand equal to factor supply $AQ_i = E_i$. The summation of this equation over all countries produces $AQ_w = E_w$. Then, identical homothetic tastes imply that the consumption vectors C_i of each country are proportional to each other and also proportional to world output Q_w: $C_i = Q_w \alpha_i$. Country i's trade is $T_i = Q_i - C_i$, and the factors embodied in trade are $AT_i = A(Q_i - C_i) = E_i - AQ_w \alpha_i = E_i - E_w \alpha_i$.

The set of equations (1) serves as a logically sound foundation for a study of trade-revealed factor abundance. Two of these equations describe the relationship between capital and labor endowments and the implicit trade in capital and labor services:

$$K_T = K_i - \alpha_i K_w, \qquad (2a)$$

$$L_T = L_i - \alpha_i L_w, \qquad (2b)$$

where (K_T, L_T) are capital and labor embodied in net exports, (K_i, L_i) are the factor endowments of country i, and (K_w, L_w) are the world's factor endowments.

We take the following definition of factor abundance.

Definition: Capital in country i is said to be abundant in comparison with labor if and only if the share of the world's capital stock located in i exceeds the share of the world's labor force: $K_i/K_w > L_i/L_w$.

Factor abundance is revealed by trade through a comparison of the vector of factors used to produce various vectors of commodities. These vectors may be defined as follows.

Definition: The vector of factors embodied in the vector of commodities z is Az, where A is the matrix of total factor requirements.

The following result establishes necessary and sufficient conditions for trade to reveal an abundance of capital.

Corollary 1

Capital is revealed by trade to be abundant relative to labor if and only if

$$K_i/(K_i - K_T) > L_i/(L_i - L_T). \qquad (3)$$

Proof: Equations (2a) and (2b) can be rewritten as

$$K_w = (K_i - K_T)/\alpha_i,$$

$$L_w = (L_i - L_T)/\alpha_i.$$

Thus

$$K_i/K_w = \alpha_i K_i/(K_i - K_T),$$

$$L_i/L_w = \alpha_i L_i/(L_i - L_T),$$

from which (3) is a consequence.

There are three useful ways of rewriting (3). If K_c is the amount of capital embodied in the commodities used in country i, then $K_i - K_T = K_c$ and, similarly, $L_i - L_T = L_c$. Then (3) is equivalent to

$$K_i/L_i > K_c/L_c, \tag{3a}$$

which means that a country is revealed to be capital abundant if its production is more capital intensive than its consumption.

Another way to rewrite (3) is $K_i(L_i - L_T) > L_i(K_i - K_T)$, or

$$-K_iL_T > -L_iK_T. \tag{3b}$$

If L_T is positive, then this inequality becomes $K_T/L_T > K_i/L_i$, or $K_T/K_i > L_T/L_i$. Thus a country which is an exporter of both labor services and capital services is revealed by trade to be relatively capital abundant if trade is more capital intensive than production or, equivalently, if the share of capital exported exceeds the share of labor exported. Similarly, if L_T is negative the inequalities are reversed, and a country which is an importer of both labor services and capital services is revealed by trade to be relatively capital abundant if trade is less capital intensive than production or, equivalently, if the share of capital imported is less than the share of labor imported.

Yet another possibility is to rewrite (3b) as $-(K_c + K_T)L_T > -(L_c + L_T)K_T$, or

$$-K_cL_T > -L_cK_T. \tag{3c}$$

Thus a country which is an exporter of both labor services and capital services is revealed by trade to be relatively capital abundant if the capital intensity of net exports exceeds the capital intensity of consumption, $K_T/L_T > K_c/L_c$, and a country which is an importer of both capital and labor services is revealed by trade to be capital abundant if the capital intensity of net exports is less than the capital intensity of consumption, $K_T/L_T < K_c/L_c$.[1]

Inequalities (3a), (3b), and (3c) identify three equivalent ways of computing trade-revealed factor abundance. Trade even more directly reveals relative capital abundance if the services of one factor are exported and the services of the other are imported, since in-

---

[1] It may be observed that Williams (1970) uses (2) to form his equation (23): $(K_w - K_i)/K_i = (1/\alpha_i) - [(K_T + \alpha_iK_i)/\alpha_iK_i]$, which he calls the "plentifulness ratio." This formula suggests erroneously that the consumption share α_i is necessary to infer the relative abundance of capital. Moreover, Williams (1970, p. 121) reports that "the percentage of United States net capital, labour and natural resources exported as 7.14, 4.24, and 3.55, respectively. Intuition would suggest that, under these circumstances the United States must be implicitly plentiful in capital." Actually, this is enough (see his eq. 36) to establish the capital abundance of the United States, given $K_T > 0$, $L_T > 0$. This is discussed further below.

equality (3b) is satisfied if $K_T > 0$ and $L_T < 0$ and is violated if $K_T < 0$ and $L_T > 0$. For reference, this will be stated as a corollary.

Corollary 2

If the net export of capital services and the net export of labor services are opposite in sign, then the factor with positive net exports is revealed to be the relatively abundant factor.

Corollaries 1 and 2 imply that one should be examining the factor content of *net* exports, but the tradition beginning with Leontief is to distinguish exports from imports. In some cases, this is an equivalent procedure.

Corollary 3

Given that the net export of capital services and the net export of labor services are opposite in sign, then the capital per man embodied in exports (K_x/L_x) exceeds the capital per man embodied in imports (K_m/L_m) if and only if the country is relatively abundant in capital, $K_i/K_w > L_i/L_w$.

Proof: Suppose first that $K_T > 0$ and $L_T < 0$; then by corollary 2, $K_i/K_w > L_i/L_w$. But $0 < K_T = K_x - K_m$ implies $K_x/K_m > 1$, and $0 > L_T = L_x - L_m$ implies $1 > L_x/L_m$. Thus $K_x/K_m > L_x/L_m$, and $K_x/L_x > K_m/L_m$. Similarly $K_T < 0$ and $L_T > 0$ imply both $K_i/K_w < L_i/L_w$ and $K_x/L_x < K_m/L_m$.

A substantial practical defect of corollary 3 is that it assumes that K_T and L_T are opposite in sign. In fact, using Leontief's 1947 data, K_T and L_T are both positive: The United States exported both capital services and labor services. In that event, the ordering $K_x/L_x < K_m/L_m$ reveals nothing about the relative magnitudes of K_i/K_w and L_i/L_w.

Corollary 4

If there are more than two commodities, the ordering of exports and imports by factor intensity, say $K_x/L_x > K_m/L_m$, is compatible with either order of factor abundance, $K_i/K_w < L_i/L_w$ or $K_i/K_w > L_i/L_w$.

Proof: An example of the "paradoxical" case $K_x/L_x < K_m/L_m$ and $K_i/K_w > L_i/L_w$ will suffice. Let the factor requirements matrix be given as

$$A = \begin{bmatrix} 4 & 1 & 1 \\ 3 & 2 & .5 \\ 1 & 0 & 3 \end{bmatrix}$$

where the first row corresponds to capital inputs, the second row to labor inputs, and the third to land inputs. Suppose that the output vectors are given by

$$Q_i = (8, 16, 5)'$$

and

$$Q_w = (12, 68, 52)'.$$

The endowment vectors are then

$$AQ_i = E_i = (53, 58.5, 23)'$$

and

$$AQ_w = E_w = (168, 198, 168)'.$$

If the prices of the commodities are all one, then trade balance, $0 = 1'T_i$, implies

$$\alpha_i = \frac{1'Q_i}{1'Q_w} = \frac{29}{132} = .22.$$

Using this, and the endowment vectors, we can compute the excess factor supplies

$$(E_i - \alpha_i E_w)' = (53, 58.5, 23) - .22(168, 198, 168)$$

$$= (16.04, 14.94, -13.96).$$

Therefore, country i, on net, exports the services of both capital and labor and imports the services of land. The commodity trade vector implied by the above system is

$$T_i = (5.36, 1.04, -6.44)'.$$

Partitioning this into two vectors, exports (X_i) and imports (M_i), we obtain

$$X_i = (5.36, 1.04, 0)'$$

and

$$M_i = (0, 0, 6.44)'.$$

Computing the factor content of exports and imports separately we have

$$AX_i = (22.48, 18.16, 5.36)'$$

and

$$AM_i = (6.44, 3.22, 19.32)'.$$

Thus, for example, country i exports 22.64 units of capital and imports 6.44 units. Computing the capital-labor content ratio we obtain

$$\lambda = \frac{(K_x/L_x)}{(K_m/L_m)} = \frac{1.24}{2} = .62,$$

which is less than one. From this we might, as does Leontief, erroneously conclude that capital is scarce relative to labor in this country. However, the true ordering of factor abundance is given by the ratio of country i's endowment to the world's endowment. Computing these ratios for each factor we obtain

$$\frac{K_i}{K_w} = .315,$$

$$\frac{L_i}{L_w} = .295.$$

This ranking indicates that contrary to the inference based on λ, the country is *abundant* in capital relative to labor.

Corollary 4 indicates that Leontief's method of computing trade-revealed factor abundance orderings is erroneous. However, in the unlikely world of two commodities, it is a correct method.

Corollary 5

If there are only two commodities, and if one is exported and the other is imported, the ordering of exports and imports by capital intensity is the same as the ordering of factor abundance; that is, $K_x/L_x \geqslant K_m/L_m$ if and only if $K_i/K_w \geqslant L_i/L_w$.

Proof: It is necessary to show that a capital-abundant country exports the capital-intensive good, assuming one good is exported and the other is imported. If X and M are the quantity of exports and imports, then equation (1) can be written as

$$A_{Kx}X - A_{Km}M = K_i - \alpha_i K_w,$$

$$A_{Lx}X - A_{Lm}M = L_i - \alpha_i L_w.$$

The ordering $K_i/K_w \geqslant L_i/L_w$ is equivalent to $(A_{Kx}X - A_{Km}M)/K_w \geqslant (A_{Lx}X - A_{Lm}M)/L_w$, which can be rewritten as

$$X\left(\frac{A_{Kx}}{A_{Lx}} - \frac{K_w}{L_w}\right) \geqslant M\left(\frac{A_{Km}}{A_{Lm}} - \frac{K_w}{L_w}\right)\left(\frac{A_{Lm}}{A_{Lx}}\right).$$

The world's capital-labor ratio K_w/L_w must be between the industry intensity ratios A_{Kx}/A_{Lx} and A_{Km}/A_{Lm}, which implies that the left or right sides of the inequality above are opposite in sign, which is compatible only with $A_{Kx}/A_{Lx} > A_{Km}/A_{Lm}$. Thus $K_i/K_w \geqslant L_i/L_w$ is equivalent to $A_{Kx}/A_{Lx} > A_{Km}/A_{Lm}$.

II. Leontief's Data Reexamined

Tables 1, 2, and 3 contain information extracted from Leontief (1954) and from Travis (1964). Table 1 is Leontief's basic summary table, which reveals that $K_x/L_x < K_m/L_m$. But table 2 indicates that the United States in 1947 was a net exporter of both capital services and labor services. For this reason, the information contained in table 1 does not reveal the relative factor abundance of capital and labor (see corollary 4). The appropriate comparison, as described in corollary 1, is reported in table 3. Since net exports are much more capital intensive than consumption, the United States is revealed by its trade to be relatively well endowed in capital compared with labor.[2]

Finally, it is necessary to comment on why the United States had such a large trade surplus according to the data in table 2. This is partly due to the fact that "noncompeting" imports, such as coffee, tea, and jute, have been eliminated from the vector of imports. It is difficult to find a theoretically sound justification for this procedure. The HOV theorem uses the factor-price-equalization theorem, which requires incomplete specialization. It is necessary, therefore, to imagine that the United States in fact produces at least small amounts of coffee, tea, and jute, and so forth. It is natural to suppose that the

TABLE 1

DOMESTIC CAPITAL AND LABOR REQUIREMENTS PER MILLION
DOLLARS OF UNITED STATES EXPORTS AND OF
COMPETITIVENESS IMPORT REPLACEMENTS
(of Average 1947 Composition)

	Exports	Imports
Capital ($, 1947 prices)	2,550,780	3,091,339
Labor (man-years)	182.313	170.004

SOURCE.—Leontief (1954, sec. VI).

[2] Baldwin's (1971) finding that the Leontief paradox holds also for 1962 data cannot be explained away so easily. Baldwin reports capital in 1958 dollars embodied in a million (1958) dollars of imports and exports to be $2,132,000 and $1,876,000, respectively. The corresponding man-year figures are 119 and 131. Merchandise exports in millions of 1962 dollars were 20,781 and merchandise imports were 16,260. As in 1947 the United States was a net exporter of both capital services and labor services, $K_T > 0, L_T > 0$, but the ratio had fallen to $K_T/L_T = \$5,579$ in 1958 dollars per man year. This number falls below Travis's estimate of the 1947 capital per man equal to $6,949/man year and is likely to fall below any estimates for 1962 as well.

TABLE 2

ADDITIONAL INFORMATION ON TRADE AND ENDOWMENTS

Trade or Factor	Value	
Exports	$16,678.4	million
Imports (competitive)	$ 6,175.7	million
Net exports of capital services (K_T)	$23,450	million
Net exports of labor services (L_T)	1.990	million man-years
Capital-labor intensity of trade (K_T/L_T)	$11,783	/man-year

SOURCE.—Leontief (1954, table 2, n.).

TABLE 3

CAPITAL INTENSITY OF CONSUMPTION, PRODUCTION, AND TRADE

	Production	Net Exports	Consumption*
Capital	$328.519 million	$23,450 million	$305,069 million
Labor	47.273 million man-years	1.99 million man-years	45.28 million man-years
Capital/labor	$6,949/man-year	$11,783/man-year	$6,737/man-year

SOURCE.—For production figures, Travis (1964).
*Uses the identity, Consumption = Production − Net Exports.

production of these commodities uses capital, labor, and "tropical land" which is very scarce in the United States. But any capital and labor embodied in the imports of "noncompeting" goods should be included in the above calculations. May we suppose that these products are labor intensive, which works also to explain the Leontief paradox?

References

Baldwin, Robert E. "Determinants of the Commodity Structure of U.S. Trade." *A.E.R.* 61 (March 1971): 126–46.

Leontief, Wassily. "Domestic Production and Foreign Trade: The American Capital Position Re-examined." *Econ. Internazionale* 7 (February 1954): 3–32. Reprinted in *Readings in International Economics*, edited by Richard E. Caves and Harry G. Johnson. Homewood, Ill.: Irwin, 1968.

Travis, William P. *The Theory of Trade and Protection.* Cambridge, Mass.: Harvard Univ. Press, 1964.

Vanek, Jaroslav. "The Factor Proportions Theory: The N-Factor Case." *Kyklos* 21 (October 1968): 749–54.

Williams, James R. "The Resource Content in International Trade." *Canadian J. Econ.* 3 (February 1970): 111–22.

[18]

Comments

The Leontief Paradox, Continued

Richard A. Brecher and Ehsan U. Choudhri

Carleton University

I. Introduction

According to Leamer (1980), the Leontief Paradox is based on a simple conceptual misunderstanding. In a multifactor version of the Heckscher-Ohlin model, he argues that a capital-abundant country need not have its exports more capital intensive than its imports—provided that the country's commodity trade embodies a net export of both labor and capital services, as was the case for the United States in Leontief's (1954) data. For such a country, however, the model does imply that capital per worker be greater in net exports than in consumption. Leamer finds that this implication is indeed consistent with Leontief's data.

This note shows, however, that there is another feature of the trade data which is not so easily explained. The fact that the United States exported labor services is in itself paradoxical. As discussed below (Sec. II), the model which Leamer uses to explain the paradox implies that a country is a net exporter of labor services if and only if its aggregate expenditure per worker is less than that in the rest of the world. This implication is clearly inconsistent with the evidence reviewed below (in Sec. III), which shows that expenditure per worker was substantially greater in the United States than the rest of the world and yet the United States exported labor services. Therefore, a modified version of the Leontief Paradox continues to stand.

Comments and suggestions from Edward E. Leamer are gratefully acknowledged. Of course, the authors alone are responsible for any remaining errors or shortcomings.

[*Journal of Political Economy*, 1982, vol. 90, no. 4]
© 1982 by The University of Chicago. All rights reserved. 0022-3808/82/9004-0010$01.50

II. The Theory

Following Leamer, adopt Vanek's (1968) version of a Heckscher-Ohlin model with n commodities, n factors, and I countries.[1] As discussed by Leamer, this model implies the Heckscher-Ohlin-Vanek theorem that

$$AT_i = E_i - E_w \alpha_i, \qquad i = 1, \ldots, I, \tag{1}$$

where A is the $n \times n$ matrix of factor requirements (for each country) in free-trade equilibrium; T_i is the $n \times 1$ vector of net exports of country i; E_i and E_w ($\equiv \Sigma_i E_i$) are the $n \times 1$ vectors of factor endowments in country i and the world, respectively; and α_i is a scalar representing country i's relative share in world expenditure. Thus,

$$\alpha_i = C_i / C_w, \tag{2}$$

where C_i and C_w represent consumption (expenditure) in country i and the world.

Let L_x, L_m, L_T ($\equiv L_x - L_m$), and L_c represent, respectively, the amount of labor embodied in country i's exports, imports, net exports, and consumption; while K_x, K_m, K_T, and K_c represent the corresponding quantities of capital. Also, let L_i and K_i represent factor endowments of country i, while L_w and K_w represent world endowments. Using equations (1), Leamer shows that if $n > 2$ while L_T and K_T are of the same sign, the condition $K_x/L_x < K_m/L_m$ is neither necessary nor sufficient to imply that country i is abundant in labor relative to capital (i.e., that $L_i/L_w > K_i/K_w$). Leamer also shows that if both L_T and K_T are positive, a necessary and sufficient condition for capital (relative to labor) abundance of country i is that K_T/L_T be greater than K_c/L_c.

The model above also has testable implications for the sign of L_T, although these were not explored by Leamer. From the set of equations (1), trade in labor services can be written as

$$L_T = L_i [1 - (\alpha_i L_w / L_i)]. \tag{3}$$

Equations (2) and (3) imply that

$$L_T > 0 \text{ iff } C_w / L_w > C_i / L_i. \tag{4}$$

Condition (4) holds regardless of whether trade is balanced. It is interesting to note, however, that if trade is balanced for country i, its

[1] The model also assumes the same constant-returns-to-scale technology in all countries, identical homothetic tastes everywhere, no international factor mobility, perfect competition, free trade, and complete international factor-price equalization. The assumption of equal numbers of commodities and factors can be relaxed, however, as long as factor prices remain equalized.

expenditure equals income, and condition (4) can be rewritten as

$$L_T > 0 \text{ iff } L_i/L_w > Y_i/Y_w, \tag{5}$$

where Y_i and Y_w ($\equiv C_w$) represent the levels of income in country i and the world. Since, under factor-price equalization, Y_i/Y_w can be interpreted as country i's aggregate factor endowment relative to the world's,[2] condition (5) reveals country i to be abundant in labor relative to (an aggregate measure of) all other factors when $L_T > 0$.

III. The Evidence

As Leamer shows, according to Leontief's 1947 data, the net export of labor services (L_T) by the United States was equal to 1.99 million man-years. Given the U.S. labor endowment of 47.273 million man-years (Leamer 1980, table 3), equation (3) would imply that U.S. expenditure per worker was about 4 percent less than the world expenditure per worker. In fact, however, the income as well as expenditure per worker in the United States was much larger than the world level. Even in the industrialized countries of northwest Europe, according to Denison's (1967) data, income per worker in 1950 ranged from 44 to 59 percent of the U.S. level, while the corresponding range for expenditure per worker was from 45 to 61 percent.[3] Per-worker income and expenditure in other less industrialized countries are likely to have been much smaller.[4] Thus, the evidence is clearly inconsistent with conditions (4) and (5) above.

While Leontief's estimates are based only on 1947 data, Baldwin's (1971) calculations using 1958 input-output data also confirm the paradoxical result that the United States was a net exporter of labor services.[5] It is important to point out that, while there was a balance of trade surplus in Leontief's as well as Baldwin's data, both studies show the labor requirement per million dollars to be higher for exports

---

[2] Note that the aggregate endowment (of factor services) in terms of a particular factor can be defined simply as the level of income (at factor cost) divided by the price of that factor.

[3] See his table 2-5 for the income-per-worker data. We calculate expenditure per worker by combining these income estimates with the data in his table 18-1 on exports and imports of the northwestern European countries. (Note that we define expenditure as income plus imports minus exports. Also, we estimate the 1950 expenditure-income ratio for the United States to be .993, using data from the U.S. Department of Commerce [1977].)

[4] For a comprehensive discussion of international differences in terms of income per capita (as a readily available proxy for income per worker) during the 1950s, see Kuznets (1966, chap. 7).

[5] It is interesting to note that Baldwin's data do not confirm the hypothesis that $K_T/L_T > K_c/L_c$ in the United States, as Leamer himself points out.

than for imports.[6] Thus, L_T presumably would remain positive even if the U.S. trade were to be balanced.[7]

IV. Conclusion

In sum, Leontief's results about the direction of U.S. trade in labor services cannot be reconciled with Vanek's version of the Heckscher-Ohlin model. Of course, a reconciliation could be attempted along conventional lines, in terms of departures from such assumptions as factor-price equalization, free trade, identical tastes, and homogeneous labor. However, until it is demonstrated that one or more of these departures can account for the net export of labor services by the United States, the Leontief Paradox is still with us.

References

Baldwin, Robert E. "Determinants of the Commodity Structure of U.S. Trade." *A.E.R.* 61 (March 1971): 126–46.

Denison, Edward F. *Why Growth Rates Differ: Postwar Experience in Nine Western Countries.* Washington: Brookings Inst., 1967.

Kuznets, Simon. *Modern Economic Growth: Rate, Structure and Spread.* New Haven, Conn.: Yale Univ. Press, 1966.

Leamer, Edward E. "The Leontief Paradox, Reconsidered." *J.P.E.* 88, no. 3 (June 1980): 495–503.

Leontief, Wassily. "Domestic Production and Foreign Trade: The American Capital Position Re-examined." *Econ. Internaz.* 7 (February 1954): 9–38. Reprinted in *Readings in International Economics*, edited by Richard E. Caves and Harry G. Johnson. Homewood, Ill.: Irwin (for Amer. Econ. Assoc.), 1968.

U.S. Department of Commerce. *The National Income and Product Accounts of the United States 1929–74: Statistical Tables.* Washington: Government Printing Office, 1977.

Vanek. Jaroslav. "The Factor Proportions Theory: The N-Factor Case." *Kyklos* 21 (October 1968): 749–54.

[6] It should be emphasized that these factor requirements per million dollars of imports are based only on import-competing products. Leamer has suggested that noncompetitive imports are more labor intensive than competitive imports. In this case, the omission of noncompetitive imports would lead to an understatement of the amount of labor required per million dollars of imports. However, according to Baldwin, noncompetitive imports accounted for only 8 percent of total imports. Indeed, with his data, even if we make the extreme assumption that noncompetitive imports use only labor and no other factor (and calculate the labor requirement by dividing the value of noncompetitive imports by the annual wage rate), labor required per million dollars of total (competitive plus noncompetitive) imports would still be lower than the amount required per million dollars of exports.

[7] A positive L_T in this case is not a certainty, because changing α_i to balance trade could alter the composition of trade and thereby affect the labor requirements per million dollars of imports and exports.

[19]

Multicountry, Multifactor Tests of the Factor Abundance Theory

By HARRY P. BOWEN, EDWARD E. LEAMER, AND LEO SVEIKAUSKAS*

The Heckscher-Ohlin-Vanek model predicts relationships among industry input requirements, country resource supplies, and international trade in commodities. These relationships are tested using data on twelve resources, and the trade of twenty-seven countries in 1967. The Heckscher-Ohlin propositions that trade reveals gross and relative factor abundance are not supported by these data. The Heckscher-Ohlin-Vanek equations are also rejected in favor of weaker models that allow technological differences and measurement errors.

The Heckscher-Ohlin (H-O) hypothesis is most widely understood in its two-good, two-factor form: a country exports the commodity which uses intensively its relatively abundant resource. Tests of this hypothesis have been inconclusive for two reasons. First, the three pairwise comparisons required by this two × two model cannot be made unambiguously in a multifactor, multicommodity world. Most previous papers that claim to present tests of the hypothesis have used intuitive but inappropriate generalizations of the two×two model to deal with a multidimensional reality. Second, the H-O hypothesis is a relation among three separately observable phenomena: trade, factor input requirements, and factor endowments. A proper test of the hypothesis requires measurements of all three of these variables. Much prior work that claims to have tested the hypothesis has used data on only two of the three hypotheticals.

*Graduate School of Business, New York University, New York, NY 10006, and National Bureau of Economic Research; University of California-Los Angeles, Los Angeles, CA 90024; and Bureau of Labor Statistics, Washington, D.C., 20212, respectively. Bowen's work on this paper was completed while on leave as an Olin Fellow at the NBER. Sveikauskas expresses his appreciation to Rensselaer Polytechnic Institute where he conducted most of his work on this paper while on a one-year leave. The work presented here does not necessarily represent the views of the U.S. Department of Labor. This paper benefited from the comments of two referees and the participants at seminars at Harvard, MIT, and New York University. The original version of this paper was presented at the 1982 meeting of the Western Economic Association.

This paper reports conceptually correct tests of the H-O hypothesis as suggested by Edward Leamer (1980) and Leamer and Harry Bowen (1981). We use a valid multidimensional extension of the two × two model known as the Heckscher-Ohlin-Vanek (H-O-V) theorem, which equates the factors embodied in a country's net exports to the country's excess supplies of factor endowments. And we use separately measured data on trade, factor input requirements, and factor endowments to conduct the first systematic and complete evaluation of the relationships implied by the H-O-V hypothesis among these three sets of variables.

Our methods contrast sharply with traditional approaches to testing the H-O hypothesis. The classic test of the H-O hypothesis is Wassily Leontief's (1953), which compares the capital per man embodied in a million dollars worth of exports with the capital per man embodied in a million dollars worth of imports. Leamer (1980) shows this comparison does not reveal the relative abundance of capital and labor in a multifactor world. Moreover, Leontief's study uses data on trade and factor input requirements but not factor endowments and, in addition, his data are only for a single country.

A second type of purported test uses a regression of trade of many commodities on their factor input requirements for a single country (for example, Robert Baldwin, 1971; William Branson and Nicholas Monoyios, 1977; Jon Harkness, 1978, 1983; Robert Stern and Keith Maskus, 1981). If the estimated coefficient of some factor is positive, the country is inferred to be abundant in that resource. Leamer and Bowen (1981) show this also is an inappropriate inference in a multifactor world since there is no guarantee that the signs of the regression coefficients will reveal the abundance of a resource. Moreover, these studies do not use factor endowment data.[1]

A third approach used to study the sources of comparative advantage involves regression of net exports of a single commodity for many countries on measures of national factor supplies (Bowen, 1983; Hollis Chenery and Moses Syrquin, 1975; and Leamer, 1974, 1984). These papers use no measures of factor input requirements and they study the weakened hypothesis that the structure of trade can be explained by the availability of resources. This contrasts with the stricter H-O-V hypothesis studied here that factor supplies, factor input requirements, and trade fit together in a special way.

The present study computes the amount of each of twelve factors embodied in the net exports of 27 countries in 1967, using the U.S. matrix of total input requirements for 1967. The factors embodied in trade are then compared with direct measures of factor endowments to determine the extent to which the data conform to the predictions of the H-O-V theory.

We first test the traditional interpretation of the H-O hypothesis that trade reveals relative factor abundance.[2] This analysis is analogous to Leontief's attempt to determine the relative abundance of capital and labor in the United States using U.S. data alone. Our empirical results offer little support for this facet of the H-O-V model. Several types

of measurement error could account for these results. Moreover, the H-O-V model implies a set of equalities, not inequalities, among the variables. We therefore extend the analysis of the H-O-V model to a regression context, and conduct a second set of tests which examine these equalities while allowing different hypotheses about consumer's preferences, technological differences, and various forms of measurement error.

Overall, our results do not support the H-O-V hypothesis of an exact relationship between factor contents and factor supplies. Support is found for the H-O-V assumption of homothetic preferences, but estimates of the parameters linking factor contents and factor supplies are found to differ significantly from their theoretical values. The data suggest that the poor performance of the H-O-V hypothesis is importantly related to measurement error in both trade and national factor supplies across countries, and the data favor a model that allows neutral differences in factor input matrices across countries.

I. Theoretical Framework

Derivation of the relationships studied here starts with the equilibrium identity expressing a country's net factor exports as the difference between factors absorbed in production and factors absorbed in consumption.

$$(1) \qquad \mathbf{A}_i \mathbf{T}_i = \mathbf{A}_i \mathbf{Q}_i - \mathbf{A}_i \mathbf{C}_i,$$

where $\mathbf{A}_i = K \times N$ matrix of factor input requirements which indicate the total (direct plus indirect) amount of each of K factors needed to produce one unit of output in each of N industries,
$\mathbf{T}_i = N \times 1$ vector of net trade flows of country i,
$\mathbf{Q}_i = N \times 1$ vector of country i's final outputs,
$\mathbf{C}_i = N \times 1$ vector of country i's final consumption.

Full employment implies $\mathbf{A}_i \mathbf{Q}_i = \mathbf{E}_i$, where $\mathbf{E}_i$ is the $K \times 1$ vector of country i's factor

---

[1] An exception is Jon Harkness (1978, 1983), who tests the H-O-V sign and rank propositions (see below) by comparing measured factor contents with excess factor supplies that are inferred from coefficients estimated by regressing factor contents on input requirements. This analysis is suspect, however, since the estimated coefficients need not correspond either in sign or rank to a country's true excess factor supplies. See Leamer and Bowen (1981).

[2] Maskus (1985) reports conceptually correct tests of this interpretation of the H-O-V theorem for the United States using 1958 and 1972 data.

supplies. Thus, the vector of factors embodied in net trade is

$$(2) \qquad \mathbf{A}_i \mathbf{T}_i = \mathbf{E}_i - \mathbf{A}_i \mathbf{C}_i.$$

This identity is transformed into a testable hypothesis by making one or more of the following three assumptions:

(A1) Assumption 1: *All individuals face the same commodity prices.*

(A2) Assumption 2: *Individuals have identical and homothetic tastes.*

(A3) Assumption 3: *All countries have the same factor input matrix,* $\mathbf{A}_i = \mathbf{A}$.

Ordinarily, the assumption of identical input matrices (A3) would be replaced by the assumption of factor price equalization and internationally identical technologies. The alternative to factor price equalization permitted here is that input requirements are technologically fixed and identical across countries, but countries have different factor prices and therefore produce different subsets of commodities.

Assumptions (A1) and (A2) imply that the consumption vector of country i is proportional to the world output vector $(\mathbf{Q}_w)$, $\mathbf{C}_i = s_i \mathbf{Q}_w$, where s_i is country i's consumption share. The consumption share can be derived by premultiplying the net trade identity $(\mathbf{T}_i = \mathbf{Q}_i - s_i \mathbf{Q}_w)$ by the vector of common goods prices

$$(3) \qquad s_i = (Y_i - B_i)/Y_w,$$

where Y_i is GNP and B_i is the trade balance. If trade is balanced, then s_i equals country i's share of world GNP.[3]

If, in addition, the factor input matrices are identical, we can write $\mathbf{A}_i \mathbf{C}_i = s_i \mathbf{A} \mathbf{Q}_w =$

$s_i \mathbf{E}_w$, where $\mathbf{E}_w = \Sigma_i \mathbf{E}_i$ is the $K \times 1$ vector of world factor supplies. Then, (2) can be written as

$$(4) \qquad \mathbf{A} \mathbf{T}_i = \mathbf{E}_i - \mathbf{E}_w (Y_i - B_i)/Y_w.$$

Equation (4) specifies an exact relationship between factor contents and factor endowments. This relationship can be tested by measuring the net export vector $\mathbf{T}_i$, the factor input matrix $\mathbf{A}$, and the excess factor supplies $\mathbf{E}_i - s_i \mathbf{E}_w$, and computing the extent to which these data violate the equality given by (4). Such analysis requires some sensible way of measuring the distance between two matrices: the matrix with columns equal to the factor contents of trade for each country, and the matrix with columns equal to the excess factor supplies for each country. In Section II we first examine the extent to which row and column elements of these matrices conform in sign and rank without reference to any specific alternative hypotheses. In Section III we then report tests against alternatives involving nonproportional consumption, measurement errors, and differences in input matrices.

Our analysis uses data on the 367-order U.S. input-output table for 1967, and the 1967 trade and the 1966 supply of twelve resources for 27 countries.[4] The countries are those for which both occupational data and detailed trade data were available. The twelve resources are net capital stock, total labor, professional/technical workers, managerial workers, clerical workers, sales workers, service workers, agricultural workers, production workers, arable land, pastureland, and forestland.

Net capital stocks were computed as the sum of discounted real investment flows in domestic currency and converted to U.S. dollars using 1966 nominal exchange rates. Industry capital requirements (plant, equipment, and inventories) were constructed from data on U.S. industry capital stocks.

The seven labor categories are those defined at the one-digit level of International

---

[3] If factor prices are equalized, s_i can also be derived by premultiplying (2) by the vector of factor prices. If factor prices are unequal, (2) can still be premultiplied by the vector of factor prices prevailing in country i to obtain an expression analogous to (3), but with both internal and external factor earnings evaluated only in terms of country i's factor prices.

[4] The Data Appendix provides detailed discussion of the data.

Standard Classification of Occupations. Total labor is a country's economically active population. Input requirements for each type of labor were constructed using occupational data from the 1971 *U.S. Survey of Occupational Employment* and the 1970 *U.S. Census of Population*. Labor data are measured in numbers of people.

The three land types conform to the definitions used by the Food and Agricultural Organization. Industry land requirements were based on the U.S. input-output table; I/O sector 1 was used for pastureland, I/O sector 2 was used for arable land, and I/O sector 3 (forest and fisheries) was used for forestland. Land is measured in hectares.

Finally, data on each country's trade in 1967 were obtained at the four- and five-digit level of the Standard International Trade Classification (SITC) and concorded to input-output sectors to perform the required vector multiplications.

II. Tests of Qualitative Hypotheses

The traditional implication of the H-O theory is that factor abundance determines which commodities are exported and which are imported, in other words, the sign of net exports. In this section we report tests of the analogous qualitative implications of the H-O-V equations concerning the sign and ordering of the factor content data.

A typical kth element of (4) can be written as

$$(5) \quad (F_{ki}^A/E_{kw})/(Y_i/Y_w)$$
$$= [(E_{ki}/E_{kw})/(Y_i/Y_w)] - 1,$$

where F_{ki} is the kth element of the factor content vector $F_i = AT_i$, and $F_{ki}^A = (F_{ki} - E_{kw}B_i/Y_w)$ is the factor content if trade were balanced. The quantity on the right-hand side of (5) is a measure of the relative abundance of resource k. If this equation is accurate, the factor content of trade can be used as an indirect measure of factor abundance. We study here two qualitative implications of (5); first, that trade reveals the abundance of resources compared with an

average of all resources, and second, that trade reveals the relative abundance of resources.

The income share in (5) is an average of the resource shares weighted by world earnings: $(Y_i/Y_w) = \Sigma_k[w_k E_{ki}/\Sigma_k w_k E_{kw}] = \Sigma_k[(w_k E_{kw})(E_{ki}/E_{kw})/\Sigma_k w_k E_{kw}]$, where w_k is the world price of factor k. If equation (5) is accurate, then the sign of the net trade in factor services, corrected for the trade imbalance, will reveal the abundance of a resource, compared with other resources on the average.[5] This sign proposition is tested for each factor (country) by computing the proportion of sign matches between corresponding elements in each row (column) of the matrix of adjusted factor contents and the matrix of factor abundance ratios. In addition, Fisher's Exact Test (one-tail) is used to test the hypothesis of independence between the sign of the factor contents and of the excess factor shares against the alternative of a positive association.

Equation (5) also implies that trade reveals the relative abundance of resources when considered two at a time. If equation (5) is accurate, the adjusted net exports of country i of factor k exceed the adjusted net exports by country i of factor k', $(F_{ki}^A/E_{kw})/(Y_i/Y_w) > (F_{k'i}^A/E_{k'w})/(Y_i/Y_w)$, if and only if factor k is more abundant than factor k', $(E_{ki}/E_{kw})/(Y_i/Y_w) > (E_{k'i}/E_{k'w})/(Y_i/Y_w)$; and the adjusted net exports by country i of

---

[5] Other definitions of factor abundance are possible. In an earlier version of this paper, we wrote (5) without adjusting the left-hand side for the trade imbalance as $F_{ki}/s_i E_{kw} = (E_{ki}/E_{kw}) - s_i$, where s_i is the consumption share $(Y_i - B_i)/Y_w$. In this form the theory can be said to imply that the sign of the net trade in factor services reveals the abundance of a factor compared with the consumption share. Equivalently, the right-hand side of this equation takes the sign of the difference between world output per factor input and the domestic consumption per factor input. This form of comparison is made by Richard Brecher and Ehsan Choudhri (1982) who point out that Leontief's findings of a positive net trade in labor services is inconsistent with the relatively high consumption per worker of the United States. Though this comparison is appropriate, we have opted here for the comparison suggested by equation (5), because it is based on a more appealing notion of factor abundance. See Kohler (1987) for a related discussion.

TABLE 1—RATIO OF ADJUSTED NET TRADE IN FACTOR TO NATIONAL ENDOWMENT

Country	Capital	Labor	Prof/Tech	Manager	Clerical	Sales	Service	Agriculture	Production	Arable	Forest	Pasture
Argentina	1.32	−0.30	−1.64	−2.60	−1.07	−0.62	−0.83	4.30	−1.46	21.24	−6.94	2.40
Australia	−3.77	−0.41	−2.95	−1.79	−1.68	0.21	−0.11	18.10	−3.65	17.15	−13.68	0.80
Austria	−2.03	3.01	2.74	5.64	2.91	3.81	3.20		2.59	−80.74	13.52	24.35
Bene-Lux	−2.36	1.81	0.88	1.82	1.90	1.36	2.39	−4.26	2.76	−364.25	−922.53	53.27
Brazil	−5.54	−0.27	−0.85	−0.49	−0.82	−0.32	−0.23	−0.04	−0.61	2.10	−0.04	−0.02
Canada	1.82	−3.49	−3.40	−2.23	−4.00	−2.73	−1.88	4.00	−6.84	12.13	6.16	2.84
Denmark	−4.89	5.82	2.37	8.70	4.25	5.08	4.51	24.56	1.21	33.57	803.73	1763.42
Finland	4.69	2.14	0.49	4.22	1.78	1.94	1.89	1.26	3.21	−24.44	30.48	434.70
France	−4.07	0.82	0.70	1.17	1.02	0.90	1.06	0.16	1.04	−21.33	−198.68	1.79
Germany	−1.05	−0.43	1.01	1.34	0.51	−1.08	−1.05	−11.86	2.07	−323.61	−377.64	−124.77
Greece	−5.50	2.93	4.48	14.95	5.37	4.49	4.68	2.20	2.02	46.92	−61.16	1.08
Hong Kong	−46.06	4.52	5.24	3.68	8.10	3.48	3.03	−14.19	6.46	−21568	−30532	−91627216
Ireland	−1.93	6.73	4.49	13.84	7.19	6.10	8.07	10.59	2.67	17.31	−129.98	72.68
Italy	−7.03	0.74	1.25	4.67	1.42	0.39	1.27	−1.73	1.87	−39.91	−431.67	−131.90
Japan	−5.47	0.10	0.44	0.48	0.33	−0.05	−0.03	−1.54	1.18	−341.42	−268.58	−1998.58
Korea	−30.51	0.61	1.53	2.85	1.81	0.76	1.73	0.27	0.85	−42.34	−29.42	1206.60
Mexico	−0.78	0.57	0.19	0.47	0.51	0.80	0.70	0.87	−0.21	12.40	5.69	0.97
Netherlands	−4.56	4.61	3.49	6.36	3.65	4.72	5.53	22.78	1.41	82.74	−719.88	330.86
Norway	−5.54	5.57	3.75	6.15	7.98	10.22	10.58	14.59	−0.06	−125.48	105.96	660.35
Philippines	−13.94	−0.10	−0.59	−0.36	−0.81	0.03	0.06	0.14	−0.81	10.47	−8.43	−17.03
Portugal	−10.31	1.92	3.92	10.85	3.75	2.83	2.72	0.63	2.49	−28.46	24.79	12.03
Spain	−6.19	3.04	4.56	13.88	4.36	4.13	3.89	2.45	2.23	−2.74	−12.00	4.92
Sweden	0.79	1.36	0.59	2.26	1.05	1.09	1.44	−0.66	2.18	−67.23	30.93	48.00
Switzerland	−5.72	3.42	4.46	11.57	3.52	5.42	4.13	−0.79	3.04	−862.95	−352.36	−12.18
UK	−12.86	0.63	1.77	2.04	1.37	1.30	1.32	−18.57	1.11	−313.42	−2573.99	−91.89
US	0.08	−0.25	0.23	−0.11	−0.19	−1.10	−0.68	1.54	−0.34	19.45	−23.82	−1.63
Yugoslavia	−3.15	0.68	0.39	1.59	1.12	2.05	1.15	0.46	0.76	−0.08	2.81	14.24

Note: Numbers in percent. Factor content data are for 1967; endowment data are for 1966.

factor k exceeds the adjusted net exports by country i' of factor k, $(F_{ki}^A/E_{kw})/(Y_i/Y_w) > (F_{ki'}^A/E_{kw})/(Y_{i'}/Y_w)$, if and only if country i is more abundant in factor k than country i', $(E_{ki}/E_{kw})/(Y_i/Y_w) > (E_{ki'}/E_{kw})/(Y_{i'}/Y_w)$. More generally, for each country and factor, the ranking of adjusted net factor exports F_{ki}^A/E_{kw} should conform to the ranking of factors by their abundance. This rank proposition is tested for each country (factor) by computing the Kendall rank correlation between corresponding columns (rows) of the matrix of adjusted factor content and the matrix of factor abundance ratios. In addition, we compute the proportion of correct rankings when the corresponding elements of the columns (rows) of the two matrices are compared two at a time.[6]

[6]Subsequent tests of the rank and sign propositions based on the proportion of "successes" do not refer to any specific alternative hypothesis and thus leaves unclear the choice of significance level. Without knowing the proportion of successes expected under a specific alternative hypothesis, judging the relative performance of the H-O-V model is largely impressionistic. The

Table 1 summarizes the factor content data by listing for each country the ratio of adjusted net exports of each factor in 1967 to the endowment of the corresponding factor in 1966, $100 \times F_{ki}^A/E_{ki}$. According to these data, the United States exports .08 percent of the services of its capital stock, .23 percent of the services of its professional/technical workers but imports labor services amounting to .25 percent of the services of its labor force. Thus, among these resources, U.S. trade reveals the United States to be most abundant in professional and technical workers, capital, and then labor. Among all resources, however, the United States is revealed most abundant in arable land, followed by agricultural workers.

Leamer (1980) computed these factor content ratios using Leontief's 1947 data and found that U.S. trade revealed the United

absence of alternative hypotheses when testing the sign and rank propositions is, in large part, the motivation for our subsequent tests of the H-O-V equations in a regression framework.

States to be abundant in capital compared to labor, thus reversing Leontief's paradoxical finding. Likewise, no "Leontief paradox" is evident in Table 1 since the United States exports capital services but imports labor services, and this ordering conforms to the ordering of the U.S. shares of world capital (41 percent) and world labor (22 percent). This result, and others like it, would lead us to accept the H-O theorem on the basis of a rank test.

Although a rank test supports the two-factor version of the H-O theorem for the United States, a contrary finding is that while the United States is a net exporter of capital services, the U.S. share of world income (47 percent) exceeds its share of world capital, which implies that there is a measured scarcity of capital in the United States. This result, and others like it, would lead us to reject the H-O theorem using a sign test.

Some obvious anomalies in Table 1 are that, after adjusting for trade imbalances, Denmark, Finland, Korea, the Netherlands, and Norway export more than 100 percent of the services of their pastureland. These anomalies probably reflect difficulties in applying U.S. input-output coefficients to other countries. For example, Denmark is a substantial exporter of agricultural products and U.S. input coefficients apparently overstate the amount of pastureland used per unit of output in Denmark. The analysis conducted in Section III will formally test the assumption of identical input coefficients, but it is clear from the anomalies in Table 1 that assumption (A3) is not entirely accurate.[7]

Formal tests of the conformity of the adjusted net factor export data (F_{ki}^A/E_{kw}) with the factor abundance data $[(E_{ki}/E_{kw})/(Y_i/Y_w)-1]$ are reported in Tables 2 and 3. The first column of Table 2 lists the proportion of sign matches between adjusted net factor exports and the abundance ratios

[7] These anomalous data values may also reflect errors of measurement in either the factor contents or endowments. In particular, Denmark and Norway probably export more than 100 percent of their forestland because these countries export fish and fish products, and fisheries are included in the input-output coefficients for forestland.

TABLE 2—SIGN AND RANK TESTS, FACTOR BY FACTOR

Factor	Sign Test[a]	Rank Tests[b]	
Capital	.52	0.140	.45
Labor	.67	0.185	.46
Prof/Tech	.78	0.123	.33
Managerial	.22	−0.254	.34
Clerical	.59	0.134	.48
Sales	.67	0.225	.47
Service	.67	0.282[c]	.44
Agricultural	.63	0.202	.47
Production	.70	0.345[c]	.48
Arable	.70	0.561[c]	.73
Pasture	.52	0.197	.61
Forest	.70	0.356[c]	.65

[a] Proportion of 27 countries for which the sign of net trade in factor matched the sign of the corresponding factor abundance.
[b] The first column is the Kendall rank correlation among 27 countries; the second column is the proportion of correct rankings out of 351 possible pairwise comparisons.
[c] Statistically significant at 5 percent level.

for each factor. The first column of Table 3 lists comparable percentages for each country. For example, the sign of adjusted net capital exports and of excess capital shares matched in 52 percent of the countries.

In general, the proposition of conformity in sign between factor contents and excess factor shares receives relatively little support when tested for each factor (Table 2). Although the proportion of sign matches exceeds 50 percent for eleven resources, the proportion of sign matches is 70 percent or greater for only four of the twelve factors with the highest proportion of sign matches for professional and technical workers (78 percent). Moreover, using Fisher's Exact Test, the hypothesis of independence between the sign of the factor contents and of the excess factor shares can be rejected (results not shown) at the 95 percent level for only one resource—arable land.

Similar results are obtained when the sign proposition is tested for each country (Table 3). The proportion of sign matches exceeds 50 percent for 18 countries, and exceeds 90 percent for five countries (Greece, Hong Kong, Ireland, Mexico, and the UK). However, the proportion of sign matches is below 70 percent for 19 of the 27 countries. In addition, the hypothesis of independence

TABLE 3—SIGN AND RANK TESTS, COUNTRY
BY COUNTRY

Country	Sign Tests[a]	Rank Tests[b]	
Argentina	.33	0.164	.58
Australia	.33	−0.127	.44
Austria	.67	0.091	.56
Belgium-Luxembourg	.50	0.273	.64
Brazil	.17	0.673[c]	.86
Canada	.75	0.236	.64
Denmark	.42	−0.418	.29
Finland	.67	0.164	.60
France	.25	0.418	.71
Germany	.67	0.527[c]	.76
Greece	.92	0.564[c]	.80
Hong Kong	1.00	0.745[c]	.89
Ireland	.92	0.491[c]	.76
Italy	.58	0.345	.69
Japan	.67	0.382	.71
Korea	.75	0.345	.69
Mexico	.92	0.673[c]	.86
Netherlands	.58	−0.236	.38
Norway	.25	−0.236	.38
Philippines	.50	0.527[c]	.78
Portugal	.67	0.091	.56
Spain	.67	0.200	.62
Sweden	.42	0.200	.62
Switzerland	.67	0.382	.69
United Kingdom	.92	0.527[c]	.78
United States	.58	0.309	.67
Yugoslavia	.83	−0.055	.49

[a] Proportion of 12 factors for which the sign of net trade in factor matched the sign of the corresponding excess supply of factor.

[b] The first column is the Kendall rank correlation among 11 factors (total labor excluded); the second column is the proportion of correct rankings out of 55 possible pairwise comparisons.

[c] Statistically significant at the 5 percent level.

between the classification of signs is rejected (95 percent level) for only four countries: Greece, Ireland, Hong Kong, and the United Kingdom.[8] Finally, for the entire sample, the proportion of sign matches out of a possible 324 is only 61 percent.

The sign proposition deals with the abundance of a resource compared with a value-weighted average of other resources (that is, Y_i/Y_w), but we can also compare resources two at a time. For example, the data in Table 1 indicate the United States is more abundant in capital than labor while the

[8] No variation was observed in the sign of factor abundance for Yugoslavia (each was positive).

U.S. resource share data (not shown) also indicate an abundance in capital compared to labor. The many possible pairwise comparisons are summarized by the rank proposition, which states that the order of adjusted factor contents and the order of the resource abundance ratios conform.

Two formal measures of the conformity between the factor content and factor abundance rankings are shown in Tables 2 and 3. The second column in these tables shows the Kendall rank correlation between the rankings while the third column shows the proportion of correct orderings when the comparisons are made two at a time.[9] For example, the results for capital in Table 2 indicate that we cannot reject (5 percent level) the hypothesis of a zero-rank correlation and that the proportion of correct orderings when the ranking between the net exports of capital services and the capital abundance ratios is compared for all pairs of countries is 45 percent.

In general, the rank proposition receives little support when tested for each factor (Table 2). The hypothesis of a zero-rank correlation is rejected (95 percent level) for only four resources (service workers, production workers, arable land, and forestland) and one of the correlations (managerial workers) is of the wrong sign. Little support is also found for the rank proposition when the comparisons are made among all possible pairs of countries. Specifically, the proportion of correct orderings exceeds 50 percent only for the three land variables.

The rank proposition also receives little support when tested country by country (Table 3). The hypothesis of a zero-rank correlation is rejected for only eight of the 27 correlations (95 percent level) and five of the correlations are of the wrong sign. Somewhat greater support is found for the rank proposition when pairwise comparisons are considered: for 22 of the 27 countries, the proportion of correct orderings exceeds 50 percent. That the rank proposition re-

[9] These proportions are interpreted as the probability, for a given factor (country), that the ranking of factor contents will match the ranking of factor abundance for a randomly selected pair of countries (factors).

ceives relatively more support when tested country by country suggests that something is affecting all the data similarly, since adding a number that is constant within a country would not affect the country rank test results but would alter the other three tests. A possible source of this kind of problem would be differences in factor input matrices across countries.

Overall, the results for the sign and rank propositions offer little support for the H-O-V model. However, the tests of these propositions do not refer to specific alternative hypotheses and may cast doubt on the H-O-V hypothesis for a variety of reasons, including nonproportional consumption, various kinds of measurement error, and differences in factor input matrices. These alternatives can be studied by regressions of factor contents on endowments as described below.

III. Tests of the H-O-V Equations

The tradition since Leontief's study has been to examine only propositions concerning factor rankings. But as shown in Section I, the H-O-V model actually implies an equality between factor contents and resource supplies. A study of this system of equations has the advantage that it allows explicit consideration of alternative hypotheses—a practice that has generally been absent in empirical tests of trade theory. Here we consider three reasons why the H-O-V equations may be inexact: nonproportional consumption, measurement errors, and technological differences.

A. Alternative Hypotheses

We first consider an alternative to the assumption of proportional consumption (A2). The general hypothesis of nonidentical, nonhomothetic tastes cannot be allowed since then trade, which is the difference between production and consumption, would be completely indeterminate.[10] Instead, we

study a specific alternative to assumption A2:

(Ã2) *All individuals have identical preferences with linear Engel curves; within each country, income is equally distributed.*

The modification of (4) implied by (Ã2) is derived by noting that (Ã2) implies that per capita consumption is a linear function of per capita income. Therefore, we can write country i's total consumption of commodity j (C_{ij}) as a linear function of its population L_i and its total expenditure ($Y_i - B_i$):[11]

$$(7) \quad C_{ij} = \lambda_j L_i + \psi_j\big((Y_i - B_i) - L_i y^0\big),$$

where λ_j = per capita "autonomous"

consumption of commodity j,

ψ_j = marginal budget shares, $\sum_j \psi_j = 1$,

$y^0 = \sum_j \lambda_j$.

Summing (7) over i gives the marginal budget shares ψ_j:

$$(8) \quad \psi_j = (Q_{wj} - \lambda_j L_w)/(Y_w - L_w y^0),$$

where L_w is world population. Inserting (8) into (7) and premultiplying by the kth row of $A(a_k)$, the amount of factor k absorbed in consumption $a_k C_i$ is

$$(9) \quad a_k C_i = (\varphi_k - \beta_k y^0) L_i + \beta_k Y_i,$$

where

$$\varphi_k = \sum_j a_{kj} \lambda_j,$$

$$\beta_k = \left(\sum_j a_{kj} Q_{wj} - \sum_j a_{kj} \lambda_j L_w\right)$$

$$/(Y_w - L_w y^0),$$

$$\beta_k = (E_{kw} - \varphi_k L_w)/(Y_w - L_w y^0).$$

---

[10] In the sense that complete information on each country's preferences would be required to determine trade.

[11] Equation (7) is based on the Linear Expenditure System.

Equation (9) implies that equation (4) can be written

(10) $\qquad \mathbf{F}_i = \mathbf{E}_i - \theta L_i - \beta(Y_i - B_i),$

where θ and β are $K \times 1$ vectors with elements $\theta_k = (\varphi_k - \beta_k y^0)$ and β_k, respectively. Given (10), assumption (A2) amounts to restricting $\theta = 0$ and $\beta_k = E_{kw}/Y_w$.

Next we allow for measurement errors. We assume measurement of net trade differs from its true value by a constant plus a random error

(M̃1) $\qquad \mathbf{T}_i^m = \omega + \mathbf{T}_i + \mathbf{T}_i^e,$

where the vector $\mathbf{T}_i^m$ is the measured value of the vector $\mathbf{T}_i$, ω is an $N \times 1$ vector of constants, and $\mathbf{T}_i^e$ is the error vector. The null hypothesis is that there is no measurement error bias

(M1) $\qquad\qquad \omega = 0.$

Assumption (M̃1) implies the factor content vector is also measured with error:

(11) $\quad \mathbf{F}_i^m = \mathbf{A}\mathbf{T}_i^m = \mathbf{A}\omega + \mathbf{A}\mathbf{T}_i + \mathbf{A}\mathbf{T}_i^e$

$\qquad\quad = \alpha + \mathbf{F}_i + \mathbf{F}_i^e,$

where $\mathbf{F}_i^m$ is the measured value of $\mathbf{F}_i$, $\alpha = \mathbf{A}\omega$ is a $K \times 1$ vector of unknown constants, and $\mathbf{F}_i^e$ is the error vector with covariance matrix that is assumed diagonal for convenience.

The measurements of the endowments are also assumed to be imperfect but in a different way:

(M̃2) $\qquad\qquad E_{ki} = \gamma_k E_{ki}^m,$

where E_{ki}^m is the measured value, E_{ki} the true value, and γ_k is a positive error multiplier. The null hypothesis of no measurement errors is

(M2) $\qquad\qquad \gamma_k = 1$ for all k.

The form of the measurement error contained in (M̃2) is also chosen for convenience since random-measurement errors in more than one variable would force us into consid-

eration of an "errors-in-variables" model, which entails regressions in more than one direction. With our assumptions, factor contents are always the dependent variable.

A third source of measurement error we consider is the incomplete coverage of countries. World endowments and world GNP are estimated here by summing across the sample of countries. The resulting underestimates of the world totals would not affect our analysis if excluded countries had total endowments proportional to the sample totals. As an alternative to this assumption, we can assume that the calculated totals contain no information about world totals. This latter assumption can be stated formally as

(M̃3) $\qquad\qquad E_{kw} = \sigma_{kS} E_{kS}.$

$\qquad\qquad\qquad Y_w = \phi_S Y_S.$

The subscript S refers to the subset of countries in the sample; σ_s is a set of unknown positive elements; and ϕ_s is an unknown positive scalar. The null hypothesis is

(M3) $\quad \sigma_{kS} = 1$ for all k and $\phi_S = 1$.

Combining the assumption of nonproportional consumption (Ã2) with the measurement error assumptions M̃1–M̃3, the expression for country i's net trade in factor k becomes

(12) $\qquad F_{ki} = \alpha_k + \gamma_k E_{ki} - \theta_k L_i$

$\qquad\qquad\qquad - \beta_k(Y_i - B_i) + F_{ik}^e,$

where the superscript "m" is suppressed for notational convenience.

The third source of alternative hypotheses is technological differences. The alternative to the assumption of identical input matrices (A3) that we consider is the assumption that input matrices differ by a proportional constant. This amounts to assuming neutral differences in technology across countries.[12]

---

[12] The specification of neutral technological differences was chosen because of its tractability in estimation.

TABLE 4—ALTERNATIVE ASSUMPTIONS AND PARAMETER RESTRICTIONS

Hypothesis	Assumptions[a]						Parameter Restrictions				
	A1	A2	A3	M1	M2	M3	θ_k	δ_i	α_k	γ_k	β_k
HG	*										
H1	*	*	*			*	0	1			E_{ks}/Y_s
H2	*	*		*	*	*	0		0	1	E_{ks}/Y_s
H3	*	*				*	0				E_{ks}/Y_s
H4	*	*	*	*	*		0	1	0	1	
H5	*	*	*				0	1			
H6	*	*		*	*		0		0	1	
H7	*	*					0				
H8	*		*	*	*			1	0	1	
H9	*		*					1			
H10	*			*	*				0	1	

[a]Absence of an asterisk indicates selection of the alternative $\tilde{A}_i$ or $\tilde{M}_i$. Each parameter restriction is listed in the same order as the corresponding assumptions A2–M3.

Definitions: A1 = identical commodity prices; A2 = identical and homothetic tastes; A3 = identical input intensities; M1 = unbiased measurement of factor contents; M2 = perfect measurement of endowments; and M3 = complete coverage of countries.

Since we calculate factor contents using the U.S. input matrix, the proportional difference in input matrices is measured relative to the U.S. input matrix. This assumption can be written

$$(\tilde{A}3) \qquad A_{us} = \delta_i A_i,$$

where $\delta_i > 0$ and $\delta_{us} = 1$.

Assumption ($\tilde{A}3$) implies that the parameters θ_k and β_k, and the values F_{ki}, are now θ_k/δ_i, β_k/δ_i and F_{ki}^{us}/δ_i, respectively, where F_{ki}^{us} is country i's net trade in factor k computed using the U.S. input matrix. Substituting these new values into (12) gives

$$(13) \quad F_{ki}^{us}/\delta_i = (\alpha_k/\delta_i) + \gamma_k E_{ki}$$
$$- (\theta_k/\delta_i)L_i - (\beta_k/\delta_i)(Y_i - B_i)$$
$$+ F_{ki}^e/\delta_i.$$

The γ_k are not scaled by δ_i since the endowments are measured independent of the input matrix. Multiplication of (13) by δ_i yields the bilinear form

$$(14) \quad F_{ki}^{us} = \alpha_k + (\delta_i\gamma_k)E_{ki} - \theta_k L_i$$
$$- \beta_k(Y_i - B_i) + F_{ki}^e.$$

Equation (14) identifies our most general model,[13] which we estimate using an iterative maximum likelihood procedure discussed below.

In addition to the general hypothesis contained in (14) (hereafter denoted HG), we consider ten alternative hypotheses H1–H10 selected from the set of possibilities corresponding to different choices from the list of assumptions about the theory and the nature of measurement errors. Table 4 states each alternative in terms of the restrictions it imposes on the parameters of (14).

Data limitations prevented us from considering more general specifications, such as allowing input requirements to differ across industries and countries.

[13] This specification was selected after testing it against the more general specification

$$F_{ki}^{us} = \pi_k + \delta_i[\alpha_k + \gamma_k E_{ki}] - \theta_k L_i - \beta_k(Y_i - B_i) + F_{ki}^e,$$

where π_k is an unknown constant.

Hypotheses HG–H10 each maintain the assumption of common goods prices (A1). Hypotheses H1–H7 further maintain the assumption of proportional consumption while allowing tests of the assumptions of identical input matrices (A3), measurement error in trade and the endowments, and incomplete coverage of countries. The hypotheses of special interest are: H4, which leaves only β_k unrestricted and corresponds to the H-O-V hypothesis that the parameter-linking factor contents and national factor supplies is unity; H3, which maintains the assumptions of proportional consumption (A2) and complete coverage of countries (M3); H9, which maintains only the assumption of identical technologies (A3); and H10, which maintains the hypothesis that both trade and the endowments are measured without error (M1 and M2).

B. Measuring Performance and Estimation Issues

Given estimates of the unrestricted parameters in (14) under each hypothesis, a method is required to determine the overall performance of each alternative. One possibility is to form indexes based on the maximized value of the likelihood function associated with (14)

$$(15) \qquad L = (\text{ESS})^{-(NK/2)},$$

where ESS is the error sum-of-squares (summed over countries and factors) and NK is the total number of observations. Values of L, like an R^2, necessarily increase as the number of parameters increases and some form of degrees of freedom correction is required. We adopt the asymptotic Bayes' formula proposed in the context of regression by Leamer (1978, p. 113) and more generally by G. Schwarz (1978):

$$(16) \qquad L^* = L(NK)^{-(p/2)},$$

where p is the number of parameters estimated under a given hypothesis. Given an alternative hypothesis j and a null hypothesis i, we form the ratio

$$(17) \qquad \Lambda = \mathbf{L}_j^*/\mathbf{L}_i^*$$

$$= (\text{ESS}_i/\text{ESS}_j)^{(NK/2)}(NK)^{(p_i - p_j)/2}.$$

The evidence is then said to favor the alternative if $\Lambda > 1$. If the parameter values associated with each hypothesis are considered equally likely a priori, then Λ is interpreted as the posterior odds in favor of the alternative.

The variances of the residuals in equation (14) are assumed to be different for different factors. Processing of the data would be relatively easy if these variances were all equal. For example, if the endowments were measured without error ($\gamma_k = 1$), then equation (14) could be estimated by ordinary least squares with dummy variables. But the assumption of equal variances makes little sense unless the data are scaled in comparable units. To achieve comparability, we scale all the data by the sample "world" endowment levels E_{kS}. Furthermore, to eliminate heteroscedasticity associated with country size, we also divide by the adjusted GNP: $Y_i - B_i$. After these adjustments, equation (14) becomes

$$(18) \qquad F_{ki}^{u s} S_{ki} = \alpha_k S_{ki} + \gamma_k \delta_i (E_{ki} S_{ki})$$

$$- \theta_k (L_i S_{ki}) - \beta_k E_{kS}^{-1} + F_{ki}^{e*},$$

where $S_{ki} = [(Y_i - B_i)E_{ks}]^{-1}$. The errors F_{ki}^{e*} are assumed to be normally distributed with mean zero and variance σ^2.

Given observations on factor contents, resource supplies, and population, the parameters in (18) are estimated using an iterative procedure, which solves the set of first-order conditions for maximizing the likelihood function (15). Given estimates δ_i^0 ($=1$ initially), estimates α_k^0, γ_k^0, θ_k^0, and β_k^0 are obtained from a regression equation for each factor as

$$(19) \qquad F_{ki}^{u s} S_{ki} = \alpha_k S_{ki} + \gamma_k \left(\delta_i^0 E_{ki} S_{ki} \right)$$

$$- \theta_k (L_i S_{ki}) - \beta_k E_{ks}^{-1} + F_{ki}^{e*}.$$

The estimates α_k^0, γ_k^0, θ_k^0, and β_k^0 are then used to obtain new estimates δ_i^0 from a regression equation for each country as

$$(20) \qquad W_{ki} = \delta_i(\gamma_k E_{ki}/E_{kS}),$$

where $W_{ki} = F_{ki}^{us}S_{ki} - \alpha_k^0 S_{ki} - \theta_k^0(L_i S_{ki}) - \beta_k^0 E_{ks}^{-1}$. Prior to using the new estimates of δ_i obtained from (20) to re-estimate (19), each estimate of δ_i is divided by the estimated value for the United States to maintain the restriction that $\delta_{us} = 1$. The process of iteratively estimating (19) and (20) continues until the value of (15) converges.

The above two-step procedure is used to estimate the parameters in (18) under hypotheses HG, H3, and H7 since each involves the specification that $\gamma_k \neq 1$ and $\delta_i \neq 1$. Estimates of the unrestricted parameters under hypotheses H1, H5, and H9 are estimated using OLS while the parameters under hypotheses H2, H4, H6, H8, and H10, which restrict $\gamma_k = 1$, are estimated using a dummy variables model applied to the data set pooled across countries and factors, and imposing the restriction $\delta_{us} = 1$.

C. Analysis

Table 5 reports information on the performance of each hypothesis. The second column of Table 5 indicates the value of the error sum-of-squares (ESS) for each hypothesis. The ESS is of course smallest for the least-restricted model (HG), although hypotheses H3 and H7 do almost as well. The corresponding log-likelihood values are reported in the next column.

Conventional hypothesis testing would compare the difference between these log-likelihood values with χ^2 values at arbitrarily selected levels of significance. For example, the χ^2 statistic for testing H3 against the unrestricted hypothesis is 58.6 ($= 2[-41.1 - (-70.4)]$), which would be compared against a number like 33.92, the upper 5 percent of a χ^2 random variable with 22 degrees of freedom (the number of restrictions). The suggested conclusion is then that the restrictions embodied in hypothesis H3 can be rejected in comparison with the unrestricted model HG. But this kind of treatment inadequately deals with the power of the test, which is

inappropriately allowed to grow with the sample size while the significance level is held fixed. This emphasis on power leads to tests that avoid type II errors merely by rejecting the alternative hypothesis and it creates a serious tendency to reject restrictions as the sample size grows. This problem is alleviated here through the use of the asymptotic Bayes' factor (17), which has a certain arbitrariness in construction, but nonetheless has the effect of lowering the significance level as the sample size grows and thus maintaining some reasonable relationship between the significance level and the power.

The fifth column of Table 5 reports the log-likelihood values adjusted for the dimensionality of the parameter space according to (16). A constant has been added to these numbers so that they are all nonnegative. The corresponding Bayes' factors (or odds ratios) are reported in the last column. The clear winner is hypothesis H3, which allows neutral differences in factor input matrices, biased measurements of factor contents, and multiplicative errors in the endowments,[14] but maintains the assumptions of identical homothetic tastes and complete coverage of countries. Second best (though far behind) is hypothesis H7, which weakens H3 by allowing for incomplete coverage of countries. The third-best hypothesis is HG, the unrestricted model. The other hypotheses are essentially "impossible," given the data evidence. Such extreme values for the Bayes' factors are not uncommon, and should

---

[14] To examine the potential extent of measurement error in the endowments, we compared measured U.S. endowments with the amount of each factor absorbed directly and indirectly in producing the 1967 vector of U.S. final demand in both manufacturing and services (a total of 354 sectors). The ratio of the amount absorbed in production to the endowment for each factor was: capital 2.1; total labor, .88; prof/tech, .62; managerial, .45; clerical, .92; sales, 1.41; service, .68; agricultural, .98; production, .99. The discrepancy for capital likely occurs because the depreciation rates used in computing industry capital stocks were typically lower than the rate used to compute national capital stocks. The discrepancy for managerial workers likely reflects the exclusion of government employees in calculating industry input requirements.

TABLE 5—PERFORMANCE STATISTICS FOR ALTERNATIVE HYPOTHESES

Hypothesis	ESS[a]	ln(L)	Number of Parameters	Adjusted[b] ln(L)	Odds of Hypothesis[c] Relative to H3
HG	1.32	−41.1	71	808.1	3.15E-15
H1	6.63	−280.9	22	707.8	nil
H2	14.56	−397.7	27	576.8	nil
H3	1.61	−70.4	49	841.5	1.0
H4	961.80	−1020.0	11	0.0	nil
H5	6.35	−274.6	33	682.8	nil
H6	11.85	−367.2	38	576.0	nil
H7	1.51	−60.9	60	819.6	32.20E-10
H8	492.39	−920.6	22	68.1	nil
H9	6.25	−272.1	44	653.9	nil
H10	11.58	−363.7	49	548.1	nil

[a] In millions.
[b] Adjusted ln(L) = ln(L) − ($p/2$)ln(297) + 1051, where p = number of parameters and 1051 is the value of equation (16) under hypothesis H4.
[c] Odds = exp[adjusted ln(L) − 841.5]. "Nil" entries indicate a value less than 10^{-50}.

probably be viewed with suspicion since they depend on a number of assumptions, normality being a potentially important example.

Although hypothesis H3 is favored, it does not lead to sensible estimates of many of the parameters. Table 6 reports estimates of the technological differences δ_i. The hypothesis that the technology is the same as that of the United States, $\delta_i = 1$, can be rejected for all but three countries (Australia, Canada, and Mexico),[15] but most of the estimates are wildly different from one, and eight take on implausible negative values. Furthermore, 15 countries have estimated δ's in excess of one, indicating that their factors are more productive than those of the United States.

It is possible that these peculiar estimates are due to one or more "rogue" observations. Table 1 indicates that eight countries with negative estimates all have large imports of the services of one or more of the land factors: arable land, forestland, and pastureland, and accounting for these extreme values

[15] The Bayes' criterion in equation (17) implies a critical t-value of 2.19. The critical value is computed as $[(T-k)(T^{1/T}-1)]^{1/2}$, where T is the number of observations (297) and k is the number of parameters (49). See Leamer (1978, p. 114) for discussion.

TABLE 6—H-O-V REGRESSIONS AND COUNTRY COEFFICIENTS UNDER HYPOTHESIS H3

Country	δ_i[a]	Standard Error	t-Statistics[b]
Argentina	1.5769	0.0941	6.129
Australia	1.1315	0.0751	1.751
Austria	3.9479	0.8720	3.380
Belgium-Luxembourg	−7.1774	2.7668	−2.955
Brazil	0.1327	0.0474	−18.281
Canada	0.9431	0.1225	−0.463
Denmark	7.2536	0.6196	10.092
Finland	4.4885	0.2966	11.758
France	−0.7803	0.7591	−2.345
Germany	−16.9248	2.0573	−8.712
Greece	6.1582	0.2809	18.357
Hong Kong	−174.4016	24.7673	−7.081
Ireland	13.4523	0.4147	30.024
Italy	−1.5930	0.7419	−3.494
Japan	−21.3424	2.2211	−10.059
Korea	3.0928	0.2646	7.906
Mexico	1.1999	0.1121	1.782
Netherlands	18.5644	3.2888	5.340
Norway	13.0655	0.8802	13.706
Philippines	2.2965	0.1057	12.258
Portugal	1.9940	0.1640	6.060
Spain	0.3709	0.2131	−2.950
Sweden	2.9687	0.7193	2.736
Switzerland	−16.2249	5.0798	−3.390
United Kingdom	−17.4481	2.0614	−8.949
United States	1.0000	NA	NA
Yugoslavia	1.7798	0.1524	5.115

Note: Number of observations = 297.
[a] Values are divided by U.S. estimate ($\delta_{us} = 1.0012$).
[b] Asymptotic t-values for testing δ_i is unity. The critical t-value based on equation (17) is 2.19.

may require a dramatic alteration of the H-O-V model. However, contrary to the suggested importance of these observations, re-estimation of the model for each hypothesis with the land variables excluded produced few changes in the estimated parameters (results not shown). Hypothesis H3 remained most favored, followed by hypothesis H7 and then HG. Under hypothesis H3, seventeen of the estimated technological differences δ_i exceeded unity and the number of countries with negative values of the technological difference parameter increased from eight to ten.[16] We thus remain confused about the exact source of the peculiar estimates.

The estimates reported in Table 7 are also cause for concern. The predicted values of the factor supplies can be found by inserting the observed values into these estimated equations. A negative value of γ_k indicates that the observed endowment and the "corrected" endowment are negatively correlated. This happens for four of the labor endowments, although three of these coefficients have large enough standard errors that the sign remains in doubt. This leaves production workers as the anomaly: the number of production workers embodied in trade is negatively related to the measured number of production workers.[17]

Overall, our results cast doubt on the hypothesis that the H-O-V equations are exact in favor of a model that allows neutral differences in factor input matrices and measurement errors in both trade and national resource supplies. This finding suggests that technological differences and measurement errors are also significant reasons for the relatively poor performance of the

TABLE 7—H-O-V REGRESSIONS AND FACTOR COEFFICIENTS UNDER HYPOTHESIS H3

Resource	Parameters	
	α_k[a]	γ_k[b]
Capital	− 990620794	13.431
	(− 6.665)	(2.142)
Labor		
Agricultural	− 7853	13.631
	(− 1.376)	(2.721)
Clerical	− 4628	− 1.111
	(− 1.426)	(− 0.386)
Prof/Tech	− 4376	− 0.360
	(− 1.866)	(− 0.128)
Managerial	− 1815	− 0.528
	(− 1.587)	(− 0.370)
Production	− 19608	− 2.671
	(− 1.997)	(− 2.152)
Sales	− 1214	0.216
	(− 0.515)	(0.175)
Service	− 1302	0.053
	(− 0.498)	(0.052)
Land		
Arable	− 2570651	1718.648
	(− 62.891)	(52.545)
Forest	− 2454843	833.206
	(− 21.263)	(20.427)
Pasture	− 202638	199.930
	(− 2.275)	(9.163)

[a]Asymptotic t-values in parentheses. The critical t-value based on equation (17) is 2.19.
[b]Values of γ_k scaled by 10^3.

sharp hypotheses contained in the rank and sign propositions considered previously. However, our results do support the assumptions of proportional consumption[18] and complete coverage of countries. However, these conclusions are rendered suspect by the peculiar point estimates that are produced by the favored hypothesis.

IV. Concluding Remarks

This paper has reported conceptually correct tests of the Heckscher-Ohlin proposition that trade in commodities can be explained

---

[16] The estimate for Belgium-Luxembourg switched from negative to positive, while the estimates for the Netherlands, Norway, and Spain switched from positive to negative.

[17] Parameter estimates for the unrestricted model HG were very similar to those reported for hypothesis H3. In particular, of the eight countries with negative values of δ_i in Table 6, only the value for France was positive. In addition, the signs and levels of significance of the parameters γ_k paralleled those shown in Table 7.

[18] This contrasts with Yutaka Horiba's (1979) test of the proportional consumption assumption using data on U.S. regional trade. Using a specification similar to ours, he rejected the assumption in terms of the value of β_k but not its sign.

in terms of an interaction between factor input requirements and factor endowments. An exact specification of this interaction in a multicountry, multicommodity, multifactor world was derived in the form of the Heckscher-Ohlin-Vanek (H-O-V) theorem, which equates the factors embodied in net trade to excess factor supplies. The H-O-V theorem was weakened to allow nonproportional consumption and technological differences and was supplemented with various assumptions about measurement errors. Using 1967 trade and input requirements, we tested the null hypothesis that the H-O-V equations are exact against several of these weaker alternatives. In addition, we examined sign and rank corollaries of the H-O-V theorem analogous to those implicitly studied by Leontief.

The Leontief-type sign and rank propositions, whether examined across countries or across factors, were generally not supported. The sign of net factor exports infrequently predicted the sign of excess factor supplies and therefore does not reliably reveal factor abundance. The ranking of factor contents infrequently conforms to the ranking of factor abundance ratios, as examined through either rank correlations or pairwise rankings.

The hypothesis that the H-O-V equations are exact was also not supported. The data suggest errors in measurement in both trade and national factor supplies, and favor the hypothesis of neutral technological differences across countries. However, the form of the technological differences favored by the data involves a number of implausible estimates, including some in which factors yield strictly negative outputs.[19] Thus, to a

considerable extent, the conclusions that come from a study of the sign and rank propositions apply to the more promising regression study: The Heckscher-Ohlin model does poorly, but we do not have anything that does better. It is easy to find hypotheses that do as well or better in a statistical sense, but these alternatives yield economically unsatisfying parameter estimates.

These generally negative conclusions concerning the empirical validity of the H-O-V model appear to contrast sharply with Leamer's (1984) conclusion that "the main currents of international trade are well understood in terms of the abundance of a remarkably limited list of resources. In that sense the Heckscher-Ohlin theory comes out looking rather well." However, the present paper tests a different set of hypotheses. Leamer (1984) studies the weakened hypothesis that the structure of trade can be explained by the availability of resources. This paper examines the stricter H-O-V hypothesis that factor supplies, factor input requirements, and trade interact in a particular way. In addition, the present results suggest that there are important differences in selected input intensities between the United States and the other countries. Leamer's (1984) study may come to a more optimistic conclusion because he makes no commitment to the U.S. input intensities.[20]

DATA APPENDIX

Data on 1966 factor and 1967 trade endowments were collected for 27 countries. The twelve resources are capital, total labor, professional/technical workers, managerial workers, clerical workers, sales workers, service workers, agricultural workers, production workers, arable land, pastureland, and forestland. In accordance with this *Review's* policy of ensuring clear documentation of data, Table A1 lists the data on countries' population, GNP, and trade balance, as well as their trade and endowment of each factor. The following provides a concise discussion of data sources and methods, and includes citation to previously published work which contains further information on these data.

Factor endowment data were obtained from Bowen (1980, 1983). Net capital stocks for each country were

---

[19]Although the assumption of factor price equalization is not explicit in our analysis, the performance of hypothesis H3 together with the results shown in Table 6 could be taken as evidence against the assumption of factor price equalization. Factor price differences might help explain the variability in the estimates of δ_i since such differences would imply nonneutral differences in factor input matrices. We intend to examine the possibility of nonneutral technological differences in later research.

[20]See also Anderson's (1987) review of Leamer (1984).

TABLE A1 — DATA BASE

(1)	(2)	(3)	Country		(4)	(5)	(6)	(7)
22.0	2.17431E10	4.68938E8	Argentina	E	2.40180E10	8496000	1342368	953251
				T	8.67853E8	77647	79417	1701
11.6	2.27360E10	−1.16039E8	Australia	E	3.50530E10	4727000	461828	702905
				T	−1.45799E9	−44830	78226	−14787
7.3	1.01688E10	−6.44060E8	Austria	E	1.56530E10	3363000	605340	393135
				T	−1.07484E9	−40112	−10955	−4982
9.8	1.89645E10	−3.45010E8	Bene-Lux	E	2.25630E10	3764000	236379	477652
				T	−9.38096E8	−7454	−26037	293
83.9	2.90170E10	2.45233E8	Brazil	E	3.04760E10	26463000	12696947	1267578
				T	−1.39899E9	−18704	6813	−4128
20.0	5.68412E10	4.24574E8	Canada	E	7.65370E10	7232000	690656	984998
				T	1.88821E9	−158932	47260	−28570
4.8	1.11664E10	−5.88141E8	Denmark	E	1.30180E10	2230000	304618	249760
				T	−1.32815E9	805	47564	−4358
4.6	8.64730E9	−2.20552E8	Finland	E	1.39290E10	2176000	574029	173862
				T	3.94420E8	−1796	−3009	−2530
49.2	1.08118E11	−9.53400E8	France	E	1.46052E11	21233000	3709405	2299534
				T	−7.06224E8	−34336	−38160	−736
59.7	1.22675E11	2.11160E9	Germany	E	1.81079E11	26576000	2854262	4217611
				T	5.72919E7	349286	−240808	75288
8.6	6.72160E9	−8.16871E8	Greece	E	7.22300E9	4314000	2065975	250212
				T	−1.35709E9	−52749	7616	−7373
3.6	1.97080E9	−4.43437E8	Hong Kong	E	2.08700E9	1525000	78842	104462
				T	−1.48229E9	−28429	−31726	−2834
2.9	2.93960E9	−3.84555E8	Ireland	E	3.37000E9	1109000	346895	90273
				T	−5.16958E8	−9731	18912	−3303

Note: See notes at end of table for column definitions.

Country		(8)	(9)	(10)	(11)	(12)	(13)	(14)	(15)
Argentina	E	588773	161424	2948112	927763	956650	30248000	60130000	145802000
	T	−998	−12	−6990	2886	1645	6561280	−3745350	3835996
Australia	E	443865	300164	2018429	369651	355470	39614000	35151000	447208000
	T	−15213	−6415	−82554	−1348	−2767	6762249	−4913655	3498840
Austria	E	260969	68941	1362688	261978	357487	1686000	3203000	2249000
	T	−4728	−1852	−14008	−1885	−1710	−1546894	−156822	87684
Bene-Lux	E	426461	145290	1778490	409900	275148	981000	687000	818000
	T	−2621	−436	22601	−805	−451	−3672691	−6653807	189337
Brazil	E	1098214	727732	5440793	1595719	2344622	31910000	522600000	141400000
	T	−4805	−1407	−14172	−646	−363	741997	15142	152291
Canada	E	868563	625568	2438630	496115	770208	43404000	322271000	20957000
	T	−21686	−10161	−134350	−5712	−5798	5389052	20253445	899259
Denmark	E	231474	35680	861226	224784	247530	2701000	472000	326000
	T	−5349	−2138	−34661	570	−824	737315	3254944	5328684
Finland	E	224998	32640	797286	165811	207590	2753000	21930000	110000
	T	−2960	−587	8710	−846	−579	−736283	6481551	320649
France	E	2344123	626373	7905046	1751722	1783572	20214000	12714000	13632000
	T	−1197	−1145	9304	−1872	−527	−4585442	−26133156	−437494
Germany	E	2479541	728182	11153947	2320085	2551296	8228000	7184000	5802000
	T	64071	28574	392143	13849	16244	−26018409	−25195922	−5730951
Greece	E	198444	29335	1134582	289901	309314	3851000	2608000	5239000
	T	−6174	−2893	−39697	−2046	−2187	1571541	−2343192	−526643
Hong Kong	E	77927	76097	755180	180102	247660	13000	10000	1
	T	−4095	−1153	14839	−1916	−1547	−2931651	−3459434	−1232976
Ireland	E	87278	14417	370739	109569	87611	1199000	208000	3554000
	T	−3175	−1431	−19559	−407	−769	96740	−622571	2308561

TABLE A1—CONTINUED

(1)	(2)	(3)	Country		(4)	(5)	(6)	(7)
52.0	7.96580E10	−5.39406E8	Italy	E	9.04360E10	19998000	4527547	1763824
				T	−6.98937E9	28922	−103119	11262
98.9	1.10388E11	2.53711E8	Japan	E	1.65976E11	49419000	11905037	6478831
				T	−8.78167E9	107388	−172142	27674
29.1	4.13000E9	−4.87021E8	Korea	E	3.02500E9	9440000	4936176	370048
				T	−1.49530E9	−49392	−9346	−5712
44.1	2.21625E10	−5.61792E8	Mexico	E	2.16390E10	12844000	5878699	910640
				T	−8.28121E8	−50163	25306	−9625
12.5	2.08090E10	−1.26535E9	Netherlands	E	2.99410E10	4699000	388607	657390
				T	−2.85259E9	−60964	29917	−8221
3.8	7.65510E9	−8.39611E8	Norway	E	1.28830E10	1464000	223699	125758
				T	−1.70045E9	−102657	−6254	−11350
32.7	6.18600E9	−1.04685E8	Philippines	E	6.59700E9	12470000	6660227	379088
				T	−1.04236E9	−35637	4721	−5728
9.3	4.26650E9	−4.03294E8	Portugal	E	3.75700E9	3381000	1166445	196436
				T	−8.61326E8	−23677	−11321	−2897
32.0	2.82285E10	−2.31879E9	Spain	E	3.47920E10	11849000	3673190	940811
				T	−4.87847E9	−148941	−17365	−17993
7.8	2.35715E10	−3.01150E8	Sweden	E	3.15550E10	3450000	368805	375705
				T	−1.03381E8	−19339	−16365	−3741
6.0	1.50576E10	−6.65988E8	Switzerland	E	2.33150E10	2843000	263546	457723
				T	−2.11706E9	−48845	−32919	−870
54.7	1.06534E11	−2.55290E9	United Kingdom	E	1.10717E11	25396000	891400	3512267
				T	−1.72415E10	−400012	−283790	−16862
196.5	7.62700E11	4.34870E9	United States	E	7.85933E11	76595000	3707198	2515623
				T	5.76114E9	258625	87377	
19.7	8.60700E9	−3.55350E8	Yugoslavia	E	1.40230E10	8837000	4539567	451571
				T	−8.59292E8	−17986	4413	−4003

Country		(8)	(9)	(10)	(11)	(12)	(13)	(14)	(15)
Italy	E	1181882	185981	8233177	2225777	897910	15258000	6099000	5147000
	T	4838	3877	112909	−1250	435	−62445355	−26821582	−7174026
Japan	E	2826767	1433151	16940833	5757313	3553226	5839000	25400000	157000
	T	16998	9108	220165	1543	4057	−19862383	−67987781	−2956563
Korea	E	244496	75520	1666160	927008	465392	2293000	6656000	18000
	T	−5232	−2186	−23143	−1903	−1873	−1111149	−2404532	−130644
Mexico	E	624218	245320	2766598	1075043	1344767	26000000	78000000	72100000
	T	−9184	−3865	−48936	−1760	−2103	3061733	3920090	297403
Netherlands	E	535686	123114	1823682	467550	429019	946000	292000	1299000
	T	−4618	−3443	−71238	−1260	−2084	417979	−3260982	3394099
Norway	E	158551	50508	653676	122390	129271	841000	7300000	158000
	T	−9529	−4377	−64732	−2976	−3447	−1297301	6966388	443706
Philippines	E	448920	342925	2035104	746953	872900	8330000	14100000	830000
	T	−4561	−2158	−24600	−1722	−1595	842059	1283864	−216082
Portugal	E	109206	24005	1103220	225513	273185	4070000	3400000	530000
	T	−3159	−990	−3460	−1060	−791	−1274623	473446	−224250
Spain	E	596005	98347	4397164	893415	1071150	20156000	13600000	12000000
	T	−15604	−7010	−79483	−5828	−5650	−1221046	−3755719	−1066016
Sweden	E	566835	77625	1390350	317745	334305	3158000	22794000	525000
	T	−2183	−926	7287	−2105	−1317	−2210020	6774374	36931
Switzerland	E	307613	48900	1205432	209245	307897	401000	981000	1778000
	T	1446	−278	−14405	−948	−876	−3652367	−4066582	−692250
United Kingdom	E	2450714	789816	12027546	2460872	3088154	7480000	1829000	12107000
	T	−3730	−6651	−62500	−15201	−11232	−24179333	−49416509	−12948250
United States	E	9911393	7284184	28799720	5108886	9275654	177550000	306850000	258000000
	T	102628	30444	235781	24053	25598	35789032	−69100970	−1108796
Yugoslavia	E	609753	98974	2212785	269528	534638	8266000	8812000	6450000
	T	−4187	−1595	−10469	−1032	−1117	−108893	−78267	664739

Notes: E = 1966 endowment. T = 1967 net trade in factor. Units of T are those of the corresponding endowment. Columns are: 1) Population (mil.); 2) GNP (1966; $US); 3) Trade Balance (1966, $US); 4) Capital (1966, $US); Labor: 5) Total; 6) Agricultural; 7) Clerical; 8) Professional/Technical; 9) Managerial; 10) Production; 11) Sales; 12) Services; Land (hectares): 13) Arable; 14) Forest; 15) Pasture.

computed by summing annual real gross domestic investment flows starting in 1949 with annual depreciation assumed to be 13.33 percent. The underlying investment data were derived from the World Bank's *Economic and Social Data Bank* tape and appear in the World Bank publication *World Tables*. Detailed discussion of the methods used to construct net capital stocks appears in Bowen (1982).

Labor endowments were derived from issues of the International Labour Office (ILO) publication *Yearbook of Labor Statistics*. The labor categories are those defined at the one-digit level of the ILO's International Standard Classification of Occupations (ISCO). Total labor is defined as a country's total economically active population. For each country, the number of workers in each ISCO category was computed by multiplying the share of a country's total labor belonging to a category times its total labor. Since occupational data are not regularly collected, the share of each labor type in each country in 1966 was derived from a time-series regression of the available share data against time. Bowen (1982) provides discussion of this method and presents the years for which occupational data were available for each country.

Land endowments were taken from issues of the Food and Agricultural Organization (FAO) publication *Production Yearbook*. The definitions of arable land, pastureland, and forestland are those used by the FAO.

The total content (direct plus indirect) of each factor embodied in net trade was calculated by premultiplying each country's net trade vector by a matrix of total factor input requirements. Total factor input requirements were calculated from data on direct and indirect factor input requirements for each industry according to the 367-order U.S. input-output table for 1967. Data on each country's trade in 1967 were obtained from the U.N. Trade Data Tapes at the four- and five-digit level of the SITC and concorded to the input-output sectors to perform the required vector multiplications. The concordances are available from the authors upon request.

On the production side, capital (plant, equipment, and inventories) input requirements were constructed from data prepared by the Bureau of Labor Statistics Economic Growth Project, which provided industry capital stock figures measured in 1958 dollars. Industry occupation requirements, measured in number of persons, were based upon the 1971 Survey of Occupational Employment and the 1970 Census of Population. These data were reclassified, to the extent possible, to be consistent with the one-digit occupational categories defined by ISCO. (It was often not feasible to translate industry skill requirements into the ILO definitions; white-collar employment in certain nontraded sectors was a particular difficulty.) Sveikauskas (1983, Appendix) and especially Sveikauskas (1984) provide a complete description of the factor requirements data and a detailed table listing the input requirements data that can be made available.

Land inputs were constructed from information contained in the U.S. input-output table. Arable land is defined as proportional to total purchases from I/O sector 2; pastureland as proportional to total purchases

from I/O sector 1 and forestland as proportional to total purchases from I/O sector 3 (which includes fisheries). This method of measuring land (natural resource) inputs corresponds to a rent definition of quantity and has been used by Baldwin (1971) and Harkness (1978), among others.

Land input coefficients are measured in dollars, whereas land endowments are measured in hectares. To adjust for this difference in units of measurement, the net trade in each land type was deflated using an imputed price. The prices were derived by dividing the total value of each type of land input absorbed in producing total U.S. output in 1967 by the corresponding U.S. endowment of each type of land in 1966. The prices, in 1967 dollars, are: arable land, $142.767 per hectare; pastureland, $108.942 per hectare; forestland, $5.688 per hectare.

REFERENCES

Anderson, James E., "Review of *Sources of International Comparative Advantage: Theory and Evidence*, by Edward E. Leamer," *Journal of Economic Literature*, March 1987, *25*, 146–47.

Baldwin, Robert E., "Determinants of the Commodity Structure of U.S. Trade," *American Economic Review*, March 1971, *61*, 126–46.

Bowen, Harry P., *Resources, Technology and Dynamic Comparative Advantage: A Cross-Country Test of the Product Cycle Theory of International Trade*, unpublished doctoral dissertation, UCLA, 1980.

_____, "Statistical Appendix to *Sources of International Comparative Advantage*," published, in part, as Appendix B of *Sources of International Comparative Advantage*, by Edward E. Leamer, Cambridge: MIT Press, 1982.

_____, "Changes in the International Distribution of Resources and Their Impact on U.S. Comparative Advantage," *Review of Economics and Statistics*, August 1983, *65*, 402–14.

Branson, William and Monoyios, Nicholas, "Factor Inputs in U.S. Trade," *Journal of International Economics*, May 1977, *7*, 111–31.

Brecher, Richard and Choudhri, Ehsan, "The Leontief Paradox, Continued," *Journal of Political Economy*, August 1982, *90*, 820–23.

Chenery, Hollis and Syrquin, Moses, *Patterns of Development, 1950–1970*, New York and

VOL. 77 NO. 5   BOWEN ET AL.: FACTOR ABUNDANCE THEORY   809

London: Oxford University Press for World Bank, 1975.

Harkness, Jon, "Factor Abundance and Comparative Advantage," *American Economic Review*, December 1978, *68*, 784–800.

_____, "The Factor-Proportions Model with Many Nations, Goods and Factors: Theory and Evidence," *Review of Economics and Statistics*, May 1983, *65*, 298–305.

Horiba, Yutaka, "Testing the Demand Side of Comparative Advantage Models," *American Economic Review*, September 1979, *69*, 650–61.

Kohler, Wilhelm K., "A Note on the Meaning of Leontief-Type Paradoxa," unpublished paper, 1987.

Leamer, Edward E., *Sources of International Comparative Advantage: Theory and Evidence*, Cambridge: MIT Press, 1984.

_____, "The Leontief Paradox Reconsidered," *Journal of Political Economy*, June 1980, *88*, 495–503.

_____, *Specification Searches*, New York: Wiley & Sons, 1978.

_____, "The Commodity Composition of International Trade in Manufactures: An Empirical Analysis," *Oxford Economic Papers*, November 1974, *26*, 350–74.

_____ and Bowen, Harry P., "Cross-Section Tests of the Heckscher-Ohlin Theorem: Comment," *American Economic Review*, December 1981, *71*, 1040–43.

Leontief, Wassily, "Domestic Production and Foreign Trade: The American Capital Position Re-Examined," *Proceedings of the American Philosophical Society*, 1953, *97*, 332–49.

Maskus, Keith V., "A Test of the Heckscher-Ohlin-Vanek Theorem: The Leontief Commonplace," *Journal of International Economics*, November 1985, *9*, 201–12.

Schwarz, G., "Estimating the Dimension of a Model," *Annals of Statistics*, 1978, *6*, 461–64.

Stern, Robert M. and Maskus, Keith V., "Determinants of the Structure of U.S. Foreign Trade, 1958–76," *Journal of International Economics*, May 1981, *11*, 207–24.

Summers, Robert, Kravis, Irving and Heston, Alan, "International Comparisons of Real Product and Its Composition: 1950–1977," *The Review of Income and Wealth*, March 1980, *26*, 19–66.

Sveikauskas, Leo, "Science and Technology in United States Foreign Trade," *Economic Journal*, September 1983, *93*, 542–54.

_____, "Science and Technology in Many Different Industries: Data for the Analysis of International Trade," *Review of Public Data Use*, June 1984, 133–56.

Vanek, Jaroslav, "The Factor Proportions Theory: The *N*-Factor Case," *Kyklos*, October 1968, *21*, 749–55.

International Labour Office, *Yearbook of Labor Statistics*, Geneva: International Labour Office, various years.

U.S. Department of Labor, Bureau of Labor Statistics (1974), *Survey of Occupational Employment*, Series of Reports 430, Occupational Employment in Manufacturing, 1971, Washington, D.C.

U.S. Bureau of the Census, U.S. Department of Commerce, *1970 Census of Population*, Occupation by Industry. PC(2)-7C, Washington: USGPO, 1972.

World Bank, *World Tables*, Baltimore: Johns Hopkins University Press for the World Bank, various years.

[20]

JOURNAL OF THE JAPANESE AND INTERNATIONAL ECONOMIES **1**, 62–81 (1987)

Imperfect Competition and International Trade: Evidence from Fourteen Industrial Countries

ELHANAN HELPMAN*

Department of Economics, Tel Aviv University, Ramat-Aviv, Tel Aviv 69978, Israel

Received May 16, 1986; revised June 1986

Helpman, Elhanan—Imperfect Competition and International Trade: Evidence from Fourteen Industrial Countries

Three hypotheses that emerge from a theoretical model are discussed. Two of them concern the behavior of the share of intraindustry trade while the third concerns the volume of trade. One is that in cross-country comparisons the larger the similarity in factor composition, the larger the share of intraindustry trade. The second is that in time series data the more similar the factor composition of a group of countries becomes over time, the larger the share of intraindustry trade within the group. The third is that changes over time in relative country size can explain the rising trade–income ratio. All three hypotheses are consistent with the data. *J. Japan. Int. Econ.*, March 1987, **1**(1), pp. 62–81. Department of Economics, Tel Aviv University, Ramat-Aviv, Tel Aviv 69978, Israel. © 1987 Academic Press.

1. INTRODUCTION

Recent developments in the theory of international trade in the presence of economies of scale and imperfect competition have shed new light on observed trade patterns. Particularly useful in this respect has been the

* I am very grateful to Per Skedinger and Peter Sellin, of the Institute for International Economic Studies, University of Stockholm, who performed most of the computations for this study. The last stages of the project were carried out with the aid of the Foerder Institute for Economic Research. I thank the Bank of Sweden Tercentenary Foundation for financing the acquisition of the data set and parts of the computations, the Foerder Institute, and especially the NEC for financing most of this research through a grant to the Kennedy School of Government.

62

0889-1583/87 $3.00
Copyright © 1987 by Academic Press, Inc.
All rights of reproduction in any form reserved.

work on monopolistic competition in differentiated products (see Lancaster, 1980; Dixit and Norman, 1980, Chap. 9; Krugman, 1981; Helpman, 1981). For example, this theory explains the existence of larger volumes of trade among similar countries with a factor proportions view of intersectoral trade flows.

Although the success of the new models in explaining stylized facts is encouraging, it is very desirable to examine more carefully their consistency with the data. There are at least two reasons for this. First, there exist empirical hypotheses that are implied by these models and that have not been tested (see, for example, Helpman, 1981). Second, by subjecting the implications of models to empirical testing, one may hope to discover weak points that need further theoretical development.

This paper reports evidence on three empirical hypotheses that emerge from models of international trade that are based on monopolistic competition in differentiated products. Two of these hypotheses concern the behavior of the share of intraindustry trade. The third hypothesis concerns the behavior of the volume of trade. The theoretical derivation of these hypotheses relies on Helpman and Krugman (1985, Chap. 8). The theory and evidence concerning the volume of trade are presented in Section 2, while the theory and evidence concerning the share of intraindustry trade are presented in Section 3.

2. THE VOLUME OF TRADE

The factor proportions theory contributes very little to our understanding of the determination of the volume of trade in the world economy, or the volume of trade within groups of countries. The Ricardian view of comparative advantage is also of little help in this respect. Nevertheless, there seem to exist certain regular relationships between income levels of trading partners and the volume of trade that economists have tried to explain for many years (see Deardorff, 1984). Models of monopolistic competition in differentiated products can contribute to the explanation of these links.

Consider a $2 \times 2 \times 2$ economy, in which capital and labor are the only factors of production. If sector X and Y both produce homogeneous products with constant returns to scale, then the factor price equalization set is represented by the parallelogram OQO^*Q' shown in Fig. 1, where OQ is the vector of employment in X and QO^* is the vector of employment in Y in an equilibrium that would have resulted if labor and capital could move freely across countries as they do across industries within a given country. The origin of the home country is O and the origin of the foreign country is O^*.

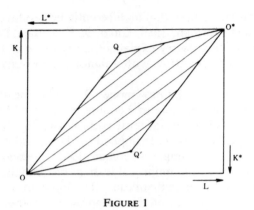

FIGURE 1

In a trading equilibrium without international factor mobility allocations in OQO^* make the home country import Y and export X. The
volume of trade is defined to be the sum of exports. Assuming identical
homothetic preferences and free trade, the volume of trade is given by

$$V = p_x(X - s\overline{X}) + p_y(Y^* - s^*\overline{Y}),$$

where s (s^*) is the share of the home (foreign) country in world spending;
X is the output level of X in the home country; Y^* is the output level of Y
in the foreign country; and $\overline{X}$ and $\overline{Y}$ are world output levels of X and Y,
respectively. Assuming balanced trade, the volume of trade is equal to

$$V = 2p_x(X - s\overline{X}) \qquad \text{for endowments in } OQO^*. \qquad (1)$$

Now, at all endowment points in the factor price equalization set p_x is
constant and both X and s are linear functions of the endowment point.
Hence, the iso-volume-of-trade curves that correspond to this model are
straight lines. Moreover, they have to be parallel to the diagonal OO^*,
and they are, therefore, represented by the lines within the parallelogram
of Fig. 1 (see Helpman and Krugman, 1985, Chap. 8). The farther from the
diagonal a line is, the larger the volume of trade that it represents.

It is clear from Fig. 1 that in this model larger volumes of trade are
associated with larger differences in factor composition. Differences in
relative country size, on the other hand—as measured by GDP—have no
particular effect. This prediction, which is inconsistent with the evidence
(see Deardorff, 1984), does not change when the model is extended to
many countries and goods.

Next, let us change the model, and suppose that X is a differentiated

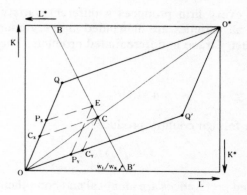

FIGURE 2

product. There are economies of scale in the production of every variety, and monopolistic competition prevails in the industry. In the equilibrium attained with free factor mobility industry X is occupied by a large number of firms, each one producing a different variety, and each one making zero profits. Suppose that all varieties are equally priced and produced in the same quantity. The vectors OQ and QO^* still represent employment in sectors X and Y, respectively. But this time OQ is employed by n firms, each one producing a different variety. Contrary to the constant returns to scale model, here the number of firms n is well determined and of great importance for many issues. The world output level of x, $\overline{X}$, is still a valid measure of aggregate output in the industry, but this time it consists of $\overline{n}$ varieties, with output per variety

$$x = \overline{X}/\overline{n}.$$

OQO^*Q' remain the factor price equalization set for trading equilibria without international factor mobility.

Figure 2 reproduces the relevant features of Fig. 1. Suppose E is the endowment point; the home country is relatively capital-rich. Then full employment with factor price equalization is attained when the home country employs OP_X in the differentiated product sector and OP_Y in the homogeneous product sector. By drawing through E a downward-sloping line BB', the slope of which equals the wage-rental ratio, we obtain point C, which represents the distribution of income across the two countries. Then, if trade is balanced, OC_Y represents consumption of Y in the home country and OC_X represents aggregate consumption of X in the home country, provided we normalize units of measurement so that $\overline{X} = OQ$ and $\overline{Y} = OQ'$. It is clear from the figure that the home country imports Y and it is a *net* exporter of X.

66   ELHANAN HELPMAN

The fact that every firm produces a different variety of X and the assumption that all varieties are demanded in every country imply that there is intraindustry trade in differentiated products. The home country produces

$$n = \overline{OP}_x/x$$

varieties and the foreign country produces

$$n^* = \overline{P_xQ}/x$$

varieties. Provided preferences are identical and homothetic in both countries, the value of X-exports from the home country is

$$s^*p_xnx$$

and the value of X-exports from the foreign country is

$$sp_xn^*x.$$

Hence, there is two-way trade in X products. The volume of trade is now equal to

$$V = s^*p_xnx + sp_xn^*x + p_y(Y^* - s\overline{Y}).$$

Again assuming balanced trade, this reduces to

$$V = 2s^*p_xnx \quad \text{for } E \in OQO^*. \tag{2}$$

It is shown by Helpman and Krugman (1985, Chap. 8) that the curves on which (2) obtains constant values look like the curves in Fig. 3. They are tangent on BB' (which passes through the center of OO^*) to rays through O. The farther from the diagonal a curve is, the larger the volume of trade that it represents. In OQO^* the volume of trade is maximized at E, when the difference in factor composition is largest for countries of equal size. By comparing Fig. 3 with Fig. 1 it is seen clearly how the existence of a differentiated product introduces a new dimension to the determinant of the volume of trade, i.e., relative country size. Now the volume of trade is larger, the larger the difference in factor composition and the smaller the difference in relative size.

Relative country size becomes *the* determinant of the volume of trade when both X and Y are differentiated products. In this case the volume of trade is

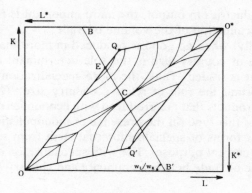

FIGURE 3

$$V = s(p_x X^* + p_y Y^*) + s^*(p_x X + p_y Y).$$

Given balanced trade this yields

$$V = 2ss^*\overline{GDP}, \qquad (3)$$

where $\overline{GDP}$ is gross domestic product in the world economy. Hence the volume of trade depends on ss^*, or relative country size. Figure 4 describes the corresponding equal-volume-of-trade curves. They are downward-sloping lines with the slope equal to the wage–rental ratio. The farther from BB' (which represents countries of equal size) a line is, the lower the volume of trade that it represents.

Figures 1, 3, and 4 make the point that the larger the share of differenti-

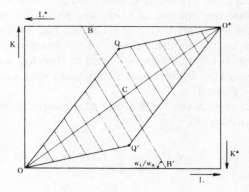

FIGURE 4

68   ELHANAN HELPMAN

ated product industries in output, the more important is relative country size in the determination of the volume of trade.

More generally, when no good is produced in more than one country, the distribution of country size is the sole determinant of the share of world GDP that is traded. Thus, the more specialization in production, the more important the role of relative country size. The existence of differentiated products that are produced with economies of scale leads to specialization of this type (in the presence of monopolistic competition). However, other forms of specialization that stem from scale economies will also do for current purposes. For with specialization of this type, the bilateral volume of trade between country j and country k is

$$V^{jk} = s^j GDP^k + s^k GDP^j,$$

where s^j is the share of country j in world spending and GDP^j is gross domestic product of country j. Assuming balanced trade this yields

$$V^{jk} = 2s^j s^k \overline{GDP}. \tag{4}$$

This provides a theoretical explanation of the gravity equation (see Anderson, 1979; Krugman, 1980), which has been estimated successfully using data on bilateral trade flows (e.g., Linnemann, 1966). Moreover, this has an important implication for the relationship between the ratio of world trade to GDP on the one hand, and the distribution of country size on the other. By direct calculation we obtain (see Helpman, 1983)

$$\frac{V}{\overline{GDP}} = \frac{1}{2} \sum_j \sum_{k \neq j} s^j s^k = \left[1 - \sum_j (s^j)^2 \right]. \tag{5}$$

Equation (5) suggests a possible explanation of the observed fact that in the postwar period the volume of trade has grown faster than income; during this period the relative size of countries has declined, so that the dispersion index on the right-hand size of (5) has grown over time. In order to examine this hypothesis, we need to develop a formula that is applicable to *groups* of countries and that takes into account trade imbalances. This is done next.

Let A be a set of indexes for a group of countries. Then the group's gross domestic product is

$$GDP^A = \sum_{j \in A} GDP^j$$

and we define

COMPETITION AND INTERNATIONAL TRADE 69

$$e^j_A = \frac{GDP^j}{GDP^A}, \qquad e_A = \frac{GDP^A}{GDP}$$

as the share of country j in the group's GDP, and the share of the group in world GDP, respectively.

Also, define T^j to be the excess of exports over imports in country j and

$$t^j_A = \frac{T^j}{GDP^A}, \qquad t_A = \sum_{j \in A} t^j_A.$$

Then the within-group volume of trade is

$$V^A = \sum_{\substack{j \in A}} \sum_{\substack{k \in A \\ k \neq j}} s^j GDP^k$$

$$= \sum_{\substack{j \in A}} \sum_{\substack{k \in A \\ k \neq j}} s^j e^k_A GDP^A = GDP^A \sum_{j \in A} s^j (1 - e^j_A).$$

However,

$$s^j = \frac{e^j_A GDP^A - T^j}{GDP} = e_A(e^j_A - t^j_A).$$

Hence,

$$\frac{V^A}{GDP^A} = e_A\left[1 - t_A + \sum_{j \in A} e^j_A t^j_A - \sum_{j \in A} (e^i_A)^2\right]. \qquad (6)$$

In this case the intragroup trade volume grows faster than its combined income if the adjusted size dispersion index, given by the bracketed term on the right-hand side of (6), grows over time (given a constant share of the group in world income).

Table I contains the calculations of the trade imbalance unadjusted size dispersion index and the trade imbalance adjusted size dispersion index for a group of 14 industrial countries during the years 1956–1981. It is clear from the table that trade imbalance adjustments do not change the time series properties of this index significantly. The reason for this is that trade imbalances as a proportion of income were quite small for those countries, including the external imbalances that were generated by the oil shocks and the shocks to primary commodity prices. Table I also presents the time series of the ratio of intragroup trade to the group's income. It is evident from these data that during this period the ratio of trade to income has risen and so has our dispersion index (the latter

70   ELHANAN HELPMAN

TABLE I

CALCULATIONS OF TRADE IMBALANCE UNADJUSTED
AND ADJUSTED SIZE DISPERSION INDEXES[a,b]

| | Trade imbalance size dispersion index | | |
	Unadjusted (1)	Adjusted (2)	Trade–income ratio (3)
1956	0.631	0.634	0.048
1957	0.638	0.640	0.049
1958	0.643	0.643	0.045
1959	0.645	0.638	0.048
1960	0.654	0.655	0.051
1961	0.670	0.670	0.052
1962	0.672	0.675	0.052
1963	0.680	0.677	0.053
1964	0.690	0.686	0.056
1965	0.691	0.686	0.057
1966	0.696	0.691	0.059
1967	0.695	0.690	0.058
1968	0.691	0.686	0.062
1969	0.723	0.718	0.070
1970	0.715	0.710	0.068
1971	0.725	0.725	0.069
1972	0.744	0.738	0.071
1973	0.767	0.763	0.080
1974	0.773	0.776	0.092
1975	0.782	0.776	0.083
1976	0.776	0.776	0.088
1977	0.778	0.778	0.088
1978	0.791	0.788	0.088
1979	0.799	0.805	0.097
1980	0.804	0.811	0.100
1981	0.776	0.777	0.092

[a] The countries in the sample are Canada, the United States, Japan, Austria, Belgium–Luxembourg, Denmark, France, Germany, Ireland, Italy, the Netherlands, Sweden, Switzerland, and the United Kingdom.

[b] The calculations were made by converting all national currency variables into U.S. dollars by means of the average exchange rate (row *af* in the IFS). (1) This index is $[1 - \Sigma_{j \in A} (e^j_A)^2]$. This index is $[1 - t_A - \Sigma_{j \in A} e^j_A t^j_A + \Sigma_{j \in A} (e^j_A)^2]$. (3) The trade–income ratio is the within-group volume of trade divided by the group's income.

resulting from a reduction in relative country size). The trade imbalance adjusted size dispersion index is plotted in Fig. 5 against the trade–income ratio. It is clear from the figure that they are positively related. Thus, the decline in relative country size contributes to some extent to the

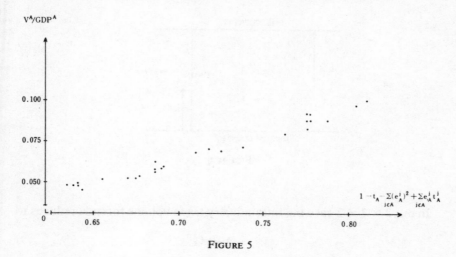

FIGURE 5

explanation of the differential rates of trade and income growth for this group of countries. However, two warnings are in order. First, this evidence is no substitute for a proper statistical test of the hypothesis. And second, the evidence is sensitive to country composition. If the United States and Japan are excluded from the sample then the link between the size dispersion index and the trade–income ratio is substantially weakened.

3. SHARE OF INTRAINDUSTRY TRADE

We have seen in the discussion of the $2 \times 2 \times 2$ model that when sector X produces differentiated products (and it is relatively capital-intensive), the relatively capital-rich country imports Y as well as varieties of X that are produced abroad, and it exports domestically produced varieties of X. The value of its X-exports exceeds the value of its X-imports so that it is a net exporter of differentiated products (assuming balanced trade). This pattern of trade is described by the arrows in Fig. 6, where $p = p_x/p_y$. The volume of trade is equal to the sum of these arrows. The volume of intraindustry trade is defined as the matching two-way flow of goods within every industry. Generally, it is

$$V_{\text{i-i}} = \sum_j \sum_k \sum_i \min(E_i^{jk}, E_i^{kj}) = 2 \sum_j \sum_{k>j} \sum_i \min(E_i^{jk}, E_i^{kj}),$$

where E_i^{jk} is exports of country j to country k of i-products.

72   ELHANAN HELPMAN

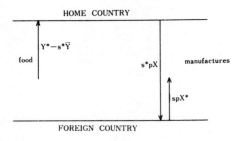

HOME COUNTRY

FOREIGN COUNTRY

FIGURE 6

In our $2 \times 2 \times 2$ case the intraindustry trade volume formula reduces to

$$V_{\text{i-i}} = 2spn^*x. \tag{7}$$

This can be used to calculate the share of intraindustry trade as the ratio $V_{\text{i-i}}/V$. Using (2) and (7) this ratio is

$$S_{\text{i-i}} = \frac{sn^*}{s^*n}. \tag{8}$$

It was shown by Helpman (1981) that $S_{\text{i-i}}$ is a declining function of the capital–labor ratio in the relatively capital-rich country and an increasing function of the capital–labor ratio in the relatively capital-poor country.

Constant intraindustry-share curves are depicted in Fig. 7 for endowments in the factor price equalization set (see Helpman and Krugman,

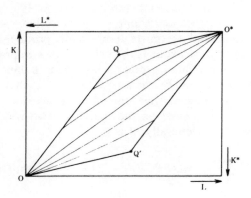

FIGURE 7

COMPETITION AND INTERNATIONAL TRADE 73

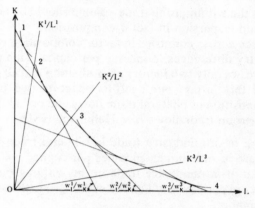

FIGURE 8

1985, Chap. 8 for a proof of the properties of these curves). The diagonal represents a share equal to one, while $O*Q$, represents a share equal to zero. The farther from the diagonal a curve is, the lower the share. It is clear from this figure that larger differences in factor composition are associated with smaller shares of intraindustry trade, and that the larger the country that is a net exporter of differentiated products the smaller the share of intraindustry trade. The second relationship may, however, be rather weak.

More insight into the determination of the share of intraindustry trade can be obtained by considering a many-country many-goods environment with only two factors of production, this time allowing for unequal factor rewards. A case of three countries and four industries is depicted in Fig. 8 by means of a Lerner diagram (strictly speaking, this diagram is valid only when production functions are homothetic; for details see Helpman and Krugman, 1985, Chap. 8). Every isoquant represents a dollar's worth of output and every downward-sloping line represents a dollar's worth of factor costs. Superscripts indicate countries (e.g, w_L^j/w_K^j is the wage–rental ratio in country j), while the rays through the origin describe the capital–labor ratios available in the three countries.

Given the structure described by the figure, country 1 produces products 1 and 2, country 2 produces products 2 and 3, and country 3 produces products 3 and 4. If these are differentiated products, then there exists intraindustry trade between countries 1 and 2, and between countries 2 and 3, but there is no intraindustry trade between countries 1 and 3. This insight can be generalized to state that with unequal factor rewards and many countries the share of intraindustry trade in the *bilateral* volume of trade should be larger for countries with more similar factor compositions. On the other hand, for a group of countries, the share of intrain-

74   ELHANAN HELPMAN

dustry trade in the within-group trade volume should be larger the smaller the within-group dispersion in factor composition.

The difference across countries in factor composition can be measured by cross-country differences in income per capita. This method is accurate when there are only two factors of production and all goods are freely traded. Given this proxy, our analysis suggests two hypotheses, one about the composition of bilateral trade flows and one about the composition of within-group trade flows (see Helpman, 1981):

(a) The share of intraindustry trade in bilateral trade flows should be larger for countries with similar incomes per capita.

(b) The share of intraindustry trade in the within-group trade volume should be larger in periods in which the within-group dispersion of income per capita is smaller.

In order to examine the consistency of these hypotheses with the data, I have calculated bilateral and within-group intraindustry trade shares for the 14 industrial countries in the sample, and for every year from 1970 to 1981. The bilateral shares were calculated as

$$S_{1\text{-}i}^{jk} = \frac{2 \sum_{i} \min(E_i^{jk}, E_i^{kj})}{\sum_{i} (E_i^{jk} + E_i^{kj})}. \tag{9}$$

This was done for every pair of countries in every year.

It is well known that this index is biased in the presence of trade imbalance (see Aquino, 1978). The bias can be seen in Fig. 6. If the trade imbalance is due to the home country's exporting less of X (thus having a trade deficit), then this will reduce the denominator of (9) but will not change the numerator, therefore yielding a larger share of intraindustry trade. If, on the other hand, the foreign country exports fewer differentiated products, $S_{1\text{-}i}^{jk}$ will be smaller. Finally, if the foreign country exports less of Y, then $S_{1\text{-}i}^{jk}$ will be larger. We see, therefore, that the bias that is generated by trade imbalance depends on its source, and no simple adjustment is possible. For this reason, I report results that were estimated using (9).

In order to test the consistency of the data with the hypothesis concerning the bilateral trade flows, I have estimated the following equation on the cross-section data for every year from 1970 to 1981,

$$S_{1\text{-}i}^{jk} = \alpha_0 + \alpha_1 \log \left| \frac{GDP^j}{N^j} - \frac{GDP^k}{N^k} \right|$$

$$+ \alpha_2 \min(\log GDP^j, \log GDP^k) + \alpha_3 \max(\log GDP^j, \log GDP^k),$$

COMPETITION AND INTERNATIONAL TRADE 75

TABLE II

	α_1	α_2	α_3	R^2
1970	−0.044	0.055	−0.014	0.266
	(−3.141)	(4.153)	(−1.105)	
1971	−0.041	0.053	−0.016	0.271
	(−3.495)	(4.003)	(−1.260)	
1972	−0.029	0.056	−0.018	0.223
	(−2.311)	(4.036)	(−1.393)	
1973	−0.017	0.048	−0.019	0.146
	(−1.389)	(3.390)	(−1.428)	
1974	−0.033	0.038	−0.020	0.146
	(−2.236)	(2.744)	(−1.471)	
1975	−0.032	0.039	−0.18	0.148
	(−2.252)	(2.602)	(−1.185)	
1976	−0.040	0.035	−0.021	0.141
	(−2.516)	(2.379)	(−1.381)	
1977	−0.021	0.033	−0.018	0.084
	(−1.361)	(2.109)	(−1.150)	
1978	−0.000	0.043	−0.018	0.076
	(−0.005)	(2.617)	(−1.137)	
1979	−0.023	0.034	−0.011	0.1000
	(−1.860)	(2.079)	(−0.715)	
1980	−0.022	0.027	−0.013	0.064
	(−1.397)	(1.641)	(−0.812)	
1981	−0.006	0.027	−0.020	0.039
	(−0.370)	(1.686)	(−1.283)	

Note. Estimates of the equation

$$S_{1-i}^{jk} = \alpha_0 + \alpha_1 \log \left| \frac{GDP^j}{N^j} - \frac{GDP^k}{N^k} \right| + \alpha_2 \log \min(GDP^j, GDP^k)$$

$$+ \alpha_3 \log \max(GDP^j, GDP^k),$$

where S_{1-i}^{jk} has been calculated on the basis of sectors in the four-digit SITC. The sample comprises the 14 industrial countries cited in Table I. t values are given in parentheses.

where N^j is the population of country j. The minimum and maximum of GDP levels were introduced in order to capture the importance of relative size (Loertscher and Wolter (1980), who estimated a similar equation for manufacturing industries, emphasized the importance of the combined size of the trading countries as represented by their joint GDP). The equation was estimated on four-digit SITC data, using manufacturing as well as nonmanufacturing sectors. The results are presented in Table II, with t values appearing in parentheses.

It is seen from Table II that there does, indeed, exist in the sample a negative partial correlation between the share of intraindustry trade and dissimilarity in income per capita, which has weakened toward the end of the sample period. It is also interesting to observe that the size of the smaller country has a positive effect and the size of the larger country has a negative effect on the share of intraindustry trade, which is consistent with the hypothesis that the more similar countries are in size the larger the share of intraindustry trade. Moreover, since the estimates of $\alpha_2 + \alpha_3$ are positive, the joint size of two countries has a positive effect on the share of intraindustry trade between them. These results justify the use of a combined size variable, as has been done by Loertscher and Wolter (1980), although caution should be exercised in this interpretation because α_3 is not different from zero at the usual significance levels.

In order to examine directly the separate effects of combined size and relative size, Table III reports estimates of the equation

$$S_{\text{i-i}}^{jk} = \alpha_0' + \alpha_1' \log \left| \frac{GDP^j}{N^j} - \frac{GDP^k}{N^k} \right| + \alpha_2' \log(GDP^j + GDP^k)$$

$$+ \alpha_3' \log \left[1 - \left(\frac{GDP^j}{GDP^j + GDP^k} \right)^2 - \left(\frac{GDP^k}{GDP^j + GDP^k} \right)^2 \right].$$

These results support the previous conclusion, although the effect of combined size appears to be rather weak in the second half of the sample period. The coefficient α_3' represents the effect of relative country size.

In order to examine the second hypothesis, we need to calculate the share of intraindustry trade in the within-group volume of trade, and a measure of the within-group dispersion of income per capita. This has been done as follows. The within-group total volume of trade has been calculated by adding up bilateral exports within the group; i.e., as

$$V^A = \sum_{j \in A} \sum_{k \in A} \sum_i E_i^{jk},$$

while the within-group volume of intraindustry trade has been calculated as

$$V_{\text{i-i}}^A = \sum_{\substack{j \in A}} \sum_{\substack{k \in A \\ k \neq j}} \sum_i \min(E_i^{jk}, E_i^{kj}) = 2 \sum_{j \in A} \sum_{\substack{k \in A \\ k > j}} \sum_i \min(E_i^{jk}, E_i^{kj}).$$

Then, the within-group share of intraindustry trade has been calculated as

$$S_{\text{i-i}}^A \equiv \frac{V_{\text{i-i}}^A}{V^A} = \frac{2 \sum_{j \in A} \sum_{\substack{k \in A \\ k > j}} \sum_i \min(E_i^{jk}, E_i^{kj})}{\sum_{j \in A} \sum_{k \in A} \sum_i E_i^{jk}}. \tag{10}$$

TABLE III

	α_1'	α_2'	α_3'	R^2
1970	−0.044	0.041	0.065	0.254
	(−3.108)	(3.003)	(3.728)	
1971	−0.041	0.037	0.065	0.262
	(−3.483)	(2.716)	(3.697)	
1972	−0.029	0.037	0.068	0.213
	(−2.290)	(2.646)	(3.738)	
1973	−0.017	0.028	0.059	0.138
	(−1.403)	(1.893)	(3.199)	
1974	−0.033	0.017	0.048	0.141
	(−2.251)	(1.157)	(2.662)	
1975	−0.032	0.021	0.048	0.142
	(−2.248)	(1.267)	(2.443)	
1976	−0.040	0.014	0.044	0.136
	(−2.507)	(0.862)	(2.278)	
1977	−0.022	0.015	0.041	0.078
	(−1.383)	(0.867)	(1.989)	
1978	−0.000	0.024	0.053	0.069
	(−0.029)	(1.337)	(2.445)	
1979	−0.023	0.022	0.040	0.095
	(−1.885)	(1.283)	(1.875)	
1980	−0.023	0.013	0.031	0.057
	(−1.414)	(0.773)	(1.424)	
1981	−0.005	0.007	0.035	0.034
	(−0.343)	(0.444)	(1.621)	

Note. Estimates of the equation

$$S_{i\text{-}i}^{jk} = \alpha_0' + \alpha_1' \log \left| \frac{GDP^j}{N^j} - \frac{GDP^k}{N^k} \right| + \alpha_2' \log(GDP^j + GDP^k)$$

$$+ \, \alpha_3' \log \left[1 - \left(\frac{GDP^j}{GDP^j + GDP^k} \right)^2 - \left(\frac{GDP^k}{GDP^j + GDP} \right)^2 \right],$$

where $S_{i\text{-}i}^{jk}$ has been calculated on the basis of sectors in the four-digit SITC. The sample comprises the 14 industrial countries cited in Table I. t values are given in parentheses.

The time series of these calculations, for the years 1970–1981, is reported in the first column of Table IV. The values are based on the four-digit SITC data and they were calculated for the sample of the 14 industrial countries that are listed at the bottom of Table I, using *all* sectors in the calculation (not the manufacturing vectors only).

One feature of the shares $S_{i\text{-}i}^A$ reported in Table IV is that they are smaller than other available calculations. Havrylyshyn (1983), for example, reports a share of 0.638 for a group of industrial countries in 1978. This is about 1.5 times larger than the figure reported in Table IV.

78 ELHANAN HELPMAN

TABLE IV

	$S_{i\text{-}i}^A$	$\sigma^A/\bar{g}^A$
1970	0.342	0.373
1971	0.346	0.354
1972	0.356	0.306
1973	0.367	0.260
1974	0.362	0.257
1975	0.378	0.245
1976	0.379	0.268
1977	0.386	0.246
1978	0.387	0.213
1979	0.394	0.201
1980	0.389	0.180
1981	0.375	0.192

$$S_{i\text{-}i}^A = \frac{2 \sum\limits_{\substack{j\in A}} \sum\limits_{\substack{k\in A \\ k>j}} \sum\limits_{i} \min(E_i^{jk}, E_i^{kj})}{\sum\limits_{j\in A} \sum\limits_{k\in A} \sum\limits_{i} E_i^{jk}}.$$

$$\frac{\sigma^A}{\bar{g}^A} = \frac{\sqrt{\sum\limits_{j\in A} \pi_j^A (g_j - \bar{g}_j^A)^2}}{\sum\limits_{j\in A} \pi_j^A g_j}.$$

There are three reasons for the differences between my results and those of others: (a) Typical calculations (including Havrylyshyn, 1983) are based on manufacturing industries only, therefore biasing the results upward. However, from a theoretical point of view, the hypotheses that have been derived at the beginning of this section are based on *all* sectors. Therefore, the appropriate index of intraindustry trade for the examination of these hypotheses is to consider all sectors, not the manufacturing industries only. (b) Typical calculations of within-group intraindustry trade shares average out single-country intraindustry trade shares in their trade volume with *the rest of the world,* using one or another system of weights. This procedure is *not* equivalent to calculating (10), and it introduces a bias the direction and magnitude of which depend on the weighting system. However, (10) seems to be the variable suggested by the theory. (c) Typical calculations are done at the three-digit disaggregation, while I have used the four-digit disaggregation.

In order to examine the relationship between the within-group share of intraindustry trade and the degree of dispersion in income per capita, we need a dispersion index. For current purposes it seems appropriate to use the ratio of the standard deviation of income per capita to its mean. Thus, taking g_j to be income per capita in country j, our index is

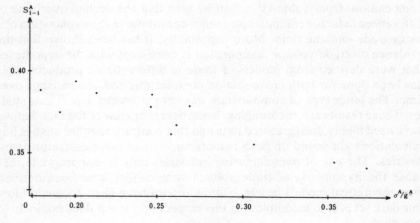

FIGURE 9

$$\frac{\sigma^A}{\bar{g}^A} = \frac{\sqrt{\sum\limits_{j \in A} \pi_j^A (g_j - \bar{g}_j^A)^2}}{\sum\limits_{j \in A} \pi_j^A g_j}, \qquad (11)$$

where π_j^A is the share of country k in the group's population (i.e., $\pi_j^A = N^j/\Sigma_{k \in A} N^k$) and $\bar{g}^A$ is equal to the denominator of the right-hand side of (11).

The second column of Table IV presents the time series of (11) for the 14 countries in the sample. It is clear from a comparison of the two columns of Table IV that the share of intraindustry trade is negatively correlated with dispersion in income per capita, as suggested by the second hypothesis. This relationship is exhibited in the scatter diagram of Fig. 9.

In summary, both hypotheses concerning the behavior of the share of intraindustry trade—one applying to bilateral trade flows and the other applying to within-group trade flows (the former applying to cross-section data and the latter applying to time series data)—find support in the evidence produced for the 14 industrial countries during the seventies.

4. Concluding Comments

It has been shown that changes over time in relative country size can contribute to the explanation of rising trade–income ratios. On the other hand, using the index of dispersion in income per capita (i.e., in factor

80   ELHANAN HELPMAN

composition) from Table IV, it can be seen that the decline over time of differences in factor composition cannot contribute to the explanation of a rising trade–income ratio. More importantly, it has been shown that the evidence on trade volume composition is consistent with the hypotheses that were derived from models of trade in differentiated products. This has been done for both cross-section comparisons and comparisons over time. The latter type of comparisons was not performed in previous studies. These results are encouraging, in particular in view of the fact that we have used highly disaggregated data and that contrary to other studies our calculations are based on both manufacturing and nonmanufacturing industries. The use of manufacturing industries only is inappropriate, because the hypotheses of trade volume composition have been derived from theoretical models in which all industries have been accounted for. Our data set is also incomplete in this respect because it does not include services.

One interesting conclusion that emerges from this analysis is that in bilateral trade flows the link between the share of intraindustry trade and differences in factor composition has weakened over time. This trend may be the result of data contamination by differential trends in inflation rates and exchange rate movements. However, it may well be the result of real economic developments, and it deserves careful investigation. One possibility is that it is a result of the rising share of multinational corporations in world trade. This would be consistent with the theoretical findings of Helpman and Krugman (1985, Chaps. 12, 13). However, at this stage it remains an open question.

REFERENCES

ANDERSON, J. E. (1979). A theoretical foundation of the gravity equation, *Amer. Econ. Rev.* **69**, 106–116.

AQUINO, A. (1978). Intra-industry trade and inter-industry specialization as concurrent sources of international trade in manufactures, *Weltwirtsch. Arch.* **114**, 275–296.

DEARDORFF, A. V. (1984). Testing trade theories and predicting trade flows, *in* "Handbook of International Economics," Vol. I (R. W. Jones and P. B. Kenen, Eds.), North-Holland, Amsterdam.

DIXIT, A., AND NORMAN, V. (1980). "Theory of International Trade," Cambridge Univ. Press, London/New York.

HAVRYLYSHYN, O. (1983). The increasing integration of newly industrialized countries in world trade, mimeo, October.

HELPMAN, E. (1981). International trade in the presence of product differentiation, economies of scale, and monopolistic competition: A Chamberlin–Heckscher–Ohlin approach, *J Int. Econ.* **11**, 305–340.

HELPMAN, E. (1983). A note on the relationship between the rate of GDP growth and the rate of growth of the volume of trade, mimeo, October.

COMPETITION AND INTERNATIONAL TRADE 81

HELPMAN, E., AND KRUGMAN, P. R. (1985). "Market Structure and Foreign Trade," MIT Press, Cambridge, MA.

KRUGMAN, P. R. (1980). Differentiated products and multi-lateral trade, mimeo.

KRUGMAN, P. R. (1981). Intra-industry specialization and the gains from trade," *J. Polit. Econ.* **89**, 959–973.

LANCASTER, K. (1980). Intra-industry trade under perfect monopolistic competition, *J. Int. Econ.* **10**, 151–175.

LINNEMANN, H. (1966). An Econometric Study of International Trade Flows," North-Holland, Amsterdam.

LOERTSCHER, R., AND WOLTER, F. (1980). Determinants of intra-industry trade: Among countries and across industries, *Weltwirtsch. Arch.* **8**, 280–293.

Part IV
International Factor Movements
and Multinational Corporations

[21]

Journal of International Economics 14 (1983) 341–356. North-Holland Publishing Company

FACTOR MOVEMENTS AND COMMODITY TRADE
AS COMPLEMENTS

James R. MARKUSEN*

University of Western Ontario, London, Ontario N6A 5C2, Canada

Received August 1982, revised version received January 1983

Several models are presented in which factor mobility leads to an increase in the volume of world trade. The models share the common characteristic that the basis for trade is something other than differences in relative factor endowments. These alternative bases for trade include returns to scale, imperfect competition, production and factor taxes, and differences in production technology. Taken together, the models suggest a more general idea: the widely held notion that trade in goods and factors are substitutes is in fact a rather special result which is a general characteristic only of factor proportions models.

1. Introduction

It is probably fair to say that international trade theory has devoted far more attention to commodity trade than to factor movements. Perhaps this largely reflects the relative importance of the two in the volume of international economic activity. Yet perhaps it also reflects a deeply ingrained notion that trade in commodities and factor movements are substitutes. By this I mean the concept that trade is caused by unequal factor endowments across countries and thus the tendency of factor movements to equalize endowments will lead to a reduction in commodity trade. Gains from trade can be realized either through the movement of goods or factors, the two being equivalent.

The first formal exposition of this idea is credited to Mundell (1957), who presented a two-good, two-factor treatment of the problem. Mundell noted that in the presence of tariffs, the relatively low priced factor in each country will be that country's abundant factor. Factor mobility in response to these international factor price differences would thus lead to the elimination of trade via the elimination of the factor proportions basis for trade. More importantly, perfect factor mobility was shown to produce an international equilibrium in which factor prices and commodity prices were identical to

*This paper was presented in workshops at the Institute for International Economic Studies, Stockholm, and at the Graduate Institute for International Studies, Geneva, during the summer of 1982. The author would like to thank participants in those workshops for helpful comments and suggestions.

0022-1996/83/$03.00 © 1983 Elsevier Science Publishers B.V. (North-Holland)

those characterizing a free-trade equilibrium in which factors were immobile. Thus, commodity trade and factor movements are substitutes in both a welfare sense and a volume-of-trade sense. With respect to the former, a world Pareto-optimal allocation can be obtained either by free trade in goods or factors. In the latter sense an increase in factor trade substitutes for or leads to a reduction in goods trade.

All of this is not to say that factor movements have no interesting characteristics. Recent papers by Bhagwati (1973), Brecher and Diaz-Alejandro (1977), and Markusen and Melvin (1979), for example, note that tariff-generated factor movements may (locally) reduce the real income of one country or even the real income of the world as a whole. Yet even these results rely on goods and factor trade being substitutes. As is clear from Jones (1967), tariffs imply that any reduction in imports at a constant terms of trade reduces national income (the 'volume-of-trade effect'). This follows from the fact that the benefits derived from an additional unit of the import good (given by the domestic price ratio) exceed the cost of obtaining an additional unit (given by the world price ratio) due to the tariff. If tariff-generated factor movements have the Mundell effect of reducing trade, they thereby reduce income in the absence of a favorable terms-of-trade change.

The purpose of this paper is to examine a number of situations in which factor movements and trade in commodities are complements in the volume of trade sense; that is, factor movements between two economies lead to an increase in the volume of commodity trade. Consider the following set of assumptions:

(a) countries have identical relative factor endowments;
(b) countries have identical technologies;
(c) countries have identical homothetic demand;
(d) production is characterized by constant returns to scale;
(e) production is characterized by perfect competition; and
(f) there are no domestic distortions in either country.

Under these assumptions, two countries will not wish to trade. If we relax assumption (a), we will have the Heckscher–Ohlin model and the Mundell property noted above.

What I wish to demonstrate in this paper is that if we retain (a), and instead relax any of assumptions (b), (d), (e), or (f), we will have a very different relationship between commodity trade and factor trade. Thus, the next five sections of the paper presents a series of simple models, each of which introduces an alternative non-factor-proportions basis for trade.

In all of these cases it is shown that the initial trading equilibrium is not characterized by factor-price equalization. While this is generally well known, the contribution here is to show that each equilibrium involves a country having the relatively high price for the factor used intensively in the production of its export good. Thus, factor mobility must lead to an inflow (outflow) of the factor used intensively in the production of the export (import) good. This adds a factor-proportions basis for trade which complements the other basis for trade. It is then shown by a simple Rybczynski argument that this factor mobility must lead to an increase in the volume of trade, at least up to the point at which one or both countries are specialized.

In all cases examined, factor prices cannot be equalized between countries until at least one country is specialized. While this is also widely understood for the bases analyzed, this paper makes the further point that for factor-price equalization to occur, each country must be relatively well endowed with the factor used intensively in the production of its export good. In the' Heckscher–Ohlin model, this is the *cause* of trade in commodities. In the present model, it is the *result* of trade in factors. If some factors are permitted to move, differences in factor endowments will emerge endogenously in response to other determinants of comparative advantage.

2. Differences in production technology

In this section we consider differences in production technology as a basis for trade and examine a set of circumstances under which this implies a complementarity between goods and factor trade. It is assumed that two goods (X and Y) are produced from two factors (L and K) in each of two countries (h and f) which have identical factor endowments. In this section and in all subsequent sections, it is assumed that total factor supplies are fixed. Denoting countries with superscripts, the production sectors are summarized as follows:

$$Y^i = G(L_y^i, K_y^i); \qquad \bar{L} = L_x^i + L_y^i,$$
$$\qquad\qquad\qquad\qquad\qquad\qquad\qquad i = f, h, \qquad\qquad (1)$$
$$X^i = \alpha^i F(L_x^i, K_x^i); \qquad \bar{K} = K_x^i + K_y^i,$$

where G, F, $\bar{L}$ and $\bar{K}$ are assumed to be identical across countries. Industries are competitive, and F and G are characterized by constant returns to scale. Countries differ only in the technical efficiency parameter α^i attached to the production function for X. We will arbitrarily assume $\alpha^h > \alpha^f$, indicating superior technology in country h. Throughout the paper, it is assumed that demand in the two countries can be represented by a set of identical, homothetic, community indifference curves.

Fig. 1 shows the model in output space with $\bar{Y}\bar{X}^f$ and $\bar{Y}\bar{X}^h$ denoting the efficient production frontiers of countries f and h, respectively. Fig. 2 shows the model in input space with $O_x \bar{L} O_y \bar{K}$ representing the identical Edgeworth boxes for the two countries (the smaller box is not relevant to this section).

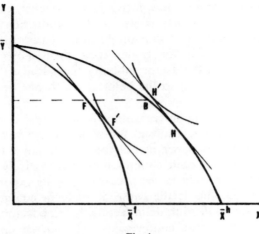

Fig. 1.

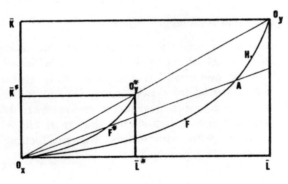

Fig. 2.

Three results need to be established and since they are very straightforward perhaps I can simply state them and dispense with the algebra.

First, the contract curves $[(O_x FAHO_y)$ in fig. 2] and the marginal rates of substitution (MRS) at the same point on these curves are identical for the two countries. Country h has a Hicks-neutral technical advantage over f which simply renumbers but does not displace the X-isoquants for h. Thus, point F in fig. 2 is an efficient production point for both countries and involves the same MRS and competitive factor-price ratio. As reflected in fig. 2, X is arbitrarily assumed to be labour-intensive.

Second, for the same factor allocation in the two countries, the marginal rate of transformation (MRT) between outputs $(-dY/dX)$ will be less in h than in f. Corresponding to the identical input bundles F in fig. 2 are the output bundles F and B in fig. 1 for f and h, respectively (countries are producing the same amount of Y). It follows that the point on $\bar{Y}\bar{X}^h$ that has the same MRT as F on $\bar{Y}\bar{X}^f$ must be 'downhill' of B at a point like H [Findlay and Grubert (1959)].

Third, in a free trade equilibrium, country h will export X and country f will export Y, as shown in fig. 1. This follows from the previous point that the production ratio (Y^f/X^f) exceeds (Y^h/X^h) when prices are equalized, coupled with the assumption of identical homothetic demand.

Let H and F in fig. 2 thus correspond to the output bundles H and F in fig. 1. Let p^* denote the world price of X in terms of Y and let w^i and r^i denote the prices of L^i and K^i in terms of Y. Competitive equilibrium implies that the price of each factor equals the value of the factor's marginal product:

$$w^i = p^* \alpha^i F_l = G_l, \qquad r^i = p^* \alpha^i F_k = G_k. \tag{2}$$

The differences in equilibrium factor prices follow directly from the equations $w^i = G_l$ and $r^i = G_k$. Since (K_y/L_y) at H in fig. 2 exceeds (K_y/L_y) at F in that diagram, it follows that G_l at H exceeds G_l at F,, and vice versa for G_k. Thus, $w^h > w^f$ and $r^h < r^f$ in terms of both goods since commodity prices are the same in the two countries.[1]

If we now allow factors to move between countries, L will migrate to country h and/or K will migrate to country f. Each country will be receiving more of the factor used intensively in the production of its export good. This adds a Heckscher–Ohlin basis for trade which acts to reinforce the direction of trade produced by the differences in production technology.

The fact that this must lead to increased trade offers at the existing terms of trade follows from the Rybczynski theorem and from the assumption of homothetic demand. Holding commodity prices constant, *either* an increase in $\bar{L}^h$ or a decrease in $\bar{K}^h$ must move the production point H in fig. 1 to the southeast.

Fig. 3 shows an increase in $\bar{L}^h$ moving production from H to H^* at constant terms of trade. Fig. 4 shows a movement of production from H to H^* in response to a decrease in $\bar{K}^h$. Homotheticity in demand implies an outward shift in consumption from H' to $H^{*'}$ in fig. 3 and a corresponding inward shift in consumption from H' to $H^{*'}$ in fig. 4. If $\bar{L}$ has increased (fig. 3), desired exports of X will increase since production of X has expanded relatively more than the demand for X. If instead $\bar{K}$ has decreased (fig. 4), desired exports will also increase since consumption of X decreases while production of X increases. Thus, in both figs. 3 and 4, the trade vector $H^*H^{*'}$ exceeds the trade vector HH'. Similar comments apply to country f.

---

[1] This non-equalization result with differences in production technology is reminiscent of the usual non-equalization result in Ricardian trade models. See, for example, Caves and Jones (1973).

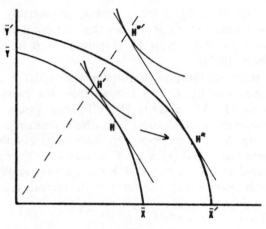

Fig. 3.

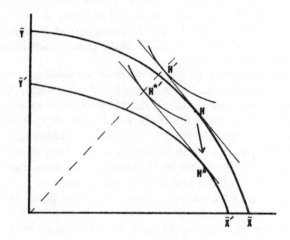

Fig. 4.

Repeating this experiment at all terms of trade leads to the conclusion that these factor movements lead to an outward shift in the offer curve of each country.

Outward shifts in both offer curves do not of course guarantee that the new trading equilibrium will be characterized by increased trade in both goods. With differences in technology, backward bending sections, etc. the equilibrium terms of trade may shift so strongly that trade in one good (but not both) decreases. It seems to me that there is little to be gained by presenting a taxonomy of possibilities which would take several pages of analysis. Perhaps the point is sufficiently established by the simple conclusion that factor movements will lead each country to increase its trade offer at the existing terms of trade.

Factor movements can only come to an end after h has specialized in X and/or f has specialized in Y. It is only after such specialization occurs that $(w/r)^h$ can begin to fall relative to $(w/r)^f$ as should be clear from the discussion following eq. (2).

It should be noted that once a country is specialized, further factor movements may decrease the volume of trade. (Indeed, in the very special case in which all factors are perfectly mobile, one country could eventually disappear.) Once H^* in fig. 4 hits the X axis, further capital outflows will cause H^* to move toward the origin. The trade offer will contract if not outweighed by labour inflow. Thus, the trade expansion result here is not global, but will always be true in a neighbourhood about the initial equilibrium provided that both countries are initially diversified.

3. Production taxes

Complementarity of goods and factor trade as a result of production taxes was treated briefly in a paper by Melvin (1970).[2] Since factor mobility was only a side issue addressed by Melvin, I would like to expand upon his idea here. Assume a two-good, two-factor, Heckscher–Ohlin production model with identical production functions and factor endowments across countries. Production is competitive and characterized by constant returns. The identical product transformation curves for countries h and f are given by YX in fig. 5. The large factor box in fig. 2 continues to represent the problem in input space. Assume, finally, that country f institutes a tax, T, on the production of X. Denoting the producer price of X in terms of Y as p^i in country i, and the consumer price of X in terms of Y as q^i, price relationships are given as follows:

$$p^f/(1-T)=q^f=p^*, \qquad p^h=q^h=p^*, \qquad p^h>p^f. \tag{3}$$

Given our demand assumptions and given $p^i=(MRT)^i$, the free-trade equilibrium must be as shown in fig. 5. Countries h and f produce at H and F and consume at H' and F', respectively. Identical transformation curves together with (3) imply that h produces more X and less Y relative to F. Combined with homothetic demand and equal consumer prices, this in turn

---

[2]Results of this section might in fact apply to a wide variety of situations in which there are domestic distortions, or at least to those situations in which free trade does not equalize domestic marginal rates of transformation. Standard references include Bhagwati and Ramaswami (1963) and Bhagwati (1971). See also Melvin (1970) for a discussion of the difference between production and consumption taxes in the open economy.

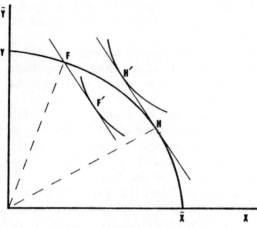

Fig. 5.

implies that country h exports X and country f exports Y. Production taxes can in this manner form a basis for trade. It also follows from the Stolper–Samuelson theorem that the real price of the factor used intensively in the production of X is higher in h than in f and vice versa for the other factor. Since X is labour-intensive by assumption (fig. 2), $w^h > w^f$ and $r^h < r^f$. Each country has the higher real price for the factor used intensively in the production of its export good.

If factors are permitted to move, L will flow into h and/or K will flow into f. The Rybczynski analysis of figs. 3 and 4 remains essentially valid given that the 'wedge' between p^* and $(MRT)^f$ is constant. Since the Rybczynski theorem is based on a constant MRT, the output changes described in figs. 3 and 4 continue to be valid, except that the world price ratio cuts the transformation surface in country f at a constant angle.[3] The result is shown in fig. 6, where country f experiences an inflow of capital. Production must shift to the northwest (from F to F^*) at the existing terms of trade, while consumption will expand or contract along a ray from the origin.[4] The arguments of the preceding section then continue to hold: each country will wish to trade more at any world price ratio and thus the volume of trade will increase subject to the caveat on offer curves mentioned in the previous section.

[3]This same property is used by Brecher and Diaz-Alejandro (1977) in analyzing a tariff-induced capital flow for a small open economy.
[4]The only difference between the distorted and non-distorted cases is that $F^*F^{*\prime}$ in fig. 6 need not lie outside FF' depending on whether or not the world price ratio is greater than the slope of the Rybczynski line (the slope of the cord connecting F and F^*). Fig. 6 shows the case where p^* is less than the slope of the Rybczynski line. If the opposite was true, welfare would deteriorate following the capital inflow, but the volume-of-trade result we are interested in here would continue to hold.

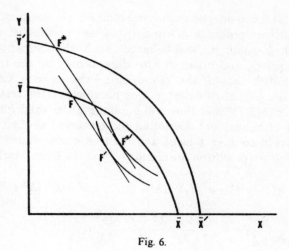

Fig. 6.

Once again, factor prices will not equalize until after h specializes in X and/or f specializes in Y.[5] When a country is diversified, it is well known that factor prices depend only on producer prices in this type of model. This results in the factor-price equalization theorem when producer prices are equalized by trade. In the present situation, the relative producer price of X is always higher in h and thus the real price of L (K) is always higher in h (f) provided that both countries are diversified. Factor prices only begin to converge when h specializes in X and/or f specializes in Y.

4. Monopoly

One of the first formal treatments of monopoly as a basis for trade was that of Melvin and Warne (1973). Their analysis was extended by Markusen (1981) to explicitly treat oligopolistic interdependence. Neither paper is however concerned with factor mobility and what I shall do here is show how their models can imply a complementarity between goods and factor trade.

The two-good, two-factor, Heckscher–Ohlin model with constant returns and X labour-intensive is employed once again. Initially, the X-sector in country f is assumed to be monopolized with all other sectors competitive. Factor endowments are initially assumed to be identical between the two countries. Both assumptions are relaxed below.

Several assumptions and results are borrowed from Melvin and Warne

[5]The fact that specialization is necessary for factor-price equalization follows from Mundell (1957). Brecher and Diaz-Alejandro show that quite different welfare effects occur before and after specialization is reached.

and Markusen: (a) factor markets are competitive such that production takes place on the efficient production frontier; (b) the monopolist cannot price discriminate; (c) demand is 'well-behaved' such that demand elasticities depend only on prices, and prices in turn depend only on the ratio of world commodity outputs;[6] and (d) the monopolist behaves in a Cournot–Nash fashion, taking the output of country h as parametric [the results will only rely on $(MRT)^f < (MRT)^h$ and thus will continue to be valid for Stackelberg and other types of behaviour]. Denoting the perceived elasticity of demand of the monopolist in country f as η_x^f and the true world elasticity of demand as η_x, the equilibrium condition for country f follows from Markusen (1981):

$$p^*(1 - 1/\eta_x^f) = p^*(1 - \sigma^f/\eta_x) = (MRT)^f, \qquad \sigma^f = X^f/(X^h + X^f),$$

(4)

$$\frac{1}{\eta_x^f} = -\frac{X^f}{p^*}\frac{\mathrm{d}p^*}{\mathrm{d}X} = -\frac{X^f}{X^h + X^f}\frac{X^h + X^f}{p^*}\frac{\mathrm{d}p^*}{\mathrm{d}X} = \frac{\sigma^f}{\eta_x}.$$

$1/\eta_x^f$ is thus equal to f's market share (σ^f) times the true (inverse) elasticity of demand.

Graphically, the free-trade equilibrium looks the same as the production tax equilibrium shown in fig. 5. The equilibrium world price ratio is tangent to the production frontier for country h but cuts the frontier for country f. Given the Heckscher–Ohlin production structure and competitive factor markets, the real price of labour is higher in h and the real price of capital is higher in f assuming again that X is labour-intensive. The demand assumptions together with equalized consumer prices imply that country h must export X.

Factor mobility will again result in an inflow of the factor used intensively in the production of each country's export good. While the Rybczynski analysis is no longer valid (σ^f/η_x is a variable), a reaction curve analysis as in Markusen (1981) essentially leads to the same conclusion about the volume of trade. Again, factor-price equalization will not occur as long as both countries are diversified, so a specialized equilibrium will be the outcome if factors are perfectly mobile (h specialized in X and/or f in Y). This has an interesting sidelight which I am not sure has been pointed out before: in the open economy, factor mobility can effectively limit product-market monopoly power.

As a final point, I might note that the basic result here often continues to hold in a wide variety of more complex situations. In my earlier paper [Markusen (1981)], for example, I consider the situation where X is monopolized in both countries, again using the assumption of Cournot–Nash behaviour. If the countries are identical, the equilibrium condition in (4)

---

[6]Melvin and Warne and Markusen show that all of these properties can be satisfied by a CES utility function with an elasticity of substitution greater than one.

would hold for both countries. The equilibrium would be symmetric and would involve both countries producing equal outputs at equal factor prices. Suppose, however, that country f has an absolutely (but not relatively) larger endowment. With the eq. (4) applying to both countries, the solution must involve $\sigma^f > \sigma^h$ but $(MRT)^f < (MRT)^h$. Country f will produce more X, but proportionately less X [Markusen (1981)].

Given our demand assumptions and equal consumer prices across countries, it must follow that h exports X and f exports Y at the Cournot–Nash equilibrium. Heckscher–Ohlin assumptions again imply a higher real rental rate in f. Factor mobility will result in an inflow of the factor used intensively in the production of each country's export good.

5. External economies of scale

External or agglomeration economies of scale as a basis for trade have been examined by Jones (1968), Melvin (1969), Herberg and Kemp (1969), and Markusen and Melvin (1981). This literature assumes that firms are competitive and individually produce with constant returns to scale technology. Industry production functions are however characterized by increasing returns. Suppose we again use the two-good, two-factor, Heckscher–Ohlin production model with perfect competition and constant returns in the Y sector. The production function of the ith firm in the X industry is given as follows

$$X_i = (X^T)F(L_{ix}, K_{ix}), \qquad X = \sum_i X_i, \qquad 0 < T < 1, \tag{5}$$

where the subscript i denotes the private inputs of firm i. F is assumed to be characterized by constant returns. (X^T) is the industry-wide external economy which is viewed as parametric by firm i. Firms thus behave as price-takers and produce with constant returns in their private inputs. Private marginal products can be shown to equal social average products and thus all output is exhausted in factor payments.

Herberg and Kemp (1969), Kemp (1969), and Markusen and Melvin (1981) have established the following properties of this type of production model. First the production frontier must be convex in the neighbourhood of $X = 0$ (figs. 7 and 8). If production frontiers are everywhere convex, specialization is the likely outcome (fig. 7).[7] Second, at an interior competitive equilibrium, the price ratio will not equal the MRT due to the non-internalized production externality. The equilibrium relationship between the two will be

[7]The production frontier can have more than one inflection point. Since we cannot get into a taxonomy of possibilities here, we will restrict ourselves to the two cases shown in figs. 7 and 8. Markusen and Melvin (1981) in fact show that these are the only two possibilities if both production functions are Cobb–Douglas.

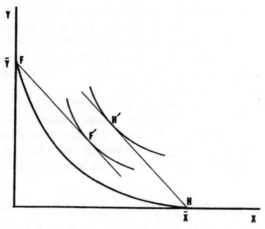

Fig. 7.

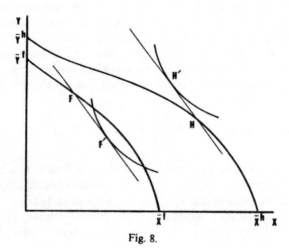

Fig. 8.

$p^*(1-T)=(MRT)$ [Markusen and Melvin (1981)]. The price ratio thus cuts the production frontier, as shown in fig. 8. As in the production tax case, the wedge between p^* and the MRT is constant, implying that equal commodity prices imply equal MRT.

Third, if countries differ in size but have identical relative factor endowments, the MRT along a given ray from the origin will be smaller in the large country. In fig. 8, country h is assumed to be the larger country, and thus at free-trade prices, h produces absolutely more X ($X^h>X^f$) and relatively more X ($X^h/Y^h>X^f/Y^f$). It then follows that h exports X and f exports Y at a free-trade equilibrium, as shown in fig. 8.

Fourth, at equal commodity prices and MRT, the real price of the factor used intensively in the production of X will be higher in the country producing more X. Let the smaller and larger factor boxes in fig. 2 refer to countries f and h, respectively, reflecting the assumption of equal relative factor endowments. Assume that F^* in fig. 2 is the competitive equilibrium factor allocation corresponding to point F in fig. 8. If this is true, then point A in fig. 2 cannot be the allocation for country h. Small movements up the respective contract curves from F^* and A generate the same dY, but a larger dX at A due to the returns to scale in X. Thus, the MRT at F^* is greater than the MRT at A. The allocation for h corresponding to H in fig. 8 must be at a point like H in fig. 2. Markusen and Melvin (1981) demonstrate that F and H in fig. 2 are related by $w^h > w^f$, $r^h < r^f$. Each country has the higher real price for the factor used intensively in the production of its export good. If both countries are specialized (fig. 7), each country will have a factor-price ratio equal to the ratio of marginal products of the good produced evaluated at the factor-endowment ratio. With equal relative or identical (fig. 7) factor endowments, w will be relatively higher in the country specializing in the labour-intensive good and vice versa for capital (the direction of trade is arbitrary).[8]

Finally, the Rybczynski effect not only holds in this model, but is actually strengthened provided that the production frontier is locally concave (the production set is convex) over the relevant region (fig. 8). At a given output ratio, adding labour to country h not only lowers the MRT for the usual Rybczynski reason, but also because of the added scale economies captured in X. Removing capital from h similarly raises the MRT at a given output ratio not only because of the Rybczynski effect but also because of the loss of scale economies in X.[9]

6. Factor market distortions

Since the results of sections 3 (production taxes) and 4 (monopoly) were based on product market distortions, it should come as no surprise that corresponding results can be obtained in a wide variety of situations involving factor market distortions. The problem from an analytical point of view is that the algebra of factor market distortions is generally much more complicated. In addition to distortions between prices and MRT, as per sections 3 and 4, the production frontier itself is generally distorted [Magee

[8]There is one possible difference between the specialization case of fig. 7 and the other cases analyzed. If returns to scale are strong and the differences in factor intensities small, the real price of both factors may be higher in the country specializing in the increasing returns good when one or both countries are specialized. We will assume that this is not the case here.

[9]Another difference between the specialized case of fig. 7 and the other cases is that the Rybczynski effect is irrelevant to the former. Thus, if for example only one factor moves, the country losing that factor will decrease its trade offer.

(1971, 1973), Herberg and Kemp (1971), Feenstra (1980), McCulloch and Yellen (1980), and Markusen and Robson (1980)].

One analytical model which does not involve such complications is the sector-specific-factors model introduced by Jones (1971) and developed by Caves (1971), Mussa (1974), Mayer (1974), and Neary (1978). In that model, there is an immobile stock of capital in each of two sectors, with labour the only factor mobile between the two sectors. With only one mobile factor, production is always technically efficient, and thus the only distortion is that between the price ratio and the marginal rate of transformation.

The implication of this simplification is that fig. 5 above can be used to represent various factor market distortions such as (a) a tax on labour used in the production of X in f or (b) monopsony power in the purchase of labour in the X-sector in country f. Assume again that factor endowments are identical in the two countries. In the specific-factors model, the MRT is simply given by the ratio of the marginal products of labour in the two sectors $(MRT = MP_{ly}/MP_{lx})$. Either factor market distortion just mentioned can be shown to imply $(MP_{ly} < p^*MP_{lx})$; that is, the value of labour's marginal product is greater in X than in Y. This in turn implies that $p^* > (MRT)^f$ which produces the trading equilibrium shown in fig. 5.

Differences in factor prices follow from Jones (1971), Mayer (1974), and Mussa (1974). Capital sector-specific to Y will command a higher price in f relative to h since it is combined with more labour in the former. The opposite applies to capital sector-specific to X. Capital mobility would then result in an inflow into each country of capital specific to the production of the export good (and vice versa for the other type of capital).

While the Rybczynski theorem is no longer valid here, the biased shifts in production needed to generate the trade expansion result continue to remain valid. An inflow of capital specific to Y, for example, will lead to an increase (but not a more-than-proportional increase) in the production of X as some additional labour is combined with capital in Y. This is really all that is assumed in constructing figs. 3, 4, and 6. The formal Rybczynski result that Y must expand more than in proportion to capital inflow is not really needed.

7. Summary and conclusions

The purpose of this paper was to present a number of models in which factor movements generated by international factor-price differences lead to an increase in the volume of world trade. These models share the characteristic that the basis for trade is something other than differences in factor proportions between countries. As noted in the Introduction, these models taken together suggest a fairly important idea: the notion that trade in goods and factors are substitutes may be a rather special result which is generally true only for the Heckscher–Ohlin basis for trade.

If there is a key here, I think that it might lie in the fact that the distribution of factors necessary for factor-price equalization is inherently arbitrary in the Heckscher–Ohlin model if commodity prices are equalized by trade. It simply does not matter where we locate factors, provided that endowments lie in the cone of diversification. In all of the models presented here, the distribution of factors matters very much. More specifically, factor-price equalization requires relative factor endowments to be different among countries. Factor-price equalization requires a country to have more of the factor used intensively in the production of any good for which that country possesses a special advantage (i.e. the export good). This was the case in the models based on differences in production technology and on returns to scale. Similarly, factor-price equalization requires a country to have less of the factor used intensively in the production of any good for which the country possesses a special disadvantage. This was the case in the production tax, monopoly, and factor market distortion models.

Thus, beginning with equal relative endowments, factors move to make endowments unequal and make each country relatively abundant (scarce) in factors used intensively in the production of domestically advantaged (disadvantaged) goods. In a sense, factor mobility creates a factor. proportions basis to reinforce the other basis for trade. In all of the models presented here, factor mobility leaves countries relatively well endowed with the factor used intensively in the production of the export good. In the Heckscher–Ohlin model, this is of course the cause of trade in goods, whereas in the present models it is the result of trade in factors. One empirical implication of this finding is that it suggests that there is an identification problem inherent in simple tests of the Heckscher–Ohlin theorem. Suppose that we find that labour (capital) abundant countries do indeed export labour (capital) intensive goods. This paper suggests that we should not conclude that differences in factor endowments are anything more than the proximate cause of trade. To the extent that capital and labour have moved in response to other bases for trade, it is these underlying determinants rather than differences in capital–labour endowments that constitute the more primitive determinants of production and trade.

References

Bhagwati, Jagdish N., 1971, The generalized theory of distortions and welfare in: J.N. Bhagwati et al., eds., Trade, balance of payments and growth: Essays in honor of Charles P. Kindleberger (North-Holland, Amsterdam).
Bhagwati, Jagdish N., 1973, The theory of immiserizing growth: Further applications, in: Michael B. Connolly and Alexander K. Swoboda, eds., International trade and money (University of Toronto Press, Toronto) 45–54.

Bhagwati, Jagdish N. and V.K. Ramaswami, 1963, Domestic distortion, tariff and the theory of optimum subsidy, Journal of Political Economy 71, 44–50.

Brecher, Richard A. and Carlos Diaz-Alejandro, 1977, Tariffs, foreign capital, and immiserizing growth, Journal of International Economics 7, 317–322.

Caves, Richard E., 1971, International corporations: The industrial economics of foreign investment, Economica 38, 1–27.

Caves, Richard E. and Ronald W. Jones, 1973, World trade and payments, 1st edn. (Little, Brown and Company, Boston).

Feenstra, R.C., 1980, Monopsony distortions in the open economy: A theoretical analysis, Journal of International Economics 10, 213–236.

Findlay, Ronald and H. Grubert, 1959, Factor intensities, technological progress and the terms of trade, Oxford Economic Papers, 111–121.

Herberg, Horst and Murray C. Kemp, 1969, Some implications of variable returns to scale, Canadian Journal of Economics 2, 403–415.

Herberg, Horst and Murray C. Kemp. 1971, Factor market distortions, the shape of the locus of competitive outputs, and the relation between product prices and equilibrium prices, in: J.N. Bhagwati et al., eds., Trade, balance of payments and growth: Essays in honor of Charles P. Kindleberger (North-Holland, Amsterdam).

Jones, Ronald W., 1967, International capital movements and the theory of tariffs, Quarterly Journal of Economics 81, 1–38.

Jones, Ronald W., 1968, Variable returns to scale in general equilibrium theory, International Economic Review 9, 261–272.

Jones, Ronald W., 1971, A three factor model in theory, trade and history, in: J.N. Bhagwati et al., eds., Trade, balance of payments and growth: Essays in honor of Charles P. Kindleberger (North-Holland, Amsterdam) 22–48.

Kemp, Murray C., 1969, The pure theory of international trade and investment (Prentice-Hall, New York).

Magee, Stephen P., 1971, Factor market distortions, production, distribution and the pure theory of international trade, Quarterly Journal of Economics 75, 623–643.

Magee, Stephen P., 1973, Factor market distortions, production, and trade: A survey, Oxford Economic Papers 25, 1–43.

Markusen, James R., 1981, Trade and the gains from trade with imperfect competition, Journal of International Economics 11, 531–551.

Markusen, James R. and James R. Melvin, 1979, Tariffs, capital mobility and foreign ownership, Journal of International Economics 9, 395–410.

Markusen, James R. and James R. Melvin, 1981, Trade, factor prices, and the gains from trade with increasing returns to scale, Canadian Journal of Economics 14, 450–469.

Markusen, James R. and Arthur Robson, 1980, Simple general equilibrium and trade with a monopsonized sector, Canadian Journal of Economics 13, 668–682.

Mayer, W., 1974, Short-run and long-run equilibrium for a small open economy, Journal of Political Economy 82, 955–968.

McCulloch, R. and J.L. Yellen, 1980, Factor market monopsony and the allocation of resources, Journal of International Economics 10, 237–248.

Melvin, James R., 1969, Increasing returns to scale as a determinant of trade, Canadian Journal of Economics 2, 389–402.

Melvin, James R., 1970, Commodity taxation as a determinant of trade, Canadian Journal of Economics 3, 62–78.

Melvin, James R. and Robert D. Warne, 1973, Monopoly and the theory of international trade, Journal of International Economics 3, 117–134.

Mundell, R., 1957, International trade and factor mobility, American Economic Review 47, 321–335.

Mussa, Michael, 1974, Tariffs and the distribution of income: The importance of factor substitutability and intensity in the short and long run, Journal of Political Economy 82, 1191–1204.

Neary, J. Peter, 1978, Short-run capital specificity and the pure theory of international trade, Economic Journal 88, 488–510.

[22]

International Corporations: The Industrial Economics of Foreign Investment[1]

By Richard E. Caves

As trade follows the flag, so does applied economics follow the newspapers. Urgent issues of public policy have in the past decade or so called forth a great deal of new factual evidence on the international corporation, as the chief conduit for foreign direct investment.[2] It has been studied as a channel for the international transfer of technology, as a business organization serving more than one national sovereign master, and as a force influencing the international financial flows recorded in a country's balance of payments. Yet relatively little emphasis has fallen on what might seem the two principal economic features of direct investment by the international corporation: (1) it ordinarily effects a net transfer of real capital from one country to another; and (2) it represents entry into a national industry by a firm established in a foreign market. This neglect is unfortunate, because recognition of these features lets one bring to bear on the causes and consequences of direct investment two important bodies of economic analysis—the pure theory of international trade and the conceptual structure and evidence of market behaviour reposing in the field of industrial organization.

Briefly, the argument of this paper is that foreign direct investment occurs mainly in industries characterized by certain market structures in both the "lending" (or home) and "borrowing" (or host) countries. In the parlance of industrial organization, oligopoly with product differentiation normally prevails where corporations make "horizontal" investments to produce abroad the same lines of goods as they produce in the home market. Oligopoly, not necessarily differentiated, in the home market is typical in industries which undertake "vertical" direct investments to produce abroad a raw material or other input to their production process at home. Direct investment tends to involve market conduct that extends the recognition of mutual market dependence—the essence of oligopoly—beyond national boundaries. Likewise it tends broadly to equalize the rate of return on (equity) capital throughout a

---

[1] An earlier version of this paper was prepared as the Royer Lectures, University of California, Berkeley, December 1969. Valuable comments were received from Professors J. S. Bain, M. Brunt, H. G. Johnson and R. W. Jones, as well as members of seminar audiences at the University of York, Catholic University of Louvain, and Graduate Institute of International Studies, Geneva.

[2] Some of the principal sources of empirical evidence are: E. R. Barlow and I. T. Wender, *Foreign Investment and Taxation*, Englewood Cliffs, N.J., 1955; US Department of Commerce, Office of Business Economics, *US Business Investments in Foreign Countries*, supplement to *Survey of Current Business*,

1

given industry in all countries where production actually takes place. This common profit rate may well exceed a "normal" or competitive one, however, since persistent oligopoly—national or world-wide—is marked by barriers to entry of new firms and, perforce, to the inflow of capital; direct investment thus does not necessarily tend to equalize rates of return in any country as between industries.

With the character and allocative consequences of foreign direct investment identified within the industry, we can proceed to a simple general-equilibrium model that develops the consequences of high international coupled with low inter-industry mobility of capital.

I. DIRECT INVESTMENT AS MARKET BEHAVIOUR

Direct investment tends to occur only in certain of its possible institutional forms, and within only a few of the many industries found in the developed countries. This section seeks to identify and explain the prevalence of these special features. Its empirical aim is to explain the relative importance among industries of the outstanding stock of international corporations or foreign subsidiaries (or of their shares of assets or markets), and not the short-term flow (either across industries or over time). And I shall be concerned with traits intrinsic to the industry, and not those that might accidentally mark the firms belonging to it.

A. *Foreign direct investment and the international corporation*

Direct investment and the international corporation do not overlap completely although they are often identified with each other. Direct investment can occur without a single corporation carrying on business in more than one country, and without any net international flow of capital having occurred—although not without a net flow of equity capital. As defined for purposes of international investment statistics, direct investment requires merely the control of an enterprise located in one country by persons who are not its citizens. A company could thus be foreign-controlled because its founders or subsequent native owners chose to sell a controlling portion of its equity capital to citizens of another country. Although a few firms are controlled abroad without the existence of a specific foreign corporate parent, they are rare birds and seem to be growing proportionally rarer over time; nearly all new direct investments involve a foreign corporate parent.

Washington, DC., 1960; J. H. Dunning, *American Investment in British Manufacturing Industry*, 1958; W. B. Reddaway *et al.*, *Effects of UK Direct Investment Overseas: Final Report*, University of Cambridge, Department of Applied Economics, Occasional Paper no. 15, Cambridge, 1968; D. T. Brash, *American Investment in Australian Industry*, Canberra, 1966; A. E. Safarian, *Foreign Ownership of Canadian Industry*, Toronto, 1966; A. Stonehill, *Foreign Ownership in Norwegian Enterprises*, Samfunnsokonomiske Studier, no. 14, Oslo, 1965; J. N. Behrman, *Some Patterns in the Rise of the Multinational Enterprise*, Research Paper no. 18, Graduate School of Business, University of North Carolina, Chapel Hill, N.C., 1969.

An economist setting out to explain differences in the net flows of direct investment among the industrial countries would naturally turn to the hypothesis that they move from countries well endowed to those poorly endowed with equity capital. Certainly this hypothesis is often assumed to hold, as when importers of equity capital such as Canada engage in national self-flagellation for an alleged lack of home-bred willingness to bear commercial risks.[1] Yet a superficial review of the evidence hardly uncovers compelling support: capital seems to flow toward high-profit countries (or industries, at least), but the countries which export large flows are not obviously low-profit areas. One should not prejudge a test of the capital-abundance hypothesis before it has been performed, but reference to the role of the international corporation would at least render its failure unsurprising. Its investments transmit equity capital, entrepreneurship, and technological or other productive knowledge in an industry-specific package. The influence of national endowments of equity capital need not dominate or even significantly influence its actions.

The prevalent forms of direct investment are restricted not just to transactions of the international corporations, but further to certain kinds of diversification of its activities. A firm's expansion into a new, geographically segregated production facility can take any of three forms: horizontal extension (producing the same goods elsewhere), vertical extension (adding a stage in the production process that comes earlier or later than the firm's principal processing activity), or conglomerate diversification. The overwhelming portion (by value) of direct investments involves either horizontal expansion to produce the same or a similar line of goods abroad, or vertical integration backwards into the production of raw material. (An important numerical proportion of foreign subsidiaries or branches takes the form of sales agencies, representing a vertical integration forward; the capital invested in them is small, however, and they will be neglected here as comprising adjuncts to their parents' export sales activities unless they undertake production and become "horizontal".) Product diversification across national boundaries is almost unknown,[2] however, and there is some evidence that the industries and firms most active in conglomerate mergers in the United States are not among the most prominent foreign investors.

The international corporation's plans to make horizontal and vertical investments abroad are directly comparable to business decisions opting for familiar forms of domestic expansion. Horizontal integration amounts to the acquisition of multiple plants by a firm operating in an industry with sub-markets that are regionally segmented, as by heavy transportation costs. From the viewpoint of rivals in the invaded sub-market, horizontal direct investment amounts to a market

---

[1] Cf. Hugh G. J. Aitken, *American Capital and Canadian Resources*, Cambridge, Mass., 1961, pp. 119–21.
[2] Barlow and Wender, *op. cit.*, p. 159.

entry by an established firm. Vertical foreign investments afford an exact analogy to "backwards" vertical integration in the home market. As seen by competing sellers at the processing stage where the entry takes place, it amounts to removal of part of the former open market for the output of this stage; that is, competing independent suppliers of raw materials will expect that the firm now served by its own subsidiary will be less likely than before to undertake or expand purchases from them in response to a given concession from the going market price. Thus the analogy of each type of foreign direct investment to firms' manoeuvres in a domestic market offers potential assistance both for explaining why the manoeuvres are undertaken and establishing their consequences for performance in the market. I now turn to the former problem; the effects of direct investment on market equilibria are discussed below in Section II.

B. *Horizontal foreign investments*

Why corporations undertake horizontal investments abroad to produce the same general line of goods as they produce at home has been explained in several ways. Hymer and others have suggested the importance of some unique asset of the firm—a patented invention or a differentiated product—on which it can earn maximum profits in foreign markets only through foreign production.[1] Several empirical studies have pointed to the influence of tariffs excluding exports from foreign markets.[2] Behrman and others have pushed the notion (not entirely free of circularity) that the corporations which invest abroad are those with international decision horizons.[3] Each of these propositions may have some explanatory power. I wish to focus on the first while taking account of the second and third.

For the possession of some special asset to lead the firm to invest abroad, two conditions must be satisfied. First, the asset must partake of the character of a public good within the firm, such as knowledge fundamental to the production of a profitably saleable commodity. Any advantage embodied in knowledge, information or technique that yields a positive return over direct costs in the market where it is first proven can potentially do the same in other markets without need to incur again the sunk costs associated with its initial discovery.[4] Knowledge would seem to be the prototypical asset displaying the character of a public

[1] Stephen H. Hymer, "International Operations of National Firms—A Study of Direct Foreign Investment", unpublished Ph.D. dissertation, Massachusetts Institute of Technology, 1960.

[2] H. C. Eastman and S. Stykolt, *The Tariff and Competition in Canada*, Toronto, 1967; Brash, *op. cit.*, ch. 3; Barlow and Wender, *op. cit.*, p. 116. For statistical evidence of the influence of the height of the foreign tariff see Thomas O. Horst, "A Theoretical and Empirical Analysis of American Exports and Direct Investment", unpublished Ph.D. dissertation, University of Rochester, 1969, chs. 3–5.

[3] E.g. Barlow and Wender, *op. cit.*, ch. 2. For a survey of these and other hypotheses, see C. P. Kindleberger, *American Business Abroad*, New Haven, Conn., 1969, ch. 1.

[4] This idea is explored by H. G. Johnson, "The Efficiency and Welfare Implications of the International Corporation", *The International Corporation*, ed. C. P. Kindleberger, Cambridge, Mass., 1970, ch. 2.

good proprietary to the firm, but it is not the only one. The essential feature of an asset conducive to foreign investment is not that its opportunity cost should be zero, but that it should be low relative to the return attainable via foreign investment. The significance of this qualification will become clear below. Second, the return attainable on a firm's special asset in a foreign market must depend at least somewhat on local production.

The necessary character of these two properties becomes clear when we recognize that the native entrepreneur always enjoys an advantage over a foreign rival from his general accumulation of knowledge about economic, social, legal and cultural conditions in his home market and country. The foreign enterprise must pay dearly for what the native either has acquired at no cost to the firm (because it was part of the entrepreneur's general education) or can acquire more cheaply (because, as it were, the native knows where to look).[1] Thus the firm investing abroad must not only enjoy enough of an information advantage in its special asset to offset the information disadvantage of its alien status; it must also find production abroad preferable to any other means of extracting this rent from a foreign market, such as exporting or licensing an established native producer. The net advantage could of course swing to direct investment on account of the unattractiveness of the alternatives, but the general *positive* reason favouring the service to a market by local production is some complementarity between such production and the rents attainable from local sales.

These requirements, taken together, point to a particular trait of market structures—product differentiation—as one necessary characteristic of industries in which substantial direct investment occurs. A "differentiated product" is a collection of functionally similar goods produced by competing sellers, but with each seller's product distinguishable from its rivals by minor physical variations, "brand name" and subjective distinctions created by advertising, or differences in the ancillary terms and conditions of sale.[2] Differentiation is inherent in many products because of the number of minor options available in their physical design and fabrication, or because they are subject to taste diversity inherent in "style"; but to some extent it is a (wasting) capital asset created by the firm through advertising outlays. Its principal consequences for market behaviour are to render the cross-elasticities of demand between rival sellers less than infinite, and to open the possibility of rivalry among sellers occurring through advertising and product variation.

In the nature of differentiation, a successful (rent-yielding) product variety is protected from exact imitation by trade marks, high costs of physical imitation, or both. Because of varying success in differentiation firms in such a market will generally not earn the same rate of profit on

[1] Cf. H. C. Eastman and S. Stykolt, *op. cit.*, p. 80.
[2] The classic discussion is Edward H. Chamberlin, *The Theory of Monopolistic Competition*, Cambridge, Mass., 1933, ch. 4.

tangible assets, and the excess profits will be at least partly immune from competitive pressure. Here is the link to the basis for direct investment: the successful firm producing a differentiated product controls knowledge about serving the market that can be transferred to other national markets for this product at little or no cost. This is clearly so for the patented good or the product embodying a particularly apt bundle of traits.[1] The proposition probably holds even for differentiation created through advertising; not only does the advertising to some extent spill across national boundaries,[2] but also successful differentiation through advertising is normally accompanied by some accumulation of unique knowledge about marketing the product and adapting it to users' tastes.

Differentiation does not encompass all forms of rent-yielding knowledge available to the firm, but—and this helps greatly to explain why differentiation and direct investment occur in the same industries—it probably does include most forms for which local production *per se* increases the rents yielded by a market. For instance, knowledge in the form of process patents or unique managerial skills in the securing of inputs (e.g., finance) or the organizing of production creates neither differentiation nor any complementarity between local production and rents per unit of sales. Transferable knowledge about how to serve a market (and differentiate a product) probably accounts for most of the advantages which Servan-Schreiber describes as the organizational skill of American corporations in *The American Challenge*.[3] Pure organizational skill would explain the successful foreign investments by American management consulting firms, but not by American manufacturing firms; an enterprise blessed with managerial excess capacity and organizational skills not related to a particular product market would tend to prefer conglomerate expansion at home, since alien status always imposes some penalty on managerial effectiveness.

To conclude this line of analysis, consider explicitly the determinants of the choice which the firm makes among serving a foreign market by export, licensing or direct investment.[4] The choice between production at home and abroad (own or licensed) will of course be affected by national comparative advantage (absolute advantage to the firm) as well as by transport costs and tariffs.[5] The balance of net delivered costs

[1] Various studies have noted the tendency of the international corporation to keep its basic research activities at its home location, on account of scale economies, and undertake research in its foreign subsidiaries mainly to adapt its products to local conditions. See Brash, *op. cit.*, ch. 6; Safarian, *op. cit.*, pp. 183–6.

[2] Eastman and Stykolt, *op. cit.*, p. 89, correctly argue that advertising rates may well capture the value of these spillovers for the advertising media; nonetheless, a positive influence of advertising outlays on profitability has been reported by W. S. Comanor and T. A. Wilson, "Advertising and the Advantages of Size", *American Economic Review*, vol. 59 (1969), pp. 87–98.

[3] J. J. Servan-Schreiber, *The American Challenge*, New York, 1968.

[4] For a formal model exploring the choice between exporting and production abroad, see Horst, *op. cit.*, ch. 1.

[5] The empirical evidence is particularly convincing on the influence of tariffs; see the sources cited on p. 4, n. 2.

of imported and locally-produced goods in a foreign market is not always decisive, however. Survey evidence shows that firms very frequently test a foreign market by exports but then switch to local production through a subsidiary, for better adaptation of the product to the local market or the superior quality (or lower cost) of ancillary service that can be provided. Note that these advantages of local production hold for producer as well as consumer goods; although the heights of differentiation are found in the latter, they are not necessarily absent in the former, and the marketing advantages of having production facilities at hand may be particularly great for producer goods. The exporter's disadvantage may lie solely in the fact that his foreign customers feel that a source of supply which must cross oceans and national boundaries is inherently more risky than one at home, and for that reason should be avoided. American firms have reported substantially increased foreign sales solely for this reason when they shift to local production.[1]

The alternative of licensing a foreign producer[2] can match the profitability of direct investment only in certain cases, namely where the rent-yielding advantage of the parent firm lies in some one-shot innovation of technique or product,[3] such as a new method for making plate glass or the secret ingredient of a successful soft drink. Only in these cases can the information on which the parent's advantage rest be easily transferred intact to the foreign firm. In other cases, either the information cannot be transferred independently of the entrepreneurial manpower, or uncertainty about the value of the knowledge in the foreign market will preclude agreement on the terms of a licensing agreement that will capture the full expected value of the surplus available to the licensor.[4] Finally, the relatively high fixed costs of securing the information necessary to undertake a foreign investment predispose the small firm to settle for licensing. Research on the use of licensing by American firms shows that it is employed by relatively small companies; conversely, the prevalence of large firms among those with direct investments abroad has often been noted.[5]

Empirical research on the inter-industry determinants of foreign investment has not yet provided a full test of the hypothesis ventured

---

[1] Behrman, *op. cit.*, p. 3.

[2] On licensing, see R. F. Mikesell, ed., *US Private and Government Investment Abroad*, Eugene, Ore., 1962, ch. 5; Kingman Brewster, *Antitrust and American Business Abroad*, New York, 1958, ch. 7.

[3] H. G. Johnson, *Comparative Cost and Commercial Policy Theory for a Developing World Economy*, Wicksell Lectures, Stockholm, 1968.

[4] Information might not be fully transferable where the knowledge consists of entrepreneurial skill in serving a differentiated market; a profit-maximizing licensing agreement might not be feasible where the process of product innovation requires continuous market testing, and the value imputed to one innovation depends on how it is combined with others.

[5] US Senate, Committee on the Judiciary, Subcommittee on Antitrust and Monopoly, *International Aspects of Antitrust*, Hearings pursuant to S. Res. 191, Washington, DC., 1967, p. 198. The choice between licensing and direct investment can also be influenced by a number of factors less central to the concerns of

here about the role of product differentiation, but casual inspection of several sets of data does seem to support it. For the United States a high rank correlation seems to exist between the extent of product differentiation[1] and the proportion of firms in an industry having foreign subsidiaries. If we calculate the portion of the larger firms in various American industries having foreign subsidiaries, the list is headed by automobiles, other consumer durables, scientific instruments, chemicals and rubber. At the bottom come primary metals, leather, lumber, paper and textiles. The same pattern emerges if we examine countries that are important gross importers of capital, such as Canada or the United Kingdom, and calculate the portion of production in various industries accounted for by subsidiaries of foreign firms.[2] A formal statistical analysis has been provided for Canada by Eastman and Stykolt, whose results I would interpret as showing that the portion of foreign ownership in a sample of industries is significantly related to product differentiation and other sources of advantage to the multi-plant firm.[3]

Of course, differentiation may not be the only industrial attribute explaining the incidence of direct investment. It has been noted, for instance, that the research-intensity of American industries (measured by expenditures on research and development as a percentage of sales) is positively related to the relative importance of sales by American subsidiaries in Western Europe (measured by the ratio of subsidiary sales to American exports to non-affiliated companies); this relation does not hold except for Western Europe.[4] Also, research and develop-

---

this paper. As Giorgio Basevi and others have suggested, opting for direct investment implies that the parent firm adds a capital asset to its portfolio denominated in foreign currency, while licensing gives rise only to a claim on the yield of such an asset. Exchange-rate expectations and considerations of portfolio balance thus may influence the choice.

[1] The assumption that products or industries can be ranked in terms of the extent of product differentiation is a controversial one, and the issue cannot receive full consideration here. In the absence of empirical information on the divergence between price elasticities facing the firm and its industry, one must resort to ranking industries by various traits of the product and its conditions of sale and use. Rankings by these various traits need not coincide, and there is no obvious formal method of weighting the various traits in order to consolidate the rankings. My view is that economists who have studied the market behaviour attributable to product differentiation in various industries would agree in general on these rankings and their aggregation.

[2] See Barlow and Wender, *op. cit.*, p. 41; Dunning, *op. cit.*, table 2, p. 58; and Irving Brecher and S. S. Reisman, *Canada–United States Economic Relations*, Studies for Royal Commission on Canada's Economic Prospects, Ottawa, 1957, p. 105.

[3] Eastman and Stykolt, *op. cit.*, ch. 4. Their own interpretation is rather different, primarily because they view multi-plant development as a consequence of firms' struggles against the disadvantages of owning plants of suboptimal scale, and thus do not recognize the direct connection noted above between differentiation and the advantages of local production to serve the market. Their measure of differentiation fails to emerge as a statistically significant determinant of foreign investment, but it is highly collinear with their proxy for advantages to the multi-plant firm (which is significant).

[4] W. Gruber, D. Mehta and R. Vernon, "The R & D Factor in International

ment expenditures on new products have been found related to the outflow of new direct investment from the United States.[1] Once one recognizes that the bulk of industrial research expenditure is on new products and product development, it becomes probable that these results for all practical purposes coincide with the line of analysis advanced previously. The current *flow* of direct investment should then occur predominantly in industries where a high current rate of research expenditure in knowledge creation adds rapidly to their stock of exportable knowledge and biases the choice among means of exporting this knowledge towards direct investment. Formal research expenditures are not the only means of building differentiation, however, and the industrial pattern of the flow of direct investment thus need not (and does not) coincide with the pattern of the accumulated stock.

The relation of differentiation to the influence of tariffs on foreign investment also calls for comment. The impact of tariffs is shown not only by direct survey evidence cited above, but also by the data revealing that subsidiaries in the import-competing manufacturing sectors of such countries as Australia and Canada often report higher production costs than those incurred by their parents at home.[2] Will tariffs cause the establishment of foreign subsidiaries in industries where differentiation is absent? Where potential rents exist for companies making direct investments abroad, tariffs are likely to increase those rents at the same time as they cut the profitability of exporting, and thus encourage the inflow of direct investment. By contrast, a tariff protecting a purely competitive industry with unimpeded entry of domestic capital would foster no direct investment; a foreign entrepreneur contemplating entry could expect only transient windfall profits to stack against the innate disadvantages of being a foreign entrepreneur.[3]

But what if barriers to entry are present and excess profits can and do prevail in the long run? The case of long-run excess profits in a foreign market, associated with oligopoly protected by entry barriers, does provide a definite theoretical exception to the preceding argument for the necessary role of product differentiation. Consider the following plausible circumstances for a large firm located in an undifferentiated oligopoly market. It might enjoy excess profits and a flow of internal funds greater than the amount needed to support a profit-maximizing rate of expansion in its home market. It might possess managerial excess capacity which, combined with its stock of technological and

---

Trade and International Investment of U.S. Industries", *Journal of Political Economy*, vol. 75 (1967), pp. 20–37.

[1] Evidence on this point is summarized in Robert Lacroix, "Pour une théorie de l'investissement direct étranger dans l'industrie manufacturière", unpublished ms., University of Montreal, 1970, ch. 2.

[2] This should be due to the tariff, since the same surveys indicate that the subsidiaries tend to be profitable relative to their parents. Brash, *op. cit.*, ch. 7; Safarian, *op. cit.*, pp. 201–3.

[3] Countries such as Canada and Australia offer pervasive tariff protection to their manufacturing sectors, yet direct investment in such protected but undifferentiated industries as textiles and steel is uncommon.

production knowledge, assure that it could establish a plant abroad at no serious disadvantage in long-run average unit costs relative to local firms of efficient scale. In this case foreign investment could clearly occur without differentiation and without any specific complementarity between local production and the profitability of foreign sales. The rate of return attainable through foreign investment to its excess liquidity, technological knowledge and under-utilized managerial resources might exceed what it could earn *either* through pooling these resources for conglomerate diversification in the domestic market *or* through the piecemeal disposal of these assets at home or abroad. The role of seller concentration and entry barriers is thus marked as important for explaining the distribution of foreign direct investment, and these factors will be considered directly in Section II.

C. *Vertical direct investments*

Foreign investment in a vertically related stage of production invites analysis in terms of the theoretical determinants of optimal vertical integration. A glance at the prevalent types of vertical investments quickly shows, however, that they represent a particular type—preparation of raw-material inputs—and thus call for a less general analysis. No gain arises from the physical integration of processes when, say, a steel company establishes an iron-ore mine, since the technology at the two stages of production has nothing in common. The corporation may integrate backwards to produce raw materials in less-developed countries where they might otherwise not be forthcoming, due to shortages of local social overhead capital and entrepreneurship; but this line of argument fails to explain extensive vertical direct investments in countries like Canada and Norway which seem well endowed with railroads and local entrepreneurs.

The motives for vertical investments among the industrial countries seem to turn heavily on the avoidance of oligopolistic uncertainty and the erection of barriers to the entry of new rivals—as in the case of domestic markets.[1] In the absence of technological complementarity, such investments would not be expected in a competitive raw-materials industry, unless due to some special difference between the raw-materials producers and the subsequent processors in time horizons, discount rates and the like. Where both the buyers and sellers of the raw material are few in number, where the profitability of investments by both buyer and seller depends heavily on the prices expected to prevail over a long period of time, where these investments are large in absolute size, and where the raw material has neither alternative uses nor substitutes in its sole use, much uncertainty can be eliminated through common ownership of the two vertically related stages. In the case of established

[1] M. G. de Chazeau and A. E. Kahn, *Integration and Competition in the Petroleum Industry*, New Haven, 1959, ch. 3; E. T. Penrose, *The Large International Firm in Developing Countries: The International Petroleum Industry*, 1968, pp. 46–50, 253–9.

arm's-length buyers and sellers, the long-term contract offers an alternative to vertical integration. At the time when a natural resource is first developed, however, these arrangements are not necessarily alternatives, since the processing firm making a direct investment in resource-based production may well reach such a contractual relationship with the natural-resource owner.

Another motive for vertical integration besides risk-avoidance arises when the processing industry is populated by relatively few sellers. By controlling their input sources, the existing firms may raise substantial barriers to the entry of new competitors. If the resource is not a ubiquitous one, and known supply sources are tied up through vertical integration, a new entrant to the processing industry must endure the extra costs and uncertainties of finding and developing his own source of raw materials. The going firms can enjoy higher than competitive profit rates without attracting new rivals.[1]

Both sets of motives point to the same determinants of the incidence of vertical direct investments among industries. High seller concentration would seem critical at the production stage from which the foreign investment is initiated. It directly generates uncertainty in the market for the raw material. It is also necessary to motivate the *firm* to take actions aiming to raise entry barriers to the *industry*. Furthermore, for the processing firm to undertake a foreign investment involving an enormous financial commitment, in the face of the prevailing influence of lenders' risk on the capital markets, it must initially be of large absolute size. Besides size and concentration in the processing industry, other predictors of vertical direct investment emerge from the other factors tending to increase market uncertainty: the minimum scale and durability of the resource investment and the existence of alternative uses.

The statistical evidence on foreign investment does not lend itself readily to testing these predictions beyond the recital of examples, though these instances do seem to provide considerable support. One additional implication—that vertical direct investment will comprise a greater portion of the total direct outflow from a country with a smaller domestic resource base—has been confirmed by a comparison of the United States and the United Kingdom.[2]

II. DIRECT INVESTMENT AND MARKET BEHAVIOUR

The total impact of foreign investment within the industry depends both on the forces which induce decisions to establish foreign subsidiaries and the consequences these subsidiaries have for market behaviour

---

[1] See Joe S. Bain, *Barriers to New Competition*, Cambridge, Mass., 1956. The same motives can operate to explain forward integration by a manufacturer into distribution. For several reasons, however, this seems a less fruitful way to erect barriers to entry, and strong elements of bilateral oligopoly and uncertainty are seldom present.

[2] R. E. Krainer, "Resource Endowment and the Structure of Foreign Investment", *Journal of Finance*, vol. 22 (1967), pp. 49–57.

and resource allocation. This section pursues these effects to the level of the industry, national and international, and the following section employs international-trade models to extend them into general equilibrium. The discussion will be confined largely to horizontal investments.

The preceding section adduced two features that should characterize any industry in which substantial horizontal direct investment occurs: product differentiation and oligopoly. The latter emerged only indirectly, and thus needs some supplemental explanation. It was established that the fixed information costs associated with planning a direct investment bias large firms towards preferring this method of extracting rents from a foreign market. Also, the theory of the multiplant firm and the likelihood of scale economies in national sales promotion (for differentiated products) suggest that a firm would not invest abroad while profitable opportunities remained for the exploitation of scale economies in production or sales in the home market. For these reasons a firm that invests abroad will be relatively large and face relatively few competitors at home, since the same structural forces probably determine the sizes of its rivals.[1]

These traits combine to nominate differentiated oligopoly as the most likely market environment for direct investment. This and other concepts drawn from the field of industrial organization can serve to predict and explain the industrial consequences of direct investment. In particular, it seems fruitful to consider a model of a national industry which, when blown up to the level of a "world industry", would capture the chief characteristics of differentiated oligopoly with direct investment. This is the national oligopoly with regional sub-markets, found commonly in national product markets where transport costs or the need to adapt output to local demand characteristics call for decentralized production, and barriers to entry constrict the number of sellers. Examples in the United States are the petroleum refining and brewery industries, which contain both national ("international") and regional ("national") sellers. Horizontal direct investment becomes the equivalent of entry into a regional sub-market by a firm established in at least one other sub-market.

The barriers to entry into a national market by an international firm can readily be compared with those identified for new domestic entrants

[1] The affinity of direct investment for industries of oligopolistic market structure has been documented extensively. In the United Kingdom, Dunning found that two-thirds of the subsidiaries covered in his survey operated in markets of tight-knit oligopoly. *Op. cit.*, pp. 155–7. Also, a significant relation has been found between the level of seller concentration (portion of sales accounted for by the five largest firms) and foreign participation for a sample of 277 manufacturing industries. This holds for American subsidiaries as well as all foreign-owned firms, and examination of a sub-sample suggests that the foreign presence typically consists of two or more firms rather than a single subsidiary. See M. D. Steuer *et al., The Economic Effects of Inward Investment in the United Kingdom: A Preliminary Report*, 1970, ch. 4. Rosenbluth reports similar findings for Canada, but shows that the association between foreign ownership and concentration can be viewed as resulting solely from the excess of the absolute size of foreign firms

in these same markets.[1] Indeed, the international firm holds advantages against each of the major sources of entry barriers. If scale economies are significant but prevail at only one stage of fabrication, the foreign firm may be able to carry out that process at a single location and transplant only the others ("assembly operations") to its subsidiary. Thus, foreign subsidiaries are typically less integrated vertically than the domestic firms with which they compete, and the manufacturing operations of subsidiaries less integrated than home production by the parent enterprise.[2] Product-differentiation barriers are, on the argument of the preceding section, definitionally offset by the rent-yielding attributes of the firm that has established itself in a differentiated market abroad. Finally, important among the sources of "absolute cost" barriers are high capital charges imposed by the market for finance when a large absolute volume of funds is sought. The foreign entrant is able to tap earnings retained abroad and having relatively low opportunity cost, as well as to enjoy a good credit rating. Formally, the international firm can buy factors of production either in the host or the home country, and thus enjoys the intrinsic advantage over the domestic firm that comes from the opportunity to trade at either of two different sets of factor prices.[3]

Against the advantage that the foreign firm enjoys in hurdling conventional barriers weigh disadvantages created by national boundaries. As was mentioned above, the entrant must incur additional costs of gathering information that are fixed in the sense that they do not vary proportionally with the amount of resources that the firm might stake abroad. A second barrier reposes in the additional risks of investment

over domestic firms. See G. Rosenbluth, "The Relation between Foreign Control and Concentration in Canadian Industry", *Canadian Journal of Economics*, vol. 3 (1970), pp. 14–30; and also E. L. Wheelwright, "Overseas Investment in Australia", *The Economics of Australian Industry*, ed. Alex Hunter, Melbourne, 1963, pp. 155–6.

[1] Joe S. Bain, *op. cit.*; H. H. Hines, "Effectiveness of 'Entry' by Already Established Firms", *Quarterly Journal of Economics*, vol. 71 (1957), pp. 132–50.

[2] Some data are available on subsidiaries' relative shares of value-added and cost of materials, and can be used to assess their degree of vertical integration, although caution is required. Brecher and Reisman (*op. cit.*, table 29, p. 107) show that the share of cost of materials is slightly higher in Canadian sudsidiaries of American companies than in their domestic competitors. Although the difference is small, it seems indicative; if the subsidiaries' productivity were higher than their competitors', they would tend to report a large value-added share (smaller cost-of-materials share) than their domestic competitors even if the physical degrees of vertical integration were the same. Another study, T. R. Gates and F. Linden, *Cost and Competition: American Experience Abroad*, New York, 1961, finds the cost-of-materials share in European subsidiaries higher than in their American parents, which strongly suggests less vertical integration in overseas operations than at home; the conclusion which the authors draw, however, is that the cost of material inputs relative to labour is higher in Europe.

[3] Evidence of the influence of factor prices abroad on subsidiaries' behaviour can be found to two recent studies: G. L. Reuber and F. Roseman, *The Takeover of Canadian Firms, 1945–61: An Empirical Analysis*, Economic Council of Canada, Special Study no. 10, Ottawa, 1969; and G. V. G. Stevens, "Fixed Investment Expenditures of Foreign Manufacturing Affiliates of U.S. Firms: Theoretical Models and Empirical Evidence", *Yale Economic Essays*, vol. 9 (1969), pp. 137–200.

in a foreign rather than in a home market. In part, this extra risk is the obverse of the high cost of information about foreign markets: where information costs more, one will settle for less of it, and, as a result, put up with more uncertainty. But extra risks for foreign investors are also associated with exchange-rate changes, political actions by a foreign government that serves one's competitor but not oneself, and the like. Noting that foreign subsidiaries retain and plough back a much larger portion of their earnings than do domestic firms, Barlow and Wender have hypothesized that firms tend to view profits realized from risky foreign ventures as "gambler's earnings" and plough them back in the subsidiary even when no export of funds originating in the home market would take place in their absence.[1]

These differences between barriers to entry by the new domestic and the established international firm contribute in several ways to explaining patterns of foreign investment and business performance. All of them help to explain the prevalence of large firms as foreign investors— even the greater risk of foreign investment, since the large firm may be able to pool the risks of several subsidiaries abroad while the small firm can contemplate establishing only one.[2] The preference of small American firms for investing in closer and more familiar countries such as Canada is thus easily explained. Finally, the greater risk of foreign investment rationalizes the survey evidence showing that a significant minority of firms insist on a higher expected rate of return before approving a foreign-investment project than they would on a comparable domestic investment, and that those who succeed earn more than their competitors in the host country.[3]

This analysis of entry barriers also suggests some traits of market structures in industries containing a significant population of foreign subsidiaries. The existence of scale economies makes it likely that a firm producing and selling in numerous sub-markets will hold a larger share in the average market than the typical competing firm operating in a single market. A seller is unlikely to expand production in a second region while scale economies remain to be exploited in the first. The more important are scale economies, relative to the size of regional

[1] Barlow and Wender, *op. cit.*, pp. 164–7. For evidence on high rates of profit retention by subsidiaries, see e.g. Brash, *op. cit.*, ch. 4. Risk-avoidance regarding the exchange rate is demonstrated by the tendency of subsidiaries to undertake substantial local borrowing, helping to balance their local-currency claims and liabilities. See Mikesell, *op. cit.*, pp. 95–8.

[2] R. A. Shearer, "Nationality, Size of Firm, and Exploration for Petroleum in Western Canada, 1946–1954", *Canadian Journal of Economics and Political Science*, vol. 30 (1964), pp. 211–27; M. D. Steuer, *American Capital and Free Trade: Effects of Integration*, 1969, pp. 33–6.

[3] The greater profitability of going foreign subsidiaries probably reflects as well the common practice of transferring the implicit rents from the use of trade marks, technical know-how and the like in the form of profits rather than service charges. For evidence on the superior profit performance of subsidiaries over domestic firms, see Brash, *op. cit.*, ch. 10; J. H. Dunning, *The Role of American Investment in the British Economy*, PEP Broadsheet no. 507, 1969, pp. 130–3; and A. E. Safarian, *The Performance of Foreign-Owned Firms in Canada*, Montreal and Washington, 1969, chs. 6, 7.

markets, the less often will a seller produce in more than one region, and the more likely is a firm expanding into a new region to pick the one with the largest market.[1] Where the existence of local production facilities gives the firm a competitive edge in marketing its product, multi-regional production may be carried to a greater extent than would minimize costs of production for the industry, and oligopolistic firms which are in active "product rivalry"—if not price competition— with one another will tend to make parallel moves in extending production to new regions.

Whatever the market structure that results from the influence of direct investment, it can be argued that entry by a foreign subsidiary is likely to produce more active rivalrous behaviour and improvement in market performance than would a domestic entry at the same initial scale. The subsidiary tends to enjoy advantages in unit cost and profitability that stem from the same factors which lower the entry barriers that it faces.[2] Furthermore, as a newcomer it has not settled into the sort of stable pattern of oligopolistic interdependence or mutual accommodation that will normally evolve among a market's long-term tenants. In any case, its experience with such patterns of accommodation derives from another market in which the game may be played quite differently. Hence its pricing and product strategies are likely to stir up established conduct patterns and increase the amount of independent (as opposed to interdependent) behaviour. The "gambler's earnings" hypothesis implies that the subsidiary playing for a big win may shun safe conformity in the interests of limited joint maximization of industry profits; but one must also note that the innate riskiness of direct investment could be taken to predict a cautious course that abjures independent action.

These influences of direct investment on market structure and conduct are too diverse to yield any summary prediction about what patterns are most likely to prevail in an industry that has received a heavy inflow of direct investment. We can, however, note one particular model said to fit a number of Canadian industries.[3] It assumes an import-competing differentiated oligopoly receiving significant tariff protection and affected by scale economies that are significant relative to the size of the national market. The selection and maintenance of an industry price is easily effected by taking the world (external) price plus the tariff. If this price would allow more than a competitive profit rate to producers

[1] These conclusions are drawn from the Sylos–Bain model, which also identifies a high elasticity of demand as a factor favouring direct investment. For an account see F. Modigliani, "New Developments on the Oligopoly Front", *Journal of Political Economy*, vol. 66 (1958), pp. 215–32.

[2] A possible source of these advantages in profitability beyond those already mentioned arises if the subsidiary improves the performance of local suppliers from whom it buys and the local distribution channels through which it sells, widening its profit margin in the short run and raising the pay-out for it of greater penetration of the market.

[3] Eastman and Stykolt, *op. cit.*; H. E. English, *Industrial Structure in Canada's International Competitive Position*, Montreal, 1964, esp. ch. 4.

whose plants are large enough to exhaust plant scale economics, both domestic and foreign firms of sub-optimal size tend to populate the industry. Differentiation causes each seller to be confronted with a downward-sloping demand curve. This fact discourages price warfare to drive our rivals (and permit the predator to expand to efficient scale), as does the fact that rivals which are subsidiaries have potential access to the "deep pockets" of their parents. Entry will continue through the establishment of foreign subsidiaries until the rate of return that a new entrant expects falls short of his target, which would equal the (higher than competitive) rate of profit earned by this industry in countries where its international firms are domiciled.[1]

Empirical evidence strongly supports the relevance of this model, confirming both the phenomenon of pricing up to the tariff and a strong dependence of the proportion of plants of sub-optimal size on the size of the national market.[2] This result seems impossible to explain without reference to product differentiation.

As a general proposition, the difficulty of predicting the effects of foreign direct investment on market structure is seen in the suggestion that entry by foreign firms may actually raise seller concentration in the host-country market. Mergers might be induced among the domestic firms, pressed by new competition, leaving the total number of firms smaller than before. This possibility cannot be denied,[3] but its significance is somewhat obscure. If the mergers involve economies, why is the stimulus of a foreign entrant needed? If not, then they probably signal retreat from the market before a rival capable of higher productivity and (possibly but not necessarily) may coincide with an improvement in the industry's productivity and market performance.

It is tempting to proceed to market models that embody mutual dependence recognized among oligopolists in a "world industry". Tacit understandings may commit firms to refrain from investing in each other's main national markets, and breakdowns of such understandings may be marked by reciprocal invasions of the home territories.[4]

---

[1] This analysis abstracts from differences that are to be expected among the rates of return on tangible assets earned by firms in a differentiated industry. It also assumes that, these differences apart, the "limit price" that bears a critical relation to entry in the Sylos–Bain model can be translated into a "limit rate of return".

[2] Eastman and Stykolt, *op. cit.*, chs. 1, 3. The same dependence of plant size on national market size is revealed in figures given by Bain which tend to show that median plant size (measured by employment) in manufacturing industries varies strongly with the size of the domestic market. See J. S. Bain, *International Differences in Industrial Structure*, New Haven, 1966, p. 39.

[3] There is no fully satisfactory evidence on this or the contrary hypothesis. Rosenbluth (*op. cit.*, p. 28) reports no association between changes in seller concentration and in foreign control for Canadian industries over the period 1954–64. Steuer *et al.* (*op. cit.*, ch. 4) found a significant negative association between the *level* of foreign participation in UK industries in 1963 and the absolute change in concentration 1958–63, which casts doubt on the hypothesis stated in the text; but they were without a measure of the *change* in foreign participation over this period.

[4] See Corwin D. Edwards, "Size of Markets, Scale of Firms, and the Character of Competition", *Economic Consequences of the Size of Nations*, E. A. G. Robinson, ed., New, York, 1960, pp. 117–30.

The tightness of oligopoly in national markets may influence the extent to which domestic firms take account of the threat of foreign entry and select their price and product strategies in the spirit of a "limit price" that will just fail to tempt foreign entry. Such theorizing quickly dwindles into taxonomy, however, and the available empirical evidence is insufficient to reveal what shape an effective array of the possibilities would take.

Most models of direct investment in a "world industry" seem to predict an important tendency for direct investment to equalize rates of return on equity capital in a given industry in all countries where production occurs. This consequence does not depend on the absence of tariffs and other impediments to trade,[1] and, indeed, the hope of import-competing domestic producers that a tariff will raise their profit rates proves illusory in the long run unless that rate lies below what "sector-specific" capital earns in the capital-exporting countries. This does not mean, however, that direct investment tends to establish a *competitive* rate of return to capital in each industry where it occurs. Because of the oligopoly and entry barriers (and neglecting the effect of differentiation on the variance of firms' profit rates), each industry's common rate of return is likely to lie above a competitive rate to a degree that reflects barriers to entry into the world industry and the attained degree of mutual dependence recognized within it. This hypothesized outcome will receive further theoretical analysis in the next section.

III. The International Corporation in General Equilibrium

A. *The impact of sector-specific capital*

The analysis to this stage has been concerned with micro behaviour and allocative results at the level of the firm and the industry. Certain features of the industrial structures resulting from direct investment can be built into a simple general equilibrium model.[2] I shall concentrate on the sector-specificity of direct investment, conspiring with entry barriers to equate rates of return between countries in a given industry but not between industries in a given country. This invokes the concept of the "specific factor of production", long familiar in trade theory, and allows use to be made of recent theoretical work on specific factors in a simple general-equilibrium model.[3] In the spirit of the Heckscher–Ohlin model, assume two countries, X and Y, capable of producing two products, A and B. Each country is endowed with a labour supply, L_x and L_y,

[1] As it does in the conventional Heckscher–Ohlin model giving rise to factor-price equalization.
[2] And certain others readily cannot—product differentiation and the rent-yielding advantages of the firm undertaking direct investment. No empirical test or defence of the hypothesis of sector-specific capital is offered here beyond suggesting that its theoretical significance is worth exploring.
[3] R. W. Jones, "A Three-Factor Model in Theory, Trade and History", *Trade, Balance of Payments, and Growth: Essays in Honor of C. P. Kindleberger*, J. Bhagwati *et al.*, eds., Amsterdam, 1971.

2

that is homogeneous and perfectly mobile between industries but does not move across national boundaries. Symmetrically, stocks of capital K_a and K_b are potentially mobile across national boundaries but specific to the two respective industries. If the usual assumptions about production functions and trade barriers necessary to produce factor-price equalization were satisfied in this model, but capital were not mobile internationally, equalization would of course not occur. Rendering *one* type of sector-specific capital perfectly mobile does cause equalization, however, if both countries remain incompletely specialized. If K_a moves freely between countries, its return is equalized directly. Competitive factor and product markets assure that this also equates the marginal products of labour in both countries' A industries and in their B industries as well. With the marginal product of labour the same in both B industries, the marginal product, and thus the rent, of K_b must be the same in both countries. Three international price links suffice to equate the rewards to three factors. If both K_a and K_b were internationally mobile, a redundant fourth link would be created, and one country could be expected to specialize completely and contain none of the stock of one type of capital.

One disturbance that can be explored in this three-factor model is the effect of an exogenous transfer of capital (say K_a) from Y to X. I do not now assume all conditions necessary for factor-price equalization, but wish instead to explore the effect of this disturbance on national factor prices and the incentive for international capital transfers. Jones has shown that an increase in the endowment of one specific factor, holding product prices constant, raises the wage of L_x as the increase in X's production of A draws L_x from B. The marginal product of K_a falls as that of L_x rises, lowering the rent to K_a. But the rent to K_b must also fall, and indeed will fall more than that of K_a if the initial share of wages in total costs for the B industry exceeds that of wages in total costs for the A industry. Symmetrical adjustments will take place in Y. Thus the exogenous flow of K_a to X lowers the rent to K_b in X and raises it in Y. Whatever the mobility of K_b, the incentive for its movement from X to Y is increased, and one has an explanation of why direct investment tends to be cross-hauled between countries. If product differentiation were allowed among firms in the A industry, it is also clear that an exogenous flow of K_a to X would tend to induce a reverse flow of K_a initiated by producers resident in X.

This three-factor model also generates some conclusions about the effects of tariffs on income distribution and welfare. In the absence of capital transfers, imposing a tariff on imports of A to X will raise the rent to K_a and lower that to K_b. In contrast to the Stolper–Samuelson conclusion for the two-factor case, the change in the real wage of L_x can be either positive or negative. As L_x is transferred to the A industry, its marginal product falls in A, the domestic price of which has been raised by the tariff, and rises in the production of B, the relative price of which has fallen; the effect on the real wage is indeterminate. If we allow K_a to flow into X in response to this rise in its rent, however, the increase in its marginal product in X's A industry is restricted. An inflow sufficient to keep its marginal product from rising more than proportionally to the tariff-induced increase in A's price would keep the marginal product of L_x from falling in the A industry. (I neglect any product and factor-price changes induced in Y.) With labour's marginal product rising in B and constant in A, its real wage increases. We may have here an explanation, in contrast to the Stolper–Samuelson theorem, of why labour in countries like Canada and Australia seems willing to support tariff protection for capital-intensive manufacturing industries.[1]

Finally, this three-factor model can be related to the welfare conclusions concerning the taxation of trade and capital flows that have been worked out for the two-factor case.[2] If each country produces only a single good, then a nation facing an imperfectly elastic foreign supply of (demand for) capital will benefit from imposing a tax on capital flows, analogous to the "optimum tariff" on trade. With incomplete specialization, however, either the optimum tariff or the optimum tax on capital (but not both) may be negative. Suppose that X imports capital from Y (not sector-specific, for the moment), and that Y's import-competing industry (B) is relatively capital-intensive. Then X may benefit from subsidizing capital imports. Such a subsidy drives up the rent to capital in Y and the total cost of foreign borrowing to X, but it also raises the price in Y of the capital-intensive B good, which is X's export. X's terms of trade thus improve, and this improvement can offset the loss in higher capital costs if X's burden of international indebtedness is small enough relative to X's receipts from export sales. This possibility will remain if we again assume capital to be sector-specific. The condition necessary to make the optimal tax on a flow of one type of capital negative will become more stringent, however. The relation (in Y) between relative factor and product prices, essential to the result, survives but is weakened.

B. *Interrelation of trade flows and capital movements*

Some additional general relations between trade and foreign investment can be uncovered if we switch to a different trade model involving more extensive descriptive assumptions and capable of generating results that have been suggested by Burenstam Linder, Drèze and Vernon. I shall sketch briefly the assumptions which in common underlie their work and indicate some predictions they imply about direct investment.[3]

The descriptive assumptions are the following:

1. The countries which enjoy higher average incomes per capita

---

[1] Sector-specific (and immobile) natural resources could be assumed in place of K_b.

[2] Ronald W. Jones, "International Capital Movements and the Theory of Tariffs and Trade", *Quarterly Journal of Economics*, vol. 81 (1967), pp. 1–38.

[3] A somewhat similar analysis, but concentrating on trade flows, appears in Harry Johnson's Wicksell Lectures, *op. cit.*

are those endowed with relatively more capital (in all its forms) per head.

2. Consumers' taste patterns can be described as consisting of certain wants or needs, each of which can be served by a variety of different goods. Consumers largely agree on a ranking of all goods produced in terms of their desirability for satisfying any given want, with the ranking running down from the most desirable and costly.[1] These rankings are similar among the various industrialized countries. When real income per head is growing, consumers raise their standards of living through trading up to more strongly preferred goods.

3. The long-term rise in standards of living tends to bias the search for new consumer goods toward those which will be highly ranked and thus consumed initially by high-income countries and groups. (Some discoveries of course will tend to truncate these rankings by rendering obsolete goods that cost more to produce but rate lower in consumer preferences.) The search for new producer goods is biased in just the same way toward innovations which initially are chosen by entrepreneurs facing high costs of labour relative to capital. This results from the long-term rise in the value of labour-time, the counterpart of increasing real income per head.

In addition, I assume that the determinants and consequences of direct investment operate as suggested in the preceding analysis. One conclusion was that firms selling in a differentiated market would establish their quasi-rent-yielding assets in the native economy of the entrepreneur before venturing abroad. This requires no assumption beyond the information-cost advantage of a native in establishing an asset in the form of market-oriented knowledge. Burenstam Linder's proposition that a commodity must first be sold in an extensive domestic market before it can be exported[2] thus gains credence for some industries. He also suggests that exports of manufactured goods will be destined disproportionately to other countries at similar levels of income per capita, a proposition that also follows for differentiated goods if we make the second assumption listed above about consumers' taste patterns. Drèze offers the related proposition that a small industrial country will tend to find its comparative advantage lying in undifferentiated manufactures, because scale economies in sales promotion put the differentiated producer in the small market at a capital-cost disadvantage in product design and the attainment of marketing experience.[3] This hypothesis gains empirical support from Belgium's trade pattern but holds less obviously for the other small industrial countries. Furthermore, it is a decidedly partial proposition, in that

[1] This description draws upon J. S. Duesenberry, *Income, Saving, and the Theory of Consumer Behavior*, Cambridge, Mass., 1949, ch. 2.
[2] Staffan Burenstam Linder, *An Essay on Trade and Transformation*, New York and Stockholm, 1961, pp. 87–123.
[3] J. Drèze, "Quelques reflexions sereins sur l'adaptation de l'industrie Belge au Marché Commun", *Comptes rendues des Travaux de la Société Royale d'Economie Politique de Belgique*, no. 275 (1960).

would-be exporters of differentiated goods compete in the sense of comparative advantage not against foreign sellers of similar products but against other domestic industries which would employ the same stock of factors of production.

Finally, Vernon has suggested that product innovations are likely to be discovered and initially produced in high-income countries, then diffused to others through trade, foreign investment and imitation.[1] The third assumption stated above explains the predominant origin of discovery in wealthy countries. The contact needed in the early stages between the producer and his market and suppliers and the presumed price-inelasticity of demand for a "novelty" call for the initial location of production in the high-income country whatever long-run comparative advantage may indicate. Initial exploitation of foreign markets will be through export; but costs eventually tell, and production spreads abroad if cost minimization so indicates. If the innovation represents a new product variety, especially a patentable one, the diffusion of production abroad is likely to be through direct investment. If the innovation is primarily one of producer goods or production technology, licensing or imitation is probable.

These propositions, primarily about trade patterns, can also be made to yield predictions about the international structure of foreign direct investment, in particular about a country's balance of international direct investment: the ratio of the book value of enterprise capital abroad controlled by its citizens to the value of capital within its borders controlled by foreigners. The deductions depend primarily on recalling the influence of comparative cost (absolute cost to the producer) on the choice between serving a foreign market by export and by direct investment, and on noting that the international mobility of capital tends to remove its influence as a determinant of national patterns of comparative advantage. Thus, the country with high efficiency wages will tend to be a relatively small importer of direct investment. Whether it is a large net exporter of equity capital, however, will depend on the sorts of commodities it exports. If its comparative advantage lies in undifferentiated manufactures or natural resource-intensive goods, it will show little tendency to export direct investment, even though it might be a net capital exporter through portfolio investments abroad. High efficiency wages may be due to a nation's role as an innovator, causing its exchange rate (and thereby its money cost level, relative to costs in other countries) to be elevated by a significant volume of "technological gap" exports. Apart from the tendency for some direct investment to occur ultimately as the manufacture of new products is diffused, such a country will also tend to be an exporter of direct investment from other industries. This is because the

[1] Raymond Vernon, "International Investment and International Trade in the Product Cycle", *Quarterly Journal of Economics*, vol. 80 (1966), pp. 190–207; also Louis T. Wells, Jr., "Test of a Product Cycle Model of International Trade: U.S. Exports of Consumer Durables", *Quarterly Journal of Economics*, vol. 83 (1969), pp. 152–63.

elevation of efficiency wages biases the choice of other producers of differentiated goods (besides the innovators) towards production abroad rather than exports.

Large size of a country's domestic market, other things equal, will favour inflows of direct investment because the foreign firm contemplating an investment will not be deterred by problems of securing an efficient level of output; against this, however, cuts a "composition effect", in that the absolute capital requirements of efficient scale (for marketing) in a large country will be onerous to foreign firms if they are based in smaller markets. Finally, the countries with a relatively cosmopolitan culture will tend to swap direct investments with each other. So will countries at similar levels of income per capita, by expansion of Burenstam Linder's argument.

These predictions are capable of a certain amount of superficial testing by example. Several of them help to explain the position of the United States as a large net exporter of direct investment, and that of Britain as a large gross importer and exporter. For other countries, however, the various criteria tend to cut against one another. As has been noted before, it often seems necessary to involve political and cultural factors in explaining bilateral patterns of foreign investment.[1]

IV. SOME WELFARE IMPLICATIONS

The remainder of this paper considers selected welfare implications of the preceding analysis, particularly for the character of welfare gains from direct investment and their distribution between the lending and borrowing countries. I shall not discuss the numerous popular and political concerns about foreign investment which have received attention elsewhere.[2]

In the absence of externalities and market imperfections, the case for free movement of direct investment as a means of maximizing world welfare is simply the case for allowing any factor or product to flow towards locations where it has the greatest excess of marginal value over marginal cost. Theoretical attention has recently focused on the more complex question of national welfare, and the theory of bilateral monopoly has been employed to identify the general interest of both lending and borrowing country in restricting capital flows when the influence of their volume on the price received or paid can be perceived. The second-best aspects of the taxation of capital flows have been explored at both the general-equilibrium and micro levels, as well as the strategic situation arising from the discordant interests of the lending and borrowing countries.[3] I have argued in the preceding sections that

---

[1] S. Chakravarty, "A Structural Study of International Capital Movement", *Economia Internazionale*, vol 14 (1961), pp. 377–402.

[2] Brecher and Reisman, *op. cit.*, ch. 8; Kindleberger, *op. cit.*, *passim*.

[3] See M. C. Kemp, "The Gains from International Trade and Investment: A Neo-Heckscher–Ohlin Approach", *American Economic Review*, vol. 56 (1966), pp. 788–809; K Hamada, "Strategic Aspects of Taxation on Foreign Investment

the bulk of direct investment can be characterized in ways somewhat different from the general assumptions commonly employed in recent theoretical work. Do the differences alter the results of this theoretical analysis, or make them more specific?

The interpretation of the international corporation as an exporter of sector-specific capital in an oligopolistic market clearly conflicts with the assumption of independent, competitive supply and demand curves for international capital transactions at the national level. To the extent that capital-exporting firms in a national industry recognize their impact on their industry's rate of return from foreign investments, the lending country's interest in monopolistic restriction of capital outflows is looked after privately; a nationally optimal level of capital exports would be achieved if sellers in each industry sent abroad the amount that would maximize their private joint profits, in the absence of complementarity or substitutability among the various industry outputs in the foreign market. Thus the exception in the United States' anti-trust laws allowing collusion in export sales through joint selling agencies is rational from a nationalistic viewpoint.[1] It is an interesting confirmation of the role of differentiated oligopoly in foreign trade and investment, however, that such agencies in fact are rare, and persist only in export industries characterized by small firms producing a homogeneous product such as paper, phosphate or carbon black.[2] One would expect price-fixing agreements and joint selling agencies to be either not feasible or else unnecessary vehicles for collusion in industries of tight-knit differentiated oligopoly.

What of the interests of the borrowing countries? Even if they face a supply of foreign equity capital already restricted through collusion among foreign corporations, further monopolistic restriction will nevertheless raise their welfare if the supply of direct investment is, in effect, less than perfectly elastic (i.e. the rate of return can be pushed down). But the analysis of differentiated oligopoly raises the possibility that this inelasticity may be lacking. If the firms dominating a "world industry" would all experience the same net revenue per unit of sales in any subsidiaries they established in this borrowing country, and if they all adhered to "limit pricing" through insistence on a common target rate of return, then they would confront the borrowing country with a perfectly elastic supply curve of capital. The chances of this outcome should not be exaggerated, however, because the failure of the first of these necessary conditions to hold is quite likely in a differentiated industry.[3]

Income", *Quarterly Journal of Economics*, vol. 80 (1966), pp. 361–75; Jones, "International Capital Movements and the Theory of Tariffs and Trade", *op. cit.*, and W. M. Corden, "Protection and Foreign Investment", *Economic Record*, vol. 43 (1967), pp. 209–32, and earlier references cited in these papers.

[1] See US Senate, *International Aspects of Antitrust, op. cit.*, p. 153.

[2] US Senate, Committee on the Judiciary, Subcommittee on Antitrust and Monopoly, *International Aspects of Antitrust, 1967*, Hearings pursuant to S.Res. 26, Washington, DC., 1967, pp. 34–46.

[3] Some evidence that Britain's *aggregate* supply of foreign investment is less than perfectly elastic appears in Reddaway's finding that post-tax rates of return on

Given some dispersion in the profit rates which foreign international corporations can earn in a borrowing country's markets, its most satisfactory instrument for capturing some of the gains from foreign investments might be an excess profits tax on rates of return beyond what is deemed to be the "limit" rate.

Given these doubts about the extent of gains available to the borrowing country, other sources of potential gains to it, and empirical evidence of their importance, merit examination. The three main possibilities are corporation income taxes, benefits from manpower training, and uncaptured productivity spillovers.

Analysis of the corporation income tax, generally applied to the net incomes of domestic firms and foreign subsidiaries alike, has shown that, if borrowing and lending countries applied the same (marginal) rate, general neutrality would exist between home and foreign investments for the lender and between subsidiary and domestic production for the borrower.[1] Actual rates do show a tendency to cluster just under 50 per cent., so that this neutrality is rather nearly attained in practice. This depends, of course, upon some convention whereby either the borrower or the lender, but not both, apply the common tax rate to the net incomes of foreign subsidiaries. The well-established practice is that the borrower gets first crack, with subsidiaries' tax liabilities to the host government credited against tax liability on the same profits to the home government. This tax flow guarantees a substantial source of real benefits from foreign investment to the borrower. As Hamada has shown, it also offers the virtue of avoiding the "prisoner's dilemma" game situation likely to result from any other convention. Differential tax rates on the net incomes of domestic and foreign-owned corporations, or on corporate income from domestic and foreign sources, appear quite uncommon, so that tax-induced distortions in the international allocation of equity capital are likely to be minor (apart from distortions that may result from the existence of the corporate income tax itself). The virtues of this situation lie not only in its contribution to world welfare but also in the unedifying nature of the alternative: to the extent that capital is sector-specific, a different tax rate in every industry would be optimal from a national viewpoint.

Apart from tax revenues, benefits to the borrower from direct investment depend on the inability of the foreign subsidiary to capture the full social product resulting from the capital, managerial skills and technological knowledge that it transplants to the host country. Two sources of leakage command particular interest, manpower training and productivity gains to domestic firms induced by the subsidiary's market behaviour.

Benefits from labour training will *not* redound to the host economy if

UK direct investments are lower in those countries imposing relatively high corporation taxes. Cf. Reddaway *et al.*, *op. cit.*, pp. 219–20.
[1] L. B. Krause and K. W. Dam, *Federal Tax Treatment of Foreign Income*, Washington, DC., 1964, ch. 4.

the following conditions hold: (1) workers invest in their own training up to the point where its marginal costs to them equal the present discounted value of its marginal benefits; (2) corporations provide training to the extent that maximizes their profits. The survey evidence on foreign subsidiaries is rather various but does suggest that they operate with some frequency in environments where these assumptions may fail to hold. The scale of labour-training programmes that are undertaken is sometimes very extensive, especially in countries such as Brazil and Mexico where the alternative opportunities for labour to acquire this training may be quite limited.[1] Even in an industrial country the foreign subsidiary may offer the domestic labour force some unique opportunities for training in association with the "differentiation" advantage that makes the direct investment profitable in the first place. This training would presumably be in managerial and technical or scientific lines. Finally, the chances seem reasonably high that a subsidiary, especially if establishing a production activity new to a country, would invest in labour training *ex post* to an extent greater than that which maximizes its private profits. This is so because of asymmetry in the risks of running short of skills, on the one hand, and over-estimating personnel turnover, on the other. If this asymmetry exists (and if employees under-invest in training on their personal initiative), then net social benefits from training will increase with the mobility of the labour force out of the foreign subsidiary. This mobility in turn will increase with the following factors: the number of domestic firms producing goods or using processes similar to those of the foreign firm; the extent to which the training is not specific to the subsidiary's particular processes or activities; and the physical proximity of the subsidiary to domestic employers.[2]

High productivity in a subsidiary, if captured in the firm's profits, yields no direct social benefit to the host country apart from the extra tax revenue. The empirical studies do suggest, however, a number of ways in which the subsidiary may fail to capture the full value of its social product. One instance overlaps with the factor of labour training. To the extent that the firm instructs in unique skills, particularly for managerial labour, employees who switch to domestic firms may transplant knowledge that provides a basis for imitative productivity gains there without real resource cost. Productivity gains may leak out from subsidiaries by channels other than the transfer of personnel,

---

[1] Lincoln Gordon and E. L. Grommers, *United States Manufacturing Investment in Brazil: The Impact of Brazilian Government Policies, 1946–1960*, Boston, 1962, ch. 8.

[2] In Britain, American subsidiaries show some tendency to move into depressed areas, where labour-training benefits might be significant, but to bid away trained employees from domestic firms rather than train their own. See Steuer *et al.*, *op. cit.*, pp. 43–4, and R. M. Jones, "The Direction of Industrial Movement and its Impact on Recipient Regions", *Manchester School*, vol. 36 (1968), pp. 149–72. Substantial net benefits could still accrue in this case, since the elevated skill wages confer a rent to skilled employees, and the domestic firms may be induced to undertake socially productive training programmes.

however. Studies of United States subsidiaries in both Britain and Australia have shown that they sometimes take the lead in improving the productivity of their domestic suppliers or the domestic distribution channels through which they sell, passing along techniques of inventory and quality control, standardization and the like.[1] In markets where the domestic firms engage in gentlemanly competition, the arrival of a foreign subsidiary may spur greater efforts to raise productivity among the local firms if, as was suggested above, the subsidiary does not find its profits maximized by conforming to existing patterns of restricted competition.[2] These gains may accrue either through copying the subsidiary's production or marketing techniques or through an increased outlay of managerial effort in response to shrivelled profits.[3] Finally, even without induced productivity gains, increased competition triggered off by the subsidiary will convey a benefit in the form of increased consumers' surplus.

Any net social benefits to the host country from labour training or productivity spillovers would weigh in the balance with all other factors in determining whether a tax or subsidy for foreign investment might be appropriate. Since these sources of social benefit may prove large in some cases, however, it is worth inquiring whether their accrual to the host country is likely to deny equivalent benefits to the home country, when equity capital moves abroad rather than choosing the best available domestic alternative.[4] The industrial analysis offered above suggests a negative answer. The international firm probably already occupies a significant share of its domestic market. Its competitive impact and any external benefits that may result from its presence there have already been unleashed. In any case, in an oligopoly market there is no reason to expect that denying it the opportunity to invest abroad will lead it to raise output in its main product line at home, driving down its rate of return in the process. Diversification into other home industries is more likely, but its presence in other domestic industries may yield fewer positive externalities than its presence abroad in its principal line of activity, for the same reasons that it enjoys the advantage of lowered barriers to entry in horizontal expansion to a new foreign market.

This section has so far addressed itself primarily to horizontal direct investments. In closing, let me consider briefly the special features of vertical foreign investments in the extraction and processing of raw

[1] Brash, *op. cit.*, ch. 8; Dunning, *op. cit.*, ch. 7.
[2] T. Scitovsky, "International Trade and Economic Integration as a Means of Overcoming the Disadvantages of a Small Nation", in Robinson, ed., *op. cit.*, ch. 18.
[3] W. M. Corden has recently explored the economic implications of a relation between profits and efficiency in "The Efficiency Effects of Trade and Protection", Conference on International Trade, Monash University, September 11–13, 1969.
[4] For a theoretical analysis of adverse effects on the landing country, see Marvin Frankel, "Home vs. Foreign Investment: A Case against Capital Export", *Kyklos*, vol. 18 (1965), pp. 411–33.

materials for export as they relate to the sources of benefit to the host country.

One difference arises in the welfare significance of taxation by the host country of subsidiaries' profits, because the (accounting) profits of the extractive subsidiary are likely to include both a pure return to capital and an intra-marginal rent on the natural-resource deposit which it exploits. If the rent is not separately captured by a native holder of resource rights for the domestic income stream, a case exists for taxing the subsidiary's profits even if equity capital (as a separate factor of production) is in perfectly elastic foreign supply. The large scale of resource deposits which attract foreign investments and the fewness of potential bidders for rights mean that great uncertainty will constrain the ability of the resource owner (private or public) to strike a prior agreement that will succeed in capturing all forthcoming rents. This poor bargaining position of the native resource-holder would naturally cause resentment, and thus it is not surprising that American firms with extractive subsidiaries abroad report much greater concern over expropriation than do firms with horizontally related manufacturing subsidiaries.[1]

Spillover benefits to the domestic economy from extractive subsidiaries, while not totally absent, are likely to be smaller than for horizontal investment in manufacturing. The subsidiary is likely to be capital-intensive, offering fewer opportunities for the training of the local labour force for an equivalent amount of capital transferred. It sells largely on world markets and buys few local inputs, so that little pressure for efficiency gains is put on competing or supplying domestic firms. Its physical location is likely to be remote from the locations of domestic firms which might be favourably affected by its presence. Its remoteness may convey an advantage, however, if its draft on the labour supply in a thin local market generates significant rents for its employees.[2]

Harvard University.

---

[1] Barlow and Wender, *op. cit.*, p. 128.
[2] Stonehill, *op. cit.*, pp. 151–2. Cf. Kindleberger, *op. cit.*, pp. 107–10. For an excellent study of the effects of extractive foreign investment in a less-developed country, see R. E. Baldwin, *Economic Development and Export Growth: A Study of Northern Rhodesia 1920–60*, Berkeley and Los Angeles, 1966.

[23]

Single-Product Firms

Three main themes have emerged so far from our attempts to explain trade patterns. First, under a large variety of industrial structures the predictive power of the factor proportions trade theory remains valid for the intersectoral pattern of trade and, in particular, for the factor content of trade flows. Second, in the presence of economies of scale large volumes of trade are consistent with small differences across countries in the composition of factor endowments. Third, the decomposition of trade volumes into an intraindustry and an intersectoral component can be related to fundamental characteristics of the countries whose trade flows are examined. In this and in the following chapter we extend the theory in order to describe an additional component of international trade. This is intrafirm trade, that is, trade among affiliates of the same multinational enterprise.

The introduction of multinational firms into the study of trade flows is desirable even if one is not interested in intrafirm trade per se, because the behavior of other major trade variables, like the volume of trade and the share of intraindustry trade, is influenced by the existence of multinational corporations, which have grown in importance in the conduct of world trade. In the United States, for example, at the all-manufacturing level multinational corporations accounted in 1970 for 62 percent of exports and 34 percent of imports (see U.S. Tariff Commission 1973, p. 322). Hence a full explanation of existing trade structures cannot be provided without taking account of the role of multinationals.

Our theory builds on two main premises: that there is product differentiation and economies of scale in some industries, and that there are inputs—such as management, marketing, and product-specific R & D—that are highly specialized and that can be located in one country and serve product lines in another country. These premises have emerged from the large descriptive literature on multinational corporations and from empirical studies of the incidence of multinationality (see Caves 1982).

In this chapter the theory deals with single-product firms; we deal with vertically integrated firms in the next chapter. Firms maximize profits and therefore make cost-minimizing location choices of product lines. This feature brings about the emergence of multinational corporations as a response to tendencies of factor rewards to differ across countries. Here the emphasis is on one source of pressure on relative factor rewards—differences in relative factor endowments. Transport costs and tariffs are assumed away, so production facilities are not established in order to save transport costs or in order to produce behind tariff walls. Other reasons for multinationality, like tax advantages of various forms, are also not considered.

Apart from describing in a general equilibrium system conditions that cause firms to choose multinationality, the theory provides an explanation of trade patterns in which the multinational corporations play a central role. There is intersectoral, intraindustry, and intrafirm trade. However, since in this chapter we deal only with single-product firms, the intrafirm trade component consists only of trade in invisibles, that is, in "headquarter services"; we deal with intrafirm trade in intermediate inputs in the next chapter.

12.1 The Basic Model

In this chapter we employ a modified version of the $2 \times 2 \times 2$ model from chapter 7 in which one sector produces differentiated products. It is assumed that there are two factors of production; labor, L, and capital, K. Food is produced by means of a standard linear homogeneous production function with the associated unit cost function $c_Y(w_L, w_K)$, where w_l is the reward to factor l. A producer of food has to employ all inputs in the same location. In a competitive equilibrium the price of food, taken to be the numeraire, equals unit costs:

$$1 = c_Y(w_L, w_K). \tag{12.1}$$

The structure of production of manufactured products is more complicated. Manufacturers require inputs of labor, capital, and headquarter service H. Headquarter services is a differentiated product, and a firm has to adapt it in order to make it suitable for the production of its variety of the finished good. Once adapted, this input becomes a firm-specific asset in the sense used by Williamson (1981), and it is *tied* to the entrepreneurial unit. However, it can serve many plants, and it need not be located within a plant in order to serve its product lines. In particular, it can serve plants that are located in other countries (see Hirsch 1976, Helpman 1984, and Markusen 1984). Inputs that fit this description are management, distribution, and product specific R & D. The

importance of such assets in the operation of multinational corporations is
described in Caves (1982, chapter 1).

Let $C^P(w_L, w_K, h, x)$ be the costs required to produce x units of a variety of
the differentiated product in a single plant when h units of H have been
adapted for its particular use. A possible form of this function is C^P
$= f(w_L, w_K) + g(w_L, w_K, h, x)$, where $f(\cdot) > 0$ and $g(\cdot)$ is positively linear
homogeneous in (h, x). Here $f(\cdot)$ generates a plant-specific fixed cost and the
variable cost component exhibits constant returns to scale. In general, we
assume that $C^P(\cdot)$ is associated with an increasing returns to scale production
function in which h is essential for production. Also we let $C^H(w_L, w_K, h)$ be the
minimum costs required in order to produce h in the desired variety, where
$C^H(\cdot)$ is associated with a nondecreasing returns to scale production function.
Then the firm's single-plant cost function is

$$C(w_L, w_H, x) = \min_h [C^P(w_L, w_K, h, x) + C^H(w_L, w_K, h)].$$

This function has obviously the standard properties of cost functions
associated with increasing returns to scale production functions. One can also
define cost functions for larger numbers of plants, but we do not need it for
what follows. The point worth noting, however, is that the firm or corporation
has fixed costs that are corporation specific but not plant specific (the cost of
producing h and adapting it); it has plant-specific fixed costs and plant-
specific variable costs.

The assumption that $C^P(\cdot)$ is associated with an increasing returns to scale
production function implies that it pays to concentrate production in a single
plant, unless there are transportation costs or differences across locations in
product prices. Since impediments to trade are not considered, the previously
described single-plant cost function is what is relevant for what follows. All
varieties will be assumed to have the same cost structure.

It is assumed that there is Chamberlinian-type monopolistic competition in
the differentiated product sector with unrestricted entry. Hence firms equate
marginal revenue to marginal cost, and free entry brings about zero profits in
every firm. In a symmetrical equilibrium these two conditions can be written
as

$$p = c(w_L, w_K, x), \tag{12.2}$$

$$R(p, \bar{n}) = 0(w_L, w_K, x), \tag{12.3}$$

where p is the price of every variety of the differentiated product;
$c(w_L, w_K, x) \equiv C(w_L, w_K, x)/x$ is average cost, $R(\cdot)$ is our measure of the degree
of monopoly power, $\bar{n}$ is the number of varieties available to consumers, and

$\theta(\cdot)$ is our measure [using $C(\cdot)$] of the degree of returns to scale in the production of manufacturers. The formal conditions of industry equilibrium (12.1) (12.3) are identical to conditions (7.12)–(7.14) from chapter 7. The important difference lies in the interpretation of the technology available to corporations in the differentiated product industry.

As in most trade theory we will assume that factors of production do not move across national borders. However, due to the technology available in the manufacturing sector, the firm-specific asset h can serve product lines in plants located in countries other than the country where the headquarters are located. The specificity of h also implies that arm's-length trade in headquarter services is an inferior organizational form to a multinationally integrated firm (see Klein, Crawford, and Alchian 1978). We will call the country where the headquarters are located the parent country of the corporation and the country where the subsidiary is located the host country.

12.2 Equilibrium in an Integrated Economy

As a first step toward the study of international trade between economies of the type described earlier we discuss in this section the equilibrium of an integrated economy. The features of the integrated economy will then be used to derive the relationship between patterns of cross-country distributions of the world's endowment of labor and capital, on one side, and trade patterns and volumes of trade, on the other.

In an integrated economy factor prices are the same everywhere, and all the firms operating in the sector that produces differentiated products have the same structure. Every firm produces one variety, and there is no overlap in varieties produced by different firms. All firms employ the same quantity of capital and labor, charge the same price for every variety, and produce the same final output and the same quantity of appropriate headquarter services. Free entry into the industry brings profits down to zero. The number of corporations $\bar{n}$ is treated as a continuous variable.

Apart from (12.1)–(12.3) the equilibrium conditions consist of equilibrium conditions in factor and commodity markets. Following the procedure discussed in chapter 7, we arrive at the equilibrium conditions in factor markets:

$$a_{LY}(w_L, w_K)\bar{Y} + a_{LX}(w_L, w_K, x)\bar{X} = \bar{L}, \tag{12.4}$$

$$a_{KY}(w_L, w_K)\bar{Y} + a_{KX}(w_L, w_K, x)\bar{X} = \bar{K}, \tag{12.5}$$

where $a_{lY}(w_L, w_K) = \partial c_Y(w_L, w_K)/\partial w_l$, $l = L, K$, is the cost-minimizing input of factor i per unit output of food; $a_{lX}(w_L, w_K, x) = \partial c(w_L, w_K, x)/\partial w_l$, $l = L, K$, is the cost-minimizing input of factor l per unit output of manufactures, $\bar{L}$ and $\bar{K}$ are the quantities of labor and capital available in the world economy, $\bar{Y}$ is the output of food and $\bar{X}$ is the output of manufactures, defined as

$$\bar{X} = \bar{n}x. \tag{12.6}$$

Finally, the commodity market-clearing condition [see (7.17)] is

$$\alpha_Y(p, \bar{n}) = \frac{\bar{Y}}{(\bar{Y} + p\bar{X})}, \tag{12.7}$$

where $\alpha_Y(\cdot)$ is the share of spending allocated to food. Conditions (12.1)–(12.7) represent the equilibrium conditions of the integrated economy. They implicitly define equilibrium values for factor rewards (w_L, w_K), pricing and output of manufacturing varieties (p, x), industry output levels $(\bar{Y}, \bar{X})$, and the numbers of varieties available to consumers $(\bar{n})$.

In what follows, we assume that the food industry is relatively labor intensive; namely

$$\frac{a_{KX}}{a_{LX}} > \frac{a_{KY}}{a_{LY}}.$$

Under this assumption the allocation of resources in the integrated equilibrium can be described by means of the box diagram in figure 12.1, which is analogous to figure 7.1. The vector OQ describes employment in the manufacturing sector, and the vector OQ' describes employment in the production of food.

12.3 The Pattern of Trade

In the standard $2 \times 2 \times 2$ Heckscher-Ohlin model, in which there are no factor-intensity reversals and preferences are homothetic and identical across countries, the set of endowment allocations can be divided into two subsets. In one subset there is factor price equalization and no specialization in production. In the other subset every country pays a lower reward to the factor of production with which it is relatively well endowed and a higher reward to the other factor of production, and at least one country specializes in the production of the good which is a relatively heavy user of its cheaper factor of production. If figure 12.1 were to describe feasible allocations across countries for a standard Heckscher-Ohlin-type economy, then the set of factor price equalization would be represented by OQO^*Q' and the other set by its complement.

The results that emerge in the present model are richer. It is useful to

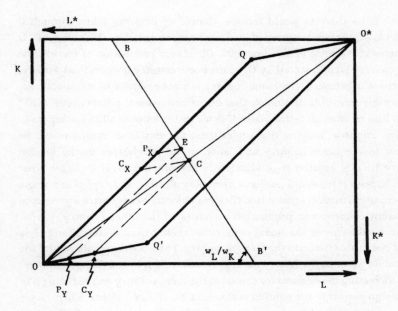

Figure 12.1

describe them by starting with intercountry factor allocations in the set OQO^*Q' of figure 12.1. Due to the symmetry in structure it is sufficient to analyze endowment points above the diagonal OQ^* where the home country is relatively capital rich. Allocations in this set were discussed in chapter 7, and we can therefore be brief.

Take, for example, the factor endowment point E. It is straightforward to see that with this world structure there is an equilibrium with factor price equalization. In this equilibrium firms based in one country have no incentive to open subsidiaries in the other country in order to locate product lines there. Assuming that under these circumstances all operations of a firm will be concentrated in the parent country, the output levels of food and manufactures in the home country are described by $\overline{OP}_Y$ and $\overline{OP}_X$, given a choice of units such that $\overline{Y} = \overline{OQ}'$ and $\overline{X} = \overline{OQ}$. The output levels in the foreign country are given by $\overline{P_YQ}'$ and $\overline{P_XQ}$.

Now, due to the fact that profits are zero, all income is factor income. Hence, by drawing through E a line BB' whose slope is $-w_L/w_K$, this line represents the cross-country income distribution. The relative income of the home country is $\overline{OC}$ divided by $\overline{CO}^*$. Since both countries have the same spending pattern, the home country consumes a proportion s of the world's output $\overline{Y}$, where s is its share in world income. Hence, by drawing a line through C parallel to OQ, its consumption of food can be represented by $\overline{OC_Y}$, where C_Y is the intersection point of this line with OQ'. Since production of food in the home country is represented by $\overline{OP_Y}$, the home country imports food. Finally, since trade is balanced, the home country is a net exporter of manufactures.

It is clear from this discussion that factor endowment points *above* OQO^* would lead to unequal factor prices if firms had to employ all factor inputs in the same country. Suppose that under these circumstances capital would be cheaper in the home country and labor would be cheaper in the foreign country (this is assured if production is homothetic). Now consider what would happen if firms did not have to employ all labor and capital at a single location; in particular, assume that they could locate headquarter activities in the parent country and production activities in the other country. Corporations would choose the home country as their parent country, and they would open subsidiaries in the foreign country. These moves would reduce the demand for labor in the home country and increase it in the foreign country, while increasing the demand for capital in the home country and reducing it in the foreign country. An equilibrium would be attained either when factor prices were equalized or the home country became the parent of all corporations (with unequal factor prices all headquarters are located in the capital-cheap country).

When factor price equalization obtains, there are many equilibrium configurations with various degrees of foreign involvement of the corporations in the differentiated product industry, just as there are many such configurations in the factor price equalization set OQO^*. In the latter case we adopted the convention that firms do not decentralize their activities unless this is necessary to achieve factor price equilization. In the current case such decentralization *is* necessary, but we maintain the spirit of the first convention by minimizing the extent of decentralization. The rule to be adopted is to consider equilibria with the smallest number of multinational corporations. This choice can be justified as the limit of a sequence of economies in which it is costly to locate plants abroad, but these costs tend to zero.

Our discussion of the decomposition of a firm's activities into headquarters and production can now be cast into a somewhat more formal framework in order to bring out as clearly as possible the analogy between previous derivations of trade patterns and the derivation of trade patterns with active multinational corporations.

Recall that h was chosen so as to minimize overall costs. The first-order condition of this cost minimization problem is

$$-C_h^P(w_L, w_K, h, x) = C_h^H(w_L, w_K, h).$$

The right-hand side represents the cost of a marginal expansion of headquarter activities, and the left-hand side represents cost savings from such an expansion. Given the values of factor rewards and output per firm in the integrated equilibrium, this condition determines the equilibrium level of headquarter activity h.

Now, using the equilibrium value of h, employment levels per unit output at headquarters and plants are given by

$$a_{lH}(w_L, w_K, h) = \frac{\partial}{\partial w_l} C^H(w_L, w_K, h)/h,$$

$$a_{lP}(w_L, w_K, h, x) = \frac{\partial}{\partial w_l} C^P(w_L, w_K, x)/x,$$

for $l = L, K$. The relationship between these input-output ratios and the a_{li}'s used in (12.4)–(12.5) is

$$a_{lX}(w_L, w_K, x) = a_{lP}(w_L, w_K, h, x) + a_{lH}(w_L, w_K, h)\frac{h}{x}, \quad l = L, K.$$

The headquarter and plant input-output ratios can be used to rewrite the factor market-clearing conditions in a form that underlines the different nature of a corporation's activities. Namely

$$a_{LY}(w_L, w_K)\bar{Y} + a_{KP}(w_L, w_K, h, x)\bar{X} + a_{KH}(w_L, w_K, h)\bar{H} = L, \tag{12.4'}$$

$$a_{KY}(w_L, w_K)\bar{Y} + a_{KP}(w_L, w_K, h, x)\bar{X} + a_{KH}(w_L, w_K, h)\bar{H} = K, \tag{12.5'}$$

where $\bar{H} = \bar{n}h$. Thus there are three outputs: food $\bar{Y}$, manufactures $\bar{X}$, and headquarter services $\bar{H}$.

In figure 12.2 the employment vector in the manufacturing sector OQ is decomposed into headquarter employment OD and plant employment DQ. The assumption is that headquarter activities are the most capital intensive, that plant activities in the manufacturing sector are of intermediate capital intensity, and that food production is the least capital intensive (in Helpman 1984, plant activities in the manufacturing sector are the least capital intensive). It is clear from our discussions in previous chapters that if arm's-length trade was possible in Y, X, and H, then $ODQO^*D'Q'$ would have been the factor price equalization set. However, since H services are specialized and every firm supplies its own requirements, they are not traded at arm's length. Hence points in the shaded areas of figure 12.2 are consistent with factor price equalization only when firms go multinational. In OQO^*Q' there is factor price equalization with national firms.

We have therefore identified the conditions that lead to the formation of

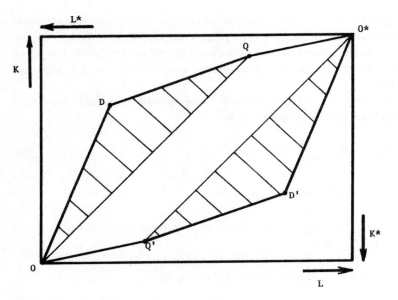

Figure 12.2

multinational corporations. Multinational corporations develop whenever the endowment allocation lies outside the parallelogram OQO^*Q', and they bring about factor price equalization in the shaded areas of figure 12.2.

Now consider what happens at endowment points in the shaded areas of figure 12.2. In particular, consider points E in ODQ of figure 12.3, which reproduce the relevant features from figure 12.2. If all the resources of the home country are employed in the production of manufactures, and if its corporations employ in the foreign country the vector EE_m in plant production (where E_m is the intersection point with OQ of a line drawn through E parallel to DQ), then the aggregate world equilibrium corresponds to the equilibrium of the integrated economy. The employment vector EE_m describes the smallest equilibrium foreign involvement of domestic multinationals consistent with full employment.

The structure of employment is as follows. In the home country the vector OE_H is employed in the production of headquarter services, and the vector $E_H E$ is employed in plant production of differentiated products. Home multinationals employ in the foreign country the vector $E_m E$ in plant production of differentiated products. Also foreign-based firms employ the vector QE_m in the manufacturing sector and the vector O^*Q in food production.

More precisely, since $Y = O$ and $Y^* = \bar{Y}$, the numbers of corporations n and

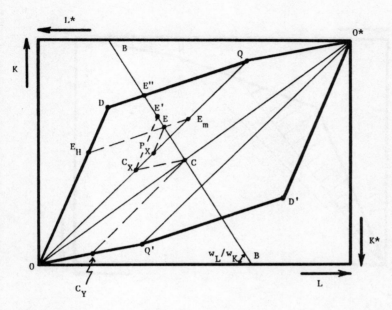

Figure 12.3

n^*, and the number of foreign subsidiaries μ located in the foreign country are obtained from the following factor market-clearing conditions:

$$a_{LP}(n - \mu)x + a_{LH}nh = L, \quad a_{LY}\bar{Y} + a_{LP}(n^* + \mu)x + a_{LH}n^*h = L^*,$$

$$a_{KP}(n - \mu)x + a_{KH}nh = K, \quad a_{KY}\bar{Y} + a_{KP}(n^* + \mu)x + a_{KH}n^*h = K^*.$$

Clearly the number of varieties produced in the home and foreign country does not equal n and n^*. The number of varieties produced in the home country is $M = n - \mu$, and the number of varieties produced in the foreign country is $M^* = n^* - \mu$.

To summarize, we have seen that endowment points in the set ODQ lead to an equilibrium with factor price equalization and the emergence of multinational corporations. Under our assumption about locational tendencies of corporations, in this set the home country (which is relatively capital rich) specializes in the production of manufactured products and in headquarter activities, and it serves as a base for the multinational corporations. It imports the homogeneous product, and there is intraindustry trade in differentiated products. Part of the intraindustry trade is carried out by multinationals.

At point E in figure 12.3 the home country is a net exporter of differentiated products. This can be seen as follows. Draw through E the line BB' whose slope

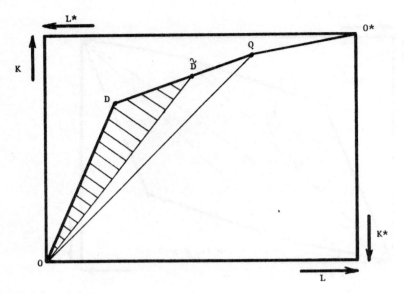

Figure 12.4

is $-w_L/w_K$, in order to obtain C. Now construct a parallelogram between O and C, using the slopes of OQ and OQ', to obtain C_X and C_Y. Home country consumption of food is represented by $\overline{OC}_Y$, and its consumption of manufactures is represented by $\overline{OC}_X$. By drawing through E a line which is parallel to OD, we obtain P_X, with $\overline{OP}_X$ representing home production of manufactures. Hence the home country's net exports of manufactures equals $\overline{C_X P_X}$. However, the home country need not be a net exporter of manufactures. Figure 12.4 describes a division of ODQ into two subsets by means of the line $O\tilde{D}$. At endowment points in the shaded area the home country is a *net importer* of manufactured products. The dividing line $O\tilde{D}$ is constructed as follows. Draw in figure 12.3 a line through C_X parallel to OD and denote its intersection point with BB' by E'. Then it is clear from the figure that at endowment points on $E'C$ the home country is a net exporter of manufactures and that at endowment points on $E''E'$ the home country is a net importer of manufactures. Now, by drawing a ray through O and E', we obtain $O\tilde{D}$ in figure 12.4. Algebraically the home country is a net importer of manufactured products if and only if $sM^* > s^*M$.

It is also clear from figure 12.3 that C represents the factor content of consumption. Therefore EC is the vector of the factor content of net imports (including invisibles). This vector is consistent with the prediction of the Heckscher-Ohlin theory; the relatively capital-rich country is a net exporter of capital services and a net importer of labor services.

Finally, observe that at E there is intrafirm trade in headquarter services. The existence of intrafirm trade is of course well documented in the empirical literature (e.g., see U.S. Tariff Commission 1973, chapter 2, and Buckley and Pearce 1979). This takes the form of imports of the parent firm from its subsidiaries as well as exports of the parent firm to its subsidiaries. Much of this trade stems from vertical integration, which we cover in the next chapter. However, there is one genuine component of intrafirm trade that is well represented by our model—the invisible exports of the parent to its subsidiaries of headquarter services.

Observe that due to the zero profit condition (12.2) plant costs are lower than the revenue obtained from sales. This means that a typical multinational corporation is making "profits" in its subsidiary, because the subsidiary hires in the host country only labor and capital for plant operation. This means that the "profits" of the subsidiary are just sufficient to cover the cost of headquarter services produced and located in the parent country. The difference between revenue and plant costs of all subsidiaries is $\mu(w_L a_{LH} + w_K a_{KH})h$. This can be considered to be either profits repatriated by the parent firms or payments by the subsidiaries for services rendered by the parent firms (a major issue in discussions of transfer pricing). From an economic point of view the second interpretation is the appropriate one. Hence μc_H, where $c_H = (w_L a_{LH} + w_K a_{KH})h$, represents intrafirm trade.

12.4 The Volume of Trade

We have seen how the trade pattern is related to the distribution of the world's endowment of factors of production. As is clear from the partition of the endowment set into the subsets in which different patterns of trade obtain, the pattern of trade depends on two factors: relative country size in terms of GNP, and the difference in relative factor endowments. For example, if the home country is relatively small and it has a relatively large endowment of capital, then the endowment point is in $OD\bar{D}$ of figure 12.4. Then there are multinational firms based in the home country, the home country exports manufactures and invisible headquarter services to its subsidiaries, it imports food, and it is a net importer of manufactures.

Differences in relative factor endowments and the relative size of countries are observable economic variables of major interest. We therefore provide in this section a description of the effects that these two variables have on the volume of trade. Our findings are summarized by the equal volume of trade curves in figure 12.5.

Start by considering endowment points in the set OQO^*. In this region there

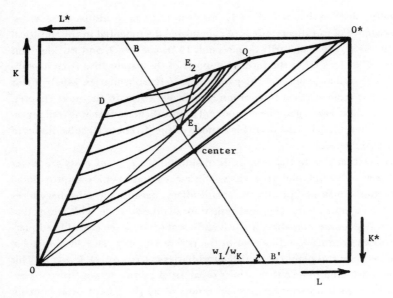

Figure 12.5

are no multinational firms. The volume of trade is defined in the usual way as
the sum of exports, where the summation is over countries and sectors. Due to
balanced trade this is equal in a two-country world to twice the exports of one
of the countries. We showed in the first section of chapter 8 that in this set the
volume of trade increases with differences in relative factor endowments and
decreases with differences in relative country size (the latter applying when
the manufacturing sector is sufficiently large). The equal volume of trade
curves were shown there to have the shape exhibited in figure 12.5.

For endowment points in ODQ the foreign country exports the homogeneous good (because it is the only producer of it) and M^* varieties of the differentiated product. some of the varieties that it exports are produced by firms
based in the foreign country, and μ of them are produced by subsidiaries of
multinational corporations based in the home country. This means that a proportion s of its output of food and manufactures is exported and that the volume of trade can be represented as

$$VT = 2s(\bar{Y} + pxM^*), \quad \text{for } E \in ODQ, \tag{12.8}$$

where s is the share of the home country in spending, which is equal to its
share in GNP. In this definition of the volume of trade we include the volume

of trade in headquarter services. It is therefore the total volume of trade and not only the component of trade in goods.

Condition (12.8) implies that given the relative country size, the volume of trade increases with the number of varieties produced in the foreign country, and given the number of varieties produced in the foreign country, the volume of trade increases with the relative size of the home country.

It is useful to pause at this stage in order to observe that depending on accounting practices the foreign country may record a difference between its gross domestic product and its gross national product. The point is of course that headquarter services of multinational corporations are traded within the firms, so that the value of output of goods in the host country is larger than its GNP. If the value of output of goods is taken to be GDP, then a discrepancy between GNP and GDP arises. If, however, imports of headquarter services are treated as imports of intermediate inputs (which they should be from an economic point of view), then there will be no discrepancy between GNP and GDP. The problem that arises is not only due to the fact that these intermediate inputs are services but that they are also not traded at arm's length and are therefore not directly recorded in trade statistics.

Now, since in ODQ both s and M^* are linear functions of (L, K), the proof from the appendix to chapter 8 can be applied to (12.8) in order to show that equal trade volume curves in ODQ are quasi concave and have therefore the shape exhibited in figure 12.5.

Moreover, since

$$Y + pxM^* = GNP^* + c_H\mu = s^*\overline{\overline{GDP}} + c_H\mu$$

where $c_H = (w_L a_{LH} + w_K a_{KH})h$ is the value of headquarter services supplied by a typical parent firm to its foreign country subsidiary, μ is the number of subsidiaries located in the foreign country, and $\overline{\overline{GDP}}$ is world GDP, then (12.8) can be rewritten as

$$VT = 2(ss^*\overline{\overline{GDP}} + c_H s\mu), \quad \text{for } E \in ODQ. \tag{12.9}$$

This representation shows that for $\mu = 0$, the volume of trade is maximized when countries are of equal size (point E_1 in figure 12.5), as we have shown also in chapter 8, and that the larger μ is, the larger the relative size of the home country for trade volume maximization. Maximizing VT for a given μ yields

$$s = \frac{1}{2}\left(1 + \frac{c_H\mu}{\overline{\overline{GDP}}}\right), \quad \text{for } E \in ODQ. \tag{12.10}$$

Points that satisfy (12.10) are represented by the line $E_1 E_2$ in figure 12.5. Since endowments that generate the same degree of multinationality μ are represented by lines parallel to OQ, as in figure 12.6, then the equal volume of trade

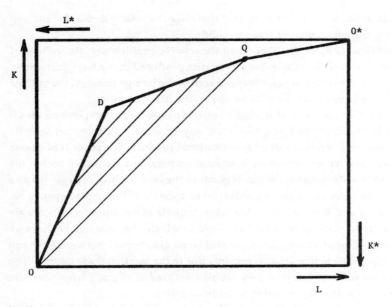

Figure 12.6

lines in figure 12.5 have a constant slope on $E_1 E_2$, and this slope equals the slope of OQ. The volume of trade is largest at E_2.

In summary, figure 12.5 represents a fairly detailed description of the relationship between factor endowments and the volume of trade. It shows that in some sense the larger the difference in relative factor endowments, the larger is the volume of trade. On the other hand, relative country size has an ambiguous effect on the volume of trade in the region that leads to the emergence of multinational corporations. Although a small upward bias in the relative size of the relatively capital-rich country increases the volume of trade, too much of this bias will reduce it. Thus the presence of multinational corporations weakens the link between the volume of trade and the degree of dispersion in relative country size. This suggests an empirical hypothesis: the larger the role of multinationals in the world economy, the weaker the effects of relative country size dispersion on the volume of trade.

12.5 Intraindustry and Intrafirm Trade

In this section we investigate the dependence of the shares of intraindustry and intrafirm trade on cross-country differences in relative factor endowments.

The volume of intraindustry trade is defined as the total volume of trade minus the sum over all sectors of the absolute value of the difference between imports and exports [see (8.14)]. In the current model this reduces to

$$VT_{i-i} = 2px \min(sM^*, s^*M). \tag{12.11}$$

The definition of the volume of intrafirm trade is more complicated. Exports of the parent firms of headquarter services are undoubtedly part of this volume of trade. The problem arises with the treatment of the final differentiated products. If parent firms serve as importers of the finished products that are manufactured by their subsidiaries, then this appears in the data as intrafirm trade, and similarly, if subsidiaries serve as importers of the differentiated products that are manufactured by parent firms. In some cases the treatment of these flows of goods as intrafirm trade has no economic justification because it is more the consequence of bookkeeping practices than true economic calculus. In the present model there is no natural choice—much depends on the implicit assumptions about the marketing technology. We choose therefore to define intrafirm trade as trade in headquarter services:

$$VT_{i-f} = c_H/t, \tag{12.12}$$

where $c_H = (w_L a_{LH} + w_K a_{KH})h$.

We have shown in section 8.3 that for endowment points in OQO^* the share of intraindustry trade is a declining function of the difference in relative factor endowments and that relative country size has no particularly strong independent affect. The share of intrafirm trade is zero in OQO^*, because in this region there are no multinational corporations.

Using (12.8) and (12.11), we obtain

$$S_{i-i} = \frac{px \min(sM^*, s^*M)}{s(\overline{Y} + pxM^*)}, \quad \text{for } E \in ODQ.$$

We have shown, however, that ODQ can be divided into two subsets, described in figure 12.4, such that in $O\tilde{D}Q$ the home country is a net exporter of manufactured products ($s^*M > sM^*$), whereas in $ODD̃$ the foreign country is a net exporter of manufactured products ($sM^* > s^*M$). Hence

$$S_{i-i} = \frac{pxM^*}{\overline{Y} + pxM^*}, \quad \text{for } E \in O\tilde{D}Q,$$

$$S_{i-i} = \frac{s^*pxM}{s(\overline{Y} + pxM^*)}, \quad \text{for } E \in OD\tilde{D}.$$

It is immediately clear from the first formula that in $O\tilde{D}Q$ the share of

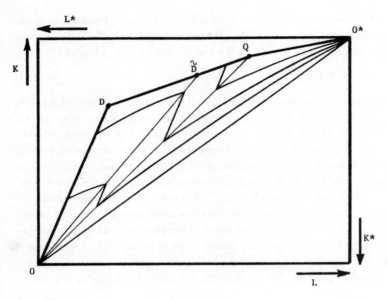

Figure 12.7

intraindustry trade is constant on lines parallel to OD, because on these lines M^* is constant. It can also be shown that the second formula implies constant S_{i-i} curves in $OD\tilde{D}$ that have the shape depicted in figure 12.7. Figure 12.7 describes constant S_{i-i} curves in the factor price equalization set. In OQO^* they are taken from figure 8.7 and are straight lines in $O\tilde{D}Q$.

It is clear from figure 12.7 that the emergence of multinational corporations changes in an important way the link between differences in relative factor endowments and the share of intraindustry trade. In OQO^* there is a negative association between them. However, when the difference in factor composition becomes large enough so as to bring about the emergence of multinational corporations, this association turns positive, as long as the capital-rich country is a net exporter of manufactures. When the difference in composition of factor endowments becomes large enough so that the capital-rich country begins to be a net importer of manufactures (concentrating a large part of its resources in producing headquarter services), the negative association between factor dispersion and the share of intraindustry trade is restored. It can also be seen from the figure that this pattern requires the capital-rich country to be sufficiently small, and this is the major way in which relative size affects these results.

Now consider the share of intrafirm trade. Using (12.8) and (12.12), this is calculated to be

$$S_{i-f} = \frac{VT_{i-f}}{VT} = \frac{c_H \mu}{2s(\bar{Y} + pxM^*)}.$$

However, due to balanced trade

$$s(\bar{Y} + pxM^*) = s^* pxM + c_H \mu,$$

where the right-hand side describes foreign country imports, which consist of differentiated products and headquarter services. Therefore

$$S_{i-f} = \frac{1}{2} \frac{c_H \mu}{s^* pxM + c_H \mu}.$$

It is easy to see from figures 12.3 and 12.6 that for constant relative country size an increase in the difference in factor composition increases the number of multinational corporations and reduces the number of varieties produced in the home country. Hence larger differences in factor composition are associated with larger shares of intrafirm trade.

The broad picture that emerges from this analysis is that for a given relative country size the share of intrafirm trade is larger, the larger the difference in relative factor endowments, but that in the presence of multinational corporations no clear-cut relationship exists between the share of intraindustry trade and differences in relative factor endowments. Hence we find that a link that is quite strong in the absence of multinational corporations is weaker in their presence. It suggests the hypothesis that the larger the involvement of multinational corporations in the world economy, the weaker the affect of changes in the degree of dispersion in income per capita on the share of intraindustry trade.

References

Buckley, P. J., and Pearce, R. D. "Overseas Production and Exporting by the World's Largest Enterprises: A Study in Sourcing Policy." *Journal of International Business Studies* 10 (1979): 9–20.

Caves, Richard E. "International Corporations: The Industrial Economics of Foreign Investment." *Economica* 38 (1971): 1–27.

Caves, Richard E. *Multinational Enterprise and Economic Analysis.* Cambridge, England: Cambridge University Press, 1982.

Dixit, Avinash, and Norman, Victor. *Theory of International Trade.* Cambridge, England: Cambridge University Press, 1980.

Helpman, Elhanan. "A Simple Theory of International Trade with Multinational Corporations." *Journal of Political Economy* 92 (1984): 451–471.

Hirsch, Seev. "An International Trade and Investment Theory of the Firm." *Oxford Economic Papers* 28 (1976): 258–270.

Klein, Benjamin, Crawford, Robert, and Alchian, Arman A. "Vertical Integration, Appropriable Rents, and the Competitive Contracting Process." *Journal of Law and Economics* 21 (1982): 297–326.

Markusen, James R. "Multinational, Multi-Plant Economies, and the Gains from Trade." *Journal of International Economics* 16 (1984): 205-226.

U.S. Tariff Commission. *Implications of Multinational Firms for World Trade and Investment and for U.S. Trade and Labor.* Washington, D.C.: Government Printing Office, 1973.

Williamson, Oliver E. "The Modern Corporation: Origins, Evolution, Attributes." *Journal of Economic Literature* 19 (1981): 1537–1568.

[24]

European Economic Review 31 (1987) 89–96. North-Holland

STRATEGIC INVESTMENT, MULTINATIONAL CORPORATIONS AND TRADE POLICY

Alasdair SMITH*

University of Sussex, Brighton BN1 9QN, UK

1. Introduction

In the model of the multinational corporation presented here, the principal focus is on how a foreign firm operating in a host market might choose to become a multinational rather than exporting its product, and how this choice may be influenced by government policy. Foreign direct investment typically plays a strategic role in oligopolistic competition: in particular, it may serve as an entry-deterrent in the style of Dixit (1980).

The effects of trade policy on foreign direct investment are very different in an oligopolistic model than in a competitive model, and it seems plausible that many markets in which multinationals are important participants are better described by oligopolistic than competitive behaviour. The effects of trade policy turn out to be very sensitive to the nature of the equilibrium; and, in particular, it is possible for a tariff to deter foreign direct investment, contrary to the conventional wisdom.

2. The model

The model offers an extremely simple characterisation of the technological advantage that a multinational firm may possess over a host-country rival: in order to make production possible, a firm-specific fixed cost must be incurred, in addition to the plant-specific fixed cost associated with the establishment of a plant in any particular location. This characterisation of multinationality has its origins in the work of Hirsch (1976). A dynamic version is presented by Horstmann and Markusen (1983) whose central objective is the analysis of the strategic timing of investment in a growing market by a multinational faced by potential competition from host-country rivals. The model of this paper does not have this dynamic aspect, and as a result is somewhat simpler than that of Horstmann and Markusen.

*I am grateful for comments and remarks by Avinash Dixit, Gene Grossman and Kala Krishna.

0014-2921/87/$3.50 © 1987, Elsevier Science Publishers B.V. (North-Holland)

In its home country the multinational has a plant where it has incurred a firm-specific sunk cost F and a plant-specific sunk cost. It produces output at constant average variable cost c. If it exports its output to the host country, a constant transport cost of s per unit must also be incurred. If it establishes a plant in the host country, it must incur the plant-specific fixed cost G, but not the firm-specific fixed cost F, and the marginal cost of output in this plant will also be constant and equal to c. We study the effects of trade policy; which is modelled as a per-unit import tax t, added to the transport cost s. The multinational chooses between exporting and foreign direct investment by comparing the cost of establishing a foreign plant with the transport and tariff costs of exporting.

A host-country firm may also enter production of the good. It must, however, incur both the plant-specific fixed cost G and the firm-specific fixed cost F before it can produce, but when these costs have been incurred, it can produce at the same constant marginal cost as the multinational. (In fact, it would make very little difference to allow cost differences between the firms.) One can think of the firm-specific fixed cost as the cost of R&D required to gain access to the technology for producing the good, with any firm that has incurred it being as efficient as any other firm. This is admittedly a very crude characterisation of R&D.

The host country market for the good is described by a concave revenue function $P(X)X$, and it will be assumed that the properties of this function are such that the multinational always finds it profitable to supply the host market, whether or not it faces a rival firm.

Some limitations of the model should be noted. (i) The possibility that the host country firm, if it enters production, will then export to the multinational's home market or even will itself become a multinational by establishing a plant in the multinational's home country are not considered here. (ii) There is only one multinational and only one potential host country rival in the market. (iii) The model does not address the internalisation issue and the possibility of licensing as an alternative to foreign direct investment (although from the viewpoint of the welfare economics of trade policy, licensing and foreign direct investment are rather similar, and without too much difficulty one could reinterpret the model as one of the choice between licensing and exporting).

For the sake of simplicity of terminology, I refer throughout to the foreign firm as 'the multinational' even though strictly speaking it may be only a potential multinational.

3. The multinational as monopolist

If the multinational faced no threat of competition, it could export and would choose the export level X_E which maximises $P(X)X - (c + s + t)X$.

Alternatively, it could invest in the host country and then would choose the output level X_H to maximise $P(X)X - cX - G$. These choices are illustrated in fig. 1, from which it is immediately evident that, because of the concavity of $P(X)X$, $X_E < X_H$.

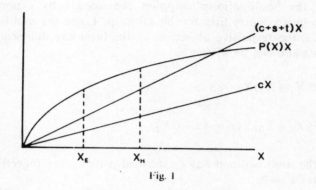

Fig. 1

The firm will choose foreign direct investment rather than exporting if and only if

$$P(X_H)X_H - cX_H - G > P(X_E)X_E - (c+s+t)X_E,$$ (1)

and the choice is influenced by the balance between G and $(s+t)X$. Specifically, as is clear from fig. 1 or from the definitions of the two optimal output levels, a sufficient condition for exporting to be the preferred option is that $G \geqq (s+t)X_H$, while a sufficient condition for direct investment to be superior is that $G \leqq (s+t)X_E$.

4. The multinational as duopolist

If there is potential entry from a single domestic producer, the model now takes the form of a multi-stage game. In the initial stages, the multinational decides whether to sell, and, if so, whether to export or to invest, while the domestic firm decides whether to enter. For the moment, let us not identify the order in which the different firms' entry decisions are made. At the final stage of the game the firms compete, if both have entered, and output levels get determined. I assume that the decisions at earlier stages of the game are made in the knowledge of the equilibria of later stages, so the equilibrium is perfect.

The equilibrium is solved by working backwards. In the event that the domestic firm does not enter, we know from the previous section what are the payoffs to the alternative actions open to the multinational.

If both firms enter the market, I assume that they act as Cournot duopolists, and it should be noted that an implication of the analysis of Fudenberg and Tirole (1984) is that the results will not be robust, at least in detail, to changes in the nature of the competitive interaction at this stage of the game. If the 'multinational' supplies the market by exporting, then, indicating the host country firm by the subscript 1 and the multinational by the subscript 2, the respective objectives of the firms are independent of the now-sunk costs and can be written

$$\max_{X_1} P(X_1 + X_2)X_1 - cX_1,$$

$$\max_{X_2} P(X_1 + X_2)X_2 - (c + s + t)X_2,$$

while, when the multinational has established a plant, the objectives are the same but with $s + t = 0$.

If we suppose only that the demand function $P(X_1 + X_2)$ is sufficiently well behaved so that the reaction curves slope and cross in the way shown in fig. 2, then an increase in $s + t$ moves the multinational's reaction curve in to the left, and the equilibria in both situations are as illustrated in fig. 2. The presence of transport costs and tariffs drives the equilibrium away from the symmetric duopoly solution (X_{HH}, X_{HH}), to a lower level of sales X_{EH} for the exporting firm, and a higher level of output X_{HE} for the host country firm. It is easily seen also that the *variable* profits of the host country firm are higher and of the multinational lower when the multinational is an exporter than when it is a direct investor. It is also obvious that a firm will make greater profits as a monopolist than as a duopolist.

Note how the choice between exporting and investing is different in duopoly from in monopoly. A monopolist simply compares the fixed cost of

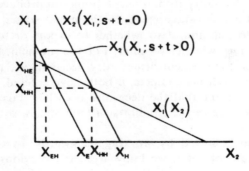

Fig. 2

investment with the transport and tax costs of exporting. A duopolist, whose output level, other things equal, is less than that of a monopolist, might be expected to be more likely to choose the export option. But this is to ignore the strategic value of making the fixed investment which lowers variable unit cost by $s+t$, and thereby, with Cournot competition, expands the multinational's output and profit while contracting its rival's output.

5. Tariffs and entry decisions

With the assumption that the multinational can make positive profits as an exporter, so that it will never choose to stay out of the host country market, the multinational must choose between exporting and investing, while the host country chooses between entering and not entering. The payoffs to the various decisions derive from the Cournot equilibria of the post-entry games discussed in the previous section and are set out in table 1, where H is the host country firm, M the (potential) multinational, and in each payoff pair, M's payoff is given first.

Table 1

M	H	
	Not enter	Enter
Export	$A, 0$	$C_E, C_H - F - G$
Invest	$B - G, 0$	$D - G, D - F - G$

The payoffs A, B, C_E, C_H, and D are given by

$$A = P(X_E)X_E - (c+s+t)X_E,$$

$$B = P(X_H)X_H - cX_H,$$

$$C_E = P(X_{EH} + X_{HE})X_{EH} - (c+s+t)X_{EH},$$

$$C_H = P(X_{EH} + X_{HE})X_{HE} - cX_{HE},$$

$$D = P(X_{HH} + X_{HH})X_{HH} - cX_{HH}.$$

We have assumed that $C_E > 0$ and we know that $B > A > C_E$ and that $B > C_H > D > C_E$.

The effect of a tariff increase on the market equilibrium will depend on which equilibrium is chosen and unfortunately the above inequalities are not

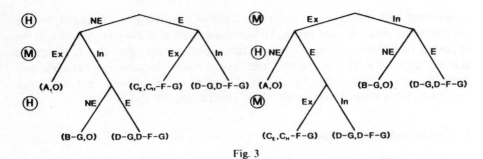

Fig. 3

sufficient to narrow down greatly the range of possible equilibria. I shall here consider only some of the possibilities; and I shall confine attention to the effects of an anticipated tariff.

It is natural to model firms' entry decisions as being sequential, and it is important, in doing this, to observe that only a decision to sink entry costs – investment by M, entry by H – is an irreversible commitment. A decision by M to export or by H not to enter is a decision which could be reversed after the rival firm has made its entry decision. Fig. 3 illustrates these entry decisions as a pair of decision trees, the first corresponding to the game in which H moves first, the second with M moving first. In each game, if the first mover makes a revocable decision at the first stage, and this is followed by an irrevocable decision by the other firm, the first mover then has an opportunity to change its decision.

5.1. The multinational as monopolist

In the event that $F + G > C_H(> D)$, H will choose not to enter, whether or not it makes its entry decision before M and whatever entry decision M makes. M will undertake foreign direct investment if $B - G > A$. In this case, imposition of a tariff has no effect. If, however, $A > B - G$ when $t = 0$, M would choose to be an exporter. After the imposition of a tariff, if M remains an exporter, it will have reduced profits, while consumption in the host market will be reduced and the host government will gain tariff revenue. Alternatively, the tariff could reduce A below $B - G$ and lead to M switching from exporting to investment, giving a simple example of tariff-induced investment.

5.2. The multinational as duopolist

In the event that $(C_H >)D > F + G$, H will choose to enter whatever entry decision M has made or will make. M will choose foreign direct investment if $D - G > C_E$ and in this event a tariff can have no effect. However, if $C_E > D - G$

when $t = 0$, M chooses to be an exporter, and the imposition of a tariff may either leave M as an exporter but change the balance of power within the duopoly in favour of H, or, if the tariff reduces C_E below $D - G$ and leads to M becoming a direct investor, there is tariff-jumping investment.

5.3. The multinational as strategic investor

In the event that $C_H > F + G > D$, H makes a positive profit from entering only if M is an exporter. Let us suppose that $A > B - G > C_E > D - G$, and let M move first. M prefers to be an exporter to an investor, for any given strategy of H. However, by choosing investment, as can be seen from the right panel of fig. 3, it deters entry by H and obtains profits of $B - G$. The monopoly (variable) profit B exceeds the sum of the duopoly variable profits $C_H + C_E$, so $B - G > C_E + (C_H - G) > C_E$ and entry-deterrence is optimal.

5.4. Tariff-induced disinvestment

Suppose that, in the absence of a tariff, $F + G > C_H > D$, but that the tariff raises C_H above $F + G$. In contrast with the case discussed in 5.3, let H move first. Suppose also that when $t = 0$, $C_E > D - G$ and $A < B - G$; a plausible pair of inequalities since transport costs are more likely to outweigh the cost of direct investment when M has the larger sales associated with monopoly. So long as the tariff does not reduce C_E below $D - G$, it will induce H to enter and M will be an exporter. In the absence of the tariff, H would not have entered and M would have been a direct investor. The effect of an anticipated tariff in this case is to induce entry by the host-country firm, to shift the market equilibrium from monopoly to duopoly, with consequent gains to consumers, and to deter direct investment by the multinational!

5.5. The anti-competitive tariff

Continuing the case analysed in 5.4, suppose that we start from the situation where $C_H > F + G > D$, and have $C_E > D - G$ and $A < B - G$, with H moving first, so that H enters and M exports. If a tariff now reduces C_E below $D - G$, then M would choose investment in response to entry by H, and therefore H will not enter. Now the tariff does induce foreign direct investment, and also has the effect of reducing competition.

5.6. The welfare economics of tariffs

The welfare effects of tariffs in each of the above cases (and in the cases not considered above) may easily be derived. Since, however, some of the results of the above analysis are dependent on the assumption that post-entry competition is Cournot [see Fudenberg and Tirole (1984) and Eaton and Grossman (1986)] it would be a mistake to attach too much significance to any individual result. More significant may be the very multiplicity of cases with different results. Tariffs may or may not induce foreign direct investment, they may or may not change the market structure, and they may have pro- or anti-competitive effects.

References

Dixit, Avinash K., 1980, The role of investment in entry-deterrence, Economic Journal, Mar.
Eaton, Jonathan and Gene M. Grossman, 1986, Optimal trade and industrial policy under oligopoly, Quarterly Journal of Economics.
Fudenberg, Drew and Jean Tirole, 1984, The fat-cat effect, the puppy-dog ploy, and the lean and hungry look, American Economic Review, Papers and Proceedings, May.
Hirsch, Seev, 1976, An international trade and investment theory of the firm, Oxford Economic Papers, July.
Horstmann, Ignatius and James R. Markusen, 1983, Strategic investments, firm-specific capital and the development of multinationals, Mimeo, July (University of Western Ontario, London).

[25]

Journal of International Economics 32 (1992) 109–129. North-Holland

Endogenous market structures in international trade (natura facit saltum)

Ignatius J. Horstmann

University of Western Ontario, London, Ontario, N6A 5C2, Canada

James R. Markusen*

University of Colorado, Boulder, CO 80309, USA, and National Bureau of Economic Research

Received September 1989, revised version received December 1990

Almost all of the large literature on international trade with imperfect competition assumes exogenous market structures. The purpose of this paper is to develop a simple model that generates alternative market structures as Nash equilibria for different parameterizations of the basic model. Equilibrium market structure is a function of the underlying technology. Familiar configurations such as a duopoly competing in exports or a single multinational producing in both markets arise as special cases. Small tax-policy changes can produce large welfare effects as the equilibrium market structure shifts, implying discontinuous jumps in prices, quantities, and profits.

> *Natura non facit saltum* (Nature does not proceed by leaps)
> [Alfred Marshall (1890, Title Page, *Principles of Economics*)].[1]

1. Introduction

There now exists a large literature on trade and trade policy under conditions of imperfect competition and increasing returns to scale. Almost all of this literature assumes an exogenously specified market structure. The situation in which a single domestic firm competes against a single foreign firm producing a perfect or imperfect substitute product is perhaps the best known of these market structures. Papers by Markusen (1981), Brander and Krugman (1983), Dixit (1984), Brander and Spencer (1985), and Eaton and Grossman (1986) are a few examples of this approach. Free entry versions of

---

*The authors wish to thank Knick Harley and two anonymous referees for helpful comments and suggestions. Of course, the usual caveat applies.
[1]This quote is originally attributed to Carl von Linné Linnaeus (1707–1777) and, in slightly different form, to Jacques Tissot (1613).

0022-1996/92/$05.00 © 1992—Elsevier Science Publishers B.V. All rights reserved

this model are found in Krugman (1979), Helpman (1981), Venables (1985), and Horstmann and Markusen (1986). Here again, though, the underlying structure of production is exogenous to the analysis. Markusen and Venables (1988) analyze free entry versus oligopoly and segmented versus integrated markets, but do not attempt to analyze how these regimes might arise as equilibrium phenomena.

Most of the formal analysis of the multinational enterprise (MNE) can be characterized in a similar fashion. Helpman (1984) essentially imposes a structure of domestic and branch plant production (i.e. multinationality is assumed). Markusen (1984) considers a MNE monopoly with one plant in each of two countries versus a duopoly between two single-plant firms, but no attempt is made to establish which is the equilibrium market structure. In a previous paper [Horstmann and Markusen (1987)], we have partially endogenized market structure, but not in a way that permits the (non-MNE) oligopoly equilibria discussed in the previous paragraph to emerge. Levinsohn (1989) shows how a tariff or quota can induce a shift in market structure by causing an exporter to enter the market as a multinational, but the paper does not focus on the positive economics of what determines initial market structure in the first place. Dixit and Kyle (1985) consider how policies can induce or prevent entry, but the option of serving a foreign market by a branch plant versus exports is not considered.

The purpose of this paper is two-fold: (i) to develop a simple model in which market structure is determined endogenously as the outcome of plant location decisions by firms, and (ii) to illustrate the impact on optimal trade policy analysis of endogenous market structure models. The assumed production technology is similar to that in Markusen (1984) and Horstmann and Markusen (1987) in that production results in both firm-specific and plant-specific fixed costs. Firm-specific costs create assets that are joint inputs across plants (e.g. blueprints) in that additional plants may be opened for the plant-specific costs only. Marginal costs are constant and identical across countries, while exports bear a constant unit transport cost.

Given this technology, and Cournot–Nash behavior by firms, we demonstrate the existence of three equilibria: (1) the two-firm, single-plant (exporting) duopoly familiar from the literature; (2) the one-firm, two-plant (MNE) monopoly; and (3) the two-firm, two-plant (MNE) duopoly. We show that, roughly speaking, equilibrium (1) emerges when plant-specific costs are large relative to firm-specific costs and transportation costs. We switch to the asymmetric equilibrium (2) when firm-specific costs and transport costs are raised such that duopoly generates negative profits. Equilibrium (3) is obtained by lowering plant-specific costs so that the MNE duopoly is both profitable and dominates the exporting duopoly. *Market structure is thus a function of the technology.*

Next we conduct a simple tax and welfare analysis of the model to illustrate the impact on optimal policy calculations of allowing the market structure to be endogenous. This analysis demonstrates that small policy changes can produce large welfare effects when equilibrium market structure shifts. Such shifts imply discontinuous jumps in prices, quantities, profits, and therefore welfare. Analysis of an import tariff shows that market structure shifts from the exporting duopoly one long before the 'optimal' tariff and welfare levels are reached. Analysis of a producer excise tax shows three changes in market structure as the tax rate increases.

2. Technology and equilibrium market structure

Suppose that the world consists of two countries, home and foreign (h and f), and that each country is endowed with an identical amount of a single homogeneous factor, labor. Each country can produce a homogeneous good Z, with units chosen such that $Z = L_z$. Z or labor is numeraire. A firm in country h can produce a good X with increasing returns to scale and a firm in country f can produce a symmetric substitute good Y. Scale economies are assumed to be large relative to demand such that the market will support at most one X and one Y firm. The (potential) X and Y producers have the following identical technologies, given as costs in units of labor (or Z):

$$F = \text{firm-specific fixed costs,}$$

$$G = \text{plant-specific fixed costs,}$$

$$m = \text{constant marginal cost,} \tag{1}$$

$$s = \text{unit transport cost.}$$

The firm-specific fixed cost is intended to represent knowledge-based assets, such as those obtained from R&D, that are joint inputs across plants [Markusen (1984)]. Multi-plant economies of scale arise in this formulation in that the fixed costs of a two-plant firm are $2G + F$, while the fixed costs of two one-plant firms are $2G + 2F$. The MNE thus offers the world productive efficiency. This having been said, however, it should be noted that a MNE monopoly will also generally involve a larger market power distortion than a duopoly, so that the welfare effects of MNE production are not clear cut. Furthermore, the mere fact that MNE production is technically efficient should not lead one to conclude that it must arise as an equilibrium industry structure (as will be illustrated below).

In order to bring out the important features of the analysis in as straightforward a fashion as possible, we adopt a very simple demand structure.[2] All consumers in both countries have identical quadratic utility functions given by

$$U(X, Y, Z) = aX - (b/2)X^2 + aY - (b/2)Y^2 - cXY + Z. \tag{2}$$

Let p_x and p_y denote the prices of X and Y in terms of Z (or L), respectively. Let L denote each country's total endowment of labor, and let π_x (π_y) denote the X producer's (Y producer's) profit in terms of Z. The aggregate budget constraint for the home country is simply

$$L + \pi_x = p_x X + p_y Y + Z. \tag{2a}$$

Profits are of course net of transport costs, as we note below, so labor devoted to this activity is reflected in π_x. Maximization of (2) with respect to (2a) gives the income-inelastic inverse demand functions:

$$p_x = a - bX - cY, \qquad p_y = a - bY - cX, \tag{3}$$

with corresponding functions for country F. We assume that $b \geq c$, with $b = c$ being the case where X and Y are perfect substitutes. The technology in (1) combined with the demand functions in (3) and the resource constraint $L = L_z + L_x + L_y$ (both X and Y are not necessarily produced in a country) complete the specification of the general equilibrium model. We assume that L is large enough to support production of the X and Y demanded from (3).

The equilibrium market structure is determined in a two-step procedure corresponding to a two-stage game. In stage one, the two firms (X and Y producers) make a choice over three options: (a) no entry, referred to as the zero plant strategy; (b) serving both the home and foreign markets from one plant, referred to as the one-plant strategy; or (c) becoming a MNE, by building plants in both countries, referred to as the two-plant strategy. In stage two, the X and Y producers play a one-shot Cournot game. Moves in stage one are assumed to be simultaneous.

The game is solved backwards in the usual fashion. We first solve for the maximized value of profits for each firm for each of the three 'capacity' choices given the capacity choice of the other firm. We illustrate this procedure by solving for maximized profits under the assumption that both firms are MNEs; that is, they both choose to maintain plants in both countries. Let X and X^* denote the X firm's sales in the home country and foreign country, respectively, and let Y and Y^* be similarly defined (e.g. Y^* is the foreign firm's sales in the foreign country). Profits for the home firm are given by

---

[2]Robustness of the results for more general demand structures is considered in section 5 below.

$$\pi_x = (a - bX - cY)X + (a - bX^* - cY^*)X^* - m(X + X^*) - 2G - F. \tag{4}$$

We assume that markets are segmented so that firms may price independently in each market. The first-order conditions corresponding to (4) under the Cournot assumption are then

$$\partial \pi_x / \partial X = a - 2bX - cY - m = 0,$$

$$\partial \pi_x / \partial X^* = a - 2bX^* - cY^* - m = 0. \tag{5}$$

Similar equations hold for Y and Y^*. Exploiting this symmetry, we can solve for Cournot outputs:

$$X = X^* = Y = Y^* = (a - m)/(2b + c). \tag{6}$$

Eq. (6) allows us to solve for prices using (3) and then for profits using (4). Maximized profits under the two-plant strategies are

$$\pi_x = 2b \left[\frac{a - m}{2b + c} \right]^2 - 2G - F = b(X^2 + X^{*2}) - 2G - F, \tag{7}$$

$$\pi_y = 2b \left[\frac{a - m}{2b + c} \right]^2 - 2G - F = b(Y^2 + Y^{*2}) - 2G - F, \tag{8}$$

Should the X and Y producers each maintain only a single plant and export to the other market, then profits and first-order conditions for the X producer are

$$\pi_x = (a - bX - cY)X + (a - bX^* - cY^*)X^* - mX - (m + s)X^* - G - F, \tag{9}$$

$$\partial \pi_x / \partial X = a - 2bX - cY - m = 0,$$

$$\partial \pi_x / \partial X^* = a - 2bX^* - cY^* - (m + s) = 0. \tag{10}$$

Again exploiting the symmetry in the problem $(X = Y^*, X^* = Y)$, Cournot outputs are

$$X = Y^* = (a - m + cd)/(2b + c), \qquad d = s/(2b - c), \tag{11}$$

$$X^* = Y = (a - m - 2bd)/(2b + c), \qquad d = s/(2b - c), \tag{12}$$

and equilibrium profits by $\pi_x = b(X^2 + X^{*2}) - G - F$ and $\pi_y = b(Y^2 + Y^{*2}) - G - F$. Relative to (7) and (8), variable profits here are lower due both to the transport cost, $sX^*(sY)$, and to the fact that the loss of sales on the foreign market outweighs gains domestically $(2b > c)$. However, fixed costs are reduced by G from $(2G + F)$ to $(G + F)$. Thus the relationship between G and s will clearly influence whether the MNE duopoly or the exporting duopoly generates more profits.[3]

Other market configurations can be derived using (6), (11), and (12). For example, if X is a two-plant MNE while Y is a one-plant exporter, then (given segmented markets) X is given by (11) and X^* by (6). Y^* is given by (6) while Y is given by (12).

This procedure allows us to derive the profits from the different choices over the number of plants. These profits, in turn, are the payoffs in the game for which the strategy space is the number of plants. The Nash equilibrium of this game in number of plants determines the equilibrium market structure for the model. Market structures are denoted (i, j), where i is the number of the X-producer's plants and j the number of the Y-producer's plants.

To obtain some insight into the types of market structures that may arise in equilibrium and what factors influence the equilibrium outcome, it is useful to consider first some example games. Table 1 provides four such games. In each the goods are assumed to be imperfect substitutes $(c = b/2)$ and marginal cost is zero. Neither assumption is important to the results. The four examples hold s constant at $s = 2$, and vary the levels of F and G. The first number of each pair is the payoff to the home country firm (the X producer) while the second number is the payoff to the Y producer. Payoffs in each case are the equilibrium profits associated with the given market structure.

In case 1 of table 1 $(F = 27, G = 7)$, there is a single Nash equilibrium with each firm producing for both markets from a single plant. Neither firm can improve profits by building a branch plant or by exiting. Inspection will show that no other proposed solution has this best-response property.

In case 2, the firm-specific costs are increased to $F = 28$ while G remains 7. Now there are three equilibria, the exporting duopoly as before but also the case in which X is a two-plant MNE and Y does not enter and the corresponding outcome with Y the MNE and X not entering. The difference from the previous case is that now a firm makes negative profits playing one plant against a two-plant (MNE) rival. If X plays two plants, Y makes negative profits from either two or one plants, so the best response is to not enter. The equilibrium with Y as the monopoly MNE has the same property.

In case 3, F is raised to 29 and G lowered to 6. The effect of this change is

---

[3]However, the relationship between these profit levels does not necessarily determine the equilibrium market structure as we shall show. See also note 2 to table 1.

Table 1
Example: $a = 16$, $b = 2$, $c = 1$, $m = 0$, $s = 2$.

		Country *F*		
		2 plants	1 plant	0 plants
Case 1: $G = 7$, $F = 27$, Nash equilibrium (1, 1)				
Country *II*	2	$(-0.04, -0.04)$	$(1.71, 0.74)$	$(23.0, 0)$
	1	$(0.74, 1.71)$	$(2.45, 2.45)*$	$(22.5, 0)$
	0	$(0, 23.0)$	$(0, 22.5)$	$(0, 0)$
Case 2: $G = 7$, $F = 28$, Nash equilibria (1, 1), (2, 0), (0, 2)				
Country *II*	2	$(-1.04, -1.04)$	$(0.71, -0.26)$	$(22.0, 0)*$
	1	$(-0.26, 0.71)$	$(1.45, 1.45)*$	$(21.5, 0)$
	0	$(0, 22.0)*$	$(0, 21.5)$	$(0, 0)$
Case 3: $G = 6$, $F = 29$, Nash equilibria (2, 0), (0, 2)				
Country *II*	2	$(-0.04, -0.04)$	$(1.71, -0.26)$	$(23.0, 0)*$
	1	$(-0.26, 1.71)$	$(1.45, 1.45)$	$(21.5, 0)$
	0	$(0, 23.0)*$	$(0, 21.5)$	$(0, 0)$
Case 4: $G = 5$, $F = 30$, Nash equilibrium (2, 2)				
Country *II*	2	$(0.96, 0.96)*$	$(2.71, -0.26)$	$(24.0, 0)$
	1	$(-0.26, 2.71)$	$(1.45, 1.45)$	$(21.5, 0)$
	0	$(0, 24.0)$	$(0, 21.5)$	$(0, 0)$

Notes

1. In all cases, fixed costs are sufficiently high that no third firm can enter.

2. When each firm chooses one plant, it will always locate in different countries given the symmetry in the model. We can prove that if firms locate together, competition increases and profits fall. If they are initially together, it is always in the interests of one firm to move to the other country. Transport costs essentially 'insulate' the firms from competition. In order to save space, we do not demonstrate this here. Locating together does become a possibility when taxes destroy symmetry, as we show in section 3.

3. An asterisk indicates a Nash equilibrium structure.

to increase the profitability of two-plant production while leaving the profitability of single plant production unchanged. The net effect is to eliminate the exporting duopoly as an equilibrium. At that allocation, *X* has an incentive to shift to branch-plant production and similarly for *Y*. The two MNE monopoly equilibria are the only Nash equilibria. It is interesting to note here that in a completely symmetric game, the only equilibria are non-symmetric in the sense that the market will only have a single firm. Prices for the good will be the same in the two countries, but since profits of the single firm are positive (23.0 in the example), the firm's home country (assuming that is where the shareholders are located) will enjoy higher welfare.

In case 4, the plant-specific cost is lowered to $G = 5$. This allows the market to support two, two-plant MNEs and indeed this emerges as the only equilibrium. Note that in case 4 the MNE duopoly equilibrium is inferior from the point of view of both firms to the exporting duopoly (profits equal 0.96 at the former versus 1.45 at the latter). This emphasizes that we cannot ignore the strategic aspects of market structure and simply infer market structure by comparing profit levels under various strategies.

Moving through from cases 1 to 4 of table 1, we see that these games suggest a certain relationship between equilibrium market structure and the relative sizes of firm-specific and plant-specific costs. Relatively low values of F and relatively high values of G generate an equilibrium market structure that corresponds to the export-duopoly case analyzed in the paper mentioned in the first paragraph of the introduction above. The asymmetric MNE monopoly of cases 2 and 3 results from increasing F relative to G, and corresponds to the situation analyzed by Markusen (1984) who compares this market structure from a welfare point of view to the exporting duopoly (case 1). The symmetric MNE duopoly of case 4 occurs from additional increases in F relative to G and corresponds closely to Helpman (1984).

The general results are summarized in figs. 1 and 2 which show the possible equilibrium market structures for various (F, G) and (F, s) pairs, respectively.[4] To understand the way that these two diagrams work, it is simplest to consider the way in which the various boundaries are generated. Consider, for instance, fig. 1. Let $\pi_x(i, j)$ denote X's profits under market structure (i, j) and let $\pi_y(i, j)$ be similarly defined. $\pi_x(2, 2)$ is given in (7), for example, and $\pi_x(1, 1)$ from (11), (12) and the following line. The boundary between the regions $(2, 2)$ and $(1, 1)$ gives the (F, G) for which the home (foreign) firm is indifferent between one-plant and two-plant production. More specifically, this boundary defines the (F, G) for which the home firm is indifferent both between the market structures $(2, 2)$ and $(1, 2)$ and between the structures $(2, 1)$ and $(1, 1)$. In both cases, the difference in home-firm profits between two-plant and one-plant production is

$$\pi_x(2, 2) - \pi_x(1, 2) = b\left[\left(\frac{a-m}{2b+c}\right)^2 - \left(\frac{a-m-2bd}{2b+c}\right)^2\right] - G$$

$$= \pi_x(2, 1) = \pi_x(1, 1).$$

Because this expression is independent of F, the boundary is a vertical line with

$$G = \alpha = 2b\left[\left(\frac{a-m}{2b+c}\right)^2 - \left(\frac{a-m-2bd}{2b+c}\right)^2\right] > 0.$$

---

[4]Figs. 1 and 2 are drawn for the parameter values of table 1, but the existence, shape, and relative position of the regions are valid for all admissible parameter values $[a, b, c, m, s(G)]$.

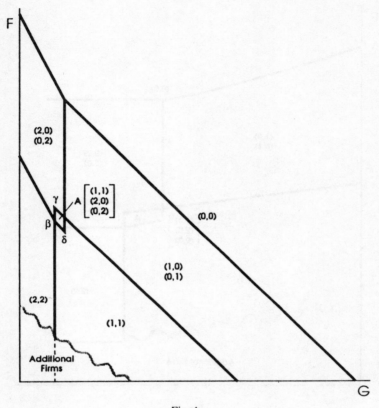

Fig. 1

For (F, G) pairs to the left of the boundary, the home (foreign) firm prefers two-plant production to one-plant production whether the foreign (home) firm has one or two plants. Therefore, subject to non-negative profit considerations, only $(2, 2)$ can be an equilibrium. To the right of the boundary, one plant production is preferred to two-plant production so only $(1, 1)$ can be an equilibrium (again subject to the structure generating non-negative profits).

The (F, G) pairs for which the structures $(1, 1)$ and $(2, 2)$ result in non-negative profits are delineated by the northern boundaries of these two regions, respectively. That is, the northern boundary or the region $(2, 2)$ gives the (F, G) for which $\pi_x(2, 2) = \pi_y(2, 2) = 0$. This boundary will also be a straight line but with slope -2. Similarly, the northern boundary of $(1, 1)$ gives the (F, G) for which $\pi_x(1, 1) = \pi_y(1, 1) = 0$. This boundary will also be a straight line but with slope -1. For (F, G) below the respective boundaries,

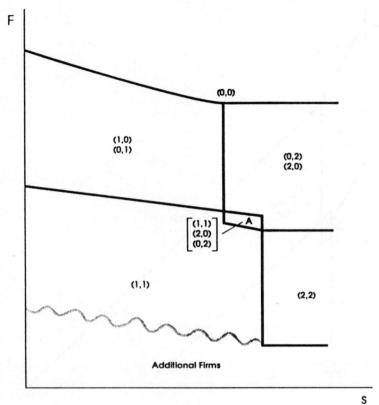

Fig. 2

profits for the given market structure are positive, while for (F, G) above the boundary profits are negative.

Much of the remainder of the diagram is straightforward. If neither of the structures $(2, 2)$ or $(1, 1)$ yield non-negative profits, then the only possibility left is a monopoly market structure [one of $(1, 0)$, $(0, 1)$, $(2, 0)$, $(0, 2)$]. Whether a firm chooses a one-plant or two-plant monopoly structure depends on whether the difference $\pi_x(2, 0) - \pi_x(1, 0)$ $[\pi_y(0, 2) - \pi_y(0, 1)]$ is positive or negative. The eastern boundary between the regions $(2, 0)$ and $(1, 0)$ gives the (F, G) for which the difference is zero. Because this difference is also independent of F, the boundary will be vertical with

$$G = \delta = b\left[\left(\frac{a-m}{2b}\right)^2 - \left(\frac{a-m-s}{2b}\right)^2\right] > 0.$$

To the left of this boundary, $\pi_x(2,0) > \pi_x(1,0)$ so that $(2,0)$, $(0,2)$ is the market structure, while to the right $\pi_x(1,0) > \pi_x(2,0)$ giving $(1,0)$, $(0,1)$ as the structure. Again, this result is subject to a non-negative profit constraint. This constraint defines the northernmost boundary of the diagram.

Two qualifications to these results are necessary. Some tedious algebra shows that, in this model, $\delta > \alpha$. This fact means that, for (F,G) with $\alpha < G < \delta$, $\pi_x(2,2) = \pi_y(2,2) < 0$ is not sufficient to guarantee that $(2,0)$ $[(0,2)]$ is an equilibrium. Because the foreign firm, for instance, finds the market structure $(2,1)$ more profitable than $(2,2)$ when $G > \alpha$, the fact that $\pi_y(2,2) < 0$ does not rule out the possibility that $\pi_y(2,1) > 0$. Clearly, should $\pi_y(2,1)$ be positive, then $(2,0)$ would not be an equilibrium market structure.

Therefore, for (F,G) with $\alpha < G < \delta$, it is necessary to check whether $\pi_x(1,2)$ is positive or negative. The southern boundary of the region A gives the (F,G) for which $\pi_x(1,2) = 0$. This boundary is a straight line with slope -1. Furthermore, since competing against exports is more profitable than competing against a domestic producer, the boundary must be everywhere below the $\pi_x(1,1) = 0$ locus (implying that $\gamma > \beta$ in fig. 1). Finally, since at $G = \alpha$, $\pi_x(1,2) = \pi_x(2,2)$, this boundary lies above the $\pi_x(2,2) = 0$ locus whenever $\alpha < G < \delta$. Together, these facts imply the existence of a region like A, characterized by (F,G) for which $(1,1)$ [below the $\pi_x(1,1) = 0$ locus] and $(2,0)$ [above both the $\pi_x(1,2) = 0$ and $\pi_x(2,2) = 0$ loci] are equilibrium market structures. Thus the region A of fig. 1 is the region of multiple equilibria illustrated by case 2 of table 1.

The second qualification is that, for sufficiently low F or G, a third (or more) firm can enter. Space does not permit us to treat this problem here, so we simply 'chop off' figs. 1 and 2 with a wavy line.

A similar process can be employed to construct the boundaries for fig. 2 in (F,s) space. The two vertical boundaries are the same as in fig. 1 in that they define the points of indifference between one-plant and two-plant production. Similarly, the other boundaries are the appropriate zero-profit loci.

A moment's consideration of fig. 1 serves to confirm the intuition gained from table 1 regarding the relationship between market structure and the costs F and G. For a given s, MNEs arise when F is large relative to G, with the asymmetric MNE monopoly occurring when F becomes sufficiently large. Exporting equilibria arise when G is large relative to F, with the asymmetric monopoly emerging when G (or $F + G$) becomes sufficiently large.

Fig. 1 is also useful in that it illustrates the asymmetric roles of the fixed costs F and G. Suppose we begin with F and G both small such that $(2,2)$ is the initial equilibrium. Increases in F increase the cost of existing as a firm but do not affect the attractiveness of branch-plant production versus exporting. Increases in G affect the relative cost of branch-plant production versus exporting as well as the cost of existing as a firm.

Fig. 2 provides insight into the impact of transport costs on the equilibrium market structure. Specifically, as firm-specific costs, F, and transport costs, s, are small relative to plant-specific costs, G, exporting is the equilibrium structure. When F and s are both large relative to G, then the asymmetric MNE monopoly structure arises. These results are analogous to those reported in Horstmann and Markusen (1987).

3. Trade policy and equilibrium market structure

In this section we analyze the effect of a tariff and a production tax/subsidy with market structure endogenous. The analysis in this section is carried out in the context of two of the games given in table 1. The results derived for these games regarding the impact of specific policies on market structure can be generalized by methods analogous to those used for figs. 1 and 2.

To proceed, let T denote a specific import tariff on Y in the home country. Assume the parameter values of case 1 of table 1 so that the symmetric exporting duopoly is the initial unique Nash equilibrium market structure. Expressions for utility, income, and profits are repeated as follows:

$$U = U(X) + U(Y) - cXY + Z,$$

$$L + \pi_x + TY = p_x X + p_y Y + Z, \tag{13}$$

$$\pi = p_x X + p_x^* X^* - m(X + X^*) - sX^* - G - F.$$

Substitute the latter two equations in the utility function and recall that, with segmented markets and constant marginal cost, foreign prices and sales will not be affected by the home-country import tariff. Differentiating, we have

$$\frac{dW}{dT} = (a - bX - cY)\frac{dX}{dT} + (a - bY - cX)\frac{dY}{dT} - m\,dX$$

$$-(p_y - T)\frac{dY}{dT} - Y\frac{dp_y}{dT} + Y\frac{dT}{dT},$$

$$\frac{dW}{dT} = (p_x - m)\frac{dX}{dT} + T\frac{dY}{dT} - Y\frac{d\hat{p}_y}{dT}, \tag{14}$$

where the second equation follows from $p_y = a - bY - cX$, $p_x = a - bX - cY$, and $p_y - T = \hat{p}_y$. The three terms in the second equation of (14) are familiar from the imperfect competition literature. The first is the excess of price over marginal cost (marginal cost is zero in our numerical examples) times the

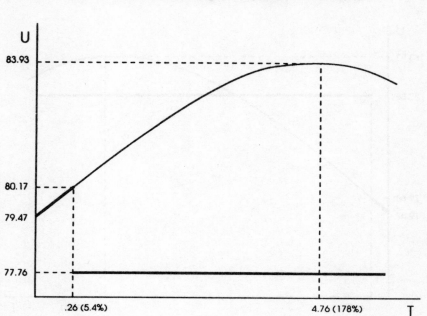

Fig. 3

change in output. This is a 'Harberger triangle' effect: with price in excess of marginal cost, increases in output are beneficial. The second term is a volume-of-trade effect: with domestic price in excess of the cost of imports ($T = p_y - \hat{p}_y$), increases in imports increase welfare at constant terms of trade. The third term is the terms-of-trade effect. Solving for X and Y as functions of T [the same as (11) and (12) with $d = (s + T)/(2b - c)$] and differentiating, we get

$$\mathrm{d}X/\mathrm{d}T = 1/15, \qquad \mathrm{d}Y/\mathrm{d}T = -4/15, \qquad \mathrm{d}\hat{p}_y/\mathrm{d}T = -8/15 \qquad (15)$$

for the parameter values of table 1: $b = 2$, $c = 1$, and $m = 0$. Substituting these expressions and the values of X and Y into (14), the optimal tariff sets (14) equal to zero, yielding a value of $T = 4.67$ (converts to 178 percent in ad valorem terms). The welfare function yields a value of 83.9 at the optimal tariff assuming that the exporting duopoly continues to be the equilibrium market structure.

These results are shown in figs. 3 and 4 where the heavy and then light curve gives welfare as a function of the specific rate of tariff T (ad valorem rate in parentheses) for the exporting duopoly market structure.[5] But with

---

[5]The scale on the horizontal axis in figs. 3 and 4 is $T^{0.75}$.

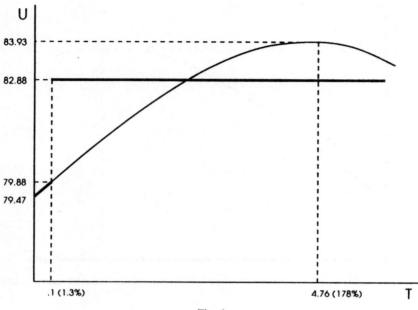

Fig. 4

market structure endogenous, we have to check if the reduced profits to the *Y* producer cause him to change strategies. Indeed, they do change and two cases are considered in figs. 3 and 4. In fig. 3 we assume that the foreign firm must have a plant in its own country. For the case 1 parameters, profits of the *Y* producer fall to 1.71 when the tariff reaches 0.26 (5.4 percent). Referring to table 1, case 1, we see that at this point the *Y* producer will enter the home market with a branch plant [the (1, 2) allocation]. The *X* producer will not have an incentive to alter its one-plant strategy, so (1, 2) is the new Nash equilibrium. The home country's welfare is reduced to 77.76, a level lower than what it was at the initial zero-tariff equilibrium. At the new equilibrium, lower *X* profits outweigh an increase in consumer's surplus so that the home country loses. Home country welfare is thus given by the (discontinuous) heavy line in fig. 3: welfare initially rises and then falls when market structure switches and remains constant thereafter (further increases in the tariff are irrelevant).

Fig. 4 considers the case where we do not constrain the foreign firm to have to produce in its own market. In this case it may pursue a strategy not considered before because it was always irrelevant: the *Y* producer can maintain one plant in the home country and serve its own country by exports. Using case 1 parameters, the profits from this strategy (the home firm also maintains a single plant in the home country) are 2.16. At a tariff rate of only 1.3 percent, the *Y* producer thus abandons his base and produces from a single home-country plant. For case 1 parameters, the home firm has no incentive to change its strategy, so this new allocation is the Nash equilibrium. Fig. 4 graphs welfare as a function of the specific tariff rate as in fig. 3. At a rate of 1.3 percent, the foreign firm enters the home market and welfare jumps to 82.88 and remains constant thereafter. There is no difference in consumer surplus after the market structure changes in figs. 3 and 4. The difference lies in profits earned by the home firm in the foreign market. In fig. 3 the profits are lower because the *X* producer is competing with a domestic (low cost) *Y* producer, whereas in fig. 4 the *Y* producer bears the transport cost to the foreign market as well and hence produces a lower quantity.

Now consider a producer excise tax in the home country. Producers of *X* and *Y* inside the country bear the tax, while we assume that import of *Y* and possibly *X* are not taxed (i.e. there is no import duty). We assume the parameter values of case 4 of tables 1 and 3 so that the symmetric two-plant MNE market structure is the Nash equilibrium. Home-country welfare as a function of the specific excise tax is shown in fig. 5. The initial welfare level is 80.68. The tax is distortionary and reduces welfare despite the fact that there is a positive terms-of-trade effect forcing down the import price of *Y*.

When the tax reaches a level of 0.38 (12.1 percent), profits for both *X* and *Y* producers are reduced to zero. Invoking a 'tie breaking' rule in favor of the domestic firm, the *Y* producer exits, and the equilibrium moves to $(2,0)$ as shown in case 4 of table 1. Welfare rises to 89.23 owing to the large increase in profits that outweighs the loss of consumer surplus. Further increases in the tax reduce the output of *X* and hence domestic welfare. But this reduction in *X* means that the demand price of *Y* is rising. At a tax rate of 0.42 (5.4 percent of the monopoly price), the foreign firm can profitably export to the home country (recall that imports bear no tax) and so the equilibrium in table 1 shifts a second time, in this case to $(2,1)$. This has an unfavorable welfare effect as the loss in profits to the *X* producer outweighs the gain in consumer surplus.

Increases in the tax beyond 0.42 continue to reduce welfare and the profits of the *X* producer. At a tax rate of 0.79 (6.3 percent of p_x), the *X* producer abandons his home-country plant and serves the home market from his plant in the foreign country. The equilibrium involves two, one-plant firms, both located in the foreign country. Welfare falls further, as shown in fig. 5, owing to the higher price of *X* and corresponding loss of consumer surplus.

5. Robustness of results

The model used in this paper is obviously restrictive in its use of functional forms. In this section we briefly describe how alternative assump-

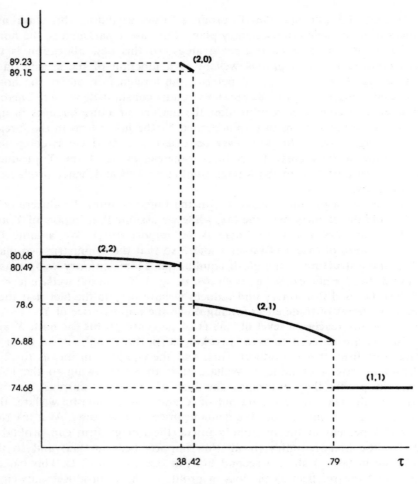

Fig. 5

tions affect the results.. We do this in terms of fig. 1, the 'general case' given the demand and cost functions assumed in this paper. Three alternative assumptions will be considered individually: (a) non-linearity of the demand curves; (b) increasing marginal cost; and (c) a positive income elasticity of demand for X and Y. The fixed-cost assumptions and the assumption of Cournot behavior in the post-entry game are retained.

The first result to note is that none of these three alternative assumptions affects the shape and general position of the zero-profit boundaries in fig. 1 (the sloping 'northern' boundaries of the regions). As we noted in connection with this diagram, the slopes of those boundaries are determined entirely by the tradeoff betwen firm-specific and plant-specific costs. Thus the boundary between $(2, 2)$ and $(2, 0)/(0, 2)$ and that between $(2, 0)/(0, 2)$ and $(0, 0)$ has a constant slope of -2: with two plants, a decrease in F of 2 cancels an increase in G of 1. The boundary between $(1, 1)$ and $(1, 0)/(0, 1)$ and that between $(1, 0)/(0, 1)$ and $(0, 0)$ similarly has a constant slope of -1.

The second result is that assumption (a) does not alter the fact that the boundary between regions $(2, 2)$ and $(1, 1)$ is vertical in fig. 1 and that there is no region in between. The same result applies to the boundary between regions $(2, 0)/(0, 2)$ and $(1, 0)/(0, 1)$. The 'eastern' boundary of region $(2, 2)$ is determined by the equality $\pi_x(2, 2) = \pi_x(1, 2)$. Assumption (a) does not alter the fact that the solution to this equation is found at a unique value of G that is independent of F, hence the vertical boundary [nor does assumption (b) for that matter; alternative assumption (c) does change this result as we will indicate below]. The 'western' boundary of region $(1, 1)$ in fig. 1 is defined by the equality $\pi_x(1, 1) = \pi_x(2, 1)$ and is again found at a unique value of G that is independent of F. Finally, the result shown in fig. 1 that the eastern boundary of region $(2, 2)$ and the western boundary of region $(1, 1)$ are the same is also independent of alternative assumption (a) [but not (b), see below]. This boundary is defined by indifference between exporting to the other country or serving it by a branch plant. Given the segmented markets assumption (which does matter) and constant marginal cost, this indifference is independent of the market structure in one's own country.

There are two qualitative differences that alternative assumptions (a) and (b) introduce into fig. 1. First, assumption (a) alone may result in the relative positions of the $(2, 2)$-$(1, 1)$ and $(2, 0)/(0, 2)$-$(1, 0)/(0, 1)$ boundaries being reversed, with the latter now occurring at the lower value of G. This leaves a parallelogram similar to A in fig. 1. Points within this new parallelogram will have the following characteristics:

(i) $\pi_x(1, 0) > \pi_x(2, 0) > 0$;

(ii) $\pi_x(1, 1) > 0$;

(iii) $\pi_x(2, 1) > \pi_x(1, 1) > 0$;

(iv) $\pi_x(1, 2) < \pi_x(2, 2) < 0$.

Similar inequalities apply to Y (i.e. replace π_x with π_y).

Given these inequalities, it is then relatively easy to see that the new equivalent to parallelogram A in fig. 1 is a region of non-existence of (pure strategy) equilibrium rather than a region of multiple equilibrium. Suppose, for example, that we start with an allocation $(1,0)$. Y will enter with one plant moving the allocation to $(1,1)$ [(ii) above]. X will in turn shift to branch-plant production abroad, moving the allocation to $(2,1)$ [(iii) above]. Y now makes negative profits from either one or two plants and exits [(iv) above], making the market structure $(2,0)$. But now X eliminates the branch plant moving back to the starting allocation $(1,0)$ [(i) above].

Assumption (b), either alone or in conjunction with (a), will in general result in there being a region between the $(2,2)$ and $(1,1)$ regions in fig. 1. This additional region arises due to the fact that, while the equation $\pi_x(1,2) = \pi_x(1,2)$ has a unique solution in G, the value of G that solves the equation is generally different from the one that solves $\pi_x(2,1) = \pi_x(1,1)$ when costs are increasing. That is to say, when marginal cost is not constant, the profitability of an additional plant depends on the number of plants the competing firm operates. The reason for this outcome is simple. Consider a situation in which the foreign firm operates two plants rather than one. Then, marginal cost at a given level of foreign country production is smaller in the two-plant case than in the one-plant case (assuming the foreign firm also produces for the home-country market). This lowered marginal cost in turn implies that the foreign firm's equilibrium output, even in its own market, will differ when it operates two plants rather than one. This fact, in turn, means that the profitability of an additional plant for the home firm will differ depending on whether the foreign firm operates one or two plants.

The form of the equilibrium in the new region is relatively easy to determine. Should an additional plant be more profitable when the competing firm operates a single plant rather than two plants [i.e. the G that solves $\pi_x(2,1) = \pi_x(1,1)$ is larger than the G solving $\pi_x(1,2) = \pi_x(2,2)$], then the new region has the property that, for all (F,G) pairs in the region, the configuration $(1,2), (2,1)$ is the unique equilibrium configuration. Should the reverse be true, then both $(2,2)$ and $(1,1)$ become equilibrium configurations. In any event, assumption (b) makes possible the asymmetric configuration $(1,2), (2,1)$ as an equilibrium outcome.

Finally, the assumption that there is a positive income elasticity of demand for X and Y makes more of a difference to the map shown in fig. 1. Not only may the $(2,2)$–$(1,1)$ and $(2,0)$–$(1,0)$ boundaries be reversed as just discussed, but they are clearly not vertical. An increase in F for constant G reduces the maximum possible quantities of X, Y, and Z that can be produced, and thus reduces income. At constant prices, demand for all three will fall, which is like contracting the size of the market for X and Y. This in turn implies that the critical value of G at which $\pi_x(2,2) = \pi_x(1,2)$ and $\pi_x(2,0) = \pi_x(1,0)$ falls as we increase F. The $(2,2)$–$(1,1)$ and $(2,0)$–$(0,2)$ boundaries in fig. 1 are negatively sloped with unknown curvature. These boundaries must, however, have a slope less than -2 (more negative), since at this value income is not in fact falling in two-plant production (the changes in G and F cancel). They thus continue to intersect the zero-profit boundaries 'from below', as shown in fig. 1.

We confirmed this intuition by replacing Z in (2) above with $(Z-(e/2)Z^2)$. The boundaries just mentioned are negatively sloped, with the $(2,0)-(1,0)$ boundary steeper (i.e. its slope is more negative) than the $(2,2)-(1,1)$ boundary. The latter boundary lies to the right of the former, as in fig. 1, although we were able to prove this only for small values of e. In summary, for small values of e and U quadratic in Z as well as in X and Y, fig. 1 remains qualitatively similar except that the $(2,2)-(1,1)$ and $(2,0)-(1,0)$ boundaries are negatively sloped (less than -2) and non-linear.

6. Summary and conclusions

The purpose of this paper is to show, via a simple model and associated numerical examples, how imperfectly competitive market structures can be endogenized in trade models. In keeping with some of the literature, the world is assumed to consist of two identical countries so that no comparative-advantage basis for trade exists. Each country produces a homogeneous consumption good with constant returns and perfect competition and one good with increasing returns to scale. There are firm-specific fixed costs as well as plant-specific fixed costs, with the former acting as joint inputs across plants [Markusen (1984)]. The single (due to the size of the market) imperfectly competitive firm in each country chooses among three options in the first stage of a two-stage game: (a) maintaining a plant in both countries, i.e. becoming a MNE; (b) serving both markets from a single home plant; or (c) not entering the market at all. If firms enter in both countries, they play a Cournot–Nash game in outputs in the second stage given their first-stage choice of modes.

Market structure (b), the two-firm, exporting duopoly is probably the most familiar in the trade literature (references noted in the Introduction). We show that this structure tends to arise as the equilibrium when plant-specific fixed costs are large relative to firm-specific fixed costs and tariff/transport costs. Two equilibria of type (a) can exist: one with only a single firm entering with two plants [as in Markusen (1984)] and one with both firms entering [similar to Helpman (1984)]. Both type (a) equilibria arise when plant-specific costs are low relative to firm-specific costs, with the second arising when the total of the two is relatively lower (so that the market can support two, two-plant firms).

Several general points arise from these results and examples. The first is an elementary point from simple game theory, but perhaps not sufficiently appreciated in trade theory. Equilibrium market structure cannot be inferred from profit levels in this type of non-cooperative game (as in the simple prisoners' dilemma). In one situation (case 4 of table 1) the equilibrium is not the profit-maximizing choice of structure. The equilibrium depends in particular on the payoffs associated with non-equilibrium strategies. Payoffs from all strategies must be evaluated in order to solve the game. Second, the results emphasize that non-symmetric outcomes are possible in an initially perfectly symmetric game.

The tax analysis shows that small tax changes can generate large welfare changes by changing equilibrium market structure. The market structure changes involve large, discontinuous changes in prices, outputs, profits, and hence welfare. In an import tariff example with an exporting duopoly as the initial market structure, the foreign firm switches to serving the domestic market with a branch plant long before the 'optimal' import tariff is reached. In one case (fig. 3), this shift causes domestic welfare to fall below the initial no-tariff level.

An example of a producer excise tax with the MNE duopoly as the initial market structure is more complex. We present an example in which there are three changes in industry structure as the tax rate increases. First, the foreign firm exits production entirely. Second, the foreign firm re-enters the domestic market by exporting to it. Third, the domestic firm abandons the domestic market, produces in the foreign country, and exports back home.

In all these cases the welfare consequences of tariffs are dramatically different from those obtained from traditional Pigouvian marginal analysis with market structure exogenous. The negative point for public policy is that the ability of firms to change plant configurations seriously limits the applicability of 'optimal' tax results found in public finance and international trade theory. A more positive implication, not explored here, is that manipulating industry structure can itself become a tool of public policy in addition to the more traditional tool of manipulating marginal price/output decisions.

References

Brander, J.A. and P.R. Krugman, 1983, A reciprocal dumping model of international trade, Journal of International Economics 15, 313–321.

Brander, J.A. and B.J. Spencer, 1985, Export subsidies and international market share rivalry, Journal of International Economics 18, 83–100.

Dixit, A.K., 1984, International trade policy for oligopolistic industries, Economic Journal, Supplement, 1–16.

Dixit, A.K. and A.S. Kyle, 1985, The use of protection and subsidies for entry promotion and deterrence, American Economic Review 75, 139–152.

Eaton, J. and G.M. Grossman, 1986, Optimal trade and industrial policy under oligopoly, Quarterly Journal of Economics, 383–406.

Helpman, E., 1981, International trade in the presence of product differentiation, economies of scale and monopolistic competition. A Chamberlinian–Heckscher–Ohlin approach, Journal of International Economics 11, 304–340.

Helpman, E., 1984, A simple theory of international trade with multinational corporations, Journal of Political Economy 92, 451–471, in: J. Bhagwati, ed., International trade: Selected readings, 2nd ed. (MIT Press, Cambridge, MA).

Horstmann, I.J. and J.R. Markusen, 1986, Up the average cost curve: Inefficient entry and the new protectionism, Journal of International Economics 20, 225–248.

Horstmann, I.J. and J.R. Markusen, 1987, Strategic investments and the development of multinationals, International Economic Review, 109–121.

Krugman, P.R., 1979, Increasing returns, monopolistic competition, and international trade, Journal of International Economics 9, 469–479.

Levinsohn, J.A., 1989, Strategic trade policy when firms can invest abroad: When are tariffs and quotas equivalent?, Journal of International Economics 27, 129–146.

Markusen, J.R., 1981, Trade and the gains from trade with imperfect competition, Journal of International Economics 11, 531–551.

Markusen, J.R., 1984, Multinationals, multi-plant economies, and the gains from trade, Journal of International Economics 16, 205–226, in: J. Bhagwati, ed., International trade: Selected readings, 2nd edn. (MIT Press, Cambridge, MA).

Markusen, J.R. and A.J. Venables, 1988, Trade policy with increasing returns and imperfect competition: Contradictory results from competing assumptions, Journal of International Economics 24, 299–316.

Venables, A.J., 1985, Trade and trade policy with imperfect competition: The case of identical products and free entry, Journal of International Economics 19, 1–20.

[26]

Increasing Returns and Economic Geography

Paul Krugman

Massachusetts Institute of Technology

This paper develops a simple model that shows how a country can endogenously become differentiated into an industrialized "core" and an agricultural "periphery." In order to realize scale economies while minimizing transport costs, manufacturing firms tend to locate in the region with larger demand, but the location of demand itself depends on the distribution of manufacturing. Emergence of a core-periphery pattern depends on transportation costs, economies of scale, and the share of manufacturing in national income.

The study of economic geography—of the location of factors of production in space—occupies a relatively small part of standard economic analysis. International trade theory, in particular, conventionally treats nations as dimensionless points (and frequently assumes zero transportation costs between countries as well). Admittedly, models descended from von Thünen (1826) play an important role in urban studies, while Hotelling-type models of locational competition get a reasonable degree of attention in industrial organization. On the whole, however, it seems fair to say that the study of economic geography plays at best a marginal role in economic theory.

On the face of it, this neglect is surprising. The facts of economic geography are surely among the most striking features of real-world economies, at least to laymen. For example, one of the most remarkable things about the United States is that in a generally sparsely populated country, much of whose land is fertile, the bulk of the population resides in a few clusters of metropolitan areas; a quarter of the inhabitants are crowded into a not especially inviting section of the East Coast. It has often been noted that nighttime satellite

[*Journal of Political Economy*, 1991, vol. 99, no. 3]
© 1991 by The University of Chicago. All rights reserved. 0022-3808/91/9903-0005$01.50

photos of Europe reveal little of political boundaries but clearly suggest a center-periphery pattern whose hub is somewhere in or near Belgium. A layman might have expected that these facts would play a key role in economic modeling. Yet the study of economic geography, at least within the economics profession, has lain largely dormant for the past generation (with a few notable exceptions, particularly Arthur [1989, 1990] and David [in press]).

The purpose of this paper is to suggest that application of models and techniques derived from theoretical industrial organization now allows a reconsideration of economic geography, that it is now time to attempt to incorporate the insights of the long but informal tradition in this area into formal models. In order to make the point, the paper develops a simple illustrative model designed to shed light on one of the key questions of location: Why and when does manufacturing become concentrated in a few regions, leaving others relatively undeveloped?

What we shall see is that it is possible to develop a very simple model of geographical concentration of manufacturing based on the interaction of economies of scale with transportation costs. This is perhaps not too surprising, given the kinds of results that have been emerging in recent literature (with Murphy, Shleifer, and Vishny [1989a, 1989b] perhaps the closest parallel). More interesting is the fact that this concentration of manufacturing in one location need not always happen and that whether it does depends in an interesting way on a few key parameters.

The paper is divided into four sections. Section I sets the stage with an informal discussion of the problem. Section II then sets out the analytical model. In Section III, I analyze the determination of short-run equilibrium and dynamics. Section IV analyzes the conditions under which concentration of manufacturing production does and does not occur.

I. Bases for Regional Divergence

There has been fairly extensive discussion over time of the nature of the externalities that lead to localization of particular industries. Indeed, Alfred Marshall's original exposition of the concept of external economies was illustrated with the example of industry localization. Most of the literature in this area follows Marshall in identifying three reasons for localization. First, the concentration of several firms in a single location offers a pooled market for workers with industry-specific skills, ensuring both a lower probability of unemployment and a lower probability of labor shortage. Second, localized industries can support the production of nontradable specialized inputs. Third, informational spillovers can give clustered firms a better production function than isolated producers. (Hoover [1948] gives a particularly clear discussion of agglomeration economies.)

These accounts of industry localization surely have considerable validity. In this paper, however, I shall offer a somewhat different approach aimed at answering a somewhat different question. Instead of asking why a particular industry is concentrated in a particular area—for example, carpets in Dalton, Georgia—I shall ask why manufacturing in general might end up concentrated in one or a few regions of a country, with the remaining regions playing the "peripheral" role of agricultural suppliers to the manufacturing "core." The proposed explanation correspondingly focuses on generalized external economies rather than those specific to a particular industry.

I shall also adopt the working assumption that the externalities that sometimes lead to emergence of a core-periphery pattern are *pecuniary* externalities associated with either demand or supply linkages rather than purely technological spillovers. In competitive general equilibrium, of course, pecuniary externalities have no welfare significance and could not lead to the kind of interesting dynamics we shall derive later. Over the past decade, however, it has become a familiar point that in the presence of imperfect competition and increasing returns, pecuniary externalities matter; for example, if one firm's actions affect the demand for the product of another firm whose price exceeds marginal cost, this is as much a "real" externality as if one firm's research and development spills over into the general knowledge pool. At the same time, by focusing on pecuniary externalities, we are able to make the analysis much more concrete than if we allowed external economies to arise in some invisible form. (This is particularly true when location is at issue: how far does a technological spillover spill?)

To understand the nature of the postulated pecuniary externalities, imagine a country in which there are two kinds of production, agriculture and manufacturing. Agricultural production is characterized both by constant returns to scale and by intensive use of immobile land. The geographical distribution of this production will therefore be determined largely by the exogenous distribution of suitable land. Manufactures, on the other hand, we may suppose to be characterized by increasing returns to scale and modest use of land.

Where will manufactures production take place? Because of economies of scale, production of each manufactured good will take place at only a limited number of sites. Other things equal, the preferred sites will be those with relatively large nearby demand, since producing near one's main market minimizes transportation costs. Other locations will then be served from these centrally located sites.

But where will demand be large? Some of the demand for manufactured goods will come from the agricultural sector; if that were the whole story, the distribution of manufacturing production would essentially form a lattice whose form was dictated by the distribution of agricultural land, as in the classic schemes of Christaller (1933) and Lösch (1940). But it is not the whole story: some of the demand for manufactures will come not from the agricultural sector but from the manufacturing sector itself.

This creates an obvious possibility for what Myrdal (1957) called "circular causation" and Arthur (1990) has called "positive feedback": manufactures production will tend to concentrate where there is a large market, but the market will be large where manufactures production is concentrated.

The circularity created by this Hirschman (1958)–type "backward linkage" may be reinforced by a "forward linkage": other things equal, it will be more desirable to live and produce near a concentration of manufacturing production because it will then be less expensive to buy the goods this central place provides.

This is not an original story; indeed, a story along roughly these lines has long been familiar to economic geographers, who emphasize the role of circular processes in the emergence of the U.S. manufacturing belt in the second half of the nineteenth century (see in particular Pred [1966] and Meyer [1983]). The main goal of this paper is to show that this story can be embodied in a simple yet rigorous model. However, before we move on to this model, it may be worth pursuing the intuitive story a little further to ask two questions: How far will the tendency toward geographical concentration proceed, and where will manufacturing production actually end up?

The answer to the first question is that it depends on the underlying parameters of the economy. The circularity that can generate manufacturing concentration will not matter too much if manufacturing employs only a small fraction of the population and hence generates only a small fraction of demand, or if a combination of weak economies of scale and high transportation costs induces suppliers of goods and services to the agricultural sector to locate very close to their markets. These criteria would have been satisfied in a prerailroad, preindustrial society, such as that of early nineteenth-century America. In such a society the bulk of the population would have been engaged in agriculture, the small manufacturing and commercial sector would not have been marked by very substantial economies of scale, and the costs of transportation would have ensured that most of the needs that could not be satisfied by rural production would be satisfied by small towns serving local market areas.

But now let the society spend a higher fraction of income on nonagricultural goods and services; let the factory system and eventually mass production emerge, and with them economies of large-scale production; and let canals, railroads, and finally automobiles lower transportation costs. Then the tie of production to the distribution of land will be broken. A region with a relatively large nonrural population will be an attractive place to produce both because of the large local market and because of the availability of the goods and services produced there. This will attract still more population, at the expense of regions with smaller initial production, and the process will feed on itself until the whole of the nonrural population is concentrated in a few regions.

This not entirely imaginary history suggests that small changes in the parameters of the economy may have large effects on its qualitative behavior. That is, when some index that takes into account transportation costs, economies of scale, and the share of nonagricultural goods in expenditure crosses a critical threshold, population will start to concentrate and regions to diverge; once started, this process will feed on itself.

The story also suggests that the details of the geography that emerges—which regions end up with the population—depend sensitively on initial conditions. If one region has slightly more population than another when, say, transportation costs fall below some critical level, that region ends up gaining population at the other's expense; had the distribution of population at that critical moment been only slightly different, the roles of the regions might have been reversed.

This is about as far as an informal story can take us. The next step is to develop as simple a formal model as possible to see whether the story just told can be given a more rigorous formulation.

II. A Two-Region Model

We consider a model of two regions. In this model there are assumed to be two kinds of production: agriculture, which is a constant-returns sector tied to the land, and manufactures, an increasing-returns sector that can be located in either region.

The model, like many of the models in both the new trade and the new growth literature, is a variant on the monopolistic competition framework initially proposed by Dixit and Stiglitz (1977). This framework, while admittedly special, is remarkably powerful in its ability to yield simple intuition-building treatments of seemingly intractable issues.

All individuals in this economy, then, are assumed to share a utility function of the form

$$U = C_M^\mu C_A^{1-\mu}, \tag{1}$$

where C_A is consumption of the agricultural good and C_M is consumption of a manufactures aggregate. Given equation (1), of course, manufactures will always receive a share μ of expenditure; this share is one of the key parameters that will determine whether regions converge or diverge.

The manufactures aggregate C_M is defined by

$$C_M = \left[\sum_{i=1}^{N} c_i^{(\sigma-1)/\sigma} \right]^{\sigma/(\sigma-1)}, \tag{2}$$

where N is the large number of potential products and $\sigma > 1$ is the elasticity of substitution among the products. The elasticity σ is the second parameter determining the character of equilibrium in the model.

There are two regions in the economy and two factors of production in each region. Following the simplification suggested in Krugman (1981), each factor is assumed specific to one sector. Peasants produce agricultural goods; without loss of generality we suppose that the unit labor requirement is one. The peasant population is assumed completely immobile between regions, with a given peasant supply $(1 - \mu)/2$ in each region. Workers may move between the regions; we let L_1 and L_2 be the worker supply in regions 1 and 2, respectively, and require only that the total add up to the overall number of workers μ:[1]

$$L_1 + L_2 = \mu. \tag{3}$$

The production of an individual manufactured good i involves a fixed cost and a constant marginal cost, giving rise to economies of scale:

$$L_{Mi} = \alpha + \beta x_i, \tag{4}$$

where L_{Mi} is the labor used in producing i and x_i is the good's output.

We turn next to the structure of transportation costs between the two regions. Two strong assumptions will be made for tractability. First, *transportation of agricultural output will be assumed to be costless.*[2]

___

[1] This choice of units ensures that the wage rate of workers equals that of peasants in long-run equilibrium.

[2] The reason for this assumption is that since agricultural products are assumed to be homogeneous, each region is either exporting or importing them, never both. But

The effect of this assumption is to ensure that the price of agricultural output and, hence, the earnings of each peasant are the same in both regions. We shall use this common agricultural price/wage rate as numeraire. Second, transportation costs for manufactured goods will be assumed to take Samuelson's "iceberg" form, in which transport costs are incurred in the good transported. Specifically, of each unit of manufactures shipped from one region to the other, only a fraction $\tau < 1$ arrives. This fraction τ, which is an inverse index of transportation costs, is the final parameter determining whether regions converge or diverge.

We can now turn to the behavior of firms. Suppose that there are a large number of manufacturing firms, each producing a single product. Then given the definition of the manufacturing aggregate (2) and the assumption of iceberg transport costs, the elasticity of demand facing any individual firm is σ (see Krugman 1980). The profit-maximizing pricing behavior of a representative firm in region 1 is therefore to set a price equal to

$$p_1 = \left(\frac{\sigma}{\sigma - 1}\right)\beta w_1, \tag{5}$$

where w_1 is the wage rate of workers in region 1; a similar equation applies in region 2. Comparing the prices of representative products, we have

$$\frac{p_1}{p_2} = \frac{w_1}{w_2}. \tag{6}$$

If there is free entry of firms into manufacturing, profits must be driven to zero. Thus it must be true that

$$(p_1 - \beta w_1)x_1 = \alpha w_1, \tag{7}$$

which implies

$$x_1 = x_2 = \frac{\alpha(\sigma - 1)}{\beta}. \tag{8}$$

That is, output per firm is the same in each region, irrespective of wage rates, relative demand, and so forth. This has the useful implication that the number of manufactured goods produced in each region

---

if agricultural goods are costly to transport, this would introduce a "cliff" at the point at which the two regions have equal numbers of workers and thus at which neither had to import food. This is evidently an artifact of the two-region case: if peasants were spread uniformly across a featureless plain, there would be no discontinuity.

is proportional to the number of workers, so that

$$\frac{n_1}{n_2} = \frac{L_1}{L_2}. \tag{9}$$

It should be noted that in zero-profit equilibrium, $\sigma/(\sigma - 1)$ is the ratio of the marginal product of labor to its average product, that is, the degree of economies of scale. Thus although σ is a parameter of tastes rather than technology, it can be interpreted as an inverse index of equilibrium economies of scale.

I have now laid out the basic structure of the model. The next step is to turn to the determination of equilibrium.

III. Short-Run and Long-Run Equilibrium

This model lacks any explicit dynamics. However, it is useful to have a concept of short-run equilibrium before we turn to full equilibrium. Short-run equilibrium will be defined in a Marshallian way, as an equilibrium in which the allocation of workers between regions may be taken as given. We then suppose that workers move toward the region that offers them higher real wages, leading to either convergence between regions as they move toward equality of worker/peasant ratios or divergence as the workers all congregate in one region.

To analyze short-run equilibrium, we begin by looking at the demand within each region for products of the two regions. Let c_{11} be the consumption in region 1 of a representative region 1 product, and c_{12} be the consumption in region 1 of a representative region 2 product. The price of a local product is simply its free on board price p_1; the price of a product from the other region, however, is its transport cost–inclusive price p_2/τ. Thus the relative demand for representative products is

$$\frac{c_{11}}{c_{12}} = \left(\frac{p_1\tau}{p_2}\right)^{-\sigma} = \left(\frac{w_1\tau}{w_2}\right)^{-\sigma}. \tag{10}$$

Define z_{11} as the ratio of region 1 *expenditure* on local manufactures to that on manufactures from the other region. Two points should be noted about z. First, a 1 percent rise in the relative price of region 1 goods, while reducing the relative *quantity* sold by σ percent, will reduce the *value* by only $\sigma - 1$ percent because of the valuation effect. Second, the more goods produced in region 1, the higher their share of expenditure for any given relative price. Thus

$$z_{11} = \left(\frac{n_1}{n_2}\right)\left(\frac{p_1\tau}{p_2}\right)\left(\frac{c_{11}}{c_{12}}\right) = \left(\frac{L_1}{L_2}\right)\left(\frac{w_1\tau}{w_2}\right)^{-(\sigma-1)}. \tag{11}$$

Similarly, the ratio of region 2 spending on region 1 products to spending on local products is

$$z_{12} = \left(\frac{L_1}{L_2}\right)\left(\frac{w_1}{w_2\tau}\right)^{-(\sigma-1)}. \tag{12}$$

The total income of region 1 workers is equal to the total spending on these products in both regions. (Transportation costs are included because they are assumed to be incurred in the goods themselves.) Let Y_1 and Y_2 be the regional incomes (including the wages of peasants). Then the income of region 1 workers is

$$w_1 L_1 = \mu\left[\left(\frac{z_{11}}{1+z_{11}}\right)Y_1 + \left(\frac{z_{12}}{1+z_{12}}\right)Y_2\right], \tag{13}$$

and the income of region 2 workers is

$$w_2 L_2 = \mu\left[\left(\frac{1}{1+z_{11}}\right)Y_1 + \left(\frac{1}{1+z_{12}}\right)Y_2\right]. \tag{14}$$

The incomes of the two regions, however, depend on the distribution of workers and their wages. Recalling that the wage rate of peasants is the numeraire, we have

$$Y_1 = \frac{1-\mu}{2} + w_1 L_1 \tag{15}$$

and

$$Y_2 = \frac{1-\mu}{2} + w_2 L_2. \tag{16}$$

The set of equations (11)–(16) may be regarded as a system that determines w_1 and w_2 (as well as four other variables) given the distribution of labor between regions 1 and 2. By inspection, one can see that if $L_1 = L_2$, $w_1 = w_2$. If labor is then shifted to region 1, however, the relative wage rate w_1/w_2 can move either way. The reason is that there are two opposing effects. On one side, there is the "home market effect": other things equal, the wage rate will tend to be higher in the larger market (see Krugman 1980). On the other side, there is the extent of competition: workers in the region with the smaller manufacturing labor force will face less competition for the local peasant market than those in the more populous region. In other words, there is a trade-off between proximity to the larger market and lack of competition for the local market.

As we move from short-run to long-run equilibrium, however, a third consideration enters the picture. Workers are interested not in nominal wages but in real wages, and workers in the region with the larger population will face a lower price for manufactured goods. Let $f = L_1/\mu$, the share of the manufacturing labor force in region 1. Then the true price index of manufactured goods for consumers residing in region 1 is

$$P_1 = \left[fw_1^{-(\sigma-1)} + (1 - f)\left(\frac{w_2}{\tau}\right)^{-(\sigma-1)} \right]^{-1/(\sigma-1)} ; \qquad (17)$$

that for consumers residing in region 2 is

$$P_2 = \left[f\left(\frac{w_1}{\tau}\right)^{-(\sigma-1)} + (1 - f)w_2^{-(\sigma-1)} \right]^{-1/(\sigma-1)} . \qquad (18)$$

The real wages of workers in each region are

$$\omega_1 = w_1 P_1^{-\mu} \qquad (19)$$

and

$$\omega_2 = w_2 P_2^{-\mu}. \qquad (20)$$

From (17) and (18), it is apparent that if wage rates in the two regions are equal, a shift of workers from region 2 to region 1 will lower the price index in region 1 and raise it in region 2 and, thus, raise real wages in region 1 relative to those in region 2. This therefore adds an additional reason for divergence.

We may now ask the crucial question: How does ω_1/ω_2 vary with f? We know by symmetry that when $f = \frac{1}{2}$, that is, when the two regions have equal numbers of workers, they offer equal real wage rates. But is this a stable equilibrium? It will be if ω_1/ω_2 decreases with f, for in that case whenever one region has a larger work force than the other, workers will tend to migrate out of that region. In this case we shall get regional convergence. On the other hand, if ω_1/ω_2 *increases* with f, workers will tend to migrate *into* the region that already has more workers, and we shall get regional divergence.[3] As we have seen, there are two forces working toward

---

[3] This description of dynamics actually oversimplifies in two ways. First, it implicitly assumes that ω_1/ω_2 is a monotonic function of f, or at least that it crosses one only once. In principle, this need not be the case, and there could be several stable equilibria in which both regions have nonzero manufacturing production. I have not been able to rule this out analytically, although it turns out not to be true for the numerical example considered below. The analytical discussion in the next section simply bypasses the question. Second, a dynamic story should take expectations into account. It is possible that workers may migrate into the region that initially has fewer workers because they expect other workers to do the same. This kind of self-fulfilling prophecy can occur, however, only if adjustment is rapid and discount rates are not too high. See Krugman (1991) for an analysis.

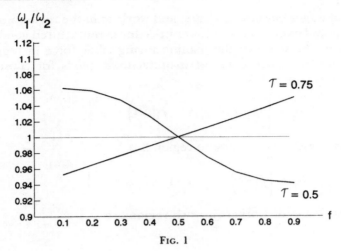

FIG. 1

divergence—the home market effect and the price index effect—and one working toward convergence, the degree of competition for the local peasant market. The question is which forces dominate.

In principle, it is possible simply to solve our model for real wages as a function of f. This is, however, difficult to do analytically. In the next section an alternative approach is used to characterize the model's behavior. For now, however, let us simply note that there are only three parameters in this model that cannot be eliminated by choice of units: the share of expenditure on manufactured goods, μ; the elasticity of substitution among products, σ; and the fraction of a good shipped that arrives, τ. The model can be quite easily solved numerically for a variety of parameters. Thus it is straightforward to show that depending on the parameter values we may have either regional convergence or regional divergence.

Figure 1 makes the point. It shows computed values of ω_1/ω_2 as a function of f in two different cases. In both cases we assume $\sigma = 4$ and $\mu = .3$. In one case, however, $\tau = .5$ (high transportation costs); in the other, $\tau = .75$ (low transportation costs). In the high-transport-cost case, the relative real wage declines as f rises. Thus in this case we would expect to see regional convergence, with the geographical distribution of the manufacturing following that of agriculture. In the low-transport-cost case, however, the slope is reversed; thus we would expect to see regional divergence.

It is possible to proceed entirely numerically from this point. If we take a somewhat different approach, however, it is possible to characterize the properties of the model analytically.

IV. Necessary Conditions for Manufacturing Concentration

Instead of asking whether an equilibrium in which workers are distributed equally between the regions is stable, this section asks whether a situation in which all workers are concentrated in one region is an equilibrium. This is not exactly the same question: as noted above, it is possible both that regional divergence might not lead to complete concentration and that there may exist stable interior equilibria even if concentration is also an equilibrium. The questions are, however, closely related, and this one is easier to answer.

Consider a situation in which all workers are concentrated in region 1 (the choice of region of course is arbitrary). Region 1 will then constitute a larger market than region 2. Since a share of total income μ is spent on manufactures and all this income goes to region 1, we have

$$\frac{Y_2}{Y_1} = \frac{1 - \mu}{1 + \mu}. \tag{21}$$

Let n be the total number of manufacturing firms; then each firm will have a *value* of sales equal to

$$V_1 = \left(\frac{\mu}{n}\right)(Y_1 + Y_2), \tag{22}$$

which is just enough to allow each firm to make zero profits.

Now we ask: Is it possible for an individual firm to commence production profitably in region 2? (I shall refer to such a hypothetical firm as a "defecting" firm.) If not, then concentration of production in region 1 is an equilibrium; if so, it is not.

In order to produce in region 2, a firm must be able to attract workers. To do so, it must compensate them for the fact that all manufactures (except its own infinitesimal contribution) must be imported; thus we must have

$$\frac{w_2}{w_1} = \left(\frac{1}{\tau}\right)^{\mu}. \tag{23}$$

Given this higher wage, the firm will charge a profit-maximizing price that is higher than that of other firms in the same proportion. We can use this fact to derive the value of the firm's sales. In region 1, the defecting firm's value of sales will be the value of sales of a representative firm times $(w_2/w_1\tau)^{-(\sigma-1)}$. In region 2, its value of sales will be that of a representative firm times $(w_2\tau/w_1)^{-(\sigma-1)}$, so the total value of the defecting firm's sales will be

$$V_2 = \left(\frac{\mu}{n}\right)\left[\left(\frac{w_2}{w_1\tau}\right)^{-(\sigma-1)} Y_1 + \left(\frac{w_2\tau}{w_1}\right)^{-(\sigma-1)} Y_2\right]. \qquad (24)$$

Notice that transportation costs work to the firm's disadvantage in its sales to region 1 consumers but work to its advantage in sales to region 2 consumers (because other firms must pay them but it does not).

From (22), (23), and (24) we can (after some manipulation) derive the ratio of the value of sales by this defecting firm to the sales of firms in region 1:

$$\frac{V_2}{V_1} = \frac{1}{2}\tau^{\mu(\sigma-1)}[(1 + \mu)\tau^{\sigma-1} + (1 - \mu)\tau^{-(\sigma-1)}]. \qquad (25)$$

One might think that it is profitable for a firm to defect as long as $V_2/V_1 > 1$, since firms will collect a constant fraction of any sales as a markup over marginal costs. This is not quite right, however, because fixed costs are also higher in region 2 because of the higher wage rate. So we must have $V_2/V_1 > w_2/w_1 = \tau^{-\mu}$. We must therefore define a new variable,

$$\nu = \frac{1}{2}\tau^{\mu\sigma}[(1 + \mu)\tau^{\sigma-1} + (1 - \mu)\tau^{-(\sigma-1)}]. \qquad (26)$$

When $\nu < 1$, it is unprofitable for a firm to begin production in region 2 if all other manufacturing production is concentrated in region 1. Thus in this case concentration of manufactures production in one region is an equilibrium; if $\nu > 1$, it is not.

Equation (26) at first appears to be a fairly unpromising subject for analytical results. However, it yields to careful analysis.

First note what we want to do with (26). It defines a *boundary:* a set of critical parameter values that mark the division between concentration and nonconcentration. So we need to evaluate it only in the vicinity of $\nu = 1$, asking how each of the three parameters must change in order to offset a change in either of the others.

Let us begin, then, with the most straightforward of the parameters, μ. We find that

$$\frac{\partial\nu}{\partial\mu} = \nu\sigma(\ln\tau) + \frac{1}{2}\tau^{\sigma\mu}[\tau^{\sigma-1} - \tau^{-(\sigma-1)}] < 0. \qquad (27)$$

That is, the larger the share of income spent on manufactured goods, the lower the relative sales of the defecting firm. This takes place for two reasons. First, workers demand a larger wage premium in order to move to the second region; this "forward linkage" effect is reflected

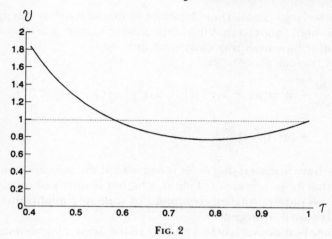

FIG. 2

in the first term. Second, the larger the share of expenditure on manufactures, the larger the relative size of the region 1 market and hence the stronger the home market effect. This "backward linkage" is reflected in the second term in (27).

Next we turn to transportation costs. From inspection of (26), we first note that when $\tau = 1$, $v = 1$; that is, when transport costs are zero, location is irrelevant (no surprise!). Second, we note that when τ is small, v approaches $(1 - \mu)\tau^{1-\sigma(1-\mu)}$. Unless σ is very small or μ very large, this must exceed one for sufficiently small τ (the economics of the alternative case will be apparent shortly). Finally, we evaluate $\partial v/\partial \tau$:

$$\frac{\partial v}{\partial \tau} = \frac{\mu \sigma v}{\tau} + \frac{\tau^{\mu\sigma}(\sigma - 1)[(1 + \mu)\tau^{\sigma-1} - (1 - \mu)\tau^{-(\sigma-1)}]}{2\tau}. \quad (28)$$

For τ close to one, the second term in (28) approaches $\mu(\sigma - 1) > 0$; since the first term is always positive, $\partial v/\partial \tau > 0$ for τ near one.

Taken together, these observations indicate a shape for v as a function of τ that looks like figure 2 (which represents an actual calculation for $\mu = .3$, $\sigma = 4$): at low levels of τ (i.e., high transportation costs), v exceeds one and it is profitable to defect. At some critical value of τ, v falls below one and concentrated manufacturing is an equilibrium, and the relative value of sales then approaches one from below.

The important point from this picture is that at the critical value of τ that corresponds to the boundary between concentration and nonconcentration, $\partial v/\partial \tau$ is negative. That is, higher transportation costs militate against regional divergence.

We can also now interpret the case in which $\sigma(1 - \mu) < 1$, so that $v < 1$ even at arbitrarily low τ. This is a case in which economies of scale are so large (small σ) or the share of manufacturing in expenditure is so high (high μ) that it is unprofitable to start a firm in region 2 no matter how high transport costs are.

Finally, we calculate $\partial v/\partial\sigma$:

$$\frac{\partial v}{\partial\sigma} = \ln(\tau)\{\mu v + \tfrac{1}{2}\tau^{\mu\sigma}[(1 + \mu)\tau^{\sigma-1} - (1 - \mu)\tau^{-(\sigma-1)}]\}$$

$$= \ln(\tau)\left(\frac{\tau}{\sigma}\right)\left(\frac{\partial v}{\partial\tau}\right). \tag{29}$$

Since we have just seen that $\partial v/\partial\tau$ is negative at the relevant point, this implies that $\partial v/\partial\sigma$ is positive. That is, a higher elasticity of substitution (which also implies smaller economies of scale in equilibrium) works against regional divergence.

The implications of these results can be seen diagrammatically. Holding σ constant, we can draw a boundary in μ, τ space. This boundary marks parameter values at which firms are just indifferent between staying in a region 1 concentration and defecting. An economy that lies inside this boundary will not develop concentrations of industry in one or the other region; an economy that lies outside the boundary will. The slope of the boundary is

$$\frac{\partial\tau}{\partial\mu} = -\frac{\partial v/\partial\mu}{\partial v/\partial\tau} < 0.$$

If we instead hold μ constant and consider changing σ, we find

$$\frac{\partial\tau}{\partial\sigma} = -\frac{\partial v/\partial\sigma}{\partial v/\partial\tau} > 0.$$

Thus an increase in σ will shift the boundary in μ, τ space outward.

Figure 3 shows calculated boundaries in μ, τ space for two values of σ, 4 and 10. The figure tells a simple story that is precisely the intuitive story given in Section I. In an economy characterized by high transportation costs, a small share of footloose manufacturing, or weak economies of scale, the distribution of manufacturing production will be determined by the distribution of the "primary stratum" of peasants. With lower transportation costs, a higher manufacturing share, or stronger economies of scale, circular causation sets in, and manufacturing will concentrate in whichever region gets a head start.

What is particularly nice about this result is that it requires no appeal to elusive concepts such as pure technological externalities: the external economies are pecuniary, arising from the desirability of selling to and buying from a region in which other producers are

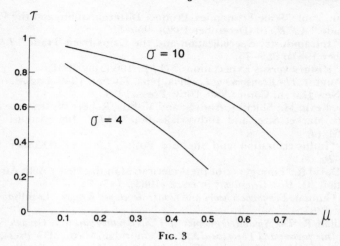

FIG. 3

concentrated. It also involves no arbitrary assumptions about the geographical extent of external economies: distance enters naturally via transportation costs, and in no other way. The behavior of the model depends on "observable" features of the tastes of individuals and the technology of firms; the interesting dynamics arise from interaction effects.

Obviously this is a vastly oversimplified model even of the core-periphery issue, and it says nothing about the localization of particular industries. The model does illustrate, however, how tools drawn from industrial organization theory can help to formalize and sharpen the insights of a much-neglected field. Thus I hope that this paper will be a stimulus to a revival of research into regional economics and economic geography.

References

Arthur, W. Brian. "Competing Technologies, Increasing Returns, and Lock-in by Historical Events." *Econ. J.* 99 (March 1989): 116–31.

———. "Positive Feedbacks in the Economy." *Scientific American* 262 (February 1990): 92–99.

Christaller, Walter. *Central Places in Southern Germany.* Jena: Fischer, 1933. English translation by Carlisle W. Baskin. London: Prentice-Hall, 1966.

David, Paul. "The Marshallian Dynamics of Industrialization: Chicago, 1850–1890." *J. Urban Econ.* (in press).

Dixit, Avinash K., and Stiglitz, Joseph E. "Monopolistic Competition and Optimum Product Diversity." *A.E.R.* 67 (June 1977): 297–308.

Hirschman, Albert O. *The Strategy of Economic Development.* New Haven, Conn.: Yale Univ. Press, 1958.

Hoover, Edgar M. *The Location of Economic Activity.* New York: McGraw-Hill, 1948.

Krugman, Paul. "Scale Economies, Product Differentiation, and the Pattern of Trade." *A.E.R.* 70 (December 1980): 950–59.

———. "Intraindustry Specialization and the Gains from Trade." *J.P.E* 89 (October 1981): 959–73.

———. "History versus Expectations." *Q.J.E.* 106 (May 1991).

Lösch, August. *The Economics of Location.* Jena: Fischer, 1940. English translation. New Haven, Conn.: Yale Univ. Press, 1954.

Murphy, Kevin M.; Shleifer, Andrei; and Vishny, Robert W. "Income Distribution, Market Size, and Industrialization." *Q.J.E.* 104 (August 1989): 537–64. (*a*)

———. "Industrialization and the Big Push." *J.P.E* 97 (October 1989): 1003–26. (*b*)

Meyer, David R. "Emergence of the American Manufacturing Belt: An Interpretation." *J. Hist. Geography* 9, no. 2 (1983): 145–74.

Myrdal, Gunnar. *Economic Theory and Under-developed Regions.* London: Duckworth, 1957.

Pred, Allan R. *The Spatial Dynamics of U.S. Urban-Industrial Growth, 1800–1914: Interpretive and Theoretical Essays.* Cambridge, Mass.: MIT Press, 1966.

von Thünen, Johann Heinrich. *The Isolated State.* Hamburg: Perthes, 1826. English translation. Oxford: Pergamon, 1966.

Part V
Uncertainty

[27]

The Protective Effect of a Tariff under Uncertainty

Elhanan Helpman
Tel-Aviv University and University of Rochester

Assaf Razin
Tel-Aviv University

We examine the protective effect of a tariff in a small economy with uncertainty and a stock market in which shares of firms are traded. In a deterministic economy, the allocation of resources is governed by commodity prices; in our economy, it is governed by equity prices and is dependent on commodity prices only to the extent that they influence equity prices. We show that in the absence of international trade in securities a tariff need not protect the import competing sector. In the presence of international trade in securities, a tariff always protects the import competing sector.

It is well known that in the standard deterministic two-sector economy the imposition of a tariff induces a resource flow from the export industry to the import competing industry if the external terms of trade do not change. This is the small-country case. It is also known that in the large-country case, that is, in the case in which a country's import (export) volume influences its external terms of trade, an imposition of a tariff may induce a resource flow out of the import competing industry and into the export industry. This is known as the Metzler Paradox (see Metzler 1949). In the small-country case, the imposition of the tariff necessarily reduces the internal terms of trade because the external terms of trade do not change. Since domestic competitive-resource allocation is governed by the internal terms of trade, the deterioration in the internal terms of trade which follows the tariff leads to an expansion of the import competing industry and to a contraction of the export industry. Hence, the tariff is protective in this case. In the large-country case, the imposition of a tariff may increase the external terms of trade at a rate which exceeds the rate of tariff, in which

Partial support from the Ford Foundation is gratefully acknowledged.

[*Journal of Political Economy*, 1978, vol. 86, no. 6]
© 1978 by The University of Chicago. 0022-3808/78/8606-0007$01.02

case the internal terms of trade will improve, thereby reversing the direction of resource flow. If this happens, the tariff is said to protect the export industry and not the import competing industry.

It is the purpose of this paper to show that in the presence of uncertainty a tariff need not provide protection to the import competing industry even in the small-country case. The situation in which this may occur is one in which there is international trade in commodities but no international trade in securities. If there is international trade in securities, a tariff does provide conventional protection.

Our analysis relies on the model developed in Helpman and Razin (1978a, 1978b). In this model there is a stock market in which shares of firms are traded. The allocation of the factors of production is governed by equity prices and depends on commodity prices only to the extent that they influence equity prices. In the absence of international trade in securities, domestic equity prices are internally determined, since domestic risks are then fully borne by domestic residents. Now, the imposition of a tariff in a small country worsens necessarily the internal commodity terms of trade in every state of nature. However, its impact on relative equity prices, which determines the interindustry resource flow, depends on whether the tariff will shift the demand for equities toward the import competing sector or away from it. If tariff proceeds are not redistributed back to consumers, then the shift in the demand for equities is ambiguous. We provide an example in which demand shifts toward the equities of the exportable industry; in this case, the tariff does not protect the import competing industry. We also show that when tariff proceeds are redistributed back to consumers in the form of lump-sum transfers, a "small" tariff protects the import competing industry if both goods are normal in consumption. (The difference between the two cases—with and without tariff proceeds redistribution—is explained at the end of the example.) This contrasts with the deterministic small-country case in which the redistribution policy is not important for the protective effect of a tariff (it is important though for the large-country case).

I. The Model

Our small economy consists of firms and consumers who operate in an uncertain environment generated by random production technology or random world prices. These random elements produce an incentive to develop financial capital markets, whose existence—in the form of stock markets—we assume. Domestic financial capital markets may or may not be integrated into the world's capital markets. If domestic capital markets are not integrated into the world's capital markets (i.e., there exists no international trade in securities), they enable risk sharing only among domestic residents. However, if domestic capital markets are integrated into the world's capital markets (i.e., there exists international trade in securities), they permit international risk sharing. Since we deal with international trade, we assume that there is international trade in commodities.

Input decisions have to be made before the resolution of uncertainty. As a result, firms face random profits and cannot undertake profit maximization. Instead, we assume—following Diamond (1967)—that firms choose their input levels so as to maximize their net value on the stock market; this procedure is equivalent to profit maximization whenever the relevant random elements become degenerate (i.e., their value becomes known with certainty). After the resolution of uncertainty, returns are realized and distributed to the firm's final stockholders.

Individuals play a double role in this economy. In the first stage—before the resolution of uncertainty—individuals choose a portfolio by means of trading in the stock market. An equity in a firm entitles the stockholder to a share in the firm's random return. This share equals the inverse of the number of the firm's outstanding equities. This is the stage in which individuals play the role of investors.

In the second stage—after the resolution of uncertainty—individuals use the proceeds from portfolios to purchase commodities. This is the stage in which they play the role of consumers.

Clearly, the two roles are interrelated. The ultimate goal of a portfolio chosen in the first stage is to provide consumption in the second stage. Hence, portfolio choice depends on preferences over consumption goods, but it also depends on probability beliefs, price expectations, and attitudes toward risk.

Firms

Consider a two-sector economy which produced two commodities, X_1 and X_2, by means of labor and capital. Each sector is composed of identical firms, and the output of each firm depends on its employment of capital and labor and on the state of nature that realizes. In particular, in every state α, where $\alpha = 1, 2, \ldots, S$, the output of firm j is

$$Q_j(\alpha) = \theta_j(\alpha) f_j(L_j, K_j), \qquad \alpha = 1, 2, \ldots, S \qquad (1)$$

where θ_j = a positive-valued random variable, $f_j(\cdot)$ = a standard neo-classical linear homogeneous production function, L_j = labor input in firm j, K_j = capital input in firm j, and Q_j = output of firm j, which is also random. Since all firms in a given sector are identical and $f_j(\cdot)$ is linear homogeneous, equation (1) also describes the output of the sector to which firm j belongs if L_j and K_j are interpreted as total factor inputs in this sector. We use this aggregation procedure and from now on use sectors as the production units. The index j is used to denote sectors: $j = 1, 2$.

Assuming the existence of a stock market, it is explained in Helpman and Razin (1978a, 1978b) that by selling shares in the stock market a firm in sector j can be viewed as selling real equities of type j, where one real

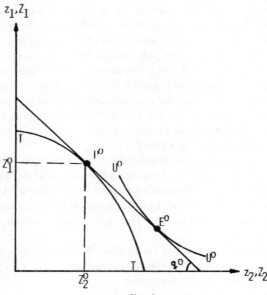

FIG. 1

equity of type j provides the bundle $[\theta_j(1), \theta_j(2), \ldots, \theta_j(S)]$ of commodity X_j. The output of real equities of type j by industry j is $Z_j = f_j(L_j, K_j)$, and we can draw a transformation curve between real equities— TT in figure 1. The curve TT has all the usual characteristics of a Heckscher-Ohlin type transformation curve.

It was shown in Helpman and Razin (1978*a*, 1978*b*) that, given the relative price of type 2 real equities q^o (q^o is the price of type 2 real equities divided by the price of type 1 real equities), net-value-maximizing firms choose in an equilibrium a point on the transformation curve TT at which the MRT (marginal rate of transformation) between Z_2 and Z_1 is equal to q^o. Hence, given q^o, production of real equities takes place at point P^o in figure 1. Corresponding to point P^o, there is an equilibrium wage rate and rental rate on capital and an equilibrium allocation of the fixed supplies of labor and capital between the sectors. Given P^o, the output of commodities is not uniquely determined; it depends on the state of nature. If state α realizes, the output of commodity i will be $\theta_i(\alpha)Z_i^o$, $i = 1, 2$.

By varying q along TT, we trace out the general equilibrium supply functions:

$$Z_j = Z_j(q), \qquad j = 1, 2. \tag{2}$$

Clearly, for q which does not result in complete specialization, $Z_2(\cdot)$ is an increasing function of q (i.e., $Z_2'[q] > 0$), and $Z_1(\cdot)$ is a decreasing function of q (i.e., $Z_1'[q] < 0$). In addition,

$$Z_1'(q) + qZ_2'(q) \equiv 0. \tag{3}$$

Consumers

Let $v(p, I)$ be the representative consumer's indirect utility function, where p is the price of X_2 in terms of X_1 and I is income in terms of X_1. All consumers are assumed to be identical. Then, it is shown in Helpman and Razin (1978*b*, eq. [7]) that the consumer's portfolio choice is in equilibrium:

$$\max_{z_1, z_2 > 0} Ev[p(\alpha), \theta_1(\alpha)z_1 + p(\alpha)\theta_2(\alpha)z_2],$$

$$\text{subject to } z_1 + q^o z_2 \le \mathcal{Z}_1(q^o) + q\mathcal{Z}_2(q^o), \tag{4}$$

where z_i is the purchase of type i real equities and E is the expectations operator based on subjective probability beliefs. Commodity prices, which may be state dependent, $p(\alpha)$, are assumed to be given to our small country. It is assumed in equation (4) that individuals know the price ratio $p(\alpha)$ in every state (i.e., their price expectations are correct) but that they do not know which state will realize.

Assuming risk aversion, we can draw a set of assets-indifference curves convex to the origin, where an assets-indifference curve is defined as all combinations of (z_1, z_2) for which the expected utility is constant. Then, the solution to equation (4) can be represented by the tangency of an assets-indifference curve to an assets-budget line, like point E^o in figure 1. The curve $U^o U^o$ represents here the highest affordable expected utility level. Observe that points P^o and E^o in figure 1 represent an equilibrium in which there is international trade in equities and in which the rest of the world produces a perfect substitute for domestic type 2 real equities, which are imported. If there is no international trade in equities, the equilibrium domestic relative price q will be such as to make $z_i = \mathcal{Z}_i(q)$, $i = 1, 2$. Such an equilibrium is represented in figure 2 by point P at which an assets-indifference curve is tangent to the transformation curve. Notice, however, that we are still assuming international trade in commodities after the realization of a state of nature at the prevailing world prices $p(\alpha)$.

At this point, the reader should note that the assets-indifference curves depend on the distribution of relative commodity prices. A shift in the price distribution pivots the entire assets-indifference map.

II. Protection under Uncertainty

Consider an ad valorem tariff on the second commodity, assuming that the second commodity is imported in every state of nature. The effect of the tariff on the allocation of resources between the two sectors differs according to whether international trade in securities takes place. We begin with the case of no international trade in securities, in which domestic residents bear all domestic risks.

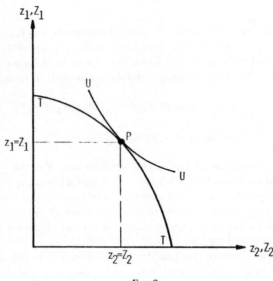

FIG. 2

A. *No International Trade in Securities*

The tariff-inclusive assets-indifference curves (which, along with the production possibilities curve, help determine the economy's production) are given by

$$Ev[(1 + t)p(\alpha); \theta_1(\alpha)z_1 + (1 + t)p(\alpha)\theta_2(\alpha)z_2 \\ + T(\alpha, t)] = \text{constant}, \tag{5}$$

where t = the tariff rate (assumed to be state independent) and $T(\alpha, t)$ = state α expected lump-sum transfer payments. If tariff proceeds are redistributed back to consumers, $T(\alpha, t)$ is assumed to equal tariff proceeds in state α. The consumer treats $T(\alpha, t)$ as a state-dependent lump-sum transfer; he does not relate it to the volume of imports, just like in the deterministic model. If tariff proceeds are not redistributed, $T(\alpha, t)$ equals zero in every state of nature. This is the relevant case if, for example, the government uses tariff proceeds in order to purchase commodities. (If the government's spending is related to the provision of public goods, our analysis is unaltered if we assume that the direct utility function is additively separable in private and public goods.) In the small-country deterministic case, a tariff protects the import competing industry independently of the way in which the tariff revenue is disposed of. In the present framework this is not so, which makes our distinction between the two extreme cases of the use of tariff revenue relevant.

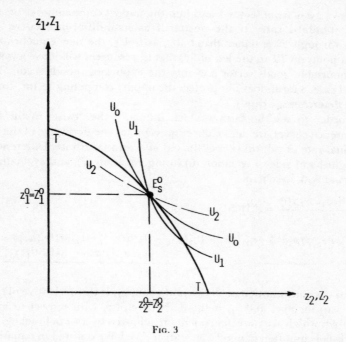

FIG. 3

The tariff-inclusive marginal rate of substitution (MRS) between real equity 2 and real equity 1 is given by

$$\text{MRS}(z_1, z_2; t) \equiv$$
$$\frac{E(1+t)\,p(\alpha)\theta_2(\alpha)v_I[(1+t)\,p(\alpha);\theta_1(\alpha)z_1 + (1+t)\,p(\alpha)\theta_2(\alpha)z_2 + T(\alpha,t)]}{E\overline{\theta}_1(\alpha)v_I[(1+t)\,p(\alpha);\theta_1(\alpha)z_1 + (1+t)\,p(\alpha)\theta_2(\alpha)z_2 + T(\alpha,t)]}.$$
(6)

Let us start with a discussion of the case in which tariff proceeds are not distributed back to consumers. In this case, individuals choose a portfolio expecting (correctly) no transfers after the realization of a state of nature.

$$T(\alpha, t) = 0 \text{ for all } t \text{ and } \alpha = 1, 2, \ldots, S.$$
(7)

From equations (6) and (7) it is readily verified that a change in the tariff rate twists the assets-indifference curves at every point (z_1, z_2) and changes the MRS between real equities 2 and 1. This is because the tariff changes the mean as well as higher moments (such as the variance) of the distribution of the relative internal price of good 2.

In figure 3, point E_s^o denotes the pretariff stock market equilibrium in which the pretariff assets-indifference curve U_oU_o is tangent to the production possibilities curve TT. If the posttariff assets-indifference curve, which passes through the initial point E_s^o, is steeper than U_oU_o, as U_1U_1, the new equilibrium must be at a point on TT to the right of E_s^o; that is, resources will move away from sector 1 and into the import competing sector, sector 2 the standard case. If the posttariff assets-indifference curve which passes through E_s^0 is flatter than U_0U_0, as U_2U_2, the new equilibrium will be at a point on TT to the left of E_s^0; that is, resources will move away from the importable goods sector and into the exportable goods sector. In the second case, a tariff does not protect the import competing sector, contrary to the deterministic case.

In order to see the factors which influence the "twist" in the assets-indifference curves, we derive the expression for the derivative of the assets' marginal rate of substitution evaluated at a zero tariff rate. Differentiating the right-hand side of equation (6), using equation (7), and evaluating the result at $t = 0$, we obtain

$$\frac{\partial MRS(z_1, z_2; 0)}{\partial t} = MRS$$

$$+ \frac{Ev_1(\alpha)\, p(\alpha)\, \{-c_{2I}(\alpha) + |c_2(\alpha) - \theta_2(\alpha)z_2][-v_{II}(\alpha)/v_I(\alpha)|\}}{Ev_I(\alpha)\theta_1(\alpha)} \frac{|p(\alpha)\theta_2(\alpha) - MRS\theta_1(\alpha)|}{}, \quad (8)$$

where c_2 is consumption of the second good, c_{2I} is the derivative of c_2 with respect to income, and v_{II} is the derivative of v_I with respect to income. Variables which are state dependent are followed by an α in brackets. Thus, $c_2(\alpha)$ is consumption of good 2 in state α. We have omitted in equation (8) functional representations of variables in order to gain clarity.

The first term on the right-hand side of equation (8) represents the direct effect of a tariff on the assets MRS. This effect is positive, implying that the direct effect is always protective. The second term summarizes the indirect effects which stem from changes in the marginal utility of income in every state of nature. The tariff affects the marginal utility of income via two routes: a direct income effect which arises from an increase in the return on type 2 real equities and a conventional price effect. The indirect effects are quite complicated, and they depend on marginal propensities to spend, import volumes, attitudes toward risk, etc. (Observe that $-v_{II}[\alpha]/v_I[\alpha]$ is the absolute measure of risk aversion, and $c_2[\alpha] - \theta_2[\alpha]z_2$ equals imports if we evaluate eq. [8] at the initial equilibrium point at which $z_2 = \bar{z}_2$.) The question that arises is whether the net indirect effect can be negative and sufficiently large in absolute value so as to outweigh the positive direct effect. The answer to this question is in the affirmative, as shown by the following example.

Example

Let the utility function be $u = \log(c_2 + \log c_1)$. This yields the indirect utility function $v = \log\{[I/(1 + t)p] - 1 + \log[(1 + t)p]\}$, where I stands for the consumer's disposable income in terms of good 1. This implies (using eqq. [6] and [7]) that MRS $(z_1, z_2; t) \equiv \{E[\theta_1(\alpha)(1+t)^{-1}p(\alpha)^{-1}$ $z_1 + \theta_2(\alpha)z_2 - 1 + \log(1+t)p(\alpha)]^{-1}\theta_2(\alpha)\}/E[\theta_1(\alpha)(1+t)^{-1}p(\alpha)^{-1}z_1$ $+ \theta_2(\alpha)z_2 - 1 + \log(1+t)p(\alpha)]^{-1}\theta_1(\alpha)(1+t)^{-1}p(\alpha)^{-1}$. Assume now that $\theta_2(\alpha) = 1$ for all α, $p(\alpha) = 1$ for all α, $\theta_1(\alpha) > 1$ for all α, and that at the initial equilibrium $t^o = 0$ and $z_1^o = z_2^o = 1$. Since for $t^o = 0$ we have $c_1^o = p(\alpha) = 1$, the assumption $\theta_1(\alpha) > 1$ assures that good 1 is initially exported and good 2 imported in all states. The stockholders' choice of these real equity holdings can be assured by an appropriate choice of production technologies and factor endowments. Then, the derivative of MRS with respect to t, evaluated at the initial equilibrium, is (see eq. [8]) ∂MRS $(z_1^o, z_2^o; t^o)/\partial t = E[1/\theta_1(\alpha)] - \{E[1/\theta_1(\alpha)]^2 - [E 1/\theta_1(\alpha)]^2\} = E[1/\theta_1(\alpha)]$ $-\text{var}[1/\theta_1(\alpha)]$, where var stands for variance. Thus, $E[1/\theta_1(\alpha)] = \text{MRS}$ is the direct effect, while $-\text{var}[1/\theta_1(\alpha)]$ is the net indirect effect. Clearly, the net indirect effect is negative, and it dominates the direct effect for sufficiently large variances of $1/\theta_1(\alpha)$. Hence, for var $[1/\theta_1(\alpha)]$, sufficiently large $\partial\text{MRS}(z_1^o, z_2^o; t^o)/\partial t < 0$, implying that, for a "small" tariff, U_2U_2 in figure 3 is the posttariff assets-indifference curve. Therefore, in this case, the imposition of the tariff leads to a contraction of the import competing industry and an expansion of the export industry.

In the absence of uncertainty, the variance of $1/\theta_1(\alpha)$ is zero, and the paradoxical result does not arise. In the presence of uncertainty, the paradoxical result can arise because of the negative effect that an increase in t has on the demand for type 2 real equities, holding their returns constant. This can be seen as follows. Write the indirect utility function as $v = \log$ $\{\theta_1(\alpha)(1+t)^{-1}z_1 + z_2 - 1 + B(t)\}$, where $B(t) = \log(1+t)$. It can be shown that an increase in B reduces the demand for type 2 real equities. Now, an increase in the tariff rate has two effects. It increases B, resulting in a decline in the demand for type 2 real equities, and increases the return on type 2 real equities, resulting in an increase in their demand. The first effect dominates when var $[1/\theta_1(\alpha)]$ is sufficiently large.

Consider now the case in which tariff proceeds are redistributed back to consumers. In this case, state α transfers (i.e., the tariff rate × the value of imports) are implicitly given by

$$T(\alpha, t) \equiv tp(\alpha)\{c_2[(1+t)p(\alpha); \theta_1(\alpha)z_1 + (1+t)\theta_2(\alpha)p(\alpha)z_2 \\ + T(\alpha, t)] - \theta_2(\alpha)\mathcal{Z}_2[q(t)]\}, \tag{9}$$

where $c_2(\cdot)$ = the second commodity demand function, $\theta_2(\alpha)\mathcal{Z}_2(\cdot)$ = the local output of good 2 in state α, and $q(t)$ is the equilibrium relative price of real equity 2 which is a function of the tariff rate. Notice that from equation (9), we get

$$T(\alpha, 0) = 0,$$
$$\frac{\partial T(\alpha, 0)}{\partial t} = p(\alpha)\{c_2[p(\alpha); \theta_1(\alpha)z_1 + \theta_2(\alpha)p(\alpha)z_2] - \theta_2(\alpha)\mathcal{Z}_2(q)\}. \tag{10}$$

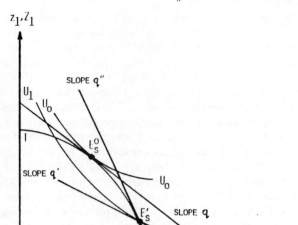

FIG. 4

That is, a zero tariff rate gives rise to a zero amount of tariff proceeds, and the rate of change in the tariff proceeds for a small tariff is equal to imports evaluated at world prices. Individuals choose a portfolio expecting to receive a lump-sum transfer of $T(\alpha, t)$ in state α, $\alpha = 1, 2, \ldots, S$ (they are not aware of the relationship given in eq. [9]).

Now we show that if both goods are normal the paradoxical result cannot appear in the case of a small tariff. In order to see this, differentiate equation (6) with respect to t and evaluate it at $t = 0$, using equation (10), to obtain $\partial \mathrm{MRS}(z_1, z_2; 0)/\partial t = [1/Ev_1(\alpha)\theta_1(\alpha)]\{Ev_I(\alpha)p(\alpha)\theta_2(\alpha) + Ev_{Ip}(\alpha)[p(\alpha)]^2\theta_2(\alpha) + Ev_{II}(\alpha)[p(\alpha)]^2c_2(\alpha)\theta_2(\alpha) - \mathrm{MRS}(z_1, z_2; 0)[Ev_{Ip}(\alpha)p(\alpha)\theta_1(\alpha) + Ev_{II}(\alpha)p(\alpha)c_2(\alpha)\theta_1(\alpha)]\}$, where v_{Ip} is the derivative of v_I with respect to its first argument.

Since $v_{Ip} = v_{pI} = \partial(-v_Ic_2)/\partial I = -v_{II}c_2 - v_Ic_{2I}$ and $pc_{2I} = 1 - c_{1I}$, we can substitute these relationships in the above expression to obtain $\partial \mathrm{MRS}(z_1, z_2; 0)/\partial t = [1/Ev_I(\alpha)\theta_1(\alpha)][Ev_I(\alpha)p(\alpha)\theta_2(\alpha)c_{1I}(\alpha) + \mathrm{MRS}(z_1, z_2; 0)Ev_I(\alpha)\theta_1(\alpha)p(\alpha)c_{2I}(\alpha)]$. If both goods are normal, the marginal propensities to spend on them are positive and the above expression is positive. This means that for normal goods a small tariff will twist the assets-indifference curves in figure 3 so as to make them steeper, like from U_oU_o to U_1U_1 and thus provide protection to the importable goods sector.

Finally, observe that an equity subsidy—i.e., a subsidy given to an industry at the financing stage—will unambiguously induce the expansion of that industry. In figure 4 we reconstruct the initial equilibrium shown in figure 3, the real equity-price ratio being q. A subsidy to sales of real equity 2 decreases to q' the relative price of real equity 2 to investors and drives a wedge between that relative price and the marginal rate of transformation q'', leading to a new equilibrium E'_s. In this case, resources will move away from sector 1 and into sector 2.

B. *International Trade in Securities*

Now consider the case in which the economy trades with the outside world in both commodities and securities. By the small-country assumption, without a tariff, commodity prices and security prices are given to the home country. A tariff raises the local price of the importable goods, but how does a tariff affect the importable-good industry's stock market value? It is explained in Helpman and Razin (1978*b*) that a tariff at a rate of $100t$ percent, which increases the price of the second commodity by $100t$ percent in every state of nature, increases by $100t$ percent the return on each unit of domestic type 2 real equities. This will result in a $100t$ percent increase in the price of local type 2 real equities in order to eliminate profitable arbitrage. The local type 2 real equity provides a return of $(1 + t)\theta_2(\alpha)p(\alpha)$ in state α while the foreign type 2 real equity provides a return of $\theta_2(\alpha)p(\alpha)$ in state α. Hence, one unit of a local type 2 real equity is now equivalent to $(1 + t)$ units of foreign type 2 real equities. This means that the price of local type 2 real equities increases from q to $(1 + t)q$. Thus, following a tariff, resources will move necessarily away from the exportable-good industry and into the importable-good industry, as in the deterministic case.

References

Diamond, Peter A. "The Role of a Stock Market in a General Equilibrium Model with Technological Uncertainty." *A.E.R.* 57 (September 1967): 759–76.
Helpman, Elhanan, and Razin, Assaf. "Uncertainty and International Trade in the Presence of Stock Markets." *Rev. Econ. Studies* 45 (June 1978): 239–50. (*a*)
————. "Welfare Aspects of International Trade in Goods and Securities." *Q. J. E.* 92 (August 1978): 489–508. (*b*)
Metzler, Lloyd A. "Tariffs, the Terms of Trade and the Distribution of National Income." *J.P.E.* 57, no. 1 (February 1949): 1–29.

Journal of International Economics 11 (1981) 239–247. North-Holland Publishing Company

THE HECKSCHER–OHLIN AND TRAVIS–VANEK THEOREMS UNDER UNCERTAINTY

James E. ANDERSON*

Boston College, Chestnut Hill, MA 02167, USA

Received January 1980, revised version received December 1980

The Heckscher–Ohlin theorem is valid under uncertainty of the special benchmark sort modelled by Helpman–Razin. Their pessimism over its validity is vanquished by more structure: rational expectations are imposed on consumers and identical and constant relative aversion to income risk is assumed. Under these circumstances, with free commodity trade, the Heckscher–Ohlin theorem holds for the international exchange of equities.

1. Introduction

Recent work on the theory of international trade under uncertainty has called into question the basic theorems of the Heckscher–Ohlin model. Helpman and Razin (1978) have brilliantly demonstrated that with the presence of a Diamond stock market (1967), international trade in equities restores all save the Heckscher–Ohlin theorem. This paper will show that the Heckscher–Ohlin theorem and its higher dimension generalization, the Travis–Vanek theorem, are also restored by international trade in equities.

Section 2 briefly reviews the Helpman–Razin model. Section 3 then shows how the Heckscher–Ohlin and Travis–Vanek theorems immediately follow with rational expectations under a specialization of the usual certainty case restriction that indifference curves over commodity bundles be identical and homothetic. Formally, the usual case allows a utility indicator to be any monotonic increasing function of a homogeneous quasi-concave function which is identical across countries. The specialization imposed here is that 'any monotonic increasing function' is reduced to any positive power function (and, inessentially, any increasing linear transform of a positive power function). This condition is necessary and sufficient for homothetic indifference curves over commodities to translate into homothetic indifference curves over equities. Furthermore, to ensure that identical homothetic

*I would like to thank John Riley for helpful comments. Elhanan Helpman's assistance was invaluable.

0022–1996/81/0000–0000/$02.50 © North-Holland Publishing Company

commodity preferences imply *identical* homothetic equity preferences, a sufficient condition is that the power function must be in the same degree across countries. In other words, the utility indicator must be identical and homogeneous up to a linear transform. This is equivalent to restricting behavior to display constant relative and identical aversion to income risk. Helpman–Razin overlooked this result in part because they failed to utilize the restrictions imposed by rational expectations, and in part because they considered the relative factor price definition of relative factor abundance, which does not sufficiently restrict preferences.

2. The Helpman–Razin model

Helpman and Razin adapt Diamond's stock market model for trade theory purposes. There are two stages of decision-making (or two periods). One is ex post, after all uncertainty is resolved. The other is ex ante, before values of random variables are known. The two-sector production model has technological uncertainty of the Hicks-neutral multiplicative variety. Resources are allocated ex ante, before the technological uncertainty is resolved. The Diamond stock market stipulates that, ex ante, firms produce and sell equities in a competitive market. Helpman–Razin offer a convenient interpretation. One unit of activity in sector j provides an ex post basket of outputs of commodity j, $(\theta_{j1},\ldots,\theta_{jS})$, one output for each state of nature s: $s = 1,\ldots, S$. Thus, one unit of equity in sector j entitles the owner to the basket $(\theta_{j1},\ldots,\theta_{jS})$. Equities are produced by firms under the usual competitive production model conditions and subject to a given real price of equities (q_j). The real equity price is revealed by the stock market; it equals the stock market value of the industry divided by its activity level. Competitive firms in the industry take it as a parameter. Firms (and with constant returns the industries) hire resources to solve the program

$$\max_{L_j, K_j} q_j f_j(L_j, K_j) - wL_j - rK_j,$$

where $Z_j = f_j(L_j, K_j)$ is the neoclassical production function, w and r are input prices, and L_j, K_j are labor and capital inputs in j. This is very similar to profit maximization. For the general equilibrium, the allocation problem depends only on relative equity prices, and the production of equities can be depicted in the usual diagram.

On the demand side of the stock market, ex ante, consumers identical in tastes and endowments purchase equities out of income received from the sale of labor and capital services and of initial equity holdings. Ex post, the consumers hold endowments $(\theta_{1s}Z_1, \theta_{2s}Z_2)$ and seek to exchange them to optimize a quasi-concave utility function over commodity bundles $\psi(C_1, C_2)$.

In Helpman–Razin, ψ is concave, which excludes the case of risk preference. Exchange equilibrium determines the ex post relative commodity price P_s and thus numeraire income $P_s\theta_{1s}Z_1 + \theta_{2s}Z_2$. Each state of nature s implies a different outcome for relative price and income given the real equity holdings (i.e. resource allocation). Consumers have knowledge of the distribution of the relative price, but not its dependence on activity levels Z. Forming the indirect utility function V, the arguments of which are relative price and income, outcomes may be ranked over selection of equity holdings (Z_1, Z_2) given the state of nature. Imposing the expected utility axioms, the consumers' ex ante objective function (the assets utility function) is the expectation of indirect utility:

$$U(Z_1, Z_2 \mid \phi_P) = \sum_{s=1}^{S} \pi_s V(P_s, P_s\theta_{1s}Z_1 + \theta_{2s}Z_2), \tag{1}$$

where π_s = probability of state s, and the ϕ_P under $U(\cdot)$ denotes a given distribution of the relative price. Given concavity of ψ, U is concave in Z_1, Z_2. The ingenious simplification of Helpman–Razin is to note that the ex ante equity purchase problem of consumers combined with the value maximization equity sale problem of firms yields a stock market analysis very much like the usual commodity allocation problem in the certainty case.

In fig. 1, Z_1 and Z_2 are units of activity in industries 1 and 2. $\bar{Z}_1$ units of activity in industry 1 will yield $\theta_{1s}\bar{Z}_1$ units of output of good 1 in state of the

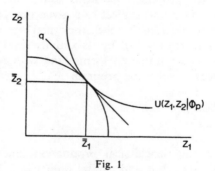

Fig. 1

world s. Z_1 and Z_2 are also the number of equities produced in industries 1 and 2. $\bar{Z}_1$ units of equity will yield $P_s\theta_{1s}\bar{Z}_1$ dollars worth of income in state of the world s, using good 2 as the numeraire. For this claim to uncertain income, consumers pay $q\bar{Z}_1$ ex ante where q is the relative equity price using good 2 as the numeraire. Portfolio and firm value maximization agree in the stock market equilibrium of fig. 1. The transformation locus of fig. 1 will, for our purposes, be taken to reflect the Heckscher–Ohlin production model.

3. The Heckscher–Ohlin and Travis–Vanek theorems

For the $2 \times 2 \times 2$ certainty case, the Heckscher–Ohlin theorem states that a country will increase production of and export the commodity relatively intensive in its relatively abundant factor. With the quantity definition of relative factor abundance, the possible offsetting effect of demand conditions is neutralized with the assumption of identical homothetic preferences. In fig. 2, relative supply functions are drawn for two countries. Z_1 and Z_2 are certain outputs. With good 1 relatively capital intensive and country A relatively capital abundant, the Rybczynski theorem guarantees that A's relative supply function lies to the right of B's. Identical homothetic preferences guarantee that a single relative demand function represents both countries' preferences. Isolation equilibria must lie at $P_B > P_A$. With the introduction of free trade, and thus a common commodity price, the Heckscher–Ohlin production and trade prediction follows.

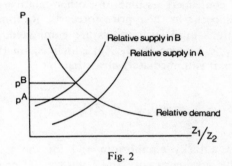

Fig. 2

For the uncertainty case, we can show that free trade in equities and commodities recreates the analysis of fig. 2. The vertical axis measures q, the relative price of equities. The horizontal axis measures relative supply of equities as in fig. 1. The Heckscher–Ohlin theorem for the case of uncertainty then follows: a country will increase production of and export that equity which is relatively intensive in its relatively abundant factor.

The trick is to show that under the identical homogeneous restriction the relative demand function of fig. 2 is the same for both countries in isolation and for the world in free trade. First note that the identical technology assumption of the Helpman–Razin version of the H–O model includes the uncertain portion. Thus, θ_{1s} is the shift parameter in industry 1 for state s in all countries. The assets utility function of consumers is $U(Z_1, Z_2 \mid \phi_P)$. Holding the price distribution constant implies a fixed assets production (Z_1^0, Z_2^0), so only $U(Z_1^0, Z_2^0 \mid \phi_P)$ is consistent with closed economy equilibrium. A change in production will change the price distribution and imply another family of asset indifference curves with a complex relation to the first family. As Helpman–Razin noted, this shifting of indifference curves appears to rule out the Heckscher–Ohlin theorem under any but very restrictive conditions.

Fortunately there is an envelope relation on the set of assets utility functions (one for each price distribution) which will establish the Heckscher–Ohlin theorem under the identical homogeneous commodity preferences restriction. Define the rational expectations (closed economy equilibrium) assets utility function:

$$W(Z_1, Z_2) \equiv U(Z_1, Z_2, \phi_P(Z_1, Z_2)). \tag{2}$$

$W(Z_1, Z_2)$ stipulates that, in equilibrium, rational consumers must know and act on the correct relative price distribution, though they are not aware of its dependence on Z_1, Z_2. In any state s, $P_s(Z_1, Z_2)$ is the actual ex post market clearing price based on activity of Z_1, Z_2. $\phi_P(Z_1, Z_2)$ is the price distribution based on Z_1, Z_2. If consumers assume any other relative price distribution, systematic error will occur in their price forecasts. Rational consumers will revise their expectations until such errors are eliminated, and the assumed distribution is $\phi_P(Z_1, Z_2)$. Since $W(Z_1, Z_2)$ is defined on the basis of closed economy equilibrium, it is immediately clear that

$$W(Z_1, Z_2) = \sum_{s=1}^{S} \pi_s \psi(\theta_{1s} Z_1, \theta_{2s} Z_2)$$

for each country in autarky equilibrium and for the world in free trade equilibrium. Also, the quasi-concavity and homogeneity properties of ψ carry through to W. Finally, we have the following lemma:

1. The indifference curve $W(Z_1, Z_2) = \bar{W}$ is the outer envelope of the set of indifference curves $U(Z_1, Z_2 | \phi_P) = \bar{W}$, where each member of the set has a different price distribution.
2. With $\psi(C_1, C_2) = F(G(C_1, C_2))$ being any homogeneous increasing function $F(\cdot)$ of a quasi-concave increasing homogeneous function $G(\cdot)$, $U(Z_1, Z_2 | \phi_P)$ is homogeneous and convex (concave) as ψ is homogeneous of degree greater (less) than one.

With $\psi(C_1, C_2)$ being homogeneous and identical in both countries, the rational expectations indifference curves $W(Z_1, Z_2)$ are identical and homogeneous. In fig. 2, a single rational expectations (or closed economy equilibrium) relative assets demand function is drawn which represents the tastes of both countries. It is downward sloping due to the quasi-concavity of W and independent of scale due to the homogeneity of W. The Heckscher–Ohlin theorem compares two autarky equilibria with a world free trade (closed world economy) equilibrium. With rational expectations, the diagram shows that the free trade relative equity price must lie between the autarky relative equity prices which in turn have the Heckscher–Ohlin ranking. The consumer's relative assets demand functions are not shown on fig. 2. At each of the three equilibria, given the price distributions implied by Z_1/Z_2, a relative assets demand function is defined which will intersect the rational expectations equilibrium relative assets demand function at the equilibrium relative equity price. The only restriction on their shape is that they cannot cross the rational expectations equilibrium assets demand function more than once and their elasticity must be algebraically greater in the neighborhood of the intersection.

A more intuitive argument relating the two sorts of demand functions at equilibrium is instructive. At any of the three closed equilibria, ex post relative commodity prices in state s are

$$P_s = \frac{\psi_1(\theta_{1s}Z_1, \theta_{2s}Z_2)}{\psi_2(\theta_{1s}Z_1, \theta_{2s}Z_2)}.$$

Equilibrium relative equity prices are

$$q = \frac{W_1(Z_1, Z_2)}{W_2(Z_1, Z_2)} = \frac{\sum_{s=1}^{S} \pi_s \psi_1(\theta_{1s}Z_1, \theta_{2s}Z_2)\theta_{1s}}{\sum_{s=1}^{S} \pi_s \psi_2(\theta_{1s}Z_1, \theta_{2s}Z_2)\theta_{2s}}$$

along the rational expectations relative assets demand function of fig. 2. The consumer's assets relative demand function is derived from

$$q = \frac{U_1(Z_1, Z_2 \mid \phi_P)}{U_2(Z_1, Z_2 \mid \phi_P)} = \frac{\sum_{s=1}^{S} \pi_s V_I(P_s, P_s\theta_{1s}Z_1 + \theta_{2s}Z_2)P_s\theta_{1s}}{\sum_{s=1}^{S} \pi_s V_I(P_s, P_s\theta_{1s}Z_1 + \theta_{2s}Z_2)\theta_{2s}},$$

where V_I is the marginal utility of income. Substituting in the true ex post expression for P_s and noting that $V_I = \psi_2$, and $V_I P_s = \psi_1$, we see that with correct expectations, the consumer's relative assets demand function agrees with (intersects) the rational expectations assets demand function.

The usual restriction on tastes in the certainty case is that indifference curves in commodity space be identical and homothetic. Formally, the utility indicator $\psi(C_1, C_2)$ must be able to be written as $F(G(C_1, C_2))$, where $G(C_1, C_2)$ is quasi-concave, homogeneous and identical across countries, and $F(G)$ is any monotonic increasing function, possibly different across countries. For the uncertainty case, for W to have identical and scale-free indifference curves across countries, it is sufficient to restrict $F(G)$ to the class of positive power functions and impose identical F across countries.[1]

It remains to prove the lemma.

Proof of 1. Let activity levels be Z_1^0, Z_2^0. In ex post commodity space, the realized utility in state s is $\psi_s^0 = \psi(\theta_{1s}Z_1^0, \theta_{2s}Z_2^0)$. The assumed realized utility in state s is $V(P_s, P_s\theta_{1s}Z_1^0 + \theta_{2s}Z_2^0) = V_s^0$. Let $P_s(Z_1^0, Z_2^0)$ be the realization in state s of the market clearing relative price based on activity of (Z_1^0, Z_2^0). For $P_s \neq P_s(Z_1^0, Z_2^0)$, $\psi_s^0 \leq V_s^0$ since an infeasible (but beneficial) exchange is implicitly assumed by consumers. For $P_s = P_s(Z_1^0, Z_2^0)$, $\psi_s^0 = V_s^0$. By definition

$$U(Z_1, Z_1 \mid \phi_P) = \sum_{s=1}^{S} \pi_s V(P_s, P_s\theta_{1s}Z_1 + Z_2)$$

and

$$W(Z_1, Z_2) = \sum_{s=1}^{S} \pi_s \psi(\theta_{1s}Z_1, \theta_{2s}Z_2),$$

so we have $U(Z_1, Z_2 \mid \phi_P) \geq W(Z_1, Z_2)$, with equality where $\phi_P = \phi_P(Z_1, Z_2)$. Since W and U are quasi-concave, $W(Z_1, Z_2) = \bar{W}$ must be the outer envelope of a family of asset indifference curves $U(Z_1, Z_2 \mid \phi_P) = \bar{W}$.

Proof of 2. Let $\psi(C_1, C_2) = F(G(C_1, C_2)) = [G(C_1, C_2)]^k$, where $G(\cdot)$ is a concave homogeneous (of degree one without loss of generality) function. Homogeneity of $\psi(C_1, C_2)$ implies that the ex post demand functions are homogeneous of degree one in income: $C_i(P_s, \lambda I_s) = \lambda C_i(P_s, I_s)$, $i = 1, 2$. The indirect utility function is $V(P_s, I_s) = V(C_1(P_s, I_s), C_2(P_s, I_s))$. Evidently $V(P_s, \lambda I_s) = \lambda^k V(P_s, I_s)$. With $I_s = P_s\theta_{1s}Z_1 + \theta_{2s}Z_2$, V is homogeneous of degree k in (Z_1, Z_2). Since the assets utility function is

$$U(Z_1, Z_2 \mid \phi_P) = \sum_{s=1}^{S} \pi_s V(P_s, I_s),$$

it is also homogeneous of degree k in (Z_1, Z_2). Evidently V (and hence U) is convex (concave) in income (hence activities) as $k > (<) 1$.

The restriction that $F(G)$ be a positive power function is sufficient for homothetic preferences over commodities to imply homothetic preferences over equities, but also nearly necessary. For F to reflect well-behaved

[1]For the case where G is Cobb–Douglas, F can differ across countries, so identical behavior towards risk is not always necessary.

preferences, it must be continuous. The necessary restriction on F which permits the theorem is that it be any positive linear transform of a positive power function, and linear transformations are irrelevant to behavior under the expected utility axioms. $\psi(C_1, C_2)$ is homothetic if and only if $\psi(C_1, C_2) = F(G(C_1, C_2))$, where G is quasi-concave homogeneous and F is monotonic increasing. $W(Z_1, Z_2)$ is homothetic if and only if $W(Z_1, Z_2) = H(J(Z_1, Z_2))$ where analogous restrictions apply to H and J:

$$W(Z_1, Z_2) = \sum_{s=1}^{S} \pi_s \psi(\theta_{1s} Z_1, \theta_{2s} Z_2) = \sum_{s=1}^{S} \pi_s F(G(\theta_{1s} Z_1, \theta_{2s} Z_2)).$$

With the continuity condition on F holding, it can be arbitrarily well approximated as an nth order polynomial in G:

$$F(G) = a + b_1 G + b_2 G^2 + \ldots + b_n G^n.$$

Only when all but one of the b_i are zero can $W(Z_1, Z_2)$ be written as a monotonic transformation of a homogeneous function.[2]

The lemma evidently generalizes readily to higher dimensions. Thus, we can demonstrate that the Travis–Vanek theorem generalizes to trade in equities.

For the certainty case of n goods, r factors, $n \geq r$, the Travis–Vanek theorem states that in free trade factor price equalization equilibrium, embodied factor trade relative to world endowments will follow the ordering of home factor endowments relative to world factor endowments. It follows from identical homothetic preferences, implying that home consumption (hence embodied factor consumption) is proportional to world consumption (hence embodied factor consumption = world endowments). If A is the unit factor requirements matrix at free trade prices,

$$F^A - AC^A \equiv T, \tag{3}$$

where T = embodied factor trade, C^A = country A's consumption vector, and F^A = country A's factor endowment vector. With identical homothetic preferences,

$$C^A = b(C^A + C^B) = b(X^A + X^B), \tag{4}$$

where b is a fraction, and X denotes production. Substituting in (3) we

---

[2]In an earlier version of this paper I committed the possibly not uncommon error of defining homotheticity following Lancaster: $F(x)$ is homothetic iff $F(\lambda x) = f(\lambda) F(x)$. Kats (1970) shows this definition does not include all radial expansion path functions and, moreover, the only admissible form for $f(\lambda)$ is λ^k. Thus, this approach reduces to that in the text.

obtain

$$F^A - bA(X^A + X^B) = T = F^A - b(F^A + F^B).\qquad(5)$$

The Travis–Vanek theorem follows when (5) is multiplied by a diagonal matrix with $1/F_i^A + F_i^B$ on the diagonal for all i. Evidently the proposition that identical homogeneous commodity preferences imply identical homothetic rational expectations asset preferences carries the Travis–Vanek theorem through to the case of uncertain technology, provided there is free trade in equities and commodities. Simply reinterpret C and X as purchase and production of equities. Factor trade embodied in the international exchange of equities will follow the ordering of home factor endowments relative to foreign factor endowments.

References

Diamond, Peter A., 1967, The role of a stock market in a general equilibrium model with technological uncertainty, American Economic Review 57, 759–776.

Helpman, Elhanan and Assaf Razin, 1978, A theory of international trade under uncertainty (Academic Press, New York).

Kats, Amoz, 1970, Comments on the definitions of homogeneous and homothetic functions, Journal of Economic Theory 2, 310–314.

Lancaster, Kelvin, 1968, Mathematical economics (Macmillan, New York).

[29]

Review of Economic Studies (1984) LI, 1–12
0034-6527/84/00010001$00.50
© 1984 The Society for Economic Analysis Limited

Pareto Inferior Trade

DAVID M. G. NEWBERY
Churchill College, Cambridge, and The World Bank

and

JOSEPH E. STIGLITZ
Princeton University

The paper shows that between two competitive but risky economies with no insurance markets, free trade may be Pareto inferior to no trade. The model is simple enough to show clearly the role prices play in transferring and sharing risk when there is an incomplete set of markets, but rich enough to exhibit the resulting inefficiencies dramatically.

The belief that free trade is Pareto optimal is one of the few tenets of economics which, at least until recently, would have received almost universal assent. The object of this paper is to demonstrate that this belief may not be well founded. We construct a simple model which lacks a complete set of risk markets but which in all other respects satisfies the conventional assumptions of a competitive economy, and show that free trade may be Pareto inferior to no trade.

The basic idea behind our model is simple. There are two countries (regions) both of which grow a risky agricultural crop and a safe crop. The output in the two regions is perfectly negatively correlated. (The model can easily be extended to cases where the correlation is zero or even positive, so long as the correlation is not perfect.) In the absence of trade, price rises whenever output falls. If demand functions have unitary price elasticity the price variations provide perfect income insurance for the farmer. With free trade the variations in the output of the risky crop offset each other and stabilize the price, which no longer varies to offset output variations. Consequently, the revenue from the risky crop now varies and the risk faced by the farmers is increased. This induces farmers to shift production away from the risky crop, raising its average price. Since consumers have unit price elasticity and thus spend a constant amount on both crops, the mean income of the farmers remains constant with the opening of trade while its riskiness increases. Consequently, farmers welfare necessarily decreases, as shown in Figure 1.

Whereas before trade was opened, consumers bore all the risk, with free trade they bear none, and, other things being equal, this would make them better off. However, the increased riskiness of the risky crop induces farmers to shift their production to the safe crop, and the consequent rise in the average price of the risky crop can make consumers worse off. Near autarky, the risk benefit dominates this allocation effect, as shown in Figure 1, but near free trade the opposite is the case. If the change in supplies and prices is sufficiently large (which it will be if producers are sufficiently risk averse), and if the consumer risk benefits are sufficiently small (which they will be if consumers are not very risk averse), then consumers will be made worse off by opening trade. Since producers are necessarily worse off (in this model), it follows that free trade is Pareto inferior to autarky.

The reconciliation of our results with the standard theorems of Welfare Economics in which free trade is Pareto efficient is straightforward—the conventional argument

2   REVIEW OF ECONOMIC STUDIES

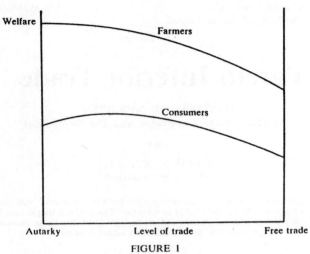

FIGURE 1
Welfare consequences of opening trade

requires not only that markets be competitive (as we assume), but also complete. In our model there must be a complete set of insurance markets enabling farmers to purchase both price and output insurance. For a variety of reasons such as moral hazard and adverse selection the set of markets is not complete. In our example autarky provides farmers with income insurance, and opening a new market (international trade in the risky commodity) has the same affect as closing these implicit insurance markets. With a complete set of markets each market provides one, and only one, marketing service, but with an incomplete set some markets may be providing several services, allocating both goods and risk. Institutional change may change the number of services provided by a particular market, and in our example such changes can make everyone worse off. Welfare analysis which assumes that each market serves only one function can be seriously misleading in these cases.

The model we shall analyze has been kept simple to make the main points as clearly as possible. In particular, we choose very special functional forms—unit price elasticity—for consumer demand which allow us to employ the concept of mean preserving changes in risk, and which thus allow a very intuitive explanation of our results. It will become clear from our model that any other specification would greatly complicate the analysis, since changes in trade will in general lead to changes in both mean income and its risk.[1] The result that free trade is Pareto inefficient is, however, quite general, and relies on three critical assumptions. First, there must be some agents who, on average, are net sellers of the risky good (in our model, the farmers) and others who are net buyers (consumers). Since these individuals must engage in trade, their welfare is affected by the price distribution.[2] Second, neither producers nor consumers can buy insurance for the risks (the variability of output of the risky crop and of its price) which they face. Changes in the level of trade change the price distribution and the risks that individuals face. If they could perfectly insure, then there would be no change in risk, and hence no adverse consequences. However, we would argue that it is more realistic to assume that individuals cannot perfectly insure themselves, and that therefore risk, and changes in risk, do matter. Third, output in the different countries cannot be perfectly correlated, for then (under our assumptions that the countries are otherwise identical) opening up trade would leave the price distribution unaffected. Thus, although we assume that outputs in the two countries are perfectly negatively correlated, all that is required is the absence of perfect positive correlation.

These three assumptions distinguish our paper from earlier studies of trade and uncertainty. These other studies have (for the most part) employed the concept of a representative consumer–producer, assumed the price distribution was given exogenously, rather than determined endogenously, assumed outputs are perfectly correlated across countries, and/or focused on the case where there are perfect risk markets, so farmers can diversify out of the risks they face.[3] The closest in spirit to the present study is the excellent work of Helpman and Razin (1978a, b) which dealt with general equilibrium effects. However, they assume a perfect equities market (a weaker assumption than a perfect risk market), perfect correlation, and they make use of the concept of a representative consumer–producer.[4]

The paper is divided into two parts. In Section 1 we develop the basic model and derive the conditions under which free trade is Pareto inferior to no trade. In Section 2 we show that the results are more robust than the simple model developed in Section 1. We discuss the critical assumptions, present an alternative interpretation of the model, and suggest extensions to the analysis.

1. COMPARISON OF AUTARKY AND FREE TRADE

We construct a simple model with two regions which are identical, except that their output of a risky agricultural commodity is perfectly negatively correlated. Each region has n identical farmers and m identical consumers. We first describe the farmers, then the consumers, and finally the market equilibria with and without trade. We then compare the two equilibria and establish conditions under which free trade is Pareto inferior to no trade.

A. Producers

Each of the n identical producers owns one unit of land. A typical farmer allocates a fraction x of his land to growing a risky crop, which we denote by subscript r, and the remainder, $1-x$, to the safe crop, denoted by subscript s. Output per acre of the risky crop is θ, a random variable, with mean unity and variance σ^2. The output of the safe crop is always unity. (These are just normalizations.)

Farmers are risk averse; they choose x before they know θ (the weather) to maximize the expected utility of profits:[5]

$$EU(\pi), \qquad U' > 0, \qquad U'' < 0, \tag{1}$$

where

$$\pi = xp\theta + q(1-x) \tag{2}$$

are the profits, p is the price of the risky crop, and q is the price of the safe crop.

Farmers are assumed to know the relationship between the price and θ, but since each farmer is small, he assumes he has no effect on price (in any state of nature).[6] Our analysis thus focuses on competitive rational expectations equilibria. The expected utility maximizing choice of x is given by the solution to

$$EU'(\pi)(p\theta - q) = 0. \tag{3}$$

4   REVIEW OF ECONOMIC STUDIES

B. *Consumers*

It is convenient to represent the respresentative consumer by his indirect utility function $V = V(I, p, q)$ where I is income which is constant.[7] For most of the analysis we shall make use of a special parameterization of the utility function. We let

$$
V = \begin{cases} \dfrac{(Ip^{-a}q^{-b})^{1-\rho}}{1-\rho} & \text{for } \rho \neq 1, \qquad (4) \\[2ex] \log I - a \log p - b \log q & \text{for } \rho = 1, \qquad (5) \end{cases}
$$

where ρ is the coefficient of relative risk aversion. These yield aggregate demand functions for the two commodities which have unitary price and income elasticities:

$$
Q_r = \frac{amI}{p}, \qquad Q_s = \frac{bmI}{q} \qquad (6)
$$

where Q_i is aggregate demand for commodity i (risky or safe), and mI is aggregate consumer income.

This specification of the utility function is chosen for several reasons: it greatly simplifies the calculations; it is the utility function for which consumer surplus calculations employed in conventional welfare analysis are valid;[8] and it implies that there will be no income redistribution effects in the policy changes which we shall consider,[9] and thus this specification enables a simple separation of the efficiency and distributional consequences of trade policy. Moreover, demand functions with unitary price elasticity play a critical borderline role in the analysis of risk with more than one commodity; if the elasticity of substitution between the two commodities is less than unity, the induced price variability results in farmers treating the safe commodity as if it were riskier than the risky commodity. (See Stiglitz (1972).) Finally, the utility function exhibits constant relative (income) risk aversion, ρ, and in the special case of unitary risk aversion of equation (5):

$$
V_{Ip} = V_{Iq} = 0, \qquad (7)
$$

so changes in price do not affect the marginal utility of income.

C. *Market equilibrium without trade*

The structure of the equilibrium is simple:

(a) Producers decide on a crop allocation, x, *given* that their expectations about the relationship between price and θ is in fact the one that emerges.

(b) After the crop is harvested, the crops are marketed competitively. Market prices equate demands (given by equation (6)) to supplies (which depend on x and θ). If all farmers act alike then market clearing prices are

$$
p = \frac{ay}{x\theta}, \qquad q = \frac{by}{1-x}, \qquad (8)
$$

where $y = mI/n$, consumer income per farmer. Equation (8) implies both crops yield perfectly safe returns, which must be identical if both crops are to be grown:

$$
p\theta = q. \qquad (9)
$$

NEWBERY & STIGLITZ   PARETO INFERIOR TRADE   5

Equations (8) and (9) imply that

$$\frac{ay}{x} = \frac{by}{1-x},$$ (10)

and give the equilibrium solution

$$x = \frac{a}{a+b}, \qquad q = (a+b)y, \qquad p = (a+b)y/\theta.$$ (11)

Producer profits are $\pi = q$ (using (9) and (2)) so producer welfare is simply $U\{(a+b)y\}$. The representative consumer's average welfare in the logarithmic case (5) is

$$EV = V_0 + aE \log \theta, \qquad V_0 = \log I - (a+b) \log \{(a+b)y\},$$ (12)

where V_0 is the utility without risk.[10]

Note that the unit elastic consumer demands transfer all the risk from farmers to consumers. Fluctuations in the supply of the risky crop affect only its price and not that of the safe crop. Except in this special case, production risk for one commodity will spill over to generate price risk for other commodities. (Stiglitz (1972)).

D. Market equilibrium with free trade

Now suppose that, to the east on the other side of a mountain range there is another region, identical to the one described above in every respect save one—the weather.[11] When it rains in the West it is dry in the East, and vice versa. The output of the risky crop is perfectly negatively correlated between the two regions. Formally, let $\theta^E + \theta^W = 2$. Initially there is no trade between East and West, but there is a pass through the mountains which permits virtually costless exchange. If it is opened, there will be competitive free trade; if not, the regions will remain autarkic. Is free trade desirable?

The strong symmetry assumptions ensure there is always a symmetric equilibrium, but there may be additional asymmetric equilibria in which each country relatively specializes in one crop. If farmers are not too risk averse there will be a unique symmetric equilibrium, and for most of the paper we shall concentrate on this.

In the symmetric free trade equilibrium, each region allocates the same fraction x of land to the risky crop, $1-x$ to the safe crop, yielding total supplies:

$$Q_r = nx\theta + nx(2-\theta) = 2nx, \qquad Q_s = 2n(1-x).$$ (13)

Prices will be perfectly stabilized at

$$\bar{p} = \frac{ay}{x}, \qquad \bar{q} = \frac{by}{1-x},$$ (14)

and so total profits are now

$$\pi = \bar{p}x\theta + (1-x)\bar{q} = (a\theta + b)y,$$ (15)

and farmers' income is now risky, though it has the same mean as before. The allocation of land between the two crops is given by the solution to equation (3):

$$EU'\{y(a\theta + b)\}\left(\frac{a\theta y}{x} - \frac{by}{1-x}\right) \equiv EM(\theta, x) = 0.$$ (16)

6   REVIEW OF ECONOMIC STUDIES

E. *Comparison of free trade and autarky*

Denote the equilibrium values of x, p, q, with free trade by $\{\bar{x}, \bar{p}, \bar{q}\}$ and in autarky by $\{\hat{x}, \hat{p}, \hat{q}\}$. Proposition 1 compares the allocations of the equilibria in the two situations:

Proposition 1. *If farmers are risk averse, the safe crop is cheaper and the land devoted to the risky crop smaller with free trade than autarky.*

Proof. With free trade and risk averse farmers the average return to the risky crop must exceed that of the safe crop:

$$E\bar{p}\theta = \bar{p} > q \quad or \quad \frac{ay}{\bar{x}} > \frac{by}{1-\bar{x}}$$

from (14). A comparison with the autarky equilibrium (10) imples $\hat{x} > \bar{x}$ and hence $\bar{q} < \hat{q}$. ∥

More generally, if $\Delta x = \hat{x} - \bar{x}$ is the fall in land allocated to the risky crop in moving from autarky to free trade, then Proposition 2 identifies two of the critical parameters determining the magnitude of Δx.

Proposition 2. (a) *The more risk averse are farmers the greater is Δx. (Diamond and Stiglitz (1974)); (b) The greater the riskiness of θ (in the sense of Rothschild–Stiglitz (1970)), the greater is Δx, provided*
   (i) *the range of θ is not too great, or*
   (ii) *there is constant relative risk aversion R with $R < 1$.*

Either of these conditions ensure that the expression $M(\theta, x)$ is concave in θ,[12] and ensures the result.

F. *Welfare analysis*

The next result follows immediately from equation (15):

Proposition 3. *Farmers are always worse off as a result of the opening of trade. In the new equilibrium mean income is unchanged but risk is increased.*[13]

Consumers now face no risk. This makes them better off but in return there is a change in x, which makes them worse off. To see this, we ask what allocation x maximizes consumer welfare

$$V = V\left\{ I\left(\frac{ay}{x}\right)^{-a} \left(\frac{by}{1-x}\right)^{-b} Z(\theta) \right\} \tag{17}$$

where $Z(\theta) > 0$ depends on trade policy. Thus under autarky $Z = \theta^a$ whilst in free trade $Z = 1$. However, for *any* $Z(\theta) > 0$, we observe that the solution is

$$x = \frac{a}{a+b} = \hat{x}, \tag{18}$$

the farmers' choice under autarky. Any other choice makes the consumer worse off. Hence, the change in consumer welfare in moving from autarky to free trade will depend

NEWBERY & STIGLITZ   PARETO INFERIOR TRADE   7

on the magnitude of the resource shift, Δx, and on the consumer gain from the elimination of the risk he faces.

From Proposition 2, Δx depends on the size of the risk and the degree of farmers' risk aversion, while the consumers' benefit from risk reduction depends on the size of risk, and the degree of consumers' risk aversion.

It therefore looks as though consumers will be worse off with free trade provided farmers are sufficiently risk averse, and this is indeed true when comparing the symmetric free trade equilibrium with autarky. However, above a critical level of farmer risk aversion, the symmetric free trade equilibrium ceases to be the unique equilibrium, and multiple equilibria appear. Typically, the existence of multiple equilibria raises issues of stability, though of course stability can only be examined in the context of a particular adjustment process. Elsewhere (Newbery and Stiglitz (1982c)) we show that for one reasonable adjustment process the symmetric equilibrium is stable if it is the unique equilibrium, but unstable otherwise. Any particular adjustment process will doubtless appear *ad hoc* to some readers, and we shall therefore sidestep the issue by asking whether there is a critical value for the farmer's risk aversion below which the symmetric equilibrium is the unique equilibrium and for which free trade is Pareto inferior to autarky.

Since farmers are always worse off in a free trade equilibrium, free trade will be Pareto inferior to autarky if consumers are worse off under free trade, i.e., if

$$E\frac{(\bar{p}^{-a}\bar{q}^{-b})^{1-\rho}}{1-\rho} < E\frac{(\hat{p}^{-a}\hat{q}^{-b})^{1-\rho}}{1-\rho}. \tag{19}$$

In the symmetric equilibrium, substituting for prices, this is equivalent to

$$\frac{\bar{x}}{\hat{x}}\frac{1-\bar{x}^{b/a}}{1-\hat{x}} < \{E\theta^{a(1-\rho)}\}^{1/a(1-\rho)}. \tag{20}$$

The R.H.S. is a monotonically decreasing function of consumer's relative risk aversion ρ while the L.H.S. is a monotonically decreasing function of farmers' relative risk aversion R. It follows that there is a monotonically increasing critical function $R = f(\rho)$ for which consumers are indifferent between autarky and the symmetric free trade equilibrium, and it can be shown that $f(0) \equiv R_0 > 0$, where the value of R_0 depends on the form of the utility function, the nature of risk, and other parameters. The crucial question is whether $R_0 < R^*$, the critical value at which the symmetric equilibrium ceases to be the unique equilibrium.

The values of R_0 and R^* depend on the parameters a, b, the distribution of θ, and the form of the farmer's utility function, but its value can be easily calculated for constant absolute or relative risk aversion utility functions and a two point distribution 'for $\theta = 1 \pm \sigma$.[14]

For values of $\sigma = 0.9$ there is a wide range of values of a and b for which $R_0 < R^*$: $0.2 \leqq a \leqq 0.8$; $a+b \leqq 0.9$, for both constant absolute and relative risk aversion utility functions. R_0 increases with b, decreases with a, and is less than 3.0 for $a \geqq 0.4$. However, for $\sigma \leqq 0.8$ there are very few such configurations, and hence for free trade to be Pareto inferior to autarky, the degree of risk must be quite extreme.

These computer solutions allow us to assert

Proposition 4.   *There exist sets of parameter values for which the unique free trade equilibrium is Pareto inferior to autarky.*

The simulations suggest that the range of values of (R, ρ) for which this is true increases with σ, a, and b. There is a larger range of values of (R, ρ) for which free trade is potentially Pareto inferior to autarky in the sense that though consumers would be better off with free trade, they would not be willing to pay the fixed sum needed to compensate producers for accepting free trade.

2. EXTENSIONS AND LIMITATIONS

The previous section of the paper used an extremely simple model to establish a strong result: free trade may be Pareto inferior to no trade. To what extent are the results dependent on the special parameterizations we have employed? And to what extent do they depend on the particular institutional assumptions we have made? The critical assumption in our analysis, we contend, is the absence of perfect risk markets, an assumption which, though not justified within the context of the model, seems empirically more plausible (at least in the context investigated here) than the other polar assumption conventionally employed, that risk markets are perfect.[15]

To see why this is important, let us consider briefly the nature of equilibrium under alternative assumptions.

A. *Financial markets*

First, we note that in the central case of consumers having logarithmic utility functions, there is no scope for future markets in the no trade situation; for then $V_{Ip} = 0$, the marginal utility of income is the same independent of the state of nature, and hence market equilibrium requires that if a small futures market were introduced, it be actuarially fair. But for producers, profits are constant, and they too would require an actuarially fair futures market. Hence the only equilibrium is one where there is no trade on the futures market. With perfect negative output correlation, there would be no scope for a futures market in the free trade situation either, since prices would not vary.

The consequences of opening up a market for ownership shares in farms is more serious. (We ignore all the problems of moral hazard, which are fundamental to an understanding of why such markets might not exist.) If farmers could purchase shares in each others' farms, then income of farmers would be constant; they would thus be indifferent between the opening of trade and autarky, but consumers would be unambiguously better off. Thus, the standard result that free trade is preferable to no trade is restored, if there is a complete set of securities markets.

B. *Structure of demand*

The major reason that the unit price elasticity assumption is employed is that it avoids the confusion between transfer and risk effects. If the elasticity of demand is not unity, a mean quantity preserving change in the price distribution will change the mean income of farmers. (Newbery and Stiglitz (1981).) In particular, if demand curves have constant elasticity greater than unity, farmers' revenue is a convex function of consumption, so, at each value of x, mean income is higher under autarky than with free trade. Although in autarky, producers' income is variable, it is less variable than output, and hence less variable than income under free trade. It can thus be shown that (i) a slight increase in trade from the no trade position always increases producers' welfare; (ii) provided the elasticity is not too large, a slight restriction on trade from the free trade position also increases producers' welfare.

The effect on consumers is more difficult to analyze. There are now three effects: (i) the risk effect; as before, opening trade reduces consumer risk; (ii) the transfer effect; because of the change in the distribution of prices, mean expenditure of consumers is increased, which makes them worse off; (iii) the allocation effect; because of the transfer effect, the allocation effect will be smaller, and may actually be positive rather than negative.

Similarly, if the elasticity of demand is less than unity the reduction is price variability *reduces* producers' mean income, and, if the elasticity is greater than 0.5, opening trade increases the variability of their income. Thus, producers are unambiguously worse off. Again, the effects on consumers are more complicated: now the transfer effect is positive, but the allocation effect is larger. Thus there are a large variety of possible patterns.

If the price elasticity is very small (less than 0.5), then pre-trade income variability is greater than post-trade income variability, in which case the opening of trade may be Pareto superior even without direct compensation schemes.

For elasticities of demand near unity, however, the qualitative properties remain unaffected: free trade may be Pareto inferior to no trade, provided farmers are sufficiently risk averse; if the elasticity is greater than unity, a slight liberalization of trade from the no trade position is Pareto improving; if the elasticity is less than unity, producers are strictly worse off; a slight restriction on trade from the free trade position is Pareto improving provided producers are sufficiently risk averse.

C. *Imperfectly correlated risk*

One of the three crucial assumptions which drives our model is that output in the different countries is not perfectly correlated, for otherwise opening up trade would leave the price distribution unaffected. For simplicity we took the polar alternative assumption of perfect negative correlation as this allowed us to use a single parameter, θ, to describe the state of the world. However, the results continue to hold for imperfectly correlated risk, and elsewhere (Newbery and Stiglitz (1982c)) we have analysed the case of symmetric risk, in which country 1 in state θ is indistinguishable from country 2 in state θ', and vice versa. This allows for imperfect output correlation whilst preserving symmetry and hence analytic tractability. With this extension it is possible to examine less extreme forms of trade policy than choosing between autarky and perfectly free trade, and to show that neither extreme is Pareto efficient.

D. *The theory of comparative advantage*

Specialists in traditional trade theory have, on a number of occasions, expressed an uneasiness with our analysis, on the grounds that it appears to ignore the principle of comparative advantage which underlies conventional trade theory. Note that this is not quite correct. Although there is no long run comparative advantage, each of the countries having precisely the same endowments and tastes, every period there is a significant comparative advantage, depending simply on the weather.

This, in fact, we would claim is one of the attractive features of our analysis: There is considerable evidence that much trade cannot be explained solely on the basis of factor

10   REVIEW OF ECONOMIC STUDIES

endowments or tastes. It seems, accordingly, desirable to explore models in which there is trade without long run comparative advantage.[16]

We can, nonetheless, easily incorporate elements of traditional comparative advantage theory within our framework. Although we leave the formal development of such a synthesis to another occasion, let us briefly show how it may be done. Assume, for simplicity, that there are two factors, say capital and labour. Assume that the safe crop is labour intensive. For simplicity, let us assume that the two countries have the same factor endowments. Clearly, there is again no long run comparative advantage. We can ask, however, what happens as a result of the opening up to trade. Our previous analysis applies almost identically, except now farmers do not face a straight line production possibilities schedule, but face a concave production possibilities schedule. It is still true, however, that the opening up of trade will lead to an increase in the production of the safe crop (labour intensive). Assume, now, that the two countries have slightly different factor endowments. There will now be two effects: in the absence of risk, the opening up of trade will lead to the equalization of factor prices, a decrease in the price of labour in one country, and an increase in its price in the other. Now, however, there is an additional risk effect, which will tend to shift production toward the safe crop (more, presumably, in the country which has a comparative advantage in its production). This effect may outweigh the first effect, so that, still, the price of labour in both countries rises; it is even possible that factor price differentials widen.

CONCLUDING REMARKS

Free trade, which arbitrages prices in different countries, can stabilize prices. Buffer stocks, which arbitrage prices at different dates, also stabilize prices, and our analysis therefore bears on the question of the desirability of leaving commodity price stabilization to private speculators.

There is an argument, popular with economists, that if markets are competitive and agents well informed, then government intervention will lead to inefficiency. This argument has been used both to argue against restrictions on trade and against the establishment of international commodity stabilization schemes.

Our analysis questions the premises of this reasoning. We show that there is no presumption that free markets will be Pareto optimal. But our analysis is not simply negative. We have shown how to decompose the risk and allocative effects of changes in the market structure, and shown that they may conflict. A change in trade policy such as the opening of trade can have a significant effect on the risk borne by producers, who respond by changing their allocation of resources. The resulting changed pattern of output in turn affects consumers, who also experience a change in risk as a result of the trade policy. Whilst the resulting transfer of risk from consumers to producers may by itself make consumers better off, the allocative response by producers can make them worse off. Returning to the buffer stock analogy, it is possible that the opening of trade between two dates which perfectly stabilizes prices may be Pareto inferior to having no trade, and that it is thus desirable to restrict the arbitrage activities of speculators (see also Newbery and Stiglitz (1981, 1982b)).

Of course, it does not follow that government intervention is automatically justified by the absence of a complete set of markets, but it does suggest that simplistic arguments for free trade based on the competitive complete market paradigm are often far from persuasive.

NEWBERY & STIGLITZ   PARETO INFERIOR TRADE   11

First version received July 1981; *final version accepted October* 1983 (Eds.).

The research reported here was supported in part by the United States Agency for International Development and is an extension of Appendix E of Newbery and Stiglitz (1977). We are grateful to L. Perez and his colleagues to USAID for their comments. We are also indebted to the editor, to participants at seminars at Warwick, University of Dublin, The World Bank, Princeton and to Roy Ruffin and Robert Lindsey for their helpful comments. Financial support from the National Science Foundation, the Social Science Research Council of the U.K., and IBM are gratefully acknowledged. Revisions to the paper were completed whilst Newbery was on leave from Cambridge University at the World Bank. The view presented are those of the authors alone and do not necessarily reflect those of the World Bank or USAID. Earlier versions of this paper which include discussions of Trade Policy appeared as Economic Theory Discussion Paper No. 23, July 1979, Cambridge, England, Econometric Research Program Research Memorandum No. 281, May 1981, Princeton, and DRD Discussion Paper 50, January 1983, World Bank, Washington, DC.

NOTES

1. Elsewhere (Newbery and Stiglitz (1982a)) we have demonstrated the inefficiency (except under very stringent conditions) of competitive (i.e., free trade) equilibria for a more general model.

2. Thus, if individuals are all identical, the changes in price distribution which are central to our analysis have no welfare consequences.

3. For an extensive survey of the recent literature on trade and uncertainty, see Pomery (1979). Among the studies focusing on the small country case with the price distribution given exogenously are those of Batra and Russell (1974, 1975) and Ruffin (1974a, b). The Batra and Russell and Ruffin papers also assumed producers had no output variability whereas the relationship between the variability of output and prices plays a crucial role in our analysis.

4. Even when there are perfect equities markets, the assumption of identical consumers is crucial. Stiglitz (1982) has shown, for instance, that while the stock market equilibrium with multiplicative uncertainty and two commodities is always a constrained Pareto optimum with identical consumers, it essentially never is if consumers differ, either in their preferences for goods or their attitudes towards risk.

5. An inessential simplification of this analysis is that producers do not consume what they produce; their welfare depends only on what they obtain from selling their crops.

6. In our simple model, since the only source of price variability is supply variability, price will be a deterministic function of θ; in more general models, it would be a stochastic function.

7. I is the consumer's endowment of a third good (or a Hicksian composite commodity, representing all other goods), which is taken to be the numeraire.

8. See Samuelson (1942).

9. For other utility functions mean income of farmers will increase or decrease as a result of the opening of trade. See Section 2.B below.

10. The dollar value of the loss from the randomness in θ is approximately $(a/2)\sigma^2$. In the case of constant relative risk aversion not equalling unity

$$EV = E\frac{\theta^{a(1-\rho)}V_0}{1-\rho}, \qquad V_0 = \left\{\frac{n}{m(a+b)}\right\}^{(1-\rho)(a+b)} I^{(1-\rho)(1-a-b)}.$$

The dollar value of the loss from risk is then approximately $\frac{1}{2}a\{1-a(1-\rho)\}\sigma^2$ which agrees with the logarithmic case for $\rho = 1$.

11. This rules out the conventional reasons for trade and allows us to concentrate on the risk aspect alone. Regions have a comparative advantage in weather alone in this model. Obviously, this heavily qualifies any policy conclusions which might be drawn from the study. See also 2.D below.

12. Since

$$M = U'[(a\theta + b)y]\left(\frac{ay}{x}\theta - \frac{by}{1-x}\right),$$

and $R \equiv -\pi U''(\pi)/U'(\pi)$,

$$\frac{\partial M}{\partial \theta} = ayU'\left\{\frac{1}{x} - \frac{R}{a\theta + b}\left(\frac{a}{x}\theta - \frac{b}{1-x}\right)\right\}$$

$$\frac{\partial^2 M}{\partial \theta^2} = \frac{Ra^2 U'y}{(a\theta + b)^2}\left[-\frac{a\theta}{x} - b\left(\frac{2}{x} + \frac{1}{1-x}\right) + \left\{R - \frac{R'\pi}{R}\right\}\left(\frac{a\theta}{x} - \frac{b}{1-x}\right)\right].$$

If the range of θ is small, $(a\theta/x) - b/(1-x)$ will be small, so $\partial^2 M/\partial\theta^2 < 0$.
Alternatively, if $R' = 0$ and $R \leq 1$, $\partial^2 M/\partial\theta^2 < 0$. Clearly, these conditions can be weakened.

## 12					REVIEW OF ECONOMIC STUDIES

13. A quantitative estimate of their welfare loss expressed as a percentage of mean income is provided by Taylor Series approximation:

$$\frac{\Delta U}{(a+b)yEU'} = \frac{U\{(a+b)y\} - EU\{(a\theta+b)y\}}{(a+b)yEU'} \approx \frac{1}{2}\left(\frac{a}{a+b}\right)^2 R\sigma^2.$$

14. Details available from Newbery on request.

15. Brazilian coffee growers do not as a rule own shares in Kenyan coffee farms, or conversely. Although we have not explained this absence of perfect risk markets, it would not be difficult to construct a model which is consistent with our analysis and which would at the same time have the property that there is imperfect risk sharing.

16. Of course, there are other possible models, emphasizing economies of scale and monopolistic competition; again, in such models, opening trade need not be Pareto improving. See, for instance, Arnott and Stiglitz (1981).

REFERENCES

ARNOTT, R. and STIGLITZ, J. E. (1982), "Equilibrium in Competitive Insurance Markets: The Welfare Effects of the Moral Hazard" (mimeo).

BATRA, R. N. and RUSSELL, W. R. (1974), "Gains from Trade Under Uncertainty", *American Economic Review*, 64, (6) 1040–1048.

BATRA, R. N. (1975), "Production Uncertainty and the Heckscher–Ohlin Theorem", *Review of Economic Studies*, 42, 259–268.

DASGUPTA, P. and STIGLITZ, J. E. (1977), "Tariffs vs. Quotas as Revenue-Raising Devices under Uncertainty", *American Economic Review*, 67, 975–981.

DIAMOND, P. A. and STIGLITZ, J. E. (1974), "Increases in Risk and Risk Aversion", *Journal of Economic Theory*, 8, 337–360.

FISHELSON, G. and FLATTERS, F. (1975), "The (Non-) Equivalence of Optimal Tariffs and Quotas under Uncertainty", *Journal of International Economics*, 5, 385–393.

HELPMAN, E. and RAZIN, A. (1978a) "Uncertainty and International Trade in the Presence of Stock Markets", *Review of Economic Studies*, 45(2), 239–250.

HELPMAN, E. and RAZIN, A. (1978b) *A Theory of International Trade Under Uncertainty* (New York).

HELPMAN, E. and RAZIN, A. (1980), "Protection and Uncertainty", *American Economic Review*, 70, (4), 716–731.

NEWBERY, D. M. G. and STIGLITZ, J. E. (1977) *The Economic Impact of Commodity Price Stabilization* (Washington, D.C.: USAID).

NEWBERY, D. M. G. and STIGLITZ, J. E. (1981) *Theory of Commodity Price Stabilization* (Oxford University Press).

NEWBERY, D. M. G. and STIGLITZ, J. E. (1982a), "The Choice of Techniques and the Optimality of Market Equilibrium with Rational Expectations", *Journal of Political Economy*, 90(2), 222–246.

NEWBERY, D. M. G. and STIGLITZ, J. E. (1982b), "Risk Aversion, Supply Response, and the Optimality of Random Prices: A Diagrammatic Analysis", *Quarterly Journal of Economics*, 97(1), 1–26.

NEWBERY, D. M. G. and STIGLITZ, J. E. (1982c), "Pareto Inferior Trade and Optimal Trade Policy" (Econometric Research Program Memorandum No. 281, Princeton).

POMERY, J. (1979), "Uncertainty and International Trade", Chapter 4 of Dornbusch and Frankel (eds.) *International Economic Policy*.

ROTHSCHILD, M. and STIGLITZ, J. E. (1970), "Increasing Risk I: A Definition", *Journal of Economic Theory*, 2, 225–243.

RUFFIN, R. J. (1974a), "International Trade under Uncertainty", *Journal of International Economics*, 4, 243–259.

RUFFIN, R. J. (1974b), "Comparative Advantage under Uncertainty", *Journal of International Economics*, 4, 261–273.

SAMUELSON, P. A. (1942), "Constancy of the Marginal Utility of Income", reprinted in *Collected Scientific Papers*, Vol. 1, 37–53 (M.I.T. Press).

STIGLITZ, J. E. (1972), "Taxation, Risk Taking and the Allocation of Investment in a Risky Economy", M. C. Jensen (ed.) *Studies in the Theory of Capital Markets* (New York.)

STIGLITZ, J. E. (1982), "The Inefficiency of the Stock Market Equilibrium", *Review of Economic Studies*, 49(2), 241–261.

[30]

Journal of International Economics 23 (1987) 201–220. North-Holland

TRADE AND INSURANCE WITH MORAL HAZARD

Avinash DIXIT*

Princeton University, Princeton, NJ 08544, USA

Received November 1986, revised version received March 1987

Previous literature on the use of trade policy for insurance has relied implicitly on moral hazard and adverse selection as the reasons for the failure of private markets for risk-bearing. This paper begins with the observation that such forces should be incorporated explicitly into the models to ensure a fair comparison between markets and governments. For the case of moral hazard, it is found that market equilibrium given exclusive insurance is an informationally constrained Pareto optimum. In one case of non-exclusive insurance, a systematic role for government insurance is found, but the scope of trade policy is ambiguous.

1. Introduction

It is often argued that in the absence of complete markets for risk-sharing, trade policy can have a second-best role in providing insurance. The most prominent exponents of this view are Newbery and Stiglitz (1984) and Eaton and Grossman (1985). The former construct an example where autarky is Pareto superior to free trade. The latter examine a more general model using numerical simulation methods, and find that the optimal policy usually involves some protection, i.e. has an anti-trade bias. Both pairs of authors appeal to moral hazard and adverse selection to motivate the absence of insurance markets. However, they do not include these forces explicitly in their models.

This procedure constitutes an unfair comparison between market equilibria and policy optima. First, the government's conduct of trade policy is assumed to be free from problems that would plague the market. Second, neither moral hazard nor adverse selection necessarily implies a total collapse of insurance markets or other risk-sharing arrangements.

To make a fair comparison, one should construct a trade model with moral hazard or adverse selection, allow markets as much play as they can

*I am very grateful to the firm of (Gene M.) Grossman and (Sanford J.) Grossman for helpful advice, and the National Science Foundation for research support under grant No. SES-8509536. I also thank Norman Ireland and Kala Krishna for useful comments on an earlier draft.

0022–1996/87/$3.50 © 1987, Elsevier Science Publishers B.V. (North-Holland)

have under the circumstances, and then ask if and how policy can improve upon the outcome. The purpose of this paper is to initiate this research program, for the case of moral hazard. Adverse selection will be treated in a separate forthcoming paper.

Some general issues of economic policy under moral hazard and adverse selection have been examined in this rigorous way, for example by Greenwald and Stiglitz (1986) and Arnott and Stiglitz (1986). They have identified some market failures, and examined how policy can act upon them. My aim is more specific; I shall construct a model that is closely related to those familiar in trade theory, and see which of the market failures have relevance for it.

My focus is on the role of trade and tax-transfer policies when there is uncertainty with moral hazard. To highlight the issue, I use a model where such policies would have no role in the absence of such problems: a small economy without distributive conflicts. To simplify the analysis, I keep the model small: two sectors, one being safe and the other risky, and one mobile factor of production, labor. The set-up is quite similar to Grossman's (1984) model of occupational choice, with some inessential details omitted, and moral hazard added.

Within this framework, we can have alternative assumptions about risk and insurance. Risk may be purely individual, or it may have an aggregate (systematic) component. As for insurance, if the total coverage purchased by an individual can be observed, then moral hazard is better controlled by making each insurance contract contingent upon the total coverage for that individual. The effect is just the same as requiring each person to buy all his insurance from the same (competitive) firm. This is called the exclusivity requirement; see Shavell (1979, fn. 8) and Arnott and Stiglitz (1986, pp. 3–4) for a full discussion. Thus, we have another choice: to assume exclusivity, or not to. The alternative assumptions about the nature of risk and the kind of insurance give rise to four separate cases. In the next three sections I shall examine three of these in detail; the fourth is then easy to consider by analogy.

In all the cases, some features are common, and it is convenient to state them here. The economy has N identical workers. Each has an indirect utility function $V(I, p)$ for goods' consumption with the following properties: I is disposable income in terms of the safe good (Y), p is the relative price of the good produced in the risky sector (X), and V is increasing and concave in I.

Each individual must choose the sector in which to work before any uncertainty is resolved. Let M denote the number who choose the safe sector. There is an increasing concave production function $Y = F(M)$. The wage is determined competitively:

$$w = F'(M). \tag{1}$$

The residual profits,

$$\Pi = F(M) - MF'(M), \tag{2}$$

are assumed to accrue to the government, and then enter consumers' incomes via the tax-transfer policies. It would make no difference to give each consumer a $(1/N)$th share of the profits directly. I could also stipulate a separate landlord class, and redistributive tax-transfer instruments to maximize workers' utility while holding landlords' utility constant, as in Grossman (1984). But that would give equivalent results and merely complicate the algebra.

The economy is small, and the world price of good X relative to good Y is fixed at p^*. The government's trade policy can maintain a domestic price p different from p^*. If $p > p^*$ the X-sector is favored by the policy, which is an import tariff or an export subsidy of $(p - p^*)$ depending on the direction of trade.

Other policy instruments pertaining to the risky sector will be described later. Any net revenue required by the government is raised by means of a uniform lump-sum tax t on each worker. Note that t must be determined as part of the equilibrium.

2. Individual risk, exclusive insurance

There are $(N - M)$ workers in the risky sector. It is perhaps simplest to think of them as independent household farms or firms. Each of them chooses his level of effort e, measured by utility units, before the uncertainty is resolved. The probability distribution of outcomes depends on e. The expected net utility of a worker in the risky sector is thus $u_x = \mathrm{E}V(I, p) - e$, where E is the expectation operator.

For algebraic simplicity, I shall assume that there are just two possible outcomes: low output x_L and high output x_H. The probability of the high outcome is $\pi(e)$, an increasing and concave function of e. The probabilities are independent across individuals. With a large number of workers, the per capita output is riskless.

The important assumption is that the range of possible outcomes, here the set $\{x_L, x_H\}$, does not vary with e. If they did, there would be events whose occurrence would reveal the chosen e exactly. Then contracts that mete out sufficiently severe punishments in such events could control moral hazard fully or almost fully, i.e. achieve or approximate the full-information first best. Therefore the assumption of invariance is the natural one to make in a model that sets out to examine the problems caused by moral hazard.

Otherwise, nothing hinges on the special structure. One could allow a continuum of possible outcomes x and a probability density function $f(x, e)$

at the cost only of analytical complexity; see the discussions in Hart and Holmstrom (1986). Similarily, one could allow hired labor or material inputs, making the entrepreneur the recipient of profits, as in Grossman (1984). Since the results are unaffected, the simplest structure is the best for my purpose.

The government makes net transfers of g_L, g_H to each X-sector worker who realizes low and high output respectively. This specification can cover many policies. If $g_L > 0 > g_H$, we have some publicly provided insurance. If $g_L = g_H > 0$, we have a reward for undertaking the risky activity. If $g_L > 0 = g_H$, we have an income-support scheme.

There is private insurance, defined by each worker's net receipts z_L and z_H in the respective states. Recall that total coverage can be observed and controlled under the exclusivity assumption of this section. Therefore the individual cannot freely choose the scale of coverage at a given ratio of z_L/z_H.

The income of each X-sector worker in the two states is

$$I_L = px_L + g_L + z_L - t, \tag{3}$$

$$I_H = px_H + g_H + z_H - t. \tag{4}$$

The expected utility is

$$u_X = (1 - \pi(e))V(I_L, p) + \pi(e)V(I_H, p) - e. \tag{5}$$

Given the government policies and the insurance contract, the worker chooses e to maximize u_X. Assuming an interior solution $(e > 0)$ the first-order condition is

$$\pi'(e)[V(I_H, p) - V(I_L, p)] = 1. \tag{6}$$

The private insurer's zero profit condition is

$$(1 - \pi(e))z_L + \pi(e)z_H = 0. \tag{7}$$

Although each person must sign up with just one insurer (exclusivity), there is competition among alternative potential insurers for clients. Therefore each insurer will choose (z_L, z_H) to maximize profit subject to providing the competitive level of expected utility u_X, and in equilibrium the profit will equal zero. It is equivalent and simpler to regard the choice of (z_L, z_H) as maximizing u_x subject to the zero profit constraint (7). The insurers are also aware of the moral hazard, i.e. the dependence of e on (z_L, z_H) via (6). Therefore we can formally regard them as choosing e as well, subject to (6) treated as a constraint on the optimization problem. The Lagrangian for the problem is

$$\mathcal{L} = (1 - \pi(e))V(I_L, p) + \pi(e)V(I_H, p) - e$$
$$- \lambda_X[(1 - \pi(e))z_L + \pi(e)z_H] + \mu\pi'(e)[V(I_H, p) - V(I_L, p)]. \tag{8}$$

The first-order conditions are

$$(1 - \pi(e))[V_I(I_L, p) - \lambda_X] - \mu\pi'(e)V_I(I_L, p) = 0, \tag{9}$$

$$\pi(e)[V_I(I_H, p) - \lambda_X] + \mu\pi'(e)V_I(I_H, p) = 0, \tag{10}$$

$$\lambda_X\pi'(e)(z_L - z_H) + \mu\pi''(e)[V(I_H, p) - V(I_L, p)] = 0. \tag{11}$$

The multiplier for the zero profit constraint is called λ_X because it is the marginal utility of a unit of sure income to an X-sector worker.

For readers unfamiliar with moral hazard problems, here is a brief characterization of the solution. First, we must have $\mu > 0$. To prove this, suppose $\mu \leqq 0$. Then (9) and (10) give

$$V_I(I_L, p) = \lambda_X/[1 - \mu\pi'(e)/(1 - \pi(e))] \leqq \lambda_X,$$

$$V_I(I_H, p) = \lambda_X/[1 + \mu\pi'(e)/\pi(e)] \geqq \lambda_X.$$

Then $V_I(I_H, p) \geqq V_I(I_L, p)$, so $I_H \leqq I_L$ and $V(I_H, p) \leqq V(I_L, p)$. Then (6) cannot hold.

With $\mu > 0$, we have $V_I(I_L, p) > \lambda_X > V_I(I_H, p)$. Then $I_L < I_H$, and insurance is incomplete. This represents the tradeoff between effort and insurance under moral hazard.

Now (11) can be written as

$$z_L - z_H = \frac{-\mu\pi''(e)}{\lambda_X\pi'(e)}[V(I_H, p) - V(I_L, p)] > 0.$$

Combining this with (7), we find $z_L > 0 > z_H$. Thus, some insurance is offered despite moral hazard. For a detailed discussion of these issues, see Shavell (1979).

Now we can complete the description of the equilibrium. In the safe sector each worker has disposable income

$$I_Y = w - t, \tag{12}$$

and utility

$$u_Y = V(I_Y, p). \tag{13}$$

Equilibrium of occupation choice gives

$$u_X = u_Y. \tag{14}$$

It remains to ensure the consistency of the tax policy. Let the consumption of the X-good by each Y-sector worker be c_Y, and that by each X-sector worker, with respectively low and high incomes, be c_L and c_H. In fact, by Roy's Identity,

$$c_i = -V_p(I_i, p)/V_I(I_i, p), \quad i = Y, L, H.$$

Then total lump-sum tax receipts equal the requirements of the grant or insurance policies in the risky sector, minus the safe sector's profits, minus the trade tax revenues. So

$$Nt = -[F(M) - MF'(M)] + (N - M)[(1 - \pi(e))g_L + \pi(e)g_H]$$

$$-(p - p^*)\{(N - M)[(1 - \pi(e))(c_L - x_L) + \pi(e)(c_H - x_H)] + Mc_Y\}. \tag{15}$$

Given the data N, x_L, x_H, and the policies p, g_L, g_H, we have to determine M, w, z_L, z_H, I_L, I_H, I_Y, e, u_X, μ, λ_X and t. We have the right number of equations (thirteen) in (1), (3)–(7) and (9)–(15). For my purpose, equilibrium is determinate.

In Shavell's (1979) model of moral hazard, the competitive equilibrium with exclusive insurance is constrained Pareto optimal. That is, a social planner facing the same information constraint – unobservable effort levels – cannot improve upon the market equilibrium. The simple reason is that the risky activity is the whole economy, and therefore a competitive insurer and the social planner must solve exactly the same constrained optimization problem. Here we have another sector, and labor and funds can be moved between them. The question is whether trade restrictions or public insurance policies can do so in a beneficial way. The answer is no; the competitive equilibrium with exclusive insurance remains constrained Pareto optimal.

In the text I shall develop this argument in an intuitive way; appendix A contains the formal proof. To keep the exposition simple, consider just one policy measure, namely a reward for undertaking the risky activity. Suppose each of the $(N - M)$ workers in the X sector is given a small lump sum Δg. This induces migration to that sector. As M falls, the Y sector wage rises, which eventually re-equates the utilities from working in the two sectors. But there are further effects. To finance the grant, we must raise the lump-sum tax on all workers by $\Delta g \cdot (N - M)/N$. Furthermore, as the Y sector wage rises by Δw, the profits there change downward by $\Delta \Pi < 0$, and each worker bears his $(1/N)$th share of that. Bearing in mind all these effects, we have

$$\Delta u_{X} = \lambda_{X}[\Delta g - \Delta g \cdot (N - M)/N + \Delta \Pi/N] \tag{16}$$

and

$$\Delta u_{Y} = \lambda_{Y}[\Delta w - \Delta g \cdot (N - M)/N + \Delta \Pi/N], \tag{17}$$

where λ_{Y} is the sure marginal utility of income in the Y sector. In the new equilibrium, we have $\Delta u_{X} = \Delta u_{Y}$. Let $K = \lambda_{X}/\lambda_{Y}$, and note that $\Delta \Pi = - M \Delta w$ by Hotelling's Lemma. Then (16) and (17) give

$$K[\Delta g \cdot M/N - \Delta w \cdot M/N] = \Delta w \cdot (1 - M/N) - \Delta g \cdot (1 - M/N).$$

This simplifies to $\Delta w = \Delta g$, and then (16) and (17) become $\Delta u_{X} = \Delta u_{Y} = 0$. Thus, the initial passive policy satisfies the first-order conditions for social optimality. Trade policy is similarly powerless.

As usual in optimal taxation theory, e.g. Diamond and Mirrlees (1971), second-order conditions are difficult to verify. However, we can be confident that we have found a maximum by observing that some special cases of the model are familiar ones where the market equilibrium is known to be Pareto optimal. Most simply, if moral hazard is vanishingly small, so $\pi(e)$ is flat at its equilibrium value, then we have a standard Arrow–Debreu model. More importantly, if the safe sector is vanishingly small, we have Shavell's (1979) model where the equilibrium is evidently constrained Pareto optimal, as we saw above.

The intuitive argument above showed how the policy favoring the risky sector was defeated by the induced migration. This bears out the general belief that if the government supports risky activities, too much risk will be taken. The principle should have wider validity than the trade context studied here.

3. Individual risk, unconstrained insurance

When an individual's total insurance coverage cannot be observed, exclusivity cannot be enforced. People are tempted to expand coverage, and that in turn reduces their incentive to make effort. In this case, if a competitive equilibrium exists, it must have zero effort and complete insurance. To see this, suppose the equilibrium level of each individual's effort is e. With perfect competition, $\pi(e)/(1 - \pi(e))$ units of low-state income can be purchased by giving up each unit of high-state income. If the individual purchases z such contracts,

$$I_{L} = px_{L} + g_{L} - t + z\pi(e)/(1 - \pi(e)), \tag{18}$$

$$I_H = px_H + g_H - t - z. \tag{19}$$

Then z is chosen to maximize

$$(1 - \pi(e))V(I_L, p) + \pi(e)V(I_H, p) - e.$$

This gives the first-order condition:

$$V_I(I_L, p) = V_I(I_H, p), \tag{20}$$

which implies $I_L = I_H$ (complete insurance) and $V(I_L, p) = V(I_H, p)$. Then the choice of effort can only be optimal if $e = 0$. Arnott and Stiglitz (1986) call this the normal case in absence of exclusivity.

Suppose the economy is in such an equilibrium. What role can our policy instruments p, g_L and g_H play? None of them can alter the zero level of effort or the completeness of insurance: those properties were derived above for arbitrary p, g_L and g_H. Thus, we have in effect an economy with effort level fixed at zero, a fixed accident probability $\pi(0)$, no moral hazard, and full insurance. Standard theorems ensure that the competitive equilibrium is Pareto optimal (conditional on the effort level), and the policies can do no better. Interested readers can derive the result formally by methods similar to those of section 2.

What this situation needs is a different kind of policy – a tax at a suitably chosen rate τ on the purchase of insurance. Then giving up a unit of high-state income will get you only $(1 - \tau)\pi(e)/(1 - \pi(e))$ units of low-state income. People will purchase incomplete insurance, and make some effort. See Arnott and Stiglitz (1986) for a full discussion. Of course to tax insurance purchase the government must observe it, and then a simpler policy may be to enforce exclusivity.

The outcome with zero effort and full insurance may be the most natural one in the absence of exclusivity, but it is not the only one. Moral hazard contributes a non-convexity to indifference curves in a state-contingent consumption space. In section 2, exclusivity permitted the use of quantity-constrained insurance, i.e. non-linear budget sets, that overcame the problem. Now, in the absence of exclusivity, that cannot be done, and a competitive equilibrium may not exist. Some new possibilities arise. Stiglitz (1983) discusses them in detail. There may be an equilibrium involving randomized insurance contracts. There may be a non-market-clearing equilibrium with a sticky benefit–premium ratio. Finally, there may be a reactive or so-phisticated conjecture equilibrium with no insurance. Each insurer is tempted to offer a contract with a small coverage that will be profitable on its own. But each realizes that when others act similarly, the resulting coverage will be much greater, the effort level will be much lower, the probability of the bad state will be much higher, and the profit on his contract will become negative.

This last possibility is not a Nash equilibrium, and therefore its intellectual foundation is shaky. But it is the only case where moral hazard is the cause of a complete cessation of private insurance, which was the staring point of the ad hoc incomplete-markets models of Newbery and Stiglitz (1984) and Eaton and Grossman (1985). Therefore I shall examine it in some detail to see how trade and tax-transfer policies by themselves can cope with moral hazard.

The model is the same as that of section 2, except of course z_L and z_H are fixed ar zero, λ_X and μ are irrelevant, and correspondingly we drop the four equations (7) and (9)–(11).

With private markets absent, some government insurance (g_L, g_H) can be provided on an exclusive basis. If private insurance remains absent or can be prohibited, the government can trivially implement the constrained Pareto-optimal level of public insurance. More interesting is the role of trade policy. Once again, I shall offer an informal reasoning here, relegating the details to appendix B.

Suppose the domestic price is changed by Δp. Since an X-sector worker who realizes the high state produces x_H and consumes c_H, his real income rises by $(x_H - c_H)\,\Delta p$. Similarly, we have $(x_L - c_L)\,\Delta p$ for an unlucky X-sector worker. The offsetting effect on the per capita tax for everyone is a weighted average of the two, say

$$\gamma_H(x_H - c_H)\,\Delta p + \gamma_L(x_L - c_L)\,\Delta p.$$

where γ_H and γ_L are positive and sum to one.

The purpose of insurance is to shift some income from the high state to the low state. Therefore we want

$$(x_L - c_L)\,\Delta p - [\gamma_H(x_H - c_H)\,\Delta p + \gamma_L(x_L - c_L)\,\Delta p] > 0$$

and

$$(x_H - c_H)\,\Delta p - [\gamma_H(x_H - c_H)\,\Delta p + \gamma_L(x_L - c_L)\,\Delta p] < 0.$$

These simplify to

$$[(x_L - c_L) - (x_H - c_H)]\,\Delta p > 0. \tag{21}$$

To see what (21) implies for trade policy, note the budget constraint for each state $i = L, H$:

$$pc_i + d_i = px_i - t,$$

where d_i is the consumption of the Y-good. Then $(x_i - c_i) = (d_i + t)/p$, and (21) becomes:

$$(d_L - d_H) \Delta p > 0. \tag{21'}$$

If the safe sector good is normal in demand, $d_L < d_H$ and so (21') requires $\Delta p < 0$. The domestic price of the risky good should be kept below its world price. Therefore in this model, trade policy provides insurance by being *counter*-protective. This may sound paradoxical. The point is that the policy is in the first instance taking away more real income from those who realize high output than from those who get low output. The average is then returned to everyone by means of the lump-sum transfer. The net result is that those in the bad state are net gainers and those in the good state are net losers; this is how insurance is generated.

Other means of collecting or disbursing revenues will have different consequences. In a similar context, but without moral hazard, Grossman (1984) uses a proportional income tax and finds that free trade is the constrained optimum, provided preferences are homothetic. Now moral hazard has no first-order effect on utility because of the Envelope Theorem, and on government revenue because the initial point has $(p - p^*)$, g_L and g_H all zero. Therefore Grossman's result would continue to hold if proportional taxes were used in my model.

If the marginal shift of the tax schedule that is used for collecting or disturbing incremental revenues is progressive (a feature that can be quite independent of the progressivity of the schedule for fixed revenue requirements), then a small positive tariff will be beneficial. My conclusion from all this is that the role of tariffs as second-best insurance schemes, when risk-sharing markets shut down because of moral hazard, is ambiguous at best, and depends on an accidental conjunction between trade policy and income taxation. It is much simpler to find and implement a welfare-improving public insurance scheme.

4. Aggregate risk, exclusive insurance

In this section I reimpose the exclusivity requirement on insurance, but introduce some systematic or aggregate risk. It would not make sense to remove individual risk entirely. For suppose one person's output is a function of his own effort e and an economy-wide random variable θ. Then relative outputs across people convey precise information about their relative effort levels. The full-information first best can be achieved, or closely approximated, by payments schemes based on relative performance. If moral hazard is to have some role, some individual risk is essential.

I shall therefore suppose that for each X-sector worker the probability π of high output is a function of his effort e and an economy-wide random variable θ, and that for each given θ, these events are independent across workers. Let $\phi(\theta)$ be the density function of θ. (There is a fully equivalent model with discrete values θ_i and probabilities ϕ_i. Also, a slight change of notation allows us to treat the world price p^* itself as a systematic random variable; the results below are unaffected.)

Even in this setting, relative performance schemes have some scope. In my model, it is possible to do even better by conditioning everything on θ, as we shall see in a moment. Hart (1983) constructs a model where a competitive market itself works like a relative performance scheme. That cannot happen here because the economy is small and p is fixed.

Remember that my ground-rule of fairness requires that we give the markets for risk-sharing their full role. Now the large numbers assumption ensures that, conditional on θ, the output per worker in the X-sector is riskless and is given by

$$\bar{x}(\theta) = (1 - \pi(e, \theta))x_{L} + \pi(e, \theta)x_{H}. \tag{22}$$

Since the equilibrium value of e can be computed, and output can be observed ex post, we can infer θ ex post. Therefore all ex ante contracts and policies can be conditioned on it. So we can have a trade policy defined by a function $p(\theta)$, and transfer or insurance policies $g_{L}(\theta)$, $g_{H}(\theta)$, with the associated lump-sum tax $t(\theta)$. Exclusive private insurance contracts can be similar functions $z_{L}(\theta), z_{H}(\theta)$.

People can also trade contingent claims to purchasing power, or Arrow's securities. I shall write $q(\theta)\phi(\theta)$ for the price of a claim to a unit of the numéraire if θ occurs. This is a harmless renaming that simplifies the notation by making budget constraints expectations with respect to θ. The equilibrium profile $q(\theta)$ can be found from the conditions of market-clearing for claims for each θ; fortunately we do not need the explicit solutions.

A new feature is that with p and t dependent on θ, the Y-sector workers are also exposed to risk. They will therefore participate in the contingent claims market. Suppose their purchases are $b_{Y}(\theta)$. Then

$$I_{Y}(\theta) = w + b_{Y}(\theta) - t(\theta). \tag{23}$$

Suppose the wage w, although sure, is paid ex post. (The alternative assumption is a mere algebraic reformulation with identical results.) Then the budget constraint while trading in contingent claims is

$$\int q(\theta)\phi(\theta)b_{Y}(\theta) \, d\theta = 0.$$

I shall write this more compactly as

$$E_\theta[q(\theta)b_Y(\theta)] = 0, \tag{24}$$

where E_θ denotes expectation with respect to θ. The maximand is

$$u_Y = E_\theta[V(I_Y(\theta), p(\theta))]. \tag{25}$$

This problem has the first-order conditions:

$$V_I(I_Y(\theta), p(\theta)) = \lambda_Y q(\theta), \tag{26}$$

for all θ. With no moral hazard in this sector, we have first-best risk allocation.

In the X-sector, we can likewise write:

$$I_L(\theta) = p(\theta)x_L + g_L(\theta) + z_L(\theta) + b_X(\theta) - t(\theta), \tag{27}$$

$$I_H(\theta) = p(\theta)x_H + g_H(\theta) + z_H(\theta) + b_X(\theta) - t(\theta), \tag{28}$$

and

$$u_X = E_\theta[(1 - \pi(e, \theta)) V(I_L(\theta), p(\theta)) + \pi(e, \theta)V(I_H(\theta), p(\theta)) - e]. \tag{29}$$

Begin with the optimum choice of e, given all the other things. The first-order condition is

$$E_\theta[\pi_e(e, \theta)[V(I_H(\theta), p(\theta)) - V(I_L(\theta), p(\theta))]] = 1. \tag{30}$$

Observe that $b_X(\theta)$ has an effect on e, that is to say a moral hazard aspect, just as do $z_L(\theta)$ and $z_H(\theta)$. Therefore we should apply exclusivity to all three, thus requiring each X-sector worker to get all his insurance for aggregate *and* individual risk from the same insurer. [An equivalent model can be had if $b_X(\theta)$ must be committed before $z_L(\theta)$ and $z_H(\theta)$ are determined.]

The insurer's zero-profit constraint is

$$E_\theta\{[(1 - \pi(e, \theta))z_L(\theta) + \pi(e, \theta)z_H(\theta) + b_X(\theta)]q(\theta)\} = 0. \tag{31}$$

He chooses $z_L(\theta)$, $z_H(\theta)$ and $b_X(\theta)$ for all θ to maximize (29) subject to (30) and (31). The first-order conditions for $z_L(\theta)$ and $z_H(\theta)$, respectively, are

$$(1 - \pi(e, \theta) - \mu\pi_e(e, \theta))V_I(I_L(\theta), p(\theta)) - \lambda_X(1 - \pi(e, \theta))q(\theta) = 0, \tag{32}$$

$$(\pi(e, \theta) + \mu\pi_e(e, \theta))V_I(I_H(\theta), p(\theta)) - \lambda_X\pi(e, \theta)q(\theta) = 0. \tag{33}$$

The condition for $b_X(\theta)$ is just the sum of these two and therefore redundant; this is obvious since the insurer could always dispense with $b_X(\theta)$ as such and just add it on to each of $z_L(\theta), z_H(\theta)$. The condition for e is

$$E_\theta\{\mu\pi_{ee}(e, \theta)[V(I_H(\theta), p(\theta)) - V(I_L(\theta), p(\theta))]$$

$$+ \lambda_X\pi_e(e, \theta)[z_L(\theta) - z_H(\theta)]\} = 0. \qquad (34)$$

The remaining equilibrium conditions are: the requirement of indifference in occupation choice,

$$u_X = u_Y, \qquad (35)$$

and the state-by-state government budget balance condition,

$$Nt(\theta) = -[F(M) - MF'(M)]$$

$$+ (N - M)[(1 - \pi(e, \theta))g_L(\theta) + \pi(e, \theta)g_H(\theta)]$$

$$- (p(\theta) - p^*)[(N - M)[(1 - \pi(e, \theta))(c_L(\theta) - x_L)$$

$$+ \pi(e, \theta)(c_H(\theta) - x_H)] + Mc_Y(\theta)]. \qquad (36)$$

Policy changes in this model consist of shifts of the whole functions $p(\theta)$, etc. Although this is an added degree of complexity, the structure of the model is very similar to the case of individual risk in section 2. Therefore it is no surprise that trade and tax-transfer policies are once again incapable of improving upon the market equilibrium. Even with systematic risk and moral hazard, competitive and exclusive insurance and state-contingent claims achieve a constrained Pareto optimum. The details are in appendix C; the intuition is similar to that developed in section 2.

I hope that cases with aggregate risk and non-exclusive insurance may now be left to the reader. If equilibrium has zero effort, full insurance for the individual risk and first-best allocation of aggregate risk, then trade and transfer policies are powerless. If the market shuts down, trade policies have the same kind of complex role, and publicly provided insurance a simpler role, as in section 3.

5. Concluding comments

These results should not create the impression that moral hazard never matters. We know from the works of Stiglitz and his co-authors cited throughout the paper that it does. There are important externalities and nonconvexities associated with moral hazard. Complicating my model will introduce some of them.

(1) If there are several risky activities with moral hazard, there can be externalities through their interaction, although such effects can be internalized by extending the exclusivity requirement.

(2) If the economy is large, producer prices in free trade are endogenous. Changes in them affect producers' profits which become consumers' incomes; this alters the incentives to make efforts to reduce the risk. The standard monopoly optimum tariff can handle that.

(3) If there is distorting commodity taxation for some other reason such as income redistribution or the provision of public goods, then there can be similar income effects via the tax revenue.

(4) If an individual's probability of success is a function not only of his unobservable effort, but also of his anonymous purchase of a commodity, then welfare could be increased by subsidizing the consumption of that commodity. However, this is not a case for tariffs, i.e. for taxing domestic production and imports of the commodity differently.

(5) I have not considered non-market-clearing equilibria. These and other problems will enlarge the scope for beneficial policy interventions, although I believe the role of trade policy will remain complex and ambiguous.

All these limitations are significant, and indicate the need for more research. But I think the paper points out even more serious limitations of previous work on trade policy under uncertainty. Using models very similar or identical to those of the earlier authors, but taking explicit account of one of the causes of incomplete risk-sharing markets on which they tacitly rely, I have found that their ad hoc assumption of missing insurance markets does indeed drive their activist policy conclusions. This is yet another instance of the need for a 'level playing field' when economists compare the performance of markets and governments.

Appendix A

The model considered in this appendix is that of section 2, with individual risk and exclusive insurance. The subject is the formal analysis of the effects of the policies represented by p, g_L and g_H on the equilibrium. Starting from an initial position where none of these policies is used, i.e. $p = p^*$ and $g_L = g_H = 0$, consider a small change Δp, Δg_L and Δg_H. This will in general change all the magnitudes, e.g. M by ΔM, t by Δt, etc.

First, focus on the problem of devising the equilibrium insurance contract. This takes p, g_L, g_H and t as parametric, and chooses z_L, z_H and e to maximize u_X as given by (5), subject to the constraints (6) and (7). When the parameters change, the first order change in u_X is found using the Envelope Theorem. We calculate the *partial* effect of the parameters on the Lagrangian

$\mathscr{L}$ defined in (8), i.e. the effect holding the choice variables and the multipliers unchanged, and then evaluate the result at the optimum. Therefore we have

$$\Delta u_X = (1 - \pi(e) - \mu\pi'(e))[V_I(I_L, p)(x_L \Delta p + \Delta g_L - \Delta t) + V_p(I_L, p) \Delta p]$$

$$+ (\pi(e) + \mu\pi'(e))[V_I(I_H, p)(x_H \Delta p + \Delta g_H - \Delta t) + V_p(I_H, p) \Delta p]$$

$$= (1 - \pi(e) - \mu\pi'(e))V_I(I_L, p)[(x_L - c_L) \Delta_p + \Delta g_L - \Delta t]$$

$$+ (\pi(e) + \mu\pi'(e))V_I(I_H, p)[(x_H - c_H) \Delta p + \Delta g_H - \Delta t]$$

$$= \lambda_X\{(1 - \pi(e))[(x_L - c_L) \Delta p + \Delta g_L]$$

$$+ \pi(e)[(x_H - c_H) \Delta p + \Delta g_H] - \Delta t\}. \tag{A.1}$$

The first step follows from the Envelope Theorem, the second from Roy's Identity, and the third from the first-order conditions (9) and (10). Note that if we conduct the thought-experiment of giving a sure dollar to an X-sector worker, i.e. formally set $\Delta g_H = \Delta g_L = 1$ and $\Delta p = \Delta t = 0$, we get $\Delta u_X = \lambda_X$. This proves that λ_X is the marginal utility of sure income in the X-sector.

Turning to the Y-sector, we have

$$\Delta u_Y = V_I(I_Y, p)(\Delta w - \Delta t) + V_p(I_Y, p) \Delta p$$

$$= \lambda_Y(F''(M) \Delta M - \Delta t - c_Y \Delta p). \tag{A.2}$$

Now we can set $\Delta u_X = \Delta u_Y$. Define K as λ_X/λ_Y, the ratio of marginal utilities in the two sectors. Then we find

$$F''(M) \Delta M = \Delta t + c_Y \Delta p + K\{(1 - \pi(e))[(x_L - c_L) \Delta p + \Delta g_L]$$

$$+ \pi(e)[(x_H - c_H) \Delta p + \Delta g_H] - \Delta t\}. \tag{A.3}$$

Finally, differentiating the government's budget constraint around the initial point of $g_L = g_H = 0, p = p^*$, we have

$$N \Delta t = M F''(M) \Delta M + (N - M)[(1 - \pi(e)) \Delta g_L + \pi(e) \Delta g_H]$$

$$- \Delta p\{(N - M)[(1 - \pi(e))(c_L - x_L) + \pi(e)(c_H - x_H)] + M c_Y\}. \tag{A.4}$$

Substituting for $F''(M) \Delta M$ from (A.3) and simplifying yields:

$$\Delta t = (1 - \pi(e)) \Delta g_L + \pi(e) \Delta g_H$$

$$+ [(1 - \pi(e))(x_L - c_L) + \pi(e)(x_H - c_H)] \Delta p. \qquad (A.5)$$

Then (A.1) becomes $\Delta u_X = 0$, and so of course $\Delta u_Y = 0$. Workers' utilities are stationary with respect to small policy changes around the initial passive position.

Appendix B

Here we have individual risk, but insurance is not constrained by exclusivity. Begin with the passive policy and consider small changes.

Differentiating the expression (5) for u_X, and remembering that e is chosen to maximize u_X (the Envelope Theorem again), we have

$$\Delta u_X = (1 - \pi(e)) [V_I(I_L, p)(x_L \Delta p + \Delta g_L - \Delta t) + V_p(I_L, p) \Delta p]$$

$$+ \pi(e) [V_I(I_H, p)(x_H \Delta p + \Delta g_H - \Delta t) + V_p(I_H, p) \Delta p]$$

$$= (1 - \pi(e)) \lambda_L [(x_L - c_L) \Delta p + \Delta g_L - \Delta t]$$

$$+ \pi(e) \lambda_H [(x_H - c_H) \Delta p + \Delta g_H - \Delta t], \qquad (B.1)$$

where I have defined

$$\lambda_L = V_I(I_L, p), \qquad \lambda_H = V_I(I_H, p) \qquad (B.2)$$

as the marginal utilities of contingent income in the two states. With $I_L < I_H$, we have $\lambda_L > \lambda_H$. The marginal utility of sure income is

$$\lambda_X = (1 - \pi(e)) \lambda_L + \pi(e) \lambda_H. \qquad (B.3)$$

For the Y-sector workers, we have (A.2), namely

$$\Delta u_Y = \lambda_Y (F''(M) \Delta M - \Delta t - c_Y \Delta p) \qquad (B.4)$$

as before. Now we set $\Delta u_X = \Delta u_Y$ and simplify. Writing $K_L = \lambda_L / \lambda_Y$ and $K_H = \lambda_H / \lambda_Y$, we find

$$F''(M)\,\Delta M = \Delta t + c_Y\,\Delta p$$

$$+\,[K_L(1-\pi(e))(x_L-c_L)+K_H\pi(e)(x_H-c_H)]\,\Delta p$$

$$+\,[K_L(1-\pi(e))\,\Delta g_L + K_H\pi(e)\,\Delta gH]$$

$$-\,[K_L(1-\pi(e))+K_H\pi(e)]\,\Delta t. \tag{B.5}$$

Differentiating the government's budget constraint gives us the same equation (A.4) as before. Using (B.5) in it, and collecting terms, gives:

$$[N-M+MK_L(1-\pi(e))+MK_H\pi(e)]\,\Delta t$$

$$=[(1-\pi(e))(N-M+MK_L)(x_L-c_L)$$

$$+\,\pi(e)(N-M+MK_H)(x_H-c_H)]\,\Delta p$$

$$+\,(1-\pi(e))(N-M+MK_L)\,\Delta g_L$$

$$+\,\pi(e)(N-M+MK_H)\,\Delta g_H. \tag{B.6}$$

This can be written in a more transparent form as

$$\Delta t = \gamma_L[(x_L-c_L)\,\Delta p+\Delta g_L]+\gamma_H[(x_H-c_H)\,\Delta p+\Delta g_H], \tag{B.7}$$

where the weights γ_L and γ_H are readily defined by reference to (B.6), and add up to unity.

Finally, combining (B.1) and (B.6), we find that, leaving out some positive constants,

$$\Delta u_X \sim (\lambda_L-\lambda_H)\{[(x_L-c_L)-(x_H-c_H)]\,\Delta p+\Delta g_L-\Delta g_H\}. \tag{B.8}$$

With $\lambda_L>\lambda_H$, we see that utility *can* be increased by suitable policies that start from the passive stance of $p=p^*$ and $g_L=g_H=0$. The general principle is that it is desirable to provide *some* insurance despite the moral hazard. Thus, tax-transfer policies that have $\Delta g_L>0$ and/or $\Delta g_H<0$ can increase welfare. Note that if the latter is used on its own, we have $\Delta t=\gamma_H\,\Delta g_H<0$, so

$$\Delta I_L = -\gamma_H\,\Delta g_H>0,$$

$$\Delta I_H = (1-\gamma_H)\,\Delta g_H<0.$$

That is how income is transferred in the desirable direction by such a policy.

What about the role of tariffs as insurance? The desirable direction of change, from (B.8), is to make

$$[(x_L - c_L) - (x_H - c_H)] \Delta p > 0. \tag{B.9}$$

This can be understood in terms of the changes in the state-contingent *real* incomes, namely $(\Delta I_L - c_L \Delta p)$ and $(\Delta I_H - c_H \Delta p)$. When trade policy is on its own, using (B.7), we have

$$\Delta I_L - c_L \Delta p = \gamma_H [(x_L - c_L) - (x_H - c_H)] \Delta p,$$

$$\Delta I_H - c_H \Delta p = -\gamma_L [(x_L - c_L) - (x_H - c_H)] \Delta p.$$

Therefore income is shifted toward the worse state when (B.9) is satisfied.

Appendix C

Here we have some aggregate risk, but exclusive insurance. Start with passive trade and transfer policies, i.e. $p(\theta) = p^*$ and $g_L(\theta) = g_H(\theta) = 0$ for all θ, and consider a small change $\Delta p(\theta)$, $\Delta g_L(\theta)$ and $\Delta g_H(\theta)$. By these I mean shifts of the whole functions $p(\theta)$, etc. and *not* movements along them such as $p'(\theta) \Delta \theta$.

Calculation of the effects on utilities proceeds as in appendix A, complicated only slightly by the need to take expectations with respect to θ. Thus,

$$\Delta u_Y = E_\theta \{ V_I(I_Y(\theta), p(\theta)) [\Delta w - \Delta t(\theta)] + V_p(I_Y(\theta), p(\theta)) \Delta p(\theta) \}$$

$$= E_\theta \{ V_I(I_Y(\theta), p(\theta)) [\Delta w - \Delta t(\theta) - c_Y(\theta) \Delta p(\theta)] \}$$

$$= \lambda_Y E_\theta \{ q(\theta) [\Delta w - \Delta t(\theta) - c_Y(\theta) \Delta p(\theta)] \}$$

$$= \lambda_Y \{ \Delta w - E_\theta [q(\theta) \Delta t(\theta)] - E_\theta [c_Y(\theta) q(\theta) \Delta p(\theta)] \}. \tag{C.1}$$

The first step uses the Envelope Theorem, the second, Roy's Identity, and the third, the first-order condition (25). The last step uses the fact that $E_\theta q(\theta)$, being the price of a claim that pays a unit of the numéraire in every state, must equal one.

The expression for Δu_X gets far too lengthy. Therefore I shall omit the arguments θ, and indicate the points where V_I and V_p are evaluated simply by L and H as appropriate. Then similar steps give

$$\Delta u_X = E_\theta\{[1-\pi-\mu\pi_e][V_I(L)(x_L\,\Delta p+\Delta g_L-\Delta t)+V_p(L)\,\Delta p]$$

$$+(\pi+\mu\pi_e)[V_I(H)(x_H\,\Delta p+\Delta g_H-\Delta t)+V_p(H)\,\Delta p]\}$$

$$=E_\theta\{(1-\pi-\mu\pi_e)V_I(L)[(x_L-c_L)\Delta p+\Delta g_L-\Delta t]$$

$$+(\pi+\mu\pi_e)V_I(H)[(x_H-c_H)\,\Delta p+\Delta g_H-\Delta t]\}$$

$$=\lambda_X\,E_\theta\{(1-\pi)q[(x_L-c_L)\,\Delta p+\Delta g_L-\Delta t]$$

$$+\pi q[(x_L-c_L)\,\Delta p+\Delta g_L-\Delta t]\}$$

$$=\lambda_X\,E_\theta\{q[(1-\pi)(x_L-c_L)+\pi(x_H-c_H)]\,\Delta p$$

$$+q[(1-\pi)\,\Delta g_L+\pi\,\Delta g_H]-q\,\Delta t\}. \tag{C.2}$$

As before, define $K=\lambda_X/\lambda_Y$, set $\Delta u_X=\Delta u_Y$, and rearrange terms. This yields:

$$F''(M)\,\Delta M=E_\theta[q\,\Delta t]-E_\theta[c_Y\,\Delta p]$$

$$+K\,E_\theta\{q[(1-\pi)(x_L-c_L)+\pi(x_H-c_H)]\,\Delta p$$

$$+q[(1-\pi)\,\Delta g_L+\pi\,\Delta g_H]-q\,\Delta t\}. \tag{C.3}$$

Differentiation of (36) for fixed θ gives

$$N\,\Delta t=MF''(M)\,\Delta M+(N-M)[(1-\pi)\,\Delta g_L+\pi\,\Delta g_H]$$

$$-\Delta p[(N-M)[(1-\pi)(c_L-x_L)+\pi(c_H-x_H)+Mc_Y]],$$

where once again I have omitted the arguments θ or (e,θ). On multiplying by $q(\theta)$ and taking expectations,

$$N\,E_\theta[q\,\Delta t]=MF''(M)\,\Delta M+(N-M)\,E_\theta[q[(1-\pi)\,\Delta g_L+\pi\,\Delta g_H]]$$

$$+(N-M)\,E_\theta[q[(1-\pi)(x_L-c_L)+\pi(x_H-c_H)]\,\Delta p]$$

$$-M\,E_\theta[c_Y\,\Delta p]. \tag{C.4}$$

Finally, substitute for $F'''(M)\,\Delta M$ from (C.3) into (C.4) and simplify to get

$$E_\theta[q\,\Delta t] = E_\theta[q[(1-\pi)(x_L - c_L) + \pi(x_H - c_H)]\,\Delta p]$$

$$+ E_\theta[q[(1-\pi)\,\Delta g_L + \pi\Delta g_H]]. \qquad (C.5)$$

When we use (C.5) in expression (C.2) we find $\Delta u_X = 0$.

References

Arnott, Richard and Joseph Stiglitz, 1986, The welfare economics of moral hazard, Queen's University Discussion Paper no. 635.

Diamond, Peter and James Mirrlees, 1971, Optimal taxation and public production I–II, American Economic Review 61 (1) March and (2) June, 8–27, 261–278.

Eaton, Jonathan and Gene Grossman, 1985, Tariffs as insurance: Optimal commercial policy when domestic markets are incomplete, Canadian Journal of Economics 18 (2), May, 258–272.

Greenwald, Bruce and Joseph Stiglitz, 1986, Externalities in economies with imperfect information and incomplete markets, Quarterly Journal of Economics 101 (2), May, 229–264.

Grossman, Gene, 1984, International trade, foreign investment and the formation of the entrepreneurial class, American Economic Review 74 (4), Sept., 605–614.

Hart, Oliver, 1983, The market mechanism as an incentive scheme, Bell Journal of Economics 14 (2), Autumn, 366–382.

Hart, Oliver and Bengt Holstrom, 1986, The theory of contracts, in: Truman Bewley, ed., Advances in economic theory, 1985 (Cambridge University Press) forthcoming.

Newbery, David and Joseph Stiglitz, 1984, Pareto inferior trade, Review of Economic Studies 51 (1), Jan., 1–12.

Shavell, Steven, 1979, On moral hazard and insurance, Quarterly Journal of Economics 94 (4), Nov., 541–562.

Stiglitz, Joseph, 1983, Risk, incentives and insurance: The pure theory of moral hazard, Geneva Papers on Risk and Insurance 8, no. 26, Jan., 4–33.

Part VI
Real Foundations of International Macroeconomics

Part VI

[31]

INTERNAL AND EXTERNAL BALANCE:
THE ROLE OF PRICE AND EXPENDITURE EFFECTS

This paper[1] illustrates by means of variations on one simple diagram certain features of the relationship between internal and external balance. Its object is merely to indicate the intimate relationships between price and expenditure effects in reconciling full employment policy with balance of payments policy.

For the major part of the argument the terms of trade are assumed unaffected by domestic policies, such as devaluation or deflation. Secondary terms of trade effects caused by repercussions of domestic policies on other countries receive only brief consideration in the latter part of the paper.

This procedure may be justified on two grounds. The first is the simple methodological argument for breaking up a complex problem into its component parts. The second is more practical. Whatever may be the case in economies playing a major role in world trade, in a dependent economy such as Australia no great damage is done if secondary terms of trade effects are neglected. Variations in the terms of trade—although frequent and often disastrous—are determined almost exclusively by conditions abroad; while the effects of Australian policies on the terms of trade are generally thought to be small.[2] Therefore there is a case for treating the terms of trade as given—a fact to which we in Australia must adjust our policies—and taking full advantage of the very considerable simplications this allows in the analysis of our international trading problems.[3]

I

Divide total production and total expenditure into two categories: traded goods and non-traded goods. This distinction corresponds broadly to sheltered and unsheltered industries. Traded goods are those with prices determined on world markets. They consist of exportables, of which the surplus over home consumption is exported; and importables, of which the deficiency between consumption and home production is imported. Non-traded goods are those which do not enter into world trade; their prices are determined solely by internal costs and demand. It is assumed, quite unrealistically, that these two categories do not shade into each other.

The procedure of treating exportables and importables as a single class of good (traded goods) is quite legitimate so long as the terms of trade are unaffected by events inside Australia.[4] The reason is that

1. This paper owes much to T. W. Swan's "Longer Run Problems of the Balance of Payments" (A.N.Z.A.A.S. paper 1955). I am also indebted to W. M. Corden for valuable advice.
2. See J. E. Meade: "The Price Mechanism and the Australian Balance of Payments", *Economic Record*, No. 63 (November 1956), p. 248.
3. The proposition that changes in the terms of trade play a minor role in restoring balance of payments equilibrium has been argued *generally* by I. F. Pearce in a paper shortly to be published.
4. The formal assumption is a perfectly elastic world demand for exports, and a perfectly elastic world supply of imports.

any quantity of exportables may be exchanged for importables at the relative price determined by the given terms of trade. Therefore, since trade allows exportables to be transformed into importables, and vice versa, it is a matter of indifference so far as the balance of payments is concerned whether an increased production of traded goods is achieved by means of greater production of exportables or greater home production of importables.

From a different viewpoint, the device of treating exportables and importables as a single class of good is equivalent to regarding the home production of both as being sold on the world markets for foreign exchange (tariffs becoming export subsidies), and then using this foreign exchange to buy back the importables we have sold, the part of our exportables we wish to consume, and imports from other countries. In other words, home produced importables are treated as a special class of exportables: goods which could be sold on world markets, but in fact are not, for we should only have to buy them back.[5]

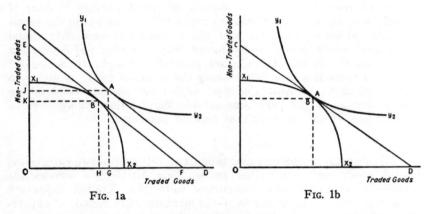

FIG. 1a   FIG. 1b

In Figure 1a the quantity[6] of traded goods is measured on the horizontal axis; and the quantity of non-traded goods on the vertical axis. The line CD represents total expenditure. OD is the amount of traded goods which could be purchased with this expenditure, given their prices; and OC is the amount of non-traded goods which could be purchased, given their prices. The slope of CD, therefore, represents the relative price of non-traded goods compared to traded goods. It corresponds broadly to an index of domestic prices compared to

5. This procedure effectively "collapses" the three-dimensional transformation function relating exportables, importables, and non-traded goods into a two-dimensional function. The assumption of constant terms of trade means that the three-dimensional function *after trade* contains a straight line in the plane relating importables and exportables—i.e. any combination of exportables and importables can be transformed into any other combination by trade. It is the existence of this straight line—which stems from our special assumption—that makes possible the reduction to two dimensions.

6. For a precise measure of quantity it is easiest to think of traded goods as measured in units of either importables or exportables, the one being translated into the other at the given terms of trade.

world prices. The indifference curve y_1y_2 represents consumers' preferences between traded and non-traded goods. The point of tangency, A, indicates the goods which will be demanded, given the level of expenditure and relative prices represented by CD.

So much for the demand side. On the supply side, x_1x_2 is the transformation curve which traces out all possible combinations of traded and non-traded goods which may be produced, given home factor supplies, technical knowledge, natural resources, etc.[7] EF is that special level of expenditure equal to full-employment production, given home and overseas prices. The slope of EF (subsequently known as the income line) is again determined by the relative prices of traded and non-traded goods. The point B represents the most profitable proportions for producing each type of good at these relative prices (marginal costs proportional to relative prices).

The situation portrayed in the diagram is one of external and internal disequilibrium. At the given level of expenditure and relative prices the community wishes to consume OG traded goods but produces only OH. There is consequently a balance of payments deficit.[8] Internally, OJ non-traded goods are demanded but only OK are produced and there is excess demand at home—a situation of overfull employment and a rising price level.

This particular diagram portrays only one of many possible disequilibrium positions. Depending upon the positions of A and B, the diagram may be generalized to trace Professor Swan's "four zones of economic unhappiness".[9] In general, if A is to the right of B, the situation is one of current account balance of payments deficit; and to the left, one of surplus. If A is above B there is home over-employment; and below B, under-employment. There are thus four zones—

A above and to the right of B: Balance of payments surplus and over-full employment (zone I).

A below and to the right of B: Balance of payment surplus and under-employment (zone II).

A above and to the left of B: Balance of payments deficit and over-full employment (zone III).

A below and to the left of B: Balance of payments deficit and under-employment (zone IV).

It is important to note that all such positions are ex ante disequilibrium positions in which the economy is always in the process

7. The given terms of trade are an element determining the shape and position of both the transformation and indifference curve. In the transformation curve they partly determine the proportions in which resources devoted to traded goods are used to produce importables and exportables, as well as the terms on which exportables may be transformed by trade into importables (or vice versa). Similarly, in the indifference curve they partly determine the ratio at which exportables and importables are translated into the combination appropriate to consumers' tastes at each point on the curve. The question is considered further in Section III below.

8. Balance of payments deficit = exports — imports = production less home consumption of exportables — consumption less home production of importables = production of importables plus exportables — consumption of importables plus exportables = production minus consumption of traded goods.

9. T. W. Swan, *op. cit.*, p. 3.

of movement: overseas reserves are either increasing or decreasing; there is a rising or falling domestic price level; and either over- or under-full employment. Only when A coincides with B is there a stable equilibrium where both internal and external balance is achieved. Figure 1b portrays such an equilibrium. At the "kissing-tangency point", where A and B coincide, the following conditions are realized: (i) expenditure coincides with full-employment income; (ii) the demand for traded goods equals production (i.e. external balance); (iii) the demand for non-traded goods equals production (i.e. internal balance); and the marginal rate of production substitution equals the marginal rate of consumers' substitution (marginal costs equal to selling price in each sector).

Such an equilibrium is a rare and delicate creature. The following section examines three common means by which a situation of internal and external equilibrium may be turned into one of disequilibrium: excess demand, a rise in world prices, and overseas capital inflow.

II

(a) *Excess demand*

Figure 2a traces out the internal and external consequences of excess demand. In the diagram the excess demand is represented by the expenditure line CD in excess of the income line EF. A is above and to the right of B—a situation of home over-employment and a balance of payments deficit.

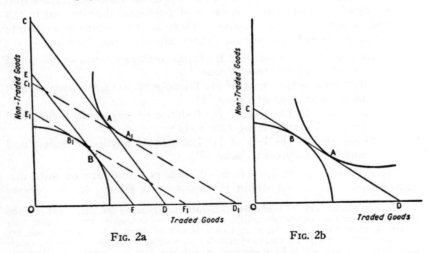

Fig. 2a   Fig. 2b

This is the first stage of excess demand where external and internal imbalance is caused wholly by expenditure effects. If this situation persists, the second stage begins as price effects come into operation. Internal excess demand raises home costs and prices, so increasing the price of non-traded goods relative to traded goods. In the diagram this is represented by the broken income and expenditure lines, E_1F_1 and

C_1D_1, which have a lesser slope compared to EF and CD. The demand and supply reactions to these second-stage price changes are as follows. On the supply side, increased prices of non-traded goods lead to an increase in their production at the expense of traded goods—a movement of resources away from production of exportables and importables to home goods. This is represented on the diagram by the movement to the left around the transformation curve from B to B_1 as EF becomes E_1F_1. The extent of this supply reaction depends upon the elasticity of substitution between traded and non-traded goods, represented by the curvature of the transformation curve.

On the demand side, the higher price of non-traded goods reduces demand for non-traded goods and adds to the demand for traded goods—a movement to the right around the indifference curve from A to A_1. Again the strength of this reaction depends upon the elasticity of demand substitution, represented by the curvature of the indifference curve.[10]

The upshot of these second-stage price effects is that production of non-traded goods increases as the demand for them declines; while the production of traded goods falls as demand increases. It is apparent, then, that after the second-stage price effects have come into operation there is no necessary reason why the original excess demand should continue to cause domestic over-employment, i.e. in terms of the diagram that A_1 should be above B_1. It is quite possible for the original excess demand to be wholly transferred via these price effects on to the balance of payments, leaving the economy in a state of internal balance (or even under-employment if A_1 falls below B_1). The reason is that the price effects of dearer non-traded goods—a greater supply and lesser demand—may offset the original expenditure effects. In other words, the part of the original excess demand which falls on home goods is met by an increasing supply and lesser demand as they become dearer, until eventually the whole excess demand falls on the balance of payments. Whether or not such a situation will occur depends, first, on the relevant elasticities—a combination of a high supply elasticity and a high demand elasticity for non-traded goods are favourable to its emergence—and, second, on the time allowed for the price effects to work themselves out.

On the other hand, excess demand must always lead to a balance of payments deficit in both the first and second stages; for here the price and expenditure effects work in the same direction so that there is no question of the one offsetting the other.

Whatever the final form of the disequilibrium, two steps are necessary to restore simultaneous internal and external balance. The first is to restore equality between expenditure and full employment equili-

10. Note that the case considered is one of "real" excess demand. The case of money excess demand may be considered by drawing the line C_1D_1 so that D and D_1 coincide—i.e. after the rise in prices of non-traded goods, fewer can be purchased with the same money expenditure. The consequent fall in real spending is reflected in the lower indifference curve tangential to this expenditure line. The monetary case differs from the real case only in that part of the original over-spending is eliminated parallel with second-stage price changes.

brium. This is the "absorption"[11] part of the problem. But this step alone is insufficient to restore equilibrium once the second-stage price effects have come into operation. An attempt to eliminate the balance of payments deficit by reducing expenditures will lead to domestic unemployment; while the maintenance of full employment involves a balance of payments deficit. This is illustrated by Figure 2b.

In Figure 2b expenditure equals full employment income. Even so the balance of payments is in deficit and there is home unemployment as the demand for non-traded goods falls short of production. The economy is still in disequilibrium because the proportions in which it is profitable to produce traded and non-traded goods do not match the proportions in which they are demanded. The only remedy is a change in relative prices such that home costs and prices fall relative to overseas costs and prices—i.e. the line CD must become steeper. A free economy could achieve this price adjustment by either one, or both, of two means:

(a) By internal deflation, which, by reducing money wages and other factor prices, lowers the prices of non-traded goods relative to traded goods. The production of non-traded goods is discouraged and the demand increased; while the production of traded goods is encouraged and the demand decreased. Eventually full equilibrium would be achieved (although total real expenditure would almost certainly fall below full employment levels in the process of this painful cost and price adjustment).

(b) If the exchange rate is free, the demand for foreign exchange exceeds supply, and the rate would fall. The prices of non-traded goods would fall relative to traded goods, and by a process similar to (a) internal and external balance would be achieved.[12]

A directed economy faces a similar choice: devaluation or deflation. But, whatever the method, home prices and costs must fall relative to overseas prices and costs before full employment can be reconciled with balance of payment equilibrium.

Further, as these changes in relative prices take place, additional cuts in expenditure are necessary to achieve the "kissing-tangency point" which denotes full equilibrium. For, at the new set of relative prices the expenditure line will exceed the income line. This reaction, in particular, emphasizes the intimate relation between expenditure and price effects in reconciling internal and external balance.

(b) *A rise in overseas prices*

This case, the converse of (a), is portrayed in Figure 3a. Increased overseas prices lead to higher prices of traded goods relative to non-

---

11. See S. S. Alexander: "Effects of Devaluation on a Trade Balance", *I.M.F. Staff Papers*, Vol. II (1951-2), pp. 263-78.

12. In the situation considered there is no question that a devaluation will not be effective; for one of the relevant elasticities—the world demand for exports—has been assumed infinite. See Meade: *The Theory of International Economic Policy*, Vol. 1, pp. 65-73.

traded goods; in the diagram this is represented by the greater slope
of CD_1 and E_1F_1 compared to the original price ratio CD. In the first
stage, the reactions are as follows. On the supply side, the higher relative price of traded goods tends to increase production at the expense
of non-traded goods—a movement around the transformation curve
from B to B_1. The demand price effects similarly lead to a movement
to the left around the indifference curve as non-traded goods are substituted for traded goods. The expenditure effects depend upon the
behaviour of domestic incomes. In the first stage when the level of

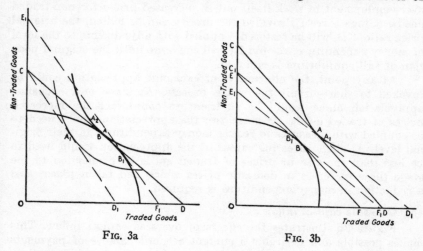

FIG. 3a   FIG. 3b

money expenditure is unchanged, the expenditure line is represented
by CD_1, i.e. after the rise in overseas prices the same level of money
expenditure will purchase only OD_1 traded goods. The fall in real
expenditure is represented by the shift to a lower indifference curve.

It is interesting to note that at this first stage A_1 could fall below
B_1. This implies that simply to maintain an unchanged level of money
expenditure may lead to home unemployment. This is because the
expenditure effects on the demand for non-traded goods of a reduced
real expenditure could more than offset the price effects as they became
relatively cheaper. In other words, if the demand elasticities are
greater than unity dearer importables and exportables may lead to
increased expenditure on such goods, so reducing the expenditure
available to purchase home goods. The implication is that maintenance
of domestic balance in the face of a rise in world prices requires a
rather more sophisticated policy than simply holding the line with
respect to expenditure. Depending on the relative strength of the income and price effects, money expenditure may need to increase or decrease simply to maintain home employment.

The second stage begins as money incomes rise under the stimulus
of increased export earnings and higher import prices. A_1 tends to
move upwards and to the right. Consider the case where money incomes
rise sufficiently to sustain the original level of real expenditure, i.e.

A_1 moves to A_2, the point on the original indifference curve tangential to a line parallel to CD_1. A_2 is above and to the left of B_1, a situation of domestic over-employment and balance of payments surplus. The balance of payments surplus is less than at stage one, but only because of increased expenditure which has also caused domestic over-spending and over-employment. Again the problem is that home costs and prices relative to world costs and prices make internal and external balance irreconcilable.

The situation could be rectified simply by allowing the domestic over-employment to work itself out in increased prices for non-traded goods. (Stage three.) Provided the process can be halted, the original price ratio, CD, will be restored. Coupled with adjustments to the level of money expenditure, A_2 and B_1 will converge until the original position of full equilibrium is restored.

At any point, the alternative of exchange appreciation could be invoked to short-circuit the whole process. At stage one, exchange appreciation alone would be sufficient to counteract the increased prices of traded goods. At stage two the appreciation would need to be coupled with measures to reduce money expenditures to their original level. At stage three the extent of the appreciation would need to be less than the rise in prices of traded goods in proportion to the stage three increases in domestic prices which had taken place; also a reduction in money expenditure is required.

(c) *Overseas capital inflow*

Figure 3b illustrates the effects of overseas capital inflow. This makes possible and desirable a current account balance of payments deficit. However, if expenditure is increased above the full employment income line EF to CD, domestic over-employment will result—A will fall above B—since at the current ratio between prices of non-traded and traded goods, a part of the extra expenditure will fall on non-traded goods. (Or, from a different viewpoint, overseas investment involves a component spent locally—on buildings, for example—which creates additional demand for non-traded goods.) If internal balance is to be maintained, structural changes are needed to transfer this additional domestic spending on to imports. Either one of two policies may be followed: the first is exchange appreciation; the second to allow domestic prices to increase. In either case the increased relative price of non-traded goods raises the demand for traded goods at the expense of non-traded goods—a movement from A to A_1—and increases production of non-traded goods relative to traded goods—a movement from B to B_1. These structural changes perform the desired task of transferring the whole of the extra expenditure on to the balance of payments, so enabling domestic balance to be reconciled with capital inflow.

III

The next step is to consider the effects of a change in the terms of trade, in the first instance an exogenous change originating overseas. For such analysis care is needed in the measurement of traded

234 THE ECONOMIC RECORD AUGUST

goods; in the following the convention has been adopted of measuring the quantity of traded goods in terms of units of importables, exportables being translated into importables at the ruling terms of trade.

In Figure 4a the unbroken transformation and indifference curves are tangential to CD and in contact, so that the economy is in a position of simultaneous internal and external balance. The terms of trade are parameters determining the shape and position of these curves, and the first step is to ask how they will respond to, say, an "adverse" movement of the terms of trade caused by a fall in the price of exportables.

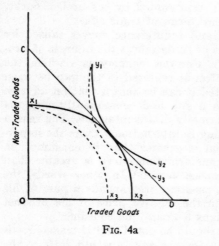

Fig. 4a

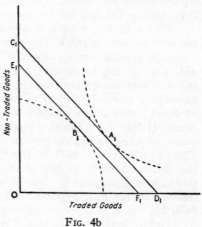

Fig. 4b

Consider first the transformation curve. At a given point on the curve certain resources are devoted to the production of traded goods. An adverse movement of the terms of trade implies that the exportables produced by these resources exchange in trade for fewer importables. Consequently the overall quantity of traded goods (measured in units of importables) produced by these resources declines, and the curve moves to the left. Two further considerations are relevant in determining this leftward movement. First, the extent is influenced by the proportions of traded and non-traded goods: greatest when all resources are devoted to traded goods; and zero when all resources are devoted to non-traded goods. Second, the movement will be partially offset by the reallocation of traded goods resources away from exportables towards home production of importables. This internal substitution within the category of traded goods, however, can only be a partial offset; for to produce importables in place of exportables implies that the comparative advantages of exportables are forgone.

The upshot is that an adverse movement of the terms of trade causes a contraction of the transformation curve to an extent determined by: (a) the extent of the adverse movement; (b) the elasticity of production substitution between importables and exportables; and (c) the proportions in which resources are devoted to traded and nontraded goods. In the diagram the new transformation curve is represented by the broken curve x_1x_3. This shift from x_1x_2 to x_1x_3 may be termed "the producers' terms of trade effect".

Similar considerations apply to the indifference curve. At a given point on the curve, fewer traded goods (measured in terms of importables) are needed to maintain the same level of "consumers' satisfaction"; for the exportables consumers require represent fewer importables. The indifference curve therefore also moves to the left. Again the extent of the shift is modified by consumers' substitution of exportables for importables, and is greater the higher the proportion of traded goods consumed. This shift, represented by the broken curve, y_1y_3, will be termed the "consumers' terms of trade effect".

Shifts in the transformation and indifference curves caused by the adverse movement of the terms of trade reflect the interest of producers and consumers respectively. For the economy as a whole, the national, or net, terms of trade effect is reflected in the gap between the new curves. As may be expected it can be shown that an adverse movement normally leads to such a gap and consequently that the national terms of trade effect is normally disadvantageous. The reason is simply that for a country engaging in international trade the importance of exportables in production is greater than in consumption. Thus the leftward shift in the transformation curve is greater than the leftward shift in the indifference curve.[13] In other words, the position is analogous to that of a producer who spends a part of his income on his own product. When the relative price of his product falls his loss qua producer outweighs his gain qua consumer.

Before leaving these shifts, it should be noted that if traded goods were measured in units of exportables, the curves would shift to the right, and the movement of the indifference curve would be more extensive than the movement of the transformation curve. However, the gap would remain, leaving the national terms of trade effect unchanged. This different behaviour is of no consequence. It is simply a reflection of the index-number problems which abound in this part of the analysis. It does, however, point to the care needed in making statements about real income and real expenditure in this context. (An adverse movement of the terms of trade causes the national income to fall when measured in terms of importables and to rise when measured in terms of exportables.)

From Figure 4a it is apparent that two steps are necessary to restore simultaneous internal and external balance. The first is a cut in expenditure equal to the national terms of trade effect. The second is a change in the relative prices of traded and non-traded goods consistent with the new point of tangency. There can be no certainty as to direction of the necessary adjustment; it depends in part on the shifts in the curves as they reflect demand and production substitution

13. There is the possibility of freak cases where the consumers' terms of trade effect outweighs the producers' effect. This would be a possibility where importables could easily be substituted for exportables on the production side, so that the producers' terms of trade effect was small.

between importables and exportables. However, when the terms of trade decline via a fall in export prices there is a relative presumption in favour of devaluation rather than appreciation. This is because the consumers' terms of trade effect encourages a shift of expenditure towards traded goods (since exportables are cheaper); while the producers' terms of trade effect encourages a movement away from the production of traded goods. From another viewpoint, a fall in export prices reduces the overall price of traded goods relative to non-traded goods; and this implies that the necessary price adjustment is rather more likely to be in the direction of devaluation than appreciation. This case is illustrated in Figure 4b. The broken curves are those of Figure 4a after the adverse movement of the terms of trade, and the slope of C_1D_1 and E_1F_1 equals the original price ratio CD. A_1 and B_1 are the points of tangency. It is apparent that, after the necessary reduction in spending (so that C_1D_1 coincides with E_1F_1), A_1 is likely to fall below and to the right of B_1. Hence to restore simultaneous internal and external balance requires an increase in the price of traded goods relative to non-traded goods.

When the terms of trade decline via a rise in import prices, the presumption is in favour of appreciation for reasons the reverse of those outlined above.

IV

While the analysis of terms of trade effect has been cast in terms of an exogenous movement, the same analysis can be applied to secondary terms of trade effects caused by domestic policies. In such cases, however, the analysis of terms of trade effects must be superimposed upon that of Section II. For example, consider a case such as that portrayed by Figure 1a—a situation of over-full employment and balance of payments deficit. The appropriate remedy is a cut in expenditure and devaluation or deflation. If application of these policies should lead to a secondary adverse movement of the terms of trade the analysis of Section III is also relevant. As has been shown, an adverse movement of the terms of trade also calls for a cut in spending, so that this part of the prescription is unaffected. Whether or not the prescription of devaluation is affected turns largely on how the secondary adverse movement of the terms of trade manifests itself—in falling export prices or rising import prices. The latter situation is unlikely for the reduced demand for imports—caused by lower expenditure and greater home production of importables—is more likely to lead to a fall in import prices. Section III shows that an adverse movement of the terms of trade reflected in lower export prices may require either devaluation or depreciation, although the presumption is in favour of devaluation. Consequently, the devaluation required to remove the original disequilibrium may need to be either more or less severe, with the presumption in favour of greater severity.

V

The analysis of the preceding sections is long-run in character; for it involves shifts in the structure of production which, in a world where factors of production are not freely mobile, take a long period to become fully effective. In the short-run, where the proportions in which traded and non-traded goods may be produced is more or less determined by the current structure of production, the transformation curve approaches a right angle. Consequently, reactions to changes in the ratio of home to overseas prices are initially only on the demand side; supply reactions, while set in motion, contribute little in the short run either to external or internal equilibrium. In such circumstances, there are three means of achieving immediate equilibrium in the balance of payments. Figures 5a, 5b and 5c illustrate the three alternatives.

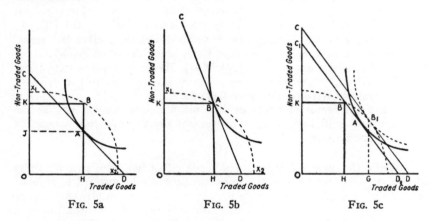

FIG. 5a   FIG. 5b   FIG. 5c

In each diagram, the broken curve is the long-run transformation curve, and the unbroken right angle KBH, the short-run transformation curve. Figure 5a illustrates the situation where the full burden of the short-run adjustment has been placed on the expenditure effect. The short-run transformation curve allows only the production of OH traded goods and OK non-traded goods to be consistent with internal and external balance. In order to reduce the demand for traded goods to OH, expenditure must be reduced to CD. However, at this level of expenditure the demand for non-traded goods OJ falls short of full employment output OK. Consequently there is domestic unemployment. This policy, then, is the familiar one of sacrificing full employment for the sake of balance of payments equilibrium.

Figure 5b illustrates the situation where the adjustment is wholly by means of relative prices. Expenditure equals full employment income; but compared to Figure 5a there has been a devaluation sufficiently great to lower the price of non-traded goods relative to traded goods to the point where the demand for each can be reconciled with the fixed short-run proportions in which they are produced. There are three objections to devaluation as a short-run remedy. First, the short-run elasticity of demand substitution between traded and non-traded goods may be so low that no conceivable exchange rate will equate demand with the fixed supply. In terms of the diagram, this is the case when the short-run indifference curve also approaches a right angle. Second, such a severe devaluation would imply that producers of traded goods are earning large excess profits while producers of non-traded goods are making losses (although covering prime costs). Even though this situation will not persist, in the short run there is considerable distortion—and, in Australian conditions, a shift in the distribution of income towards farmers. The final objection is that a situation of balance of payments surplus and home over-employment will appear as the supply reactions become effective; and this will require correction by an appreciation of the exchange rate to yield a price ratio consistent with long-run equilibrium.

Figure 5c illustrates the alternative of import licensing. The level of expenditure and the relative prices of traded and non-traded goods —represented by CD—are those consistent with a long-run equilibrium at B_1. However, in the short run production consists of OH traded goods and OK non-traded goods. Import restrictions, represented by the line BH, restrict the demand for traded goods to the level at which they are produced, so preventing a drain on overseas funds. There is consequently excess demand for imports equal to HG. To prevent this excess demand being transferred to non-traded goods and so causing domestic over-employment, expenditure must be reduced below its long-run equilibrium level to C_1D_1. Such a situation is only temporary; for the relative prices of non-traded and traded goods will induce a movement of resources into the production of traded goods—a movement along the long-run transformation curve to B_1. Provided expenditure is eventually restored to CD a full equilibrium without import restrictions will eventually be reached.

This is perhaps the only respectable argument for import-restrictions: they enable us to "buy time"[14] while long-run supply adjustments are set in motion, so avoiding the necessity for wasteful short-run measures to achieve external balance, such as unemployment or a severe devaluation which will require reversal. However, this argument for import restrictions is only valid if either one of two conditions is realized: (i) there is no long-term fundamental balance of payments disequilibrium and the short-term situation is wholly the product of volatile terms of trade; or (ii), if there is such a disequilibrium, home costs and prices are such as to encourage a sufficient shift of resources into traded goods, and expenditure is not in excess of full employment levels.

W. E. G. SALTER

Australian National University.

14. Swan, *op. cit.*, p. 4.

[32]

Journal of International Economics 4 (1974) 177–185. © North-Holland Publishing Company

TARIFFS AND NONTRADED GOODS

Rudiger DORNBUSCH*

University of Rochester, Rochester, N.Y. 14627, U.S.A.

1. Introduction

This paper discusses the effects of tariffs in a small country that consumes and produces three commodities: exportables, importables and nontraded goods. That subject has been previously studied in two altogether different ways. A general equilibrium approach in a well specified two-country model has been developed by McDougall (1970). An alternative treatment with a strong flavor of partial equilibrium analysis underlies or is implicit in a large body of applied work and policy discussions.[1] The latter approach is typically developed in terms of independent markets for imports and exports with an emphasis on nominal prices, the exchange rate and the trade balance and a de-emphasis on the role of nontraded goods.

The purpose of this paper is to reinterpret the latter approach as a special case of the general equilibrium model and to demonstrate that the analysis may be conveniently developed in the formal context of the pure theory of trade by reference to relative prices, the budget constraint and the conditions of equilibrium in the nontraded goods market. Such an analysis is useful because it highlights the crucial role of nontraded goods in the analysis and points out the implicit assumptions and theoretical basis that underlie the particular measures of the protective effects of tariffs, their welfare cost and the social cost of foreign exchange that have been developed in this model.

2. The model

The home country consumes and produces both exportables and importables as well as a nontraded good. The country is small so that the relative price of traded goods in the world market is taken as given. Income is assumed to equal

*I am indebted to J. Chipman, M. Corden, S. Engerman, R. Jones and M. Mussa for their helpful comments. I wish in particular to acknowledge the many suggestions I have received from J. Bhagwati.
[1]See, in particular, Corden (1971, ch. 5) who studies the small country case and Balassa (1971a, b) and Basevi (1968) who consider the case of variable terms of trade.

178   R. Dornbusch, Tariffs and nontraded goods

expenditure, the tariff proceeds are redistributed via lumpsum subsidies, and initial distortions are absent. The relative prices of both traded goods in terms of home goods are flexible so as to allow the nontraded goods market to clear.

The formal model may be reduced to the equilibrium condition in the home goods market. The excess demand for nontraded goods, N, is a function of the relative prices of importables and exportables in terms of home goods, P_m and P_e respectively, and real income measured in terms of home goods, I. In equilibrium the excess demand for nontraded goods will be zero:

$$N(P_m, P_e, I) = 0. \tag{1}$$

The domestic relative price of importables in terms of exportables, P_m/P_e, is determined by the given world terms of trade, P^*, and the tariff wedge, $T = (1+t)$:

$$P_m/P_e = P^*T. \tag{2}$$

To verify that equilibrium in the nontraded goods market implies trade balance equilibrium we consider the budget constraint which states that income equals expenditure or, equivalently, that the value of output plus the tariff proceeds equals expenditure and which may be written in the following manner:

$$P_e(E-P^*M)-N = 0, \tag{3}$$

where M and E denote imports and exports.[2] In this form the budget constraint states that the trade balance surplus, measured in terms of home goods, is identically equal to the excess demand for home goods. It follows that we may study the equilibrium properties of the model in terms of either the equilibrium trade balance or equilibrium in the home goods market.

3. The effects of a tariff

The effects of a tariff are derived by differentiating the market equilibrium condition in eq. (1) and noting that the redistribution of tariff proceeds implies that the imposition of a (small) tariff yields zero net income effects.[3] Define the compensated excess demand elasticities of home goods with respect to the

[2]Denoting production and consumption of the ith commodity by Q_i and C_i respectively we can write income, inclusive of tariff proceeds, as $I \equiv Q_n + P_m Q_m + P_e Q_e + (t/T)P_m M$ and expenditure as $C_n + P_m C_m + P_e C_e$. Imposing the equality of income and expenditure and using the definitions of M, E, and N as well as eq. (2) we arrive at the budget constraint as shown in eq. (3).

[3]Denoting the marginal propensity to spend on home goods by $\gamma \equiv \partial C_n/\partial I$ we can write the effect on demand of income changes and of the income effects implicit in price changes, as: $\gamma(dI - C_m dP_m - C_e dP_e)$. Noting that $dI = Q_m dP_m + Q_e dP_e + P_m M dt$, and substituting that expression we have the net income effect on demand for home goods as $\gamma(\hat{P}_e + \hat{T} - \hat{P}_m)P_m M = 0$.

relative prices of importables and exportables as θ_m and θ_e, respectively.[4] Using these elasticities and denoting a proportional change in a variable by a ^ we have:

$$\theta_m \hat{P}_m + \theta_e \hat{P}_e = 0. \tag{4}$$

Since terms of trade are given, the change in the domestic relative price of importables in terms of exportables is identically equal to the tariff:

$$\hat{P}_m - \hat{P}_e = \hat{T}. \tag{5}$$

Substituting this result in eq. (4), we can solve for the change in the equilibrium relative prices of traded goods in terms of nontraded goods:

$$\hat{P}_e = -\frac{\theta_m}{\theta_m + \theta_e} \hat{T}, \tag{6}$$

and

$$\hat{P}_m = \left[1 - \frac{\theta_m}{\theta_m + \theta_e}\right] \hat{T} = \frac{\theta_e}{\theta_m + \theta_e} \hat{T}. \tag{7}$$

The effects of a tariff as shown in eqs. (6) and (7) will depend on the substitution or complementarity relationship between home goods and the two traded goods. Consider first the case where the home good substitutes with each of the traded goods so that both the cross price elasticities of excess demand θ_m and θ_e are positive.[5] In that case the relative price of importables will increase in terms of home goods while the equilibrium relative price of exportables declines in terms of nontraded goods. Furthermore these price changes are less than proportionate to the tariff.

An interpretation of these results is offered in fig. 1. The schedule $N = 0$ shows the relative prices of exportables and importables in terms of home goods such that the nontraded goods market clears. The schedule is a blow-up of the neighborhood of the free trade equilibrium and is constructed by varying the tariff rate and redistributing the tariff proceeds so that along the schedule real income is constant. Accordingly the schedule is negatively sloped since it only reflects substitution effects. The free trade equilibrium is at point A where the ray OR,

---

[4]The compensated excess demand elasticities for nontraded goods are defined as follows: $\theta_m \equiv (\partial N/\partial P_m)(P_m/P_m M)$ and $\theta_e \equiv (\partial N/\partial P_e)(P_e/P_e E)$ and may be positive or negative depending on the substitution or complementarity relationship on the demand and supply side. Treating traded goods as a composite commodity we note that $\theta_m + \theta_e$ is the excess demand elasticity with respect to the relative price of traded goods and must be positive since traded goods as a group and home goods must be substitutes.

[5]We note that since we restrict only the sign of the *excess* demand elasticities this does not require that home goods and traded goods are substitutes both on the demand and supply side. We further note that the assumption that home goods substitute with both traded goods does not restrict the relationship between traded goods. They may be substitutes, complements or unrelated. The latter case is explored in detail in sect. 4 below.

the slope of which measures the relative price of traded goods, intersects the $N = 0$ schedule. At the free trade equilibrium the relative prices of traded goods in terms of home goods are P_m^0 and P_e^0 and associated with these prices, and indeed all points along $N = 0$, we have trade balance equilibrium.

The imposition of a tariff raises the domestic relative price of importables in terms of exportables by the amount of the tariff and accordingly rotates the ray OR to OR'. The new equilibrium will be at point D with relative prices of importables and exportables in terms of home goods P_m' and P_e' respectively. We note that the increase in the relative price of importables in terms of home goods, BA/AP_e^0, falls short of the tariff, CA/AP_e^0, and similarly for the decline in the relative price of exportables.

Fig. 1 is useful in interpreting the reference to exchange rate adjustments attendant upon a tariff that have been made in the literature.[6] For that purpose

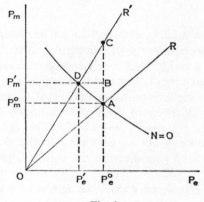

Fig. 1

we decompose the move from A to D into two steps. At the initial relative price of exportables in terms of home goods, P_e^0, the imposition of a tariff raises the price of importables in terms of both exportables and home goods by the amount of the tariff so that the economy would find itself at point C. At that point, however, there is an excess demand for nontraded goods and a matching trade balance surplus. To attain the equilibrium at point D home goods would have to appreciate in terms of *both* traded goods or, equivalently, the prices of both traded goods would have to fall equiproportionately in terms of home goods. It is the latter adjustment from point C to D that has been identified with an exchange rate appreciation, an identification that derives from the (implicit) assumption that the nominal prices of home goods are fixed so that the adjustment in relative prices has to be brought about by a decline in the nominal

[6]See, for example, Balassa (1971a, pp. 326–328) and (1971b, pp. 310–313), Basevi (1968, pp. 842–849) and Corden (1971, ch. 5).

prices of traded goods.[7] It is in this sense that the change in the equilibrium (relative) price of importables has been interpreted as the tariff, CA/AP^0_e, less the 'exchange rate appreciation' CB/AP^0_e.

Consider next the effects of tariffs in the presence of complementarity. We note that the term $(\theta_m + \theta_e)$ in eqs. (6) and (7) is positive since it is the negative of the own price elasticity of excess demand for home goods. It follows that if home goods and importables are complements, $\theta_m < 0$, the tariff causes the prices of both traded goods to appreciate in terms of home goods. This is so since at a constant price of exportables the tariff creates an excess supply of home goods and thus requires an increase in the price of both traded goods in terms of home goods to eliminate the excess supply. Conversely, if exportables and home goods are complements, $\theta_e < 0$, the prices of both traded goods decline in terms of home goods.[8]

4. A special case

A special case of the model developed so far has been widely employed in policy discussions and empirical work concerned with the resource allocation and welfare effects of a tariff. That specialization assumes that the cross price elasticity between traded goods is zero and thus implies not only that home goods and both traded goods are substitutes but also that θ_m and θ_e can be identified with the compensated elasticity of demand for imports (defined positive) and the elasticity of supply of exports respectively. This special case furthermore assumes that real income is not an argument in the demand for imports or supply of exports so that by implication the marginal propensity to spend on home goods is unity.

With these assumptions we may write the demand for imports and supply of export as follows:

$$M = M(P_m); \quad E = E(P_e). \tag{8}$$

Using the budget constraint in eq. (3) we may rewrite the equilibrium condition in eq. (1) in terms of the trade balance equilibrium condition

$$P^*M(P_m) = E(P_e), \tag{9}$$

[7]While the analogy with exchange rate changes may be suggestive, it should be emphasized that the requisite adjustment is one of relative prices and that, in this model, it is altogether immaterial whether such an adjustment comes via a change in the nominal prices of home goods at constant traded goods prices or via a change in the nominal prices of traded goods at constant nominal prices of home goods. Indeed there is nothing in this model that will determine nominal prices or an exchange rate and the frequently encountered assumption that in the 'background' monetary and fiscal policy maintain the nominal price of home goods is an unsatisfactory way of concealing what is essentially a nonmonetary economy. For a discussion of tariffs in a properly specified monetary economy see Mussa (1973).

[8]For the case of complementarity, the home goods market equilibrium schedule is positively sloped. It will intersect the OR ray from below for the case where importables and home goods are complements and intersect it from above when home goods and exports are complements.

and close the model by the relationship between prices in eq. (2), that is
$P_m = P^*P_eT$.

The particular assumptions of this model allow for simple measures of the
protective effect of a tariff, its welfare cost and the 'social cost of foreign
exchange'. These measures can be interpreted in terms of fig. 2. There we show
the supply of exports, E, and the demand for imports measured in terms of
exports at international prices, P^*M. The demand for imports is drawn as a
function of the relative price of exportables. This is possible because by eq. (2)
we can write $P_m = P^*P_eT$ so that for a given tariff the demand for imports can
be shown as a function of P_e. Initial free trade equilibrium obtains at point A
where the trade balance is in equilibrium, $P^*M = E$, and hence by eq. (3)
equilibrium obtains in the home goods market.

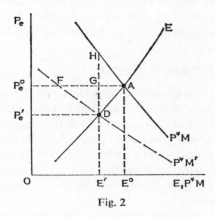

Fig. 2

The imposition of a tariff shifts the demand for imports downward to P^*M'
in the proportion of the tariff. At the initial relative price of exportables, P_e^0,
the demand for imports declines to point F and accordingly there is a trade
balance surplus equal to AF and an excess demand for home goods equal to
AF times P_e^0. The excess demand for home goods causes their relative price to
increase in terms of both traded goods until the economy reaches point D where
full equilibrium again obtains.

An indication of the direction and magnitude of resource movements is the
change in the equilibrium relative prices. The increase in the equilibrium relative
price of imports in terms of home goods measures the protection granted to that
industry. As is seen from fig. 2, the price increase, HG/GE′, falls short of the
tariff, HD/DE′, due to the depreciation of traded goods in terms of home goods.
This discrepancy between the tariff rate and the appropriate measure of protection has led in the literature to the concept of a 'net protective rate'.[9] That rate

[9] See Corden (1971, ch. 5) and Balassa (1971a, b).

is defined as the tariff less the change in the equilibrium 'exchange rate'. It follows from the preceding discussion that it is properly identified with the increase in the equilibrium relative price of imports in terms of home goods and thus for a small tariff is measured by eq. (7).

Consider now the welfare cost of a discrete tariff. To develop a formal expression we assume a social utility function $U = U(C_n, C_m, C_e)$ and substituting for consumption in terms of production and trade we have $U = U(Q_n, Q_m + M, Q_e - E)$. Next we differentiate that utility function and divide by the marginal utility of nontraded goods to obtain the change in utility measured in terms of home goods denoted by dV:[10]

$$dV \equiv dU/(\partial U/\partial C_n) = P_m dM - P_e dE. \tag{10}$$

The expression for the welfare change in eq. (10) can be related to the tariff by use of eq. (9). Differentiating that equation yields $dE = P^* dM$ which after substitution in eq. (10) and use of eq. (2) gives the following expression for the marginal welfare change:

$$dV = (t/T)P_m dM = tP_e P^* dM. \tag{11}$$

The welfare cost of a discrete tariff is given by the integral of eq. (11) and on the special assumptions of this model can be identified with the familiar 'triangle' measure HDA in fig. 2. For that identification to be correct we do require both assumptions of this model, zero cross price effects between traded goods and zero marginal propensities to spend on traded goods. These assumptions together ensure that we deal with compensated import demand and export supply schedules that will not shift in response to cross price effects or the income effects of a discrete tariff.[11]

Closely related to the welfare cost of a tariff is the concept of the 'social cost of foreign exchange' or more appropriately the shadow price of external resources.[12] To determine that shadow price we assume that the home country receives external resources, say aid, so that we can rewrite the trade balance equilibrium condition in eq. (9) as

$$P^* M(P_m) = E(P_e) + A, \tag{12}$$

where A denotes aid receipts measured in terms of exportables. Differentiating that equilibrium condition and substituting in eq. (10) yields an expression for

[10]In arriving at eq. (10) we have used the fact that from consumer maximization the ratios of marginal utilities are equated to the domestic price ratios and that producer maximization implies that the change in the value of output at domestic prices is zero, i.e., $dQ_n + P_m dQ_m + P_e dQ_e = 0$.

[11]The very restrictive assumptions underlying the triangle measure have not been sufficiently emphasized in actual applications. See, for example, Basevi (1968). This issue is nontrivial since at the level of aggregation that is considered there is no reason to expect that the assumptions should be a good approximation of the real world.

[12]For a survey article on the social cost of foreign exchange see Bacha and Taylor (1971). Sec. 3 of that paper deals with the measure that is developed here.

F

the shadow price as the welfare gain per unit of aid, both measured in terms of home goods:

$$\frac{dV}{P_e dA} = 1 + tP^* \frac{dM}{dA}. \tag{13}$$

We note from eq. (13) that the shadow price will differ from unity by a factor that will depend on the given tariff and the change in imports induced by aid. The latter term can be derived by differentiating the trade balance equilibrium condition in eq. (12) holding constant the tariff and hence the domestic relative price of traded goods. Performing that operation and using the definition of the elasticity of demand for imports we obtain $P^* dM/dA = \theta_m/(\theta_m + \theta_e)$ and hence the expression for the shadow price becomes:

$$\frac{dV}{P_e dA} = 1 + t \frac{\theta_m}{\theta_m + \theta_e}. \tag{14}$$

The second term in eq. (14) constitutes the rationale for shadow pricing and has a straightforward interpretation. Under a tariff imports are socially overpriced and welfare will increase if the public can be induced to expand imports over the existing distortion.[13] Aid receipts will produce such an expansion in imports since they raise expenditure on nontraded goods raising their relative price and hence by the substitution effect increasing imports.[14] The increase in imports per unit of aid, given by the ratio $\theta_m/(\theta_m + \theta_e)$, multiplied by the distortion in the form of the tariff accordingly measures the excess benefit of aid.[15]

---

[13]This line of argument is obviously familiar from the literature on distortions, for a review see in particular Bhagwati (1971).

[14]The argument can readily be interpreted in terms of fig. 2. Aid receipts are added to the supply of exports and accordingly shift that schedule to the right. At the initial equilibrium price there is trade balance surplus and matching excess demand for nontraded goods. To restore equilibrium the relative price of traded goods in terms of home goods has to decline thereby increasing imports and decreasing exports.

[15]The measure in eq. (14) requires zero marginal propensities to spend on traded goods; it does not require, however, zero cross price elasticities. This is so because we maintain constant the relative price of traded goods.

References

Bacha, E. and Taylor, L., 1971, Foreign exchange shadow prices: A critical review of current theories, Quarterly Journal of Economics 85, no. 2, 197–224.

Bhagwati, J., 1971, The generalized theory of distortions and welfare, in: J. Bhagwati et al., Trade, balance of payments and growth (North-Holland, Amsterdam) 69–90.

Balassa, B., 1971a, The structure of protection in developing countries (Johns Hopkins Press, Baltimore).

Balassa, B., 1971b, Effective protection in developing countries, in: J. Bhagwati et al., Trade, balance of payments and growth (North-Holland, Amsterdam) 300–323.

Basevi, G., 1968, The restrictive effect of the US tariff and its welfare value, American Economic Review 58, no. 4, 840–852.

Corden, M., 1971, The theory of protection (Clarendon Press).
McDougall, I.A., 1970, Non-traded commodities and the pure theory of international trade, in: A. McDougall and R.H. Snape, eds., Studies in International Economics (North-Holland, Amsterdam) 157–192.
Mussa, M., 1973, Tariffs and the balance of payments: A monetary approach, unpublished manuscript (University of Rochester).

[33]

Determinants of the Equilibrium Real Exchange Rate

The importance of the equilibrium real exchange rate, the relative price of non-traded to traded goods consistent with balance-of-payments equilibrium, has long been recognized.[1] However, no simple, compact derivation of the determinants of the real exchange rate in a multicommodity framework appears to be available.[2] Section I below attempts to fill this gap, and Section II notes the implications of the main result for a number of applied questions.

I. Theory

I assume a small open economy producing arbitrary numbers of traded and nontraded goods under competitive conditions. The world prices of traded goods are exogenously given, and, without loss of generality, I take one of the traded goods as numeraire so that domestic prices are measured in terms of foreign currency. Since I consider only situations of balance-of-payments equilibrium, it is immaterial whether this is achieved by adjustment of a floating exchange rate or by monetary inflows and outflows under a fixed exchange rate. I assume that there are n nontraded goods, whose prices, denoted by the vector p, are endogenously determined so as to equate domestic demand and supply. The determination of equilibrium may be illustrated in a compact manner by making use of the *trade expenditure function*.[3] This equals the excess of home expenditure, determined by a standard expenditure function, $e(p, u, \alpha)$, over home income from production, determined by a GNP function, $g(p, \beta)$, plus any additional income received by the private sector, γ. In symbols:

$$(1) \qquad E(p, u, \phi) = e(p, u, \alpha) \\ - g(p, \beta) - \gamma.$$

Here $\phi = (\alpha, \beta, \gamma)$ is a vector of shift parameters whose interpretation will vary with the particular shocks under consideration. For example, α may include the prices of non-numeraire traded goods as well as taste parameters; β may include both factor endowments and technology parameters; and γ may include redistributed tax or tariff revenue as well as direct transfers from abroad. The scalar u measures home utility, which can be interpreted either as the actual utility of a single aggregate consumer or as the level of social welfare attained when optimal redistribution is continually carried out by means of lump-sum transfers. Relaxing this assumption to allow for different individuals in the economy with optimal lump-sum redistribution not carried out would introduce additional complications that, though potentially important in practice, are not central to the applications of the model discussed below. In any case, these considerations have been widely discussed in other contexts.[4]

*University College, Belfield, Dublin 4, Ireland, and Queen's University, Kingston, Ontario K7L 3N6 Canada. An earlier version of this paper was circulated as Discussion Paper No. 209 of the Centre for Economic Policy Research, London, and was presented at the Econometric Society European Meetings in Copenhagen in August 1987. I am grateful for helpful comments to participants on that occasion and to Mick Devereux, Lars Svensson, Scott Taylor, Stephen Yeo, and a referee.

[1] Peter Oppenheimer (1974) documents early writings on models with nontraded goods, whereas W. E. G. Salter (1959) and Michael Bruno (1976) are representative of the voluminous modern literature.

[2] By contrast, the building blocks of such a derivation are well known. See, in particular, Richard Caves and Ronald Jones (1985, pp. 494–98), Avinash Dixit and Victor Norman (1980, ch. 5), and Alan Woodland (1982, chs. 8 and 10).

[3] The detailed properties of this function have been examined by Dixit and Norman (1980, pp. 90–91), who call it the "excess expenditure function," and Woodland (1982, p. 170), who calls its negative the "maximum net revenue function."

[4] To give only two examples, Dixit and Norman (1986) examine the problems that arise in measuring

The great convenience of the trade expenditure function is that, for fixed ϕ, its properties resemble those of the usual expenditure function, $e(p, u, \alpha)$. In particular, it is increasing in u, it is concave in p, and its partial derivatives with respect to p equal the Hicksian or utility-compensated excess demand functions for nontraded goods:[5]

$$(2) \quad E_p(p, u, \phi) = e_p(p, u, \alpha) - g_p(p, \beta).$$

The function E is homogeneous of degree zero in the prices of all goods, traded as well as nontraded. However, since p denotes the prices of nontraded goods only, the matrix of second partial derivatives of E with respect to p will be nonsingular provided there is some substitutability in either demand or supply between traded and nontraded goods. I assume this henceforward and denote the negative of this matrix by S:

$$(3) \quad S = - E_{pp}(p, u, \phi).$$

Because of the properties of e and g, S is symmetric and positive definite.

It is now straightforward to characterize equilibrium. First, balance of payments equilibrium requires that aggregate expenditure equal aggregate income:[6]

$$(4) \quad E(p, u, \phi) = 0.$$

Second, commodity market equilibrium requires that excess demand for each nontraded good be zero:

$$(5) \quad E_p(p, u, \phi) = 0.$$

The $n + 1$ equations (4) and (5) determine the values of the $n + 1$ endogenous variables, p and u, as functions of the parameters ϕ.

To solve the model, first totally differentiate (4) to obtain

$$(6) \quad du = - E_\phi' d\phi \equiv d\Phi.$$

Here, I have used (5) to eliminate a term in dp and have chosen units of measurement for utility such that $E_u = e_u = 1$. I have also introduced the scalar parameter Φ to denote the aggregate effect of any given combination of exogenous shocks: $d\Phi$ measures the net change in utility arising from changes in all the exogenous variables. Next, totally differentiate (5) to obtain:

$$(7) \quad - S dp + E_{pu} du = - E_{p\phi} d\phi$$

$$\equiv - E_{p\Phi} d\Phi.$$

The two terms on the left-hand side of (7) measure respectively the substitution effects of price changes and the income effects of utility changes on the excess demand for nontraded goods. The right-hand side measures the effects of changes in exogenous variables on excess demand; as in (6), it is convenient to aggregate these effects, with each element of the vector $E_{p\Phi}$ giving the net increase in excess demand for each nontraded good as a result of changes in exogenous variables.[7] Combining (6) and (7) and solving for the vector of changes in nontraded goods prices yields

$$(8) \quad dp = S^{-1}(E_{pu} + E_{p\Phi}) d\Phi.$$

The final step is to aggregate the price changes of individual nontraded goods to obtain the change in the real exchange rate. I define the latter as a fixed-weight index number of the relative prices of nontraded goods divided by a price index for traded goods,

---

welfare changes when lump-sum redistribution is not feasible, and Lance Taylor (1974) considers the positive implications of intranational differences in spending propensities in a model with traded and nontraded goods.

[5] Throughout, terms such as E_p denote the vector of partial derivatives of E with respect to p, and terms such as E_{pp} denote the matrix of second partial derivatives. All vectors are column vectors, and a prime denotes a transpose.

[6] In a multiperiod model, a payments imbalance could be consistent with full intertemporal equilibrium. I ignore such considerations in what follows.

[7] Thus, the ith component of the vector $E_{p\Phi}$ equals $-\Sigma_j E_{ij} d\phi_j / \Sigma_j E_j d\phi_j$, where E_{ij} is shorthand for $\partial^2 E / \partial p_i \partial \phi_j$.

p_T:[8]

(9) $$\pi \equiv x'p/p_T,$$

where the elements of the vector x are the base-period consumption (and production) levels of individual nontraded goods. Totally differentiating, with p_T assumed constant, and combining with (8) gives the principal result of this note:

(10) $$d\pi = x'S^{-1}(E_{pu} + E_{p\Phi})\,d\Phi/p_T.$$

The interpretation of this result is facilitated if the parameters are expressed in proportional terms. This may be done by introducing a diagonal matrix P, the ith element on the principal diagonal of which is the price of the ith nontraded good. Straightforward manipulations now allow (10) to be rewritten as follows:

(11) $$\hat{\pi} = \omega'\bar{S}^{-1}(\mu - \sigma)\,d\Phi.$$

Here $\hat{\pi}$ equals $d\pi/\pi$; ω equals $Px/x'p$, the vector of individual commodity weights in the nontraded goods price index; $\bar{S}$ equals PSP, a simple transformation of the substitution matrix defined in (3); μ equals PE_{pu}, the vector of *marginal propensities to consume* nontraded goods; and σ equals $-PE_{p\Phi}$, which may be interpreted as the vector of *marginal propensities to produce* nontraded goods. Of course, the values of the latter depend on the particular shock under consideration, as the examples in the next section illustrate.

II. Applications

Equation (11) may be interpreted as implying that any exogenous shock will raise π and so lead to a *real appreciation* if the demand effects of the shock outweigh the supply effects. The coefficient of $d\Phi$ in (11)

is a weighted sum of the differences between the marginal propensities to consume and to produce each nontraded good. The weights equal the elements of the vector $\omega'\bar{S}^{-1}$ and so reflect both the relative importance of each good in consumption and the difficulty of substituting it for other goods. While there is no guarantee that all these weights must be positive,[9] the fact that $\bar{S}$ is a positive definite matrix justifies the statement that a real appreciation will occur provided the elements of ω and $(\mu - \sigma)$ are positively correlated. The significance of this result is best seen by considering a number of applications.

A. *Effects of a Transfer*

An incoming transfer, such as foreign aid, is necessarily effected in terms of traded goods. Hence, at initial prices, it does not affect the output of nontraded goods and so all the elements of σ are zero. It follows (assuming nontraded goods are normal in demand) that a transfer is likely to induce a real appreciation, a prediction that has been confirmed empirically by Michael Michaely (1981).

B. *The "Dutch Disease"*

A sector-specific boom has effects identical to those of a transfer if it occurs in an "enclave" traded-good sector, which has no production links with the rest of the economy. (Natural resource sectors are an obvious example.) Such a boom has a "spending effect" only (in the terminology of Max Corden and myself [1982]) and necessarily leads to a real appreciation. Real national income and so potential welfare rises, although the loss of competitiveness experi-

---

[8] These price indices may be given a rigorous justification for large as well as small changes if the trade expenditure function is homothetically separable in the prices of traded and nontraded goods.

[9] One special case in which the weights must be positive is where all goods are substitutes in aggregate excess demand. Then S has positive diagonal entries and negative off-diagonal entries, and (from the homogeneity restrictions on excess demand) SP has a dominant diagonal. It follows that all the elements of $(SP)^{-1}$ are positive, which implies that the same must be true of the elements of $\bar{S}^{-1}$.

enced by nonbooming traded sectors may pose problems of adjustment and may lead to loss of learning-by-doing gains in those sectors. These potentially harmful side effects of a boom have come to be known as the "Dutch Disease." The effect on the real exchange rate is less clear-cut if the booming sector is integrated with the rest of the economy so that the boom also has a "resource movement effect." In particular, if the boom, through general-equilibrium interactions, encourages more production of nontraded goods at initial prices (i.e., the elements of $g_{p\beta}$ and hence of σ are positive), then a real appreciation is not inevitable.[10] Expressed in the terminology of Sir John Hicks (1953), the more home-market biased is the sectoral pattern of economic growth, the less likely is a real appreciation. In the neutral benchmark case of "balanced growth" and homothetic tastes, μ_i and σ_i are equal for each nontraded good; hence all relative prices, including the real exchange rate, are unaffected by growth.

C. *International Comparisons of Purchasing Power Parity*

The doctrine of purchasing power parity may be expressed as the prediction that price levels should be equal across countries when compared by means of equilibrium exchange rates. However, there is ample evidence against this hypothesis and in favor of the view that nontraded goods are relatively cheaper in low-income countries. (See Irving Kravis, Alan Heston, and Robert Summers, 1978.) Bela Balassa (1964) and Paul Samuelson (1964) argue that such deviations from purchasing power parity are to be expected because higher-income countries have higher relative productivity in the production of traded goods. This implication follows clearly from (11): $\hat{\pi}$ and $d\Phi$ may be reinterpreted as the differences between a high-income and a low-income country in the real exchange rate and the level of real income

respectively, and μ and σ may be reinterpreted as the differences between the two countries in *average* propensities to consume and produce nontraded goods at constant prices. If international productivity differences are smaller in the production of nontraded goods (such as services) than in the production of traded goods, the elements of σ are likely to be small or even negative,[11] and so the higher-income country will have a higher real exchange rate (a higher relative price of services). This effect will be reinforced if nontraded goods are superior in demand (so that the elements of μ are positive and relatively large). Although cross-section evidence in favor of this productivity-differential hypothesis is not strong (see Balassa, 1964, and Lawrence Officer, 1976), David Hsieh (1982) shows that it is confirmed by time-series tests.[12] His suggestion that this occurs because country-specific factors such as tastes vary relatively little over time is fully in keeping with equation (11).

D. *Changes in the Terms of Trade*

Although I have so far assumed that the prices of all traded goods are given, $d\Phi$ may be interpreted as the change in income arising from a change in the terms of trade. Suppose that export prices rise so that the terms of trade improve. In this application μ denotes the marginal propensities to consume nontraded goods as before, but σ must be reinterpreted as the cross-price effects on excess supply of nontraded goods of the terms of trade improvement. These must be

---

[10] See Peter Neary and Sweder van Wijnbergen (1986) for further theoretical and empirical elaboration.

[11] For example, in a two-sector model, if the higher-income country has a Hicks-neutral technological superiority in the traded sector only, then it must produce relatively less of the nontraded good at given prices (i.e., σ must be negative) in either the Heckscher-Ohlin or specific-factors model. With more general forms of technological differences, σ may be positive (see Ronald Findlay and Harry Grubert, 1959; Ronald Jones, 1970; and Neary, 1981) but there is still a presumption that it will be low or negative.

[12] Of course, the results of such tests should be interpreted with care, since strictly speaking the hypothesis applies only to steady-state comparisons in which balance of payments equilibrium holds continually.

negative if every traded good is a substitute for every nontraded good, thus reinforcing the income effect. This gives the conclusion that, except where complementary relationships dominate, a terms of trade improvement tends to lead to a real appreciation.[13]

III. Conclusion

The approach adopted in this paper shows that a number of results in the literature on small open economies are special cases of a general phenomenon: changes in exogenous variables are more likely to lead to a real appreciation the greater their effect on the demand for and the smaller their effect on the supply of nontraded relative to traded goods. Unfortunately, this paper throws no light on one of the most difficult problems facing all students of the open economy—theorists, applied economists, and policymakers alike—namely, determining how far actual real exchange rates diverge from their equilibrium values.

[13] Rudiger Dornbusch (1980, ch. 6) gives a three-commodity exposition of this result. If the terms of trade improvement arises from a fall in import prices, the income and substitution effects work in opposite directions. Since σ_t equals $p_i \Sigma_j E_{ij} \, dq_j / \Sigma_j E_j \, dq_j$, where the denominator (which equals $- d\Phi$) is negative following a terms of trade improvement and the E_{ii} terms are positive by assumption, the sign of σ_t depends on the sign of the price changes dq_j.

REFERENCES

Balassa, Bela, "The Purchasing-Power Parity Doctrine: A Reappraisal," *Journal of Political Economy,* December 1964, *72,* 584–96.

Bruno, Michael, "The Two-Sector Open Economy and the Real Exchange Rate," *American Economic Review,* September 1976, *66,* 566–77.

Caves, Richard E. and Jones, Ronald W., *World Trade and Payments,* 4th ed., Boston: Little, Brown, 1985.

Corden, W. Max and Neary, J. Peter, "Booming Sector and Deindustrialisation in a Small Open Economy," *Economic Journal,* December 1982, *92,* 825–48.

Dixit, Avinash K. and Norman, Victor, *Theory of International Trade: A Dual, General Equilibrium Approach,* Welwyn: James Nesbit, 1980.

———— **and** ————, "Gains from Trade without Lump-Sum Compensation," *Journal of International Economics,* August 1986, *21,* 111–22.

Dornbusch, Rudiger, *Open-Economy Macroeconomics,* New York: Basic Books, 1980.

Findlay, Ronald and Grubert, Harry, "Factor Intensities, Technological Progress, and the Terms of Trade," *Oxford Economic Papers,* February 1959, *11,* 111–21.

Hicks, John R., "An Inaugural Lecture: 2. The Long-Run Dollar Problem," *Oxford Economic Papers,* June 1953, *5,* 121–35.

Hsieh, David A., "The Determination of the Real Exchange Rate: The Productivity Approach," *Journal of International Economics,* May 1982, *12,* 355–62.

Jones, Ronald W., "The Role of Technology in the Theory of International Trade," in R. Vernon, ed., *The Technology Factor in International Trade,* New York: NBER, 1970, 73–92.

Kravis, Irving, Heston, Alan and Summers, Robert, *International Comparisons of Real Product and Purchasing Power,* Baltimore: Johns Hopkins Press, 1978.

Michaely, Michael, "Foreign Aid, Economic Structure and Dependence," *Journal of Development Economics,* December 1981, *9,* 313–30.

Neary, J. Peter, "On the Short-Run Effects of Technological Progress," *Oxford Economic Papers,* July 1981, *33,* 224–33.

———— **and van Wijnbergen, Sweder,** eds., *Natural Resources and the Macroeconomy,* Oxford: Basil Blackwell and Cambridge, MA: MIT Press, 1986.

Officer, Lawrence H., "The Productivity Bias in Purchasing Power Parity: An Econometric Investigation," *International Monetary Fund Staff Papers,* November 1976, *23,* 545–79.

Oppenheimer, Peter, "Non-Traded Goods and the Balance of Payments: A Historical Note," *Journal of Economic Literature,*

September 1974, *12*, 882–88.

Salter, W. E. G., "Internal and External Balance: The Role of Price and Expenditure Effects," *Economic Record*, August 1959, *35*, 226–38.

Samuelson, Paul A., "Theoretical Notes on Trade Problems," *Review of Economics and Statistics*, May 1964, *46*, 145–54.

Taylor, Lance, "Short-Term Policy in Open Semi-Industrialized Countries: The Narrow Limits of the Possible," *Journal of Development Economics*, September 1974, *1*, 85–104.

Woodland, Alan D., *International Trade and Resource Allocation*, Amsterdam: North-Holland, 1982.

[34]

The Terms of Trade and the Current Account: The Harberger-Laursen-Metzler Effect

Lars E. O. Svensson

University of Stockholm

Assaf Razin

Tel-Aviv University

The paper examines the effect of terms-of-trade changes on a small country's spending and current account, assuming optimizing behavior in an intertemporal framework with perfect international capital mobility. A temporary (future) terms-of-trade deterioration implies a deterioration (improvement) of the trade balance, whereas a permanent terms-of-trade deterioration has an ambiguous effect, depending on the rate of time preference. Nominal and real variables are considered via exact price indexes. Two periods and an infinite horizon are examined.

I. Introduction and Summary

In two classic articles, Harberger (1950) and Laursen and Metzler (1950) postulated that saving out of any given level of income decreases with a deterioration of the terms of trade—the *Harberger-*

Revision of Seminar Paper no. 170, Institute for International Economic Studies, University of Stockholm, March 1981. We have benefited from comments by participants in the seminars at the Institute for International Economic Studies, the departments of economics at Columbia University and at MIT, and the joint Hebrew–Tel Aviv Universities Workshop in International Economics. In particular we wish to thank Avinash Dixit (who discovered a major error in the first draft), M. June Flanders, Jacob Frenkel, Elhanan Helpman, Nancy Marion, Torsten Persson, Hans Tson Soderstrom, and an anonymous referee.

[*Journal of Political Economy*, 1983, vol. 91, no. 1]
© 1983 by The University of Chicago. All rights reserved. 0022-3808/83/9101-0004$01.50

Laursen-Metzler effect.[1] Their argument was relatively straightforward: A terms-of-trade deterioration decreases "real income," and the decrease in real income reduces saving out of any given income, both measured in terms of exportables. Thus, if investment is constant and there is no government deficit, the change in saving is equal to the change in the current-account surplus, and hence the Harberger-Laursen-Metzler effect implies that the current account will deteriorate in response to a terms-of-trade deterioration (if income, measured in terms of exportables, is held constant).

The Harberger-Laursen-Metzler effect played an important role in the discussion of the relative merits of the elasticity and absorption approaches to the effect of a devaluation on the trade balance and balance of payments (Alexander 1952; Tsiang 1961). It continues to appear in the discussion of the transmission of disturbances in open-economy macroeconomics (e.g., Mussa 1979; Dornbusch 1980).

The macroeconomic effects of terms-of-trade changes have met renewed interest since the oil price increases began in the early seventies. The conventional wisdom is that, given limited substitution possibilities in production, an increase in the price of an imported intermediate input leads to a current-account deterioration (see, e.g., Schmid 1976; Findlay and Rodríguez 1977; Buiter 1978; and Bruno and Sachs 1979). This response is consistent with the Harberger-Laursen-Metzler effect, although the effect is not always used in deriving it.[2]

---

[1] The literature persists in labeling the effect by the names of Laursen and Metzler only, ignoring Harberger's contribution. His derivation of the effect is more rigorous than Laursen and Metzler's (1950), and his article was published first. However, each article refers to the other. In Harberger's (1950) discussion of the effect on the trade balance of a devaluation in a Keynesian model where the income level was demand determined, he found that the Harberger-Laursen-Metzler effect implies that the standard Marshall-Lerner condition for a devaluation to improve the trade balance, or alternatively the condition for "exchange stability" (that the sum of the two countries' price elasticities of import exceeds one), is modified to become more restrictive in that the sum must exceed one with a margin. Laursen and Metzler were discussing the transmission of business cycles between countries and flexible exchange rates. In so doing, they derived the same modified condition for exchange stability. Their main point, though, was that because of the Harberger-Laursen-Metzler effect, flexible exchange rates would not insulate a country from foreign business cycles, and they showed that an expansion abroad would lead to a domestic contraction. The Harberger-Laursen-Metzler effect aroused considerable controversy. Laursen and Metzler's argument was disputed by White (1954), and Harberger was criticized by Day (1954), Pearce (1955), and Spraos (1955). The simplifying assumptions Harberger and Laursen and Metzler used were scrutinized, and both the sign and the size of the effect were disputed. Meade's (1951) neglect of the effect caused severe criticism of his work by Johnson (1951). Johnson (1956) includes a brief survey of the controversy.

[2] Rodríguez (1976) criticizes the most simpleminded variant of the monetary approach to balance of payments, where the effect of an exogenous increase in any produced tradable good—net exported or imported—leads to an improvement in the balance of payments. He suggests an alternative formulation where real expenditure depends on "real permanent income" (see an additional remark in Sec. VI).

Very recently the conventional wisdom has been challenged by Obstfeld (1980, 1982). Obstfeld argues that a deterioration of the terms of trade will result in increased saving and an improvement, rather than a deterioration, in the current account; consequently, the general validity of the Harberger-Laursen-Metzler effect is questioned.

Although the early critics of Harberger and Laursen and Metzler clarified several obscure points, they did not succeed in providing a complete analysis of the effect of terms-of-trade changes on spending, saving, and the current account. Presumably they lacked a satisfactory theory of saving, consistent with intertemporal utility-maximizing behavior. Later authors (e.g., Jones 1960; Tsiang 1961; and Dornbusch 1980) have used a simplified approach to the determination of the Harberger-Laursen-Metzler effect, but, as we shall see, this approach is not generally consistent with intertemporal utility maximization. Obstfeld (1982) discusses the Harberger-Laursen-Metzler effect in an intertemporal utility-maximizing framework, but, as we shall also see, he deals only with a special case.

The purpose of this paper is to examine rigorously the effect of terms-of-trade changes on spending and the current account. Our approach is to use an intertemporal model, somewhat similar to Razin (1980), of a small, open economy facing given world prices and a given world rate of interest. Our general approach enables us to point to the crucial role of the relative sizes of the marginal propensity to spend, in the present and in the future, for the effects of terms-of-trade changes on the current account. Our approach also integrates the use of different effects that have been mentioned separately in earlier literature. We will emphasize the difference between the trade balance responses to temporary and permanent terms-of-trade changes.

The changes in the nominal (in terms of some unit of account) trade balance due to a terms-of-trade deterioration can be separated into three different effects: (i) a direct effect, consisting of a revaluation of the net export vector; (ii) a wealth effect on consumption, since a terms-of-trade deterioration reduces wealth; and (iii) a pure substitution effect on consumption, due to relative price changes within and between the periods. In general, the sum of these effects is of ambiguous sign, although the direct plus wealth effect is unambiguously negative (positive) for a temporary (future) terms-of-trade deterioration.

Under appropriate assumptions (namely, that preferences are homothetically weakly separable) we can obtain additional results. We can then define exact price indices that enable us, in turn, to define the real trade balance and the real rate of interest. We find that the effect on the real trade balance consists of (i) a direct change in the real value of output equal to what we usually call a real terms-of-trade effect, (ii) a wealth effect on real spending, and (iii) an intertemporal substitution effect. The wealth effect on real spending is due to the change in welfare from a terms-of-trade deterioration. The change in welfare consists of static terms-of-trade effects, both in the present and in the future, as well as an intertemporal terms-of-trade effect due to a change in the real rate of interest. The substitution effect on real spending is due to the change in the real rate of interest. All these effects are rigorously derived and graphically shown in familiar diagrams.

A *temporary* deterioration in the terms of trade generates two effects: a temporary fall in real income and a change in the real interest rate. The fall in real income leads to a negative direct plus wealth effect and hence a deteriorated trade balance, since the fall in spending is just a fraction (the marginal propensity to spend out of wealth) of the fall in real income. This is an example of spending smoothing behavior. The change in the real interest rate leads to a substitution effect on spending. If the real interest rate falls, the substitution effect reinforces the direct plus wealth effect and the current account must unambiguously deteriorate.

In order to isolate the effect of the change in the terms of trade from other dynamic effects, we examine a stationary state for the case where preferences concerning consumption bundles within each period are the same. In a stationary state relative spot prices are the same in the present and in the future, and the net export vector is also the same in the present and in the future. A *permanent* terms-of-trade deterioration that leaves the real rate of interest constant then causes a deterioration or improvement in the real trade balance, depending on whether the marginal propensity to spend in the future exceeds or falls short of the propensity to spend in the present or, equivalently, whether the rate of time preference decreases or increases respectively with the level of welfare. On a priori grounds, neither alternative—decreasing or increasing rate of time preference—can be excluded. In the extension of our analysis to an infinite horizon, we observe that a necessary and sufficient condition for stability of the stationary state is that the rate of time preference increases with the level of welfare. As we will show, however, we do not consider stability of the stationary state more reasonable on a priori grounds than instability.

One conclusion from our analysis is that export-oriented or import-substitution policies, which alter the internal terms of trade faced by domestic consumers and producers, in general have ambiguous effects on the current account. That is, the level of spending is not directly related to changes in the terms of trade, internal or external, while spending is more directly related to policy-induced changes in wealth and interest rates (see also Helpman and Razin 1981; Razin and Svensson 1982).

When investment is incorporated into the framework, the effect of terms-of-trade deterioration on the current account becomes more complex, depending on the detailed input-output structure of the economy. This is discussed in the earlier version of this paper (Svensson and Razin 1981).

The present paper is organized in the following manner. The basic model is set up in Section II, and the general effect of a terms-of-trade deterioration on nominal spending and the nominal trade balance is reported. The details are presented in the Appendix. In Section III, further assumptions are made that enable us to discuss the determinants of real spending and the real trade balance, and a convenient graphical illustration is presented. The effect of a permanent deterioration in the terms of trade on the trade balance in a stationary state is discussed in Section IV. Our results are extended to an infinite horizon in Section V. Section VI discusses the relationships between our results and those of the previous literature.

II. The Model, Nominal Spending, and the Nominal Trade Balance

We will consider a small country in an intertemporal framework. Let there be two periods, indexed $t = 1$ and 2, and n goods, indexed $i = 1, \ldots, n$. We assume that the country can trade all goods in the world market at given spot prices and also that it has free access to the world credit market, with a given rate of interest. Let the n-vector $\mathbf{P}^t$ denote period t's nominal spot prices of goods and let D denote the nominal discount factor (equal to one over one plus the nominal rate of interest). These nominal values are measured in some arbitrary unit of account.[3] The country is represented by a single consumer whose utility function is $U(\mathbf{c}^1, \mathbf{c}^2)$, where $\mathbf{c}^1$ and $\mathbf{c}^2$ denote period 1 and period 2 vectors of consumption, respectively. It will be convenient to use the corresponding (present value) expenditure function $E(\mathbf{P}^1, D\mathbf{P}^2, u)$. We recall that the expenditure function is defined as

$$E(\mathbf{P}^1, D\mathbf{P}^2, u) = \min \{\mathbf{P}^1 \mathbf{c}^1 + D\mathbf{P}^2 \mathbf{c}^2 : U(\mathbf{c}^1, \mathbf{c}^2) \geq u\}, \qquad (1)$$

where $\mathbf{P}^t \mathbf{c}^t$ denotes the inner product $\Sigma_i P_i^t c_i^t$. That is, the expenditure function gives the minimum present value of consumption in the two periods required to reach a given utility level, at given spot prices and discount factor.[4] For the sake of simplicity, let us assume that period

[3] Since our model is a real model, however, only relative prices will matter.
[4] See Dixit and Norman (1980) on the properties of the expenditure function.

t's output bundle, the n-vector $\mathbf{x}^t$, is given. Positive components correspond to outputs and negative components to inputs of intermediate products. This means that the analysis allows a terms-of-trade effect arising from an increase in prices of intermediate goods such as oil. There is no investment.

The equilibrium of the small country can be represented by the intertemporal budget constraint

$$E(\mathbf{P}^1, D\mathbf{P}^2, u) = \mathbf{P}^1\mathbf{x}^1 + D\mathbf{P}^2\mathbf{x}^2 \equiv Y^1 + DY^2 \equiv W, \qquad (2)$$

where $Y^t = \mathbf{P}^t\mathbf{x}^t$ denotes nominal income in period t, that is, value added in production, and W denotes nominal wealth, that is, the present value of total income in both periods. The equation states that the present value of expenditure is equal to wealth. It expresses the welfare level u as an implicit function of the given world prices, the discount factor, and output levels in the two periods. Note that u is the overall (intertemporal) welfare level resulting from consumption in both periods.

A well-known property of the expenditure function is that its derivative, with respect to the price of a good, equals the Hicksian compensated demand function for that good. It follows that equilibrium consumption, and the net export (vectors) $\mathbf{e}^1$ and $\mathbf{e}^2$, are given by

$$
\begin{aligned}
\mathbf{c}^1 &= \mathbf{E}_1(\mathbf{P}^1, D\mathbf{P}^2, u), \\
\mathbf{c}^2 &= \mathbf{E}_2(\mathbf{P}^1, D\mathbf{P}^2, u), \\
\mathbf{e}^1 &= \mathbf{x}^1 - \mathbf{c}^1, \\
\mathbf{e}^2 &= \mathbf{x}^2 - \mathbf{c}^2,
\end{aligned}
\qquad (3)
$$

where $\mathbf{E}_1$ and $\mathbf{E}_2$ denote vectors of derivatives $(\partial E/\partial P^1_1, \ldots, \partial E/\partial P^1_n)$ and $[\partial E/\partial(DP^2_1), \ldots, \partial E/\partial(DP^2_n)]$ and where the welfare level that fulfills (2) is substituted into (3). Hence, equations (2) and (3) define the equilibrium of the country as a function of world prices, the discount factor, and the output vectors.

Nominal spending in period 1, Z^1, is then given by

$$Z^1 = \mathbf{P}^1\mathbf{c}^1, \qquad (4)$$

the value of consumption, and the trade balance surplus in period 1 is defined by

$$B^1 = \mathbf{P}^1\mathbf{e}^1 = \mathbf{P}^1\mathbf{x}^1 - \mathbf{P}^1\mathbf{c}^1, \qquad (5)$$

the value of the net export vector—the trade balance. Since there is no initial debt and hence no interest payments to or from the rest of the world, the trade balance is equal to the current-account surplus, or the excess of income over spending. In the absence of domestic investment, it is also equal to savings and to the accumulation of foreign assets.

We want to know the effect on spending and the trade balance of a terms-of-trade deterioration. In this n-good setup, we define a terms-of-trade deterioration in period t as a change $d\mathbf{P}^t$ in nominal prices that fulfills

$$\mathbf{e}^t d\mathbf{P}^t < 0. \tag{6}$$

That is, we require that the net export weighted price changes should be negative. In a two-good situation, where one good is exported and the other is imported, this corresponds to the usual definition of a decrease in the relative price of exports in terms of imports. We also distinguish a temporary, a future, and a permanent terms-of-trade deterioration. (i) A temporary terms-of-trade deterioration fulfills $\mathbf{e}^1 d\mathbf{P}^1 < 0$ and $d\mathbf{P}^2 = 0$; that is, there is a terms-of-trade deterioration only in period 1. (ii) A future terms-of-trade deterioration fulfills $d\mathbf{P}^1 = 0$, $\mathbf{e}^2 d\mathbf{P}^2 < 0$; that is, there is a terms-of-trade deterioration only in period 2. And (iii) a permanent terms-of-trade deterioration occurs when there is terms-of-trade deterioration in both periods.

To find the effects on spending and the trade balance of a terms-of-trade deterioration, we can now differentiate (4) and (5) for price changes fulfilling (6), taking into account (2) and (3). The details are shown in the Appendix (see also Svensson and Razin 1981). The outcome is that the changes in spending and the trade balance can be separated into three effects: (i) a direct effect, consisting of a revaluation of the consumption and net export vectors, respectively; (ii) a wealth effect on spending or, more precisely, a welfare effect, because the change in world prices changes welfare, which corresponds to an equivalent change in wealth at constant prices; and (iii) substitution effects, due to changes in spending because of changes in relative prices within and between periods, at a constant welfare level.

The direct and wealth effects can in some cases be unambiguously signed, whereas the substitution effects are more ambiguous. In particular, the sum of the direct and wealth effects on the trade balance is negative for a temporary terms-of-trade deterioration. For a period 2 terms-of-trade deterioration, the direct effect is zero and the wealth effect is positive. Thus, if the substitution effect is disregarded, the trade balance will deteriorate for a temporary current, and improve for a future, terms-of-trade deterioration. For a permanent terms-of-trade deterioration, the direct and wealth effects on the trade balance are in general ambiguous.

This is as far as we can go on a general level. In order to get more precise results for the determinants of spending and the trade balance, we shall make more specific assumptions.

III. Price Indices, Real Spending, and the Real Trade Balance

We wish to be able to identify something that can be interpreted as "real" spending and the real trade balance surplus. Remember that so far only nominal aggregates have been considered (in terms of some arbitrary unit of account). This requires constructing appropriate price indices, by which nominal aggregates are deflated. With these price indices, we can also define a real rate of interest.

A consistent way of doing this is to assume that the utility function is weakly separable,

$$U(\mathbf{c}^1, \mathbf{c}^2) = \bar{U}[z^1(\mathbf{c}^1), z^2(\mathbf{c}^2)], \tag{7}$$

and also that the subutility functions $z^1(\mathbf{c}^1)$ and $z^2(\mathbf{c}^2)$ are homothetic. Without any loss in generality, the subutility functions can then be chosen to be linearly homogeneous. The expenditure function $E(\mathbf{P}^1, D\mathbf{P}^2, u)$ can now be written $\bar{E}[\Pi^1(\mathbf{P}^1), D\Pi^2(\mathbf{P}^2), u]$, where $\bar{E}(\Pi^1, D\Pi^2, u)$ is the expenditure function corresponding to the utility function $\bar{U}(z^1, z^2)$, and $\Pi^1(\mathbf{P}^1)$ and $\Pi^2(\mathbf{P}^2)$ are expenditure functions, per unit of utility, corresponding to the subutility functions $z^1(\mathbf{c}^1)$ and $z^2(\mathbf{c}^2)$, respectively.[5]

We can rewrite the budget constraint (2) as

$$\bar{E}[\Pi^1(\mathbf{P}^1), D\Pi^2(\mathbf{P}^2), u] = W. \tag{8}$$

Nominal spending, (4), will fulfill

$$Z^1 = \Pi^1(\mathbf{P}^1)\bar{E}_1 = \Pi^1(\mathbf{P}^1)z^1, \tag{9}$$

where $\bar{E}_1$ denotes the derivative $\partial\bar{E}/\partial\Pi^1$. Hence we may interpret z^1 as the real spending in period 1 and $\Pi^1(\mathbf{P}^1)$ as the corresponding price index of real spending. That is, $\Pi^1(\mathbf{P}^1)$ is the nominal price of the period 1 subutility and similarly with respect to period 2.

Now let us define real prices (price vectors) $\mathbf{p}^t = \mathbf{P}^t/\Pi^t$ in period t, the real discount factor $\delta = D\Pi^2/\Pi^1$, and the real income $y^t = Y^t/\Pi^t = \mathbf{p}^t\mathbf{x}^t$ in period t. The real wealth is $w = W/\Pi^1 = y^1 + \delta y^2$. Note that all real magnitudes in period t are expressed in terms of units of period t subutility.

---

[5] The expenditure function $\bar{E}[\Pi^1(\mathbf{P}^1), D\Pi^2(\mathbf{P}^2), u]$ can be thought of as derived in two stages. First, period 1 spending $\mathbf{P}^1\mathbf{c}^1$ is minimized for a given level of period 1 subutility z^1, which defines the period 1 expenditure function as $\Pi^1(\mathbf{P}^1)z^1 = \min \{\mathbf{P}^1\mathbf{c}^1: z^1(\mathbf{c}^1) \geq z^1\}$. The period 1 expenditure function is linear in the period 1 subutility level due to the linear homogeneity of the period 1 subutility function. Analogously, the period 2 expenditure function is given by $\Pi^2(\mathbf{P}^2)z^2 = \min \{\mathbf{P}^2\mathbf{c}^2: z^2(\mathbf{c}^2) \geq z^2\}$. Second, the overall expenditure function $E(\mathbf{P}^1, D\mathbf{P}^2, u)$ can then be written as $\min \{\mathbf{P}^1\mathbf{c}^1 + D\mathbf{P}^2\mathbf{c}^2: U(\mathbf{c}^1, \mathbf{c}^2) \geq u\}$, which equals $\min \{\Pi^1(\mathbf{P}^1)z^1 + D\Pi^2(\mathbf{P}^2)z^2: \bar{U}(z^1, z^2) \geq u\}$, which in turn is $\bar{E}[\Pi^1(\mathbf{P}^1), D\Pi^2(\mathbf{P}^2), u]$. See Blackorby, Primont, and Russell (1978) or Goldman and Uzawa (1964) on separability and price indices.

TERMS OF TRADE 105

The real discount factor is expressed in units of period 1 subutility per units of period 2 subutility. Since the expenditure function is linearly homogeneous in prices, we can rewrite the budget constraint

$$\bar{E}(1, \delta, u) = \mathbf{p}^1\mathbf{x}^1 + \delta\mathbf{p}^2\mathbf{x}^2 = y^1 + \delta y^2 = w. \tag{10}$$

Real spending and the real trade balance surplus in the two periods, b^1 and b^2, are now given by the following four equations:

$$\begin{aligned}
z^1 &= \bar{E}_1(1, \delta, u), \\
z^2 &= \bar{E}_\delta(1, \delta, u), \\
b^1 &= y^1 - z^1, \\
b^2 &= y^2 - z^2.
\end{aligned} \tag{11}$$

A change in the nominal prices, $d\mathbf{P}^t$, in each period will change the real prices and the discount factor according to

$$\begin{aligned}
d\mathbf{p}^t &= (d\mathbf{P}^t/\Pi^t) - \mathbf{p}^t\hat{\Pi}^t, \\
d\delta &= \delta(\hat{\Pi}^2 - \hat{\Pi}^1),
\end{aligned} \tag{12}$$

where $\hat{\Pi}^t$ denotes the relative change in the price index in period t, which is given by

$$\hat{\Pi}^t = d\Pi^t/\Pi^t = \Sigma_i(P_i^t c_i^t/Z^t)(dP_i^t/P_i^t), \tag{13}$$

that is, the usual consumption share weighted relative price changes.[6] The changes in the real prices lead to changes in the real income in period t,

$$dy^t = \mathbf{x}^t d\mathbf{p}^t = \mathbf{e}^t d\mathbf{p}^t, \tag{14}$$

where we have used the condition that the real prices fulfill $\mathbf{c}^t d\mathbf{p}^t = 0$.[7] That is, the change in real income in period t is equal to what we, by analogy with (6), call the real terms-of-trade effect in period t.

To find the effects on real spending and the real trade balance, we first differentiate (10) to get

$$\bar{E}_u du = dy^1 + \delta dy^2 + b^2 d\delta. \tag{15}$$

This means that the change in the level of welfare is proportional to the change in the present value of real income (the change in real wealth) at a constant discount factor, plus the real current-account

---

[6] We have $d\Pi^t/\Pi^t = \Sigma_i[(\partial\Pi^t/\partial P_i^t)dP_i^t/\Pi^t] = \Sigma_i[(c_i^t/z^t)dP_i^t/\Pi^t] = \Sigma_i[(P_i^t c_i^t/\Pi^t z^t)dP_i^t/P_i^t]$, with $\Pi^t z^t = Z^t = \Sigma_i P_i^t c_i^t$.

[7] We have $\mathbf{c}^t d\mathbf{p}^t = \mathbf{c}^t d[\mathbf{P}^t/\Pi^t(\mathbf{P}^t)] = (\mathbf{c}^t d\mathbf{P}^t/\Pi^t) - (\mathbf{p}^t\mathbf{c}^t d\Pi^t/\Pi^t)$. But by n. 6, $d\Pi^t = (\mathbf{c}^t/z^t)d\mathbf{P}^t$. Furthermore, $\mathbf{p}^t\mathbf{c}^t = Z^t$, since $\mathbf{P}^t\mathbf{c}^t = \Pi^t z^t$. Note that $dy^1 = \mathbf{e}^1 d\mathbf{p}^1 = \mathbf{e}^1 d(\mathbf{P}^1/\Pi^1) = (\mathbf{e}^1 d\mathbf{P}^1/\Pi^1) - (\mathbf{p}^1\mathbf{e}^1 d\Pi^1/\Pi^1) = (\mathbf{e}^1 d\mathbf{P}^1/\Pi^1) - (b^1 d\Pi^1/\Pi^1)$. Hence, it does not follow that dy^1 is always negative if $\mathbf{e}^1 d\mathbf{P}^1$ is negative.

surplus in period 2, times the change in the real rate of interest. The latter term we call the real intertemporal terms-of-trade effect.

Next, by differentiating (11) and using (15) we get the change in real spending,

$$dz^1 = z_w^1(dy^1 + \delta dy^2 + b^2 d\delta) + z_\delta^1\delta, \qquad (16)$$

where z_w^1 is the real marginal propensity to spend out of real wealth, and z_δ^1 denotes the derivative $\partial\bar{E}_1/\partial\delta$. Hence the change in real spending consists of a wealth effect and a substitution effect, the latter corresponding to a change in the real discount factor.

Finally, the change in the real trade balance surplus is

$$db^1 = dy^1 - z_w^1(dy^1 + \delta dy^2 + b^2 d\delta) - z_\delta^1\delta, \qquad (17)$$

which consists of a direct effect on real income, a wealth effect on real spending, and a substitution effect on real spending.

Expressions (16) and (17) can be interpreted graphically as shown in figure 1. The initial real income point (y^1, y^2) is A and the initial real spending point (z^1, z^2) is C. The slope of the intertemporal budget line is equal to one over the real discount factor. The period 1 real current-account surplus is equal to the horizontal distance between A and C (the surplus is positive in the diagram). The vertical distance between A and C is the real trade balance surplus in period 2 (negative). Consider changes in world prices that lead to a real terms-of-trade deterioration in both periods. This shifts the real income point southwest to A'. The change in world prices also changes the real discount factor. In the diagram we assume that the real discount factor increases, and this twists the budget line counterclockwise through A'. The new real spending point is C'. The new real trade balance surplus in period 1 is equal to the horizontal distance between A' and C'. The change in real spending in period 1 can be decomposed into the shift from C to D along the wealth-expansion path corresponding to the wealth effect $z_w^1(dy^1 + \delta dy^2)$ and the shift from D to F corresponding to the wealth effect $z_w^1 b^2 d\delta$ caused by the intertemporal terms-of-trade effect. Finally, the shift from F to C' corresponds to the substitution effects $z_\delta^1 d\delta$.

Let us consider separately the effect of world price changes that imply a temporary real terms-of-trade deterioration ($dy^1 = \mathbf{e}^1 d\mathbf{p}^1 < 0$, $dy^2 = \mathbf{e}^2 d\mathbf{p}^2 = 0$) but hold constant the real discount factor. This amounts to a shift in the real income point west, to A'', say. The real spending point shifts southwest to D. Clearly, the real trade balance unambiguously deteriorates.

Note, however, that a temporary nominal terms-of-trade deterioration ($\mathbf{e}^1 d\mathbf{P}^1 < 0$, $d\mathbf{P}^2 = 0$) will in general also imply a change in the real discount factor. If it leads to an increase in the discount factor,

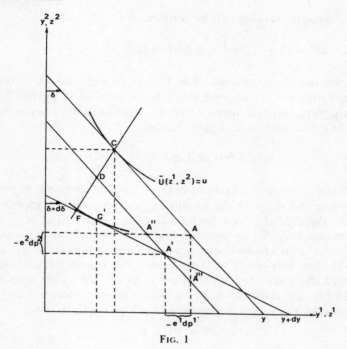

FIG. 1

the substitution effect on the trade balance is counter to the direct plus wealth effect, and the overall change on the real trade balance is of ambiguous sign.

In the diagram, we can also see the effect of the expected future real terms-of-trade deterioration, at constant real discount factor. In this case the real income point shifts south to, say, A'''. Clearly, the real trade balance will unambiguously improve. Again, a future nominal terms-of-trade deterioration will in general also imply a change in the discount factor and a corresponding substitution effect.

It follows from the above that the effect on the real trade balance of a permanent real terms-of-trade deterioration is in general ambiguous. In the next section, we examine that case more closely.

IV. A Permanent Terms-of-Trade Deterioration in a Stationary State and the Rate of Time Preference

We now consider changes in world prices that leave the real discount factor constant. Then both the intertemporal terms-of-trade effect and the substitution effect in (17) vanish and the change in the real current-account surplus can be written as

$$db^1 = (1 - z_w^1)dy^1 - \delta z_w^1 dy^2 = \delta z_w^1\left(\frac{z_w^2}{z_w^1} - \frac{dy^2}{dy^1}\right)dy^1, \qquad (18)$$

where we use the condition that $1 - z_w^1 = \delta z_w^2$ and z_w^2 is the real marginal propensity to spend (out of real wealth) in period 2. Consider a permanent real terms-of-trade deterioration. Then it is clear from (18), and also from figure 1, that

$$db^1 \gtreqless 0 \text{ if and only if } \frac{z_w^2}{z_w^1} \gtreqless \frac{dy^2}{dy^1}. \qquad (19)$$

That is, the real current account deteriorates or improves, depending on whether the slope of the wealth expansion path is greater or less than the slope of the "real income line" through A and A'.

Let us now consider a stationary state with the following properties: We assume that preferences are not only homothetically weakly separable, but identically so. This means that the subutility functions $z^1(\mathbf{c}^1)$ and $z^2(\mathbf{c}^2)$ are identical. Then the price index functions $\Pi^1(\mathbf{P}^1)$ and $\Pi^2(\mathbf{P}^2)$ are also identical. In addition, we assume that world nominal spot prices are the same in both periods, that is,

$$\mathbf{P}^2 = \mathbf{P}^1 = \mathbf{P}. \qquad (20)$$

Then, due to the linear homogeneity of the price index function, the real discount factor δ is equal to the nominal discount factor D. Furthermore, let us assume that the change in world prices is the same in both periods,

$$d\mathbf{P}^2 = d\mathbf{P}^1 = d\mathbf{P}. \qquad (21)$$

Then it follows from (12) that the real discount factor is constant. Finally, let us assume that

$$\mathbf{e}^1 = \mathbf{e}^2 = \mathbf{e}; \qquad (22)$$

that is, the net export vector is the same in both periods.

It follows from (20) and (22) that

$$b^1 = b^2 = 0; \qquad (23)$$

that is, the real trade balance surplus is zero, and hence real spending equals real income in every period. Since real prices, by (12), (20), and (21), satisfy

$$d\mathbf{p}^1 = d\mathbf{p}^2 = d\mathbf{p}, \qquad (24)$$

it particularly follows from (22) that

$$dy^1 = \mathbf{e}^1 d\mathbf{p}^1 = \mathbf{e}^2 d\mathbf{p}^2 = dy^2 = dy; \qquad (25)$$

TERMS OF TRADE

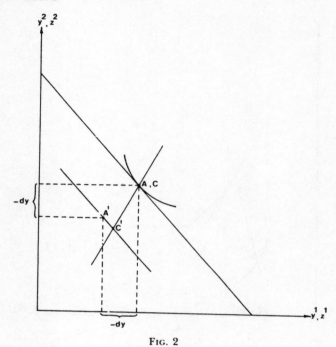

FIG. 2

that is, the changes in real income in the two periods are equal. Then, the change in the current-account surplus is much simplified. It must be equal to

$$db^1 = \delta(z_w^2 - z_w^1)dy. \tag{26}$$

For a permanent terms-of-trade deterioration, when $dy < 0$,[8] we have:

$$db^1 \lesseqgtr 0 \text{ if and only if } z_w^2 \gtreqless z_w^1. \tag{27}$$

The real current account deteriorates, or improves, depending on whether the marginal propensity to spend in period 2 exceeds, or falls short of, the marginal propensity to spend in period 1, that is, whether the slope of the wealth-expansion path is greater or less than one.

This situation is illustrated in figure 2. The initial equilibrium, with a zero current account, is A, C, where the real income and spending points coincide. The deterioration in the terms of trade shifts the real income point to A' along a line having a slope equal to one. The real spending point shifts to C', where the budget line through A' cuts the wealth-expansion path (here with a slope that exceeds one). The

[8] When $b^1 = 0$, it follows from n. 7 that $e^1 dP^1 < 0$ implies $e^1 dp^1 < 0$.

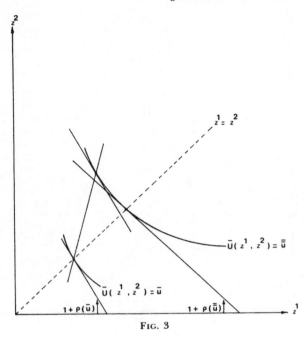

FIG. 3

current account in period 1 changes to the horizontal distance between A' and C'. Thus, here the current account deteriorates.

The condition described above concerning the marginal propensities to spend can be related also to the rate of time preference.
Define the rate of time preference as a function $\rho(u)$ of the welfare
level u by

$$\rho(u) = \frac{\bar{U}_1(z^1, z^2)}{\bar{U}_2(z^1, z^2)} - 1, \tag{28}$$

for $z^1 = z^2$ and $\bar{U}(z^1, z^2) = u$, where $\bar{U}_1$ denotes the partial derivative of
$\bar{U}$ with respect to z^1, etc. That is, the rate of time preference for a
given welfare level is equal to (the absolute value of) the slope of the
indifference curve of the utility function $\bar{U}(z^1, z^2)$ on the 45-degree
ray, minus one. Equivalently, the rate of time preference is equal to
the marginal rate of substitution between real spending in period 2
and real spending in period 1, minus one, evaluated at a point where
the real spending in the two periods is equal. Put differently, the rate
of time preference is the subjective interest rate along the 45-degree
ray. From figure 3 we can directly derive the result that a necessary
condition for the marginal propensity to spend in period 2 to exceed

(fall short of) that in period 1 is that the rate of time preference decreases (increases) with the level of welfare.[9]

Let us recall the discussion in the literature regarding the rate of time preference. Fisher (1930) assumed that the rate of time preference decreases with the level of welfare, but Fisher's arguments were criticized by Friedman (1969). Uzawa (1968), followed by Findlay (1978), specified a rate of time preference which increases with the level of welfare. Uzawa (1969) also used an alternative specification where preferences are homothetic and the rate of time preference does not change with the level of welfare. In two classic articles, Koopmans (1960) and Koopmans, Diamond, and Williamson (1964), it has been shown that consistency with some basic axioms demands that the rate of time preference be positive, but it may decrease, remain constant, or increase without violating the axioms (Koopmans et al. 1964, p. 98). Hence, it seems to us that a priori neither a decreasing nor an increasing rate of time preference can be excluded.

So far we have restricted our analysis to a two-period model. Next, we shall show how to extend our analysis to an infinite horizon.

V. An Infinite Horizon

Here we use a very simplified approach, restricting ourselves to the case where real prices, the real discount factor, and the production vector are the same in all periods. In particular, we find it convenient first to deal with a very simple case where the country is restricted to choosing between present real spending and permanently constant future spending. Then we reformulate this case to one where the country chooses between present real spending and real future wealth. Finally, we show that the analysis of the case where the country chooses an optimal sequence of real spending over time is completely analogous to the analysis of the first two special cases.

Let us assume an infinite horizon, and let there be discrete periods $t = 1, 2, \ldots$. Let preferences be identically homothetically weakly separable, such that the utility function is:

$$U(\mathbf{c}^1, \mathbf{c}^2, \ldots) = \bar{U}[z(\mathbf{c}^1), z(\mathbf{c}^2), \ldots], \qquad (29)$$

where $\mathbf{c}^t$ is period t's consumption vector and where the subutility function $z(\mathbf{c}^t)$ is homogeneous of degree one and the same in each period. We will assume that the world relative spot prices are the same in each period. Then real (spot) prices, denoted by $\mathbf{p}$, are the same in

---

[9] An alternative condition is in terms of the wealth elasticity of period 1 spending, evaluated at the stationary point. If the elasticity is larger (smaller) than one, the current account will deteriorate (improve) from the terms-of-trade deterioration.

each period. We will also assume that the real discount factor δ between any two consecutive periods is the same; that is, the real rate of interest r, given by $\delta = (1 + r)^{-1}$, is the same between any two consecutive periods. In particular, we assume that the real rate of interest is positive and hence that the real discount factor is less than one. Finally, let us assume that the production vector $\mathbf{x}$ is also the same in each period.

Then the welfare-maximizing problem in the first period can be written

$$\max_{\{z^t\}} \bar{U}(z^1, z^2, \ldots)$$

subject to

$$\sum_1^\infty \delta^{t-1} z^t \leq (1 + r^{-1})\mathbf{px}, \tag{30}$$

where $z^t = z(\mathbf{c}^t)$ denotes real spending in period t, and where we have utilized that $\Sigma_1^\infty \delta^{t-1} = 1 + r^{-1}$.

Let us assume first that the country exhibits bounded rationality in the sense that it restricts its choice to that between real spending z^1, in period 1, and permanent future real spending $\bar{z}^2$. Then let us define the bounded rationality utility function $\check{U}(z^1, \bar{z}^2) = \bar{U}(z^1, \bar{z}^2, \bar{z}^2, \ldots)$ and formulate the problem as:

$$\max_{(z^1, \bar{z}^2)} \check{U}(z^1, \bar{z}^2)$$

subject to

$$z^1 + r^{-1}\bar{z}^2 = (1 + r^{-1})\mathbf{px}, \tag{31}$$

where we have utilized that $\Sigma_2^\infty \delta^{t-1} = r^{-1}$.

The solution is shown in figure 4. The "permanent" real income point is A. Real spending in period 1 and permanent future real spending are given by point C. The real current-account surplus, identical to real net saving, is given by the horizontal distance between A and C. Since there is no initial debt, the first-period current account is also equal to the trade balance in that period.

Now, let us assume that the country solves the same problem (31) in the next period, period 2.[10] But now the permanent real income point is at D rather than A, since the country now receives interest on its accumulated foreign assets, in addition to income from production, and the relevant budget line has shifted outward. That is, the repre-

---

[10] That is, we take the utility function $\check{U}(z^t, \bar{z}^{t+1})$ to describe the preferences when decisions are made in period t, not only in period 1.

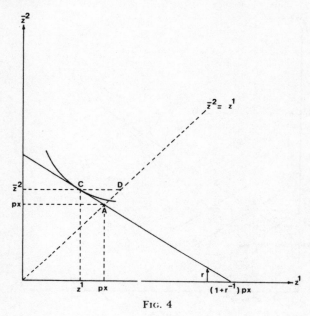

FIG. 4

sentative consumer solves the sequence of problems:

$$\max_{(z^t, \bar{z}^{t+1})} \tilde{U}(z^t, \bar{z}^{t+1})$$

subject to

$$z^t + r^{-1}\bar{z}^{t+1} = (1 + r^{-1})\bar{z}^t \tag{32}$$

for $t = 2, \ldots$. The solutions to these are illustrated in figure 5. Observe that in period 2 the current-account surplus is given by the horizontal distance between points D and E while the trade balance is measured by the horizontal distance between A and E. It is clear that real spending converges to the stationary state level z^* if and only if the wealth-expansion path FF has a slope less than one. In analogy with (28), we now define the rate of time preference function $\tilde{\rho}(u)$ as

$$\tilde{\rho}(u) = \frac{\tilde{U}_1(z^t, \bar{z}^{t+1})}{\tilde{U}_2(z^t, \bar{z}^{t+1})} - 1 \tag{33}$$

for $z^t = \bar{z}^{t+1}$ and $\tilde{U}(z^t, \bar{z}^{t+1}) = u$. Then, as before, a necessary condition for the wealth-expansion path to have a slope less than one is that the rate of time preference increases with the level of welfare.

In order to deal with a case of full rationality rather than bounded rationality, let us first restate problems (31) and (32) in terms of future

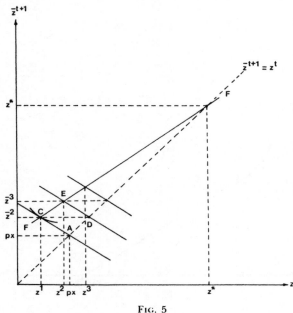

Fig. 5

wealth rather than in terms of real future permanent spending. We then define real wealth w^t in period $t = 1, 2, \ldots$, as

$$w^1 = (1 + r^{-1})\mathbf{px}$$

and

$$w^{t+1} = (1 + r)(w^t - z^t) \text{ for } t = 1, \ldots. \tag{34}$$

That is, real wealth in period 1 is equal to the present value of initial permanent real income $\mathbf{px}$, and real wealth in period t is equal to one plus the real rate of interest times that part of the real wealth in period $t - 1$ that is not spent. From (34) and the budget constraints in (32) we also have

$$w^{t+1} = (1 + r^{-1})\bar{z}^{t+1}; \tag{35}$$

that is, real wealth in period $t + 1$ is equal to the present value of real permanent future spending.

Given (35), let us define the reduced utility function $\tilde{V}(z^t, w^{t+1}, \delta)$ as

$$\tilde{V}(z^t, w^{t+1}, \delta) = \tilde{U}[z^t, w^{t+1}/(1 + r^{-1})]. \tag{36}$$

Then problems (31) and (32) can be written as

$$\max_{(z^t, w^{t+1})} \tilde{V}(z^t, w^{t+1}, \delta)$$

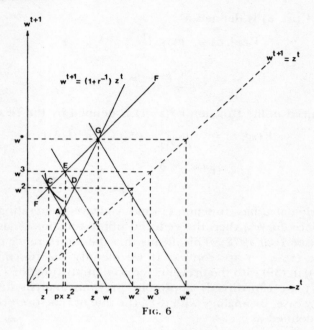

FIG. 6

subject to

$$z^t + \delta w^{t+1} = w^t. \tag{37}$$

The solutions to (37) are shown in space (z^t, w^{t+1}) in figure 6, which, given the linear relation (35), is completely analogous to figure 5. The stationary state (z^*, w^*) is stable if and only if the wealth-expansion path *FF* has a slope less than that of the "stationarity line" $w^{t+1} = (1 + r^{-1})z^t$; a necessary condition for this is that the rate of time preference increases with the welfare level.

Let us now consider the full rationality problem. Given some axioms concerning the intertemporal preference ordering (see Koopmans 1960; Koopmans et al. 1964; and Iwai 1972),[11] we can define an indirect utility as a function of wealth and the real interest rate and a reduced utility function defined in terms of present spending and next-period wealth. It is derived from the dynamic programming principle that along the optimal path decisions in the next period must be optimal with regard to the level of wealth resulting from the decision taken in the current period. The indirect utility

---

[11] We wish to thank the referee for bringing Iwai's important work to our attention.

function $V(w^t, \delta)$ is defined as

$$V(w^t, \delta) = \max_{\{z^\tau\}_t^\infty} \bar{U}(z^t, z^{t+1}, \ldots)$$

$$\text{s.t.} \sum_t^\infty \delta^{\tau-1} z^\tau = w^t. \tag{38}$$

The reduced utility function $V^*(z^t, u)$ is defined by the relation

$$V(w^t, \delta) = \max_{(z^t, w^{t+1})} V^*[z^t, V(w^{t+1}, \delta)]$$

$$\text{s.t. } z^t + \delta w^{t+1} = w^t, \tag{39}$$

$$w^1 = (1 + r^{-1})\mathbf{px}.$$

If the original utility function is quasi-concave (generating convex indifference curves) then the reduced utility function is also quasi-concave (see Iwai 1972). This means that the indifference curves in the space (z^t, w^{t+1}) are convex. If we identify the function $V^*[z^t, V(w^{t+1}, \delta)]$ in (39) with the previous reduced utility function $\bar{V}(z^t, w^{t+1}, \delta)$ in (37), we can directly apply our previous analysis to the full rationality case. By analogy with (31), the rate of time preference can then be defined as

$$\rho(u) = \frac{\partial V^*/\partial z^t}{(1 + r^{-1})(\partial V^*/\partial u)(\partial V/\partial w^{t+1})} - 1$$

along the stationarity line $w^{t+1} = (1 + r^{-1})z^t$ and for $V^*[z^t, V(w^{t+1}, \delta)] = u$.[12]

Hence, in the infinite-horizon case, a necessary and sufficient condition for stability of the stationary state is that the rate of time preference increases with the welfare level.

Let us now consider the effect of a terms-of-trade deterioration on the real current account, under the assumption of a stable stationary state. We will assume that the country is initially at the stationary state G in figure 6. Suppose that initially the country holds no foreign assets. Real prices are $\mathbf{p}^*$ and spending z^* is equal to the initial real permanent income, $\mathbf{p}^*\mathbf{x}$. The initial real wealth is $w^* = (1 + r^{-1})\mathbf{p}^*\mathbf{x}$. Now consider a real permanent terms-of-trade deterioration $\mathbf{e}d\mathbf{p}^* < 0$ that does not change the real rate of interest. This corresponds to a decrease in the initial real permanent income and a decrease in the

---

[12] By (33) and (35) we have

$$\tilde{\rho}(u) = \frac{\partial \tilde{V}/\partial z^t}{(1 + r^{-1})\partial \tilde{V}/\partial w^{t+1}} - 1.$$

Identifying $V^*[z^t, V(w^{t+1}, \delta)]$ with $\tilde{V}(z^t, w^{t+1}, \delta)$ in (37) gives $\partial \tilde{V}/\partial z^t = \partial V^*/\partial z^t$ and $\partial \tilde{V}/\partial w^{t+1} = (\partial V^*/\partial u) \cdot (\partial V/\partial w^{t+1})$.

initial real wealth given by $dw = (1 + r^{-1})ed\mathbf{p}^*$. Suppose that prices change from $\mathbf{p}^*$ to $\mathbf{p}$, real permanent income changes from $\mathbf{p}^*\mathbf{x}$ to $\mathbf{px}$, and the real wealth shifts down to the level w^1 in figure 6. This corresponds to a new feasible stationary state given by point A, with real spending equal to the new permanent income.

However, at that level of real wealth, real spending is given by point C, corresponding to a positive real current-account surplus which is equal to the horizontal distance between A and C. Since there is no initial debt this is also the trade account surplus. The surplus in the current account increases the next period's real wealth to w^2, etc. Eventually the country returns to its previous stationary state (z^*, w^*). At the stationary point the permanent spending z^* is financed by output sales $\mathbf{px}$ as well as interest receipts on accumulated assets.

We can express this by saying that the country has a long-run target wealth w^*. A real terms-of-trade deterioration from an initial stationary state decreases current real wealth below its target level. To get back to its target, the country saves by having a real current-account surplus.

However, if the rate of time preference is decreasing with the welfare level the *FF* line will intersect the stationary line from below. A deterioration in the terms of trade would lead to overspending and assets' decumulation. In an extreme case it may continue up to a point where interest payments are equal to output, $\mathbf{px}$. At that point spending ceases completely. Alternatively, there can be another stable point to which the assets' decumulation process would converge.

Hence, in the infinite-horizon case, stability of the stationary state implies that the rate of time preference increases with the welfare level and that a terms-of-trade deterioration, as above, implies an improvement in the real current account while instability implies a deterioration. We do not, however, regard stability of the stationary state as more reasonable than instability. Whether or not there is stability depends on the preferences' structure. But note that the country may, in the unstable case, become too large, thus violating the small-country assumption. The experiment investigated here is therefore only partial, with the interest rate being held constant. The present framework can obviously be embedded in a general world equilibrium in order to get a more complete view of the interactions between the current account, the terms of trade, and the rate of interest.[13]

---

[13] Stability of the stationary state is not a necessary condition for the existence of an optimal solution. Imagine that a country in an initially unstable stationary state experiences a permanent improvement in its terms of trade. The country begins to run a surplus and accumulates assets. Its spending increases over time, but as long as the wealth-expansion path is above the stationarity line its spending never exceeds its

VI. Relations to Previous Literature

In the general case, the effect on nominal spending, Z^1, of a change in world prices is given by (A.2) in the Appendix and consists of a direct, a wealth, and a substitution effect. Similarly, the effect on the nominal trade balance surplus and nominal saving, $B^1 = S^1 = Y^1 - Z^1$, is given by (A.3). Previous literature has considered (mainly) the two-good case, where the country is completely specialized in the production of one exportable good. In our framework, let $n = 2$ and let good 1 be exportable. Then the production vectors $\mathbf{x}^1$ and $\mathbf{x}^2$ and the net trade vectors $\mathbf{e}^1$ and $\mathbf{e}^2$ are:

$$
\begin{aligned}
\mathbf{x}^1 &= (x_1^1, 0), \\
\mathbf{x}^2 &= (x_1^2, 0), \\
\mathbf{e}^1 &= (x_1^1 - c_1^1, -c_2^1), \\
\mathbf{e}^2 &= (x_1^2 - c_1^2, -c_2^2).
\end{aligned}
\tag{40}
$$

Also, the literature has been concerned with spending and saving measured in terms of exportables. In our framework this corresponds to choosing the exportable good as the numeraire and hence restricting nominal prices in period 1 to fulfill

$$
\begin{aligned}
\mathbf{P}^1 &= (1, P_2^1), \\
d\mathbf{P}^1 &= (0, dP_2^1).
\end{aligned}
\tag{41}
$$

Hence under (40) and (41) we have

$$
dY^1 = \mathbf{x}^1 d\mathbf{P}^1 = 0;
\tag{42}
$$

that is, period 1 income measured in exportables is constant, and the terms-of-trade effect in that period is

$$
\mathbf{e}^1 d\mathbf{P}^1 = -\mathbf{c}^1 d\mathbf{P}^1 = -c_2^1 dP_2^1.
\tag{43}
$$

Thus, a terms-of-trade deterioration is represented by an increase in the price of importables relative to exportables.

Hence, under (42) the change in spending in terms of exportables is

$$
dZ^1 = -dS^1,
\tag{44}
$$

---

permanent income and it continues to accumulate (subject to the limits imposed by the small-country assumption and a suitable terminal condition on wealth in the limit). Nothing in principle prevents this dynamic path from being an optimal solution to (30). If the wealth-expansion curve happens to have several intersections with the stationarity line, we realize that we will have alternating stable and unstable stationary states along the stationarity line. All kinds of possibilities then arise: e.g., a terms-of-trade change can shift the country from a region in which it approaches one stable stationary state to one where it starts to approach another or where it accumulates indefinitely, and vice versa.

and the change in saving measured in terms of exportables (given by [A.3]) is

$$dS^1 = (1 - Z_W^1)\mathbf{e}^1 d\mathbf{P}^1 - Z_W^1 D\mathbf{e}^2 d\mathbf{P}^2 - \mathbf{P}^1(\mathbf{E}_{11}d\mathbf{P}^1 + \mathbf{E}_{12}D\mathbf{P}^2), \quad (45)$$

where the first term on the right-hand side is the product of the marginal propensity to save out of wealth in period 1 times the terms-of-trade effect.

Harberger (1950, pp. 52–53), in his discussion of the effect of a devaluation on the trade balance, assumed (i) that savings S, measured in terms of exportables, depend on "real consumer income" y only, and (ii) that the change in real consumer income is equal to the quantity imported times the increase in the price of importables relative to exportables; that is, in our notation,

$$S = S(y) \quad (46)$$

and

$$dy = -\mathbf{c}_2 d\mathbf{P}_2 = \mathbf{e}_2 d\mathbf{P}_2 = \mathbf{e}d\mathbf{P}, \quad (47)$$

where we have used (43). Thus, the change in saving due to a terms-of-trade deterioration is

$$dS = S_y \mathbf{e}d\mathbf{P}, \quad (48)$$

where S_y denotes the marginal propensity to save out of real income. We may thus interpret Harberger's result as including the first term in (45) while disregarding the period 2 wealth effect and the substitution effect on spending.

Laursen and Metzler (1950, p. 280) argued (i) that the ratio of savings to income, measured in terms of exportables, decreases with the fall in real income, and (ii) that a terms-of-trade deterioration decreases real income. Their argument is therefore completely analogous to that of Harberger. Consequently, a terms-of-trade deterioration should decrease saving and increase spending out of any given level of income, where all variables are measured in terms of exportables. Laursen and Metzler supported their argument with reference to Duesenberry's (1948) empirical findings that in the short run, during the business cycle, the saving ratio indeed falls with declining real income. They were subsequently criticized by White (1954), who emphasized that in the long run saving and spending out of any given level of income should be unaffected by terms-of-trade changes. This was because statistical evidence showed that the savings ratio in the long run tended to be constant with changes in real income. This point had, however, already been acknowledged in Laursen and Metzler's original article, which explicitly dealt with the short run (since their main interest was the transmission of business cycles between countries). We may thus interpret Laursen and Metzler's argument as being concerned with the first effect in (45) arising from what we have called a *temporary* terms-of-trade deterioration. White, on the other hand, is concerned with a *permanent* terms-of-trade deterioration, which may indeed, under circumstances examined in detail in Section IV above, result in a zero effect on saving. They all disregarded substitution effects on spending.

Harberger, and implicitly Laursen and Metzler, were criticized by Day (1954), Pearce (1955), and Spraos (1955) for not having considered substitution between saving and consumption and for disregarding the effect of a terms-of-trade deterioration on the real value of saving. This implies that Harberger had underestimated the loss in real income from a terms-of-trade deterioration. Pearce (1955) emphasized in particular that any substitution effect between saving and consumption would depend on changes in the real rate of interest. We may interpret this line of criticism as being concerned with the distinction between the effects of a temporary versus a permanent terms-of-trade deterioration and with the substitution effects on saving. However, they did not succeed in providing a clear-cut analysis of the problem, presumably because they did not consider an intertemporal utility-maximization model where the demand for saving is derived from the demand for future consumption.

Subsequently, Jones (1960), Tsiang (1961), and Dornbusch (1980) used a specification that regards nominal spending as a product of a price index Π, depending on nominal prices $\mathbf{P}$, and real spending z, depending on real income; that is,

$$Z = \Pi(\mathbf{P})z(y), \tag{49}$$

where real income y is nominal income Y deflated by the price index, or

$$y = Y/\Pi(\mathbf{P}). \tag{50}$$

From our analysis it follows that under the assumption of homothetical weak separability of preferences, nominal spending can indeed be written as the product of a price index and real spending. The latter will, however, in general, depend on the real discount factor δ and on the real wealth $y^1 + \delta y^2$, not only on real current income y^1. That is,[14]

$$Z^1 = \Pi^1(\mathbf{P}^1)z^1(\delta, y^1 + \delta y^2). \tag{51}$$

---

[14] In the stationary case when y^1 equals y^2 we can, of course, write $\bar{z}^1(\delta, y^1) \equiv z^1[\delta, (1 + \delta)y^1]$; and for price changes that leave the real rate of interest constant and affect real income in both periods identically, it will appear as if real spending depends on current income $y^1 = Y^1/\Pi^1$ only.

Rodríguez (1976) (who considers an alternative to the simple version of the monetary approach to the balance of payments) indeed makes real expenditure a function of real permanent income rather than real current income. On the other hand, he disregards the dependence of spending on the real interest rate.

It is clear that the questions raised by Harberger and Laursen and Metzler can satisfactorily be answered only in an explicitly intertemporal framework. This is the starting point of Obstfeld (1982), who undertakes a rigorous analysis of the issues within an infinite-horizon, continuous-time, and intertemporal utility-maximizing model along the lines of Uzawa (1968). In contrast to Harberger and Laursen and Metzler, he finds that a terms-of-trade deterioration increases rather than decreases saving and hence improves rather than deteriorates the current account.

The reason for Obstfeld's result is the following. First, he uses a discounted sum of utilities (an integral) as the intertemporal utility function. Thus he implicitly assumes identically homothetically weakly separable preferences. Second, he considers a permanent terms-of-trade deterioration leaving the rate of interest constant in an initial stationary state. Third, and crucially, he assumes that the rate of time preference increases with the welfare level (in his case it is only a function of instantaneous flow of utility). This, as we have seen above in Section V, must imply that the current account improves.

Recently, Sachs (1981) has discussed the determinants of the current account in a two-period model of a country producing, consuming, investing, and exporting a final good and importing an intermediate input, oil. He examines the effect of a terms-of-trade deterioration, that is, an increase in the relative price of oil at a constant (final goods) rate of interest. He assumes a Cobb-Douglas intertemporal utility function; hence the rate of time preference is constant. Since there is only one consumer good there are no consumption substitution effects on the trade balance. Sachs emphasizes the distinction between a temporary and a permanent terms-of-trade deterioration and shows that savings deteriorate for a temporary terms-of-trade deterioration but may remain unchanged for a permanent terms-of-trade deterioration. These results correspond to ours in Sections III and IV. Sachs also includes the effects of investment on the current account. See also Svensson (1981) for further analysis of a small oil importer's trade balance with investment and with and without full employment.

The trade balance response to oil price increases when there are nontraded goods has recently been analyzed along similar lines in explicitly intertemporal models by Marion (1981) and Bruno (1982).

Appendix

The General Effects on the Nominal Spending and the Nominal Trade Balance of a Terms-of-Trade Deterioration

In order to find the effect of a change in world prices, $d\mathbf{P}^t$, on welfare, we differentiate (2), using (3), to obtain

$$E_u du = \mathbf{e}^1 d\mathbf{P}^1 + \mathbf{e}^2 D d\mathbf{P}^2, \tag{A.1}$$

where E_u, the inverse of the marginal utility of present value income, is positive. The expression $E_u du$ is the wealth equivalent of the change in the welfare level.

We differentiate (4) and use (A.1) to obtain the effect of the world price changes on spending,

$$dZ^1 = \mathbf{c}^1 d\mathbf{P}^1 + Z_W^1(\mathbf{e}^1 d\mathbf{P}^1 + \mathbf{e}^2 D d\mathbf{P}^2) + \mathbf{P}^1(\mathbf{E}_{11} d\mathbf{P}^1 + \mathbf{E}_{12} D d\mathbf{P}^2). \tag{A.2}$$

where $Z_W^1 = \mathbf{P}^1 \mathbf{c}_W^1$ is period 1 marginal propensity to spend out of wealth, and $\mathbf{c}_W^1$ is the partial derivative with respect to W of the uncompensated demand function for goods. (The term $\mathbf{P}^1 \mathbf{E}_{1u} du$ can be written as $\mathbf{PE}_{1u} E_u^{-1} E_u du$, and $\mathbf{E}_{1u} E_u^{-1}$ is equal to $\mathbf{c}_W^1$.) The expression $\mathbf{E}_{11}$ is the matrix of substitution effects $(\partial^2 E/\partial P_i^1 \partial P_j^1) = [\partial c_i^1(\mathbf{P}^1, D\mathbf{P}^2, W)/\partial P_j^1]$, where $\mathbf{c}^1(\mathbf{P}^1, D\mathbf{P}^2, u)$ is the compensated demand for goods consumed in period 1. Similarly, $\mathbf{E}_{12}$ is the cross-periods substitution matrix $[\partial^2 E/\partial P_i^1 \partial(DP_j^2)] = [\partial c_i^1(\mathbf{P}^1, D\mathbf{P}^2, u)/\partial(DP_j^2)]$. The first term on the right-hand side of (A.2) can be called a direct effect, the second a wealth effect, and the third a substitution effect.

Finally, differentiating (5) using (A.2) yields

$$dB^1 = \mathbf{e}^1 d\mathbf{P}^1 - Z_W^1(\mathbf{e}^1 d\mathbf{P}^1 + \mathbf{e}^2 D d\mathbf{P}^2) - \mathbf{P}^1(\mathbf{E}_{11} d\mathbf{P}^1 + \mathbf{E}_{12} D d\mathbf{P}^2). \tag{A.3}$$

Thus, the effect of world price changes on the nominal trade balance surplus also consists of three effects: a direct effect, a wealth effect, and a substitution effect. We let $\mathbf{E}_{11} d\mathbf{P}^1$ denote the n vector given by the postmultiplication of the matrix $\mathbf{E}_{11}$ by $d\mathbf{P}^1$, the latter taken as a column vector, etc. Then $\mathbf{P}^1(\mathbf{E}_{11} d\mathbf{P}^1)$ denotes the inner product between $\mathbf{P}^1$ and $(\mathbf{E}_{11} d\mathbf{P}^1)$ or, equivalently, the premultiplication of the matrix $\mathbf{E}_{11}$ by $\mathbf{P}^1$ as a row vector and the postmultiplication by $d\mathbf{P}^1$ as a column vector.

Let us consider three cases:

1. *Temporary* deterioration in the terms of trade. This means that $\mathbf{e}^1 d\mathbf{P}^1 < 0$ and $d\mathbf{P}^2 = 0$. It is temporary because price changes take place only in the first period. It amounts to a deterioration because the net export weighted price changes are negative, and according to (A.1) the level of welfare decreases. The change in the trade balance surplus is given by

$$dB^1 = (1 - Z_W^1)\mathbf{e}^1 d\mathbf{P}^1 - \mathbf{P}^1(\mathbf{E}_{11} d\mathbf{P}^1). \tag{A.4}$$

The term $(1 - Z_W^1)$ is the marginal propensity to save. When all goods are normal, $-Z_W^1 = 1 - \mathbf{P}^1 \mathbf{c}_W^1 = D\mathbf{P}^2 \mathbf{c}_W^2 > 0$. Hence the first two effects (the direct effect and the wealth effect) are unambiguously negative, while the substitution effect is either positive or negative. If the first two effects dominate, the trade balance deteriorates.

2. *Anticipated future* deterioration in the terms of trade. In this case $d\mathbf{P}^1 = 0$ and $\mathbf{e}^2 d\mathbf{P}^2 < 0$. Thus (A.3) reduces to

$$dB^1 = -Z_W^1 \mathbf{e}^2 D d\mathbf{P}^2 - \mathbf{P}^1(\mathbf{E}_{12} D d\mathbf{P}^2). \tag{A.5}$$

TERMS OF TRADE **123**

If all goods are normal, the wealth effect on the trade balance is positive. However, the substitution effect is ambiguous. If the wealth effect dominates, the trade balance improves.

3. *Permanent* terms-of-trade deterioration. In this case $e^1 dP^1 < 0$ and $e^2 dP^2 < 0$. The direct effect is positive, if goods are normal, and the wealth effect is of opposite sign. The substitution effect is still ambiguous. Without some further restrictions, we cannot determine whether the trade balance improves or deteriorates.

References

Alexander, Sidney. "Effects of a Devaluation on a Trade Balance." *Internat. Monetary Fund Staff Papers* 2 (April 1952): 263–78.

Blackorby, Charles; Primont, Daniel; and Russell, R. Robert. *Duality, Separability, and Functional Structure: Theory and Economic Applications.* New York: North-Holland, 1978.

Bruno, Michael. "Adjustment and Structural Change under Raw Material Price Shocks." *Scandinavian J. Econ.* 84, no. 2 (1982): 199–222.

Bruno, Michael, and Sachs, Jeffrey D. "Macroeconomic Adjustment with Input Price Shocks: Real and Monetary Aspects." Seminar Paper no. 118. Stockholm: Inst. Internat. Econ. Studies, Univ. Stockholm, 1979.

Buiter, Willem H. "Short-Run and Long-Run Effects of External Disturbances under a Floating Exchange Rate." *Economica* 45 (August 1978): 251–72.

Day, Alan C. L. "Relative Prices, Expenditure and the Trade Balance: A Note." *Economica* 21 (February 1954): 64–69.

Dixit, Avinash K., and Norman, Victor D. *Theory of International Trade.* London: Nisbet and Cambridge Univ. Press, 1980.

Dornbusch, Rudiger. *Open Economy Macroeconomics.* New York: Basic, 1980.

Duesenberry, James S. "Income-Consumption Relations and Their Implications." In *Income, Employment and Public Policy: Essays in Honor of Alvin H. Hansen,* by Lloyd A. Metzler et al. New York: Norton, 1948.

Findlay, Ronald E. "An 'Austrian' Model of International Trade and Interest Rate Equalization." *J.P.E.* 86, no. 6 (December 1978): 989–1007.

Findlay, Ronald E., and Rodriguez, Carlos Alfredo. "Intermediate Imports and Macroeconomic Policy under Flexible Exchange Rates." *Canadian J. Econ.* 10 (May 1977): 208–17.

Fisher, Irving. *The Theory of Interest.* New York: Macmillan, 1930.

Friedman, Milton. *The Optimum Quantity of Money and Other Essays.* Chicago: Aldine, 1969.

Goldman, Steven M., and Uzawa, Hirofumi. "A Note on Separability in Demand Analysis." *Econometrica* 32 (July 1964): 387–98.

Harberger, Arnold C. "Currency Depreciation, Income, and the Balance of Trade." *J.P.E.* 58, no. 1 (February 1950): 47–60.

Helpman, Elhanan, and Razin, Assaf. "Export Subsidies and the Current Account: An Empirical Test." Sapir Center for Development, December 1981 (Hebrew).

Iwai, Katsuhito. "Optimal Economic Growth and Stationary Ordinal Utility: A Fisherian Approach." *J. Econ. Theory* 5 (August 1972): 121–51.

Johnson, Harry G. "The Taxonomic Approach to Economic Policy." *Econ. J.* 61 (December 1951): 812–32.

————. "The Transfer Problem and Exchange Stability." *J.P.E.* 64, no. 3 (June 1956): 212–25.

Jones, Ronald W. "Depreciation and the Dampening Effect of Income Changes." *Rev. Econ. and Statis.* 42 (February 1960): 74–80.

Koopmans, Tjalling C. "Stationary Ordinal Utility and Impatience." *Econometrica* 28 (April 1960): 287–309.

Koopmans, Tjalling C.; Diamond, Peter A.; and Williamson, Richard E. "Stationary Utility and Time Perspective." *Econometrica* 32 (January/April 1964): 82–100.

Laursen, Svend, and Metzler, Lloyd A. "Flexible Exchange Rates and the Theory of Employment." *Rev. Econ. and Statis.* 32 (November 1950): 281–99.

Marion, Nancy P. "Anticipated and Unanticipated Oil Price Increases." Working Paper no. 759. Cambridge, Mass.: Nat. Bur. Econ. Res., 1981.

Meade, James E. *The Theory of International Economic Policy.* Vol. 1. *The Balance of Payments.* New York: Oxford Univ. Press, 1951.

Mussa, Michael. "Macroeconomic Interdependence and the Exchange Rate Regime." In *International Economic Policy: Theory and Evidence,* edited by Rudiger Dornbusch and Jacob A. Frenkel. Baltimore: Johns Hopkins Univ. Press, 1979.

Obstfeld, Maurice. "Intermediate Imports, the Terms of Trade, and the Dynamics of the Exchange Rate and Current Account." *J. Internat. Econ.* 10 (November 1980): 461–80.

————. "Aggregate Spending and the Terms of Trade: Is There a Laursen-Metzler Effect?" *Q.J.E.* 97 (May 1982): 251–70.

Pearce, I. F. "A Note on Mr. Spraos' Paper." *Economica* 22 (May 1955): 147–51.

Razin, Assaf. "Capital Movements, Intersectoral Resource Shifts, and the Trade Balance." Seminar Paper no. 159. Stockholm: Inst. Internat. Econ. Studies, Univ. Stockholm, 1980.

Razin, Assaf, and Svensson, Lars E. O. "An Asymmetry between Import and Export Taxes." Mimeographed. Tel-Aviv: Tel-Aviv Univ., August 1982.

Rodríguez, Carlos Alfredo. "The Terms of Trade and the Balance of Payments in the Short Run." *A.E.R.* 66 (September 1976): 710–16.

Sachs, Jeffrey D. "The Current Account and Macroeconomic Adjustment in the 1970s." *Brookings Papers Econ. Activity,* no. 1 (1981), pp. 201–68.

Schmid, Michael. "A Model of Trade in Money, Goods and Factors." *J. Internat. Econ.* 6 (November 1976): 347–61.

Spraos, John. "Consumers' Behaviour and the Conditions for Exchange Stability." *Economica* 22 (May 1955): 137–47.

Svensson, Lars E. O. "Oil Prices and a Small Oil-importing Country's Welfare and Trade Balance: An Intertemporal Approach." Seminar Paper no. 184. Stockholm: Inst. Internat. Econ. Studies, Univ. Stockholm, 1981.

Svensson, Lars E. O., and Razin, Assaf. "The Terms of Trade, Spending and the Current Account: The Harberger-Laursen-Metzler Effect." Seminar Paper no. 170. Stockholm: Inst. Internat. Econ. Studies, Univ. Stockholm, 1981.

Tsiang, Sho-Chieh. "The Role of Money in Trade-Balance Stability: Synthesis of the Elasticity and Absorption Approaches." *A.E.R.* 51 (December 1961): 912–36.

TERMS OF TRADE 125

Uzawa, Hirofumi. "Time Preference, the Consumption Function, and Optimum Asset Holdings." In *Value, Capital and Growth: Papers in Honor of Sir John Hicks,* edited by J. N. Wolfe. Edinburgh: Edinburgh Univ. Press, 1968.
———. "Time Preference and the Penrose Effect in a Two-Class Model of Economic Growth." *J.P.E.* 77, no. 4, pt. 2 (July/August 1969): 628–52.
White, William H. "The Employment-insulating Advantages of Flexible Exchanges: A Comment on Professors Laursen and Metzler." *Rev. Econ. and Statis.* 36 (May 1954): 225–28.

[35]

Trade Reform, Policy Uncertainty, and the Current Account: A Non-Expected-Utility Approach

By Sweder van Wijnbergen*

Rapid and comprehensive reduction in barriers to international trade has often been followed by a sharp deterioration in the current account (Rudiger Dornbusch, 1987; Dani Rodrik, 1990).[1] The steep, $9 billion deterioration in Mexico's current account during the two years after the trade-reform process was accelerated in 1987 is only the most recent example. The macroeconomic counterpart of the deterioration has typically been a decline in private savings; no clear response pattern has been observed for private investment. Economic theory has in recent years reached clear conclusions on these matters; the problem with these conclusions is that they seem counterfactual.

The problem does not really reside with investment. The investment response will depend on relative capital intensity of the industry whose protection is removed compared to the sectors favored by trade liberalization. Putty-clay considerations would tend to strengthen the investment response, as old capital gets scrapped more quickly in response to changing relative prices. On the other hand, policy uncertainty bestows an option value on assets more liquid than physical capital (van Wijnbergen, 1985) and thus tends to depress investment. However, with no clear prediction emerging from eco-

nomic theory, the ambiguous empirical record on this score is only to be expected.

The situation is different with savings. In an elegant analysis, Assaf Razin and Lars Svensson (1983) pointed out that a permanent reduction in tariffs affects current and future goods in the same way, leaving intertemporal relative prices and private savings unchanged. Gradual tariff reduction in fact raises the price of current goods in terms of future goods and would thus tend to improve private savings (Sebastian Edwards and van Wijnbergen [1986] make a case for gradualism in the presence of capital-market imperfections on this basis). It is this body of theory that, for all its theoretical elegance, seems firmly at variance with the facts.

This paper starts from the observation that anticipated policy reversal may explain a decline in private savings for the same reason gradual tariff reduction causes private savings to go up. Temporarily low tariffs lower the relative price of current goods in terms of future goods and thus tend to depress private savings.

However, the possibility of policy reversal does more than skew intertemporal relative prices toward today rather than tomorrow; it also increases policy uncertainty per se. Is it possible that this increase in uncertainty reinforces the private-savings impact of an anticipated reversal of trade reform? This cannot really be analyzed in the standard expected-utility framework because risk aversion and intertemporal substitution, two very different attributes of consumer preferences, are arbitrarily confined to be inversely related in that framework. I show that, in the context of imperfectly credible trade reform, this inverse relation implies that policy uncertainty is unimportant when it would reduce private savings and, when

*Development Research Department, World Bank, 1818 H Street, N.W., Washington DC 20433, and CEPR, 6 Duke of York Street, London SW1Y 6LA, U.K. I am indebted to Patricio Arrau and Ravi Kanbur for helpful discussions. The opinions expressed in this paper do not necessarily coincide with those of the institutions with which I am affiliated.

[1] Dornbusch (1987) makes the point in a different context: he argues that an increase in tariffs would improve the U.S. current account. By symmetry (not an innocuous assumption), this supports the view that a decrease would deteriorate the current account.

important, would tend to increase private savings.

This conclusion depends entirely on the inverse relation between risk aversion and intertemporal substitution elasticity imposed arbitrarily by the framework of expected-utility maximization. The "ordinal certainty equivalence" (OCE) approach introduced by Larry Selden (1978) offers a way out of the straitjacket imposed by expected-utility maximization. The OCE approach allows independent parametrization of risk aversion and intertemporal substitution. Within the OCE framework, I show that, with positive risk aversion, policy uncertainty will in fact reinforce the negative savings impact of an anticipated policy reversal, especially when that negative impact is strong. This suggests that with high risk aversion and high intertemporal substitution, a rapid trade reform that is not fully credible may depress private savings significantly, with attendant negative impact on the current account. This conclusion seems to accord well with actual experience.

I. The Model

There are two periods, 0 and 1. Thus, the time-consistency problems that naive applications of the OCE approach lead to in multiperiod settings (cf. Philippe Weil, 1990) do not arise. Consumers consume home and foreign goods in each period. The home good is chosen as numeraire, and the exogenous world relative price of the foreign good in terms of the home good is normalized to 1. There is no tariff in period 0; it is the beginning of a period of complete trade liberalization. However, π, the probability that the old tariff $(t_1 - 1)$ will be restored in the next period, is larger than zero. Thus, the future local price of the foreign good, T_1, follows a binomial distribution:

$$(1) \quad T_1 = \begin{cases} t_1 & \text{with probability } \pi \\ 1 & \text{with probability } 1 - \pi. \end{cases}$$

To simplify the structure of income effects, assume that consumers have no within-period income, just wealth at the be-

ginning of period 0, W_0. Wealth is spent today or tomorrow, and within each period, on home goods h and imports m. Wealth not spent in period 0 earns a certain rate of return R (the world rate of interest) between period 0 and 1.

I assume homothetic, unit-elastic preferences across goods within a time period.[2] Consumers know the within-period tariff at the beginning of the period, before allocating expenditure over home and foreign goods. One can therefore define real consumption expenditure C_1 and the associated dual price index p_1 as

$$(2) \quad C_1 = (h_1^* + m_1^* T_1)/p_1$$

$$p_1 = T_1^\alpha.$$

(an asterisk indicates an optimally chosen quantity). C_0 is defined similarly. By assumption, the period-0 tariff is zero: $T_0 = 1$. The budget share of foreign goods in each period, α, is constant because of the assumption of a unitary within-period substitution elasticity. Under these assumptions, the within-period budget identities are

$$(3) \quad W_2 = 0 \qquad pC_1 = W_1$$

$$W_1 = (W_0 - C_0) R.$$

The consumer choice problem presented here involves both intertemporal choice for given intertemporal prices and response to risk. The standard expected-utility framework is unsatisfactory for this problem, because risk aversion and intertemporal substitution, two very different attributes of consumer preferences, are necessarily inversely related in that framework. This follows from the controversial assumption, made axiomatically, of consumer indifference with respect to the timing of resolution of uncertainty about consumption lotteries (cf. Larry Epstein and Stanley Zin, 1989; Weil, 1990).

---

[2]The assumption of unit intratemporal elasticity is made to simplify the expression for the exact period-1 consumer price index and the consumption rate of interest. Qualitatively similar results would come out with any positive intratemporal substitution elasticity.

I use the "ordinal certainty equivalence" framework (Selden, 1978) to disentangle risk aversion and intertemporal substitution. Under this approach, utility is defined over the certain period-0 consumption level and a certainty-equivalent measure of the uncertain period-1 consumption level. This utility function is characterized by an intertemporal substitution elasticity $\sigma = 1/\rho$. The certainty equivalent of period-1 consumption is based on risk aversion parametrized by the coefficient of relative risk aversion, γ, which is assumed to be strictly positive. This results in the following welfare function:

$$(4) \quad V = \left[C_0^{1-\rho} + \beta \left(EC_1^{1-\gamma} \right)^{\frac{1-\rho}{1-\gamma}} \right]^{\frac{1}{1-\rho}}$$

$$= \left(C_0^{1-\rho} + \beta C_{1,\mathrm{RA}}^{1-\rho} \right)^{\frac{1}{1-\rho}}$$

with

$$C_{1,\mathrm{RA}} = \left[E \left(C_1^{1-\gamma} \right) \right]^{\frac{1}{1-\gamma}}.$$

$C_{1,\mathrm{RA}}$ can be interpreted as the certainty equivalent of the uncertain period-1 aggregate consumption level, with γ as the relevant risk-aversion parameter. Using (2) and (3), one can derive a simplified expression for C_1:

$$(5) \quad W_0 = C_0 + \left(\frac{T_1^a}{R} \right) C_1$$

$$= C_0 + \frac{C_1}{R_{\mathrm{CRI}}} \qquad R_{\mathrm{CRI}} = \frac{R}{T_1^a}$$

$$\Rightarrow C_1 = R_{\mathrm{CRI}} (W_0 - C_0).$$

R_{CRI} is the *ex post* consumption rate of interest: the terms on which consumption today can be substituted for consumption tomorrow. Since T_1 is stochastic, R_{CRI} is stochastic too; define R_γ, the risk-adjusted consumption rate of interest, as the *ex ante*

certainty equivalent of R_{CRI}:

$$(6) \quad R_\gamma = \left(ER_{\mathrm{CRI}}^{1-\gamma} \right)^{\frac{1}{1-\gamma}}.$$

Then, the certainty equivalent of C_1, $C_{1,\mathrm{RA}}$, equals

$$(7) \quad EC_1^{1-\gamma} = (W_0 - C_0)^{1-\gamma} E \left(R_{\mathrm{CRI}}^{1-\gamma} \right)$$

$$= (W_0 - C_0)^{1-\gamma} R_\gamma^{1-\gamma}.$$

Maximizing V as defined in equation (4) subject to the budget constraints (3) and using equation (7) yields the following for period-0 consumption, C_0:

$$(8) \quad C_0 = \frac{1}{1+A} W_0.$$

That is, period-0 consumption is proportional to wealth. The proportionality factor $1/(1+A)$ depends on the risk-adjusted rate of interest R_γ, the subjective time-preference discount-factor β, and the intertemporal substitution elasticity:

$$(9) \quad A = \beta^{1/\rho} R_\gamma^{(1-\rho)/\rho}.$$

Trade-policy reversal thus affects private consumption in period 0 entirely through its impact on the risk-adjusted consumption rate of interest, R_γ. An increase in this rate affects period-0 consumption:

$$(10) \quad \frac{\partial C_0}{\partial R_\gamma} = - \frac{1}{(1+A)^2} \left(\frac{A}{R_\gamma} \right) \left(\frac{1-\rho}{\rho} \right)$$

$$= \varphi(\rho - 1) \qquad \varphi > 0.$$

If the intertemporal substitution is larger than 1 ($\rho < 1$), a higher risk-adjusted consumption rate of interest depresses private consumption.

II. Trade Reform, Future Policy Reversal, and Private Savings

Since all the effects of potential policy reversals work through the risk-adjusted consumption rate of interest, I first calculate this rate for the binomial distribution over future tariff rates of equation (1):

$$(11) \quad R_\gamma = \left[E\left(\frac{R}{T_1^\alpha}\right)^{1-\gamma} \right]^{\frac{1}{1-\gamma}}$$

$$= R\left[1 + \pi\left(t_1^{-\alpha(1-\gamma)} - 1\right)\right]^{\frac{1}{1-\gamma}}.$$

Obviously, for $\gamma = 0$ this rate equals the expected rate:

$$(12) \quad R_{\gamma=0} = (1-\pi)R + \pi t_1^{-\alpha} R$$

$$= R\left[\pi\left(t_1^{-\alpha} - 1\right) + 1\right].$$

It is instructive to separate the effect of potential future tariff increases through their impact on the *expected* consumption rate of interest from their impact on savings through increasing the variance of the consumption rate of interest. I therefore examine the case of a fully anticipated trade-policy reversal first, before introducing uncertainty about it in the next subsection.

A. Anticipated Future Trade-Policy Reversal and Private Savings

With full anticipation ($\pi = 1$), the risk-adjusted rate of interest R_γ collapses into the expected rate for $\pi = 1$:

$$(13) \quad R_\gamma = R\left[1 + \left(t_1^{-\alpha(1-\gamma)} - 1\right)\right]^{\frac{1}{1-\gamma}}$$

$$= Rt_1^{-\alpha}.$$

From (13), one can derive the impact of a fully anticipated trade-policy reversal

(higher future tariffs) on R_γ:

$$(14) \quad \frac{\partial R_\gamma}{\partial t_1} = -\alpha R t_1^{-(1+\alpha)}.$$

Equation (14) establishes the first point of this paper: an anticipated trade-policy reversal (i.e., an anticipation that future tariffs will exceed current tariffs) lowers the risk-adjusted consumption rate of interest. Combining (10) and (14) then indicates how an anticipated trade-liberalization reversal (higher future tariffs) affects current consumption:

$$(15) \quad \frac{\partial C_0}{\partial t_1} = \left(\frac{\partial C_0}{\partial R_\gamma}\right)\left(\frac{\partial R_\gamma}{\partial t_1}\right)$$

$$= -\varphi(\rho - 1)\alpha R t_1^{-(1+\alpha)}$$

$$> 0 \quad \text{if and only if } \frac{1}{\rho} > 1.$$

Equation (15) establishes the following proposition.

PROPOSITION 1 (IT Effect): *An anticipated rollback of trade liberalization leads to an increase in current consumption (a decline in private savings) if the intertemporal substitution elasticity exceeds 1 ($\rho < 1$).*[3]

B. Private Savings and Uncertainty about Future Trade Policy

Does uncertainty about future trade policy per se, for any given expected value of future tariffs,[4] have an impact on period-0 consumption? Such an effect would open up a second channel through which a trade reform with less than complete credibility could affect private savings. This could be assessed by manipulating π and t_1 so as to

---

[3] The impact on savings will be unconditionally negative if consumers anticipate the income effects of a period-1 rebate of tariff revenues.

[4] Or, more precisely, for any given expected value of the consumption discount rate.

increase the variance for given expected value of the future dual price index, p_1. However, the particular structure of the model is such that this approach is a difficult route toward establishing the link between trade-policy uncertainty and private savings. The first problem is that an increase in the variance of the expected consumption rate of interest that preserves the mean would imply a complicated nonlinear restriction on t_1 and π [it requires keeping expression (12) constant]. The second problem is more serious, since it is more than just a technical complication that could in principle be dealt with like the first. The problem is that the relation between the variance and π is quadratic under the binomial assumption made in equation (1) and has an interior maximum (the variance is proportional to $\pi[1-\pi]$). This relation can thus not be inverted to write R_γ as a function of the variance rather than of π itself. Different values of π can yield the same variance of the expected consumption rate of interest, so there is no way π can be substituted out of the expression for R_γ to write R_γ as a function of the variance instead. Moreover, changes in π will have effects on the variance of the expected rate of interest that differ in their sign depending on the initial value from which π is changing. I therefore follow a different approach.

In the OCE framework, assuming $\gamma = 0$ eliminates all impact of uncertainty, obviously without any impact on the *expected* consumption rate of interest. Thus, an analysis of the case for $\gamma = 0$ isolates the pure expected reversal effect, with no pollution by uncertainty per se. The impact of uncertainty can then be assessed by looking at the impact of increasing γ. Increasing γ leaves the expected consumption discount rate unaffected, since it only involves a change in preferences, not in the objective environment. It therefore does not have any effect on the impact of an *expected* reversal analysed in Subsection II-A; in the OCE approach, risk aversion and intertemporal substitution can be separated. Therefore, the impact of increasing γ from 0 is the impact of uncertainty at the value to which γ has

been increased. Finally, since the only uncertainty in the model is the uncertainty related to future tariffs, the entire impact of the increase in γ is due to the existing uncertainty about future trade policy. The impact of an increase in γ would be zero if there were no tariff uncertainty.

Consider how an increase in γ would affect period-0 consumption given the stochastic structure outlined in (9). Once again, the entire impact of both uncertainty and of increases in γ runs through the impact on the risk-adjusted interest rate. Thus, consider the derivative of R_γ with respect to γ. To this end, I introduce some simplifying notation. Define first the consumption discount rate in case of a zero future tariff as R_H, and in the case of a positive future tariff as R_L. Also, define k as $k = 1 - \gamma$. This yields

$$(16) \quad R_\gamma = \left[\pi R_L^k + (1-\pi) R_H^k \right]^{1/k}$$

$$= \left(E R_i^k \right)^{1/k} \qquad i = \text{L}, \text{H}.$$

E is the expectations operator over the distribution specified in equation (1). Taking logs and bringing k to the other side yields

$$(17) \quad k \log R_\gamma = \log \left(E R_i^k \right).$$

Log-differentiation yields

$$(18) \quad \left(\frac{k}{R_\gamma} \right) \left(\frac{dR_\gamma}{dk} \right) + \log R_\gamma = \frac{E\left[R_i^k \log(R_i) \right]}{E(R_i^k)}.$$

Multiplying both sides by k and rearranging terms gives

$$(19) \quad E(R_i^k) \left(\frac{k^2}{R_\gamma} \right) \left(\frac{dR_\gamma}{dk} \right)$$

$$= E\left[R_i^k \log(R_i^k) \right] - E(R_i^k) \log(E R_i^k)$$

$$> 0.$$

The inequality in (19) obtains because of convexity of the function $f(z) = z \log(z)$. Since $k = 1 - \gamma$, equation (19) establishes the result:[5]

$$(20) \quad dk = -d\gamma \Rightarrow \frac{dR_\gamma}{d\gamma} < 0 \quad \text{for all } \gamma.$$

Thus, introducing risk aversion in the presence of uncertainty about future trade reform will unambiguously lower the risk-adjusted consumption rate of interest, something that it would not have done without the trade-related uncertainty (since there is no other source of uncertainty). One can therefore conclude that uncertainty about future trade-policy reversal will lower the risk-adjusted consumption rate of interest. However, (10) states that a cut in the risk-adjusted rate of interest will depress private savings if the intertemporal substitution elasticity is larger than 1 ($\rho < 1$). Thus, combining equations (10) and (20) yields the following proposition.

PROPOSITION 2 (Uncertainty Effect): *Uncertainty about future trade policy per se (i.e., for given expected value of the tariff) will increase private consumption today if the intertemporal rate of substitution exceeds 1 ($\rho < 1$).*

Thus, under the OCE approach, the intertemporal substitution effect (IS) of Proposition 1 reinforces the uncertainty effect (UE) of Proposition 2 for all values of ρ. If intertemporal substitution is high ($\rho < 1$), both the IS effect and the UE effect increase private consumption; if intertemporal substitution is low ($\rho > 1$), both depress private consumption. Moreover, this holds for all values of the risk-aversion parameter γ. This contrasts with the expected-utility approach, in which the two effects reinforce each other only when $\gamma < 1$ (i.e., when uncertainty is relatively unimportant because risk aversion is low).

III. Conclusions

This paper starts from the observation that trade liberalization is often followed by

a strong surge of imports and an accompanying current-account deterioration. The macroeconomic counterpart of this deterioration is typically a decline in savings rather than an investment boom. I show first of all that anticipation of reimposition of tariffs in the future lowers the expected consumption rate of interest (makes current goods cheaper in terms of future goods). Therefore, an anticipated future tariff increase will increase current consumption if the intertemporal substitution elasticity is larger than 1. If consumers internalize the impact of future tariff revenues on their after-tax income, the savings impact will *always* be negative, even for an intertemporal substitution elasticity below 1.

The second result concerns the impact of policy uncertainty per se on private savings. I separate the impact of *expected* shifts in intertemporal relative prices from risk aversion by using the ordinal-certainty-equivalence approach pioneered by Selden (1978), and, for infinite horizons, by Epstein and Zin (1989) and Weil (1990). This approach relaxes the rigid inverse relationship between intertemporal substitution and risk aversion that characterizes the expected-utility approach to consumer choice under uncertainty. Within the OCE framework, I establish that policy uncertainty per se will further reduce private savings if (a) there is positive risk aversion and (b) the intertemporal substitution elasticity exceeds 1.

This is an interesting result for two reasons. First it shows how policy uncertainty about future tariffs will reinforce the negative savings impact of the direct anticipated reversal effect exactly when the latter is large (intertemporal substitution elasticity is high). The two effects will thus be in the same direction exactly when they matter most. The second observation is more academic. In the standard expected-utility approach, risk aversion is low when intertemporal substitution is high, because the relevant elasticities are each other's inverse. The consequence of this is that whenever the uncertainty effect is important, the direct anticipation effect is not and vice versa. This result is reversed in the non-expected-utility approach: the two effects are comple-

[5]This result is a special case of a general proposition in Peter Diamond and Joseph Stiglitz (1974).

mentary in the case where the direct antici-pation effect is important.

How relevant is all this from an empirical point of view? There is after all a widely held belief that the intertemporal substitution elasticity is very low (ρ very high), with some economists setting ρ as high as around 10 (Robert Hall, 1988). More recent evidence using the approach of Epstein and Zin (1989) to consumer choice under uncertainty has tended to come up with different results, however. Most relevant in this case are the results reported for Mexico in Patricio Arrau and van Wijnbergen (1991) and Gil Bufman et al. (1991), since Mexico's experience with trade reform was in fact what triggered this paper.

Arrau and van Wijnbergen (1991) and Bufman et al. (1991) find values for ρ between 0.24 and 0.8, depending on whether or not money services are accounted for in the measure of consumption, indicating a substitution elasticity well in excess of 1. With money services incorporated, the implicit estimate of the intertemporal substitution elasticity is 4.2, significantly in excess of 1. Similar results are reported by Epstein and Zin (1991) for the United States. Whether the channels explored in this paper were in fact behind the sharp deterioration in the trade balance that followed Mexico's trade reforms requires a more in-depth analysis than the evidence just mentioned, but the empirical results suggest that the channels explored in this paper could conceivably have played an important role.

These results have important policy implications. If the trade reform will not be reversed, but the government cannot credibly communicate that to the private sector, consumers effectively trade off the wrong intertemporal prices. As a consequence, private savings will be suboptimally low; this justifies policy intervention to increase private savings. This is a special case of a more general point made by Guillermo A. Calvo and Carlos A. Vegh (1990): mistaken beliefs about future policy act like a distortion and therefore justify policy intervention in principle. Increasing private savings should preferably be done through a temporary increase in consumption taxes. If that is not feasible, a case can be made for temporary tariffs as a second-best response; this would be equivalent to gradual rather than "cold turkey" trade liberalization.

A magnifying impact could come about if the private-savings response leads to such a large current-account deficit that the trade reform itself does in fact get reversed, a case of self-fulfilling prophecy.[6] This very real possibility further strengthens the case for policy intervention to increase private savings and, arguably, for external support in the early periods of trade reform, possibly through institutions like the World Bank.

REFERENCES

Arrau, Patricio and van Wijnbergen, Sweder, "Intertemporal Substitution, Risk Aversion, and Private Savings in Mexico," mimeo, World Bank, 1991.

Bufman, Gil, Leiderman, Leo and van Wijnbergen, Sweder, "Consumption and Velocity during Stabilization Programs," mimeo, World Bank, 1991.

Calvo, A. Guillermo and Vegh, Carlos A., "Credibility and the Dynamics of Stabilization Policy: A Basic Framework," unpublished paper presented at the conference "Spain and the European Monetary System" (Sixth World Congress of the Econometric Society), Barcelona, August 1990.

Diamond, Peter and Stiglitz, Joseph, "Increases in Risk and Risk Aversion," *Journal of Economic Theory*, July 1974, *8*, 337–60.

Dornbusch, Rudiger, "External Balance Correction: Depreciation or Correction?" *Brookings Papers on Economic Activity*, 1987, (1), 249–71.

_____, "Credibility and Stabilization," mimeo, Massachusetts Institute of Technology, 1989.

Edwards, Sebastian and van Wijnbergen, Sweder, "The Welfare Effects of Trade and Capital Market Liberalization," *International Economic Review*, February 1986, *27*,

---

[6]Dornbusch (1989) discusses the possibility of such self-fulfilling equilibria in the context of stabilization programs.

141–9.

Epstein, Larry and Zin, Stanley, "Substitution, Risk Aversion, and the Temporal Behavior of Consumption and Asset Returns: A Theoretical Framework," *Econometrica*, July 1989, *57*, 937–69.

_____ and _____, "Substitution, Risk Aversion, and the Temporal Behavior of Consumption and Asset Returns: An Empirical Analysis," *Journal of Political Economy*, April 1991, *99*, 263–86.

Hall, Robert, "Intertemporal Substitution in Consumption," *Journal of Political Economy*, April 1988, *96*, 339–57.

Razin, Assaf and Svensson, Lars, "Trade Taxes and the Current Account," *Economics Letters*, 1983, *13* (1), 55–7.

Rodrik, Dani, "Trade Policies and Development: Some New Issues," mimeo, Kennedy School of Government, Harvard University, 1990.

Selden, Larry, "A New Representation of Preferences over 'Certain × Uncertain' Consumption Pairs: The 'Ordinal Certainty Equivalence' Hypothesis," *Econometrica*, September 1978, *46*, 1025–45.

van Wijnbergen, Sweder, "Trade Reform, Aggregate Investment, and Capital Flight: On Credibility and the Value of Information," *Economics Letters*, 1985, *19* (4), 369–72.

Weil, Philippe, "Non-Expected Utility in Macroeconomics," *Quarterly Journal of Economics*, February 1990, *105*, 29–43.

[36]

Journal of Development Economics 27 (1987) 41–55. North-Holland

THE NARROW MOVING BAND, THE DUTCH DISEASE, AND THE COMPETITIVE CONSEQUENCES OF MRS. THATCHER

Notes on Trade in the Presence of Dynamic Scale Economies

Paul KRUGMAN

Massachusetts Institute of Technology, Cambridge, MA 02139, USA

This paper presents a model of trade in which comparative advantage, instead of being determined by underlying attributes of countries, evolves over time through learning-by-doing. In this model, arbitrary patterns of specialization, once established, tend to become entrenched over time. The model sheds light on three widely held views that do not make sense in more conventional models. First is the view that temporary protection of selected sectors can permanently alter the pattern of comparative advantage in the protecting country's favor. Second is the view that seemingly favorable developments, such as the discovery of exportable natural resources, may lead to a permanent loss of other sectors and reduce welfare in the long run. Third is the possibility that a temporary overvaluation of a currency due to tight money can lead to a permanent loss of competitiveness in some sectors.

1. Introduction

When an economist tries to talk with businessmen about international trade, he often senses a frustrating failure to make a connection. Partly this is a matter of differences in vocabulary and style, but it also reflects a more fundamental difference in outlook. Economists, schooled in general equilibrium analysis, have what we might call a 'homeostatic' view of international trade. By this I mean that they believe that there is a natural pattern of specialization and trade, determined by underlying characteristics of countries, and that automatic forces tend to restore this natural pattern. Trade policy, exchange rate movements, or other shocks may temporarily distort trade, but when these disturbing factors are removed the natural pattern will reassert itself.

Businessmen, by contrast, are schooled in the competition of individual firms, where equilibrating forces are much less apparent. A wrong decision or a piece of bad luck may result in a permanent loss of market share. Indeed, if large market share itself conveys advantages, the effects of temporary disturbances will grow rather than fade away over time. When businessmen look at international trade, they naturally tend to see competition among

0304-3878/87/$3.50 © 1987, Elsevier Science Publishers B.V. (North-Holland)

nations as competition among firms writ large. As a result, they are far more alarmist in their outlook than economists. They fear that foreign tariffs and subsidies or an overvalued exchange rate will lead to permanent loss of markets, and may indeed propagate into a general loss of competitiveness.

Now it is clear that in this case economists know something that businessmen do not – namely, that there are economy-wide resource constraints, and that as a result factor prices are endogenous. Japan cannot have a competitive advantage over the U.S. in everything, because if it did, there would be an excess demand for Japanese labor. Japanese relative wages would rise (perhaps via an exchange rate adjustment), and this would restore U.S. competitiveness in some sectors. It is precisely the recognition of resource constraints which leads economists to emphasize *comparative* rather than *absolute* advantage as the basis for trade.

Yet while businessmen are surely wrong in treating competition among nations as an enlarged version of competition among firms, economists may not have captured the whole of the story either. The homeostatic view of international competition rests ultimately on models which rule out by assumption the kinds of dynamics of competition which are the main concern of corporate strategy. Perhaps if these dynamics were allowed to play a role, something of the businessman's view of competition would turn out to make sense after all. Obviously nations are not firms – they cannot be driven altogether out of business. But perhaps a nation can be driven out of *some* businesses, so that in fact temporary shocks *can* have permanent effects on trade.

The purpose of this paper is to present a simple model of international specialization which incorporates at the national level one of the key elements of strategic analysis at the level of the firm. This is the role of the learning curve. That is, there are dynamic economies of scale in which cumulative past output determines current productivity.[1] In order to bring out the unconventional possibilities clearly, the model is both simplistic and extreme. It can, however, be used to illustrate some of the possibilities missed by more conventional approaches. In particular, I use the model to show how one might justify heterodox analyses of three current policy issues: the effects of Japanese industrial targeting, the consequences of oil discoveries for industrial competitiveness, and the long run penalties of an overvalued currency.

The paper is in seven sections. The second section sets out the model's assumptions. The third shows how comparative advantage and the pattern of specialization are determined. The next three sections then provide illustra-

---

[1]This is not the first such analysis. Bardhan (1970) analyzed trade and industrial policy in the presence of learning effects. His model was, however, oriented more towards development policy in small LDCs than towards the issues addressed in this paper.

tions of applications of the analysis. A final section draws conclusions and presents suggestions for further research.

2. A model of dynamic comparative advantage

Consider a world consisting of two countries, Home and Foreign. We will suppose that each of these countries has only one factor of production, labor. Labor can be used to produce any of n traded goods, together with a non-traded good.

At any point in time, we assume that these are constant returns to the production of each traded good,

$$X_i(t) = A_i(t)L_i(t), \quad x_i(t) = a_i(t)l_i(t), \qquad i = 1, \ldots, n, \tag{1}$$

where X_i is output of traded good i in the home country, L_i is labor devoted to that good's production, and lower case letters indicate corresponding quantities in the foreign country.

While there are constant returns at any point in time, however, we assume that there are dynamic increasing returns, taking the form of an industry learning curve. In each industry in each country, the productivity of resources depends on an index of cumulative experience,

$$A_i(t) = K_i(t)^\varepsilon, \quad a_i(t) = k_i(t)^\varepsilon, \qquad 0 < \varepsilon < 1. \tag{2}$$

I will assume in this paper that the learning curve is entirely an industry phenomenon, completely external to firms, so that perfect competition continues to prevail. This is obviously not an ultimately satisfactory formulation, and some discussion of the difference it makes will be given in the concluding section of the paper.

Discussion of external economies in trade often assumes that these economies do not spill across national boundaries. This is, however, not realistic – surely firms can learn from the experience of firms in other countries, though perhaps not as well as they can from other domestic firms. Further, it will be useful as a technical matter to allow for international diffusion of knowledge in our later analysis. Thus I will suppose that both domestic and foreign production enters into the index of experience,

$$K_i(t) = \int_{-\infty}^{t} [X_i(z) + \delta x_i(z)]\,\mathrm{d}z, \quad k_i(t) = \int_{-\infty}^{t} [\delta X_i(z) + x_i(z)]\,\mathrm{d}z, \qquad 0 \leqq \delta \leqq 1, \tag{3}$$

where δ can be interpreted as a measure of the internationalization of learning. If $\delta = 0$, we have the often assumed case of purely national learning effects; if $\delta = 1$, the learning curve should be defined in terms of aggregate world variables. In what follows I will assume that δ in fact lies somewhere between these extremes.

To complete the model, we need to specify how wages are determined, how expenditure is determined, and the composition of demand. Later in this paper we will want to explore the consequences of sticky wages and unemployment. For now, however, we will assume full employment. Each country has an exogenously given labor force at any point in time, $L(t)$ and $l(t)$, respectively. These labor forces will be assumed both to grow exponentially at the rate g.[2]

Expenditure will (until section 6) be assumed equal to income. A constant share $1 - s$ of income will be assumed spent on non-traded goods. Each traded good will receive a constant and equal share s/n of expenditure.

3. Dynamics of specialization

To analyze international specialization in this model, I proceed as follows. First I analyze the dynamics of relative productivity change, taking the allocation of resources in each country as given. Then I analyze the allocation of resources, taking relative productivities as given. Finally, as a last stage, I show how these interact.

Let us begin, then, with the determination of relative productivities over time. From (2) we know that relative productivity is simply a function of the relative experience indexes K and k,

$$A_i(t)/a_i(t) = [K_i(t)/k_i(t)]^\epsilon. \tag{4}$$

Thus we must focus on the dynamics of K and k. From (3), we have

$$\mathrm{d}K_i(t)/\mathrm{d}t = X_i(t) + \delta x_i(t), \quad \mathrm{d}k_i(t)/\mathrm{d}t = x_i(t) + \delta X_i(t). \tag{5}$$

The relative change in the experience indices can therefore be written as

$$\frac{\mathrm{d}K_i(t)/\mathrm{d}t}{K_i(t)} - \frac{\mathrm{d}k_i(t)/\mathrm{d}t}{k_i(t)} = \frac{X_i(t) + \delta x_i(t)}{K_i(t)} - \frac{x_i(t) + \delta X_i(t)}{k_i(t)}. \tag{6}$$

Now suppose that the relative labor allocation $L_i(t)/l_i(t)$ is held fixed. Then $K_i(t)/k_i(t)$ will tend to converge on a steady state. Setting the left hand side of

---

[2]A growing population, or technological progress independent of output, is necessary to make the steady state analysis of this paper possible.

(6) to zero and substituting from (1) and (2), we have

$$\left(\frac{K_i}{k_i}\right)^{\varepsilon-1} = \frac{l_i}{L_i}\left[\frac{1-\delta k_i/K_i}{1-\delta K_i/k_i}\right]. \tag{7}$$

To interpret (7), we can use fig. 1. The curve LHS represents the left hand side of (7), RHS the right hand side. Clearly, the steady state value of K_i/k_i always lies between δ and $1/\delta$ – which is not surprising given our specification of international spillovers. The steady state value does, however, depend on the allocation of resources. An increase in L_i/l_i is illustrated by the dotted line in the figure; it leads to a higher steady state relative K_i. Since the experience indices in turn determine relative productivity, this means that we can write the steady state relative productivity A_i/a_i as a function of the relative sizes of sectoral labor forces,

$$A_i/a_i = \alpha(L_i/l_i), \tag{8}$$

where the function $\alpha(\cdot)$ is implicitly defined by (7). From the analysis above it is clear that $\alpha(\cdot)$ is increasing in L_i/l_i, that $\alpha(0)=\delta$, and that $\alpha(\infty)=1/\delta$.

Now let us turn to the determination of the allocation of labor. At any point in time this model will simply be Ricardian in character. We can rank tradeable industries by their relative productivities $A_i(t)/a_i(t)$. What we then

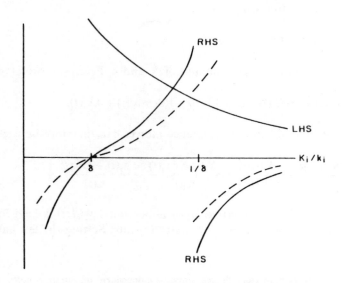

Fig. 1. Long run determination of relative productivity.

require is that for the marginal industry

$$A_i(t)/a_i(t) = W(t)/w(t),$$ (9)

where $W(t)$ is the wage rate at time t. Let $\sigma(t)$ be the share of the world tradeable sector located in the home country, i.e., the number of tradeable sectors in which the home country has a comparative advantage relative to n, the total number of tradeable sectors. Then we can, as in fig. 2, show the equilibrium condition (9) as the downward sloping schedule AA.

The other equilibrium condition is, of course, balance of payments equilibrium. In a way familiar from Dornbusch, Fischer and Samuelson (1977) we may write this condition as

$$\frac{W(t)}{w(t)} = \frac{\sigma}{1-\sigma} \frac{\bar{T}(t)}{\bar{L}(t)},$$ (10)

which yields the upward-sloping schedule BB.

We are now in a position to describe the dynamics of specialization over time. In the absence of any 'extrinsic' dynamics – that is, shocks arising from outside sources – these are very simple, almost embarrassingly so. Basically, once a pattern of specialization is established, it remains unchanged, with changes in relative productivity acting to further lock the pattern in. To see this, suppose that at some point the situation looks like that shown in fig. 2.

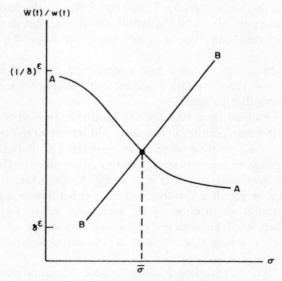

Fig. 2. Short run specialization.

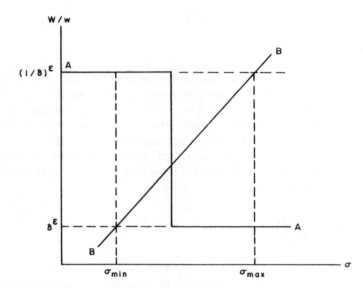

Fig. 3. Long run specialization.

Some goods are now produced in the home country, some in the foreign country. For those in the first group, we have $L_i(t) = sL(t)/\sigma(t)n$, $l_i(t) = 0$. For those in the second group, $L_i(t) = 0$, $l_i(t) = sl(t)/(1-\sigma)n$. It is immediately apparent that for the first group, productivity will rise faster in the home country, while for the second group it will rise faster in the foreign country. This means that the part of AA to the left of $\bar{\sigma}$ will rise, that part to the right of $\bar{\sigma}$ will fall. In the long run AA will come to have the 'step' shape illustrated in fig. 3.

Like a river which digs its own bed deeper, a pattern of specialization, once established, will induce relative productivity changes which strengthen the forces preserving that pattern.

Clearly, history matters here even for the long run. In particular, whatever market share $\bar{\sigma}$ the home country starts with will be preserved over time, and so therefore will be the relative wage rates associated with that share. Thus there is a whole range of possible steady state market shares. The boundaries of that range are shown as $\sigma_{\min}$ and $\sigma_{\max}$ in fig. 3. These are defined by the relative wage rates at which a country will be competitive in a sector even if it has no production experience of its own and must rely entirely on international diffusion of knowledge. Obviously the range of possible outcomes is narrower, the larger is δ – that is, the more international are the learning effects.

We have now laid out a simple model where comparative advantage is 'created' over time by the dynamics of learning, rather than arising from underlying national characteristics. In the remainder of this paper I will perform a series of thought experiments on this model. What we will see is that a model of this kind can be used to formalize a variety of heterodox arguments about international competition.

4. The narrow moving band

The economic success of Japan has been attributed by many to the industrial policies of the Japanese government, and in particular to the use of infant industry protection as a way of gradually broadening the Japanese industrial base. In an effective diatribe, Givens (1982) has described the intervention of the Japanese government as a 'narrow moving band' which slices off one industry after another, protecting an industry until it is strong enough to eliminate its U.S. competitors, then moving on to the next target.

The economic reasoning underlying this view of Japanese policy is not completely clear, but our model seems to have the necessary features. It is certainly possible in this model – within limits – for temporary protection to permanently shift comparative advantage.

Suppose that there is some good i in which the foreign country originally has a comparative advantage. Then the labor allocation will be $L_i = 0$, $l_i = s/\sigma n$. Now suppose that the home country closes its market for good i to imports. The effect will be to turn i into a non-traded good, with each country satisfying its own demand,

$$L_i = sL/n, \quad l_i = sl/n.$$

Clearly, the effect of this market closure will be to accelerate the pace of productivity change in this sector in the home relative to the foreign country. If the protection is continued long enough, this change in relative productivity growth may be enough to give the home country a cost advantage in i. At this point the protection becomes irrelevant, and trade policy has achieved a permanent shift in comparative advantage. We can imagine a government protecting a series of sectors in succession, and thus steadily increasing its market share – a process illustrated in fig. 4.

There is, however, a limit to this process. As a country acquires more industries, its relative wage rate will rise. This means that the next sector will require higher relative productivity and thus a longer period of protection to become established. In the limit, protectionist policies can at most lead to a relative productivity advantage of $\alpha(L/l)$ and thus cannot push the relative wage above $W/w = \alpha(L/l)$.

Without pursuing the story too much further, this analysis suggests that the use of temporary protection to engineer permanent shifts in comparative advantage is likely to work best when one is a country with a large labor

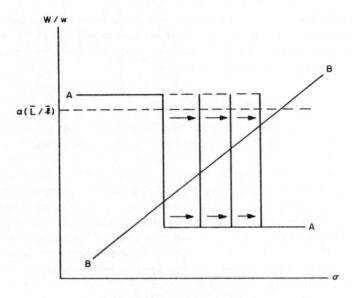

Fig. 4. The narrow moving band.

force but low wages. Small countries will find that the domestic market is not large enough for protection to yield much in the way of accelerated productivity growth; high-wage countries will find that the extra productivity is not enough to provide a cost advantage.

5. The Dutch disease

When a country discovers tradeable natural resources, such as oil, it normally experiences real appreciation of its exchange rate and thus a crowding out of its other tradeable sectors. This phenomenon first drew attention in the case of the Netherlands, where natural gas discoveries clearly hurt the competitiveness of Dutch manufacturing, but the experience is familiar from a number of examples.[3] The interesting question is why it should be regarded as a problem. In conventional trade models, countries should simply specialize in whatever is their comparative advantage. If an oil discovery shifts this comparative advantage, so be it. In practice, however, there is widespread concern that the contraction of a country's manufacturing sector which follows natural resource discoveries is a bad thing. The worry seems to be that when the natural resources run out, the lost manufacturing sectors will not come back.

[3]A number of papers have been written on the Dutch disease. See, in particular, Corden and Neary (1982) and Van Wijnbergen (1984).

Our model does not allow a role for natural resources directly. However, the discussion of the Dutch disease usually treats income earned in the natural resource sector much as if it were a pure transfer payment from abroad. So I will approximate the discussion by considering the implications of a transfer payment from the foreign to the home country.

We need first to rewrite the balance of payments equilibrium condition to take account of the transfer. Following Dornbusch, Fischer and Samuelson (1977) the condition may be written

$$\sigma(t)s[l-T] = (1-\sigma(t))s\{[W(t)/w(t)]L+T\},$$

where T is the transfer, measured in foreign wage units. This implies the relative wage equation

$$\frac{W(t)}{w(t)} = \frac{s(t)}{1-\sigma(t)} \frac{l}{L} + \frac{1-s}{s} \frac{T}{L}. \tag{11}$$

This now defines the BB schedule. As long as $s < 1$ – that is, as long as there are non-traded goods – a transfer to the home country will shift the schedule up.

The effects of this transfer depend both on its size and on its duration. Let us suppose that we are initially in or near a steady state in which each country has been specialized for a long period. Then the schedule AA will have the shape shown in fig. 5: a step function. The effect of a small transfer is illustrated by the upward shift of BB to $B'B'$; this will raise the home country's wage but without altering the pattern of specialization. A larger transfer, however, will raise the schedule to $B'B'$: the rise in the recipient's relative wages will be enough to offset its productivity advantage, so that some sectors move abroad.

The longer run implications now depend on how long the transfer payment lasts. The shift of production from home to foreign will mean declining relative home productivity in those industries over time. Thus AA will develop a middle step, which will deepen over time. The possibilities are illustrated in fig. 6. There a large transfer is assumed to shift BB up to $B'B'$, resulting in a shift of some industries from the home to foreign country. If the transfer does not last too long, when it ends and BB returns to its previous position the old pattern of specialization and relative wages will reassert itself. If the transfer lasts longer, however, some of the industries will not come back when it ends. For a transfer of sufficiently long duration, all of the industries which move abroad in the short run will remain abroad even when the transfer ends. In either of the latter cases the home country's market share and relative wage will turn out to have been permanently reduced by its temporary good fortune.

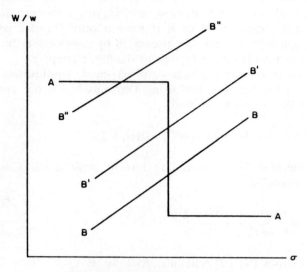

Fig. 5. Short run impacts of a transfer.

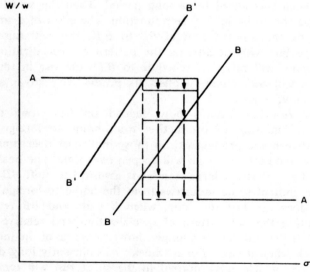

Fig. 6. Long run effects of a transfer.

6. The competitive consequences of Mrs. Thatcher

When countries pursue more contractionary monetary policies than their trading partners, one important channel through which the monetary contraction takes effect appears to be through real appreciation of the exchange rate and a resulting loss of competitiveness in traded goods production. This has been dramatically illustrated by the experience of the U.K. under Margaret Thatcher. When this happens, a major question becomes one of appropriate policy response. Given a consensus on the need for a contractionary monetary policy, say to control inflation, should the tradeable sector be required to bear as much of the burden as seems to be the case? Or should exchange market intervention, capital controls, or such trade policy instruments as tariffs and export subsidies be used to insulate the traded sectors from some of the consequences of a disinflationary transition?

The implication from conventional economic models is that traded sectors should contract along with the rest of the economy. If a certain amount of slack must be created in the economy, why should it occur only in non-traded sectors? Frankel (1983) has shown that in one simple model a floating exchange rate actually gets it exactly right, producing the optimal mix of output reduction between traded and non-traded sectors.

The counter-argument is not usually clearly expressed, but hinges on the belief that preserving competitiveness in tradeable sectors is somehow more important than maintaining output in non-traded sectors. While a model with dynamic economies of scale may not capture the whole of this belief, it does provide at least a possible way to make sense of a view that sees the international consequences of tight money as more serious and enduring than the purely domestic consequences.

To examine this issue, we need to modify our model to allow for monetary policy, and in particular for monetary policy with real effects. Once again Dornbusch, Fischer and Samuelson (1977) provide the simplest formulation. Let us assume, first, that nominal expenditure in each country is proportional to that country's money supply (both measured in units of local currency),

$$E(t) = M(t)V, \quad e(t) = m(t)v. \tag{12}$$

Let us define $R(t)$ as the exchange rate, defined as the price of foreign currency in terms of home currency. Then the balance of payments equilibrium condition may be written as

$$\sigma(t)R(t)e(t) = [1 - \sigma(t)]E(t). \tag{13}$$

For changes in monetary policy to have a real effect, there must be nominal rigidities somewhere. The simplest assumption is simply to let wage rates be exogenously fixed in local currency,

$$W(t) = \bar{W}, \quad w(t) = \bar{w}. \tag{14}$$

Combining (13) and (14), we can write an equation for relative wages measured in a common currency,

$$\frac{\bar{W}}{R(t)\bar{w}} = \frac{\sigma(t)}{1 - \sigma(t)} \frac{e(t)}{E(t)}. \tag{15}$$

This will define a *BB* schedule, just as in previous sections. The *AA* schedule continues to be defined as before.

Consider, now, the effects of a temporary reduction in the home money supply. A decline in *M* will reduce *E*, shifting *BB* up. As in the last section, if the shock is not large enough there will be no effect on the pattern of specialization. For a sufficiently large reduction in the money supply, however, market clearing will require that some industries move from the home to the foreign country.

At this point the analysis becomes entirely parallel to the analysis in the previous section. If the tight monetary policy is sustained for long enough, when it ends, specialization will remain in its new pattern instead of returning to its previous pattern. As a result the temporary rise in relative wages produced by the monetary contraction will be followed by a permanent reduction in relative wages.

This is a highly simplified model, but it does seem to capture the essentials of an argument that it is dangerous to let tight money be reflected in a very strong currency.

7. Conclusions and implications

The purpose of this paper has been to suggest that heterodox views about a variety of issues in international economics can be tied together by a single theme: the argument that dynamic economies of scale play a crucial role in international specialization. The three examples given might at first glance seem quite disparate – the use of infant industry protection to expand market share, the problems resulting from natural resource discoveries, and the long run effects of monetary policy. Yet we were able to show that alarmist concerns in each case can be given their most plausible grounding by a model in which dynamic economies of scale play a crucial role.

This is, however, an exploratory paper, and by no means intended to give blanket approval to any proposal for protection. There are at least three major reasons to be cautious about the results. Each of these reasons also provides a program for future research.

54 *P. Krugman, Narrow moving band, Dutch disease, competitiveness*

The first problem with the analysis is the assumption that dynamic scale economies are wholly external to firms. There are certainly both external and internal dynamic scale economies in reality. We have some rough idea how important the internal economies are (varying greatly across sectors); how important the external economies are is highly disputable. A major question is the extent to which the results would go through with imperfectly competitive firms and internal economies. We know from recent work that predatory trade and industrial policies, like those of section 4, are possible in a world of imperfectly competitive firms [see Brander and Spencer (1985) and Eaton and Grossman (1986)]. But it also seems to be the case that in some models the sort of multiple equilibria we have stressed here vanish when economies of scale are wholly internal to firms [see Helpman and Krugman (1985, chs. 3 and 4)]. The point is that a wage differential between countries with no fundamental differences in their technological capacity may offer a profit opportunity if the differential is not due to wholly external effects.

Second, the model here is clearly too stark in its assumption that dynamic scale economies are the only source of specialization and trade. Allowing for other forces – particularly differences in factor endowments – would surely soften the results. In particular, the complete arbitrariness of the pattern of specialization would be modified, particularly if factor prices shift over time. To return to the geological metaphor of section 3, a river may dig its own bed, reinforcing the results of past history; but eventually the larger forces of tectonics will bury that history. Britain's early pre-eminence in cotton spinning may have been self-reinforcing for the first half of the nineteenth century, but it was eventually overridden by the rising gap between wages in Britain and those in poorer countries.

Finally, while this paper has addressed policy issues, it has not contained any explicit welfare analysis. We have seen, for example, that in the model presented here a step-by-step policy of infant industry protection can succeed in making a country competitive in an enlarged range of industries. We have not, however, shown that this is necessarily a desirable policy. Formal welfare analysis is bound to be hard in the kind of world envisaged in this paper, a world of imperfect markets and dynamic effects over time. Nonetheless, we should be careful about making policy prescriptions without such analysis.

This paper, then, is an exploration rather than a definitive work. It raises more questions than it answers.

References

Bardhan, P., 1970, Economic growth, development, and foreign trade (Wiley, New York).
Brander, J. and B. Spencer, 1985, Export subsidies and international market share rivalry, Journal of International Economics 18, 83–100.

Corden, N.M. and J.P. Neary, 1982, Booming sector and de-industrialization in a small open economy, Economic Journal 92, 825–848.

Dornbusch, R., S. Fischer and P. Samuelson, 1977, Comparative advantage, trade, and payments in a Ricardian model with a continuum of goods, American Economic Review 67, 823–839.

Eaton, J. and G. Grossman, 1986, Optimal trade and industrial policy under oligopoly, Quarterly Journal of Economics, May, 383–406.

Frankel, J., 1983, The desirability of a dollar appreciation given a contractionary US monetary policy, NBER working paper no. 1110.

Givens, N.L., 1982, The US can no longer afford free trade, Business Week, Nov. 22, 15.

Helpman, E. and P. Krugman, 1985, Market structure and foreign trade (MIT Press, Cambridge, MA).

Van Wijnbergen, S., 1984, The Dutch disease: A disease after all, Economic Journal 94, 41–55.

Part VII
Trade, Technology and Growth

[37]

The Terms of Trade and Equilibrium Growth in the World Economy

By Ronald Findlay*

The extensive discussions that have been going on in connection with proposals for a New International Economic Order have focused attention on the nature of the economic relations between the advanced and less developed regions of the world economy, or the "North" and "South" as it has become customary to refer to them. Ever since the work of Raul Prebisch and Hans Singer almost three decades ago the movement of the terms of trade between these regions has been regarded as a key index of the distribution of the benefits from the international division of labor and the development prospects of the South. Although an extensive and controversial literature has developed around these issues, there has been a significant lack of rigorous formal analysis to provide a framework within which the diverse arguments and pieces of empirical evidence can be sorted out and assessed.

The objective of this paper is to present a highly stylized dynamic model in which the terms of trade emerge as the mechanism linking the growth rates of output in the North and South. The analysis attempts to forge a synthesis of three famous papers, using the neoclassical growth model of Robert Solow for the North, the "labor surplus" or "dual economy" model of W. Arthur Lewis for the South, and the Harry Johnson (Part 2) treatment of the terms of trade to serve as the link between them.

I

Imagine a world economy consisting of two regions, the North and the South. The North produces a single composite commodity, manufactures, which can be used for either consumption or investment. The

*Columbia University.

technology for manufactures is represented by a neoclassical production function with constant returns to scale and with capital and labor as the inputs. Capital consists of a stock of manufactures. The size of the labor force is given at any instant and grows over time at a constant rate. There is also labor-augmenting technological progress at a fixed rate assumed to be going on. Under these assumptions, as is well known, the production function can be expressed in terms of capital and "effective" labor, which grows over time at a fixed rate equal to the sum of the rate of natural increase and the rate of technological progress. A constant fraction of output is saved and invested. Markets are perfectly competitive and are cleared instantaneously so that there is always full employment of labor and full utilization of capacity.

These assumptions, of course, correspond exactly to the Solow neoclassical growth model. The only change is that the portion of output in the North which is not saved is spent either on manufactures or on another homogeneous commodity, representing primary products, with the proportions depending upon the relative price of the two goods. Income elasticities of demand for both goods are unity.

Primary products constitute the sole output of the South. There is again a neoclassical production function with capital and labor as the inputs governing the output of primary products. Capital consists of a stock of manufactures, just as in the North. Labor is in perfectly elastic supply from a "hinterland," which is otherwise outside the model, at a fixed real wage in terms of primary products. There is perfect competition so labor is hired up to the point at which its marginal productivity is equal to the fixed real wage. Total employment at any instant will depend upon the quantity of capital available. The capital-labor ratio is uniquely determined by the fixed real wage and in turn determines the marginal product of capital and hence the amount of profit per unit of labor. The *rate* of profit, however, cannot be determined unless the relative price of manufactures and primary products is known, since capital consists of a stock of manufactures and profits of a flow of primary products.

It is assumed that a constant fraction of profits are saved and all wages are consumed. Consumption expenditure, whether out of wages or profits, is spent on manufactures and primary products with the proportions depending upon relative prices. Income elasticities of demand for both goods are unity. Investment demand is thus purely for manufactures while consumption demand is divided between the two goods. The fraction of profits which is saved determines the increase in the stock of capital that propels the system forward.

It is apparent that this depiction of the South corresponds closely to the celebrated Lewis model of economic development with unlimited supplies of labor. The Solow economy of the North and the Lewis economy of the South are linked through international trade. It is assumed that there is no lending so that trade is always balanced. The demand for imports in each region depends upon the relative price of the two goods and real income. Johnson obtained a simple formula for the change in the terms of trade resulting from exogenously given growth rates of output in the two regions. In the present model, however, there is a feedback from the terms of trade to the growth rate of output in the South. The next section will demonstrate how the terms of trade and the growth rate of the South have to adjust to the growth rate of the "effective" labor force in the North that determines the steady-state growth of the whole interdependent dynamic system that constitutes the specification of the world economy.

II

The basic structure of the model will be presented in this section. The following notation will be used:

q = output per worker of manufactures in the North

π = output per worker of primary products in the South

L_N, L_S = employment in North and South

Y_N, Y_S = total incomes in North and South

k_N, k_S = capital-labor ratios in North and South

$\bar{w}$ = fixed wage in the South

n = fixed growth rate of effective labor in the North

θ = the terms of trade (manufactures per unit of primary products)

λ = ratio of employment in the South to employment in the North

ρ = rate of profit in the South

s = constant fraction of income saved in the North

σ = constant fraction of profit saved in the South

I_N, I_S = total imports in North and South

m = per capita imports of the North

μ = per capita consumption imports of the South

η_N, η_S = elasticities of m and μ with respect to θ and $1/\theta$, respectively.

Asterisks will denote long-run equilibrium values of the corresponding variables.

The constant returns-to-scale production function for primary products in the South is

$$(1) \qquad \pi = \pi(k_S)$$

and the profit-maximization condition is

$$(2) \qquad \pi(k_S) - \pi'(k_S)k_S = \bar{w}$$

Under the usual assumptions that $\pi'(k_S) > 0$ and $\pi''(k_S) < 0$, there is a unique k_S^* that satisfies (2). Since capital consists of a stock of manufactures and output of a flow of primary products, the rate of profit in the South is

$$(3) \qquad \rho = \theta\pi'(k_S^*)$$

while the common growth rate of total capital, output, and employment in the South is

$$(4) \qquad g = \sigma\rho$$

which is the so-called "Anglo-Italian" equation.

A necessary condition for a steady-state equilibrium in the world economy is that the growth rates of North and South should be equal. Since the natural growth rate of the North is the constant n, it follows from (3) and (4) that there is a unique value

$$(5) \qquad \theta^* = \frac{n}{\sigma \pi'(k_S^*)}$$

of the terms of trade that is consistent with balanced growth of the world economy as a whole. Notice that θ^* depends only on $n, \sigma, \bar{w}$, and the production function for the South. It is completely independent of the production function and propensity to save of the North, and of the demand for imports in the two regions.

The terms of trade must also, however, equilibrate the balance of trade. I now turn to the determination of the terms of trade in the "short run" by reciprocal supply and demand for exports and imports in the usual manner, after which it will be shown how the short- and long-run values of the terms of trade become reconciled with each other.

The production function for the North is

$$(6) \qquad Y_N = q(k_N) L_N$$

where L_N depends upon time by the relation

$$(7) \qquad L_N = L_0 e^{nt}$$

and k_N at any instant is determined by past history. The import demand function of the North is

$$(8) \qquad I_N = m\big[\theta, (1-s)q(k_N)\big] L_N$$

where it is assumed that $m'(\theta) < 0$ and that the elasticity of m with respect to per capita consumption $(1-s)q(k_N)$ is equal to unity. The import demand function for the South is

$$(9) \quad I_S = \bigg[\theta\sigma\pi'(k_S^*)k_S^* \\ + \mu\bigg(\frac{1}{\theta}, \bar{w} + (1-\sigma)\pi'(k_S^*)k_S^*\bigg)\bigg] L_S$$

where the expression in brackets is the sum of per capita imports for investment and consumption, respectively. At any price $1/\theta$ the demand for capital goods will be $\theta\sigma\pi'(k_S^*)k_S^*$ per worker employed, so that investment is always equal to the fraction σ of profits in terms of primary products, implying that the price elasticity of demand for capital goods imports is unity. Per capita import demand for consumption purposes is μ, with $\mu'(1/\theta) < 0$ and the elasticity with respect to per capita consumption $\bar{w} + (1 - \sigma)\pi'(k_S^*)k_S^*$ is equal to unity. Southern employment L_S is determined by

$$(10) \qquad k_S^* L_S = K_S$$

where the total capital stock at any instant K_S is given by past history. In the absence of international capital movements the trade balance must be zero so that

$$(11) \qquad \theta I_N = I_S$$

Substituting for I_N and I_S from (8) and (9) and letting $\lambda = L_S / L_N$ denote the ratio of employment in the two regions, (11) can be solved to obtain

$$(12) \quad \theta = \frac{\lambda\mu\bigg[\bigg(\dfrac{1}{\theta}\bigg), \bar{w} + (1-\sigma)\pi'(k_S^*)k_S^*\bigg]}{m(\theta, k_N) - \lambda\sigma\pi'(k_S^*)k_S^*}$$

In the short run λ and k_N are given by past history so that (12) determines the value of θ that equilibrates the trade balance. On the other hand, if θ is at its long-run value θ^* as determined by (5) then for each k_N there is a value of λ such that (12) is satisfied. In particular, if k_N is at the steady-state value k_N^* given by the condition

$$(13) \qquad k_N^* = \frac{sq(k_N^*)}{n}$$

then (12) determines the corresponding unique steady-state value of λ as

$$(14)$$
$$\lambda^* = \frac{\theta^* m^*(\theta^*, k_N^*)}{\bigg[\mu^*\bigg(\dfrac{1}{\theta^*}, \bar{w} + (1-\sigma)\pi'(k_S^*)k_S^*\bigg) + nk_S^*\bigg]}$$

after using (5). It is apparent that λ^* is equal to the ratio of steady-state per capita imports for the two regions.

The ratio of total incomes in the two regions is

(15) $$\frac{Y_S}{Y_N} = \frac{\theta^* \pi(k^*)\lambda^*}{q(k_N^*)}$$

In interpreting (15) it should be noted that $q(k_N^*)$ is output per unit of "effective labor." If n includes labor-augmenting technical progress then the ratio of effective to actual labor will be continually increasing in the North. The per capita income of the actual labor force will be continually rising in the North while it will be constant in the South since n is there the rate of growth of the actual labor force.

III

Having obtained the steady-state solution of the model, this section examines the question of convergence towards the steady state from arbitrary initial conditions. At any instant L_N, K_N, and K_S are all given by past history, and L_S is determined by the fixed wage $\bar{w}$ and the corresponding capital-labor ratio k_S^*. Dividing K_N and L_S by L_N, one obtains the normalized variables k_N and λ which are the state variables of the dynamic system to be studied explicitly in this section. Capital in the South K_S is not a separate state variable since it is always strictly proportional to L_S by virtue of the fixed-wage assumption. Under the assumptions about saving out of profits and wages, the common growth rate of K_S and L_S is $\sigma\pi'(k_S^*)\theta(\lambda, k_N)$. The relative rate of change of λ is therefore the difference between this rate and the fixed growth rate n of labor force in the North. The rate of change of k_N is equal to the difference between per capita saving and the requirements for maintaining the capital per head of the growing labor force.

The basic dynamic system can therefore be formulated as

(16) $$D\lambda = [\sigma\pi'(k_S^*)\theta(\lambda, k_N) - n]\lambda$$

(17) $$Dk_N = sq(k_N) - nk_N$$

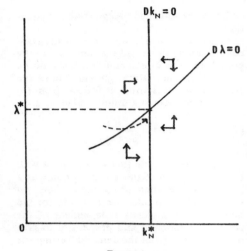

FIGURE 1

where D denotes the derivative with respect to time.

The properties of this system can be conveniently seen by means of the phase diagram constructed in Figure 1. The $Dk_N = 0$ locus is a vertical line at the value k_N^* obtained in (13). It is independent of λ. The condition for $D\lambda = 0$ is that θ should be at the value θ^* obtained earlier in (5). The $D\lambda = 0$ locus is therefore one which shows the value of λ corresponding to any value of k_N such that $\theta = \theta^*$. The positive slope of the $D\lambda = 0$ locus is derived from the relation

(18) $$\left.\frac{d\lambda}{dk_N}\right|_{\theta=\theta^*} = -\frac{\partial\theta}{\partial k_N} \bigg/ \frac{\partial\theta}{\partial\lambda}$$

which is obtained by total differentiation of (12) evaluated at θ^*, with

(19)

$$\frac{\partial\theta}{\partial k_N} = -\frac{(1-s)q'(k_N)\tilde{m}\theta}{\left[m - \lambda\sigma\pi'(k_S^*)k_S^*\right]\left(1 - \eta_S - \dfrac{\theta m}{\lambda\mu}\eta_N\right)}$$

(20)

$$\frac{\partial\theta}{\partial\lambda} = \frac{\left[\mu + \theta\sigma\pi'(k_S^*)k_S^*\right]}{\left[m - \lambda\sigma\pi'(k_S^*)k_S^*\right]\left(1 - \eta_S - \dfrac{\theta m}{\lambda\mu}\eta_N\right)}$$

The common denominator of (19) and (20) is the product of two terms, the first of which is the denominator of (12) and is positive. The second is negative if

$$(21) \qquad \eta_S + \frac{\theta m}{\lambda \mu} \eta_N > 1$$

where η_S and η_N are the elasticities of consumer import demand with respect to the terms of trade in the two regions. This is what corresponds to the familiar Marshall-Lerner stability condition in the present model, since the elasticity of demand for investment imports in the South is unity. It is apparent that (21) and the Marshall-Lerner condition are equivalent since (21) implies that η_N plus a weighted average of η_S and the unit elasticity of investment imports with $\lambda \mu / \theta m$ as the weight of η_S exceeds unity. The symbol $\tilde{m}$ in the numerator of (19) is the partial derivative of m with respect to per capita consumption expenditure $(1-s)q(k_N)$ in (8). It follows that

$$\frac{\partial \theta}{\partial k_N} > 0, \qquad \frac{\partial \theta}{\partial \lambda} < 0$$

if (21) holds, which establishes the positive slope of the $D\lambda = 0$ locus from (18). The reason for this slope is clear since an increase in k_N improves the terms of trade of the South above θ^* so that an increase in λ is required to restore this value. The intersection of the $D\lambda = 0$ and $Dk_N = 0$ loci determines the steady-state value λ^* of λ, already obtained in (14).

Examining the dynamic system (16) and (17) the "trace condition" for stability is seen to be satisfied since

$$(22) \qquad \frac{\partial(D\lambda)}{\partial \lambda} = \lambda^* \sigma \pi'(k_S^*) \frac{\partial \theta}{\partial \lambda} < 0$$

$$(23) \qquad \frac{\partial(Dk_N)}{\partial k_N} = sq'(k_N^*) - n < 0$$

at the steady-state point (λ^*, k_N^*). The condition (23) is the same as the familiar stability condition for the Solow model of a closed economy.

The "determinant condition" for stability is also fulfilled since

$$(24) \qquad \frac{\partial(D\lambda)}{\partial k_N} = \lambda^* \sigma \pi'(k_S^*) \frac{\partial \theta}{\partial k_N} > 0$$

$$(25) \qquad \frac{\partial(Dk_N)}{\partial \lambda} = 0$$

The conditions imply that λ falls at any point above the $D\lambda = 0$ locus and rises at any point below it, while k_N increases at any point to the left of the $Dk_N = 0$ locus and decreases at any point to the right. The motion of λ and k_N is indicated by the arrows in each of the quadrants. A possible trajectory from an arbitrary initial condition is indicated by the dashed curve in Figure 1. At the initial point θ is below θ^* so that the growth rate of the South is below n which means that λ falls and θ increases. When the $D\lambda = 0$ locus is reached $\theta = \theta^*$. The increase in k_N raises the terms of trade above θ^* which means that λ must now start to increase together with k_N towards the steady-state values λ^* and k_N^* while θ approaches θ^* from above. The terms of trade therefore overshoot the long-run value θ^* but then are pulled towards it. The intersection of the trajectory with the $D\lambda = 0$ locus divides the approach towards the steady state into two phases, the first in which the South grows more slowly than the North and the terms of trade continually improve, and the second in which the South grows faster than the North and the terms of trade converge toward θ^* from above.

IV

This section investigates the impact and long-run effects of variations in the parameters. The initial position will in all cases be taken as the steady-state point (λ^*, k_N^*). First, suppose that there is a shift of demand in the North towards primary products, so that m is larger for any given θ. The impact effect on θ is given by partial differentiation of (12) with respect to a shift parameter which reveals that θ would increase if the stability condition (21) holds. This raises the rate of profit in the South which causes λ to increase and θ to fall. It is

International Trade II

clear from (5) that the long-run value of θ^* is independent of the import demand function of the North, so that θ converges back towards the original θ^*, while (14) indicates that λ^* increases in the same proportion as the increase in m. In terms of Figure 1 the effect is to shift the $D\lambda=0$ schedule upwards, while leaving the $Dk_N=0$ schedule unchanged, so that λ^* rises and k_N^* remains constant.

The impact and long-run effects of the shift in import demand can be conveniently seen in terms of Figure 2. The BB curve shows the combinations of θ and λ that maintain equilibrium in the trade balance when the capital-labor ratio of the North is at its steady-state value k_N^*. The negative slope follows from the assumption that the Marshall-Lerner stability condition (21) holds. An increase in the propensity to import of the North shifts BB to the right to $B'B'$, since λ has to increase at constant θ for (12) to still hold. In the short run λ cannot change so it remains at the original value of λ^* while θ increases to the corresponding point on $B'B'$. This raises the rate of growth of the South so λ increases gradually while θ falls and the economy of the South moves down $B'B'$, approaching the point on it corresponding to the original terms of trade θ^*. The same line of reasoning indicates that a shift in the South's consumption demand towards manufactures eventually leaves θ^* unchanged but reduces λ^* by a proportion equal to the product of the increase in consumption demand and the share of imports for consumption to total imports in the South. The effects on relative income shares of these shifts in import demands are proportional to the changes in λ^*, as (15) indicates.

An increase in the propensity to save of the North raises k_N^* by virtue of (13) so that the $Dk_N=0$ schedule is shifted to the right, while (5) shows that θ^* is not affected by this change. An increase in s, for given values of θ and k_N, must lead by (12) to a reduction in λ, so that the $D\lambda=0$ schedule is shifted downwards as a result. This is because a rise in s means a shift towards manufactures and away from primary products in the demand pattern of the North, so

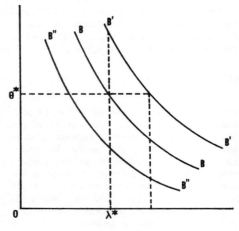

FIGURE 2

that λ must fall if there is to be equilibrium in the balance of trade with everything else held constant. The fact that the $D\lambda=0$ locus shifts down while the $Dk_N=0$ locus shifts to the right might appear to render the effect of a rise in s on λ^* ambiguous. If the North is to the left of the Golden Rule point where $q'(k_N)=n$, however, a rise in s must raise total consumption per capita $(1-s)q(k_N^*)$. It follows from (14) that λ^* must increase in the same proportion as steady-state per capita consumption in the North, since the elasticity of demand for primary products with respect to consumption expenditure is unity. It is interesting to note, therefore, that λ^* is maximized, for given values of all other parameters, when the propensity to save in the North is at the level required by the Golden Rule. The disparity in per capita consumption and income levels between North and South is of course widened by the increase in s since the levels of these variables in the South are not affected by s. The ratio of *total* incomes shown in (15) worsens for the South in spite of the increase in λ^*, since the proportionate increase of this variable is equal to $(1-s)q(k_N^*)$ which is less than that of $q(k_N^*)$ because of the rise in s. An increase in the North's propensity to save therefore raises relative employment in the South but it lowers its relative per capita income. The favorable effect on relative total income of the South of the improvement in relative employment is not sufficient to offset the decline in relative per capita incomes.

Technological change in the North can be introduced in the form of a once and for all Hicks-neutral shift in the production function $q(k_N)$, or in the form of an increase in the rate of labor-augmenting Harrod-neutral progress that results in an increase in n, the growth rate of the effective labor force. Taking the case of the Hicks-neutral shift first, it is evident that the $Dk_N = 0$ locus is shifted to the right and that k_N^* increases. For given values of θ and k_N (12) implies that λ must increase if $q(k_N)$ rises. The $D\lambda = 0$ locus is therefore shifted upward and so λ^* increases. The immediate impact of the Hicks-neutral shift in the production function of the North is for θ to increase with λ^* and k_N^* at their original steady-state values. The initial rise of θ raises the growth rate of the South above n, which causes λ to increase towards its new steady-state value, while k_N also increases because savings in the North now exceed the steady-state requirement. The fact that the South grows faster than the North means that θ falls after the initial jump in its level, and it eventually approaches its original level θ^* which, as may be seen from (5), is not affected by the shift in $q(k_N)$. It can be seen from (14) and (15) that the shift in $q(k_N)$ has no effect on the relative total incomes of the North and South since λ^* increases in the same proportion as $q(k_N)$ while θ^* remains unchanged. Relative per capita incomes of course move in favor of the North.

An increase in n shifts the $Dk_N = 0$ locus to the left and reduces k_N^*. From (5) it is clear that θ^* must rise in the same proportion as n, so that there is a permanent improvement in terms of trade of the South. For any given k_N it follows from (12) that a higher θ^* requires a lower λ to equilibrate the trade balance, so that the $D\lambda = 0$ schedule is shifted downward and λ^* falls.

A change in any of the South's parameters does not affect the $Dk_N = 0$ locus and so leaves k_N^* unchanged. The welfare of the North, however, can be altered by these parameter shifts through their effects on the terms of trade. An increase in the fixed real wage $\bar{w}$ raises the capital-labor ratio k_S^* in the South and so reduces $\pi'(k_S^*)$, the marginal productivity of capital. This results by (5) in a rise in θ^* proportionately equal to the fall in $\pi'(k_S^*)$. The South is therefore able to improve its terms of trade in the long run by an exogenous increase in the fixed real wage. The price for this, however, will be a reduction in the relative employment ratio λ^*. This can be proved by showing that an increase in $\bar{w}$ must reduce λ^* if the terms of trade are held constant, so that the improvement in the South's terms of trade must reduce it even further by virtue of the fact that $\partial\lambda/\partial\theta < 0$. The rise in k_S^* induced by the rise in $\bar{w}$, combined with the fact that the South is to the left of the Golden Rule since $\sigma < 1$ means that total consumption expenditure $\bar{w} + (1 - \sigma)\pi'(k_S^*)k_S^*$ and investment nk_S^* both rise on a per capita basis. At constant terms of trade this means an increase in the demand for imports for both consumption and investment purposes. Exports will however be constant, since the North's income is not affected, so that λ^* must fall as a result of the rise in $\bar{w}$ with θ^* held constant. But θ^* in fact rises, so that λ^* must fall even further since $\partial\lambda/\partial\theta < 0$.

An increase in σ, the propensity to save out of profits in the South, leads by (5) to a fall in θ^* in the same proportion. The effect on λ^* is obtained by logarithmic differentiation of (14) with respect to σ, using the fact that the elasticitiy of θ^* with respect to σ is minus unity. This establishes that

$$(26) \qquad \frac{\sigma}{\lambda^*} \frac{d\lambda^*}{d\sigma} \gtreqless 0$$

depending upon whether

$$(27) \qquad \frac{\theta^* m}{\lambda^* \mu} \eta_N + \eta_S \gtreqless 1 + \frac{(\theta^* - \bar{\mu})\sigma\pi'(k_S^*)k_S^*}{\mu}$$

where $\bar{\mu}$ is the additional import of manufactures for consumption resulting from an increase in total consumption expenditure in terms of primary products $\bar{w} + (1 - \sigma) \cdot \pi'(k_S^*)k_S^*$. The condition (27) on the sum of the elasticities of import demands is more stringent than the stability condition (21), since the marginal propensity to import when income in the South is measured in terms of manufactures is $\bar{\mu}/\theta^*$, which is between zero and unity, making $(\alpha^* - \bar{\mu})$ positive.

The effect of a rise in σ on λ^* at constant terms of trade is for it to be reduced, since all of the increase in saving out of profits is spent on imports while only part of what was formerly being consumed was spent on imports, requiring λ^* to fall to equilibrate the trade balance. The terms of trade worsen, however, which, if (21) holds, leads to a rise in λ^*. The necessary and sufficient condition for the induced increase in λ^* to more than offset the fall at constant terms of trade is provided by (27).

In terms of Figure 2 the increase in σ shifts the BB curve to the left to $B''B''$. In the short run λ^* remains fixed so θ falls to the corresponding point on $B''B''$. This decline, however, may be smaller or greater than the long-run decline in θ^* which must be in the same proportion as the increase in σ. The new steady-state value of λ^* will be at the point on $B''B''$ corresponding to this long-run decline in θ^* and the economy of the South moves along $B''B''$ in whichever direction is required to get to this point since $D\lambda$ will be positive or negative depending upon whether the impact effect on θ is less or more than the long-run effect.

The effect of the increase in σ is to *worsen* the relative per capita income of the South since θ^* falls while $\pi(k_S^*)$ and $q(k_N^*)$ are unchanged. The effect on relative total incomes depends in addition upon what happens to λ^*. So long as the total elasticity of λ^* with respect to σ, obtained earlier in connection with (27), does not exceed unity the relative total income of the South must also decline.

A simple way in which a once and for all technological change in the South can be introduced is by an increase in the marginal productivity of capital with the capital-labor ratio and the marginal productivity of labor unchanged. This will lower θ^* in the same proportion as the rise in the marginal productivity of capital, as implied by (5). Denoting $\pi'(k_S^*)$ by r, the effect of this type of

technical progress on λ^* is obtained by logarithmic differentiation of (14) with respect to r, using the fact that the elasticity of θ^* with respect to r is minus unity. This yields the result that

$$(28) \qquad \frac{r}{\lambda^*} \frac{d\lambda^*}{dr} \gtrless 0$$

depending on whether

$$(29) \qquad \frac{\theta^* m}{\lambda^* \mu} \eta_N + \eta_S \gtrless 1 + \frac{[\theta^* - (1-\sigma)\bar{\mu}] r k_S^*}{\mu}$$

The interpretation of (29) is analogous to that of (27). The impact and long-run effects on θ and λ can also be shown in terms of Figure 2 in a manner corresponding exactly to the preceding analysis of the increase in the propensity to save, since the increase in the South's income at constant terms of trade requires λ to be reduced, thus shifting BB to the left.

The effect of this type of technological change is to *reduce* the relative per capita income of the South. The reason is that θ^* deteriorates in the same proportion as r increases while $\pi(k_S^*)$ increases only by the share of profit times this amount. Thus the relative total income of the South would also decline unless the total elasticity of λ^* with respect to r, obtained in connection with (29), were to exceed the share of wages times the proportionate increase in r resulting from the technological change.

V

"An engine of growth" was the famous phrase that Dennis Robertson used to describe the role of international trade in the expansion of the world economy from the mid-nineteenth century to World War I, a process that has continued in the last three decades after the disruptions of the interwar years. In the model that has been presented here, trade is indeed an engine of growth for the economy of the South, but the power that drives that engine is generated by the exogenously determined natural growth rate of the North. The South does not have a given natural growth rate but an endogenous one, depending upon the value of the terms of trade since this is what determines the rate of profit in the Anglo-Italian equation. The steady-state level of the terms of trade must be whatever is necessary to make the endogenous growth rate of the South equal to the fixed natural growth rate of the North.

The structural differences in the determination of the growth rate of the two regions produces asymmetrical consequences on the terms of trade of changes in technology and the propensity to save. As demonstrated in the previous section, once and for all improvements in the production function of the North and increases in its propensity to save leave the terms of trade unchanged in the long run and increase its real per capita income. In the South, on the other hand, these shifts lead to a proportionate fall in the long-run terms of trade and a decline in real per capita income measured in terms of manufactures. These unfavorable effects, however, are compensated by an increase in the relative employment ratio if the elasticities of import demand are sufficiently high. This asymmetry is a prominent feature in the writings of Raul Prebisch and Hans Singer. The arguments put forward for this asymmetry by these writers, however, usually involve the role of monopolies and trade unions in the North and generally have not been very convincing. The present analysis obtains similar conclusions in spite of assuming perfectly competitive markets everywhere.

In conclusion some of the major limitations of the model may be noted. One of these is the absence of international capital mobility in response to differences in the rate of profit between North and South. This can readily be handled but an adequate treatment requires a separate paper. Another is the assumption of complete specialization in both regions. Two-sector open dual economics have been studied, for example in my book, Part 2, though only in the context of either constant terms of trade or an exogenously shifting demand curve for the exportable primary product. Once again, an extension of the analysis to accommodate this feature is quite feasible but would require too much space to attempt here.

The most basic assumption of all, of course, has been that the South enjoys unlimited supplies of labor at a fixed real wage. This is not intended as a permanent state of affairs, since if the growth rate of employment in the "modern" or commercialized sector exceeds the rate of population growth, the unlimited supplies of labor must become exhausted and growth will eventually produce a rise in the real wage. Structural differences between North and South would then no longer exist and the neoclassical model would come into its own the world over. Hopefully that day will come, but it has not as yet.

REFERENCES

Ronald Findlay, *International Trade and Development Theory*, New York 1973.

Harry G. Johnson, *International Trade and Economic Growth*, Cambridge, Mass. 1967.

W. A. Lewis, "Economic Development with Unlimited Supplies of Labour," *Manchester Sch. Econ. Soc. Stud.*, May 1954, *22*, 139–91.

Raul Prebisch, *The Economic Development of Latin America and its Principal Problems*, New York 1950.

D. H. Robertson, "The Future of International Trade," *Econ. J.*, Mar. 1938, *48*, 1–14.

H. W. Singer, "The Distribution of Gains between Borrowing and Investing Countries," *Amer. Econ. Rev. Proc.*, May 1950, *40*, 473–85.

R. M. Solow, "A Contribution to the Theory of Economic Growth," *Quart. J. Econ.*, Feb. 1956, *70*, 65–94.

[38]

Tariffs, Technology Transfer, and Welfare

Robert C. Feenstra

Columbia University

Kenneth L. Judd

Northwestern University

It is found that the welfare gain per unit of revenue raised is maximized for an export tariff on technology transfer, followed by an import tariff on goods, with an export tariff on goods the poorest policy alternative. These results are derived within a monopolistic competition model, where the production of any good requires some initial research and development (R&D), and technology transfer occurs when R&D is done in one country for production of goods in the other. An intuitive explanation is presented, based on the public-good nature of R&D and also the elasticity of demand for technologies from firms.

I. Introduction

It is widely recognized that the transfer of technology from developed to less developed countries has an important impact on the pattern of trade and relative incomes across countries. A positive description of such technology transfer was presented some years ago by Vernon (1966), and the hypotheses of his celebrated "product cycle" have led to numerous empirical studies. But, unfortunately, it is difficult to obtain welfare-theoretic policy implications from the product cycle

The authors thank participants at international trade workshops of the University of Chicago, NBER, Columbia, Yale, and the University of Western Ontario for helpful comments. Special thanks to Rick Brecher, in particular, whose suggestions have been included in this draft. Financial support of the National Science Foundation grant SES-80-25401 is acknowledged.

[*Journal of Political Economy*, 1982, vol. 90, no. 6]
© 1982 by The University of Chicago. All rights reserved. 0022-3808/82/9006-0003$01.50

theory, since it is not explicitly based on the optimizing behavior of economic agents. In an important contribution, Krugman (1979*b*) develops an analytical model of the product cycle and obtains several welfare implications of changes in innovation and technology transfer. In his model the levels and rates of innovation and technology transfer are treated as parameters, and so the relationship between changes in actual commercial policy instruments (such as tariffs) and these parameters is an open question. Before policy recommendations can be made, this relationship must be determined. Other analyses of technology transfer are presented by Rodríguez (1975), McCulloch and Yellen (1976), Findlay (1978), and Pugel (1980, in press).

In this paper we shall endogenously determine the level of technology transfer in an optimizing framework and examine the effects of tariffs on technology transfer and welfare. Our basic model is similar to that of the recent theoretical literature on monopolistic competition and trade (see esp. Krugman 1979*a*, 1979*b*; see also Dixit and Norman 1980; Lancaster 1980; and Helpman 1981), which can be reviewed as follows. These models assume some fixed costs of production, resulting in economies of scale. Naturally, the fixed production cost or activity uses resources of the same country in which production occurs. With a monopolistically competitive market structure, the number or variety of goods produced is solved for in the zero-profit equilibrium. A change in trade opportunities due to liberalization or commercial policy will then affect world variety, which has a welfare impact additional to the usual welfare effect with a fixed number of goods.

Our analysis differs from these fixed cost models of monopolistic competition and trade in that the "fixed" production activity need not occur in the same country where production takes place. Specifically, we shall assume that the production of any good requires some initial research and development (R&D) cost and that this R&D can be done in either country: the actual locational choice of R&D activity will be determined by the optimizing behavior of firms. We shall adopt a very simple view of R&D in which the costs to develop the technology to produce any good are a nonstochastic constant. Analytically, these R&D costs are identical to the fixed costs of the usual monopolistic competition model, except that the R&D costs are not country specific. We shall identify R&D activity done at home for production of goods abroad as "technology transfer," and the extent of this technology transfer can be measured as the number of goods developed at home but produced abroad, multiplied by the R&D cost per good.

Several limitations of our analysis can be noted at the outset. First, our model and equilibrium are static. That is, all goods are developed, produced, and consumed within the same (single) period. Equilibrium is obtained when a sufficiently large variety of goods are developed and marketed such that profits are zero. This static framework is used for convenience but is still of considerable interest for analyzing R&D and technology transfer: many of the effects we identify of tariffs on technology transfer, world variety, and welfare would undoubtedly carry over (in some form, at least) to a dynamic model. A dynamic analysis of product development under autarky is presented by Judd (1980); this material is sufficiently new to deter application to a trade model at the present time.

Second, we shall assume that the tastes of each country are represented by identical symmetric CES utility functions. Symmetry of the utility function within any industry or group is needed to use free-entry monopolistic competition as the equilibrium concept. Then when a single group of commodities and a constant elasticity of substitution are assumed, it is known that under autarky the monopolistically competitive equilibrium is identical to the social optimum.[1] That is, under autarky government intervention is not needed. Using a symmetric CES utility function is therefore both a limitation and a virtue: If tariffs are found to be desirable with trade, then this is not due to the possibility of correcting some distortion which exists under autarky, since the autarky equilibrium is socially optimal. That is, by using a CES utility function we are able to separate carefully the role of tariffs in correcting domestic distortions (which do not exist) and exploiting monopoly power in trade.

In the next section we shall determine the free trade equilibrium and show how various combinations of relative country sizes and R&D costs lead to different trade patterns. In Section III we examine the effects of tariffs on technology transfer and welfare, considering in turn a uniform import tariff on goods and an export tariff on technology transfer; the effects of an export tariff on goods can be inferred from these results. We consider only the effects of small changes in tariff rates around zero, that is, small movements away from the free trade equilibrium. In Section IV we rank the welfare impact of the various tariff instruments, again for small movements around the free trade equilibrium. Significantly, we find that the welfare gain per unit of revenue raised is maximized for the export tariff on technology transfer, followed by the import tariff on goods, with the export tariff on goods the poorest policy alternative. An

[1] Dixit and Stiglitz (1977, p. 301) work within a more general framework, where production of a homogeneous numeraire commodity occurs; this good must be omitted to obtain the result stated in the text. The result is also proved in a more general dynamic model by Judd (1980).

intuitive explanation for this result is presented, based on the public-good nature of R&D and also on the elasticity of demand for technologies from firms. In Section V we extend our analysis to include subsidization of R&D for domestic production of goods as a policy instrument; conclusions are given in Section VI. The derivations of mathematical results are gathered in the Appendix.

II. Trade Equilibrium and Patterns

We assume that labor is the only factor of production, where the endowments of the home and foreign countries are given by L and L^*. Labor in the two countries is equally efficient at producing goods, with one unit of labor required per unit of output, but has different efficiencies in the R&D activity: k units of home labor are needed to develop the technology for any good, whereas k^* units of foreign labor are required. Note that labor cannot migrate between the countries. Home and foreign wages are denoted by w and w^*, where $\mu = w^*/w$ is the relative foreign wage.

Letting v and v^* index home and foreign goods, respectively, we assume that domestic and foreign tastes are given by the identical symmetric CES utility functions

$$U = \int_0^V x(v)^c dv + \int_V^{V+V^*} x(v^*)^c dv^*, \qquad 0 < c < 1 \tag{1a}$$

and

$$U^* = \int_0^V x^*(v)^c dv + \int_V^{V+V^*} x^*(v^*)^c dv^*, \qquad 0 < c < 1, \tag{1b}$$

where V and V^* denote the variety (measure) of home and foreign goods produced, $x(v)$ and $x(v^*)$ are the quantities consumed at home of domestic and foreign goods, and $x^*(v)$ and $x^*(v^*)$ are the quantities consumed abroad of imported and local goods.[2] The parameter c of the utility function is related to σ, the elasticity of substitution, by $\sigma = 1/(1 - c)$, $\sigma > 1$.

Several known properties of the CES utility function can be reviewed (see App.). The elasticity of home, foreign, or world demand for any good is given by $\sigma = 1/(1 - c)$. It follows that the profit-maximizing prices for goods produced at home and abroad are given by w/c and w^*/c, that is, constant proportional markups over variable

---

[2] In writing these utility functions we index goods such that the foreign index v^* exceeds the home index v. As discussed below, under certain assumptions we shall find that no good is produced in both countries with trade. (An asterisk on v refers to the origin of production, while an asterisk on x refers to the origin of demand.)

cost. Thus, $\mu = w^*/w$ is the relative price of imported goods, or the inverse terms of trade, for the home country.

In writing the utility functions (1a) and (1b) we assume that no good is produced in both countries in the trade equilibrium. This assumption can be justified on the basis of positive fixed costs to transferring abroad a technology developed for use at home. That is, let k (k^*) denote the amount of home (foreign) labor needed to develop a new technology for producing a good in either country, while z (z^*) denotes the additional fixed cost needed to adapt an existing technology, used in one country, for production in the other. This structure amounts to a "putty-clay" assumption on R&D, where ex ante the costs of developing a new technology for use in either country are equal, but ex post existing technologies cannot be costlessly transferred between countries. So long as the fixed costs z and z^* are positive and tariffs on trade are infinitesimally small, then no good will be produced in both countries with trade, which can be explained as follows.

Anticipating some of our equilibrium results, we shall find that in the free trade equilibrium wages are equalized across countries, so with small tariffs wages differ only slightly. The additional return available to any firm from transferring an existing technology and producing in both countries (e.g., to "jump" a tariff barrier) clearly depends on the difference in wages, and when tariffs are infinitesimally small then so are the additional profits. In particular, the profits will be less than the fixed cost of transferring an additional technology, so this activity will not occur. Now that we have established that a single firm will not produce a good in both countries, note that two (or more) firms will never produce the same good in a single or differing countries, since with symmetry of demand and costs the monopoly profits from developing a new product always exceed the duopoly profits from developing and marketing an existing product; thus, firms will specialize in different goods. Therefore, with infinitesimally small tariffs and positive fixed costs to transferring an existing technology, no good will be produced in both countries with trade.[3]

---

[3] An alternative assumption implying that no good is produced in both countries is that in addition to the fixed costs of R&D there are fixed country-specific production costs. So long as the country-specific fixed costs are positive and tariffs are infinitesimally small, a firm will never find it profitable to produce a good in both countries, since the additional profits which could be earned by taking advantage of lower wages abroad would be less than the fixed costs of establishing the foreign plant. However, under this alternative assumption the comparative static results reported below would have to be modified slightly to take account of the domestic and foreign labor engaged in the fixed production cost activity. Under either assumption, with large tariffs firms may produce in both countries, and our model thus very naturally extends to an analysis of multinational firms.

Firms in either country will choose to develop their product technologies in the country where R&D costs wk or w^*k^* are minimized. For the moment we shall assume that wk is less than w^*k^*, so that all R&D activity is done at home; after determining the trade equilibrium we shall then establish the conditions under which this trade pattern holds. From this assumption, the extent of technology transfer is given by V^*wk, that is, the variety of goods developed at home but produced abroad, multiplied by the R&D cost per good.

If we use home labor as the numeraire (so $w \equiv 1$) and solve for commodity demands from utility maximization, the domestic and foreign profits from developing and marketing any good are given by

$$\pi = \left(\frac{1}{c} - 1\right)[x(v) + x^*(v)] - k$$

$$= (1 - c)\frac{(L + \mu L^*)}{(V + V^*\mu^{-d})} - k, \quad d = \frac{c}{1 - c}; \tag{2}$$

and

$$\pi^* = \left(\frac{\mu}{c} - \mu\right)[x(v^*) + x^*(v^*)] - k$$

$$= \mu^{-d}(1 - c)\frac{(L + \mu L^*)}{(V + V^*\mu^{-d})} - k, \tag{3}$$

where for convenience we have introduced the symbol $d = c/(1 - c) = \sigma - 1 > 0$. A more detailed derivation of these profit equations is given in the Appendix.

If we assume free entry, an equilibrium condition of our model is that the variety of goods available must be sufficiently large such that profits are nonpositive in each country. If we assume for the moment that goods are produced in both countries, from (2) and (3) the condition $\pi = \pi^* = 0$ implies

$$\mu = w^*/w = 1,$$

$$(V + V^*) = (1 - c)[(L + L^*)/k].$$

The first condition states that wages are equalized across countries. The second condition determines the extent of world variety $V + V^*$ and is shown as the line $\pi\pi^*$ in figure 1, along which profits are zero.

Aside from zero profits, the remaining equilibrium condition is that trade must be balanced. Continuing to use home labor as the numeraire, we can give the trade surplus of the home country as

$$T = [Vx^*(v)/c] + kV^* - [V^*x(v^*)\mu/c], \tag{5}$$

where $Vx^*(v)/c$ = value of home exports of goods, kV^* = value of home exports of R&D, or technology transfer, and $V^*x(v^*)\mu/c$ = value of home imports of goods.

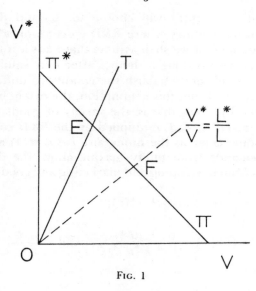

FIG. 1

If we use the condition $\mu = 1$ from (4) and substitute for commodity demands from utility maximization, the equilibrium condition $T = 0$ can be written as

$$\frac{VL^*}{(V + V^*)} + kV^* = \frac{V^*L}{(V + V^*)}. \tag{6}$$

Combining this with (4) we obtain

$$V/V^* = (cL/L^*) - (1 - c), \tag{6'}$$

which is shown as the line OT in figure 1, along which trade is balanced. Conditions (4) and (6) can be used to solve for the equilibrium varieties in the two countries:

$$V^* = \left(\frac{1 - c}{c}\right)\frac{L^*}{k}$$

$$V = (1 - c)\frac{(L + L^*)}{k} - V^* \tag{7}$$

$$= (1 - c)\frac{L}{k} - \frac{(1 - c)^2}{c}\frac{L^*}{k}.$$

These equilibrium varieties are shown at the point E in figure 1.

The dashed line in figure 1 gives those combinations of country varieties such that the variety of goods produced in each country is proportional to its size (labor force). It can be seen that at the equilibrium E the foreign country produces and exports a disproportionately large variety of goods; these exports are needed to purchase the imports of both goods and technology from the home country. Because of its technology exports, the home country produces and exports a disproportionately small variety of goods, as compared with the position F. It can be shown that F is the equilibrium of a fixed cost monopolistic competition trade model, in which $k = k^*$ and the fixed production cost or activity uses resources of the same country in which the goods are produced; that is, fixed costs are country specific.[4] At F the country varieties are given by $V = (1 - c)(L/k)$ and $V^* = (1 - c)(L^*/k)$.

So far we have assumed that R&D activity takes place only in the home country and that goods are produced in both. Since in this equilibrium wages are equalized across countries, the former assumption is satisfied if $k \leq k^*$, so that all firms will choose to develop their technologies in the home country (or be indifferent). The condition under which goods are produced in both countries can be found by inspecting (6') or (7); the equilibrium variety produced at home is nonnegative only if

$$\frac{L}{L^*} \geq \left(\frac{1-c}{c}\right) = \left(\frac{1}{\sigma - 1}\right). \tag{8}$$

Thus, both of our initial assumptions are satisfied in the region (A) of figure 2, which leads to the trade pattern of technology transfer from home to abroad and "intraindustry" trade in goods.

If $L/L^* < 1/(\sigma - 1)$, then the home country will specialize in R&D activity, with goods produced only in the foreign country. If we assume for the moment that no technologies are developed abroad, full employment at home requires that $L = kV^*$, and so the equilibrium world variety is given by $V^* = L/k$, where $V = 0$. The zero-profit condition for production of goods abroad becomes (see [3])

$$\pi^* = (1 - c)\left(\frac{L + \mu L^*}{V^*}\right) - k$$

$$= (1 - c)\left(\frac{L + \mu L^*}{L/k}\right) - k = 0, \tag{9a}$$

which implies:

$$\mu = \left(\frac{c}{1 - c}\right)\frac{L}{L^*} = (\sigma - 1)\frac{L}{L^*}. \tag{9b}$$

Note that R&D activity will take place only at home so long as $wk \leq w^*k^*$ or $k/k^* \leq \mu$. Finally, it can be shown that home profits from the production of goods are nonpositive so long as $\mu \leq 1$.

[4] This is a special case of Krugman (1979a).

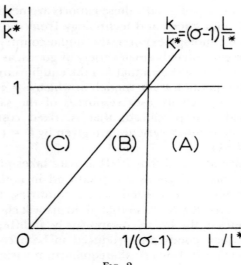

Fig. 2

In summary, the region in which the home country imports all goods and exports only technologies, while the foreign country exports all goods and imports only technologies, is shown by (*B*) in figure 2. Under this trade pattern, world variety is determined by V^* = L/k, $V = 0$, independent of the foreign country's labor force. The relative foreign wage is given by (9b) and is a decreasing function of the relative size of the foreign country. This may be contrasted with region (*A*), in which goods are produced in both countries and wages are equalized.

Last, if the home country is small relative to the foreign labor force, domestic R&D activity may be unable to support all the desired varieties produced abroad. This occurs in region (*C*) of figure 2, where the home country specializes in R&D activity but the foreign country produces both goods and technologies. Since technologies are developed in both countries we must have $wk = w^*k^*$ or $\mu = k/k^*$. Then from the zero-profit condition for production of goods abroad we have (see [3])

$$\pi^* = (1 - c)\left[\frac{L + L^*(k/k^*)}{V^*}\right] - k = 0, \qquad (10a)$$

which implies:

$$V^* = (1 - c)\left(\frac{L}{k} + \frac{L^*}{k^*}\right). \qquad (10b)$$

The condition that home profits from production of goods be non-positive is again satisfied if $\mu \leqq 1$. Thus, in region (C) the relative foreign wage $\mu = k/k^*$ is independent of country sizes, while world variety given in (10b) depends on the labor force of both countries.

This completes our description of the various trade equilibriums and patterns. If $k > k^*$ in figure 2 then we just reverse the roles of the domestic and foreign countries and consider technology transfer from abroad to home. In the following section we examine the impact of tariffs on variety, the relative wage, and welfare under the various trade patterns, focusing our attention on region (A), where R&D activity occurs only at home with goods produced in both countries.

III. Effects of Tariffs

When the home country specializes in the R&D activity, as in regions (B) and (C) of figure 2, the effect of a uniform import tariff on goods or an export tariff on technologies can be easily analyzed. So long as these tariffs do not change the pattern of specialization, then they will have no real effects, leaving home and foreign utility and technology transfer kV^* unchanged. This result is most easily seen for the import tariff: since no goods are produced at home the tariff is equivalent to a lump-sum tax on consumption, with the revenue returned, which has no equilibrium effects. A tariff on technologies can be analyzed similarly.[5]

Turning to region (A), where goods are produced in both countries but R&D occurs only at home, we shall examine the general equilibrium effects of a uniform import tariff on goods—denoted by t—and export tariff on technology transfer—denoted by τ. Due to the complexity of this comparative statics exercise (see App.), we shall examine only small changes in the tariff rates around zero, that is, small movements away from the free trade equilibrium. Note that a uniform export tariff on both goods and technologies has equivalent real effects to an equal value of the import tariff on goods; this is the Lerner symmetry theorem applied to our model. Therefore, the effects of an export tariff applied to goods on domestic and foreign variety, and the terms of trade, can be readily inferred from the comparative statics results presented below.[6]

---

[5] The tariff on technology transfer in regions (B) and (C) is analyzed in greater detail in an earlier draft of this paper (Feenstra and Judd 1981).

[6] The effects of an export tariff on goods are analyzed in greater detail in Feenstra and Judd (1981); see also the discussion at the end of this section and in the Appendix.

A. Import Tariff on Goods

Evaluated at $t = 0$, the effect of a uniform import tariff is:

$$\frac{dV}{dt} = \left(\frac{1 - c}{c}\right)\frac{LV^*}{L + L^*} > 0,$$

$$\frac{dV^*}{dt} = \frac{-LV^*}{c(L + L^*)} < 0, \qquad (11)$$

$$\frac{d\mu}{dt} = \frac{-L}{c(L + L^*)} < 0.$$

Thus, domestic variety rises, foreign variety and technology transfer kV^* fall, and the foreign wage is reduced. These results may be understood by noting that the import tariff shifts home demand toward domestic goods, which raises domestic profits and equilibrium variety, lowers foreign profits and equilibrium variety, and increases the relative demand for, and wage of, labor at home. It can also be seen that world variety $(V + V^*)$ is reduced: $(dV/dt) + (dV^*/dt) = -LV^*/(L + L^*) < 0$.

With the import tariff the domestic relative price of imports is $\mu(1 + t)$. While we expect this price to rise, according to the Metzler effect it is possible for the foreign terms of trade μ to decrease enough due to the tariff so that $\mu(1 + t)$ actually falls. Evaluated at $t = 0$, from (11) we have

$$\frac{d}{dt}[\mu(1 + t)] = 1 - \frac{L}{c(L + L^*)}, \qquad (11')$$

so that $\mu(1 + t)$ falls if $L/(L + L^*) > c$. In order for the trade equilibrium to occur in region (A) of figure 2, as assumed, condition (8) must be satisfied, which can be rewritten as

$$\frac{L}{L + L^*} > (1 - c)$$

$$> c \text{ if } c < \tfrac{1}{2}. \qquad (8')$$

Thus, if $c < \tfrac{1}{2}$ or equivalently $\sigma < 2$, a Metzler effect occurs, with the domestic relative price of imports falling due to the tariff; note that this condition is sufficient but not necessary. The elasticity of substitution and demand $\sigma = 1/(1 - c)$ applies to both domestic and foreign tastes, so $\sigma < 2$ corresponds to relatively inelastic foreign demand, bearing some resemblance to the Metzler condition in standard two-good competitive trade models.

Using (11), we can write the change in utility due to the import tariff as

$$\frac{1}{U}\frac{dU}{dt} = \left(\frac{c}{V+V*}\right)\left\{V* - \left[1 - \frac{L}{c(L+L*)}\right]V* - \left(\frac{1-c}{c}\right)\frac{V*L}{L+L*}\right\}$$

$$= \left(\frac{1}{V+V*}\right)\frac{cLV*}{L+L*} > 0. \tag{12}$$

The first term in the decomposition (12) refers to the effect of redistributed tariff revenue on utility, while the second and third terms are the effects of the change in the domestic relative price of imports $\mu(1 + t)$ and world variety $(V + V*)$, respectively. The fall in world variety has a negative impact on utility, but nevertheless the tariff is welfare improving. It is interesting to note that if we ignore the first and third terms in (12), that is, disregard the change in tariff revenue and world variety, then utility rises with the tariff if and only if there is a Metzler effect; this result can also be derived in standard two-good competitive trade models. However, if we continue to ignore the redistribution of tariff revenue but include the decrease in world variety, utility will necessarily fall with the tariff, since

$$-\left[1 - \frac{L}{c(L+L*)}\right]V* - \left(\frac{1-c}{c}\right)\frac{V*L}{L+L*} = \frac{-L*V*}{L+L*} < 0.$$

B. Export Tariff on Technology Transfer

Evaluated at $\tau = 0$, the effect of a tariff on the export of technologies is

$$\frac{dV}{d\tau} = \left(\frac{1-c}{c}\right)V* > 0,$$

$$\frac{dV*}{d\tau} = \frac{-V*}{c} < 0, \tag{13}$$

$$\frac{d\mu}{d\tau} = -\left(\frac{1-c}{c}\right) < 0.$$

Not surprisingly, the tariff reduces the amount of technology transfer $kV*$. This reduction in variety tends to raise the demand for all goods, which increases domestic profits and the equilibrium variety V produced at home; the shift in the production of goods and labor demand toward the home country lowers the relative foreign wage μ. The tariff on technology transfer also reduces world variety, $(dV/d\tau) + (dV*/d\tau) = -V* < 0$.

The impact of these effects on home utility can be written as

$$\frac{1}{U}\frac{dU}{d\tau} = \frac{(1-c)}{(V+V^*)}\left[\frac{c(L+L^*)V^*}{L} + V^* - V^*\right]$$

$$= \frac{ckV^*}{L} > 0,$$

(14)

using (4). As before, the first term in the decomposition (14) is the effect on utility of the redistributed tariff revenue, while the second and third terms are the effects of a change in the domestic relative price of imports μ and world variety $(V + V^*)$, respectively. The latter two effects cancel, and welfare is unambiguously improved due to the tariff on technology transfer.

As mentioned earlier, the effects of an export tariff on goods may be inferred from the results above using the Lerner symmetry theorem. Specifically, taking the difference between the comparative statics derivatives (11) and (13) yields the effects of the export tariff on domestic and foreign variety; taking the difference beteen (11') and (13) yields the effect on the domestic price of imports, that is, the relative foreign wage with an export tariff on goods. This dependence between the three tariff instruments will be used in the following section, where we rank the tariffs according to their impact on welfare.

Before proceeding to this, we should comment on the industry structure which has implicitly been assumed in the R&D activity. There are two possibilities. First, the R&D which occurs at home for production of goods abroad may be internally performed by home subsidiaries of foreign firms.[7] This intrafirm transfer of knowledge would be difficult to observe and monitor and, in reality, may be less than fully reflected in the balance of payments. In this case a tariff on technology exports may not be a feasible policy instrument, and to affect the level of technology transfer the home country may have to use less direct policy measures, such as tariffs on the export or import of goods.

On the other hand, it is fully consistent in theory to assume that the R&D industry is perfectly competitive and external to the goods industry. With free entry of firms into the goods industry, the demand curve for patented technologies is infinitely elastic at the level of monopoly profits earned, net of R&D costs. The supply curve of patented technologies is horizontal at the marginal cost k (or k^* abroad), and equilibrium is established when the price of a patented

---

[7] In Sec. II we ruled out the possibility of a firm producing the same good in both countries, but with multiproduct firms located in both countries we may still observe internal transfers of knowledge.

technology is k, a result which we have already used. Also, since the total duopoly profits from two firms selling an identical product within the goods industry can be assumed less than the monopoly profits, it is in the interest of both buyers and sellers to ensure that all technologies are patented, that is, can be sold to one and only one firm.

This sort of competitive sale of knowledge would be reflected in the services component of the current account and should be accessible to policy intervention. The extent to which technology transfer can be controlled in reality depends on which of the two possible industry structures is predominant.

IV. Welfare Ranking of Tariffs

The welfare effect of the tariffs analyzed in the previous section can be directly compared by computing the welfare impact, per unit of revenue raised, for each of the policy instruments. This exercise can be performed with or without the redistribution of tariff revenues, where the government may choose to withhold the revenue in order to finance some other intervention, for example, subsidization of R&D for domestic use, as analyzed in the next section. It turns out that the ranking of the tariffs according to their welfare impact is independent of whether revenues are redistributed or not, so we shall make use of our results in the previous section and report only the case where revenues are distributed back to consumers.[8]

To develop some intuition as to the comparative effects of the different tariff instruments, suppose we arbitrarily hold the terms of trade constant. Then for given varieties V and V^*, an infinitesimal import tariff on goods will have no effect on home utility: for a small country the change in utility due to a tariff evaluated at free trade is zero, which implies that the optimal tariff is zero.

Continuing to hold the terms of trade constant, let us compare this result with a small tariff on technologies.[9] The change in home utility due to such a tariff is composed of two terms: the change in tariff revenue and the change in utility due to the reduction in technology transfer, and thus variety V^*.[10] Evaluated at $\tau = 0$ the change in tariff

---

[8] For the case in which tariff revenues are not redistributed, see Feenstra and Judd (1981). With revenues withheld home utility is a decreasing function of the various tariffs, and so computing the welfare impact per unit of revenue raised corresponds to the balanced-budget incidence of the tariffs.

[9] In this exercise we hold μ constant, which is the inverse commodity terms of trade. The price of exported technologies relative to imported commodities is given by $(1 + \tau)/\mu$, which varies when we change τ while holding μ fixed.

[10] For the purpose of this intuitive exercise, we hold V constant. In fact, if we hold the terms of trade fixed, the tariff on technologies tends to increase V due to the redis-

revenue $\tau k V^*$ is just kV^*. The tariff will reduce V^* according to the elasticity of demand for technologies from foreign producers, which is denoted $e_v^* > 0$. Then the change in home utility, evaluated at free trade, is given by

$$\frac{1}{\lambda} \frac{\partial U}{\partial \tau} = kV^* - \frac{1}{\lambda} \frac{\partial U}{\partial V^*/V^*} e_v^* = kV^* \left(1 - \frac{1}{\lambda k} \frac{\partial U}{\partial V^*} e_v^* \right), \quad (15)$$

where λ is the marginal utility of income.

To determine the sign of this expression, first consider the foreign demand for technologies. In the presence of the tariff τ on technology transfer, the profits of a foreign firm are given by $\pi^* = [(\mu/c) - \mu][x(v^*) + x^*(v^*)] - k(1 + \tau)$. Since no R&D is done in the foreign country, the output of any firm is just L^*/V^*, and so

$$\pi^* = \mu \left(\frac{1 - c}{c} \right) \frac{L^*}{V^*} - k(1 + \tau).$$

Then $\pi^* = 0$ implies

$$\frac{(1 + \tau)}{\mu} kV^* = \left(\frac{1 - c}{c} \right) L^*.$$

The left-hand side is the value of technologies transferred abroad, while the right-hand side is total gross foreign profits (i.e., before R&D costs are deducted). In a zero-profit equilibrium these are equal, and since the latter are proportional to the foreign labor force and therefore fixed, the elasticity of foreign demand for technologies e_v^* is *unity*. Then, from (15), the qualitative effect of the tariff on home utility depends on whether $(\partial U/\partial V^*)(1/\lambda k)$ is greater or less than one.

For any good purchased by consumers, the marginal utility of consumption just equals its price times the marginal utility of income. Since k is the price of technologies (evaluated at $\tau = 0$ and with home wages as the numeraire), $(\partial U/\partial V^*)(1/\lambda k)$ can differ from unity only due to the special nature of technologies: while V^* enters the consumers' utility function, it is not directly purchased, and so the marginal value to consumers need not equal its price to firms or resource cost. Notice that if $(\partial U/\partial V^*)(1/\lambda k)$ did happen to equal one, as with conventional products, then from (15) a small tariff on technology transfer would have no effect on home welfare, as with a tariff on goods.

In fact, in equilibrium $(\partial U/\partial V^*)(1/\lambda k)$ is *less* than unity, which implies that a small tariff on technology transfer *raises* home utility, even when the terms of trade are held constant. This result may be

---

tribution of tariff revenues and the reduction in foreign variety, both of which increase home demand. This rise in V reinforces our conclusion below that a small tariff on technology transfer, with the terms of trade held fixed, increases home welfare.

TARIFFS

obtained as follows. Recall from Section I that the autarky monopolistically competitive equilibrium leads to the socially optimal level of variety. This means that with free trade the varieties V^* and V maximize world variety, defined as the sum of each country's welfare weighted by the inverse of its marginal utility of income. Thus, with free trade,

$$\frac{\partial[(U/\lambda) + (U^*/\lambda^*)]}{\partial V^*} = k; \qquad (16)$$

that is, the marginal value of a new foreign technology equals its marginal cost. From (16) we see that $\partial U/\partial V^* < \lambda k$, so that (15) must be positive.

Note that (16) reflects the public-good nature of technologies; that is, the number or variety of products available is identical for all consumers in both countries, where the monopolistically competitive equilibrium leads to the socially optimal or Lindahl allocation of this "public good." Together with the result that e_v^* is unity, this implies that the loss in utility due to reduced variety is less than the gain from tariff revenue. More generally, so long as the foreign elasticity of demand for technologies is inelastic, we would find from (15) that a small tariff on technologies would be welfare improving.

Holding the terms of trade constant, we have thus shown that a small tariff on technology transfer has a greater impact on home utility than a small tariff on goods. Of course, in our two-country model tariffs will cause the terms of trade to change, and this effect can be compared per unit of revenue raised by the tariffs. For the tariff on technologies, the change in revenues $R_\tau = \tau k V^*$ evaluated at $\tau = 0$ is kV^*. Dividing this into (13) we obtain the change in the inverse terms of trade per unit of revenue raised:

$$\frac{d\mu}{dR_\tau} = -\left(\frac{1-c}{c}\right)\frac{1}{kV^*}. \qquad (17a)$$

If we consider the import tariff on goods, revenue is $R_t = tx(v^*)V^*/c$ and evaluated at $t = 0$, $\partial R_t/\partial t = LV^*/(V + V^*)$.[11] Dividing this into (11) we obtain the terms-of-trade effect per unit of revenue raised for the import tariff:

$$\frac{d\mu}{dR_t} = \frac{-L}{c(L + L^*)}\frac{(V + V^*)}{LV^*} = -\left(\frac{1-c}{c}\right)\frac{1}{kV^*}, \qquad (17b)$$

since $k = (1 - c)[(L + L^*)/(V + V^*)]$ from (4). Comparing (17a) and (17b) we see that per unit of revenue raised the tariffs on technologies and goods have identical effects on the terms of trade. Combined with

[11] This expression may be derived from the demand function (A3) in the Appendix.

our earlier result in (15), this suggests that if we allow the terms of trade and variety to change in general equilibrium, a small tariff on technologies may be superior to a small tariff on goods, as we shall now examine.

For the import tariff on goods, we can divide the general equilibrium impact on utility (12) by the marginal revenue effect $\partial R_t/\partial t = LV^*/(V + V^*)$ and simplify to obtain

$$\frac{1}{\lambda}\frac{dU}{dR_t} = 1 - \left[1 - \frac{L}{c(L + L^*)}\right] - \left(\frac{1 - c}{c}\right)\frac{L}{L + L^*}$$

$$= \frac{L}{L + L^*} < 1, \tag{18}$$

where λ is the marginal utility of income. Similarly, for the tariff on technology transfer we divide (14) by the marginal revenue effect kV^* and simplify to obtain

$$\frac{1}{\lambda}\frac{dU}{dR_\tau} = 1 + \frac{L}{c(L + L^*)} - \frac{L}{c(L + L^*)} = 1. \tag{19}$$

As usual, the first terms in (18) and (19) are the effect of redistributed tariff revenue on utility, the second term reflects the change in the domestic relative price of imports, while the third term is the effect of the change in world variety. As noted in the previous section, for the import tariff the fall in utility due to reduced world variety always exceeds the rise (if any) due to a Metzler effect, so the change in utility per unit revenue (18) is *less* than unity. However, for the tariff on technologies the terms of trade and world variety effects just cancel, and so utility rises by exactly unity and thus by *more* than for the tariff on goods.

We can readily extend our analysis to include an export tariff on goods, since, as noted earlier, a combined export tariff on both goods and technologies is equivalent to an equal value of the import tariff on goods. If we measure the impact on utility per unit of revenue raised, this means that a weighted average of the utility change for the export tariffs on goods and technologies equals the utility change for the import tariff on goods, where the weights are the proportions of goods and technologies in total exports. Combined with our result above, we therefore obtain a unique welfare ranking of the three policy instruments, for small movements away from the free trade equilibrium: *The welfare gain per unit of revenue raised is maximized for the export tariff on technology transfer, followed by the import tariff on goods, with the export tariff on goods the poorest policy alternative.*

V. Subsidization of R&D for Domestic Use

A policy instrument which we have not yet considered is the subsidization of R&D done to produce goods domestically. As we now show, this policy is welfare improving. If we recall that with CES utility functions the autarky equilibrium is also the social optimum, it seems likely that the subsidization of R&D for domestic use together with tariffs on trade complete the list of desirable policy interventions.

Subsidizing the development of technologies for home use at the ad valorem rate s requires that revenue of skV be raised from domestic consumers. Note that this policy is relevant only in region (A) of figure 2. Domestic profits are given by

$$\pi = \left(\frac{1}{c} - 1\right)[x(v) + x^*(v)] - k(1 - s)$$

$$= (1 - c)\frac{(L - skV + \mu L^*)}{(V + V^*\mu^{-d})} - k(1 - s), \qquad d = \frac{c}{1 - c},$$

which can be compared with (2). Domestic profits are an increasing function of the subsidy: Evaluated at $s = 0$,

$$\frac{d\pi}{ds} = -(1 - c)k\left(\frac{V}{V + V^*}\right) + k$$

$$= (1 - c)k\left(\frac{V^*}{V + V^*}\right) + ck > 0.$$

The general equilibrium response to a change in the subsidy can be computed from the equilibrium conditions $\pi = \pi^* = 0$ and $T = 0$ (see App.). Evaluated at $s = 0$, we obtain

$$\frac{dV}{ds} = cV + \frac{(1 - c)^2}{c}V^* > 0,$$

$$\frac{dV^*}{ds} = -\left(\frac{1 - c}{c}\right)V^* < 0, \qquad (20)$$

$$\frac{d\mu}{ds} = -\left(\frac{1 - c}{c}\right) < 0.$$

As expected, subsidization of R&D for domestic use increases the variety of goods produced at home and exported. The level of technology transfer kV^* falls, while the shift in the production of goods and demand for labor toward the home country reduces the relative foreign wage. The effect of the subsidy on world variety $(V + V^*)$ is ambiguous, as $(dV/ds) + (dV^*/ds) = cV - (1 - c)V^* \gtreqless 0$.

Using (20) we can write the change in utility due to the R&D subsidy as

$$\frac{1}{U}\frac{dU}{ds} = \frac{(1-c)}{(V+V^*)}\left\{-cV\frac{(L+L^*)}{L} + [cV - (1-c)V^*] + V^*\right\}. \quad (21)$$

The first term in the decomposition (21) gives the negative impact on utility due to the revenue cost of the subsidy. The second term is the effect of changing world variety, while the third term is the positive impact on utility of the decrease in the domestic relative price of imports μ. It turns out that this positive terms-of-trade influence is large enough to dominate the first two effects; using (4) and (6) we can show that

$$\frac{1}{U}\frac{dU}{ds} = c(1-c)\frac{kV^*}{L} > 0.$$

Thus, if we start at the free trade equilibrium, a small subsidy on the development of technologies for home use is welfare improving.

VI. Conclusions

A significant conclusion of this paper is the efficacy of an export tariff on technology transfer. This result has been derived within a static framework where the level of technology transfer is endogenously determined by the optimizing behavior of firms. As discussed at the end of Section III, the feasibility of this policy intervention depends on the industry structure within the R&D activity: if R&D is internally performed by home subsidiaries of foreign firms then this technology transfer may be difficult to monitor and tax.[12] On the other hand, if technologies are developed externally to the goods industry and marketed, then policy controls applied to the sale of technologies abroad would appear to be feasible.

It is useful to compare our result with that of Rodríguez (1975, sec. 1). Using a Ricardian model with a fixed number of goods (two) and ignoring the costs of R&D, he finds that an optimal lump-sum royalty payment applied to the technology of one good is superior from the point of view of the transferring country to an optimal export tariff applied to the same good. This result, while similar to ours in that it underscores the strength of tariffs (lump-sum royalties) applied to technologies, differs substantially from our principal conclusion in its derivation. Rodríguez obtains his result from the lump-sum nature of

---

[12] In this case the government would have to use indirect methods to restrict technology transfer, such as a tax on the domestic R&D activity of foreign firms or foreign profits of home-based firms.

the royalty payment, as compared with royalties charged per unit of production or ad valorem tariffs on goods. Any monopolist can extract a greater surplus from the buyer by presenting an "all or nothing" choice on a bundle of commodities (in this case, the entire quantity produced by the transferred technology), and the transferring country acts in this way when charging the optimal lump-sum royalty. The resulting situation is Pareto optimal since product prices are identical across countries, consumers, and firms: the royalty payment has shifted the two countries along the world contract curve to the point where the country receiving the technology has the same level of welfare as in autarky and the transferring country has secured the maximum gain. This type of reasoning does not apply to our analysis, since we have examined only small tariffs around the free trade equilibrium. As shown in Section IV, our results depend on the extent of change in technology transfer when a tariff or royalty payment is applied, in addition to properties of the free trade equilibrium when the optimal variety is produced, while these considerations do not appear in Rodríguez's model. Of course, it would be interesting to extend our analysis and examine optimal tariffs, in which case the reasoning Rodríguez uses should apply, but this reasoning would be in addition to the effects we have separately identified.

Pursuing this comparison further, suppose we inquire as to the effects of small tariffs on technologies (i.e., lump-sum royalties) or goods in the Rodríguez model with a fixed number of goods and technologies. Let us assume that the royalty payments are government financed by lump-sum taxes in the receiving country, so that they have no direct effect on product prices. Then a tariff on technology transfer will affect the terms of trade simply by the transfer of royalty payments between the countries. If tastes are identical across countries, as we have assumed, then the terms of trade are not affected by this transfer, and the tariff on technologies will increase home welfare (real income) by the amount of revenue or royalty payments collected. In contrast, the welfare impact of a tariff on goods can be decomposed into the tariff revenue effect and also the change in the domestic relative price of imports. Only if the latter is zero will welfare rise by the amount of revenues collected. Otherwise, welfare will rise by more or less than the redistributed revenue, depending on whether the domestic relative price of imports falls or rises. In the absence of a Metzler effect, this price rises with the tariff on goods, and so per unit of revenue raised the tariff on technology transfer has a *greater* positive impact on welfare than the tariff on goods.

Thus, our results may be viewed as a substantial generalization of this proposition to the case of endogenous levels of variety and technology transfer, as determined in a monopolistically competitive equilibrium. Interestingly, in this framework the efficacy of a tariff on technologies as compared to goods is independent of whether a Metzler effect occurs or not, as explained by the discussion at the end of Section III*A*: with the number of goods endogenous, the reduction in world variety due to a tariff on goods implies that welfare (real income) rises by *less* than the tariff revenue, even in the presence of a Metzler effect.

Last, what may be inferred from our results concerning national policy in the United States or other technology-exporting countries? First, it would be incorrect to conclude that these countries should impose tariffs on technology transfer, since our welfare results have been derived in a static setting without consideration of tariff retaliation or more efficient instruments and organizations which could redistribute income internationally. However, it does seem valid to apply our results, for example, when evaluating the desires of groups such as U.S. labor for restrictions on technology transfer. A priori, one may question why these groups should be more concerned with the export of technologies than with the export of raw materials or intermediate products, which presumably could lead to as great an expansion of foreign output, exports, and resulting competition at home. Our results point to a special role of technologies as distinct from goods, which is quite consistent with the desires of these special interest groups and useful in forming a positive interpretation of their lobbying efforts.

Appendix

The consumer's utility maximization problem is

$$\max \int_0^V x(v)^c dv$$

subject to

$$\int_0^V p(v)x(v)dv = I, \tag{A1}$$

where $p(v)$ and $x(v)$ are the price and quantity consumed of good v, I is income, and V is the total variety (measure) of goods available; for the moment we are not distinguishing between domestic and foreign goods. The elasticity of substitution between goods is given by $\sigma = 1/(1 - c) > 1$, where $0 < c < 1$ is assumed.

The first-order conditions for (A1) are $cx(v)^{c-1} = \lambda p(v)$, $0 \leq v \leq V$, where λ is the marginal utility of income. It follows that $x(v) = [\lambda p(v)/c]^{-\sigma}$ and

$$\int_0^V p(v)x(v)dv = (\lambda/c)^{-\sigma} \int_0^V p(v)^{-d}dv = I,$$

where $d = c/(1 - c) = \sigma - 1 > 0$. The commodity demand functions are then given by

$$x(v) = [p(v)^{-\sigma}I] \Big/ \Big[\int_0^V p(v)^{-d}dv\Big]. \tag{A2}$$

Thus, the (positive) elasticity of demand for any good equals σ.

To derive the free trade profit equations (2) and (3), first note that the profit-maximizing prices for goods produced at home and abroad are given by w/c and w^*/c, respectively, since the elasticity of domestic or world demand is $\sigma = 1/(1 - c)$. Substituting these prices into (A2) and noting that $I = wL$ and $I^* = w^*L^*$, we obtain the quantities consumed:

$$x(v) = cL/(V + V^*\mu^{-d}), x(v^*) = \mu^{-\sigma}x(v), \tag{A3}$$

$$x^*(v) = \mu cL^*/(V + V^*\mu^{-d}), x^*(v^*) = \mu^{-\sigma}x^*(v),$$

where $\mu = w^*/w$, $x(v)$ and $x(v^*)$ are the quantities consumed at home of domestic and foreign goods, and $x^*(v)$ and $x^*(v^*)$ are the quantities consumed abroad of imported and local goods. Using (A3) we obtain the free trade profits given in (2) and (3).

For the case of an ad valorem import tariff on goods at rate t, with the revenue redistributed to domestic consumers, the quantities consumed (A3) are modified as

$$x(v) = c\{L + [tx(v^*)V^*/c]\}/\{V + V^*[\mu(1 + t)]^{-d}\},$$

$$x(v^*) = [\mu(1 + t)]^{-\sigma}x(v), \tag{A4}$$

$$x^*(v) = \mu cL^*/(V + V^*\mu^{-d}), x^*(v^*) = \mu^{-\sigma}x^*(v),$$

where $R_t = tx(v^*)V^*/c$ is the tariff revenue. Substituting (A4) into the profit equations

$$\pi = \Big(\frac{1}{c} - 1\Big)[x(v) + x^*(v)] - k \tag{A5}$$

and

$$\pi^* = \Big(\frac{\mu}{c} - \mu\Big)[x(v^*) + x^*(v^*)] - k,$$

we obtain expressions for the profits from product development at home and abroad.

For the case of an export tariff on goods at rate τ_x, or on technology transfer at rate τ_k, (A4) and (A5) must be modified as follows. For the export tariff on goods revenue is $R_{\tau_x} = \tau_x x^*(v)V/c$, while the relative price of imports for home and foreign consumers is μ and $(1 + \tau_x)/\mu$, respectively. For the export tariff on technologies revenue is $R_{\tau_k} = \tau_k kV^*$, the relative price of imports for home and foreign consumers is μ and $1/\mu$, while the R&D cost for foreign producers is $k(1 + \tau_k)$.

The comparative statics are performed using the equilibrium conditions $\pi = \pi^* = 0$ and trade balance. This calculation is simplified by rewriting the trade balance (surplus of the home country) T as follows:

$$T = (1 + \tau_x)[Vx^*(v)/c] + (1 + \tau_k)kV^* - [V^*x(v^*)\mu/c]$$

$$= \{\mu L^* - [V^*x^*(v^*)\mu/c]\} + (1 + \tau_k)kV^* - [V^*x(v^*)\mu/c];$$

if we use the budget constraint for foreign consumers $[V^*x^*(v^*)/c] + [Vx^*(v)(1 + \tau_x)/\mu c] = L^*$, then

$$T = -\frac{V^*\mu}{c}[x(v^*) + x^*(v^*)] + (1 + \tau_k)kV^* + \mu L^*$$

$$= -\frac{V^*}{(1-c)}[\pi^* + k(1 + \tau_k)] + (1 + \tau_k)kV^* + \mu L^*,$$

since $\pi^* = [(\mu/c) - \mu][x(v^*) + x^*(v^*)] - k(1 + \tau_k)$, then

$$T = -[\pi^*V^*/(1-c)] - [(1 + \tau_k)kV^*c/(1-c)] + \mu L^*. \tag{A6}$$

Setting $\pi^* = 0$ in (A6), we can write the equilibrium condition $T = 0$ as

$$T = \mu L^* - [(1 + \tau_k)kV^*c/(1-c)] = 0. \tag{A7}$$

The comparative statics are performed on the system: $\pi = 0, T = 0, \pi - \pi^* = 0$, where the second equation refers to (A7). Letting τ denote any of the three tariffs or the subsidy on R&D for domestic use, evaluated at $\tau = 0$, we obtain

$$\begin{pmatrix} dV \\ dV^* \\ d\mu \end{pmatrix} = -M^{-1} \begin{pmatrix} \pi_\tau \\ T_\tau \\ \pi_\tau - \pi_\tau^* \end{pmatrix} d\tau, \tag{A8}$$

where

$$M^{-1} = \frac{V^*}{L^*} \begin{bmatrix} \dfrac{-c(V + V^*)}{(1-c)} & 1 & -V^*\left[1 - \dfrac{c(2-c)}{(1-c)}\right] \\ 0 & -1 & V^* \\ 0 & 0 & 1 \end{bmatrix}$$

To complete the Appendix we must specify the values of π_τ, π_τ^*, and T_τ, which are substituted into (A8), as follows:

1. *Import tariff on goods.*—Evaluated at $t = 0$: $\pi_t = LV^*/(V + V^*)^2$, $\pi_t^* = -LV/(V + V^*)^2$, $T_t = 0$.

2. *Export tariff on goods.*—Evaluated at $\tau_x = 0$: $\pi_{\tau_x} = -L^*V^*/(V + V^*)^2$, $\pi_{\tau_x}^* = L^*V/(V + V^*)^2$, $T_{\tau_x} = 0$.

3. *Export tariff on technologies.*—Evaluated at $\tau_k = 0$: $\pi_{\tau_k} = (1-c)kV^*/(V + V^*)$, $\pi_{\tau_k}^* = [(1-c)kV^*/(V + V^*)] - k$, $T_{\tau_k} = -ckV^*/(1-c) = -L^*$.

4. *Subsidy on R&D for domestic use.*—Evaluated at $s = 0$: $\pi_s = ck + [(1-c)kV^*/(V + V^*)]$, $\pi_s^* = -(1-c)kV^*/(V + V^*)$, $T_s = 0$.

References

Dixit, Avinash K., and Norman, V. *Theory of International Trade: A Dual, General Equilibrium Approach.* Cambridge: Cambridge Univ. Press, 1980.

Dixit, Avinash K., and Stiglitz, Joseph E. "Monopolistic Competition and Optimum Product Diversity." *A.E.R.* 67 (June 1977): 297–308.

Feenstra, Robert C., and Judd, Kenneth L. "Tariffs, Technology Transfer, and Welfare." Mimeographed. Chicago: Univ. Chicago, 1981.

Findlay, Ronald. "Relative Backwardness, Direct Foreign Investment, and the Transfer of Technology: A Simple Dynamic Model." *Q.J.E.* 92 (February 1978): 1–16.

Helpman, Elhanan. "International Trade in the Presence of Product Differentiation, Economies of Scale and Monopolistic Competition: A Chamberlin-Heckscher-Ohlin Approach." *J. Internat. Econ.* 11 (August 1981): 305–40.

Judd, Kenneth L. "On the Performance of Patents." Mimeographed. Chicago: Univ. Chicago, 1980.

Krugman, Paul R. "Increasing Returns, Monopolistic Competition, and International Trade." *J. Internat. Econ.* 9 (November 1979): 469–79. (*a*)

——. "A Model of Innovation, Technology Transfer, and the World Distribution of Income." *J.P.E.* 87, no. 2 (April 1979): 253–66. (*b*)

——. "Scale Economies, Product Differentiation, and the Pattern of Trade." *A.E.R.* 70 (December 1980): 950–59.

Lancaster, Kelvin J. "Intra-Industry Trade under Perfect Monopolistic Competition." *J. Internat. Econ.* 10 (May 1980): 151–75.

McCulloch, Rachel, and Yellen, Janet L. "Technology Transfer and the National Advantage." Harvard Inst. Econ. Res. Discussion Paper no. 526. Cambridge, Mass.: Harvard Univ., 1976.

Pugel, Thomas A. "Technology Transfer and the Neo-Classical Theory of International Trade." In *Technology Transfer and Economic Development,* edited by Robert G. Hawkins and A. J. Prasad. Greenwich, Conn.: JAI, 1980.

——. "Endogenous Technical Change and International Technology Transfer in a Ricardian Trade Model." *J. Internat. Econ.* (in press).

Rodríguez, Carlos Alfredo. "Trade in Technical Knowledge and the National Advantage." *J.P.E.* 83, no. 1 (February 1975): 121–35.

Vernon, Raymond. "International Investment and International Trade in the Product Cycle." *Q.J.E.* 80 (May 1966): 190–207.

[39]

Empirica 1'88 — Austrian Economic Papers

Growth, Technological Progress, and Trade

Elhanan Helpman*)

1. Introduction

This paper deals with the relationship between international trade and economic growth. It deals, therefore, with an old question, but also a question in search to a new answer. The renewed interest in this subject has arisen as a result of a combination of events, research results (or more to the point, a lack of satisfactory research results), and the availability of new tools. As far as events are concerned, there is the decline of output growth in the 1970s that was associated with a productivity slowdown. During those years the volume of world trade declined for the first time since World War II. Despite the general slowdown, however, some countries managed to maintain relatively high growth rates. For example, the average rate of growth of the four Asian NIC — Korea, Hong Kong, Taiwan, and Singapore — remained at the high average level of 8.3 percent p. a. during 1973 to 1984. This raises the question: Why were some countries painfully affected by the adverse shocks to the world economy while others have avoided much of the damage? Naturally, an answer to this question — which refers to a particular episode — requires a detailed understanding of the episode itself. But a reliable answer also requires an understanding of the broad forces of economic growth and their relationship to international trade. This is the more so in view of the fact that as a rule, output growth is often strongly correlated with export growth (see *Michaely,* 1977, *Feder,* 1982, and *Helpman — Trajtenberg,* 1987). For example, during the years of the slowdown 1973-1984 exports of Korea and Taiwan grew at an average rate of about 15 percent.

The traditional approach to economic growth as a process of capital accumulation has provided important insights, but failed to provide a satisfactory account of the data. This brought about a shift of attention to technical progress. Viewed in broad terms, technical progress should be able to explain the residual in growth accounting. It is, however, an illusive term that needs to be filled up with concrete details in order to be useful, and this has proved to be a difficult task (see *Griliches,* 1979). Recent developments in the theory of industrial organization, which treat explicitly research and development and economies of scale, may help to fill in this gap.

On the other hand, the theory of international trade has been influenced by advances in industrial organization for close to ten years. However, the major bulck of work in this area

---

*) I would like to thank Gene Grossman for allowing me to use insights from our joint ongoing work in the preparation of this paper, and to Paul Romer and Martin Weitzman for comments on an earlier draft.

was static. The recent revival of interest in dynamic trade issues provides an opportunity to extend this work in order to deal with dynamic trade issues. It may prove helpful in explaining the long-run relationship between trade and growth. We need a theory that can address fundamental questions, such as: Does growth drive trade or is there a reverse link from trade to growth? Many authors have emphasized the role of free trade in promoting growth (see, e. g., *Bhagwati,* 1978, and *Krueger,* 1978). Nevertheless, there also exist arguments that trade policy was central in the promotion of fast growth in Japan and some of the NIC. Current theory is not suitable to deal in a satisfactory way with these alternative views.

Then there exists the question of the determinants of long-run growth. Neoclassical theory predicts declining growth rates, unless there is technical progress. On the other hand, growth rates of the most advanced countries have not been declining, and growth rates seem to be positively autocorrelated (see *Romer,* 1986A). Moreover, developed countries grow on average faster than less developed countries. Does it indicate that there are no diminishing returns to growth? And how is all this related to trade?

There is, of course, a debate concerning the proposition that productivity levels converge. *Baumol* (1986), e. g., has argued that they do (see also *Maddison,* 1987). However, his sample of countries — that builds on *Maddison's* (1982) data set — suffers from a sample selection bias that leads to this conclusion even if the proposition is wrong. More careful examination of the data suggests that convergence of productivity levels is at least doubtful (see *De Long,* 1987, and *Romer,* 1988). Is international trade an important element in these processes? Some observers believe that it is, and that international learning goes far beyond direct trade relationships (see, e. g., *Pasinetti,* 1981, ch. XI).

I cannot offer answers to all these and other related questions. What I can offer instead is a description of some recent work which helps to think in novel ways about them. Some of this work is exploratory in nature; most of it is rather fragmented. It nevertheless has a lot in common, as I will try to explain, and may eventually lead to a coherent theory. This is an exciting renewed area of enquiry. I will start with a brief description of the neoclassical aggregative approach to growth in order to set up the stage for the following discussion. I will then proceed to discuss new lines of work on the theory of economic growth that emphasize economies of scale. These studies deal with closed economies, but I will also discuss their implications for the role of international trade. This will be followed by a description of a disaggregated approach in which trade figures prominently. Finally, I will deal with the role of product cycles which have not yet been integrated into this line of research — a task awaiting to be done.

2. Aggregative approach

Every theory of economic growth builds on the saving-investment relationship. It is therefore possible, at least in principle, to build a theory in which the main driving force is either saving or investment. The neoclassical theory underlines the role of saving, in the sense that it emphasizes the desire to allocate consumption over time, making investment respond to the consumption needs. I will therefore concentrate on growth in consumption per capita. Since the role of population growth is well understood in these frameworks, I abstract from population growth altogether. With this clarification in mind, we can formulate the consumption choice problem that is at the heart of neoclassical growth theory as follows:

$$max \int_0^\infty e^{-\varrho t} u\left(c\left(t\right)\right) d\,t,$$

subject to the intertemporal budget constraint

$$\int_0^\infty e^{-R\left(t\right)} c\left(t\right) d\,t \;=\; \varOmega,$$

where ϱ is the subjective discount rate, $u\,(c)$ is the temporal utility function, c is consumption, $R\,(t)$ is the discount factor, $\varOmega$ is wealth at time zero, and t is a time index. Wealth at time zero is defined as the value of existing assets plus the present value of income from non-marketable assets (such as labour income). The wealth level is taken to be exogenous by the individual consumer, but it is in fact endogenous to the economy at large; it depends on the time pattern of wages, technological factors, and the like. Similarly for the interest factor: It is exogenous to the individual consumer but endogenous to the economy (in the context of international economics the interest factor might also be exogenous to a single country — the small country assumption — but it is endogenous to the world economy). A major difficulty in the derivation of a complete characterization of equilibrium trajectories is indeed the solution of variables that are exogenous to the individual decision maker but endogenous to the economy.

The solution to the consumer's problem yields the following equation for consumption growth:

$$(1) \quad \frac{\dot c}{c} = \beta\,(r - \varrho),$$

where β is the inverse of the elasticity of the marginal utility of consumption, defined to be positive, and $r \equiv \dot R$ is the instantaneous real interest rate. This is the fundamental equation that I will use to discuss aggregative growth. It implies that positive growth requires the real interest rate to be larger than the subjective discount rate. Since the subjective discount rate is taken as an exogenous constant, issues of growth become inseparable from factors that determine the real interest rate and its change over time. In order to concentrate on the main issues, I now assume that the elasticity of the marginal utility of consumption is constant, which amounts to assuming an isoelastic utility function.

7

The fundamental growth equation *(1)* reveals a great deal about what is possible in frameworks that rely on it. For one thing, it shows that sustained long-run growth is possible only if the real interest rate can be maintained above the subjective discount factor. But the behaviour of the real interest rate is related to the technology of production and accumulation. Therefore the possibilities of sustained long-run growth depend on the nature of these technologies.

In the one-sector neoclassical model output y is a concave function of the capital stock k (the constant labour supply is suppressed): $y = f(k)$. Abstracting from adjustment costs in capital formation, suppose that a unit of output can be converted into one unit of capital. Then at each point in time the cost of a unit of capital is 1 (in terms of output, which is the numeraire). On the other hand, without depreciation the return to the ownership of a unit of capital is the entire future stream of its marginal product value (it is also possible to specify this relationship by taking explicit account of the possibility of resale of the capital unit), with this stream depending on the time path of the economy's capital stock. No capital accumulation takes place when current costs exceed the present value of the return (assuming irreversibility of investment; otherwise divestment will take place). If, however, capital accumulation does take place at a point in time t, or it is just marginally profitable to invest, then the current value of a unit of capital, which is 1, is equal to the present value of its marginal product value,

$$(2a) \quad \int_{t}^{\infty} e^{-(R(\tau)-R(t))} f_k(k(\tau)) \, d\tau = 1.$$

In a competitive equilibrium the left-hand side of *(2a)* cannot exceed 1.

Equation *(2a)* represents a standard asset pricing equation. In the context of growth it provides a link between the real interest rate and capital accumulation. Differentiation with respect to time yields

$$(3a) \quad r(t) = f_k(k(t)),$$

namely, the real interest rate is equal to the marginal product of capital (the presence of adjustment costs generates a more complicated relationship). Since capital accumulation reduces the marginal product of capital, it also leads to a declining real interest rate. Therefore, capital accumulation cannot lead to sustained long-run growth; it leads to declining real interest rates, and when the real interest rate becomes equal to the subjective discount rate consumption growth ceases and the economy reaches a steady state. The long-run interest rate is equal to the subjective discount rate.

These results have certain implications for a system of countries. In a world economy in which there exist no international capital movements countries will grow at independent rates, as determined by their subjective discount rates, the elasticity of the marginal utility of consumption, technology, population, and initial capital stocks. However, the rate of growth of every country eventually converges to zero. In the zero-growth steady-state real interest rates differ across countries in so far as subjective discount rates differ.

In a world with integrated capital markets the real interest rate is determined by the country with the highest marginal product of capital (assuming irreversible investment). Investment is first channeled to the country with the highest marginal product of capital, until its marginal product falls to the level of the country with the next highest marginal product. From then on investment takes place in both, maintaining equality of marginal products, which also determine the real interest rate. When the marginal product of capital in these two countries falls sufficiently to equal the marginal product in the country with the third highest marginal product of capital, the third country too begins to accumulate capital. And the process continues along the same line with other countries.

The above described process of capital accumulation determines output growth, i. e., GDP. Thus, for example, the country with the lowest marginal product of capital might not experience output growth for some time (or forever). Nevertheless, its consumption and GNP may be growing. Integrated capital markets lead to equalization of real interest rates. It is therefore evident from equation *(1)* that consumption of countries with subjective discount rates below the interest rate will be rising independently of their marginal product of capital. In particular, if they have identical preferences (i. e., common values of β and ϱ), consumption will grow at a common rate, converging eventually to zero. If subjective discount rates differ but β is the same, the most patient country, i. e., with the lowest discount rate, has the fastest growing consumption, and it ends up (in the limit) consuming the entire world output. Its consumption growth ceases when the real interest rate drops to its discount rate.

It is clear from this discussion that the neoclassical growth model fails to predict sustained long-run growth as a result of capital accumulation. One way out of this predicament is to introduce technical progress. Its introduction as an exogenous process helps growth accounting, but is not satisfactory. In order to understand the evolution of economies along sustained growth trajectories and the role of trade in this process it is necessary to further explore the "unexplained residual" in growth accounting. If *(1)* is the basis of this inquiry, it is necessary to do away with the negative association between the real interest rate and the capital stock. One line of research in this direction, that has been explored by *Romer* (1986A, B) and *Lucas* (1985), breaks this link by introducing economies of scale. The essential elements of this approach are taken up in the next section.

3.   Economies of scale

The idea that economies of scale can lead to a self perpetuating process of economic growth goes back to at least *Allyn Young* (1928). Romer's contribution lies in its precise

9

formulation and linkage to neoclassical growth theory. One major obstacle to a precise formulation was associated with the usual difficulty to construct general equilibrium models
with economies of scale. In each one of the cited papers he explores a route which is by
now well known in the theory of international trade. The first is to consider economies of
scale that are external to the firm but internal to the industry; the second is to consider
economies of scale that are internal to the firm, with firms producing differentiated products and engaging in monopolistic competition. I will discuss both possibilities.

3.1   External economies

External economies have been widely discussed in international trade theory (see *Helpman*, 1984). In the static models this takes the form of a production function in which the
output level of an individual firm depends on its inputs and on the output level of the industry. This is usually referred to as Marshalian externalities. The idea is that a larger industry
supports larger industry specific public inputs, such as finer stages of specialization,
thereby benefiting all firms. Following *Arrow* (1962), Romer shifted the externality from output to capital. Namely, the output level of an individual firm depends not only on its stock of
capital, but on the stock of capital of the industry at large. In this context the stock of capital can be broadly interpreted to include human capital or knowledge. The precise interpretation dictates what would be reasonable assumptions about the production and accumulation technology, but is of no consequence for the points I wish to make here. Let us
therefore maintain the interpretation of physical capital accumulation.

The production function of a single producer is taken to be $f(k, K)$, where K is the economy's capital stock and k is the capital stock of the producer (we suppress the share of labour that the producer employs in equilibrium). All producers are alike. Suppose also that
there is a continuum of them, and that their measure is 1. Then $K = k$ at each point in
time.

A single producer takes the economy's capital stock as given. Therefore from his point of
view the marginal product value of a unit of capital is $f_k(k, K)$. If a unit of output can be
costlessly converted into a unit of capital, as we have assumed in the discussion of the
neoclassical model, then the break-even condition for profitable investment (or the asset
pricing equation) becomes

$$(2b) \quad \int_t^\infty e^{-(R(\tau)-R(t))} f_k(k(\tau), K(\tau)) \, d\tau = 1,$$

which implies

$$(3b) \quad r(t) = f_k(k(t), K(t)).$$

It is clear that in this case accumulation of capital by individual firms drives down the real interest rate via the own capital stock effect, given the concavity of $f(k, K)$ in the first argu-

10

ment. Now, however, the real interest rate is also affected by the economy wide capital stock K (with $K = k$), which represents the external effect. If an increase in the economy's capital stock raises the marginal product of capital of individual firms, capital accumulation raises the real interest rate via the external effect. The combined direct plus indirect effect of capital accumulation may therefore increase or reduce the real interest rate, depending on the nature of the production function. If $f_k (k, k)$ is rising in k, the interest rate increases; if it is declining, the interest rate falls. Of particular interest for our purposes is whether the limit of the private marginal product of capital can be bounded above the subjective discount rate when the capital stock goes to infinity. If it is, there will be sustained long-run growth. The answer to this question is in the affirmative, as shown by the following example.

Let $f (k, K) = A K \log (1 + k)$, where $A > 0$ is a constant and $\log$ indicates the natural logarithm. The social production function, defined by $F (K) \equiv f (K, K)$ exhibits increasing returns to scale, with the marginal product of capital increasing with the capital stock. The private production function $f (k, K)$ is concave in the private capital stock k, exhibiting declining marginal productivity of private capital. At each point in time the real interest is given by $f (k, K) = \dfrac{A K}{1 + k}$ (see *(3b)*). Since $K = k$ on the equilibrium path, the time pattern of interest rates is

$$r (t) = A \, \frac{k (t)}{1 + k (t)} .$$

Hence, capital accumulation leads to rising real interest rates and rising growth rates. Given $k (0)$ a sufficiently large value of A ensures $r (0) > \varrho$, so that consumption grows from the very beginning, with its rate of growth rising over time until it reaches the long-run sustainable level $\beta (A - \varrho)$.

This model with external economies of scale has two important general implications: First, the growth rate may be rising rather than falling; second, the economy may reach a sustainable positive long-run growth rate. It has also important implications for a system of countries. In the absence of international capital mobility every country grows at its own rate, depending on preferences, technology, labour, and the initial capital stock. The larger the initial capital stock the higher the growth rate, because a larger capital stock brings about a larger marginal product of capital. Growth rates do not converge necessarily to zero, and there may exist differences in the sustained long-run growth rates. In the presence of free international capital mobility real interest rates are equalized. Consequently, consumption growth rates can differ across countries only in so far as preferences differ. This is similar to the result in neoclassical growth models. Here, however, investment takes a very different course. The real interest rate is determined by the country with the highest private marginal product of capital $f_k (k, K)$, and this is the country that attracts all investment as long as its private marginal product of capital is the highest (the social marginal product of capital $F_K (K) \equiv f_k (K, K) + f_K (K, K)$ is not necessarily the highest in this country). If the private marginal product of capital is declining with the capital stock, taking into account both the direct and the external effects, then the real interest rate and the growth rate will be declining until the private marginal product of capital in this country falls to the level existing in the country with the next highest marginal product. If, however, the private marginal product is increasing in the capital stock via the joint direct and external effects, the real interest rate and the growth rate will be rising. In this case the gap in marginal productivities of capital never closes and investment is indefinitely channeled into a single country. It is now easy to see what happens when the marginal product falls in the highest marginal productivity country but is rising in the second highest, or in any other country down the line of the marginal productivity ranking. The first country down the line whose marginal private product of capital increases with the capital stock ends up accumulating capital for the world, provided its turn to invest is ever reached. Hence, there may exist agglomeration effects in capital accumulation. They may provide a significant advantage to countries that attract investment, thereby working in favour of large countries that have a large capital stock to begin with. This advantage is partly realized by means of returns to fixed factors of production, including labour (it is easy to calculate these advantages from the production function $A\,K\,log\,(1+k)$). Hence, in this type of an environment it may make sense to pursue policies that stimulate growth, including the attraction of foreign investment.

In this formulation the production function is a black box. Particularly disturbing is the lack of explicit accounting for the external effects. It is, however, possible to imagine plausible situations in which the nature of the externality depends on the firms' conduct, on market structure, and the like. Consequently, it is premature to draw policy conclusions from models that do not specify explicitly these relationships. Experience suggests that the nature of useful policies depends on those unspecified links.

3.2 Differentiated Inputs

The second route to sustain sufficiently large real interest rates in the long run, thereby ensuring long-run growth, is based on the notion of specialization refinements that was introduced by *Ethier* (1982). Ethier's original purpose was to provide a better foundation for his earlier work on international trade, in which he argued in favour of an external economy approach, but in which the output level of an individual firm depends on the size of the world's industry rather than the country's in which it is located. This was accomplished by constructing a model in which there exist differentiated intermediate inputs with which the final output is produced. These inputs are produced with economies of scale, with the market structure being monopolistic. Using a CES production function for the final good, productivity of the final good sector depends on the number of available middle products. In the context of international trade it makes the productivity level of a country's industry depend on the size of the world's industry when middle products are traded. A second benefit of this approach is that it underlines trade in intermediate inputs, which is indeed the bulk of world trade.

12

In the context of a growth model the production function of the final good can be written as

$$(4) \quad y \quad = A \int_0^n x\,(i)^\alpha\,d\,i, \qquad 0 < \alpha < 1, \quad A > 0,$$

where n is the number (measure) of available intermediate inputs (stages of specialization) and $x\,(i)$ is the quantity of variety i being employed. Labour employment is being suppressed as before (it is part of the constant A). Given prices $p\,(i)$ for intermediate inputs in terms of the final good and $A = 1$, profit maximization by producers of the final good yield the following demand functions for middle products:

$$(5) \quad x\,(i) \quad = \alpha^{1/(1-\alpha)}\,p\,(i)^{-1/(1-\alpha)}.$$

Now suppose that middle products are produced only with capital. The capital requirement for x units of output of a single variety is $g\,(x)$, where average requirement $\frac{g\,(x)}{x}$ is declining over some range so as to exhibit economies of scale. Using the demand functions *(5)* monopolistic competition with free entry into the intermediate goods industry implies mark-up pricing over marginal costs as well as average cost pricing. Hence, if r stands for the rental rate on capital these conditions yield

$$(6) \quad \alpha\,p\,(i) = r\,g'\,(x\,(i)),$$

$$(7) \quad p\,(i) = \frac{r\,g\,(x\,(i))}{x\,(i)}.$$

Given r, *(6)* and *(7)* solve prices and quantities. Clearly, all varieties are equally priced and produced in the same quantity. Taking also account of *(5)* provides a solution for r. Hence, *(5)* through *(7)* determine uniquely (x, p, r).

Finally, assume as before that a unit of the final good can be costlessly converted into a unit of capital. Then the interest rate has to equal the rental rate on capital, because the present value of the rental rates has to equal the cost of a unit of capital, which is 1. Consequently, r is the real interest rate and it is constant. If this technologically determined real interest rate is larger than the subjective discount rate the economy settles instantly on a fixed, positive, growth rate path. The rate of consumption growth equals the rate of growth of the capital stock, which equals in turn to the rate of growth of the number of intermediate inputs.

In a system of countries every country benefits from the opportunity to purchase intermediate inputs from its trading partners. If they have the same technologies, the rental rate on capital is equalized (see *(5)* through *(7)*), and so is the real interest rate, even if there is no international capital mobility. In this case there is no particular equilibrium investment pattern when capital markets are integrated; aggregate world investment can be distributed across countries in any feasible way. When capital markets are segregated savings of a country determine (as usual) its investment level. In both cases countries have common growth rates of consumption if preferences are also identical.

When production functions differ, there are richer dynamics. Suppose that only the technology to produce intermediate inputs differs across countries. Then from *(5)* through *(7)* it is seen that it will induce differences in output per variety, their price, and the rental rate. Differences in price will not eliminate the incentive to trade intermediate inputs, so that the static gains from trade will be realized. The effects of differences in rental rates depend on the degree of integration of financial markets. If there is no international capital mobility, the rental rate of every country determines its domestic real interest rate and the growth rate of its consumption, capital stock, and the number of products (with the latter two being equal to each other). Every country settles immediately on a constant growth path.

With integrated capital markets the real interest rate is determined by the country with the highest rental rate on capital. Growth rates of consumption differ only if there are differences in preferences. Since the rental rates do not change through time (they do not depend on the capital stocks; see *(5)* through *(7)*), a country that begins with the highest rental rate maintains its position forever, thereby determining forever the real interest rate. This is also the country to which investment is channeled; it is in fact the only country with capital accumulation (unless there is more than one country with the highest rental rate) and the only country that introduces new varieties of middle products. The latter, however, are used worldwide.

A comparison of the two approaches outlined in this section reveals a great degree of similarity, as well as the suitable specification of the external effects suggested by Ethier. Consider for simplicity the case in which all varieties are equally priced. Then a producer who spends resources z on producing the final good obtains an output level $y = A\,n \left(\dfrac{z}{p\,n}\right)^{\alpha}$

(see *(4)*). This output level exhibits declining marginal productivity in his resources z — which is analogous to declining marginal productivity of k in $f(k, K)$. And it increases with n — which is analogous to the external effect K. The latter is even more evident when one recognizes that n is proportional to the economy's capital stock. A special feature of the economy with intermediate inputs is that the private marginal product value of capital is independent of the capital stock. In a many country world n is proportional to the world's capital stock rather than the country's in which the producer operates, provided intermediate inputs are traded. Therefore the external effect is not country specific but rather worldwide.

Finally, I would like to point out that the fixity of the rental rate in Romer's second model is a result of the specific functional form used in *(4)* rather than the model itself. This can be seen as follows: Let q be the value of the integral on the right hand side of *(4)*, and let the production function be $\varphi(q)$. Then *(5)* is replaced by

(5a) $x(i) = \varphi'(q)^{1/(1-\alpha)} \, \alpha^{-1/(1-\alpha)} \, p(i)^{-1/(1-\alpha)}$.

Since a single producer of a variety of intermediate inputs takes q as given, this does not change the nature of *(6)* and *(7)*. From *(6)* and *(7)*, however, we obtain $\alpha = \dfrac{g'(x(i))\, x(i)}{g(x(i))}$, which fixes x at the same level for every variety. Using this result together with *(5a)*, *(7)*, and the definition of q, we obtain $r = \dfrac{\alpha\, x^\alpha\, \varphi'(n\, x^\alpha)}{g(x)}$. It is clear from here that the rental rate increases with n if and only if $\varphi''(q) > 0$. In the original specification $\varphi''(q) \equiv 0$, which explains the constancy of the rental rate. Since n is proportional to the capital stock $\Big($in fact, $n = \dfrac{K}{g(x)}\Big)$, we see that the rental rate can be increasing or declining in the capital stock, and when increasing it can reach a constant value as the stock of capital goes to infinity.

4. Acquired comparative advantage

So far I have dealt with aggregative growth issues, leaving little scope for the role of temporal trade. To be sure, intertemporal trade played a major role in this discussion, as is evident from the central role assigned to international capital mobility, which is the main channel of intertemporal trade. But what about the traditional form of trade, i. e., the exchange of goods at a point in time? A study of the dynamics of this form of trade requires a disaggregated framework.

Early work in disaggregated frameworks concentrated on the effects of growth on the terms of trade (see *Bhagwati*, 1958). This lead to an identification of conditions under which at constant prices capital accumulation or technical progress bring about an expansion of the export industry that exceeds the increase in local demand for its product. Under these conditions the terms of trade deteriorate. Later on, with the development of two-sector neoclassical growth theory, *Oniki — Uzawa* (1965) extended it to a two-country set-up in order to study the effects of capital accumulation on the pattern of trade. Since they employed a framework without international capital mobility, capital accumulation of every country was driven by the propensity to save. Consequently, saving behaviour determined the evolution of Heckscher-Ohlin comparative advantage. Work along these lines is surveyed by *Findlay* (1984) and *Smith* (1984), and its results are too well known to be repeated within the constraints of this paper. I proceed, therefore, to discuss a new line of research. There is, however, one point related to this approach that needs to be clarified at this juncture. In my discussion of the issues I pointed out that the extremely fast growth of exports in some of the NIC gives the impression that international trade plays an important role in this process. It can nevertheless be argued that the comovement of output and exports stems from internal sources that bring about output growth, which induces in turn export growth. If this is the case, then causality is from growth to trade rather than the other way around. This argument, which is made in detail in *Helpman — Trajtenberg* (1987), proceeds as follows.

Suppose there is Hicks-neutral technical progress in the exporting industries. Then at constant prices it becomes relatively more profitable to produce exportables. Consequently, resources are driven from import competing industries to exporting industries. Factor rewards adjust to this reallocation in the usual way. The result is that output of exportables rises both because they employ more resources and because their production is more efficient. Since GDP rises while the import competing industries contract, output of exportables grows necessarily faster than GDP. As long as there is no particularly strong demand bias towards exportables when expenditure rises, exports are bound to grow faster than output. This explanation seems to be consistent with the data. Moreover, by introducing a spectrum of qualities for exportables it is possible to derive conditions on cost and price structures under which this process will also be accompanied by an upgrading of the quality of exports (as, e. g., in Korea and Taiwan).

Our theoretical description fits the stylized facts. Is it the correct explanation? There is not enough evidence to form a final judgment. It is, however, my opinion that this is at best a partial explanation. For one thing it is necessary to explain why technical progress is concentrated in exporting industries. Is it just a coincident or is it after all the result of a mechanism in which foreign trade plays a major role? I tend to believe the latter. This suggests the need to explore alternative lines of research which are more explicit about productivity gains. Investigations of acquired comparative advantage are major candidates for this purpose.

Factor accumulation changes the degree of Heckscher-Ohlin type comparative advantage, and in a predictable way the pattern of trade (see the recent studies by *Leamer,* 1984, 1987). However, many changes in world trade are probably associated with acquired comparative advantage, such as the development of new products, the development of new production technologies, learning to produce existing products, and the like. Therefore, important as factor accumulation might be, it cannot explain all changes in world trade. Recent work on international trade in the presence of economies of scale and non-competitive market structures, which was static in nature, provides a suitable point of departure for the study of trade dynamics with acquired comparative advantage.

The static theory emphasizes the role of differentiated products that are produced with economies of scale, and the importance for welfare of the available number of such products (see *Helpman — Krugman,* 1985). It is, however, clear upon reflection that the development of new products cannot be satisfactorily analysed in static frameworks. A significant part of fixed costs in the production of specialized products is associated with their development and design, which takes up time and resources. Moreover, the fixed costs of R&D are not recovered instantaneously but rather through sales over prolonged periods of time. This implies that the incentive to invest in R&D depends on expectations of future profits, which depend in turn on the expected evolution of the industry (worldwide), the length of available patent protection laws, the speed of imitation by other countries (which also depends on their investment in reversed engineering and other forms of learning), and the like.

In order to take account of these complications it is necessary to construct explicit, dynamic models of international trade, in which R&D is considered as an economic activity. Their study will help to understand the evolution of trade when acquired comparative advantage plays a central role. It should also shed new light on the process of economic growth and the relationship between trade and economic growth. As I indicated before, the link between trade and growth was traditionally analysed by considering the effects of factor accumulation or technological improvement on trade. The new approach may illuminate the reverse causal link: From trade to growth. It should eventually also provide a suitable framework for a study of the role of economic policy in promoting acquired comparative advantage and growth. Such policies have been widely discussed, and used to explain the success of some of the high performance countries (such as Japan and some of the NIC). However, so far these arguments have been made without a suitable theoretical underpinning, and it is therefore difficult to evaluate their validity. Studies along the above suggested line should help to evaluate them.

An example of this line of theorizing is provided by *Grossman — Helpman* (1988). This work is limited in scope and incorporates only a few of the above listed features. It is, however, more complete than other studies in its detailed outline of dynamic economic forces. Of particular interest for our purpose is the treatment of R&D. Suppose that there exists an industrial sector that produces horizontally differentiated products. Preferences are of the Spence-Dixit-Stiglitz type and there exists a continuum of such products. There exists a technology for product development, which is represented by a cost function $c_n (w)$, where w is a vector of factor prices. An entrepreneur who incures these costs at a point in time obtains in return the know-how to produce a variety of the industrial product. This variety is unique, in the sense that no one else knows how to produce it. In principle it is possible to assume that this variety-specific knowledge is limited in time, or that the time of acquired monopoly power is uncertain, and it is possible to link it to patent laws and imitation activities of other entrepreneurs (possibly from other countries). These complications are avoided by assuming that a developer gains indefinite monopoly power for his product.

Under these circumstances it pays to develop a product if the present value of operating profits derived in the future is at least as high as current R&D costs. Competitive entry ensures that entrepreneurs break even in present value terms. Namely,

$$(2c) \quad \int_t^{\infty} e^{-(R(\tau)-R(t))} \pi(\tau) \, d\tau = c_n(w(t)),$$

17

where π (t) are operating profits at time t. This is the counterpart of the asset pricing equations *(2a)* and *(2b)*. Choosing R&D as the numeraire, c_n $(w\,(t)) = 1$ at all time periods. Then *(2c)* implies

(3c) $r\,(t) = \pi\,(t)$,

i. e., the real interest rate — measured in terms of R&D value — is equal to the instantaneous operating profit rate.

Next, if a share s_x of total spending is allocated to industrial goods, then in symmetrical equilibria the instantaneous profit rate can be shown to equal $(1-\alpha)\,s_x\dfrac{E}{n}$, where α is a parameter of the utility function over differentiated products, which has the form given in *(4)*, E is total spending, and n is the number of available varieties. The expenditure share is taken to be constant due to a Cobb-Douglas specification of upper-tier preferences for different product categories, whose number is assumed to be 2. The second is a traditional good. Assuming a unitary elasticity of substitution in consumption over time implies that aggregate consumption expenditure E (on both product categories) satisfies *(1)* with $\beta = 1$. Taken together all this yields a differential equation in spending

(6) $\quad \dfrac{\dot{E}}{E} = (1 - \alpha)\,s_x\dfrac{E}{n} - \varrho.$

For the competitively produced traditional product price equals marginal costs while for the differentiated product, whose production takes place under constant returns to scale after it is developed, price is marked up above marginal costs in the usual way. In addition there are factor market clearing conditions. All these static relationships enable one to solve prices, factor rewards, and output levels as functions of the spending level E. In particular, the level of R&D — as measured by the number (measure) of newly developed varieties — is a function of expenditure:

(7) $\quad \dot{n} = \nu\,(E).$

Equations *(6)* and *(7)* constitute an autonomous system of differential equations, which together with the initial condition on the number of products and the transversality condition from the consumer's decision problem yield a unique equilibrium trajectory for a closed economy. Provided suitable stability conditions are satisfied, an economy that begins with a small number of products will experience a rising number of products and consumption expenditure. It will, however, reach a steady state with constant consumption and a constant number of products.

In this model the number of products plays the role of a capital stock: All investment is channeled into R&D which leads to the accumulation of more and more variety. The accumulation process ceases when the profit rate — and with it the interest rate — drop to the level of the subjective discount rate. From this point of view it is similar to the neoclassical model. The reason for this similarity is further revealed by considering a one-sector representation (which is close in spirit to Romer's, although quite different in implications). Suppose there is no traditional good. Then $s_x = 1$. Suppose also that available factors of production can produce a fixed quantity Q of a resource that can be used for product development or the production of differentiated products. Let one unit of the resource develop a single variety and let α units of the resource be required to manufacture a unit of the final good. Then the market price of the resource is 1 (remember that R&D is the numeraire) and the price of the final product is 1 for all varieties (the mark-up condition implies that price is $1/\alpha$ times marginal costs). In this case *(7)* reads

$$(7a) \quad \dot{n} = Q - E,$$

which is the usual saving-investment relationship. In this form the model reduces to a variant studied by *Judd* (1985), although in a somewhat different representation. It makes clear why growth ceases: The profit rate and with it the interest rate, have to fall. But it also makes clear what is required for sustained growth; accumulation of variety is not enough to maintain indefinitely sufficiently high profit and interest rates. The introduction of new products squeezes profits. Accumulation of productive resources is required to prevent profit rates and interest rates from falling to the subjective discount rate.

Grossman — Helpman consider a two-country, two-good, two-factor version. The two factors are interpreted to be unskilled labour (or just labour) and human capital. The traditional good is the most labour intensive. Preferences are the same everywhere and so are technologies, which are of the constant coefficients type. Financial capital is mobile internationally. Within a wide range of endowment structures there is factor price equalization at each point in time. The wage rate is rising and the return to human capital is falling. The price of traditional goods is rising, while the price of manufactured differentiated products is rising slower, if at all (measured in terms of the numeraire, i. e., the R&D activity). It is necessarilly falling when manufacturing of industrial goods is more human-capital intensive than R&D. Otherwise it is rising. Investment in R&D declines through time while output of manufactures increases. Output of traditional goods increases if and only if R&D is more human-capital intensive than manufacturing of industrial goods.

The relatively human-capital rich country runs a deficit on current account at the initial stages of development (the world starts with zero variety). The rate of accumulation of new products is the same in both. Despite the existence of unbalanced trade, the human-capital rich country is a net exporter of manufactures and an importer of the traditional good at every point in time. When R&D is more human-capital intensive than manufactures, the volume of trade grows faster than consumption spending and also faster than GNP. Under the same relative intensity ranking a sufficiently large difference in factor composition brings

19

about the emergence of multinational corporations in the human-capital rich country. From this point in time the rate of product innovation is not the same in both countries and the human-capital rich country may end up importing manufactures. Multinationals develop new products and locate manufacturing activities in the labour rich country (assuming that manufacturing requires labour while headquarter services require human capital). The degree of multinationality, as measured by the number of products produced by subsidiaries, their output volume, or their employment, increases initially and also close to convergence to a steady state. This seems to be a rich model, but not rich enough to account for all unexplained phenomena. Further extensions and elaborations are required.

Studies along this line can be helpful in explaining the role of acquired comparative advantage in the dynamic evolution of trade, in the process of economic growth, and the interaction between them. This type of research is in its infancy, and it has to go a long way before its full potential is realized. Time will tell how large is this potential.

5. Product cycles

In the previous section countries were treated symmetrically and it was assumed that product developers maintain indefinite monopoly power. The latter assumption excluded the possibility of imitation which is at the heart of the product cycle approach. Also at the heart of this approach is an inherent asymmetry between the North, which knows how to develop new products, and the South that knows only how to imitate their production. *Vernon's* (1966) original insight was formalized by *Krugman* (1979) in a framework with differentiated products, and recently generalized in various directions by other authors. I will provide a brief description of Krugman's approach in order to discuss its potential and the need to merge it with the approaches outlined in the previous section. Following this discussion I will point out additional variations that are of potential interest.

Preferences for variety are the same as in the previous section, but there is only one product: Manufactures. Only the North acquires the know-how to produce new varieties and this is achieved at no cost (this is a critical and deficient assumption). The exogenous rate of innovation is i, so that i times n is the number (measure) of newly introduced products at a point in time, where n is the number of products available in the world economy. At a point in time northern producers maintain monopoly power in n_N varieties, while southern producers know how to produce n_S varieties, with $n = n_N + n_S$. These numbers are determined as follows. The South tries to imitate production of varieties in which the North has monopoly power. At each point in time it learns how to produce a proportion μ of goods in which the North has monopoly power. This too is costlessly achieved (another deficient assumption). In this case $\dot{n}_S = \mu\, n_N$ and $\dot{n}_N = i\, n - \mu\, n_N$. Namely, the number of products which the South learns how to produce equals the rate of imitation μ times the number of products in which the North maintains monopoly power while the addition to the number of products in which the North maintains monopoly power equals the overall addition to available variety minus the number of products whose production technology is acquired by the South. Denoting by s_N the share of products in which the North maintains monopoly power this calculus implies

$$(8) \quad \dot{s}_N = i - (i + \mu) \, s_N \, .$$

This is a differential equation that describes the evolution of product composition. If the initial value of the share is smaller than $\dfrac{i}{i+\mu}$ the share rises over time until it reaches the steady-state value $\dfrac{i}{i+\mu}$. If it is larger, it declines towards the steady-state value. In the steady state it is equal to the rate of innovation divided by the rate of innovation plus the rate of imitation. The larger the rate of innovation and the smaller the rate of imitation the larger the share of products in which the North maintains monopoly power in the long run. This makes, of course, sense.

So far I have described the mechanics of product innovation and imitation. These mechanics have simple and sensible properties, but little economic content. Some economic content is added by the following considerations. Suppose that goods are produced only with labour, with one unit of labour producing one unit of any variety, and that initially the wage rate is higher in the North. There is perfect competition in the South. Then the South will produce all goods for which it has the required know-how, namely, n_S . The North will produce all goods in which it maintains monopoly power. Given the suitable pricing and market clearing conditions this implies the following equilibrium relationship between relative wages and the share s_N .

$$(9) \quad \frac{w_N}{w_S} = \alpha \left(\frac{s_N \, L_S}{(1-s_N) \, L_N} \right)^{(1-\alpha)},$$

where L_j is the labour force in country j. It is clear from here that if the share s_N is rising the gap between northern and southern wages widens over time and if it is declining the wage gap narrows down. This is an important insight(1). In the steady state the wage ratio is higher the larger the rate of product innovation and the smaller the rate of imitation. This too is a sensible result.

This model has been extended by *Dollar* (1986) to allow for two factors of production and for the rate of imitation to depend on the production cost differential between North and South. Another variant, due to *Jensen — Thursby* (1987), makes the rate of innovation depend on resources devoted to R&D, but assumes that all the innovation is done by a single northern monopolist. It seems to me that future research will benefit from an integration of the approach presented in the previous section with the product cycle model. By this I mean to endogenize the rate of innovation and the rate of imitation by means of explicit economic considerations that consist of an intertemporal cost-benefit analysis. Surely, the rate of imitation depends on resources devoted to reversed engineering, learning, and the like. The incentive to engage in this activity depends on expectations of future benefits, which depend in turn on the degree of protection provided by patent laws and other devices by means of which monopoly power is preserved. Similarly for the rate of innovation. The incentive to engage in this activity depends on expected future profits, which also depend on the above mentioned factors. It is therefore clear that the equilibrium values of these rates are interrelated in important ways, and they are jointly determined with other activities that draw on an economy's resources.

An alternative product cycle model has been proposed by *Flam — Helpman* (1987) (see also *Segrstrom — Anat — Dinopoilos,* 1987). There horizontal product differentiation is replaced with vertical differentiation. Namely, goods differ in quality. Using a competitive structure they consider situations of labour growth (the only factor of production), changes in income distribution, and technical progress in manufacturing. The demand for different qualities of manufactured products is driven by differences in household incomes. Income distribution may differ across countries. They show that when the North has comparative advantage in the production of high quality products a quality based product cycle can emerge. Both North and South may be moving up the quality spectrum of produced goods, with the North introducing ever better products and the South abandoning production of its lowest quality varieties. Moreover, as the North too abandons production of its lowest quality products, the varieties that were produced in the North are eventually picked up by the South and produced there until abandoned at a later stage. This process explains an observed phenomenon. Various commodities are replaced over time with higher quality products, and the lowest qualities disappear from the market.

It should be clear from this description that introduction of vertical differentiation carries great potential in the treatment of trade and growth. Much of the increase in the standard of living has been achieved not so much by producing larger quantities as by providing higher quality products. By the same token much of international trade is an exchange of goods of different quality. It is most desirable to develop the theory along this line, paying explicit attention to the resource cost of higher quality product development and the incentive to engage in it. I will not repeat the arguments already made on this subject in reference to horizontal differentiation: They equally apply to vertical differentiation. The problem is, of course, that treatment of dynamic general equilibrium models with vertical product differentiation and noncompetitive market structures is much harder. Harder, yes, but not hopeless.

I have outlined a number of problems that require attention from international trade theorists, and which — I believe — can also greatly benefit from careful empirical studies. I have also described some recent work, trying to highlight ways in which it can be used to shed new light on these problems. It appears that the way is now open for new inquires into the relationship between international trade and economic growth, and eventually, into the possible role of trade and industrial policy in the promotion of economic growth.

22

6. References

Arrow, K. J., "The Economic Implications of Learning By Doing", Review of Economic Studies, 1962, 24, pp. 155-173.

Baumol, W. J., "Productivity Growth, Convergence, and Welfare: What The Long-Run Data Show", American Economic Review, 1986, 76, pp. 1072-1085.

Bhagwati, J. N., "Immiserizing Growth: A Geometrical Note", Review of Economic Studies, 1958, 25, pp. 201-205.

Bhagwati, J. N., Foreign Trade Regimes and Economic Development: Anatomy and Consequences of Exchange Control Regimes, Ballinger, NBER, Lexington, 1978.

De Long, B., "Have Productivity Levels Converged?", NBER Working Paper, 1987, (2419).

Dollar, D., "Technological Innovation, Capital Mobility, and the Product Cycle in North-South Trade", American Economic Review, 1986, 76, pp. 177-190.

Ethier, W. J., "National and International Returns to Scale in the Modern Theory of International Trade", American Economic Review, 1982, 72, pp. 389-405.

Feder, G., "On Exports and Economic Growth", Journal of Development Economics, 1982, 12, pp. 59-73.

Findlay, R., "Growth and Development in Trade Models", in Jones, R. W., Kenen, P. B. (Eds.), Handbook of International Economics, Vol. 1, North-Holland, Amsterdam, 1984.

Flam, H., Helpman, E., "Vertical Product Differentiation and North-South Trade", American Economic Review, 1987, 77, pp. 810-822.

Griliches, Z., "Issues in Assessing the Contribution of Research and Development in Productivity Growth", Bell Journal of Economics, 1979, 10, pp. 92-116.

Grossman, G. M., Helpman, E., "Product Development and International Trade", NBER Working Papers, 1988, (2540).

Helpman, E., "Increasing Returns, Imperfect Competition, and Trade Theory", in Jones, R. W., Kenen, P. B. (Eds.), Handbook of International Economics, Vol. 1, North-Holland, Amsterdam, 1984.

Helpman, E., Krugman, P. R., Market Structure and Foreign Trade, M. I. T. Press, Cambridge, Mass., 1985.

Helpman, E., Trajtenberg, M., Dynamic Comparative Advantage and the Hypothesis of Export-Led Growth, 1987 (mimeo).

23

Jensen, R., Thursby, M., "A Decision Theoretic Model of Innovation, Technology Transfer and Trade", Review of Economic Studies, 1987, 55, pp. 631-648.

Judd, K. L., "On the Performance of Patents", Econometrica, 1985, 53, pp. 567-585.

Krueger, A. O., Foreign Trade Regimes and Economic Development: Liberalization Attempts and Consequences, NBER, Columbia University Press, New York, 1978.

Krugman, P. R., "A Model of Innovation, Technology Transfer, and the World Distribution of Income", Journal of Political Economy, 1979, 87, pp. 253-266.

Leamer, E. E., Sources of International Comparative Advantage, M. I. T. Press, Cambridge, Mass., 1984.

Leamer, E. E., "Paths of Development in the 3-Factor, n-Good General Equilibrium Model", Journal of Political Economy, 1987, 95, pp. 961-999.

Lucas, R. E. Jr., On the Mechanics of Economic Development, The Marshall and Horowitz Lectures, 1985 (mimeo).

Maddison, A., Phases of Capitalist Development, Oxford University Press, Oxford, 1982.

Maddison, A., "Growth and Slowdown in Advanced Capitalist Economies: Techniques of Quantitative Assessment", Journal of Economic Literature, 1987, 25, pp. 649-698.

Michaely, M., "Exports and Growth: An Empirical Investigation", Journal of Development Economics, 1977, 4, pp. 49-53.

Oniki, H., Uzawa, H., "Patterns of Trade and Investment in a Dynamic Model of International Trade", Review of Economic Studies, 1965, 32, pp. 15-28.

Pasinetti, L., Structural Change and Economic Growth, Cambridge University Press, Cambridge, 1981.

Romer, P. M. (1986A), "Increasing Returns and Long-Run Growth", Journal of Political Economy, 1986, 94, pp. 1002-1037.

Romer, P. M. (1986B), "Increasing Returns, Specialization, and External Economies: Growth as Described by Allyn Young", Rochester Center for Economic Research, Working Paper, 1986, (64).

Romer, P. M., "Capital Accumulation in the Theory of Long Run Growth", Rochester Center for Economic Research, Working Paper, 1988, (123).

Segrstrom, P. S., Anat, T. C. A., Dinopoilos, E., A Schumpeterian Model of the Product Life Cycle, 1987 (mimeo).

Smith, M. A. M., "Capital Theory and Trade Theory", in Jones, R. W., Kenen, P. B. (Eds.), Handbook of International Economics, Vol. 1, North-Holland, Amsterdam, 1984.

Vernon, R., "International Investment and International Trade in the Product Cycle", Quarterly Journal of Economics, 1966, 80, pp. 190-207.

Young, A. A., "Increasing Returns and Economic Progress", Economic Journal, 1928, 38, pp. 527-542.

7. Note

(1) In the latter case the wage gap may disappear before a steady state is reached, which will eliminate the identification of the number of products produced in the South with the number of products it knows to produce. This minor point can easily be taken care of. For current purposes suppose it does not arise.

Correspondence:

Elhanan Helpman

Department of Economics
Tel Aviv University

Tel Aviv 69978
Israel

[40]

Comparative Advantage and Long-Run Growth

By GENE M. GROSSMAN AND ELHANAN HELPMAN*

We construct a dynamic, two-country model of trade and growth in which endogenous technological progress results from the profit-maximizing behavior of entrepreneurs. We study the role that the external trading environment and that trade and industrial policies play in the determination of long-run growth rates. Cross-country differences in efficiency at R&D versus manufacturing (i.e., comparative advantage) bear importantly on the growth effects of economic structure and commerical policies. (JEL 411, 111, 621)

What role do the external trading environment and commercial policy play in the determination of *long-run* economic performance? This central question of international economics has received surprisingly little attention in the theoretical literature over the years.

Previous research on trade and growth has adopted the neoclassical framework to focus on factor accumulation in the open economy. (See the surveys by Ronald Findlay, 1984, and Alasdair Smith, 1984.) This research largely neglects the effects of trade structure on rates of growth, however, addressing instead the reverse causation from growth and accumulation to the pattern of trade.[1] The direction that the research followed almost surely can be ascribed to the well-known property of the standard neoclassical growth model with diminishing returns to capital that (endogenous) growth in per capita income dissipates in the long run.

For this reason, the familiar models that incorporate investment only in capital equipment seem ill-suited for analysis of long-run growth.

The available evidence collected since the seminal work of Robert Solow (1957) also leads one to look beyond capital accumulation for an explanation of growth. Exercises in growth accounting for a variety of countries generally find that increases in the capital to labor ratio account for considerably less than half of the last century's growth in per capita incomes.[2] Although econometric efforts to explain the residual have been somewhat disappointing (see, for example, Zvi Griliches, 1979), professional opinion and common sense continue to impute much of this residual to improvements in technology.[3] We share the view, expressed by Paul Romer (1986, 1990), that a full understanding of growth in the long run requires appreciation of the economic determinants of the accumulation of knowledge.

In this paper we draw on the pioneering work by Romer to construct a model that highlights the roles of scale economies and technological progress in the growth process. As in Romer's work, our model im-

*Grossman: Woodrow Wilson School, Princeton University, Princeton, NJ 08544. Helpman: Department of Economics, Tel Aviv University, Ramat Aviv, Israel. We are grateful to Avinash Dixit, Carl Shapiro, and Lars Svensson for their comments on an earlier draft, and to the National Science Foundation and the Alfred P. Sloan Foundation for financial support. Grossman also thanks the World Bank and Helpman thanks the International Monetary Fund for providing support and a stimulating environment during part of our work on this project. These organizations are not responsible for the views expressed herein.

[1] An exception is Max Corden (1971), who studies how the opening up of trade affects the speed of transition to the steady state in a two-factor neoclassical growth model with fixed savings propensities.

[2] See Angus Maddison (1987) for a careful, recent exercise in growth accounting.
[3] The benefits of education and experience undoubtedly contribute part of the explanation for the growth residual. See, for example, Robert Lucas (1988) and Gary Becker and Kevin Murphy (1990) for growth models that highlight the role of human capital accumulation as a source of growth.

plies an endogenous rate of long-run growth in per capita income, and we study its economic determinants. Our primary contribution lies in casting the growth process in a two-country setting. We provide, for the first time, a rigorous analysis linking long-run growth rates to trade policies and other international economic conditions. Moreover, we show that recognition of cross-country differences in economic structure impinge upon conclusions about the long-run effects of domestic shocks and policies.

Our model incorporates the essential insights from Romer (1990), although we introduce some differences in detail. The building blocks are an R&D sector that produces designs or blueprints for new products using primary resources and previously accumulated knowledge, an intermediate-goods sector consisting of oligopolistic producers of differentiated products, and a consumer-goods sector in each country that produces a country-specific final output using labor and intermediate inputs. As in Wilfred Ethier (1982), total factor productivity in final production increases when the number of available varieties of differentiated inputs grows. Thus, resources devoted to R&D contribute over time to productivity in the production of final goods, as well as to the stock of scientific and engineering knowledge.

The new elements in our analysis stem from the assumed presence of cross-country differences in the effectiveness with which primary resources can perform different activities, that is, *comparative advantage*. For simplicity we specify a one-primary-factor model, and allow the productivity of this factor in the three activities to vary internationally. Similar results could be derived from a multifactor model with interindustry differences in factor intensities (see Grossman and Helpman, 1989d, and Grossman, 1989). In any event, we find that many comparative dynamic results hinge on a comparison across countries of parameters reflecting efficiency in R&D relative to efficiency in manufacturing the goods that make use of the knowledge generated by R&D. The effects of policy in a single country, of accumulation of primary resources in a single

country, and of a shift in world tastes toward the final output of one of the countries all depend upon the identity of the country in which the change originates in relation to the international pattern of comparative advantage.

We describe the economic setting in Section I below. Then, in Section II, we derive the dynamic equilibrium of the world economy and calculate two reduced-form equations that determine the steady-state growth rate. In Section III, we investigate the structural determinants of long-run growth. There, the implications for growth of variations in consumer preferences, primary-input coefficients in one or both countries, and stocks of available primary resources are considered. Section IV contains policy analysis. We study barriers and inducements to trade in consumer goods and subsidies to research and development. The analysis is extended in Section V to incorporate lags in the dissemination of knowledge and asymmetries in the speed of diffusion within and between countries. We use the extended model to reconsider the effects of trade policies on the steady-state rate of growth. Finally, Section VI provides a brief summary of our findings.

I. The Model

We study a world economy comprising two countries. Each country engages in three productive activities: the production of a final good, the production of a continuum of varieties of differentiated middle products (i.e., intermediate inputs), and research and development (R&D). A single primary factor is used in production, and is taken to be in fixed and constant supply in each country. Although we refer to this factor as "labor," we have in mind an aggregate of irreproducible resources that for any given level of technical know-how limits aggregate output.

At a point in time, output of final goods in country i is given by

$$Y_i = BA_i L_{Yi}^{1-\beta} \left[\int_0^n x_i(\omega)^\alpha \, d\omega \right]^{\beta/\alpha},$$

$$0 < \alpha, \beta < 1,$$

where L_{Yi} represents employment in the final-goods sector, $x_i(\omega)$ denotes the input of middle product ω, A_i is a country-specific productivity parameter, and n is (the measure of) the number of varieties of middle products available at that time.[4] This production function exhibits constant returns to scale for given n, but an increase in the measure of varieties of middle products raises total factor productivity. This specification, which we borrow from Ethier (1982), captures the notion that an increasing degree of *specialization* generates technical efficiency gains. The economy's potential for augmenting the degree of specialization by developing new middle products implies the existence of dynamic scale economies at the industry level that are external to the individual final-good-producing firms.

Competition in the final-goods sectors ensures marginal-cost pricing. Hence, by appropriate choice of the constant B, producer prices satisfy

$$(1) \quad p_{Yi} = \left(\frac{w_i}{A_i}\right)^{1-\beta} \left[\int_0^n p_X(\omega)^{1-\epsilon}d\omega\right]^{\beta/(1-\epsilon)},$$

$$\epsilon = \frac{1}{1-\alpha} > 1,$$

where w_i is the wage in country i and $p_X(\omega)$ is the price of variety ω. Final-good producers worldwide pay the same prices for (freely traded) middle products.

At every moment in time, the existing producers of middle products engage in oligopolistic price competition. The producer of a variety ω in country i chooses $p_X(\omega)$ to maximize profits,

$$\pi_i(\omega) = \left[p_X(\omega) - w_i a_{LXi}\right]$$

$$\times \frac{p_X(\omega)^{-\epsilon}}{\int_0^n p_X(\omega)^{1-\epsilon}d\omega}\beta\Sigma_i p_{Yi}Y_i,$$

where a_{LXi} is the unit labor requirement for production of intermediates in country i. This expression for profits comprises the product of profits per unit (in square brackets) and derived demand for variety ω, where the latter incorporates the assumption that neither the prices of competing products nor the value of final production varies with $p_X(\omega)$. The first-order condition for a profit maximum implies the usual fixed-markup pricing rule,

$$(2) \quad \alpha p_X(\omega) = w_i a_{LXi}.$$

It is clear from (2) that varieties originating from the same country bear the same price. Letting p_{Xi} represent the price of a variety produced in country i and n_i be the number of intermediate inputs produced there, equations (1) and (2) imply

$$(3) \quad p_{Yi} = \left(\frac{w_i}{A_i}\right)^{1-\beta} \left(\sum_j n_j p_{Xj}^{1-\epsilon}\right)^{\beta/(1-\epsilon)},$$

$$(4) \quad \alpha p_{Xi} = w_i a_{LXi}.$$

With these prices, profits per firm can be expressed as

$$(5) \quad \pi_i = (1-\alpha)p_{Xi}X_i/n_i,$$

where X_i is aggregate output of intermediates in country i (n_i times per-firm output) and is given by

$$(6) \quad X_i = \frac{n_i p_{Xi}^{-\epsilon}}{\sum_j n_j p_{Xj}^{1-\epsilon}}\beta\left(\sum_j p_{Yj}Y_j\right).$$

As in our 1989c paper (see also Kenneth Judd, 1985), resources devoted to research generate "blueprints" that expand the measure of differentiated products. Research outlays are made by private, profit-maximizing entrepreneurs, who appropriate some of the benefits from a new technological innovation in the form of a stream of oligopoly profits. We assume that innovators receive indefinite patent protection, but that blueprints are not tradable, so that all profits must be derived from production in

---

[4] Here, and henceforth, we omit time arguments when no confusion is caused by doing so.

the country in which a middle product has been developed. Then, with free entry by entrepreneurs, if resources are devoted to R&D in country i at time t, the present value of future operating profits from producing there—discounted to time t—must equal the current cost of R&D. We denote R&D costs by $c_{ni}(t)$ and write the zero-profit condition as

$$\int_t^\infty e^{-[R(\tau)-R(t)]}\pi_i(\tau)d\tau = c_{ni}(t),$$

where $R(t)$ is the cumulative interest factor from time 0 to time t ($R(0)=1$). Differentiating this condition with respect to t, we find

$$(7) \qquad \frac{\pi_i + \dot{c}_{ni}}{c_{ni}} = \dot{R}.$$

Equation (7) expresses a standard no-arbitrage condition. Recognizing that $c_{ni}(t)$ represents the value of an input-producing firm in country i at time t, (7) equates the instantaneous rate of return on shares in such a firm (the sum of dividends and capital gains) to the rate of interest.

We follow Romer (1990) in assuming that R&D generates a second output, which takes the form of a contribution to the stock of disembodied knowledge. Knowledge here includes all general scientific information, as well as some forms of engineering data with more widespread applicability, generated in the course of developing marketable products. Knowledge contributes to the productivity of further research efforts by reducing the amount of labor needed for an inventor to develop a new product. Due to the more general and non-patentable nature of this product of the R&D effort, appropriation of the resulting returns by the creator seems problematic. We assume to begin with that general knowledge disseminates immediately and costlessly throughout the world. This approximates a situation in which information spreads through technical journals, professional organizations, and interpersonal commercial contacts, and where literature, scientists, and business-

people move freely across international borders (see Luigi Pasinetti, 1981, ch. 11). We relax this assumption by introducing lags in the dissemination of knowledge in Section V.

With these knowledge spillovers in mind, we specify our R&D technology as follows. If L_{ni} units of labor engage in research in country i, they generate a flow of new products $\dot{n}_i$ given by

$$(8) \qquad \dot{n}_i = L_{ni}K / a_{Lni},$$

where K is the current stock of knowledge and a_{Lni} is a country-specific productivity parameter. We take the stock of knowledge to be proportional to cumulative experience in R&D; that is, there are no diminishing returns to research in adding to scientific understanding. By choosing units for K so that the factor of proportionality is unity, we have $K = n$ and

$$(9) \qquad \dot{K} = \sum_i L_{ni}K / a_{Lni}.$$

Since knowledge has been assumed to be a free input to each individual entrepreneur, the cost of product development in country i can be written as

$$(10) \qquad c_{ni} = w_i a_{Lni} / n.$$

We turn now to the demand side of the model. Consumers worldwide share identical, homothetic preferences. They view the final goods produced in the two countries as imperfect substitutes. We represent preferences by a time-separable intertemporal utility function

$$(11) \quad U_t = \int_t^\infty e^{-\rho(\tau-t)}$$

$$\times \log u[y_1(\tau), y_2(\tau)]d\tau,$$

where ρ is the subjective discount rate and $y_i(\tau)$ is consumption of final goods from country i in period τ. The instantaneous sub-utility function $u(\cdot)$ is nondecreasing, strictly quasi-concave, and positively linearly homogeneous.

A typical consumer maximizes (11) subject to an intertemporal budget constraint. With $u(\cdot)$ linearly homogeneous, this optimization problem can be solved in two stages. First, the consumer maximizes static utility for a given level of expenditure at time τ, $E(\tau)$. The solution to this subproblem generates an indirect utility function, $v[p_{Y1}(\tau), p_{Y2}(\tau)]E(\tau)$, where p_{Yi} is the price of Y_i. In the absence of barriers to trade in final goods, these prices are common to consumers in the two countries. The second-stage problem involves choosing the time pattern of expenditures to maximize

$$(12) \quad V_t = \int_t^\infty e^{-\rho(\tau - t)}\{\log v[p_{Y1}(\tau), p_{Y2}(\tau)]$$

$$+ \log E(\tau)\} \, d\tau$$

subject to

$$(13) \quad \int_t^\infty e^{-[R(\tau) - R(t)]}E(\tau)$$

$$\leq \int_t^\infty e^{-[R(\tau) - R(t)]}w(\tau)L \, d\tau + Z(t),$$

where $w(t)$ is the consumer's wage rate at time t, L is his labor supply, and $Z(t)$ is the value of his time t asset holdings. The interest factor in (13) is common to all individuals as a result of trade on the integrated world capital market, but the wage rate varies by country.

From the first-order conditions to this problem, we find that the optimal path for expenditure obeys

$$(14) \quad \frac{\dot{E}}{E} = \dot{R} - \rho.$$

Savings are used to accumulate either ownership claims in input-producing firms or riskless bonds issued by these same firms. Arbitrage ensures that the rates of return on these two assets are equal, and in equilibrium consumers are indifferent as to the composition of their portfolios.

II. Equilibrium Dynamics

During the course of the development of our model in the previous section, we provided some of the equilibrium conditions. For example, we derived pricing equations for goods and a no-arbitrage condition relating equilibrium asset returns. In this section we complete the list of equilibrium requirements by adding conditions that stipulate market clearing in factor and final-goods markets. We then derive and discuss a reduced-form system that describes equilibrium dynamics.

Static equilibrium in the markets for the two final goods implies

$$(15) \quad p_{Yi}Y_i = s_i E,$$

where $s_i(p_{Y1}, p_{Y2})$ is the share of world spending allocated to Y_i and E is world spending on consumer goods. The share function is, of course, homogeneous of degree zero. We establish below that relative commodity prices are constant in the vicinity of a steady state with active R&D sectors in both countries. For this reason, we take s_i to be constant in our subsequent analysis, and omit its functional dependence on relative prices.

The labor-market clearing conditions equate labor supply and labor demand in each country. Using (3) and Shephard's lemma, we see that final-goods producers demand $(1 - \beta)p_{Yi}Y_i / w_i$ workers. The demand for labor by middle-products manufacturers is $a_{LXi}X_i$, while (8) and the fact that $K = n$ imply demand for labor by product developers of $(a_{Lni}/n)\dot{n}_i$. Hence,

$$(16) \quad (a_{Lni}/n)\dot{n}_i + a_{LXi}X_i$$

$$+ (1 - \beta)p_{Yi}Y_i / w_i = L_i,$$

where L_i is the labor force available in country i.

Since we neglect here the monetary determinants of the price level, we may choose freely a time pattern for one nominal variable. It proves convenient to specify the numeraire as follows:

$$(17a) \qquad p_{X1} = n(a_{LX1}/a_{Ln1})^{1/\varepsilon}.$$

We show in Appendix A of our 1989a working paper that, with this normalization, a necessary condition for convergence to a steady state with positive R&D in both countries (i.e., nonspecialization) is

$$(17b) \qquad p_{X2} = n(a_{LX2}/a_{Ln2})^{1/\varepsilon}.$$

Together, (17a) and (17b) imply that relative prices of middle products are constant along the convergent path, which further implies with (4) the constancy of relative wages, and with (3) the constancy of relative prices of final goods. This last fact justifies our treatment of expenditure shares as fixed.

Let $g(t)$ denote the rate of growth of the number of products and the stock of knowledge; that is, $g \equiv \dot{n}/n = \dot{K}/K$. Then from (17) and (4) we see that prices of intermediates and wages grow at rate g, while from (10), product development costs are constant. Equations (5)–(7), (10), (15), and (17) imply

$$(18) \qquad X_i = \frac{n_i b_i^{1/\alpha}}{\sum_j n_j b_j} \frac{\beta E}{n}$$

and

$$(19) \qquad \dot{R} = \frac{1}{\varepsilon - 1} \frac{\beta E}{\sum_j n_j b_j},$$

where $b_i \equiv (a_{Lni}/a_{LXi})^\alpha$. The coefficients b_i will serve as our measures of *comparative advantage*. Country 1 enjoys comparative advantage in conducting R&D if and only if $b_1 < b_2$.

Since wages grow at the same rate as n, it proves convenient to define $e \equiv E/n$. Letting $\sigma_i \equiv n_i/n$ be the share of products manufactured in country i and noting that $g = \sum_i \dot{n}_i/n$, (16), (15), (17), (4), and (18) imply

$$(20) \qquad g = H - \frac{\beta e}{\sigma} - \frac{1 - \beta}{\alpha} se,$$

where we have defined $H \equiv \sum_i L_i/a_{Lni}$, the total *effective* labor force, $\sigma \equiv \sum_i \sigma_i b_i$, a weighted average of the comparative advantage parameters with product shares as weights, and $s \equiv \sum_i s_i/b_i$. Observe that the parameter σ, which provides a useful summary of the static intersectoral resource allocation, grows (shrinks) over time if and only if the growth rate of the number of differentiated middle products in the country with comparative *disadvantage* in R&D exceeds (falls short of) that of the other country.

We are now prepared to derive two equations that describe the dynamic evolution of the world economy. From the definition of e, we have $\dot{e}/e = \dot{E}/E - g$, or, substituting (14), (19), and (20),

$$(21) \qquad \frac{\dot{e}}{e} = \frac{\beta e}{\alpha \sigma} + \frac{1 - \beta}{\alpha} se - H - \rho.$$

Hence, the rate of increase of spending per middle product is larger the greater is spending per product and the smaller is the share of the country with comparative disadvantage in R&D in the total number of varieties.

Now, from the definition of the product shares σ_i, their rates of change are given by $\dot{\sigma}_i/\sigma_i = \dot{n}_i/n_i - \dot{n}/n$. Using (16) together with (17), (4), (18), and (20), we obtain

$$(22) \qquad \dot{\sigma}_i = h_i - \frac{s_i}{b_i} \frac{1 - \beta}{\alpha} e$$
$$- \sigma_i \left(H - \frac{1 - \beta}{\alpha} se \right),$$

where $h_i \equiv L_i/a_{Lni}$ is effective labor in country i, and $\sum_i h_i = H$. Since the evolution of the two product shares are related by $\sum_i \dot{\sigma}_i = 0$, we can replace (22) by a single differential equation in σ. Making use of the fact that $\dot{\sigma} = \sum_i \dot{\sigma}_i b_i$, we find

$$(23) \qquad \dot{\sigma} = h - \frac{1 - \beta}{\alpha} e - \sigma \left(H - \frac{1 - \beta}{\alpha} se \right),$$

where $h \equiv \sum_i h_i b_i$.

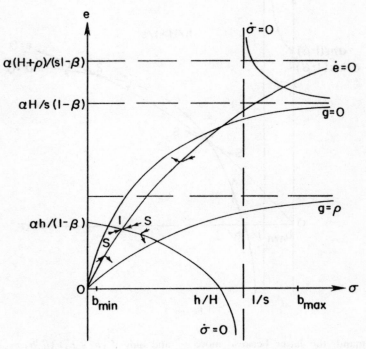

FIGURE 1

Equations (21) and (23) constitute an autonomous system of differential equations in e and σ. The solution to this system, together with (13), (20), and the definition of σ, provide a complete description of the evolution of spending and the number of products in each country. From these, the paths for outputs, employments and final-goods prices are easily derived. Thus, we shall use this two-equation system to analyze equilibrium dynamics.[5]

In Figures 1 and 2 we depict the stationary points for e. We draw the $\dot{e} = 0$ locus as increasing and concave (see (21)). To understand the positive slope of this curve, observe from (19) that the interest rate can be expressed as

$$(24) \qquad \dot{R} = \beta e / \sigma(\varepsilon - 1).$$

Thus, an increase in spending per product increases the interest rate and (from (20)) reduces the rate of growth of n (the former because the profitability of R&D rises with

---

[5]A restriction that we have not explicitly taken into account to this point is that product development must be nonnegative in each country. This condition certainly is satisfied in the neighborhood of a steady-state equilibrium with positive growth, but it need not hold all along the convergent path to such an equilibrium.

Thus, strictly speaking, the equilibrium dynamics that we describe below apply for sure only in the vicinity of a steady state.

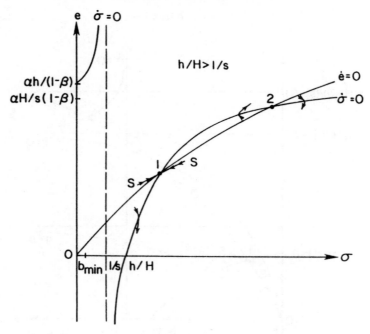

FIGURE 2

derived demand, the latter because more spending means less savings and hence less investment). Since an increase in the interest rate raises the rate of growth of nominal spending, and the rate of growth of e is just the difference between the rates of growth of E and n, it follows that an increase in e raises the growth rate of e. To compensate for this acceleration in spending per product, if e is to be stationary, σ must rise. An increase in σ lowers the interest rate and raises the rate of growth of n, thereby reducing the rate of growth of e.

Next, we distinguish two subcases depending on the relative sizes of h/H and $1/s$.[6] It can be shown that $h/H > 1/s$ if

---

[6] A borderline case arises when $b_1 = b_2$; that is, when comparative advantage is absent. Then $h/H = 1/s$, and $\sigma = b$ always. Convergence to the steady-state level of e is immediate in this case; see Grossman and Helpman (1989a).

and only if $(b_2 - b_1)(h_2 b_2/s_2 - h_1 b_1/s_1) > 0$. Therefore, the case $h/H > 1/s$, depicted in Figure 2, applies, for example, if the shares of the two countries' final outputs are in proportion to their relative *effective* labor forces; that is, $h_1/s_1 = h_2/s_2$. But a bias in size relative to budget share of final output can reverse the inequality and hence the relationship between h/H and $1/s$. This gives us the case $h/H < 1/s$, shown in Figure 1, with which we begin the discussion.

In general, both $1/s$ and h/H must lie between $b_{\min}$ and $b_{\max}$. The $\dot{\sigma} = 0$ curve in Figure 1 is everywhere downward sloping, crosses the horizontal axis at h/H, and is discontinuous at $\sigma = 1/s$. The slope of the curve is understood as follows. For $\dot{\sigma} = 0$, we must have $\dot{\sigma}_1 = 0$, which requires that the resources available for R&D in each country be just sufficient to preserve the country's *share* in the world's number of varieties. Consider country 1 and suppose for concreteness that this country has comparative advantage in R&D. Then an increase in σ lowers σ_1, thereby reducing the resources needed for production of middle products. The fall in σ_1 also reduces the amount of R&D country 1 must perform to preserve its share in the number of products. *Ceteris paribus*, σ_1 would tend to rise. An increase in e, on the other hand, diverts resources away from R&D to production of middle and final products in country 1. But it also causes the world's rate of product growth to fall, thereby diminishing the amount of R&D country 1 must undertake to maintain its share of middle products. The relative magnitudes of these two effects depend upon country 1's relative size, and on the share of its final product in aggregate spending. In the case under consideration, the second effect dominates, and so the $\dot\sigma = 0$ curve slopes downward.

In this case, there exists a unique steady state shown as point 1 in the figure. For initial values of σ not too different from that at point 1, a unique trajectory (saddlepath) converges to the steady state. This trajectory, labeled SS, fulfills all equilibrium requirements and satisfies the intertemporal budget constraint with equality. Along this trajectory (in the vicinity of the steady state), the interest rate and profit rate are declining (see (24)) and nominal expenditure E is rising. If the country with comparative advantage initially has a share of products that is smaller (larger) than its steady-state share, expenditure rises more slowly (rapidly) than the number of products.

The case depicted in Figure 2 arises when $h/H > 1/s$. Then the $\dot\sigma = 0$ schedule slopes upward. If the curve intersects the $\dot e = 0$ locus in the positive orthant at all, it must intersect it twice, as at points 1 and 2.[7] The

lower point (point 1) represents the steady state with the higher rate of growth (growth rates increase as we move down along the $\dot e = 0$ schedule, as we demonstrate below) and indeed the growth rate corresponding to point 2 may be negative. More importantly, as we show in Appendix B of our 1989a working paper, the equilibrium at point 1 exhibits saddle-path stability, whereas that at point 2 is locally unstable.[8] To the right of point 1, the saddle-path leading to that point remains trapped in the area bounded by the $\dot e = 0$ locus and the line segment joining points 1 and 2, and is everywhere upward sloping. Thus, the qualitative properties of the dynamic trajectory that leads to a stable, positive-growth equilibrium in Figure 2 mimic those of the stable saddle-path in Figure 1.

For the remainder of this paper we shall restrict our discussion to stable steady-state equilibria with positive rates of growth. That is, we focus our attention on equilibria such as those at the points labeled 1 in Figures 1 and 2. In the steady state there occurs intraindustry trade in middle products and interindustry trade in consumer goods, with the long-run pattern of trade determined by comparative advantage, productivities in the two final-goods industries, and consumer preferences.

III. Determinants of Long-Run Growth

Our model generates an endogenous rate of long-run growth. We now are prepared to explore how economic structure and economic policy affect this growth rate. In this section, we derive the implications of sec-

[7]The geometry supports this claim, once we recognize that the $\dot\sigma = 0$ curve asymptotes to the horizontal line at $\alpha H / s(1 - \beta)$, whereas the $\dot e = 0$ curve asymptotes to the horizontal line at $\alpha(H + \rho)/s(1 - \beta)$. The algebra provides confirmation, as simple manipulation reveals that the steady-state growth rate solves a quadratic equation.

[8]We strongly suspect, however, that whenever there exist two positive-growth, steady-state equilibria in the admissible range, there also exists a third (saddle-path stable) steady-state equilibrium with zero growth. We have established the existence of such an equilibrium for some parameter values, but so far have been unable to construct a general existence proof. Since the equilibrium at point 1 in Figure 2 can only be reached if the initial value of σ is less than that at point 2, we suspect that initial values of σ in excess of that at point 2 (and perhaps only these) imply convergence to a steady state with zero growth.

toral productivity levels, country sizes, and demand composition for the steady-state growth rate. The influence of trade policies and of subsidies to R&D are treated in the next section.

We derive the long-run values of e and σ by setting $\dot{e}$ and $\dot{\sigma}$ to zero in (21) and (23). The steady-state magnitudes, $\bar{e}$ and $\bar{\sigma}$, solve

$$(25) \qquad \frac{\beta\bar{e}}{\alpha\bar{\sigma}} + \frac{1-\beta}{\alpha} s\bar{e} = H + \rho;$$

$$(26) \qquad \frac{1-\beta}{\alpha}\bar{e}(1 - \bar{\sigma}s) + \bar{\sigma}H = h.$$

Whenever $1/s > h/H$, these equations provide at most one solution for $(\bar{e}, \bar{\sigma})$ consistent with $\bar{g} > 0$. When $1/s < h/H$, there may be two such solutions, in which case we select the stable equilibrium, that is, the one with the smaller values for $\bar{e}$ and $\bar{\sigma}$. Stability implies, in this latter case, that the $\dot{\sigma} = 0$ curve intersects the $\dot{e} = 0$ curve from below (see Appendix B of our 1989a working paper). We make use of this condition, namely,

$$(27) \qquad \frac{\beta\bar{e}}{(H+\rho)\bar{\sigma}^2} > \frac{\alpha H - (1-\beta)s\bar{e}}{\bar{\sigma}H - h}$$

$$\text{for} \quad 1/s < h/H,$$

in signing the comparative-dynamics derivatives that follow.

The growth rate of the number of varieties in the steady-state equilibrium can be derived from the solution to (25) and (26), together with (20). From this, we can easily calculate the growth rate of output. In the steady state, nominal expenditure grows at rate $\bar{g}$, while (3) implies that p_{Yi} grows at rate $[1 - \beta/(1 - \varepsilon)]\bar{g}$. From these facts and (15), we deduce that final output grows at rate $\beta\bar{g}/(1 - \varepsilon)$.

It is worth noting at this point that the steady-state equations (25) and (26), as well as the equation for $\bar{g}$, do not rely on our assumption of perfect capital mobility. In

the absence of capital mobility, the steady state would be the same as long as consumers worldwide share identical preferences (and therefore common subjective discount rates).[9]

It is instructive to begin the discussion with the case in which neither country exhibits comparative advantage in conducting R&D; that is, $b_1 = b_2 = b$. This case has $h = bH$ and $s = 1/b$. Then (25) and (26) provide a unique solution for $\bar{e}$ and $\bar{\sigma}$, which upon substitution into (20) yields the long-run growth rate

$$(28) \qquad \bar{g} = \frac{\beta(H+\rho)}{\varepsilon} - \rho.$$

This equilibrium growth rate shares much in common with that derived by Romer (1990) for a closed economy. In particular, the growth rate rises with effective labor H and declines with the subjective discount rate. Our measure of effective labor adjusts raw labor for productivity in R&D (recall that $H = \Sigma_i L_i / a_{Lni}$), so greater effectiveness in research in either country, as well as a larger world labor force, necessarily means faster growth. Long-run growth does not, however, depend upon coefficients that determine absolute productivity in the intermediate or final goods sectors (such as A_i or a_{LXi}). Nor do properties of the instantaneous utility function $u(\cdot)$, including the product composition of final demand, play any role in the determination of $\bar{g}$. As we shall see presently, all these features (except for the absence of an effect of A_i on $\bar{g}$) are special to a world without any comparative advantage.

Consider next the case with $1/s > h/H$. The curves $\dot{e} = 0$ and $\dot{\sigma} = 0$ in Figure 3 describe the initial situation, with a unique initial steady state at point 1. Now suppose

---

[9]The cases of perfect and imperfect capital mobility do differ in their implications for the steady-state share of each country in aggregate spending E. However, as should be clear from (25) and (26), the cross-country composition of E does not matter for the issues taken up in the present section.

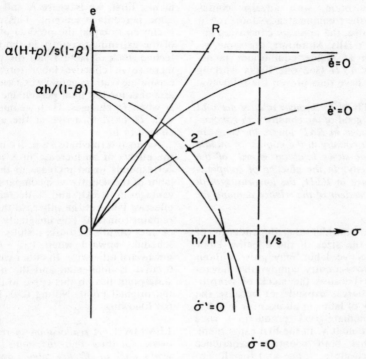

FIGURE 3

that preferences change so that s increases. This corresponds to a shift in tastes in favor of the final good produced by the country with comparative advantage in performing R&D. From (25), we see that the $\dot{e} = 0$ curve shifts down, say to $\dot{e}' = 0$ in the figure. Equation (26) implies that the $\dot{\sigma} = 0$ schedule shifts out (in the positive orthant) to $\dot{\sigma}' = 0$. The new steady state occurs at a point such as 2. But observe that all points on $\dot{e}' = 0$ to the right of its intersection with ray OR are characterized by slower steady-state growth than at point 1. This claim follows from (20) and (25), whence

$$(29) \qquad \bar{g} = \frac{\beta\bar{e}}{(\varepsilon - 1)\bar{\sigma}} - \rho.$$

Since the intersection of $\dot{\sigma}' = 0$ and $\dot{e}' = 0$ necessarily lies to the right of the intersection of the latter curve with OR, we have established that an increase in s reduces steady-state growth.

When tastes shift unexpectedly toward the final good of the country with comparative advantage in R&D, resources there must be reallocated to satisfy the relatively higher consumer demand. A process begins whereby labor there shifts out of R&D and the manufacture of middle products. Products accumulate more slowly in this country than in the other, and over time its share of middle products falls (i.e., σ rises). Output per middle product changes by the same proportion in both countries (see (18)). So, in the new steady state, the country with comparative disadvantage in R&D is responsible for a relatively larger share of the world's innovation, with adverse consequences for the common steady-state growth rate. Of course, the opposite conclusion applies when s falls. Moreover, the same results obtain at stable equilibrium points when $1/s < h/H$ (see our 1989a working paper). We have thus proven the following:

PROPOSITION 1: *Stronger relative demand for the final good of the country with comparative advantage in R&D lowers the long-run share of that country in the number of middle products and slows long-run growth of the world economy. In the absence of comparative advantage in R&D, the long-run growth rate is independent of the relative demand for final goods.*

Next we consider the dependence of growth on the sizes of the effective labor forces. Effective labor may grow without affecting cross-country comparative advantage either because the stock of irreproducible resources expands, or because the productivity of labor in all uses (or in R&D and intermediate-good production) rises equiproportionally. In the first experiment, suppose that both countries experience equiproportionate, once-and-for-all increases in the sizes of their effective labor forces. We have already seen that this change would augment world growth in the absence of comparative advantage. In our 1989a working paper we prove that the same result carries over to a world with intercountry differences in relative productivities at R&D and manufacturing. We establish the following there:

PROPOSITION 2: *An equiproportionate, once-and-for-all increase in the effective labor forces of both countries accelerates long-run growth.*

Greater resources generate faster growth in our model, as in Romer (1990), essentially because dynamic scale economies characterize long-run production.

We investigate next the effects of an increase in the effective labor force of a single country. Conceptually, it proves convenient to decompose this change into two elements. First, we increase h and H by the same percentage amount. This percentage is chosen to equal the product of the share of the expanding country in the world's effective stock of labor times the percentage increase in effective labor force that the expanding country actually experiences. This accounts for the total percentage change in H when H_i changes. Then we must adjust h with H fixed to arrive at the appropriate change in h.

As an intermediate step, let us consider the effects of an increase in h alone. This corresponds to an increase in the effective labor of the country with comparative disadvantage in R&D, and a decrease in the effective labor of the other, so that the sum remains constant. This imaginary reshuffling of the world's resources shifts the $\dot{\sigma} = 0$ schedule upward when $1/s > h/H$, and downward otherwise. In either case, the $\dot{e} = 0$ curve is unaffected and the new steady-state point lies on this curve to the right of the original point. Noting (29), this proves the following:

LEMMA 1: *A reallocation of resources between countries that maintains a constant world stock of effective labor raises the long-run growth rate and increases the long-run product share of the relatively R&D efficient country if and only if the share of this country in effective labor increases.*

When the effective labor force of only country 1 (say) increases, h rises by proportionately more or less than H, according to whether country 1 has comparative disadvantage or advantage in R&D. If country 1 has comparative advantage in R&D, then both the uniform increase in H and h and the adjustment (lowering) of h, that together comprise the effect of an increase in H_1, serve to accelerate world growth. But if country 1 has comparative disadvantage in R&D, the two effects work in opposite directions. The increase in resources, by Proposition 2, speeds growth; but the reallocation of given resources, by Lemma 1, slows growth. The net effect is ambiguous, as the numerical examples that we present in Appendix D of our 1989a working paper serve to demonstrate. We have established the following:

PROPOSITION 3: *The long-run growth rate is higher the larger is the effective labor force of the country with comparative advantage in R&D. A larger effective labor force in the country with comparative disadvantage in R&D may be associated with faster or slower growth, depending upon the extent of productivity differences. In the absence of comparative advantage, long-run growth is faster the larger is the effective labor force of either country.*

These results emphasize the novel features of growth in a world with distinct countries and intercountry differences in relative productivities. They also suggest that findings reported by Paul Krugman (1990) may be somewhat special. A country need not enjoy faster growth by joining the integrated world economy, if the country enjoys substantial comparative advantage in R&D. Moreover, growth in resources or improvements in the productivity of existing resources do not guarantee faster long-run growth in a world equilibrium with free trade. If resources expand or become more efficient in the country with comparative disadvantage in R&D, then the resulting intersectoral reallocation of resources worldwide might slow innovation and growth everywhere.

IV. Economic Policy

In this section we discuss the effects of tariffs, export subsidies, and R&D subsidies on long-run growth. In order to do so, it is necessary for us to introduce the relevant policy parameters into the equations that describe instantaneous and steady-state equilibrium. To avoid repetition of the detailed arguments presented in Section I, we present here only the necessary modifications of the model and then explain their implications for the steady-state conditions. We restrict attention to small taxes and subsidies; this restriction facilitates exposi-

tion, as the channels through which economic policies affect long-run growth can be seen more clearly. We confine our analysis of trade policies to those that impede or encourage trade in final goods.

The introduction of taxes and subsidies to the model necessitates consideration of the government's budget. As usual, we assume that the government collects and redistributes net revenue by lump-sum taxes and subsidies. In a static framework, this specification suffices to determine completely the government's budgetary policy. But in a dynamic framework the budget need not balance period by period, so budgetary policy in general must specify the intertemporal pattern of lump-sum collections and transfers. However, with perfectly foresighted and infinitely lived agents, our model exhibits the Barro-Ricardo neutrality property. Hence, we need not concern ourselves with the intertemporal structure of budget deficits so long as the present value of the government's net cash flow equals zero.

The presence of the aforementioned policies modifies the decision problem for consumers in country 1 in two ways. First, we replace the price of good i in (12) by $T_i p_{Yi}$, where $T_1 = 1$. With this formulation, p_{Yi} remains the producer price of final good i, $T_2 > 1$ represents a tariff in country 1 on imports of consumer goods, and $T_2 < 1$ represents a subsidy by country 2 on exports of final output.[10] Second, we add the present value of net taxes to the right-hand side of (13) as a lump-sum addition to consumer wealth. The amount of this collection or redistribution will differ across countries according to their policies.

These modifications do not affect (14), which continues to describe the optimal intertemporal pattern of expenditures for consumers worldwide as a function of the pattern of equilibrium interest rates. In a steady state with $\dot{e} = 0$, (14) reduces to

$$(30) \qquad \dot{R} = \bar{g} + \rho.$$

---

[10]The effects of a country 2 import tariff and a country 1 export subsidy can be derived symmetrically, so we neglect these policies here and leave the maximand for consumers in country 2 as before.

Notice that (30) implies that in any steady state in which countries grow at the same rate, long-run equalization of interest rates obtains. This property of our model holds irrespective of the presence or absence of international capital mobility and the presence or absence of tariffs or export subsidies on final goods and subsidies to research and development.

Turning to the production side, our policies do not alter equations (3)–(8) describing pricing and output relationships in the intermediate and final-goods sectors and the technology for knowledge creation. However, R&D subsidies do change the private cost of R&D. We replace (10) by

$$(10') \qquad c_{ni} = w_i a_{Lni} / n S_i,$$

where $S_i > 1$ represents subsidization of research costs in country i. It proves convenient to redefine our numeraire to normalize for the effect of the R&D subsidy on the price of intermediate inputs in country 1. Our new normalization dictates a modified equation for the price of intermediates produced in country 2 as well. Together, these relationships, which replace (17a) and (17b), can be written as

$$(17') \qquad p_{Xi} = n(S_i a_{LXi}/a_{Lni})^{1/\varepsilon}.$$

As for the market-clearing conditions, the factor-markets equation (16) is not affected, but we must replace (15) by

$$(15') \qquad p_{Yi} Y_i = \frac{s_{i1} E_1}{T_i} + s_{i2} E_2,$$

where E_i denotes aggregate spending by consumers in country i, and the shares of spending devoted to good i by residents of country 1 and country 2 are $s_{i1} = s_i(p_{Y1}, p_{Y2} T_2)$ and $s_{i2} = s_i(p_{Y1}, p_{Y2})$, respectively. Although import tariffs and export subsidies on final goods do not affect steady-state producer prices of final output in our model,[11] the direct response of

[11] This statement can be verified using equations (3), (4), and (17').

spending shares in country 1 to changes in trade policy must now be taken into account. Moreover, R&D subsidies, if introduced at different rates in the two countries, will affect the steady-state value of p_{Y1}/p_{Y2}, and may therefore influence the long-run spending shares in both countries.

This completes the necessary modifications of the equilibrium relationships. We can now use the extended model to derive the equations describing steady-state equilibrium in the presence of policy intervention. In a steady state, employment in the R&D sector is given by $a_{Lni}\dot{n}_i/n = a_{Lni}\bar{g}\bar{\sigma}_i$. Making use of (4), (5), (7), (30), (10'), and (17') (which together imply $\dot{c}_{ni} = 0$ in a steady state), we find employment in the manufacture of middle products equal to $a_{Lni}\bar{\sigma}_i(\bar{g} + \rho)(\varepsilon - 1)/S_i$. Substitution of these terms into (16) yields the steady-state labor market–clearing condition,

$$(31) \qquad \bar{g}\bar{\sigma}_i + \frac{(\varepsilon - 1)(\bar{g} + \rho)}{S_i}\bar{\sigma}_i$$
$$+ \frac{1 - \beta}{\alpha b_i S_i^{1/\varepsilon}}\bar{q}_i = h_i,$$

where $q_i \equiv p_{Yi} Y_i / n$. Next, from (4)–(7), (30), and (17'), we obtain

$$(32) \qquad (\varepsilon - 1)(\bar{g} + \rho)\left(\sum_i \frac{\bar{\sigma}_i b_i}{S_i^{\alpha}}\right)$$
$$- \beta \sum_i \bar{q}_i = 0.$$

Naturally, we also require

$$(33) \qquad \sum_i \bar{\sigma}_i = 1.$$

Finally, (15') implies

$$(34) \qquad \bar{q}_i = \frac{\bar{s}_{i1}\bar{e}_1}{T_i} + \bar{s}_{i2}\bar{e}_2.$$

It is straightforward, now, to verify that (31)–(34) imply (25) and (26) when $T_i = S_i = 1$ for $i = 1, 2$ (with $\bar{e} = \Sigma_i \bar{e}_i$). This provides a consistency check on the extended model with policy instruments.

We consider trade policies first. From (34), the ratio $\bar{q}_1 / \bar{q}_2$ satisfies

$$(35) \qquad \frac{\bar{q}_1}{\bar{q}_2} = \frac{\bar{s}_{11}\bar{e}_1 + \bar{s}_{12}\bar{e}_2}{\bar{s}_{21}\bar{e}_1 / T_2 + \bar{s}_{22}\bar{e}_2}.$$

Now, for given expenditure levels $\bar{e}_i$, equations (31)–(33) and (35)—which constitute a system of five equations—provide a solution for $(\bar{g}, \bar{\sigma}_1, \bar{\sigma}_2, \bar{q}_1, \bar{q}_2)$. In this system, the trade policy parameters appear only in (35). Therefore, the long-run effects of trade policy depend only on their effects on $\bar{q}_1 / \bar{q}_2$, taking into account the induced adjustment in the spending levels $\bar{e}_1$ and $\bar{e}_2$. Moreover, for small trade policies (i.e, with an initial value of $T_2 = 1$), the spending shares are equal across countries ($\bar{s}_{i1} = \bar{s}_{i2}$), so the effect on $\bar{q}_1 / \bar{q}_2$ of changes in the cross-country composition of aggregate spending "washes out."

Further inspection of (35) reveals that an increase in T_2 starting from free trade with $T_2 = 1$ (i.e., a small import tariff in country 1) unambiguously raises $\bar{q}_1 / \bar{q}_2$.[12] A tariff shifts demand by residents of country 1 toward home consumer products, and since relative producer prices do not change in the long run, steady-state relative quantities must adjust. The effect of this change on the steady state is qualitatively the same as for an exogenous increase in world preference for final good 1, such as we studied in the previous section when we varied s_1.

---

[12] The easiest way to see this is to write the right-hand-side of (35) as

$$(\bar{p}_{Y1}, \bar{p}_{Y2})[\phi_1(\bar{p}_{Y1}, T_2\bar{p}_{Y2})\bar{e}_1 + \phi_1(\bar{p}_{Y1}, \bar{p}_{Y2})\bar{e}_2]/$$
$$[\phi_2(\bar{p}_{Y1}, T_2\bar{p}_{Y2})\bar{e}_1 + \phi_2(\bar{p}_{Y1}, \bar{p}_{Y2})\bar{e}_2],$$

where $\phi_i(\cdot)$ is minus the partial derivative of $v(\cdot)$ from (1) with respect to its ith argument divided by $v(\cdot)$. Then an increase in T_2 with $\bar{p}_{Y1} / \bar{p}_{Y2}$ constant clearly raises demand for final good 1 in country 1 (the first component of the bracketed term in the numerator increases) and lowers the demand there for final good 2 (the first component of the bracketed term in the denominator falls).

Similarly, a small export subsidy in country 2 (a reduction in T_2 to a value slightly below one) biases country 1 demand in favor of foreign final output. So we may apply directly our results from Proposition 1 to state the following:

PROPOSITION 4: *A small import tariff or export subsidy on final goods reduces a country's steady-state share in middle products and R&D. It increases the rate of long-run growth in the world economy if and only if the policy-active country has comparative disadvantage in R&D.*

Commercial policies *do* affect long-run growth rates. They do so by shifting resources in the policy-active country out of the growth-generating activity (R&D) and into production in the favored sector. At the same time, a resource shift of the opposite kind takes place abroad in the dynamic general equilibrium. The net effect on world growth hinges on the identity of the country that favors its consumer-good industry. If import protection or export promotion is undertaken by the country that is relatively less efficient in conducting R&D, then growth accelerates; otherwise, growth decelerates.

Next, we investigate the effects of small subsidies to R&D, introduced from an initial position of *laissez faire*. For these policy experiments, $T_2 = 1$ before and after the policy change, so the expenditure levels $\bar{e}_i$ cancel from (35). Suppose, first, that both countries apply subsidies at equal *ad valorem* rates; that is, $S_1 = S_2 = S$. In this case, relative prices of final output do not change across steady states. Therefore, the spending shares $\bar{s}_{ij}$ do not change. In Appendix C of our 1989a working paper, we totally differentiate (31)–(33) and (35) with respect to S to prove the following:

PROPOSITION 5: *A small R&D subsidy by both countries at a common rate increases the rate of long-run growth in the world economy.*

This proposition is not surprising, and corresponds to a similar result for the closed economy derived by Romer (1990). Since R&D represents the only source of gains in per capita income in our model, stimulation of this activity promotes growth.

What is more interesting, perhaps, is the effect of a small R&D subsidy in a single country. As for bilateral subsidies, a unilateral subsidy promotes growth by bringing more resources into product development in the policy-active country. But now, relative final-good prices change, so the spending shares in (35) must be allowed to vary unless the utility function has a Cobb-Douglas form. Depending on whether the elasticity of substitution between final products exceeds or falls short of one, this induced change in the pattern of spending can be conducive to or detrimental to growth. Moreover, an R&D subsidy in a single country will alter the relative shares of the two countries in product development. If the subsidy is introduced by the country that is relatively less efficient at performing R&D, this effect too can impede growth. In Appendix D of our 1989a working paper we show, by means of a numerical example using a Cobb-Douglas utility function, that an R&D subsidy introduced by the country with comparative disadvantage in R&D might (but need not) reduce the world's growth rate. We also prove in Appendix C that, for the case of constant spending shares, an R&D subsidy must encourage growth if it is undertaken by the country with comparative advantage in R&D. Thus we have the following:

PROPOSITION 6: *The provision of a subsidy to R&D in one country increases long-run growth if spending shares on the two final goods are constant and the policy is undertaken by the country with comparative advantage in R&D. Otherwise, the long-run growth rate may rise or fall.*

Our results here on the long-run growth effects of government policy have no immediate normative implications, both because we perform only steady-state comparisons and because the initial *level* of utility may differ along alternative growth paths. But in our 1989b paper we conduct a complete

welfare analysis for a small country with endogenous growth generated by technological progress as here. We find that the market determined rate of growth is suboptimally low due to the presence of the nonappropriable spillovers in the process of knowledge generation. An R&D subsidy that speeds growth improves welfare for the small country until some optimal growth rate is achieved. Further increases in the subsidy rate reduce welfare even as they accelerate growth. We show also that trade policy need not raise welfare, even if it successfully speeds growth. The explanation for this lies in the presence of a second distortion in our economy, one that stems from the pricing of middle products above marginal cost. The mark-up pricing practiced by intermediate producers gives rise to suboptimal use of middle products in the production of final goods. Trade policy that accelerates growth but reduces the output of middle products in the general equilibrium can be detrimental to welfare. Conversely, commercial policy that augments the output of middle products can improve welfare even if the growth implications of such policy are adverse.

These results do not carry over immediately to the current environment, though the considerations we found to be relevant in our 1989b paper are certainly applicable here as well. Normative analysis in the present two-country setting is complicated by the terms-of-trade effects that arise when policy alters the relative price of the final goods, changes the price of intermediates (if sectoral trade in middle products is not balanced), or varies the interest rate. Because of these various terms-of-trade effects we have been unable thus far to find simple conditions under which growth-enhancing policy by one government raises that country's welfare.

V. Lags in the Diffusion of Knowledge

We have assumed all along that research and development creates as a by-product an addition to the stock of knowledge that facilitates subsequent R&D. Moreover, we supposed that the knowledge so created becomes available immediately to scientists and engineers worldwide. We now relax the latter assumption, in recognition of the fact that privately created knowledge, even if nonappropriable, may enter the public domain via an uneven and time-consuming process. Also, since legal and cultural barriers may inhibit the free movement of people and ideas across national borders, we shall allow here for the possibility that information generated in one country disseminates more rapidly to researchers in the same country than it does to researchers in the trade partner country. After extending the model we will reconsider the effects of trade policies on the steady-state rate of growth.

In place of our earlier assumption that world knowledge accumulates exactly at the rate of product innovation (equation (9)), we suppose now that R&D expenditures contribute to country-specific stocks of knowledge according to

$$(9^{\dagger}) \quad K_i(t) = \lambda_h \int_{-\infty}^{t} e^{\lambda_h(\tau - t)} n_i(\tau)$$

$$+ \lambda_f \int_{-\infty}^{t} e^{\lambda_f(\tau - t)} n_j(\tau) \, d\tau,$$

where $K_i(t)$ is the stock of knowledge capital at time t in country i. With this specification, the contribution of a particular R&D project to general knowledge is spread over time. At the moment after completion of the project, none of its findings have percolated through the scientific and professional community. After an infinite amount of time has passed, the R&D project makes, as before, a unit contribution to knowledge. After finite time, the contribution lies between these extremes of zero and one, as given by the exponential lag structure in $(9^{\dagger})$. The parameters λ_h and λ_f (with $\lambda_h \geq \lambda_f$) distinguish within-country and cross-country rates of diffusion.

The introduction of lags in the diffusion of knowledge alters two of the fundamental equations of the model. First, (8) becomes

$$(8^{\dagger}) \quad \dot{n}_i = L_{ni} K_i / a_{Lni}.$$

Second, we have in place of (10),

$$(10^{\dagger}) \quad c_{ni} = w_i a_{Lni} / K_i.$$

In a steady state with $\dot{n}_1 = \dot{n}_2 = g$, we have $n_i(\tau) = n_i(t) e^{g(\tau - t)}$, so that

$$(36) \quad K_i(t) = \frac{\lambda_h}{\lambda_h + \bar{g}} n_i(t) + \frac{\lambda_f}{\lambda_f + \bar{g}} n_j(t)$$

$$= \left[\frac{\lambda_h}{\lambda_h + \bar{g}} \bar{\sigma}_i + \frac{\lambda_f}{\lambda_f + \bar{g}} \bar{\sigma}_j \right] n(t)$$

$$\equiv \mu_i(\bar{\sigma}_1, \bar{\sigma}_2, \bar{g}) n(t).$$

So in the steady state, knowledge in each country is proportional once again to the total number of middle products. But the factor of proportionality has become country-specific and endogenous. This means that the steady-state labor-input coefficient for R&D in country i, a_{Lni}/μ_i, also is endogenous; that is, relative productivity in R&D depends now not only on relative natural abilities in performing this activity, but also on relative cumulative experience in research, as summarized by the σ_i's. This consideration leads us to draw a distinction henceforth between *natural* and *acquired* comparative advantage in R&D.

From (36) we see that when $\lambda_h = \lambda_f \to \infty$ (i.e., when diffusion lags are very short), $\mu_1 = \mu_2 \to 1$, and the extended model reverts to the earlier formulation. For $\lambda_h = \lambda_f$ finite, $\mu_1 = \mu_2$, so that the ratio of the natural-plus-acquired productivity parameters for each country is the same as for the natural productivity parameters alone. In this case, the pattern of comparative advantage cannot be reversed by endogenous learning, and all results from before continue to apply. We concentrate here on cases in which the rates of diffusion are *unequal* but the difference between them is small.[13]

---

[13]A large difference between the within-country and across-country rates of diffusion may imply that, in the steady-state equilibrium, all R&D is carried out by one country. Such specialization, which is common in mod-

We derive the long-run effects of trade policy in the extended model using equations (31)–(33) and (35), but with $S_1 = S_2 = 1$ (no R&D subsidies), with b_i replaced by b_i / μ_i^α (natural plus acquired comparative advantage in place of just natural comparative advantage), and with h_i replaced by $h_i \mu_i$ (natural plus acquired effective labor in place of natural effective labor). For clarity of exposition, we shall also assume for the remainder of this section that the spending shares s_i are constant. This assumption is valid when $u(\cdot)$ takes a Cobb-Douglas form.

The new elements that diffusion lags introduce to the analysis of policy stem from the effects of *relative size* and *demand-side bias*. Before considering these new aspects, let us suppose that labor forces are equal and demand for the two final goods is symmetric. By totally differentiating the system of steady-state equations (see Appendix E of our 1989a working paper), we establish the following:

PROPOSITION 7: *Suppose $L_1 = L_2$, $s_1 = s_2$, $a_{LX1} = a_{LX2}$, and $\lambda_h - \lambda_f > 0$, but small. Then a tariff on imports of final goods in country i raises the long-run growth rate if and only if $a_{Lni} > a_{Lnj}$.*

In this case, the effects of acquired comparative advantage necessarily *reinforce* those of natural comparative advantage. The country that is relatively more productive in creating new blueprints will attain, in the steady-state equilibrium prior to the introduction of policy, a majority share of the world's middle products. By its greater concentration in R&D, it will gain more experience in research and attain a higher steady-state stock of knowledge. Thus, the effects of learning will augment its initial comparative advantage in R&D. When policy is introduced in one country or the other,

the implications of the dynamic resource reallocation for the global efficiency of R&D will be all the more significant.

Now suppose that the two countries differ initially only in (effective) size, as measured by h_i. Recall that with equal rates of diffusion, a small tariff in either country does not affect the long-run rate of growth. Now, however, we find the following:

PROPOSITION 8: *Suppose $b_1 = b_2$, $s_1 = s_2$ and $\lambda_h - \lambda_f > 0$, but small. Then a small tariff on imports of final goods raises the long-run growth rate if and only if the policy is introduced by the country with the relatively smaller effective labor force.*

Here, the larger country will come to acquire comparative advantage in R&D, though it starts with none. The reason is as follows. With differential rates of diffusion, knowledge takes on the characteristics of a *local public good*. The larger country will have more (effective) scientists to benefit from this nonexcludable good as its share in world R&D exceeds one half. So it acquires over time a relatively larger knowledge base and hence a relatively more productive corps of researchers. Trade policy that serves to divert resources away from the R&D sector in the larger country once comparative advantage has been established must be detrimental to growth.

The effects of demand-size bias are similar. The country whose good is in relatively greater demand must devote relatively more of its resources to final-goods production. Thus, its R&D sector initially will be smaller. This country develops over time a comparative disadvantage in R&D, as its learning lags that in its trade partner country. Protection in this country will improve world efficiency of R&D and thereby speed growth.

Once we allow for lags in the diffusion of scientific knowledge and differential speeds of diffusion within versus between countries, we find a richer set of possibilities for the long-run effects of trade policy. Comparative advantage continues to play a critical role in determining whether policy in one country will speed or decelerate growth.

---

els with a national component to increasing returns to scale, necessarily occurs here if static preferences are Cobb-Douglas and $\lambda_f = 0$ (i.e., all spillovers are internal). Then the equations that we have developed to describe the steady-state equilibrium (which presume non-specialization in each country) would not be valid.

But comparative advantage now must be interpreted with care, because it reflects not only natural ability but also the (endogenous) benefits from cumulative experience.[14] Since steady-state productivity in R&D varies positively with the size of the R&D sector, all determinants of the equilibrium allocation of resources to this sector come to be important in the analysis of policy.

VI. Conclusions

In this paper, we have analyzed a dynamic, two-country model of trade and growth in which long-run productivity gains stem from the profit-maximizing behavior of entrepreneurs. We have studied the determinants of R&D, where research bears fruit in the form of designs for new intermediate products and in making further research less costly. New intermediate products permit greater specialization in the process of manufacturing consumer goods, thereby enhancing productivity in final production. In order to highlight the role of endogenous technological improvements as a source of growth we have abstracted entirely from factor accumulation. But Romer (1990) has shown that capital accumulation can be introduced into a model such as the one we have studied without affecting the analysis in any significant way.

The interesting features of our analysis arise because of the assumed presence of *cross-country differences* in efficiency at R&D and manufacturing. Considerations of comparative advantage in research versus manufacturing of intermediate goods bear importantly on the implications of economic structure and economic policy for long-run patterns of specialization and long-run rates of growth. We find, for example, that growth in world resources or improvements in R&D efficiency need not speed the rate of steady-

state growth, if those changes occur predominantly in the country with comparative disadvantage in R&D.

Concerning policy, we find for the first time a link between trade intervention and long-run growth. Any (small) trade policy that switches spending toward the consumer good produced by the country with comparative advantage in R&D will cause long-run growth rates to decline. Subsidies to R&D will accelerate growth when applied at equal rates in both countries, but need not do so if introduced only in the country with comparative disadvantage in R&D. When knowledge spillovers occur with a time lag and diffusion is faster within the country of origin than across national borders, comparative advantage becomes endogenous. Once we recognize that comparative advantage can be *acquired* as well as natural, we find a role for country size and demand-size bias in determining the long-run effects of policy.

Our emphasis on comparative advantage in research and development highlights only one channel through which trade structure and commercial policy might affect long-run growth. In other contexts, the trade environment might influence the rate of accumulation of human capital or the rate at which a technologically lagging (less developed) country adopts for local use the existing off-the-shelf techniques of production. Investigation of the links between trade regime and these other sources of growth seems to us a worthy topic for future research.

REFERENCES

Becker, Gary S. and Murphy, Kevin M., "Economic Growth, Human Capital and Population Growth," *Journal of Political Economy*, forthcoming, 1990.

Corden, W. Max, "The Effects of Trade on the Rate of Growth," in J. Bhagwati et al., eds., *Trade, Balance of Payments, and Growth: Papers in Honour of Charles P. Kindleberger*, Amsterdam: North-Holland, 1971.

Ethier, Wilfred J., "National and Interna-

[14]Endogenous comparative advantage also plays a central role in Krugman's (1987) analysis of commodity-specific learning-by-doing. There, as here, productivity increases with cumulative experience. But each good is produced in only one country in Krugman's model, so long-run comparative advantage is fully determined by the initial pattern of specialization.

tional Returns to Scale in the Modern Theory of International Trade," *American Economic Review*, June 1982, *72*, 389–405.

Findlay, Ronald, "Growth and Development in Trade Models," in R. Jones and P. Kenen, eds., *Handbook of International Economics*, Amsterdam: North-Holland, 1984.

Griliches, Zvi, "Issues in Assessing the Contribution of Research and Development in Productivity Growth," *Bell Journal of Economics*, Summer 1979, *10*, 92–116.

Grossman, Gene M., "Explaining Japan's Innovation and Trade: A Model of Quality Competition and Dynamic Comparative Advantage," National Bureau of Economic Research Working Paper No. 3194, December 1989.

_____ and Helpman, Elhanan, (1989a) "Comparative Advantage and Long-Run Growth," National Bureau of Economic Research Working Paper No. 2809, January 1989.

_____ and _____, (1989b) "Growth and Welfare in a Small, Open Economy," Woodrow Wilson School Discussion Paper in Economics No. 145, June 1989.

_____ and _____, (1989c) "Product Development and International Trade," *Journal of Political Economy*, December 1989, *97*, 1261–83.

_____ and _____, (1989d) "Quality Ladders in the Theory of Growth," National Bureau of Economic Research Working Paper No. 3099, September 1989. (*Review of Economic Studies*, forthcoming.)

_____, _____ and Razin, A., eds., *International Trade and Trade Policy*, Cambridge, MA: MIT Press, forthcoming.

Judd, Kenneth, "On the Performance of Patents," *Econometrica*, May 1985, *53*, 567–85.

Krugman, Paul R., "The Narrow Moving Band, the Dutch Disease, and the Competitive Consequences of Mrs. Thatcher: Notes on Trade in the Presence of Dynamic Scale Economies," *Journal of Development Economics*, October 1987, *27*, 41–55.

_____, "Endogenous Innovation, International Trade and Growth," *Journal of Political Economy*, forthcoming, 1990.

Lucas, Robert E. Jr., "On the Mechanics of Economic Development," *Journal of Monetary Economics*, July 1988, *22*, 3–42.

Maddison, Angus, "Growth and Slowdown in Advanced Capitalist Economies: Techniques of Quantitative Assessment," *Journal of Economic Literature*, June 1987, *25*, 649–98.

Pasinetti, Luigi, *Structural Change and Economic Growth*, Cambridge: Cambridge University Press, 1981.

Romer, Paul M., "Increasing Returns and Long-Run Growth," *Journal of Political Economy*, October 1986, *94*, 1002–37.

_____, "Endogenous Technological Change," *Journal of Political Economy*, forthcoming, 1990.

Solow, Robert M., "Technical Change and the Aggregate Production Function," *Review of Economics and Statistics*, August 1957, *39*, 312–20.

Name Index

The International Library of Critical Writings in Economics

Microeconomic Theories of Imperfect Competition
Jacques Thisse and Jean Gabszewicz

The Economics of Increasing Returns
Geoffrey Heal

The Balance of Payments
Michael J. Artis

Cost-Benefit Analysis
Arnold Harberger and Glenn P. Jenkins

The Economics of Unemployment
P.N. Junankar

Mathematical Economics
Graciela Chichilnisky

Economic Growth in the Long Run
Bart van Ark

Gender in Economic and Social History
K.J. Humphries and J. Lewis

The Economics of Local Finance and Fiscal Federalism
Wallace Oates

Privatization in Developing and Transitional Economies
Colin Kirkpatrick and Paul Cook

Input-Output Analysis
Heinz Kurz and Christian Lager

The Economics of Global Warming
Tom Tietenberg

Ecological Economics
Robert Costanza

The Economics of Energy
Paul Stevens

The Economics of the Arts
Ruth Towse

The Economics of Intellectual Property
Ruth Towse

Political Business Cycles
Bruno Frey